GOD, GUNS, AND SEDITION

A COUNCIL ON FOREIGN RELATIONS BOOK

A COUNCIL ON FOREIGN RELATIONS BOOK

The Council on Foreign Relations (CFR) is an independent, nonpartisan membership organization, think tank, and publisher dedicated to being a resource for its members, government officials, business executives, journalists, educators and students, civic and religious leaders, and other interested citizens in order to help them better understand the world and the foreign policy choices facing the United States and other countries. Founded in 1921, CFR carries out its mission by maintaining a diverse membership, with special programs to promote interest and develop expertise in the next generation of foreign policy leaders; convening meetings at its headquarters in New York and in Washington, DC, and other cities where senior government officials, members of Congress, global leaders, and prominent thinkers come together with CFR members to discuss and debate major international issues; supporting a Studies Program that fosters independent research, enabling CFR scholars to produce articles, reports, and books and hold roundtables that analyze foreign policy issues and make concrete policy recommendations; publishing *Foreign Affairs,* the preeminent journal on international affairs and U.S. foreign policy; sponsoring Independent Task Forces that produce reports with both findings and policy prescriptions on the most important foreign policy topics; and providing up-to-date information and analysis about world events and American foreign policy on its website, https://www.cfr.org.

The Council on Foreign Relations takes no institutional positions on policy issues and has no affiliation with the U.S. government. All views expressed in its publications and on its website are the sole responsibility of the author or authors.

GOD, GUNS, AND SEDITION

FAR-RIGHT TERRORISM
IN AMERICA

BRUCE HOFFMAN AND
JACOB WARE

Columbia University Press
New York

Columbia University Press
Publishers Since 1893
New York   Chichester, West Sussex
cup.columbia.edu
Copyright © 2024 Bruce Hoffman and Jacob Ware

Library of Congress Cataloging-in-Publication Data
Names: Hoffman, Bruce, 1954– author. | Ware, Jacob, author.
Title: God, guns, and sedition : far-right terrorism in America /
Bruce Hoffman and Jacob Ware.
Description: New York : Columbia University Press, [2024] | Series: A Council
on Foreign Relations book | Includes bibliographical references and index.
Identifiers: LCCN 2023024186 (print) | LCCN 2023024187 (ebook) |
ISBN 9780231211222 (hardback) | ISBN 9780231558808 (ebook)
Subjects: LCSH: Domestic terrorism—United States. | Terrorism—Political
aspects—United States. | Right-wing extremists—United States. |
Radicalism—United States.
Classification: LCC HV6432 .H635 2024 (print) | LCC HV6432 (ebook) |
DDC 363.3250973—dc23/eng/20230627
LC record available at https://lccn.loc.gov/2023024186
LC ebook record available at https://lccn.loc.gov/2023024187

Printed in the United States of America

Cover design: Noah Arlow
Cover image: Getty Images

FOR J. & M.
AND FOR ALL THOSE SUFFERING
FROM HATRED AND INTOLERANCE

CONTENTS

PREFACE

We began work on this book a month into the global COVID lockdown in April 2020. It was a dark, dangerous, and uncertain time. Conspiracy theories that had already gained widespread currency throughout the preceding years were now rampant across the internet and social media. The vilification of Jews, Asians, persons of color, and immigrants, among others, was reaching unprecedented levels. And I (Bruce Hoffman) had recently been the target of a serious hate crime. It was time to return to my analytical roots.

Violent, far-right extremism was the first "account" I worked on as a young terrorism and counterterrorism analyst when I joined the RAND Corporation's Security and Subnational Conflict Research Program in 1981. Everyone else in the program had already taken one of the more prominent left-wing and ethnonationalist and separatist terrorists active at the time, so I decided to focus on a threat that was receiving less attention. This resulted in my first professional publication and a series of additional reports and scholarly articles on the threat posed by neo-Nazi and neofascist groups in Europe.[1] Shortly afterward, however, my research shifted to focus on a similar trend then unfolding in the United States.

By the middle of the 1980s, the U.S. Department of Energy had become increasingly concerned about the rise of violent, far-right extremism and violence in this country. Because many of its nuclear-weapon research, production, and storage facilities were located in states where this activity was increasing,[2] the department asked RAND to conduct a detailed threat assessment. Between 1986 and 1995 I led a number of research projects and was the author or coauthor of several reports and articles addressing the danger of far-right terrorism in the United States.[3] One of these reports, published in 1988 and cited in this book, identified these terrorists as the most likely to perpetrate a major, future mass-casualty attack in the United States.[4] And another, published just weeks before the 1995 bombing of a federal office building in Oklahoma City that killed 168 people, again underscored the continuing threat from violent, far-right extremists in this country and offered policy recommendations on how to address it.[5]

The historical pattern and potential for future violence from far-right terrorism in the United States also featured prominently in the first edition of my book *Inside Terrorism,* published in 1998. But then the September 11, 2001, terrorist attacks occurred. And, like most other terrorism analysts, my attention was diverted to al-Qaeda and then ISIS as well as their various affiliates and branches.

Meanwhile, a succession of terrorist incidents in Oslo and Utøya, Norway, in 2011; in Charleston, South Carolina, in 2015; in Pittsburgh, Pennsylvania, in 2018; and in Christchurch, New Zealand, Poway, California, and El Paso, Texas in 2019 clearly showed that the same sanguinary ideology and hateful mindset that had fueled far-right violence during the closing decades of the twentieth century had neither disappeared nor abated.

I thus approached my friend and colleague at the Council on Foreign Relations, Jacob Ware, and proposed that we together write this book. The plot by a Michigan militia cell to kidnap and execute Democratic governor Gretchen Whitmer uncovered in October 2020 and the January 6, 2021, insurrection at the U.S. Capitol infused our work with greater urgency.

Along the way, we enjoyed the help and support of many outstanding colleagues and friends as well as institutions.

We would first and foremost like to acknowledge with deep appreciation the support and encouragement we received at the Council on Foreign Relations from Richard Haass, James Lindsay, Shannon O'Neil, and Trish Dorff. Richard and Jim carefully read and provided extensive comments on the manuscript that immeasurably sharpened and improved both our analysis and our prose. Shannon reviewed the final draft, and both Jacob and I benefited tremendously from Trish's vast knowledge of publishers and publishing. We have also been extremely fortunate at the council to enjoy the generous support of the Shelby Cullom Davis Charitable Fund and wish to thank the Davis family for their continual support of the Shelby Cullom and Kathryn W. Davis Senior Fellowship in Counterterrorism and Homeland Security in honor of Ms. Davis's long history with CFR.

Rita Katz, the executive director of the world-renowned SITE Intelligence Group, allowed us access to SITE's reporting of violent, extremist messages on the internet and social media as well as SITE's invaluable analyses. Rita's book, *Saints and Soldiers: Inside Internet-Age Terrorism, from Syria to the Capitol Siege*, also published by Columbia, is an essential companion to this work.

We are also indebted to Dr. John T. Picarelli, director of counterterrorism at the National Security Council, whose comments greatly strengthened and helped shape the concluding chapter's policy recommendations. We would be remiss, too, not to acknowledge the four, anonymous peer reviewers whose suggestions and recommendations also improved this book.

Jacob and I were able to call upon the many superb students in Georgetown University's undergraduate Center for Jewish Civilization and graduate Security Studies Program for help. Thanks are therefore due to Adam Hilleley, Molly Jaskot, Mehvish Khan, Radhika Shah, Heloise Wiart, Yebin Won, and most especially Cleary Waldo for their research assistance and support.

This book benefited immensely from the hard work of the publishing team at Columbia University Press. Special thanks to Robert Fellman, who edited the manuscript; Michael Haskell, who oversaw its production; and Caelyn Cobb, editor of global history and politics, and her assistant, Monique Laban. We are very grateful to have Eric Lupfer representing us as he is among the most patient, supportive, and effective agents any author could want. We are also indebted to Megan Posco for her critical help in publicizing the book.

I would like to thank the many longstanding friends who contributed to this book through discussions, criticism, and just by being there for me throughout the process of writing this book. Christopher Adamczyk, Joseph Bernard, Peter Bergen, David Brannan, Daniel Byman, Colin Clarke, Mark Cochrane, Christopher Costa, Richard English, Jocelyn

Flores, Brittany Fried, Joshua Geltzer, Marie Harf, Seamus Hughes, Ed Husain, Seth Jones, the late Walter Laqueur, Robert Litwak, Sean Magee, Ellen McHugh, Bethania Michael, Ami Pedahzur, Fernando Reinares, Elizabeth Stanley, Anders Stephanson, Anders Strindberg, Christopher Wall, Alison Watson, Gabriel Weimann, and Tim Wilson as well as an exceedingly generous donor who wishes to remain anonymous all helped make this book possible. For the past two decades I have had the privilege of being the George H. Gilmore Senior Fellow at the U.S. Military Academy's Combating Terrorism Center and am honored to be a part of that remarkable institution. An entirely different category of persons also made this book possible. Profound thanks to Andrew Umhau, Bruce Kressel, Assil Saleh, Agnieska Kupiec, and Hisham Barakat.

Finally, and as always, my greatest strength and joy in life comes from my wife, children, their partners, and my grandchildren. Nothing I do would be possible—or be worth doing—without them.

Bruce Hoffman
Baton Rouge, LA, and Washington, DC
July 2023

. . .

I was sixteen years old on the day a bloodthirsty white supremacist murdered dozens of children at an island summer camp near Oslo in Norway—an incident covered in these pages. As a citizen of a neighboring country who shared both an age and idealism with those murdered, the shooting shook me to the very core. This incident—coupled with my younger sister's brush with jihadist terrorism during a school trip to Toulouse in France and my own experiences as one of the school-shooting generation's earliest graduates—drove my desire to join the fight to make the world a safer and happier place and to rid our nation of the cancerous hate by which it has too often been defined.

My early counterterrorism research, in graduate school at Georgetown University, focused on more youthful networks, often composed of men and boys who had grown up in the same era I had. Like Bruce, my first report, published some thirty-seven years later with the International Centre for Counter-Terrorism in The Hague, studied the far right, providing a threat assessment of the Atomwaffen Division, a neo-Nazi group whose members were responsible for several murders in the United States.[6] By the time 2019 arrived and the trajectory of the violent far right covered in this book reached an urgent stage with outbursts of violence at Christchurch, Poway, El Paso, and beyond, I was offered the opportunity to work under the legendary Bruce Hoffman—with this book project beginning shortly thereafter. My time writing this book has been defined by an imposter syndrome inevitable to anyone working alongside the doyen of their academic field, but I have come to appreciate that it is precisely my inexperience that provides a valuable perspective. This book is a reflection of our differing worldviews. Our strength as a writing team comes from our mix of pragmatism and idealism, our blend of deep historical study and fluency in modern online culture.

In addition to the names already thanked by my coauthor (some of whom, inevitably, receive another deserved mentioned below), I would like to extend my appreciation to several individuals who have played key roles in this work. I have been blessed in my short career with wonderful mentors, teachers, and leaders. The cliché "they taught me everything I know" is embarrassingly accurate in my case. In chronological order, my thanks to Elizabeth Grimm, Jerome B., Seamus Hughes, Daniel Byman, Seth Jones, Rebecca Patterson, Farah Pandith, Ambassador John Campbell, Michael Horowitz, Joshua Kurlantzick, Chris Tuttle, and Colin Clarke. Thanks, too, to Bart Schuurman for giving me my first big opportunity and to Laura Ellsworth for the chance to help Eradicate Hate. I truly stand on the shoulders of giants.

I owe a tremendous debt to Georgetown University—particularly the Security Studies Program and Center for Jewish Civilization. A particular thank you to my Georgetown consiglieri—Yebin Won, Peyton Ritter, Gia Kokotakis, and Ella Busch—and to all my outstanding students. Thank you to Cleary Waldo for your care with our manuscript. And thank you to St. Andrews and your glorious university for all you have given me. Home is where the heart is, and my heart will forever be in Scotland.

I've also been blessed with great friends, who have tested theories, questioned assumptions, and challenged conclusions. Daniel, Emilee, Grayson, Jared, Finn, Will, Grace, Matt, Kristin, Alex, Gavin, Cam, Gibbs, Hannaka, Chris, Caspar, Lex, Millie, Tom, Liv, Gus, Nick, Will R., Jack, Emily, Hope, Ellen, and many others—thank you. Pablo Brum and Amir Asmar, I look forward to continuing to debate the topic of this book, and others, over many future meetings. Special mention to Burton Gerber; thank you for welcoming me into your life and for your service and the inspiration you provide. Thank you, too, to my family and the Pennsylvania wing for patient support over the course of this project and for decades of love.

Thank you to the wonderful team at the Council on Foreign Relations, none more than Shira Schwartz, our fearless leader and the best boss anybody could ask for. Thanks to Richard Haass, James Lindsay, and Shannon O'Neil for strengthening the manuscript and giving me the opportunity. Thanks to Radmila Jackovich for her warm and protective stewardship. Thanks to Ebenezer Obadare, Upamanyu Lahiri, and Terry Mullan for all the laughter. Thanks to Chris Brodsky, a great mentor, and to Trish Dorff, Anya Schmemann, and Jenny Mallamo and their teams for their patient shepherding of our project. Thank you to Sinet Adous, a valuable and hard-working partner-in-crime. A huge thank you, too, to Eric Lupfer, Megan Posco, and the outstanding team at Columbia University Press for believing in me, us, and the project.

I would also like to thank all the survivors, for their bravery, strength, and relentless advocacy. A special thank you to Hannah K. Your care with me on my own journey of healing and redemption will never be forgotten. Thank you, too, to Anthony Purcell, who saved my life.

But I reserve the most profound gratitude for two people. First, Bruce—my intellectual lodestar and my mentor and friend. Thank you for taking a chance on me and for many years of trust and guidance across multiple institutions and job titles. One day, you no doubt will realize I was never deserving of your faith. Until then, I hope my contributions to this work and our many other collaborations are worthy of your trust.

And finally, Sarah—my ever-present, incandescent lighthouse on sunny days and through stormy seas. Thank you for your support, love, positivity, edits, and warmth, through pandemics, illnesses, traumas, and writer's block. You are the force behind every smile and the inspiration for every fight. You will always be the light in my life.

Jacob Ware
Washington, DC
July 2023

GOD, GUNS, AND SEDITION

1

ACCELERATIONISM REBORN

We're storming the Capitol, it's a revolution!

—ELIZABETH FROM KNOXVILLE, TENNESSEE

I n the summer of 2020, the messaging across far-right American internet forums was jubilant.[1] The one-two punch of the novel coronavirus pandemic, coupled with widespread protests and nationwide unrest triggered by the murder of another unarmed African American by police, had laid the country low. Yet in this moment of collective despair, America's racists, bigots, antisemites, white supremacists, and antigovernment extremists reveled in the newfound opportunities that had emerged throughout that year. Now was the time, their hateful posts on Telegram channels and seditious summons on Facebook proclaimed, to act decisively and bring the United States to its knees.

On Facebook that April, President Donald Trump's tweets to "liberate" various states from their governors' COVID stay-at-home orders and defend Second Amendment rights had galvanized exponents of the "boogaloo"—the mass insurrection-initiated civil war meant to overthrow the U.S. government.[2] "Yo the president is boog posting," exclaimed one typical message.[3] Until Facebook removed these friend groups and their posts from the platform at the end of June 2020, its author was among over 72,000 members of such Facebook groups devoted to "boogaloo."[4] Using other colloquialisms, such as "big igloo" and "big luau," or referring to themselves as "boojahideen," they explained how "We the people need to stand up to what's right and revolt. We CAN NOT allow our freedoms to be stopped or silenced. Organize and get off our ASSES and let's take back AMERICA!!" Another announced, "This Has Been A Long Time Coming: Stand-By For Instruction," while a third showed a photograph of a loaded assault rifle with the message "I heard there was gonna be a Big Luau. Thought I'd dress appropriately."[5]

The posts on Telegram, an encrypted and anonymous chat app, were even more explicit. "Your world is crumbling around you," proclaimed one notorious user group, as the pandemic death toll rose that April.[6] A few days later, another observed that the time was opportune to unleash "pure terror" on leading public figures and other societal "elites."[7] In May, yet a third neo-Nazi online channel advised that "The name of the game is discrediting the System and making sure it's got its hands too full with others to crack down on you."[8] And as demonstrations over George Floyd's killing spread across the country, an American neo-Nazi group argued that "now is the perfect time to start doing stuff if you live in the US . . . find a lawless area, look for a small group of [N-word], fire on them from a concealed position . . . then run."[9]

While some posted and tweeted, others were spurred to take action to hasten America's collapse. A month before the 2020 presidential election, a group of antigovernment extremists who had connected over Facebook plotted to kidnap Gretchen Whitmer, the governor of Michigan.[10] According to the FBI's affidavit, one of the ringleaders—a forty-year-old man named Adam Fox—was recorded saying, "In all honesty right now . . . I just wanna make the world glow, dude. I'm not even fuckin' kidding . . . I don't fuck'n care anymore, I'm just so sick of it. That's what it's gonna take for us to take it back . . . everything's gonna have to be annihilated man. We're gonna topple it all, dude."[11] His hope was that the kidnapping of Governor Whitmer would inspire other like-minded radicals in other states to similarly kidnap their own governors and try them for treason in kangaroo courts.[12] "I can see several states takin' their fuckin' tyrants," Fox exclaimed. "Everybody takes their tyrants."[13]

On January 6, 2021, a similar intent propelled the mob that stormed the U.S. Capitol building and attempted to seize Vice President Mike Pence and coerce him into nullifying the 2020 election results. Some rioters were photographed roaming the Capitol carrying flex cuffs—the heavy-duty plastic ties used by law enforcement in place of handcuffs— reportedly to subdue members of Congress, including Speaker Nancy Pelosi and other Democratic Party leaders, whom they hoped to take hostage.[14] Among the many memorable images of that day, however, was the photograph of a scaffold with a hangman's noose erected on the mall in front of the Capitol building.[15] The scene evoked the imagined "Day of the Rope" portrayed in the dystopian 1978 novel *The Turner Diaries*, by the white supremacist William L. Pierce, when corrupt, self-serving, liberal politicians, among others, are made to account for their misdeeds.[16]

Using daring, dramatic acts of violence to create chaos and disorder to lay the path for upheaval and revolution was also the motive of another would-be insurrectionist named Seth Aaron Pendley, who, six months after he demonstrated at the U.S. Capitol on January 6, pleaded guilty to plotting to blow up the Amazon Web Services Data Center in Ashburn, Virginia. According to the Department of Justice's complaint, Pendley sought to "kill off about 70% of the internet" and thereby shut down the digital communications of the FBI, CIA, and other key federal agencies.[17] In the ensuing chaos and disorder that he hoped would follow, Pendley sought to "provoke a reaction" from the "oligarchy" that he believed controlled the United States and thereby finally "convince the American people to take action against what he perceived to be a "dictatorship."[18]

All the above conforms, ironically, to the Marxist strategy of revolution called accelerationism. Accelerationism is also the contemporary manifestation of a decades-old white power strategy to foment violent chaos as a means to seize power. Although first articulated by Karl Marx and Frederick Engels in their seminal 1848 pamphlet *Manifesto of the Communist Party*,[19] accelerationism first surfaced as a concept for a white supremacist revolution in the United States in the 1980s-era newsletter *Siege*, written by James Mason, who now lives quietly in Denver and has long been one of Pierce's most dedicated acolytes. Although mostly forgotten and never a leading figure in American white supremacism, Mason was resurrected as an avatar of contemporary far-right violent extremism by users of the notorious online message board Iron March. In 2015, that platform published a digital edition of the collection of Mason's past writings, which had been first published as a single volume in 2003. The actual concept of accelerationism does not appear until page 199, where

Mason argues that "the country isn't going but has gone MAD; that the final END of society is accelerating; that the entire foundation itself is thoroughly corroded. . . . Now isn't that the most encouraging thing anyone has reported to you in a long, long time?" As the introduction to the 2003 edition explains, "At this junction social malaise cannot be halted, only accelerated onward to the abyss."[20]

In this current usage, accelerationism is embraced by a spectrum of white supremacists, white nationalists, racists, antisemites, xenophobes, and antigovernment militants as a clarion call to revolution. They fervently believe that the modern Western liberal state is so corrupt and inept that it is beyond redemption and must be destroyed in order to create a new society and way of governance. With the West supposedly poised on the precipice of collapse, accelerationism's adherents maintain that violent insurrection is required to push democracy over the edge and into oblivion. Only by hastening its destruction can a white-dominated society and new order emerge. Fomenting divisiveness and polarization through violent attacks on racial minorities, Jews, liberals, foreign interlopers, and power elites and thereby producing a cataclysmic collapse of the existing order and provoking a second civil war, accordingly, is accelerationism's stock-in-trade.[21] "Accelerationists are especially dangerous," an analysis published in 2020 argued,

> because they believe an act of mass violence by a single individual (a "lone wolf") or small cell can trigger their desired race war. Such attacks are intended to force the white population to recognize their "true" enemy, join a revolutionary uprising, and destroy the political system. Accelerationists organize themselves to facilitate these attacks, following the principles of "leaderless resistance" and calling on individuals or small cells to perpetrate revolutionary acts of violence without centralized leadership.[22]

This was precisely the intention of both Brenton Tarrant, who perpetrated the March 2019 slaughter at two mosques in Christchurch, New Zealand, and John Earnest, who carried out an attack just weeks later at a synagogue in Poway, California. Tarrant was explicit about the repercussive intentions of his attack that killed fifty-one people and wounded forty others. His goal, he wrote:

To incite violence, retaliation and further divide [*sic*] between the European people and the invaders currently occupying European soil. To avenge those European men and women lost in the constant and never ending wars of European history who died for their lands, died for their people only to have their lands given away to any foreign scum that bother to show up. To agitate the political enemies of my people into action . . .

To show the effect of direct action, lighting a path forward for those that wish to follow. A path for those that wish to free their ancestors lands from the invaders grasp and to be a beacon for those that wish to create a lasting culture, to tell them they are not alone. To create an atmosphere of fear and change in which drastic, powerful and revolutionary action can occur. To add momentum to the pendulum swings of history, further destabilizing and polarizing Western society in order to eventually destroy the current nihilistic, hedonistic, individualistic insanity that has taken control of Western thought.[23]

Earnest was equally clear: "There is at least one European man alive who is willing to take a stand against the injustice that the Jew has inflicted upon him," he wrote before the attack in an "open letter" posted on an internet site just before the shooting.

That my act will inspire others to take a stand as well. . . . I do not seek fame. I do not seek power. I only wish to inspire others and be a soldier that has the honor and privilege of defending his race in its greatest hour of need—and have a family if possible. . . . To my brothers in blood. Make sure that my sacrifice was not in vain. Spread this letter, make memes, shitpost, FIGHT BACK, REMEMBER ROBERT BOWERS, REMEMBER BRENTON TARRANT . . .

In case you haven't noticed we are running out of time. If this revolution doesn't happen soon, we won't have the numbers to win it. The goal is for the US government to start confiscating guns. People will defend their right to own a firearm—civil war has just started.[24]

The accelerationist strategy that produced the Christchurch and Poway attacks and surfaced again in Washington, DC, on January 6, 2021, is far from new, and its sulfurous legacy can be traced back decades. This terrorist strategy is in fact part of a long tradition of extreme, destabilizing far-right violence: indeed, each of the social media posts, dangerous plots, and violent incidents recounted so far reveals the dangerous, continued resonance of the accelerationist strategy that Pierce always admitted to advocating in *The Turner Diaries*.[25] To understand why and to put those events in broader context, one has to view January 6, 2021, as another milestone in a trajectory that commenced in the late 1970s and gathered momentum throughout the 1980s. Its evolution slowed following the nationwide law enforcement crackdown that resulted from the 1995 Oklahoma City bombing but was infused with new purpose after Barack Obama was elected president in 2008 and the economic recession that stunned the country the same year. And it was subsequently weaponized in the 2010s by social media and further empowered by the febrile rhetoric and polarization of politics that continued to divide America.

Today, accelerationism is the driving force behind fears that the United States is potentially on the verge of a new civil war. In her 2022 book *How Civil Wars Start*, the renowned political scientist Barbara F. Walter argues that "we are closer to civil war than any of us would like to believe" because of a toxic mix of political extremism and polarization, social and cultural tribalism, popular embrace of conspiracy theories, proliferation of guns and well-armed militias, and the erosion of faith in government and the liberal, Western democratic state. Among the key factors she cites is accelerationism, which she describes as "the apocalyptic belief that modern society is irredeemable and that its end must be hastened, so that a new order can be brought into being."[26] Steven Simon and Jonathan Stevenson, two former National Security Council staffers with deep knowledge of sectarian conflicts in Northern Ireland and the Middle East, similarly describe a situation where the United States could easily tip into civil war. The country, they write, "now appears to be in a state of 'unstable equilibrium'—a term originating in physics to describe a body whose slight displacement will cause other forces to move it even further away from its original position," thus potentially emboldening violent action to plunge the United States into the chaos and disorder that is accelerationism's goal.[27] The most dismal assessment, though, is that of the Canadian journalist Stephen Marche, who in his 2022 book *The Next Civil War: Dispatches from the American Future* contends that a new American civil war is inevitable. "The United States is coming to an end. The question is how." To his mind, "the United States is descending into the kind of sectarian conflict usually found in poor countries with histories of violence, not the world's most enduring democracy and largest economy."[28]

As febrile and alarmist as such assertions may be, there is more than a grain of truth to these fears. A 2021 survey conducted by the University of Maryland's Center for Democracy and Civic Engagement and the *Washington Post*, for instance, found that fully a third of Democrats and slightly more Republicans believe the use of violence for political purposes is "somewhat justified." This was the highest percent response to this question in the two decades it has been asked.[29] Indeed, only five years before, no more than 8 percent of respondents from either party agreed when the same question was posed.[30] Moreover, a year later even more Republicans (41 percent compared with 36 percent) again regarded politically motivated violence as "somewhat justified." Somewhat more assuring was that the percent of Democrats responding positively when that question was again posed declined by ten points. "Overall, the new survey reflects how much the partisan wars continue to rage across the country a full year after the Jan. 6 riot," the *Washington Post* noted of the 2022 survey, and "hopes for unity have largely faded as doubts about democracy have grown."[31] These fears had only intensified by the end of the year as the United States Select Committee to Investigate the January 6 Attack on the United States Capitol concluded its work by voting to refer President Trump and his attorney, John Eastman, to the U.S. Department of Justice for prosecution.[32] A *Washington Post*–ABC News poll revealed that nearly nine in ten Americans (88 percent) were now concerned that ongoing political polarization had heightened the risk of politically motivated violence—with six in ten stating that they were "very concerned" about this development.[33]

But neither polls nor predictions are prophecy, and motive without means is inconsequential . . . until one remembers that the United States leads the world—by far—in the number of firearms in private hands. Although the United States comprises only 4 percent of the world's population, it accounts for 40 percent of the globe's firearms. There are an estimated 400 million privately held firearms in the United States—more than one gun per person. Gun ownership in the United States is higher than the total of the other top twenty-five countries in the world whose civilians possess firearms. There are approximately 121 firearms for every hundred people in the United States, compared with fifty-three in Yemen, the number-two country by proportion of population.[34] Indeed, more guns were purchased in the United States during 2020 alone—17 million— than in any other year on record.[35] This proliferation of privately held weapons in the United States, Simon and Stevenson observe, "make the leaderless resistance advocated by the late-twentieth-century militia the-oreticians and now epitomized by the far right, anti-authoritarian Boo-galoo Bois—they of the Hawaiian shirts—all the more practicable."[36] Indeed, among the most fervent defenders of Second Amendment rights are people who express their desire for a new civil war.[37] And it was this fervent embrace of gun rights that electrified the militia movement in the early 1990s and motivated the deadliest terrorist incident on American soil until the September 11, 2001, attacks—the 1995 bombing of the Alfred P. Murrah Federal Building in Oklahoma City.

For Walter, the "existential fear [that] leads to a domestic arms race" and increased firearms acquisition is an important indicator of the poten-tial for the outbreak of insurgency that can then escalate to civil war and even to genocide. "The United States is not on the verge of genocide," she hastens to explain. "But if militias were to rapidly expand . . . become more brazen, and a sense of insecurity grows, right-wing terrorism in the United States could accomplish a more immediate objective: It could shift the country even more willingly toward authoritarianism." Walter sees the United States on the verge of the open insurgency stage defined by the Central Intelligence Agency's authoritative *Guide to the Analysis of Insur-gency*, which, she claims, "means we are closer to civil war than any of us would like to believe."[38]

And even if the United States avoids an actual civil war, it is not diffi-cult to imagine a variety of dark scenarios spanning a range of politically violent potentialities that would destabilize the country, further entrench existing divisions, and severely challenge our government's ability to pro-tect its citizens. In his 2023 book on the erosion of democratic norms in America, Richard Haass, then president of the Council on Foreign Rela-tions, raised the possibility of a version of Northern Ireland's longstand-ing "Troubles" coming to the United States. "If there is a model for what we should fear," Haass warns, "it comes from Northern Ireland and the Troubles, the three-decade struggle starting in the late 1960s that involved multiple paramilitary groups, police, and soldiers and resulted in some 3,600 deaths and a sharp reduction in local economic output."[39] Haass has direct experience of the pernicious effects of that tragic conflict, having served as U.S. envoy to the Northern Ireland peace process between 2001 and 2003 and then as chair of the multiparty negotiation that led to the 2014 Stormont Agreement.[40] And leading American white supremacists, who have long been among the foremost advocates of civil war and sedition, have cited the Northern Irish exemplar and the province's preeminent terrorist organization, the Provisional Irish Republican Army (PIRA), as worthy of emulation. "Soon, our version of the 'Troubles' will be widespread," wrote Robert Miles, one of the early leaders of America's violent far-right underground, under his Norse code name "Fafnir" on a 1980s online forum. "The patterns of operations of the IRA will be seen across this land. . . . Soon, America becomes Ireland recreated."[41]

• • •

God, Guns, and Sedition excavates this long history of accelerationism, explains its emergence, and analyzes the violence it has produced over the past forty years—and the potential for the mass violence leading to civil war recounted here. In this context, we define "far-right terrorism" in the American setting broadly as a threat featuring an overlapping and evolving multitude of actors, movements, and ideological strains, ultimately united by a desire to return the United States to some long-lost halcyon days defined by hierarchies dividing people by race, gender, religion, and even regional identity—with white masculinity reigning supreme. These actors are "terrorists" because of their preparedness to use lethal violence in pursuit of that mission.[42]

We also aim to provide an important correction to the argument found in other works on this subject: that the modern iterations and characteristics of contemporary violent far-right extremism are somehow a new phenomenon. In this respect, key dimensions of this disparate movement, especially pertaining to the advent of digital technology and social media and strategies like accelerationism, have often been depicted as unique to the twenty-first-century violent extremist landscape in the United States. These developments are not, in fact, novel but are instead merely the latest manifestations of a movement and threat that have been gathering momentum since the 1970s and that have been almost hypersonically empowered by social media. Indeed, the two most consequential trends of modern terrorism—online radicalization and recruitment and lone-actor, independent acts of violence carried out by individuals or small cells in service of a broader movement (so-called lone wolf attacks)—were in fact pioneered by the American violent far right four decades ago. In this work, we show that the wave of violent, far-right extremism that swept across the Western world in 2019 and then visited the seat of America's government on January 6, 2021, was not the successful implementation of a new strategy of political violence or some serendipitous combination of planning and luck but the culmination of a long and deliberate journey, begun by movement pioneers in the early 1980s, to develop a battle plan to overthrow the U.S. government.

This work thus provides a comprehensive, narrative account of the development of violent far-right American extremism up to, including, and beyond the January 6, 2021, attack on the U.S. Capitol. Our objective is to show that the tragedies defining the modern far-right terrorist threat—from Dylann Roof's attack on a historic Charleston church to January 6—are just the latest flashpoints in a historical process that has been unfolding for decades. The contemporary American violent far right should thus be seen as a continuation, not as a break—but in a new and emerging trend known as "ideological convergence," it now brings together the converging ideologies of white supremacism, hostility to government, racism, antisemitism, xenophobia, and vast conspiracy theories. The book also draws out many of the key themes that weave their way through the narrative history of far-right terrorism in America—including the movement's adoption of cutting-edge communications technology, its pioneering embrace of leaderless resistance or lone wolf strategies, the tactics and targets that have come to define its ideology and violence, the personality traits exhibited by many of its adherents, its often symbiotic relationship with domestic American politics, and the recruitment and infiltration of U.S. military and law enforcement personnel. Each of these themes has profound counterterrorism implications.

Moreover, unlike many other forms of terrorism, the threat from modern American violent far-right extremism is more individually than organizationally driven. It is a movement where the parts are indisputably greater than the whole. Accordingly, we focus on a consistent succession of individuals who have always given the movement its momentum and vitality. There is a common thread between older far-right luminaries such as Louis Beam, William Potter Gale, Robert Mathews, and Timothy McVeigh and contemporary figures such as Dylann Roof, Robert Bowers, and John Earnest. Through them, the ideological trajectory of the radicalization and violence that has repeatedly surfaced in recent years is clear. Far from being an unfortunate symptom of today's society, the development of this threat has been systematically planned by a lineage of violent, far-right extremists who have sought to project their hateful and antidemocratic views of the world into American society. By tracing this malignant lineage, we also seek to identify the countermeasures that our leaders need to implement to smother this threat. Accordingly, this work unpacks a range of short-term, medium-term, and long-term measures to counter radicalization and violence today and build resilience among generations to come. This comprehensive counterterrorism strategy will require measures to combat extremists' free rein online, efforts to build and support longer-term initiatives to prevent new radicalization, and the establishment of new laws to counteract the challenges in prosecuting perpetrators of far-right terrorist plots.

The next four chapters of this book serve as a critical launch pad for showing the trajectory that violent far-right extremism in the United States has followed over the past four decades—and most especially the connectivity and convergence that animates this disparate movement. Chapter 2 details the emergence of the Order, a violent neo-Nazi cell, tracing its relationships with a number of white supremacist communities and organizations from year to year. In chapter 3, we outline the events leading up to the watershed 1988 Fort Smith trial, in which fourteen white supremacists were acquitted on charges of plotting to overthrow the U.S. government. Chapter 4 unpacks the rapid expansion of the militia movement in the early 1990s, paying special attention to the disastrous federal raids on a small compound in northern Idaho in 1992 and on a religious cult in Texas the following year. And in chapter 5, we revisit the radicalization of Timothy McVeigh—a decorated war hero and America's deadliest modern domestic terrorist—and assess the impact of his lethal 1995 bombing in Oklahoma City. Our intention is thus to bridge the earlier history laid out in the initial chapters with the contemporary developments that constitute the latter half of the book. Along the way, we also correct some longstanding misconceptions and falsehoods that have been inadvertently perpetuated (concerning, for instance, the dystopian, racist novel *The Turner Diaries* and some of the most important far-right terrorist plots of the 1980s).

Then, in chapter 6, we fast-forward to the election of President Barack Obama, analyzing its impact on violent extremism in the United States alongside the emergence of a new communications tool that abetted radicalization, recruitment, and mobilization. Chapter 7 assesses the consequences that the election of Donald Trump as U.S. president has had on the violent far right in America. And in chapter 8, we revisit the tumultuous years since 2020, which will be forever remembered for their effects on broader society as well as the violent, extremist fringes of American society. The book concludes with a number of counterterrorism policy recommendations needed to address this threat.

Despite the ultimately successful certification of the 2020 presidential election and subsequent unimpeded transfer of power; the arrests of over one thousand rioters who participated in the January 6, 2021, storming of the U.S. Capitol building, which has resulted in guilty pleas or convictions of at least half of those charges; and the mostly peaceful events surrounding the 2022 midterm elections, the threat from far-right terrorism in contemporary America continues unabated.[43] Given the long historical trajectory documented in this book, which culminated in the events of January 6, the continued proliferation and pervasiveness of conspiracy theories and the growing racism, antisemitism, and xenophobia that have entered the mainstream of political and social discourse in the United States, the potential for new acts of politically motivated violence—including mass shootings, attacks on critical infrastructure, bombings, and other attacks—cannot be dismissed or ignored.

2

BATTLE PLAN

September 16, 1991. *Today it finally began! After all these years of talking—and nothing but talking—we have finally taken our first action. We are at war with the System, and it is no longer a war of words.*

—EARL TURNER, IN *THE TURNER DIARIES*

Over the past four decades, advertisements for *The Turner Diaries* have repeatedly asked an apocalyptic question: "What will you do when they come to take your guns?" Its author, however, was not simply a zealous exponent of Second Amendment rights. Rather, according to the Southern Poverty Law Center, the hate-monitoring organization based in Montgomery, Alabama,[1] as founder and leader of the National Alliance—"a group whose members included terrorists, bank robbers and would-be bombers"—William Luther Pierce was "America's most important neo-Nazi for some three decades until his death in 2002" and "the movement's fiercest antisemitic ideologue."[2]

Defying the prevailing stereotype of American white supremacists as crude country bumpkins or uneducated "rednecks," Pierce graduated from Houston's prestigious Rice University in 1955 and subsequently worked at New Mexico's Los Alamos National Laboratory before studying at Caltech and obtaining his doctorate in physics from the University of Colorado. He taught at Oregon State University for a time. But Pierce's strident anticommunism and racist and antisemitic beliefs increasingly pulled him toward a career of full-time advocacy and hate-mongering. In 1974, Pierce founded the National Alliance.[3] Its goal continues to find supporters today: "We must have no non-Whites in our space and we must have open space around us for expansion. . . . We will do whatever is necessary to achieve this White living space and to keep it White. We will not be deterred by the difficulty or temporary unpleasantness involved, because we realize that it is absolutely necessary for our racial survival."[4]

The Anti-Defamation League (or ADL, formerly known as the Anti-Defamation League of B'nai B'rith), the organization founded over a century ago to "stop the defamation of the Jewish people and . . . secure justice and fair treatment to all,"[5] described the National Alliance in 1998 and again in 2000 as "the single most dangerous organized hate group in the United States today." The National Alliance earned this distinction largely as a result of Pierce's pseudonymous authorship of *The Turner Diaries* as Andrew Macdonald.[6]

No other book has had so pervasive or sustained an influence over violent far-right extremism in the United States as *The Turner Diaries.*[7] Within five years of its publication, the *New York Times* would report that Pierce's dystopian treatise of race war and revolution had become "the bible of an anti-Semitic movement" that in 1984, as we shall see, actually declared war on the U.S. government.[8] An apocryphal claim appeared on the back of the 1985 edition that similarly noted how the FBI "has labeled *The Turner Diaries* 'the bible of the racist right.'"[9] Often repeated, it was most likely penned by Pierce for publicity purposes.[10] Nonetheless, a prescient 1991 FBI memorandum described *The Turner Diaries* as "a significant work and foundation document closely embraced by the leadership as well as rank and file members of the Right-wing, White Supremist [sic] Movement, also known as the 'Christian Identity Movement.'"[11] By the time of the 1995 bombing of the Alfred P. Murrah Federal Building in Oklahoma City, which *The Turner Diaries* inspired,[12] at least two hundred thousand and perhaps as many as five hundred thousand copies of the paperback had been sold.[13] Distributed by National Vanguard Books, the National Alliance's publishing arm,[14] it could occasionally be found at book shops,[15] but more often *The Turner Diaries* was hawked by individual sellers at gun shows and venues such as the annual Soldier of Fortune

Convention in Las Vegas as well as by mail order through advertisements placed in *Shotgun News* and other gun magazines as well as the now defunct *Soldier of Fortune* magazine.[16]

The book recounts the eponymous hero's two-year struggle after he and his "fellow patriots" are forced to go underground to defend themselves when a predatory government imposes the "Cohen Act" to seize all legally held firearms. After more than eight hundred thousand of his fellow citizens are arrested, a thirty-five-year-old electrical engineer named Earl Turner joins "The Organization," the movement spearheading this revolution-cum–race war, and embarks on a concerted terrorist campaign that includes the assassination of public officials, journalists, and prominent Jews; the wholesale murder of African Americans, Latinos, and other minorities; shooting down commercial airliners; poisoning municipal water supplies; and bombing public utilities. Among the more noteworthy incidents is the "Day of the Rope," when the Organization carries out a public mass execution by hanging an expansive category of alleged "race traitors," including "the politicians, the lawyers, the businessmen, the TV newscasters, the newspaper reporters and editors, the judges, the teachers, the school officials, the 'civic leaders,' the bureaucrats, the preachers," and others.[17] In addition, chapter 6 recounts a truck bombing of the FBI's downtown Washington, DC, headquarters. "All day yesterday and most of today we watched the TV coverage of rescue crews bringing the dead and injured out of the building"—a particularly important passage in the book given its chilling similarity to the 1995 Oklahoma City bombing. "It is a heavy burden of responsibility for us to bear," it continues,

> since most of the victims of our bomb were only pawns who were no more committed to the sick philosophy or the racially destructive goals of the System than we are.
>
> But there is no way we can destroy the System without hurting many thousands of innocent people—no way. It is a cancer too deeply rooted in our flesh. And if we don't destroy the System before it destroys us—if we don't cut this cancer from our living flesh—our whole race will die.[18]

Turner is later inducted into a more elite unit within the Organization known as "The Order." That unit has seized control of the U.S. nuclear arsenal and launches missile attacks that obliterate New York City and Tel

Aviv but fails to destroy the former Soviet Union. The Soviets then launch a retaliatory strike against the United States that Turner describes as "horrendous, but spotty. They fired everything they had left at us, but it simply wasn't enough. Several of the largest American cities, including Washington and Chicago, were spared." Turner, accordingly, is ordered to carry out a kamikaze attack on the Pentagon in a small airplane containing a nuclear weapon. An "epilog" records the consequences of Turner's martyrdom: the final defeat and collapse of the United States. The Organization eventually conquers Europe and, unleashing an array of chemical, biological, and radiological weapons, defeats China and "effectively sterilize[s] . . . some 16 million square miles of the earth's surface, from the Ural Mountains to the Pacific and from the Arctic Ocean to the Indian Ocean." The "dream of a White world finally became a certainty," the book concludes—with Turner having "helped greatly to assure that his race would survive and prosper . . . and that The Order would spread its wise and benevolent rule over the earth for all time to come."[19]

Pierce denies that his intention in writing *The Turner Diaries* was to provide any kind of a blueprint or model for the violent race revolution it recounts.[20] But on numerous occasions the novel has done exactly that: inspiring emulation and imitation—with often tragic results. Among those who adopted the battle plan delineated in *The Turner Diaries* was a lifelong militant anticommunist and antigovernment firebrand named Robert Mathews. Mathews was just one rising star in a white supremacist universe that embraced *The Turner Diaries'* core tenets of racism, antisemitism, xenophobia, and sedition; it also included such prominent figures as William Potter Gale, Richard Girnt Butler, Gordon Kahl, James Ellison, Kerry Noble, and Louis Beam, who all played key roles in the emergence of this movement during the 1980s.

• • •

Born in rural Texas in 1953, Robert Mathews grew up in an otherwise unremarkable lower-middle-class household in Phoenix. He joined the militantly anticommunist John Birch Society at age eleven, became a member of the Young Republicans, and converted to Mormonism five years later. While still a teenager, Mathews cofounded the Arizona Sons of Liberty[21]—which the authoritative *Encyclopedia of White Power*, edited by Jeffrey Kaplan, one of the preeminent scholars in the field, describes as "a paramilitary underground of constitutionalist fundamentalists composed of far-right Mormons and survivalists, dedicated to counter what they perceived as the corruption of true Americanism."[22] The group's mostly low-level violent antics went unnoticed until they staged a commando-like assault on a local television station. The publicity that the barricade-and-hostage incident was designed to generate also caught the FBI's attention. Mathews was convicted of tax evasion in 1973 and after serving six months' probation left Arizona to build a new life in Washington State.[23] "I maintained then as I do now," Mathews explained in 1984, "that our people have devolved into some of the most cowardly, sheepish, degenerates that have ever littered the face of this planet." He moved to Metaline Falls,[24] a town in northeastern Washington State, and with his father's help eventually purchased eighty acres of land.[25]

Mathews paints a picture of the archetypal American frontiersman. He claims to have arrived in Washington State with only twenty-five dollars in his pocket and a desire to "work hard and be left alone, and the dream of someday acquiring my own small farm." His family subsequently followed him from Arizona to this unspoiled northern woodland paradise. Mathews got a job at a mine and a cement plant, married, and kept to himself. His spare time was devoted to learning about the malignant influences destroying Western society. Mathews cites Oswald Spengler's post–World War I lamentation on the decline of the West and William Gayley Simpson's *Which Way Western Man?* as seminal resources.[26] The Simpson book is especially noteworthy in this respect. Published by William Pierce's National Vanguard Books, it is described on Amazon as having been written by "an exceptionally deep thinker [who] traced the sickness that has overtaken the White man's world in the twentieth century to its roots in Jewish world conspiracy and its coordinated aggressive moves against us. . . . Every racially White person," the summary posted on Amazon continues, "will want this book in his collection, as it is very possibly the best book of racial philosophy originally written in the English language."[27] Mathews was by this time also a devotee of Pierce and was captivated by the National Vanguard press's other bestseller—Pierce's *The Turner Diaries*.[28]

Mathews admits to having drunk deeply from this well of white supremacy, racism, and antisemitism. The adoption of a blond-haired, blue-eyed son supposedly brought about a startling epiphany, he later recalled:

> I realized that White America, indeed my entire race, was headed for oblivion unless White men rose and turned the tide. The more I came to love my son the more I realized that unless things changed radically, by the time he was my age, he would be a stranger in his own land, a blonde-haired, blue-eyed Aryan in a country populated mainly by Mexicans, mulattoes, blacks and Asians. . . . I came to learn that this was not by accident, that there is a small, cohesive alien group within this nation working day and night to make this happen.[29]

But in point of fact, Mathews had long previously held these views.[30] And his attraction to this region of Washington where he settled was not simply a product of its isolation or rugged beauty. The region's silver mines—where Mathews found employment—for instance, had once attracted settlers from the former Confederate States of America, whose descendants still subscribed to the same racist and seditious sentiments that had led to America's civil war over a century earlier.[31] The area was in fact a magnet for other hardcore white supremacists—including a fifty-six-year-old retired aeronautical engineer and ordained cleric from California, the Reverend Richard Girnt Butler.[32]

A lifelong anticommunist—whose father blamed global Jewish conspirators for that ideology's malignant propagation—Butler had served in the Army Air Corps during World War II before settling in the Los Angeles neighborhood of Montebello.[33] There in the early 1960s he fell under the influence of two fellow Californians: a retired U.S. Army colonel named William Potter Gale and Dr. Wesley Swift, a former Methodist minister turned leader of the Church of Jesus Christ Christian.[34] Gale had served on General Douglas MacArthur's staff directing anti-Japanese guerilla operations in the Philippines during World War II. Like Mathews and Butler, Gale's hostility to communism had led him to the John Birch Society but more significantly to founding in 1970 the loosely organized, militant antigovernment movement known as Posse Comitatus.[35] Latin for "power of the county," Posse adherents disavow any form of government above the county level, advocate a return to the gold standard, oppose federal and state income taxes, reject the existence of the Federal Reserve system, and decry the supremacy of the federal judiciary over local courts.[36]

Gale introduced Butler to Swift, who is today recalled on his church's website as "the single most significant figure in the early years of the Christian Identity movement in the United States."[37] A fanatical anticommunist and reputed former Ku Klux Klan organizer, Swift preached a highly idiosyncratic interpretation of scripture derived from the nonviolent, philo-Semitic, Anglo-Israelism movement that emerged in Britain during the mid-nineteenth century.[38] Swift transformed its core tenet, that the ten lost tribes of ancient Israel were composed of Anglo-Saxons and not Jews, into an aggressively antisemitic, white supremacist dogma.[39] Adherents to Christian Identity claim:

- Jesus Christ was a Christian not a Jew;
- the United States and not Israel is the Promised Land;
- white Aryans are the true descendants of the biblical tribes of Israel and are therefore the true Chosen People, not the Jews;
- Jews are imposters—literally Satan's progeny—put on earth to undermine white Christendom through Jewish control of the global economy and media as well as the empowerment of persons of color;
- a perpetually Manichean struggle must therefore be waged between good and evil by Aryans against Jews that will someday lead to a climacteric apocalypse.[40]

Under Swift's tutelage, Butler was ordained as a Church of Jesus Christ Christian minister and succeeded him as its leader after Swift's death in 1970.[41] Like his mentor, Butler was a zealous exponent of the "two seed" theory. This mix of traditional Calvinism combined with some aspects of Mormonism and core Identity tenets holds that Adam and Eve begat Abel but that later that day Eve had sex with Satan (in the guise of the serpent in the Garden of Eden), which produced Cain—and in turn the Jews. The Jewish people, according to Identity theology, are not the children of God but are Satan's emissaries. They are thus the anti-Christ. Indeed, all the universe's nonwhite races are descended from the Jews—the "beasts of the field" referred to in Genesis 2:8.[42]

Just a year after relocating to Idaho in 1973, Butler founded the Aryan Nations to serve as an umbrella organization for the entire white supremacist movement.[43] The religious and racial purification of the United States that *The Turner Diaries* details was a central feature of its ideology. Article 8 of the "Aryan National State Platform," for instance, states that "a ruthless war must be waged against any whose activities are injurious to the common interest."[44] As Butler explained in an Aryan Nations brochure from the 1980s: "We will have a national racial state at whatever price in blood is necessary. Just as our forefathers purchased their freedom in blood, so must we." Titled *This Is Aryan Nations*, the treatise goes on to decry "the leadership of malicious, bastardizing politicians . . . [in] modern, decadent America [where] millions of whites watch in abject dismay and hopelessness as their great culture, heritage and civilization evaporates in the steaming stinking, seething milieu of so many alien races, cultures and gods."[45]

By linking Identity theology to the Aryan Nations goals and objectives, Butler sought to unite racists, antisemites, neo-Nazis, white supremacists, militant tax resisters, antifederalists, and survivalists into one coherent movement.[46] "The principles of Identity Christianity provide the divine justification for acts of violence against the government, non-Whites, homosexuals, and Jews," the University of Toronto's Tanya Telfair Sharpe explains. "It further holds that our democratic foundations of governance are the product of a global conspiracy orchestrated by Jews, capitalists, and other elites designed to control and manipulate American society for their own evil ends. Identity Christianity [*sic*] thus uses religion and scripture to sanction violence against persons who are not White, Anglo-Saxon Christians."[47] Or as Danny O. Coulson, the founding commander of the FBI's elite Hostage Rescue Team and a former deputy assistant director, recalled, "Identity was terrifying because it transformed hate into a religious duty and sanctified murder itself as an act of faith."[48]

The Aryan Nations' political agenda was further justified by the Church of Jesus Christ Christian's interpretation of scripture. Additional legitimization was provided by Butler's authority as its preeminent cleric. "Scripture says, 'There shall be bloodshed' . . . Therefore there should be war,"[49] he argued from a pulpit adorned with multiple Nazi swastikas and resurrection Christian crosses beneath a red, blue, and white stained-glass window with the Aryan Nations symbolic cross fashioned from a sword and crown.[50] In a membership form distributed during the 1980s and 1990s, Butler further explained the spiritual base of Aryan Nations' beliefs. "Aliens are pouring over as a flood into *each* of our ancestral lands, threatening dispossession of the heritage, culture, and very life blood of our posterity," he wrote. "We know that as we return to our Father's natural Life Order, all power, prosperity, and liberty again comes to us as our possession, to establish justice forever on earth."[51] *This Is Aryan Nations* articulated the religious foundations of the Aryan Nations political program:

> *WE BELIEVE* that there is a battle being fought this day between the children of darkness (today known as Jews) and the children of light (God), the Aryan race, the true Israel of the Bible. Revelations 12:10–11.
>
> *WE BELIEVE* in the preservation of our race individually and collectively as a people as demanded and directed by God. We believe a racial nation has a right and is under obligation to preserve itself and its members. . . . As His divine race, we have been commissioned to fulfill His divine purpose and plans. . . .
>
> *WE BELIEVE* that there is a day of reckoning. The usurper will be thrown out by the terrible might of Yahweh's people as they return to their roots and their special destiny. We know there is soon to be a day of judgement and a day when Christ's Kingdom (government) will be established on earth, as it is in heaven. "And in the days of these kings shall the God of heaven set up a kingdom which shall never be destroyed; and the kingdom shall not be left to other people, but it shall break in pieces and consume all these kingdoms and it shall stand forever. The saints of the Most High, whose kingdom is an everlasting kingdom, and all dominions shall serve and obey Him." Daniel 2:44; 7:18; 7:27.[52]

An article from that period of time published in the Aryan Nations' newsletter emphasized the divinely ordained dimension of its raison d'être. In "An All White Nation?—Why Not?" Reverend Roy B. Masker explains how white American Christians "are in disobedience to our Father and God, Yahwey, for allowing the Nation He gave us to become the mongrelized cesspool in which we now find ourselves. . . . Indeed, it is incumbent upon us to BUILD A NEW, ALL-WHITE NATION! We are under command to do so! All scripture demands it! Woe to those who stand in the way of the Aryan juggernaut!"[53]

This, accordingly, was the amenable environment that from 1975 Mathews called home—a fitting backdrop to establish what Nazi Germany had called *lebensraum* and the National Alliance had similarly termed "White living space."[54] A likeminded community of Church of Jesus Christ Christian congregants and retirees had already settled there a few years before. Land was relatively inexpensive, at around two hundred dollars per acre;[55] taxes were low; the region was sparsely populated; and best of all, it was desirably homogeneous.[56] Butler purchased a twenty-acre site at the edge of the Coeur d'Alene National Forest, off Rimrock Road, just north of Hayden Lake.[57] As befits "the international headquarters of the White race,"[58] he set about building a hundred-seat chapel, a combined meeting hall and communal dining room, an outdoor reviewing stand at which speakers could address large gatherings, a print shop, and a barracks—overseen by a security watchtower with armed guards, surrounded by a six-foot-high barbed wire fence, and patrolled by attack dogs. Nearby was Butler's own, simple home with its pretty flowers.[59] Surrounded by intimidating, tall Ponderosa pines and other evergreen trees, a gatehouse and raiseable barrier marked the entrance to the compound—with a prominent sign warning "White Kindred Only!"[60] Its seclusion was intended to prevent snooping from law enforcement, the media, civil rights, and other nongovernmental organizations as well as the curious public.[61]

• • •

The apple of Butler's eye and most tangible manifestation of the Aryan Nations' unification mission was what in the 1980s was advertised as its annual "Summer Congress and [N-word] Shoot."[62] Held in July,[63] the typical event, according to the University of Chicago historian Kathleen Belew, "was part organizing meeting, part church service, part summer picnic," where participants moved easily from the racist diatribes issued during the conference's plenary sessions to more casual conversation and networking over heaping plates of spaghetti served family style.[64] At its heyday in the early 1980s, perhaps as many as five hundred attendees from over a dozen different Ku Klux Klan and neo-Nazi organizations enrolled in workshops on various aspects of white supremacy, acquired survivalist skills, or undertook paramilitary training courses.[65] One obstacle course reportedly concluded with participants firing automatic weapons at a poster of Menachem Begin, Israel's prime minister, as they proclaimed, "For God, nation, race!"[66] But the real highlight for many was the climactic "SACRED CROSS LIGHTING"[67]—a fixture of Ku Klux Klan gatherings since the early 1900s.[68] The Aryan Nations' variant included the traditional tall cross, denoting "the light of this world, which is Jesus Christ," along with four smaller ones signifying for them the points of the compass and the ubiquity of the white race's historical dominance and heritage.[69]

The 1983 congress proved to be the most significant—and consequential—both for the Aryan Nations and for the American white supremacist movement more generally. This meeting laid bare the movement's violently seditious character and the actual terrorism threats it posed.[70] The killing only weeks earlier of Gordon Kahl, a sixty-three-year-old farmer and longstanding member of a North Dakota chapter of the Posse Comitatus, was the ostensible flashpoint for what an insider would later describe as "the first and only armed revolt against the government in this century"[71]—led by Robert Mathews.

Kahl reflected the uniquely multitudinous dimensions of violent, far-right extremism. Another decorated World War II veteran, Kahl had grown up in rural Heaton, North Dakota. From an early age he was taught that whites and blacks and Jews and Christians were separate peoples with whom one should not associate or mix. The fact that there were likely few opportunities to do so in tiny Heaton in the middle of that sparsely populated state during the 1920s and 1930s only reinforced his segregationist convictions. Kahl's wartime service as a turret gunner flying B-25 bombers in both Europe and the Pacific did little to modify or alter his views. Indeed, by the time Germany surrendered in 1945, Kahl had come to believe that the war he had just fought had been avoidable. Instead, a shadowy cabal of bankers, Jews, capitalists, and others had drawn President Franklin D. Roosevelt into their conspiracy to profit from the fighting. Kahl's close reading of Henry Ford's antisemitic 1920 screed *The International Jew: The World's Foremost Problem*, which promoted the Russian Czarist-era seminal antisemitic conspiratorial text *The Protocols of the Elders of Zion* (also known as *The Protocols of the Meetings of the Learned Elders of Zion*), further reinforced this malignant worldview. By the 1960s, after a brief dalliance with the John Birch Society, Kahl became involved with the grassroots militant tax protest movement that would eventually crystallize as the Posse Comitatus.[72] In 1967 he sent a letter to the Internal Revenue Service that would become the source from which all his future travails would flow. From this time forward, Kahl swore, he would not "pay tithes to the Synagogue of Satan under the second plank of the Communist Manifesto. . . . Never again will I give aid and comfort to the enemies of Christ."[73]

Kahl formally joined the Posse Comitatus in 1973. He was appointed its coordinator for Texas the following year. The IRS finally caught up with him three years later. Kahl was arrested, tried, and convicted of failure to pay income tax.[74] His appeals denied, Kahl served eight months of a year sentence at the federal penitentiary in Leavenworth, Kansas. The terms of his parole were that Kahl would henceforth agree to pay his income tax as well as refrain from involvement with either the Posse or any other organization similarly opposed to federal and state laws. He had absolutely no intention of submitting to any of those conditions. The stage was thus set for another confrontation, especially after the IRS attached a lien to eighty acres of his land—a quarter of the family farm. In March 1981, the IRS put the seized acreage up for auction; that same month, a warrant was issued for Kahl's arrest. Income taxes were a Satanic commandment that he could not abide, Kahl declared before leaving town. Kahl and his wife stayed mostly in Arkansas, where they visited the compound of a Christian survivalist group known as the Covenant, the Sword, and the Arm of the Lord (CSA). They returned to North Dakota in 1982. It was only a matter of time before his cat-and-mouse game with federal authorities would turn violent.[75]

By the early 1980s, local chapters of the Posse Comitatus had been established in almost every state in the country. The movement had also become increasingly violent, especially in the Midwest, where farmers had been hard hit by foreclosures. Posse adherents attacked local, state, and federal law enforcement officers attempting to serve subpoenas for firearms or land-use violations and enforce property seizures.[76] That some members like Kahl routinely found scriptural justification for their militant opposition to taxes and governmental authority above the county level[77] is clear from the sixteen-page letter that he sent to Richard Butler and various other friends, supporters, and journalists while on the run again in 1983. Describing himself as a "Christian patriot" intent on "put[ting] our nation back under Christian Common Law, which is another way of saying God's Law as laid down by the inspiration of God, through his prophets and preserved for us in the Scriptures," Kahl recounted how on February 13, 1983, he, his wife, his son Yorie, and three friends were "ambushed on our return to our homes." At a roadblock just north of Medina, North Dakota, a tense standoff unfolded as Kahl and Yorie, each armed with semiautomatic .223 Ruger Mini-14s, confronted four U.S. marshals—accompanied by a county deputy sheriff and a local police officer—who had come to arrest Kahl. "There was a lot of screaming and hollering going on [and] a shot rang out," the farmer-turned-militant recalled.[78] More shooting erupted. When the smoke cleared, Ken Muir, the U.S. marshal for North Dakota, and a deputy marshal, Robert Cheshire, lay dead. Another deputy marshal was wounded, as were the deputy sheriff and a police officer. Yorie had been shot in the stomach and was arrested shortly afterward at a nearby clinic. Kahl went home, changed clothes, collected some ammunition, climbed into his 1966 AMC Rambler, and disappeared.[79]

His supporters subsequently repackaged Kahl's letter into a circular to raise funds for his defense if he was captured. This was wishful thinking. Kahl was fully prepared to die for his beliefs. The killing of the marshals, his letter argued, was no different from the killing he had done during the war to protect himself and fellow crewmen. "I would have liked nothing other [than] to be left alone," Kahl reflected, "so I could enjoy life, liberty and the pursuit of happiness, which our forefathers willed to us. This was not to be after I discovered that our nation had fallen into the hands of an alien people." He saw himself as persecuted by a predatory government, in league with powerfully odious forces, and therefore as a reluctant warrior-patriot, cast on the defensive by the "enemies of Christ [who] have taken their Jewish Communist manifesto, and incorporated it into the Statutory Laws of our country, and threw our Constitution and our Christian Common Law (which is none other than the Laws of God as set forth in the Scriptures) into the garbage can." To Kahl's mind, the United States was a "conquered and occupied nation, conquered and occupied by the Jews." White Christians, accordingly, were enmeshed in a life-or-death struggle "between the people of the Kingdom of God, and the Kingdom of Satan." He placed his faith in the Lord's hands. "I have no idea where I'm going," Kahl concludes the letter, "but after some more prayer, I will go where the Lord leads me, and either live to carry on the fight, or die if that be the case, and for the present at least, I bid you all good-bye."[80]

Kahl's odyssey took him through Texas and finally back to Arkansas. The subject of a massive FBI manhunt, he evaded his pursuers for four months until a crucial tip revealed that Kahl was hiding in the house of a fellow Posse member and survivalist named Leonard Ginter. It was the perfect bolt-hole. Ginter lived in the equivalent of a concrete bunker, built in anticipation, Ginter had told a neighbor, of the "end of time," which, he believed, was coming—just as the Bible had decreed. "But Russia is going to take over this country first," he had explained.[81]

On June 13, 1983, forty FBI agents, U.S. marshals, Arkansas state police, and local law enforcement officers, accompanied by an ambulance and a fire truck, surrounded the dwelling. Another shootout erupted, and both Kahl and Gene Matthews, the county sheriff, were killed. Unsure whether Kahl had only been wounded, the authorities dropped tear gas canisters, smoke grenades, and diesel fuel down the chimney to smoke him out. Instead, a fire started that burned out of control—fueled by the thousands of rounds of high-velocity ammunition stockpiled inside. Kahl's charred remains were later discovered with a bullet hole to his skull: Matthews had managed to shoot him just before being cut down himself by two shots from the fugitive farmer's Ruger Mini.[82]

Kahl was immediately hailed as a martyr by those sharing his dark, conspiratorial worldview. The government, they now firmly believed, had declared war on them.[83] And for at least two separate groups of likeminded violent extremists, it was now time to fight back. The Aryan Nations' annual gathering a few weeks' hence would provide the ideal setting to plan and coordinate this revolution. It was with this thought in mind that James Ellison, the leader of the CSA—the survivalist community located in rural Mountain Home, Arkansas, which Kahl and his wife had visited— loaded up the car and began the two-day drive north to Idaho.[84] He had been invited to deliver the event's closing address.[85]

• • •

Ellison conformed to the country cleric–turned–white supremacist model that seemed typical of the movement's leadership during the 1980s.

Hailing from San Antonio, Texas, he had gone from Bible teacher to fundamentalist minister. In 1976, according to FBI records, Ellison, then thirty-five, purchased an isolated 220-acre farm and former resort alongside Bull Shoals Lake on the Arkansas-Missouri border, about seven miles southwest of Pontiac, Missouri.[86] Ellison named it the Zarephath-Horeb Community Church, after two ancient biblical sites, and opened a rehabilitation center for young people addicted to drugs or seeking to escape religious cults they had joined.[87] Within a few years, however, according to Kerry Noble, an ordained minister in Ellison's church and the CSA's spokesman, the man revered by his followers as the self-professed "King James of the Ozarks"[88] had begun to steer the community away from the "quiet, rural community church" it once was "into a violent, paramilitary, right-wing, white supremacist group."[89] The change was prompted by a self-proclaimed divine vision Ellison had of the Lord visiting retribution upon America's cities because of the depravity and licentiousness that had "reached heights beyond that of the Tower of Babel." In his retelling of the vision, Ellison claimed that "the only hope for America . . . is for Christians to leave the cities and organized churches and . . . build refuges in isolated sections of the country, so others will have a place to come when the Tribulation period hits."[90] As an FBI assessment explained, the CSA was described as a

> non-traditional religion which includes faith healing, speaking in tongues, and a prophecy which says that society will soon collapse in turmoil, and that the United States will suffer a collapse of economy or nuclear war. As a result, there will be chaos, and the panicked masses will rove the country looking for food and protection. Those who are not prepared will be a threat to those who have been preparing. . . . In preparation for this, the group stockpiles food and weapons and trains themselves in military and survival procedures.[91]

Between 1978 and 1979 alone, the community purchased over fifty thousand dollars' worth of firearms, ammunition, and military equipment. "Every man was issued a pistol and rifle, with full military gear," Reverend Noble recalled, and received training in marksmanship and combat skills.[92] The FBI would subsequently describe the CSA as "the best trained civilian paramilitary group in America."[93] The 100–120 men, women, and children[94] who by this time inhabited the CSA compound were tasked by Ellison "to build an Ark for God's people during the coming tribulations on the earth."[95] The "coming war," they were taught, "was a step toward God's government."[96] Then, in 1981, Ellison decreed that henceforth the community would be called the Covenant, the Sword, and the Arm of the Lord. "The Covenant speaks of all the covenants of God from Adam to Christ," he told his followers,

> and especially of the covenants He has made with us in this last hour. It also speaks to the covenant that He has made with each of you individually and that you have made with Him and with each other and with this Body.
>
> The Sword speaks of all the judgments of God from the time of the Garden, but especially of the coming judgment upon America. The Arm is those people whom God will use to administer the final end-time judgement. And we are part of that people.[97]

This accorded perfectly with the CSA's own white supremacist positions, which since at least 1979 had followed the tenets of the Identity Church.[98] Noble recounts the consequences of this transformation. "As white supremacists, we now believed that other races and those who would betray the white cause in America were destined to be destroyed in future chaos. We were now not only the elect spiritually, but racially as well." Antisemitism was at the core of their beliefs and ZOG—the Zionist Occupation Government—their ineluctable enemy. "The Jews have declared war on our race," Ellison preached, "promoting race-mixing and thereby polluting the pure seed of God."[99] As Noble explains, "As with others in the right-wing movement we blamed the Jews for the problems of the world, for pornography, the lack of morality, for the economic situation in America, for minority rights over white rights, and for kicking God out of the schools. Even though most of us had never personally known a Jew, we became convinced they were the enemies of God . . . that would one day need to be taken and destroyed."[100]

To prepare for this eventuality, the community supported itself through timber sales, a salvaging business, construction projects, and a mail-order publishing house. Among the titles they marketed were such antisemitic staples as *The Protocols of the Elders of Zion* as well as *The Holy Book of*

Adolf Hitler, The Negro and the World Crisis, Who's Who in the Zionist Conspiracy, The Jews: 100 Facts, and the *Christian Army Basic Training Manual*.[101] But there was an additional, more sinister dimension to the CSA's commercial activities. The group's gunsmiths were adept at retooling legally purchased semiautomatic weapons—Israeli Uzis, Chinese-made AK-47s, German Heckler & Koch assault rifles, and U.S.-manufactured MAC-10s and MAC-11s—into illegal, fully automatic submachine guns, whose sale they profited handsomely from. Additional income was generated from the various training courses that the CSA also offered. Among these, the most infamous was the urban warfare course taught at the group's four-block mock town dubbed "Silhouette City."[102] Patterned on the FBI Academy's storied "Hogan's Alley" training facility,[103] the CSA version featured pop-up targets of African American and Jewish people as well as police officers with a Star of David in place of their badges.[104] As the previously mentioned FBI analysis explained, the suite of CSA training courses included "instruction on organization, survival techniques, and para-military topics. Also taught are firearms and marksmanship, repelling, foraging for food, erection of such obstacles as punji sticks and barbed wire to detour [sic] looters, urban warfare, military field craft, national forest survival, home defense, Christian martial arts, Christian military truths, nuclear survival and tax protesting."[105] Kahl was among the graduates of some of these courses, which typically cost five hundred dollars.[106]

Noble recalled that Ellison returned from the Aryan Nations Congress infused with new energy and a new purpose. "Thirteen men from various right-wing organizations met in Idaho," the CSA leader recounted. "We discussed Gordon Kahl when the feds found him in Arkansas. I said I wished I'd been there, the sword is now out of the sheath, and it's ready to strike." Plans were laid, Ellison continued, to finance the revolution through counterfeiting, bank robbery, and attacking armored cars transporting cash—just like left-wing radicals had done. A hit list was drawn up of prominent capitalists, Jews, and other "people who need to be eliminated," as was a point scale created to incentivize Aryan warriors to assassinate those named on the list along with African Americans, federal agents, and others. "There was also talk about 'Silent Warriors,'" he explained, "who would go out alone and commit crimes and not tell anyone what they had done," as well as autonomous attack cells composed of no more than two to five men, to preserve operational security. "At the close of the meeting," Ellison somberly concluded, "I passed a sheet of paper for everyone to sign, which they did. Then I told them that they had just committed conspiracy and treason against the United States of America, that the revolution had begun!"[107] Another account of this private meeting convened by Butler in the compound's Aryan Hall claims that many of the signatories believed they were simply providing their names and addresses for a mailing list and not agreeing to a battle plan for sedition. Regardless, at least some of the men present at the 1983 congress had reached the irrevocable conclusion that the time for talk and bluster had passed. Among them was Robert Mathews.[108]

• • •

In July 1983 the thirty-year-old Mathews was a rising star in the white power movement. He had both impressed Butler and was sufficiently integrated into the Aryan Nations family to have had the Christian Identity pastor baptize his adopted son. Mathews had also distinguished himself as the most proactive member of Butler's personal security detail at an Aryan Nations rally held in Spokane, Washington, a month earlier. The muscular, boyish-looking Mathews was not tall, but he had a commanding presence and magnetic personality.[109] He was "enormously charismatic," one contemporary observer noted,[110] and thus was well situated in the wake of Kahl's killing to translate the movement's hate-filled and seditious rhetoric into concrete action. Mathews was particularly moved by the exhortations of one speaker at the 1983 gathering—Louis Beam, the Aryan Nations' "ambassador at large" and a former Grand Dragon of the Texas Ku Klux Klan.

With the exception of Pierce, perhaps no one has had as great an influence on the modern white power movement as Beam. A decorated U.S. Army veteran who had served an extended eighteen-month tour as a helicopter door gunner in Vietnam, Beam had grown up in a segregated company town on Texas's gulf coast. He was apparently already a committed racist while still in elementary school.[111] Classmates recall Beam boasting in the fourth grade about being a member of the Ku Klux Klan and attempting to recruit them.[112] Beam returned from Vietnam in 1968 disgruntled and disillusioned. He railed against flag-burning antiwar protestors and blamed the "communists" in the U.S. government for restraining the military in Vietnam and thus selling out him and his fellow warriors in an unwinnable war. He promptly joined the local chapter of the Ku Klux Klan.[113] Years later, Beam would blame "Post Viet Nam Stress Syndrome" for his anger toward the government. "There is no relief, and can be none," he ranted in one treatise.

> We are forever trapped in the rice paddies and skies of Vietnam. We can neither go back or go forward, but are suspended for eternity in the place that they put us. . . .
>
> I wonder if stress can be defined as wanting to machine gun all the people who sent us over there, along with the ones who spit on us when we returned. Or, is perhaps stress something more simple like crying out for justice in the name of the mangled dead, and not being heard? Or is stress more of a mathematical function, like trying to figure out how much blood 57,673 bodies can hold?[114]

In 1971 Beam was charged with the bombings of a progressive radio station and the Houston office of the Socialist Workers Party but escaped imprisonment.[115] Thereafter, he organized a series of paramilitary training courses in Texas designed "to turn Klansmen into soldiers."[116] Beam ran at least four such facilities. At "Camp Puller," a fifty-acre tract of swampland reminiscent of Vietnam's rice paddies, both teenagers and children—some reportedly as young as eight years old—received instruction in "strangulation, decapitation using a machete, hijacking airplanes, and firing automatic weapons." As Beam ascended through the Klan ranks from Grand Titan to Grand Dragon, he also created two elite, special operations–type units for his fellow Klansmen—the Texas Emergency Reserve and anti-immigrant Klan Border Watch. Beam also organized Klan recruitment drives at Fort Hood in Killeen, Texas, and rallies featuring David Duke, the smooth-talking Louisiana-based founder and leader of the Knights of the Ku Klux Klan.[117] Duke represented a new kind of hatemonger. He wore a suit and tie, came across as educated and articulate, and claimed that he was not against blacks as much as he was an advocate for the rights of white Christians.[118] This would prove to be a harbinger of a wider trend reflected in today's alt-right, for example, the polo shirts and chinos worn by neo-Nazis at the 2017 Charlottesville demonstrations and other protests.[119]

Beam was again arrested in 1979 after trying to gain entrance to the Houston hotel where Vice Premier Deng Xiaoping of China was staying. He hoped to murder Deng and thereby avenge "the 100,000 GI's" who perished because of the support China had provided to North Vietnam during the war.[120] As the state's preeminent Klan leader, Beam attracted widespread attention in February 1981 for his role in the Texas chapter's sustained harassment of Vietnamese fishermen working the gulf waters off Galveston. Within months, however, a combination of a federal court ruling specifically prohibiting such activities along with Beam's conviction on misdemeanor charges of conducting paramilitary exercises on federal land without a permit prompted him to resign as Grand Dragon and head to Idaho—supposedly on vacation. Two months later, Beam and his family were still there—living at the Aryan Nations' Hayden Lake compound. His arrival had attracted the attention of the local FBI office in Coeur d'Alene, who would soon have him under surveillance. In 1982, Butler appointed Beam the Aryan Nations' "ambassador at large."[121] This new role suited the energetic former Klansman well, and soon Aryan Nations chapters had been established in Colorado, Florida, Missouri, Tennessee, and Texas.[122]

Beam claims to have opened a business in Hayden Lake selling survival and camping gear and spent most of his time drinking coffee and changing his infant daughter's diapers.[123] In fact, his time spent in Idaho would have a lasting effect not only on future white power violence but on the trajectory of modern terrorism. Beam's lasting contribution was to rescue from obscurity the concept of clandestine, underground warfare known as "leaderless resistance." Writing in a 1983 issue of the *Inter-Klan Newsletter and Survival Alert*, which he coedited, Beam explained the principles of an approach to warfare that a World War II veteran of the Office of Strategic Services (OSS)—a forerunner of the CIA—named Colonel Ulius Louis "Pete" Amoss had developed.[124] Exasperated by the Soviet bloc's ability to penetrate and neutralize traditional, hierarchically organized partisan units and other resistance forces, the wartime spy and inveterate cold warrior concluded that "we do not need 'leaders'; we need leading ideas. These ideas would produce leaders. The masses would produce them and the ideas would be their inspiration. Therefore, we must create these ideas and convey them to the restless people concerned with them."[125]

This was music to Beam's ears. He and his fellow white power leaders were continually frustrated by the ability of government informants and undercover agents to penetrate their movement. This concept, the Aryan Nations' newly appointed ambassador-at-large now enthused, "is that any one cell can be infiltrated, exposed and destroyed, but this will have no effect on the others. . . . The efficient and effective operation of a cell system . . . of course, is dependent upon central direction which means impressive organization, [and] funding from the top." Beam identified only one significant hurdle. "At first glance, such a type of organization seems unrealistic, because the natural question is, how are the cells to cooperate with each other, when there is not intercommunication or central direction?"[126] By the time of the Aryan Nations Congress just weeks later, he would have a solution to that challenge, too.

Gordon Kahl's fate loomed large as the attendees gathered in Hayden Lake. In a stirring panegyric by Beam, the North Dakota farmer was hailed as a modern-day William Travis and Davy Crockett—akin to these brave warriors who had made the ultimate sacrifice in the fight against tyranny at the Alamo. Beam also glowingly described Kahl's imagined ascent to heaven, complete with a Viking honor guard "standing at the gate to Valhalla—arms outstretched in salute."[127] Addressing the congress, Beam was just as blunt and unequivocal. "WE ARE AT WAR," he declared.[128] An attendee would later recall that Beam's words brought tears to Mathews's eyes.[129] "I'm here to tell you that if we can't have this country," Beam continued, "as far as I'm concerned no one gets it. The guns are cocked, the bullets are in the chamber. . . . We're going to fight and live or we're going to die soon. If you don't help me kill the bastards, you're going to be required to beg for your child's life, and the answer will be no."[130]

In addition to the workshops, seminars, and plenary events, a small group of thirteen white power leaders and movement elders, along with their impatient youthful counterparts, met privately in Butler's living room—surrounded by heavily armed guards. As Ellison later told Noble, the gathering agreed that it was "time for action."[131] The battle plan that emerged reflected both Beam's leaderless resistance strategy and his proposal to utilize emerging computer networking technology to ensure the security of the movement's internal communications and support the revolution that they had agreed to commence.[132] Leaderless resistance fused with computerized bulletin board systems (BBSes) brought the movement unparalleled advantages of both real-time and clandestine connectivity—effectively concealing it from the prying eyes and attentive ears of federal authorities.[133]

It is difficult to appreciate just how singularly profound this development was. Typewriters were still a ubiquitous feature of offices everywhere, and facsimile transmission (fax) machines had only recently entered the workplace.[134] Desktop computers were both mostly unknown and expensive to acquire. At the time, these primitive machines, with their limited memory and slow processing capabilities, were far from the must-have household item they would eventually become. An Apple IIe starter system with 64k memory, for instance, cost $1,260 in 1983—about $3,315 today.[135] And modems (modulator-demodulators) to transmit BBS data over conventional telephone lines had only become affordable and hence somewhat accessible some two years earlier.[136]

The "Aryan Nations Liberty Net" that Beam created was therefore truly revolutionary and arguably marked the beginning of terrorist exploitation of digital communications for radicalization, recruitment, fundraising, the exchange of best practices, and the planning and execution of operations. In an era before the World Wide Web, much less the internet, and with primitive dial-up rather than wi-fi and broadband, Beam's system ran on Apple network software, was text only, and used 300 baud dial-up modems[137] over ordinary telephone lines to transmit information.[138] The rate of transmission of data was described as "well below reading speed."[139] It took Beam nearly a year of work before his Aryan Nations Liberty Net was finally up and running. As he had intimated in his article on leaderless resistance,[140] Beam announced this new development in the spring 1984 issue of the *Inter-Klan Newsletter & Survival Alert*. "It may very well be that American know-how has provided the technology which will allow those who love this country to save it from an ill deserved fate," he gushed.

Computers, once solely the domain and possession of governments and large corporations, are now bringing their power and capabilities to the average American. . . .

It has been said that knowledge is power, which it most assuredly is. The computer offers, to those who become proficient in its use, power undreamed of by the rulers of the past. . . .

Imagine, if you can, a single computer to which all leaders and strategists of the patriotic movement are connected. Imagine further that any patriot in the country is able to tap into this computer at will in order to reap the benefit of all accumulative knowledge and wisdom of the leaders. "Someday," you may say? How about today? Such a computer is already in existence and operation. We hereby announce Aryan Nation Liberty Net. Dial 208-772-6134, listen to the computer talk.

The article, titled "COMPUTERS AND THE AMERICAN PATRIOT," also imparted helpful buyers' advice and detailed log-on instructions. Beam provided a phone number and post office box for those who had additional questions. "At last, those who love God and their Race and strive to serve their Nation will be utilizing some of the advanced technology available heretofore only to those in the ZOG (Zionist Occupation Government) government [*sic*] and others who have sought the destruction of the Aryan people," he promised.[141]

Sponsored by the Aryan Nations, the Aryan Nations Liberty Net served five key purposes. First, it sought to tap into a new demographic and build a broader white supremacist constituency by appealing to young computer "hackers"—a newly popularized term at the time. Second, it sought to obviate restrictions on the mailing of hate literature to Canada and European countries like West Germany. Third, it identified like-minded "patriotic groups" across the country to encourage and facilitate greater networking. Fourth, it was an innovative fundraising mechanism. "The Aryan Nations computer network is designed to bring truth and knowledge to our people on the North-American continent," Butler explained in one such appeal for donations. "You may ask 'why the computer . . technology?' The answer is simple, because it is our Aryan technology just as is the printing press, radio, airplane, auto, etc., etc. We must use our own God-given technology in calling our race back to our Father's Organic

Law." Finally, it was an inexpensive, quick, and easy way to spread the movement's propaganda unhindered by government interference, intrusion, or monitoring. The site contained some repackaged material that had originally appeared in print along with files with titles like "Know Your Enemy," which contained the addresses and telephone numbers of all the ADL offices in the United States, as well as those of the branches of the U.S. Communist Party and, even more menacingly, lists of the names of "race traitors" and "ZOG informers."[142] In perhaps the first warning about far-right exploitation of new online technologies, the ADL in 1985 cautioned that the networks were "[seeking] to spread their hate propaganda among young people, surely the most vulnerable to its influence." The report also drew a direct link to violence. "More troubling," the report noted, "the use of new technology to link together hate group activists coincides with an escalation of serious talk among some of them about the necessity of committing acts of terror."[143]

As previously recounted, Beam's call to battle at the 1983 congress had deeply resonated with Mathews. The former Klansman had been unequivocal. Violence was imperative if the white race was to save itself. Mathews departed Hayden Lake infused with a newfound sense of mission and purpose.[144] Beam's powerful words in addition to everything else Mathews had heard at the gathering and likely at the private meeting in Butler's living room had convinced him, according to the journalist Stephen Singular, that "it would be the young men who commenced the battle and won the war." Mathews had in fact already reached this conclusion. Everything that he heard and saw during that visit to the Aryan Nations compound had only hardened his resolve. Earlier that year, for instance, Mathews had formed a new organization that he called the White American Bastion. Mathews recruited friends and acquaintances from the northern Idaho white supremacist milieu and with two companions had spent the summer building the group's headquarters and a living quarters on his farm.[145]

In Mathews's "Last Letter," written over a year later, he explained the logic animating his decision to wage a terrorist campaign to overthrow the U.S. government. "I have no choice," Mathews had declared. "I must stand up like a White man and do battle. A secret war has been developing for the last year between the regime in Washington and an ever growing number of White people who are determined to regain what our forefathers discovered, explored, conquered, settled, built and died for."[146]

In September 1983, Mathews addressed the National Alliance's annual conference in Washington, DC. His membership in and recruitment efforts on behalf of multiple white supremacist organizations was hardly atypical of the movement either then or now. As the journalist Peter Lake, who successfully infiltrated these groups, later explained, "It's like the difference between the Army, Navy, and Marines—they all salute the same flag."[147] Indeed, unbeknownst to the conferees listening, Mathews's message presaged the violent trajectory he was about to embark upon. "My brothers and sisters," he began,

> from the mist-shrouded forested valleys and mountains of the Pacific Northwest I bring you a message of solidarity, a call to action, and a demand for adherence to duty as members of a vanguard of an Aryan resurgence and ultimately total Aryan victory. The signs of awakening are sprouting up across the Northwest, and no more than among the two-fisted farmers and ranchers. . . . The task is not going to be easy. TV satellite dishes are springing up like poisonous mushrooms across the domain of the tillers of the soil. The electronic Jew is slithering into the living rooms of even the most remote farms and ranches. The race-destroying dogs are everywhere. In Metaline Falls, we have broken the chains of Jewish thought. . . . The future is now! So stand up like men and drive the enemy to the sea! Stand up like men and swear a sacred oath upon the green graves of our sires that you will reclaim what our forefathers discovered, explored, conquered, settled, built, and died for! Stand up like men and reclaim our soil! Look toward the stars and proclaim our destiny! In Metaline Falls we have a saying: Defeat, never! Victory forever![148]

Three weeks later, nine men styling themselves as "Aryan Warriors"[149] joined hands in a circle around a white baby girl meant to symbolize the Aryan race and its future. In appropriately reverential voices they pledged fealty to the white supremacist revolution proclaimed by Mathews.[150] "I, as a free Aryan man, hereby swear an unrelenting oath," they affirmed,

> upon the green graves of our sires, upon the children in the wombs of our wives, upon the throne of God almighty, sacred is his name, to join together in holy union with those brothers in this circle and to declare

forthright that from this moment on, I have no fear of death, no fear of foe; that I have a sacred duty to do whatever is necessary to deliver our people from the Jew and to bring total victory to the Aryan race.[151]

The FBI agent in charge of the Coeur d'Alene office, whose attention they soon attracted, found nothing particularly noteworthy about the group. They were people "much like your next door neighbor,"[152] Wayne F. Manis observed. Indeed, the youngest person around the circle, Richard Kemp, age twenty, had been a star player on his Salinas, California, high school basketball team. Andrew Barnhill was a twenty-seven-year-old former seminarian who had joined and then left the CSA before ending up dealing poker in a Montana casino. Bruce Pierce (no relation to William), at age twenty-nine, was an impetuous drifter from Kentucky who had settled in Montana and discovered Identity theology only the previous year. An invitation to visit the Aryan Nations compound in March 1983 had sufficiently impressed him that he moved his family to Hayden Lake. Two months later, Pierce was among the bodyguards surrounding Butler at the same Spokane rally where Mathews had distinguished himself. Pierce decided then and there that Mathews was the leader that the white power movement had always been waiting for.[153]

Although the prematurely balding thirty-two-year-old Randy Duey looked like a "meek accountant,"[154] he was a U.S. Air Force veteran who had studied history at Eastern Washington University, just across the Idaho state border. Duey had befriended Denver Parmenter, another mature student and a fellow veteran. Age thirty-one, Parmenter had served three years in the U.S. Army and was washing dishes and mopping floors to make ends meet when Duey introduced him to Mathews. Richard Scutari arguably had the most diverse career of the men who gathered that day at Mathews's farm. In his mid-thirties, Scutari had been a U.S. Navy diver where he supposedly gained experience "with explosives training and [became an] instructor in hand-to-hand combat as well as assault rifle and combat pistol shooting."[155] Scutari then worked as a deep-sea diver in the North Sea oil fields, owned a construction company for a time, and became expert in several different martial arts. Through his friendship with Barnhill, Scutari had done some work for the CSA's Jim Ellison and then had flown to Spokane from his home in Florida to meet Mathews and check out this new group.[156]

David Lane, age forty-three, was the eldest. An amateur golf champion who hailed from Aurora, Colorado, Lane had made a name for himself in white power circles as the state organizer for David Duke's Knights of the Ku Klux Klan and later for the Aryan Nations. He was also an accomplished propagandist, having helped turn the innocuously titled *Primrose and Cattlemen's Gazette* into a platform for his violently antisemitic rants.[157] Lane is also renowned as the author of the popular white supremacist credo known as the "14 Words," which proclaims the following mission for white supremacists everywhere: "We must secure the existence of our people and a future for White children." It is frequently cited in contemporary white power memes, publications, and communications simply as "14."[158] The only person in the circle who had done time was a twenty-seven-year old from Arizona named Gary Lee Yarbrough. While AWOL from the U.S. Marines, Yarbrough was arrested for burglary and sentenced to a five-to-eight-year prison term at the Arizona State Penitentiary in Florence. It was there that he first read about the Aryan Nations and imbibed its literature. Yarbrough headed for Idaho upon his release and found work on Butler's personal security detail and in the print shop producing hate literature.[159]

Although their ages and backgrounds varied, these men were united by the belief of an America gone wrong. Although, unlike Beam, they had not fought in Vietnam, they were patriots who were profoundly disillusioned with a government that had sent its young citizens overseas to fight a needlessly prolonged and increasingly pointless war. Their view, like Beam's, was that spineless politicians had restrained the military and squandered an opportunity to stop the spread of communism. As white men in a demographically changing United States, they also felt alienated by a population that was becoming increasingly more diverse. They were especially opposed to affirmative action efforts and other such compensatory programs and themselves felt economically ignored or disadvantaged.[160] "As adults, they came to view America as a land beset with dark forces of chaos in the forms of immigration, drugs, crime, and Ronald Reagan's 'trickle down' economy," the criminologist Mark Hamm explains. The Equal Rights Amendment, passed by the U.S. Congress in 1972, which would have constitutionally guaranteed legal gender equality for women and men had it been ratified by the requisite number of states, was also vehemently opposed by this movement. Feminism was regarded as emasculation and thus became a key dimension of white supremacism's simultaneous advocacy that relegated women back to narrow, historically gendered roles as cook, cleaner, and mother. Accordingly, Hamm notes, "Masculinity and whiteness became entwined as never before—to be a 'real' white man was to be hyper-masculine. In this way, paramilitary mythology became the path to redemption."[161]

Having sworn unremitting allegiance to the "sacred duty to do whatever is necessary" to ensure the triumph of the Aryan race, the eight men listened as Mathews outlined his plan. It was drawn entirely from *The Turner Diaries*.[162] Although at that moment these men referred to themselves simply as "the Group" or "the Company," they would soon adopt the name "the Order"—in homage to Pierce's fictional creation.[163] They also sometimes called themselves the Brüder Schweigen (German for the "Silent Brotherhood").[164] The book had in fact become Mathews's "bible," according to both Thomas Martinez, a later recruit and subsequent FBI informant, and Wayne Manis, the veteran FBI agent who had arrived in Coeur d'Alene that November to oversee the bureau's investigation of this regional hub of white supremacist activism.[165] That a novel should provide the "blueprint"[166] for the real-life Order's terrorist campaign underscores how unprepared the group was for so monumental a task as triggering an uprising that would overthrow the U.S. government. "Many of Bob's followers were in a state of shock to suddenly come to grips with the fact that they were about to leave their mundane day-to-day existence as law-abiding citizens and embark on a career of crime with the goal of overthrowing the United States government," Manis marveled. "Clearly, this would entail taking up arms and killing people who were the object of their aggression and hatred."[167] But however fantastical the Order's grandiose ambitions may have been, their fervent belief in the efficacy of violence to achieve them was completely serious. This would not be the last time that *The Turner Diaries* would fulfill the dual role of template and inspiration for violent insurrection.

Accordingly, what the Order lacked in operational skills and experience was simply to be adopted from *The Turner Diaries* and grafted onto their six-step strategy. First was organizing themselves to prosecute this revolution. The next steps of amassing a "war chest"—and then resorting to armed robbery, if necessary—had been identified two months earlier in Butler's living room.[168] Robert Miles had persuasively argued that to have any chance of success, such a venture would require ample funds. A Grand Dragon of a Michigan KKK chapter, "Pastor Bob" was a well-respected elder statesman of the white supremacist movement. He had the bona fides and gravitas that a six-year prison stint for conspiring to bomb school buses in defiance of court-ordered school desegregation efforts inevitably bestows on the self-styled community of "Aryan Warriors" in which racists like Miles circulated. Like many of its other leading figures, Miles cloaked himself in clerical authority—presiding over the Mountain Church of Jesus Christ the Savior that he founded on his seventy-acre farm in rural Cohoctah, Michigan.[169] It was in essence a Midwestern version of Butler's Church of Jesus Christ Christian, performing a similar convening and coordinating function. The ADL described the church's ethos as "violence, white supremacy, antisemitism, and racism, as well as hostility to the federal government."[170] At Butler's house that July, Miles had cited the success that left-wing terrorists in the Black Liberation Army along with remnants of the rebranded Weather Underground, now calling themselves the May 19th Communist Organization, had two years before in robbing a Brinks armored car of $1.6 million in Nyack, New York. "If we were half the men the leftists were," the fifty-eight-year-old cleric had observed, "we'd be hitting armored cars, too."[171] Hence, Mathews and his band concluded the best way to build the "war chest" they required was through armed robbery. The fourth step was to recruit more members; fifth was to commence operations with the assassination of the movement's most insidious enemies; and the sixth step would culminate in the "armed guerrilla operations"[172] by a dedicated band of clandestine warriors depicted in *The Turner Diaries*.

Less than fifteen months later, however, Mathews was dead. Twenty-four of his followers would soon be arrested. They were indicted on sixty-seven racketeering and conspiracy counts, and all but one was convicted.[173] Of these, ten received prison sentences of between twenty years and life. None of the Order's grand schemes to jumpstart their terrorist campaign with the assassinations of well-known Jewish persons such as former secretary of state Henry Kissinger; Elie de Rothschild, scion of the famous international banking family; and the renowned television producer Norman Lear; or gentiles like the prominent New York banker David Rockefeller or the civil rights advocate Morris Dees, the cofounder and chief trial counsel of the Southern Poverty Law Center, ever came to fruition. Instead, on June 18, 1984, the Order's gunmen murdered Alan Berg, a controversial Denver radio talk show host,[174] who was Jewish and had incurred the group's wrath because of his combative on-air interviews of various white power advocates. Although no one was ever specifically convicted of Berg's murder, David Lane and Bruce Pierce initially received prison sentences of forty and one hundred years, respectively, in one trial and an additional 150 years on other charges.[175] Lane had been one of the enraged persons who would call in during Berg's broadcasts.[176] Even the group's initial effort to acquire operational funds fell flat. The robbery of a Spokane video and pornography store netted only $369,[177] and an exploding dye pack concealed in a bundle of cash Mathews had just stolen from a Seattle bank had blown up in his face and either ruined or permanently stained the bank notes.[178]

But by heeding Miles's advice and focusing their attention on armored cars, the Order's fundraising efforts grew more successful. Three such heists enabled Mathews and his band to accumulate over $4 million in cash.[179] The single largest haul of $3.6 million came from the combined ambush and armed robbery of a Brinks armored car near Ukiah, California, in July 1984.[180] After the seven gunmen each pocketed $40,000 themselves as combined salary and bonus,[181] Mathews proceeded to distribute a portion of the loot to some of the white power movement's leading personages. Dan Gayman, the pastor of the Church of Israel, outside Schell City, Missouri, and an exponent of the "two seed" theory, was given $10,000; Butler and the Aryan Nations received at least $40,000; William Pierce was reportedly gifted $50,000; Frazier Glenn Miller Jr., the founder and leader of the North Carolina–based White Patriot Party, got $200,000; and $300,000 was reputedly channeled to Californian Tom Metzger for his White Aryan Resistance group, with the same amount going to Miles for his Michigan parish.[182]

Even so, the bulk of the stolen cash was neither ever recovered nor fully accounted for. As much as two-thirds of it seems to have disappeared. As of 1997, for instance, the FBI had traced only $600,000 of the Ukiah haul.[183] Mathews and other Order members appear to have variously spent, doled out, stashed, or laundered the rest of their haul into legitimate business ventures. Two government informants, for instance, maintain that Mathews gave a Denver lawyer at least $1 million and perhaps as much as $2 million to invest on behalf of the movement.[184] An additional 10 percent of the stolen cash was supposedly donated to the Aryan Nations—in addition to the sum given to Butler after the Ukiah robbery. One of Mathews's other followers claimed to have dug up $100,000 that had been secretly buried on a farm in the Pacific Northwest and to have handed it to Beam.[185] And Mathews reputedly opened a surrogate mother program and sperm bank in Portland, Oregon, to promote the propagation of the Aryan race.[186]

It was the group's counterfeiting scheme, however, that arguably led to its demise. Less than two months after the oath-taking ceremony, Bruce Pierce was arrested in Union Gap, Washington, trying to pass the group's amateurishly produced initial run of $50 banknotes. Although he jumped bail and disappeared, the FBI now had Pierce firmly in their sights.[187] A weapon inadvertently left behind by Mathews during the Ukiah armored car robbery that had been legally purchased by Andrew Barnhill in Montana provided another key lead.[188]

By September, more than a hundred FBI agents were deployed against the Order. Nearly half that number was assigned to the hitherto tiny Coeur d'Alene office, with some forty agents actively watching the last known residences of Mathews, Parmenter, and Yarbrough, among others.[189] The following month, Yarbrough spotted a U.S. Forest Service vehicle on the backwoods dirt road leading to his house. Guessing correctly that it was the FBI in disguise, he opened fire on the truck, stopping the agents in their tracks. Although Yarbrough managed to flee, the search of his house netted important evidence. By this point, all the Order's key personnel were on the run. In hopes of escaping the FBI dragnet closing in on them, Mathews, Yarbrough, Scutari, and Frank DeSilva, a recent recruit, fled to Oregon.[190]

Then, in November 1984, Thomas Martinez, whom Mathews had recruited to the group, was arrested in Philadelphia passing a phony banknote. He agreed to become an FBI informant and soon after flew west to meet with Mathews in Portland.[191] The FBI raided the motel they were staying in on November 24, 1984. Mathews and Yarbrough tried to shoot their way out. Although Mathews escaped, Yarbrough was arrested. But the net around Mathews was tightening.[192] In a desperate act of defiance, Mathews fired one last rhetorical salvo at the government that was relentlessly closing in. As Alan Berg's biographer Stephen Singular observed of the document, "Earl Turner would have been proud."[193] The Order's formal "Declaration of War," dated November 25, 1984, attacked immigration from the Southern Hemisphere as well as legalized abortion. It decried capitalists and communists as well as bankers and Jews. Kahl's heroism was lauded and the "Government agents" that "shot him in the back" decried. In words reminiscent of much contemporary discourse, Mathews proclaimed:

> We will resign ourselves no more to be ruled by a government based on mobocracy. We, from this day forward declare that we no longer consider the regime in Washington to be a valid and lawful representative of all Aryans who refuse to submit to the coercion and subtle tyranny placed upon us by Tel Aviv and their lackeys in Washington. We recognize that the mass of our people have been put into a lobotomized, lethargic state of blind obedience and we will not take party anymore in collective racial suicide!

A similarly verbose "Open Letter to the U.S. Congress" was appended. It blamed the country's elected representatives "for what has happened to America" and vowed ominously to hold each one responsible. Although neither Mathews nor Pierce nor Scutari nor Duey nor any of the three other signatories had ever served in Vietnam, they still pledged that they would exact revenge for the "betrayal of the 55,000 Americans who were sacrificed." The "anti-American 'Israel Lobby'" was castigated for its steady erosion of the Second Amendment. Fascinatingly, common cause was made with "our Arab friends," whom the U.S. government was blamed for having turned "into enemies." After citing the Vietnam War again, the letter concluded with an ominous warning. "When the Day comes, we will not ask whether you swung to the right or whether you swung to the left; we will simply swing you by the neck. . . . With these things said, let the battle begin."[194] It was over less than two weeks later.

At 4:00 AM on December 7, about a hundred FBI agents converged on a two-story wood chalet on Whidbey Island—a vacation area at the mouth of Puget Sound in Washington State. The Seattle field office had received a tip that Mathews was hiding there. He had a 9mm Uzi submachine gun, thousands of rounds of ammunition, and a gas mask. An FBI negotiator tried to talk Mathews into surrendering. "I have been a good soldier, a fearless warrior," the Order leader responded. "I will die with honor and join my brothers in Valhalla." As the siege dragged on, the following afternoon the FBI resorted to tear gas, hoping to force Mathews out of the dwelling. More than 250 canisters were fired into its upper floor, where Mathews had taken refuge, with no result. An FBI SWAT team preceded by blindingly loud flash-bang grenades gained access to the ground floor but was met with a hail of machine-gun fire and forced to retreat. As darkness fell, the FBI summoned a helicopter to illuminate the scene—which attracted more gunfire from Mathews as he attempted to shoot it down. An illumination flare was then fired into the chalet's ground floor in hopes of lighting the way for a more successful SWAT assault. The wood-frame house caught fire and was rapidly engulfed in flames. Mathews refused to leave and perished—just as he had promised.[195]

As Noble observed, "The right-wing now had its second significant martyr."[196]

3

RACE WAR

October 28, 1991. . . . *One of the major purposes of political terror, always and everywhere, is to force the authorities to take reprisals and to become more repressive, thus alienating a portion of the population and generating sympathy for the terrorists. And the other purpose is to create unrest by destroying the population's sense of security and their belief in the invincibility of the government.*

—EARL TURNER, IN *THE TURNER DIARIES*

The Order's brief but violent existence laid bare a wider conspiracy that literally stretched from north to south and from coast to coast. Just by following the money that the group had distributed from its armored car robberies and counterfeiting ventures, the FBI was able to map a network that extended far beyond the rural corner of Idaho that was home to Robert Mathews and the Aryan Nations. Its recipients included leading white supremacists and their organizations in Michigan and Missouri, California and North Carolina, Arkansas and Virginia. What federal authorities previously had regarded as a variegated but mostly isolated and individually distinct collection of likeminded hatemongers and hotheads was now seen as a far more coordinated and insidious threat.

The ground around the wood cabin where Mathews met his fiery death had barely cooled when less than two weeks later, federal attorneys from Alabama, California, Colorado, Idaho, Oregon, and Washington State met in Seattle to compare notes and plan the government's response. They were especially alarmed by how closely Mathews's strategy and the Order's actions had followed the battle plan depicted in *The Turner Diaries*. Among the evidence seized in the ongoing FBI investigations had been the blueprints for a large hydroelectric dam on the Pend Oreille River in northeastern Washington State. Given that attacks on public utilities figured prominently in the novel, this discovery evoked heightened concern. Revelations about the existence of the movement's two technologically cutting-edge Aryan Nations Liberty Net bulletin boards further underscored the ambitious coordination efforts and more wide-ranging conspiratorial dimensions of the movement.[1] Federal agents had marveled at the array of similarly off-the-shelf but high-tech equipment seized from Order members—including computers, programmable radio scanners, transceivers, and voice-stress analyzers—gear not usually found in possession of other domestic terrorists of that era.[2] Commenting on the movement in January 1985, Stanley E. Morris, the director of the U.S. Marshals Service, observed that its adherents "commit illegal acts but wrap themselves in the American flag . . . assault the police but view themselves as religious and God-fearing . . . [and] talk of freedom but support virulent racial and religious bigotry."[3] A confrontation on a quiet stretch of road in Missouri three months later would prove the acuity of his assessment.

• • •

On April 15, 1985, two state troopers, Jimmie Linegar and Allen Hines, were conducting routine traffic stops on opposite sides of an intersection outside Branson, Missouri, just north of the Arkansas border. At 1:45 PM Linegar pulled over a brown 1975 Chevy van with Nevada plates. The driver produced an Oregon driver's license in the name of Matthew Mark Samuels. Hines's patrol car was closer, so Linegar used its radio to communicate the information to a dispatcher, who fed it into the relevant law enforcement computer databases. An alert flashed that Samuels was a possible alias. Linegar signaled to Hines to come over to him, and the two men briefly conferred. The two troopers exited the vehicle and cautiously approached the van: Linegar on the driver's side and Hines on the passenger side. Seated behind the wheel, watching intently from the van's two side-view mirrors, was a man from Athol, Idaho, whose real name was David Tate. He was holding an illegally modified fully automatic MAC-10 submachine gun—the same type of weapon used to murder Alan Berg the previous June.[4]

Although only twenty-two years old, Tate had been deeply immersed in white supremacy almost his entire life. He was still a child when his family relocated from California to Idaho specifically to be near Pastor Butler and his Church of Jesus Christ Christian. They purchased a dairy farm in Careywood, about a half-hour's drive north of Hayden Lake, and became devoted parishioners. Tate and his siblings attended Butler's "Aryan Academy"—a converted trailer parked behind the Aryan Nations leader's office where the progeny of other devoted followers learned their own version of the fabled education Rs—in this case, reading, 'riting, 'rithmetic, and racism.[5] Tate was a keen student of several martial arts and had served as both the Aryan Nations' chief of security and head instructor of its unarmed combat courses. He routinely carried with him both the Bible and a pistol. Tate had also worked in the Aryan Nations print shop with his good friend, Gary Yarbrough, producing the Order's counterfeit currency.[6] Unbeknownst to either Tate or the two troopers, just three hours earlier a Seattle grand jury had indicted him and twenty-two other Order members on federal racketeering charges.[7]

Linegar spoke briefly with Tate and then ordered him to step out of the van. Hines saw the driver's side door open and turned to walk to the rear of the vehicle, where both troopers would question Tate. In that moment's distraction, however, Tate had dropped to the ground and deftly executed a shoulder roll that better positioned him to open fire. Linegar was suddenly staring down the barrel of Tate's MAC-10. A burst of gunfire ripped across the trooper's body armor, fatally piercing the unprotected parts of his torso. Hines and Tate exchanged fire—but the trooper's standard police-issue revolver was no match for a fully automatic submachine gun. Three bullets struck Hines in the shoulder, arm, and hip. Fearing the arrival of more police, Tate fled into the surrounding forest. For six days he evaded a massive search, aided by helicopter gunships flown by the Missouri National Guard, a specially-equipped FBI spy plane capable of detecting the heat signature of human beings on the ground below, and the fabled bloodhound dogs of manhunts throughout history. However, a tip from a citizen about someone behaving strangely led police and federal agents to a lake in Forsyth, Missouri, about ten miles from the crime scene, where Tate was found unarmed and hiding under a bush.[8]

A search of his brown van had revealed that Tate was transporting a small armory of machine guns, assault rifles, pistols, a sniper rifle, silencers, thousands of rounds of ammunition, hand grenades, dynamite, and a pint whiskey bottle containing nitroglycerine. Ski masks, police scanners, and four birth certificates in the names of various aliases were also discovered. Police and the FBI deduced that Tate had been en route to the Covenant, the Sword, and the Arm of the Lord (CSA) compound in Mountain Home, Arkansas—about ninety minutes from Branson. Whether the FBI knew that he had been a guest there four or five years earlier is not clear. But it would not have escaped notice that among the twenty-four Order operatives charged in Seattle were two men who had once belonged to the CSA. And, by complete coincidence, yet another Order member named in the indictment, Frank DeSilva, had been swept up in the dragnet for Tate. DeSilva was arrested at an Arkansas campground just across the Missouri border—along the highway leading to Mountain Home. This confirmed the suspicions of a CSA connection, and on April 16 the FBI applied for a warrant to arrest James Ellison, the CSA's leader, and search the compound. Among the charges listed was racketeering, kidnapping, bombing, arson, and attempted murder—along with a variety of federal firearms offenses. Edwin M. Meese, the U.S. attorney general, arrived in Arkansas the following day to supervise the expanding investigation into the white supremacist movement's myriad transnational connections.[9]

On April 19 some four hundred heavily armed FBI agents backed by other federal and state and local law enforcement personnel surrounded the CSA compound. The FBI was well aware of the armaments stockpiled there—which, in addition to machine guns, assault weapons, hand grenades, mines, and C-4 plastic explosives, included at least one U.S. military-issue light antitank weapon.[10] An internal bureau threat assessment had emphasized that CSA members were "*ARMED & EXTREMELY DANGEROUS*."[11] What they did not know was that four Order members were in fact hiding there and that two were particularly intent on celebrating Hitler's April 20 birth date—the following day—in a gunfight with the feds.[12] Back in Washington, FBI Assistant Director Oliver "Buck" Revell was thus justified in worrying that his agents were about to "walk into a firestorm [where] a lot of people will get killed." Although the agent in charge of the operation, HRT Commander Danny O. Coulson, dismissed such concerns as overwrought, he thought deeply about the potentially tragic consequences of sending his men into what he admitted could be a "meat grinder." Accordingly, the FBI's medics arranged to borrow a Huey helicopter for emergency evacuation purposes.[13] An armed personnel carrier was also summoned to support the impending assault. As Coulson later reflected, "the FBI was contemplating the biggest shootout in its history."[14] That, in fact, was also what Ellison was planning.[15]

As a survivalist collective whose purpose was to prepare for what its members believed was the coming nuclear apocalypse,[16] the CSA had enough food to last for five years and was otherwise completely self-sufficient in terms of unlimited fresh water along with ample supplies of kerosene for lamps and wood for its cooking and heating stoves. In anticipation of some future confrontation, Ellison had an armor-plated vehicle built—complete with a heavy machine gun designed for use against low-flying aircraft. "I'm preparing for war," he had told Kerry Noble, his second-in-command. "I didn't start this war, they did! But I intend to finish it."[17]

After a tense, four-day standoff, a prophecy from the divine that was communicated by Ellison's wife, Ollie, ended the siege, and Ellison and his followers surrendered peacefully.[18] Among them was a boy aged about fourteen who had previously stood his ground when confronted by federal agents surveilling the compound. Coulson later remarked that he had "never seen such a look of hatred on anyone so young." As the HRT commander's colleague and friend, Larry Bonney, reminded him: "Another time, another place, and they would kill us in a minute. We should never forget that."[19]

Following an initial sweep of the compound to dispose of dangerous ordnance and clear away any mines or booby traps, the FBI conducted a thorough search. In addition to the large quantities of arms, ammunition, explosives, and the antitank missile they had expected to find was a thirty-gallon drum of potassium cyanide. Although Ellison at first claimed that it was for pest control, he subsequently revealed the cyanide's real purpose:

to poison the reservoirs of several major American cities. Ellison would go on to testify under oath in federal court that the CSA had obtained the cyanide from the Michigan hate-monger Robert Miles. Together with two other white supremacist luminaries, Louis Beam and Richard Butler, Miles and Ellison had discussed New York City, Chicago, and Washington, DC, as potential targets.[20] The plot, as both Ellison and Noble would later also admit, was straight out of *The Turner Diaries*: "fomenting urban anarchy . . . [to] bring on the revolution."[21] In point of fact, however, that amount of cyanide dumped into a municipal water supply would have done nothing. The filtration and treatment systems at U.S. facilities would have degraded the poison's toxicity and rendered it ineffective. Moreover, to affect even an untreated reservoir lacking the protective processes standard in this country, the perpetrators would have required at least six times—ten *tons*, or 175 gallons—the amount of cyanide that the CSA possessed.[22] But Noble's repeated invocation of the divine intervention that he and the other conspirators believed would have ensured "that those who were meant to die would be poisoned"[23] spoke to a homicidal mindset justifying killing on an alarmingly mass scale, which the government had hitherto simply failed to grasp.

Accordingly, the more the authorities learned, the more concerned they became. Although the CSA standoff had been resolved without violence, this was the third such confrontation in two years with American white power militants. And this time it was not a lone gunman but an entire community of well-prepared and highly trained violent extremists wielding an astonishing array of lethal armaments that, Coulson observed, "would be the envy of any Middle Eastern terrorist group." Moreover, he was convinced that the FBI had recovered only "a fraction" of the CSA's actual weapons stockpile—which remained cleverly cached and therefore undiscovered.[24] The overlapping membership and close links forged between multiple, geographically diverse groups were also stronger and more extensive than the government had previously thought. And there was also the belated but fundamentally disquieting realization that the twenty-four Order members awaiting trial in Denver were mere foot soldiers in a planned insurrection whose leaders were still free.[25] As the historian Kathleen Belew explains: "To some extent the strategy of leaderless resistance had worked as intended, both in protecting leaders from prosecution and by isolating cells infiltrated by informants."[26]

Accordingly, in 1985 the Department of Justice launched Operation Clean Sweep—the first major coordinated effort to target the highest echelons of this movement.[27] Subsequent events would clearly show the need for such a concerted approach.

· · ·

The 1986 Aryan Nations Congress encapsulated the movement's response to this increased scrutiny from all levels of law enforcement. It attracted some three hundred to four hundred attendees over the July 12 weekend. Among them were fifteen of the most prominent proponents for what the *New York Times* described as "a white, male-dominated homeland in the Northwest"—encompassing Idaho, Montana, Oregon, Washington State, and Wyoming.[28] They hailed from across the country and Canada and included, among others, Robert Miles of the Mountain Church in Cohoctah, Michigan; the KKK state leader Bill Albers of Modesto, California; Pastor Thom Robb of the Church of Jesus Christ in Harrison, Arkansas; the Canadian Aryan Nations leaders Terry Long of Alberta and John Ross Taylor of Toronto; the White Aryan Resistance's (WAR) founder and leader Tom Metzger of Fallbrook, California;[29] Jerry Radford of Raleigh, North Carolina, representing the White Patriot Party; Greg Withrow, one of the original U.S. "skinheads" to align with white supremacism and the leader of the White Student Union of Sacramento, California;[30] Stan Witek from Los Angeles, who led the National Socialist Party; and the immensely influential author of *The Turner Diaries*, William Pierce, then living in Mill Point, West Virginia.[31]

The congress featured the typical litany of seditious speeches, homages to the Third Reich, and requisite cross burning. Racism, antisemitism, and anti-immigrant sentiments were repeatedly avowed. "You know yourself that today a white male is considered a third-class citizen by the de facto government," Butler told the gathering. "Therefore, as the posterity of those who founded this country, it is our duty to reclaim our heritage." He later explained to reporters that the movement's goal was "a return to the kind of country our forefathers wanted when they came over on the Mayflower." As more white families were immigrating to the Pacific Northwest, the Aryan Nations leader averred, the more confident he was of establishing this racially homogeneous homeland.[32] Among the paraphernalia sold at the congress was a medallion celebrating the dead and imprisoned Brüder Schweigen, another name for the group used by the Order's members. "Should you fall, my friend," the inscription on one side read, "another friend will emerge from the shadows to take your place."[33] Unbeknownst to the authorities, a successor group—calling itself the Brüder Schweigen Strike Force II, or the Order II—was already active.

Conceived most likely in 1985, the new variant also recruited members from the Aryan Nations. But unlike the original Brüder Schweigen, which, as it grew larger, became vulnerable to infiltration, the new group was kept deliberately small. It amounted to two married couples—David and Deborah Dorr, the leaders, and Edward and Olive Hawley—as well as Elden "Bud" Cutler and Kenneth Shray. At the time, David Dorr was Butler's security chief—having succeeded Cutler following the latter's conviction on federal charges of plotting to eliminate Thomas Martinez, who, as previously noted, had become an FBI informant. Dorr resumed the counterfeiting operation that Mathews had initiated. It was in fact a phony $20 bill that the Hawleys had tried to pass at the Spokane Interstate Fair that would trigger the series of arrests that effectively crippled the new group. But, in contrast to the original Order, the Brüder Schweigen Strike Force II never strayed far from home. Its first attack, in March 1986, was an unsuccessful attempt on the life of a local Jewish businessman. A pipe bomb next exploded at an auto body shop that August. Two weeks later, Dorr and Edward Hawley executed Shray, who they suspected had turned government informant. A brief respite followed when the Dorrs left for Chicago—astonishingly to appear as guests on the *Oprah Winfrey Show*. Upon their return the bombings resumed. On September 16, 1986, a pipe bomb damaged the Coeur d'Alene home of a Catholic priest leading community efforts against the Aryan Nations' continued presence in Kootenai County. Two weeks later, simultaneous blasts occurred at a local restaurant, the telephone company offices, a finance company, and the federal building. They were meant to distract attention from the group's coordinated robbery of two banks and an Idaho National Guard armory in nearby Post Falls. The operation, however, was a colossal failure. All the perpetrators were arrested. The authorities were able to persuade a relatively recent recruit, Robert Pires, to testify against the others. They were all convicted and received prison sentences of between eight to twenty years. Pires pleaded guilty to first-degree murder and three counts of detonating a bomb. Although he was sentenced to life imprisonment for these crimes, because of his cooperation, Pires was placed in the federal witness protection program and made eligible for parole once he had completed ten years of penal servitude.[34]

The purpose of their inchoate terrorist campaign had been to drive local residents and opponents of the Aryan Nations from the county. The Dorrs believed that by instigating this mass exodus they could lower property values and thus make it more affordable for other white supremacists to move to the area. More to the point, however, was Dorr's conviction—like Mathews before him—that Butler was all talk and no action and that the time had come to initiate the long-promised race war. To this end, Pires testified in federal court that Dorr had also compiled a hit list that marked federal judges, FBI agents, community leaders, and even Butler himself for assassination. As with the original Order, counterfeiting figured prominently in the Brüder Schweigen Strike Force II's ambitious plans to finance their nationwide race war and insurrection.[35]

The FBI's initial optimism that the Order's demise had crippled the movement and might also serve as a deterrent to other violently inclined, sedition-minded white supremacists[36] suffered a further blow on August 1 when a bank in the small town of Rossville, Illinois, was robbed of $44,000. Evidence found in the abandoned getaway vehicle—which was registered to Robert Miles's daughter Marion—led the FBI to conclude that one of the robbers was her fiancé, Thomas Harrelson, a known Aryan Nations member and ex-convict. The robbery immediately aroused concerns that the money was to be used to fund continued violent, seditious activities by the Order's would-be successors. Added to the FBI's infamous "Ten Most Wanted" list, Harrelson was arrested on February 19, 1987, in Drayton, North Dakota; following his trial, conviction, and time in prison, he was paroled in 2003.[37]

In Arizona, meanwhile, yet another collection of antigovernment zealots had attracted the attention of federal authorities. In December 1986, the FBI arrested six members of the so-called Arizona Patriots. They were charged with plotting to bomb the IRS office in Ogden, Utah, and the FBI field office, the Simon Wiesenthal Center (a Holocaust research center), and two offices of the militant Jewish Defense League in Los Angeles, as well as clinics legally performing abortions and a Phoenix synagogue. Additional arrests followed after the FBI learned of the group's other plans, which included an Order-inspired robbery of an armored car transporting casino receipts from Laughlin, Nevada, to Las Vegas and the assassination of Bruce Babbitt, Arizona's governor; an Arizona federal judge with a Jewish surname; and a Jewish banker living on the East Coast—in addition to plotting the bombing of various federal buildings, the demolition of bridges, and attacks on critical infrastructure in at least two states.[38]

The indictments capped a two-year FBI investigation into the group, which had first appeared in 1982 when members intentionally filed frivolous lawsuits over state driver license and vehicle registration regulations in hopes of paralyzing the court system. Its founder was a former actor named Ty Hardin. A U.S. Army veteran who had fought in the Korean War, Hardin found modest fame as the eponymous star of the 1960s television Western *Bronco*. The character played by Leonardo DiCaprio in Quentin Tarantino's 2019 movie *Once Upon a Time . . . in Hollywood* was based in part on Hardin. Sometime in the 1970s, however, he decided to abandon his acting career and moved to Prescott, Arizona. A succession of tax disputes with the IRS fueled by Hardin's growing aversion to what he claimed was "Zionist control of Hollywood" were behind his transformation to "freedom fighter" cum "ultra-fundamentalist evangelical Christian preacher."[39] The personal quotes section on Hardin's IMDb page includes a diatribe reminiscent of the language and imagery more usually associated with firebrands such as Pierce, Beam, and Butler. "There very well could be uprisings and race discrimination issues throughout our nation," Hardin fulminated.

> The floodgates of our borders have been opened for years and a population of illegals starving in our streets just might make a loud noise. We are all Americans, first and foremost, devoted to protecting our Constitution and our Christian heritage from enemies both foreign and domestic. The world globalists have no respect for God's creation and their greed and desires for total world control are now apparent to all who have opened their eyes. Martial law will be implemented and Homeland Security will protect their butts from the millions of armed patriots getting prepared to defend our Constitution.[40]

The Arizona Patriots were thus cut of the same cloth as Posse Comitatus and other 1980s antigovernment/white supremacist groups that trafficked in conspiracy theories, obsessed over questions of national religious and racial purity, and shared the same dystopian worldview. Some of its roughly two hundred or so members were among the forty-four attendees at a July 1984 meeting hosted by William Potter Gale, the founder of Posse Comitatus, at his California ranch. That gathering produced a jointly signed statement accusing various government officials of sedition and calling for the dissolution of the U.S. Congress.[41] Butler was also one of the signatories, and a few weeks later he welcomed a delegation of Arizona Patriots to that year's Aryan Nations Congress.[42] But like their counterparts in both Order iterations, this faction of the Patriots had also tired of proclamations and battle cries that never translated into action. They concluded that Hardin was no different than Butler. Striking out on their own, these militants commenced paramilitary and survivalist training at a 320-acre ranch near Kingman, Arizona, owned by a one-armed, supposed former CIA mercenary named Jack Maxwell Oliphant.[43] It was there that the FBI found the blueprints for two Colorado River dams in Arizona and one on the Missouri River in South Dakota that the group had planned to destroy.[44] Kathleen Belew quotes a U.S. government official's description of Oliphant and his associates as "cave men with bombs." But there should be no mistaking their homicidal intentions.[45] As Evelyn A. Schlatter, another scholar of American violent, far-right extremism, notes, the group "made . . . white supremacy into a jihad, or holy war, that portrays Jews as the source of all evil."[46]

Despite the gravity of charges, only Oliphant and one other conspirator, a twenty-three-year-old dishonorably discharged U.S. military veteran named Monte Ross, received prison sentences. The others were either put on probation or had their cases dismissed. In what would remain a pattern in the sentencing of white supremacists to comparatively lighter jail terms than other convicted terrorists, both Oliphant and Ross received sentences of four years each.[47] It is therefore not surprising that in the 1990s Oliphant's ranch was still a hub for paramilitary and survivalist training and related activities.[48]

• • •

By the fall of 1986, the FBI was more convinced than ever that the white supremacist threat had not abated. It was clear that the Order had not died with Robert Mathews or the incarceration of his followers but that the group was in fact spawning successors dedicated to carrying forward the original inchoate revolution. Moreover, the movement's leaders had themselves doubled down on their intention to overthrow the U.S. government. Federal prosecutors in Illinois, Colorado, California, Idaho, North Carolina, and Arkansas assigned to Operation Clean Sweep pored through voluminous affidavits, court-authorized wiretap transcripts, and the reports from nearly a dozen well-placed confidential informants to prepare grand jury indictments. The information was derived from listening devices and wiretaps that FBI agents had placed in Robert Miles's Cohoctah, Michigan, church and home. They revealed that his Mountain Church had become a central communications node for coordinating Order operations. A string of bank robberies in Illinois, Missouri, and North Dakota revealed the dimensions of a coordinated effort to raise funds in support of a range of seditious activities. They included plans to bomb federal office buildings in at least five cities as the opening bid in negotiations to gain the release of the imprisoned Order members. Another scheme hatched by a Ku Klux Klan cell entailed invading the Caribbean island state of Dominica to establish a white supremacist dictatorship. Many of the FBI's informants—among whom was Zillah Craig, Mathews's paramour and the mother of his daughter—also told of a summit meeting held by three of the movement's "generals"—Miles, Beam, and a retired U.S. Army colonel, longstanding John Birch Society acolyte, and antisemite named Gordon "Jack" Mohr—at which many of these plots were discussed. Other leading movement figures, including Metzger, William Pierce, and Frazier Glenn Miller of North Carolina, were also implicated in an FBI affidavit filed on October 2, 1986.[49]

On April 26, 1987, Department of Justice attorneys in Fort Smith, Arkansas, announced a series of sweeping indictments against fourteen white supremacists. They stood accused of seditious conspiracy, plotting to carry out assassinations and bombings of federal officers and facilities (including federal appeals court buildings in Denver, Kansas City, Minneapolis, New Orleans, and St. Louis), destroying utilities, establishing guerrilla camps, poisoning water supplies, transporting stolen money, and procuring false identification. Their plans to establish an all-white republic were alleged to have been conceived between mid-1983 and 1984 and were to be financed through armed robberies and counterfeiting. The

Dominica invasion plot, the 1983 firebombing of a Jewish community center in Bloomington, Indiana, and the sabotage of an Arkansas natural gas pipeline the following year were also cited.[50]

The seditious conspiracy charge was the most serious—and ambitious. Enacted after the U.S. Civil War to prosecute recalcitrant southerners who refused to accept the authority of the U.S. federal government and amended in 1918 for use against domestic anarchists, 18 U.S.C. §2384 provides penalties of up to twenty years' imprisonment and a $20,000 fine should it be determined that at least two or more persons had "conspire[d] to overthrow, put down, or to destroy by force the Government of the United States, or to levy war against them, or to oppose by force the authority thereof, or by force to prevent, hinder, or delay the execution of any law of the United States."[51] Beam, Butler, and Miles were the leaders charged with this offense, along with previously imprisoned Order figures such as Barnhill, Lane, Ardie McBrearty, Bruce Pierce, Scutari, an Arkansas gun dealer named Robert Smalley who had supplied the group with weapons, and Richard Snell, a member of the CSA awaiting execution for the slayings of an Arkansas state trooper and a Texarkana pawnshop owner and former policeman. Snell was also named in the murder plot targeting an FBI agent and the chief federal judge for the western district of Arkansas, as were Bill Wade, his son Ray, Lambert Miller, and David McGuire, who also belonged to the CSA. McGuire was CSA leader James Ellison's son-in-law at the time. They each faced sentences of up to ten years in prison and a $10,000 fine. Other movement luminaries such as Gale, Mohr, Metzger, and William Pierce escaped indictment.[52]

The trial lasted seven weeks and heard from 192 witnesses. The prosecution introduced over 1,200 evidentiary items,[53] but from the start it was plagued by missteps. First, the voir dire and peremptory challenges winnowed down a racially diverse jury pool to ten white male and two white female jurors. Both women would subsequently enter into romantic relationships with two of the defendants—at least one of which began during the trial with flirtatious glances that subsequently led to marriage. "I know all the stuff he's done," the juror Carolyn Slater said of the object of her affection, McGuire. "Nobody's perfect."[54]

Second, two of the prosecution's key witnesses—James Ellison and Frazier Glenn Miller—undermined their credibility by the deals they made with the government to avoid prosecution themselves or to ensure they received reduced sentences for additional crimes.[55] Ellison was further discredited by the defense, who detailed his self-anointment as "King James of the Ozarks," his claims to be in direct communication with God, and his practice of polygamy.[56] Miller, the founder and leader of the Carolina Knights of the Ku Klux Klan, which he subsequently rebranded the White Patriot Party, had been released on bond for violating a previous plea deal where he had agreed both to desist from contact with fellow white supremacists and engaging in paramilitary training. After an appeals court upheld his conviction, this former U.S. Army Green Beret with two combat tours in Vietnam behind him had gone underground.[57] In an open letter to "White Patriots" titled "Declaration of War," Miller called for a "total war" against the "Zionist Occupation Government (ZOG)" and the "[N-word], Jews, Queers, assorted Mongrels, White Race traitors, and despicable informants." The letter also invoked the name of the Order, to which Miller proudly claimed he was a "loyal member" and called for the use of the Order's "point system" as means to systematically eliminate the white man's myriad enemies.[58]

Four days after the Fort Smith indictments were announced, Miller and two accomplices were captured in Ozark, Missouri. They were found in possession of a variety of illegal weapons—including fragmentation grenades, C-4 plastic explosives, automatic weapons, and pistols. As part of a plea deal whereby he agreed to provide testimony against other members of his organization and information on other related criminal activities, Miller pleaded guilty to federal charges of mailing threatening communications and was sentenced to five years in prison.[59] Paroled after serving three years, Miller would later be sentenced to death in 2015 for murdering three people outside a Jewish community center and retirement home in Kansas.[60]

Third, seditious conspiracy is a difficult charge on which to obtain a conviction, on First Amendment grounds. Because of its conspiratorial dimension, where the intended crime(s) only had to have been discussed and not necessarily acted upon, this accusation is often refuted by claims of First Amendment protections—as the defense in this case would also argue.[61] Indeed, in his opening statement, Everett Hofmeister, Butler's attorney, emphasized that "the issue here is the right to freedom of speech. Replacing the government of the United States with another government is not conspiracy."[62] Indeed, FBI HRT Commander Danny O. Coulson had doubts about the prosecution's strategy from the start, which Hofmeister's defense validated. "Most Americans are suspicious whenever the government tries to weave a complicated conspiracy case," he later reflected, "especially one that comes close to infringing on the constitutional right of free speech, and the Fort Smith jury was no exception."[63]

The jury began its deliberations in early April 1988 and after four days told Judge Morris Arnold that they were unable to reach a verdict. Arnold refused to accept that the jurors were deadlocked and ordered them back to the jury room. The following day, April 8, they returned a not guilty verdict on all charges.[64] The jury's decision was all the more galling because many of the defendants had represented themselves.[65] "The government was going to send a message to the movement," said Thom Robb, the Ku Klux Klan's national chaplain, who had attended the trial to lend moral support to the defendants. "The movement sent a message to the Government."[66] "I think ZOG has suffered a terrible defeat here today," Beam enthused. "I think everyone saw through the charade and saw that I was simply being punished for being a vociferous and outspoken opponent of ZOG." Butler hailed the verdict as proof that Americans "still enjoy the freedom of speech, freedom of assembly, freedom of association and freedom of religion." Miles, however, was less sanguine. When asked by a reporter how the trial had affected the white supremacist movement, he had replied, "Who knows? What movement? What's left of it after this?"[67]

. . .

A 1988 RAND Corporation report—written by one of the authors of this book and published a month after the Fort Smith trial ended—described how that era's white supremacist movement had "demonstrated a remarkable resiliency to withstand pressure from heightened attention by federal, state, and local law enforcement agencies, to rebound from setbacks (such as widespread arrests of members), and to continue to try to carve out a whites-only homeland in the Pacific Northwest."[68] Indeed, as Kathleen Belew would write thirty years later, "white power activists understood the sedition trial acquittals as a green light for future violence."[69]

While it is true that after several years of escalating confrontation, bloodshed, and outright terrorism an unusual quiet suddenly descended on the movement, the same powerful forces and leading personages remained hard at work adjusting their tactics, refining their messaging, and adopting new strategies in order to broaden their appeal and attract new recruits while strengthening their existing constituencies. In fact, while he was still on trial, in September 1987 Butler had announced that the Aryan Nations would open a new "missionary/political outreach" center in Utah to supplement the existing ones in Montana and the Canadian provinces of Ontario and Alberta. Butler explained that the movement hoped to tap into Utah's predominantly white, Mormon population and intended to establish additional centers in Texas and Washington State.[70]

Another even more promising constituency Butler courted were primarily urban "skinheads"—loosely organized groups of violently inclined, shaven-headed, tattooed youths. The major skinhead gangs at the time included the Chicago-based Romantic Violence; Dallas's Confederate Hammerskins (later the Hammerskin Nation or simply Hammerskins); Detroit's SS-Action Group; the White American Skin Head (WASH) organization, based in Cincinnati; the San Francisco Bay Area Skin Head gang (BASH); and Sacramento's Aryan Youth Movement–White Student Union, founded by John Metzger, the son of the longtime white supremacist Tom Metzger, which claimed to have about thirty chapters with some three hundred members scattered across the country. Smaller skinhead communities were also active in Florida, Portland, Los Angeles, Dallas, and Denver. In point of fact, the ADL estimated the number of hardcore skinhead militants at no more than several hundred nationwide but in a 1987 report cautioned that their ranks were rapidly growing. The skinheads' glorification of violence, affinity for Nazism, and racist and antisemitic attitudes accounted for mainstream white supremacism's interest in this generally younger and even less disciplined demographic.[71]

Like the Anglo-Israelism movement that evolved into Identity theology, the skinhead phenomenon originated in Britain. From the early 1970s onward, they were identifiable by their shaved heads, numerous tattoos, chain-adorned apparel, and army surplus or black, high-top Doc Martens boots. Their militant patriotic and anti-immigrant views neatly fit the ideology of established British neo-Nazi groups such as the National Front, which began to recruit skinheads into their ranks. The skinheads soon acquired a reputation for violence and mayhem, engaging in football hooliganism (violence between fans of rival soccer teams). Skinheads had

already acquired an infamous reputation for their random and unpro-
voked attacks on Pakistani and other Asian immigrants and fire bombings of the homes and shops of various immigrant groups in the United
Kingdom. They also routinely engaged in street brawls and similar acts
of aggressive violence in London and other British cities.[72]

The British skinheads' American counterparts shared a similar mindset of xenophobia, racial and religious bigotry, and an affinity for Nazi
symbols and ideology. But according to the ADL, U.S. skinheads tended
to be more brazenly antisemitic. Indeed, throughout the 1980s they
were responsible for a succession of attacks on Jews, African Americans,
immigrants, and other people of color. Arrests of skinheads were reported
in Michigan, Illinois, Ohio, Texas, Florida, and California on charges
ranging from assault and vandalism to arson and robbery.[73] In another
parallel with Britain, the gravitational pull between skinheads and older,
well-established hate-mongers was irresistible. In 1985, for instance, Chicago skinheads joined a protest march organized by the American Nazi
Party. Two years later, skinheads from those same streets celebrated the
forty-ninth anniversary of Kristallnacht by vandalizing and destroying
suspected Jewish-owned stores on the city's North Side.[74] Skinheads
from the Detroit area also regularly attended meetings and conferences
held by Robert Miles at his racist Mountain Church of Jesus Christ the
Savior in Cohoctah. And skinhead gangs reportedly were represented at
both the 1986 and 1987 Aryan Nations Congresses.[75] As previously noted,
one of the featured speakers at the 1986 event was Greg Withrow, the
leader of the Sacramento skinhead group. In an impassioned speech at the
congress, Withrow declared, "Men, women and children, without exception, without appeal, who are of non-Aryan blood shall be terminated or
expelled. The next line of leadership shall be a generation of ruthless
predators that shall make past Aryan leadership and warriors seem pale
by comparison."[76]

Around this time, Richard Girnt Butler also ramped up the Aryan
Nations' prison outreach efforts. The first issue of *The Way*, the Church
of Jesus Christ Christian's bimonthly newsletter dedicated to its incarcerated brethren, appeared in September 1987. Its editorial manifesto
explained *The Way*'s intention "to provide a good source of Bible study
into the ISRAEL IDENTITY message and its related histories and politics for interested convicts, while also providing news and happenings of

concern to our chained brothers and sisters."[77] Scriptural interpreta-
tions and explanations were discussed along with various bits of legal
advice. *The Way* invited inmates to contribute articles and share their
thoughts. Its first two issues featured contributions by the imprisoned
Order members David Tate and David Lane.[78]

Louis Beam meanwhile hunkered down after his acquittal and focused
his efforts anew on building the solid base of support for the white supremacist revolution he always believed was inevitable. To this end, he founded
a new publication called *The Seditionist*—in reference to the criminal
charge levied against him at Fort Smith. Beam's newsletter appeared quarterly between 1988 and 1992. Its final issue introduced a new generation
of white supremacists to the strategy of leaderless resistance that Beam
had first articulated in 1983.[79]

The movement's preoccupation with cultivating new sources of recruits
and ensuring its longevity in the months following the trial was prompted
by two separate but intertwined concerns. First was the realization that
had the government proven its case, the movement would have been effectively decapitated and would likely have collapsed. Second, its core leadership was old—Butler was already seventy, and Miles was only a few years
younger.[80] Had they been convicted, both would have spent the rest of
their lives in prison. If the dream of an all-white America was to survive,
it was imperative to appeal to new constituencies and attract a broader
and younger demographic. The passing of William Potter Gale just weeks
after the trial ended and the reflections on his legacy that followed led
to an epiphany—and the resurrection of an old idea of his that would
endow the movement with fresh momentum.

• • •

Gale, as previously recounted, was a World War II veteran who had
acquired firsthand knowledge of guerrilla warfare and clandestine operations while serving on General MacArthur's staff in the Philippines. He
left the army as a lieutenant-colonel in 1950 and subsequently immersed
himself in a variety of racist, antisemitic, and seditious causes. The John
Birch Society was too moderate for Gale, who quit over its unwillingness
to employ violence.[81] Over the next three-and-a-half decades, the FBI
would amass thousands of pages of files on Gale and his indefatigable

crusade against communists, Jews, people of color, immigrants, and the U.S. government.[82]

Starting in 1955, when Gale organized a group calling itself "For America, Inc.," whose purpose, he told the FBI agent interviewing him, was to "teach Americanism as opposed to communism," Gale's activities were of ongoing interest to the bureau as he drifted from one extremist cause and group to another. Around 1958 or 1959, for instance, he was ordained by Dr. Wesley Swift in his Church of Jesus Christ Christian and subsequently became Swift's assistant.[83] Gale wholeheartedly subscribed to Identity theology and, according to his former wife, believed that America was "being taken over by the Communist Party and groups such as, the Muslims."[84] According to the FBI, he was one of the cofounders of the 1950s-era Christian Defense League (CDL), whose mission included monitoring the activities of both the ADL and NAACP as well as assembling "files on all Jews in the country."[85] A membership solicitation from 1959 presaged the arguments that groups such as the Aryan Nations would later use to attract supporters. "Christians WAKE UP!" one such letter declared.

> The N.A.A.C.P. represents the Negro. The A.D.L. represents the Jew. Who represents YOU! The truth is that an alien, anti-Christian element has invaded your land. They seek to destroy your Christian culture by waging a relentless WAR on everything Christian. . . . The preservation of our white Christian heritage is at stake.[86]

Gale's serial involvement with far-right extremism took a different turn in 1960, when he revitalized the so-called California Rangers—a prototype of the militia organizations that would emerge across the United States three decades later. He made no secret of plans to deploy "20,000 fully armed and trained men who could be put into the streets of Los Angeles within six hours after an emergency."[87] Gale's rhetoric was also becoming more extreme. A reliable source, for instance, told the FBI about a speech Gale had delivered before a gathering at the Hollywood Women's Club on May 3, 1963. "WE HAVE BEEN TALKING TOO LONG AND WE'RE NOT GOING TO TALK ANY MORE," he had reportedly declared. "WE WANT 100 PEOPLE WHO WILL GIVE US $1,000 A PIECE, WE'LL DO THE REST. THIS JOB IS GOING TO BE DONE

NOW. IF YOU DON'T UNDERSTAND THIS, YOU ARE TOO STUPID TO HEAR MY MESSAGE. THIS IS A FIGHTING MINISTRY."[88]

Gale's loose talk advocating political assassination alongside his blunt warnings that elected officials might have to be "physically" removed from office prompted FBI Director J. Edgar Hoover to write to the White House in June 1963 about Gale.[89] Even though Hoover believed neither President Kennedy nor Vice President Johnson, nor their families for that matter, were in danger,[90] two months later the head of the DOJ's Criminal Division, Assistant Attorney General Herbert J. Miller, instructed Hoover to continue to monitor Gale and "develop any information that his group intends to assassinate various government officials."[91] Gale was in fact already under investigation by the FBI over his suspected involvement in a singularly horrific act of domestic terrorism.

Few incidents of the blood-soaked history of the American civil rights movement are as infamous as the September 1963 bombing of the Sixteenth Street Baptist Church in Birmingham, Alabama. Four girls aged between eleven and fourteen were killed and twenty other people injured in the blast.[92] Gale had fallen under suspicion because of yet another racist speech he had given in July as well as a trip he had made to Mississippi and Alabama that same month.[93] An FBI informant had reported Gale's heated rhetoric when addressing another racist gathering that summer. "We must defend ourselves against this [the threat posed by communists, Jews, and people of color]," he thundered, *even if we have to take up arms and make their blood run in the streets.*"[94] A tip that Gale had been spotted in Birmingham "on or about 9/15/63"—the date of the bombing—had focused the FBI's attention on his movements and activities throughout the preceding months. Gale's involvement was eventually discounted, and the plot was linked to four members of the Ku Klux Klan.[95] Even so, FBI communications repeatedly advised that Gale "SHOULD BE CONSIDERED ARMED AND DANGEROUS."[96]

Indeed, Gale seemed to have a hand in almost every manifestation of 1960s white supremacism. As Hoover had explained in his report to the White House, Gale was obsessed with "Jews being the enemy of the world and specifically the United States."[97] In 1964 this led to Gale's unveiling of "Operation AWAKE," an acronym for Army of the White American Kingdom of Evangelists. Described in its membership solicitations as "the

Defense Division of the Church of Jesus Christ, Christian," AWAKE was led by Swift, with Gale as his trusted lieutenant.[98] In addition to Gale's role in this new organization, he remained active in both the Christian Defense League and its paramilitary arm, the California Rangers.[99] A CDL flyer from 1964 boasted of its close association with Swift, of having a thirteen-member board of directors, and of recently leasing the "entire third floor of the office building at 617 South Olive Street in downtown Los Angeles." Its purpose, according to Richard Girnt Butler, the CDL's national director who would later achieve notoriety as the Aryan Nations' founder and leader, was "to unite Christians into a powerful force to achieve the Kingdom goal . . . [and] to put Christianity back into every phase of national life, particularly in government and education."[100] Membership dues were $12 per annum. Applicants were required to affirm that not only did they "BELIEVE THAT JESUS IS THE CHRIST" and were of "THE WHITE RACE" but, in a nod to the movement's simultaneous but conflicting claims of ardent patriotism coupled with patently seditious inclinations,[101] also had to pledge to "SUPPORT THE LAWFULLY ADOPTED WRITTEN CONSTITUTION OF THE UNITED SOVERIGN STATES OF CHRISTIAN AMERICA."[102]

It therefore comes as no surprise that when a southern California incarnation of the KKK appeared around this time, the FBI identified Swift as its leader and Gale as a "principal member." Known as the Christian Knights of the Invisible Empire (CKIE), it was suspected of a 1963 arson attack on a Black-owned business in Lancaster, California. Los Angeles County Sheriff's Office deputies in fact questioned Gale about his involvement.[103] Within months, however, the CKIE ceased operation, only to resurface, according to a Los Angeles FBI field office intelligence assessment, as Gale's Operation AWAKE.[104]

But Gale's most significant and indeed lasting accomplishment was his fusion of the divinely ordained hate and intolerance emblematic of Identity theology with antigovernment and tax resistance militancy. In 1964 Gale incorporated under California state law his Ministry of Christ Church. The filing listed suburban Glendale in Los Angeles County as its location. An FBI analysis would later conclude that the church was an anodyne-sounding "cover" for what was actually an "underground army" called the Identity Group. As the leader of both, Gale was described in the memorandum as a person who "espouses hatred for Jews and Negroes and advocates assassination of FBI Agents and Internal Revenue Service agents as well as the hanging of certain judges"—thus accounting for the FBI's intensifying focus on Gale and the variegated entities associated with him.[105]

In 1972, Gale purchased one hundred acres of land outside the small rural town of Mariposa, California, near Yosemite National Park, and moved the church there.[106] The FBI's Sacramento field office consequently assumed responsibility for monitoring Gale. Within weeks its agents had produced an assessment of Gale and his activities that was even more alarming than previous ones. The new report detailed how the Ministry of Christ Church and the Identity Group were actively engaged in a variety of illegal activities, including seditious conspiracy, plotting to assault or kill federal officers, instigating rebellion or insurrection, and advocating the overthrow of the U.S. government. The significance of one detail, however, likely went unnoticed at the time, given the litany of more pressing concerns evident in the assessment. Gale had begun to call publicly for the formation "of a 'Posse Comitatus,' a voluntary group of citizens who would act in the name of local sheriffs to 'enforce' the law."[107]

The doctrine of Posse Comitatus, literally, "power of the county," rejected any form of government above the county level as a means to nullify federal and state income taxes, deny the legality of the Federal Reserve system, and challenge the supremacy of federal law over state and especially local jurisdictions. A Posse circular obtained by the FBI, for instance, explained that a "general misconception" exists in America that "any statute passed by legislators bearing the appearance of law constitutes the law of the land." According to Gale, "such an unconstitutional law is void, the general principles follow that it imposes no duties, confers no rights, creates no office, bestows no power or authority on anyone." The bottom line of Gale's idiosyncratic interpretation of American jurisprudence was that "no one is bound to obey an unconstitutional law and no courts are bound to enforce it."[108] The philosophy of the Posse movement thus revolved around Gale's argument that "since the formation of our Republic, the local County has always been the seat of government for the people. A county government is the highest authority of government in our Republic as it is closest to the people, who are in fact, the government. The County Sheriff is the only legal law enforcement office in the United States of America . . . it is his responsibility to protect

the people of his county from unlawful acts on the part of anyone including officials of the government."[109]

From the start, Gale seamlessly merged Identity theology with his messages about tax resistance and opposition to state and federal legal
supremacy. His quarterly newsletter, titled *Identity*, for instance, publicized the formation of a "U.S. Christian Posse Association" under the
Ministry of Christ Church's auspices, "to assist and provide the necessary
direction towards the formation of a Christian posse in every county in
the U.S.," as a 1975 FBI report explained. "'Identity' states that the body
of citizens constituting the sheriff's posse was titled Posse Comitatus."[110]

By offering additionally enticing publications with titles like "How to
Protect Yourself from the Internal Revenue Service (on your income
tax),"[111] Gale had tapped into a potentially limitless constituency. With
many facing bankruptcy of their businesses and foreclosure of their farms
and homes, he opened the doors of the white supremacist movement to
potential adherents whose dire economic circumstances made them more
susceptible to simplistic, highly reductionist explanations of their plight.
The Posse Comitatus's populist bombast blamed Jews, immigrants, Wall
Street, welfare cheats, and the government for all their woes. As Daniel
Levitas, an expert on white supremacism, explains, Gale "fashioned an
elaborate, American-sounding ideology that married uncompromising
anti-Semitism, anticommunism, and white supremacy with the appealing notion of the extreme sovereignty of the people." Gale seamlessly
melded racism, antisemitism, and xenophobia into an extremist antigovernment ideology of tax resistance and the preeminence of local authority as a means to ensure the superiority of the white race according to his
vision of "natural and 'lawful' rights that trumped those of a (racially) corrupt state."[112]

Convoluted legalese providing justification for not paying taxes, especially in economically depressed American farming and ranching communities during the 1970s,[113] functioned like a gateway drug that drew this
audience more deeply into the white supremacist milieu. The human
rights activist Leonard Zeskind, an expert on Christian Identity, would
later describe this approach as an ideological and theological "conveyor
belt," whereby "people come into contact with political or religious groups
looking for answers to the problems of society. Political affiliation is not
tightly compartmented and there is always overlap with other groups."[114]

Gale's approach proved remarkably successful in breathing new life into a movement with otherwise limited appeal and therefore at the risk of declining into irrelevance. Finding justification not to file income tax returns or to ignore foreclosure notices resonated more readily and widely in 1970s and 1980s America than Nazi salutes and cross burnings. The first Posse Comitatus chapter had surfaced in 1973 in Lane County, Oregon— about a two-hour drive south of Portland.[115] Within a year, it had spread to five other counties in that state, with signs of increasing Posse Comitatus activity having appeared in Washington State, Idaho, Arkansas, Ohio, Virginia, and Wisconsin.[116] By 1978, the FBI had identified seventy-eight chapters in nearly two dozen states with an estimated membership of some 12,000 people. A toxic combination of Identity ideology and white supremacism mixed with militant tax resistance and antigovernment sentiments was also beginning to coalesce, much as Gale had hoped it would.[117] Indeed, the North Dakota farmer Gordon Kahl, who was killed in the 1983 gun battle with federal agents recounted in chapter 2, was an example of how effectively Gale's message had resonated.

With the Posse Comitatus and followers like Kahl, Gale's dream of an armed, trained citizens' militia ready to resist government intrusiveness and infringement of core constitutional rights had been realized. All Gale's prior efforts—with the California Rangers, the CDL, and AWAKE, for instance—had failed to gain traction. But the bleak economic conditions in America's farming heartland during the early 1980s now provided him with a highly receptive audience. A combination of falling crop prices, poor weather, and soaring interest rates were driving farmers into bankruptcy at a rate not experienced since the Great Depression fifty years earlier.[118] And Gale milked it for all he could. Identifying himself as "the Rev. William P. Gale," he acquired a weekly platform for his "National Identity Broadcast" over KTTL radio in Dodge City, Kansas. The transcript of one show recounts Gale castigating "these judges . . . these officials of government, [and] politicians" who, he claimed, were ordering white, Christian Americans to "Turn over your inheritance to the blacks and the Asiatics, and [that accordingly] you must allow all the scum of the earth to come into your land by destruction of your immigration laws."[119] Giving voice to the accelerationist philosophy coursing more powerfully through the extreme right at the time, Gale was unabashed in his advocacy of sedition. "You're damned right I'm teaching violence," he declared in another broadcast. "God said you're going to do it that way, and it's about time somebody is telling you to get violent, whitey."[120] To this end, in March 1982 the Posse Comitatus sponsored a "survival school" in Weskan, Kansas. Gale was one of the teaching staff. Its curriculum on tax avoidance schemes, racism, and antisemitism also included instruction on the "proper explosives needed to demolish roadways, dams and bridges."[121]

Gale, it must be said, lived what he preached. Unlike Butler and some of the movement's other blowhards, this former U.S. Army officer led from the front. At age sixty-nine, when most other sexagenarians had long retired to the golf course or parked themselves at the card tables at their men's clubs, Gale along with seven followers was arrested in October 1986 on charges of conspiracy, interference with tax collection, and sending death threats to a federal judge and various IRS agents. The plotters were alleged to belong to the Committee of the States, yet another of Gale's anti-government creations.[122] In his inaugural sermon in 1982 to this latest iteration in a succession of self-styled "Christian Patriot" organizations, Gale planted the seeds of far more consequential violence in the future. "You've got an enemy government running around," he explained. "You've got a criminal government running around the land. And its source and its location is Washington, D.C. and the federal buildings they've built with your tax money all over the cities in this land."[123]

Gale was convicted in January 1987 and sentenced to a year's imprisonment. The government that he so bitterly despised, however, took pity on him. Because of his ill health, Gale was able to avoid penal servitude while appealing his sentence. He died fifteen months later of complications from emphysema.[124] Although Gale never become the icon of the violent, far-right that Kahl or Mathews are or achieved the prominence within the movement that other leaders like Richard Girnt Butler and Robert Miles arguably enjoyed, Gale's impact was even more important. "Like children grown to maturity," the scholar Daniel Levitas observes, "the forces he shaped have fueled the radical right to the present day."[125] Similarly, the historian Evelyn Schlatter describes how Gale, from the time he left the army in 1950, worked tirelessly to ensure the growth and popularity of the militia movement that some thirty years later took root across the United States. For this reason alone, she describes Gale as "one of the most influential rightist figures in the country until his death in

1988."[126] Capitalizing on seething antigovernment sentiment and a desire to avoid paying taxes, he founded the Posse Comitatus in the late 1960s and throughout the 1970s expanded the movement's reach and widened its base. Gale's infusion of Christian Identity theology into this mix created angry militants like Gordon Kahl, who were as passionate about racial and religious purity as they were about perceived government overreach. Significantly, Gale was also one of the pivotal figures responsible for popularizing the concept of armed, antigovernment citizens' militias—which now assumed greater importance for a movement seeking to reinvent itself and thereby tap into a wider and geographically even more diverse constituency.[127]

Given the centrality of global conspiracies involving Jews allied with other secret powerful forces intent on controlling the world for their own evil purposes, a concern that long animated Gale's malignant worldview, it is stunningly ironic that his own paternal grandparents were Jewish—a fact that both Gale and his father both fervently concealed and forever denied.[128]

4

ARMED AND DANGEROUS

I have never seen the whole picture so clearly. . . . We are truly the instruments of God in the fulfillment of His Grand Design.

—EARL TURNER, IN *THE TURNER DIARIES*

Extremist movements that cannot broaden their appeal and tap into new sources of recruits and support risk both their continued relevance and very existence. One of the noteworthy features of American white supremacism has been its capacity for reinvention. As with all such demagogic phenomena, a catalyst—some inciting event or events—is often needed to set this reinvigoration in motion. At the start of the twentieth century, a convergence of fortuitous circumstances revived the Ku Klux Klan—and during the 1990s similarly accounted for the rise and growth of armed, antigovernment citizens' militias.

. . .

A century before the power of social media and mass communication transformed violent extremism's reach and accessibility, the Ku Klux Klan could boast of at least four to five million dues-paying members from every state of the union.[1] The KKK of the 1910s and 1920s in fact had more adherents in the North than in the South and was more popular in the cities than the countryside. Ohio, a northern state that fought with the Union in the Civil War, claimed the largest membership—four hundred thousand. Pennsylvania, another northern state, had more than thirty thousand members in Philadelphia alone.[2] Its members, according to the historian Linda Gordon, included "both the well and the poorly educated, professionals, businesspeople, farmers, and wage workers, but the lower middle-class and skilled working-class people formed its core constituency."[3] Future president Harry S. Truman and future senator and Supreme Court justice Hugo Black belonged to the Klan, as did more than a dozen sitting governors, scores of congressmen and senators, and hundreds of state and local elected officials. The Klan sent delegations to the 1924 and 1928 national presidential conventions of both parties and helped Republican Calvin Coolidge win the 1924 election. It influenced and lobbied for the infamous Immigration Act of 1924, which was designed to exclude Jews, Italians, and Asians from settling in America and remained in force until 1965.[4] In a dramatic show of both its strength and popularity, on August 8, 1925, tens of thousands of Klansmen and Klanswomen paraded down Washington, DC's Pennsylvania Avenue, attired in their distinctive white robes and conical hats—but unmasked.[5] The Klan's twentieth-century revival and its remarkable ability to insert itself into the mainstream of American society was the product of a movie and a lynching that occurred within months of each other in 1915.

The original, Reconstruction-era Ku Klux Klan had a remarkably short-lived existence. Founded in 1866 as a fraternal organization by six Confederate Army veterans in rural Pulaski, Tennessee, it soon adopted a more aggressively political and reactionary mission. Within two years, autonomous local chapters, known as "klaverns," had spread across the South. Although the Confederate general Nathan Bedford Forrest had been elected national leader, or "Grand Wizard," the escalating violence directed mostly against emancipated slaves was uncoordinated, though widespread. The magnitude of the violence during the Reconstruction era produced staggering numbers of casualties—in just one indication of the horrendous violence, more than one thousand mostly Black Louisianans were killed in that state between the April and November elections in 1868, with another two thousand killed or wounded in the lead-up to the 1871 election. And yet, as the terrorism expert Daniel Byman reflects, "As horrible as these accounts of murder are, the number of unknown deaths is probably far greater."[6]

In 1870, the federal government intervened. The first legislative initiatives, known as the Enforcement Acts, were passed by Congress during President Ulysses S. Grant's first term in office. Interfering in elections or preventing citizens from voting became a federal offence, as did conspiring to abridge those fundamental constitutional rights. President Grant also signed into law a bill establishing the Department of Justice, allowing a stronger federal government role in investigations and prosecution. Indeed, "the department's first principal task was to secure the civil rights promised by the 13th, 14th and 15th Amendments."[7] The following year Congress enacted the Ku Klux Klan Act, again specifically to combat this movement. It gave the president the authority to order the suspension of habeas corpus and deploy the U.S. military to maintain domestic law and order. In addition, the act strengthened the powers of federal attorneys to prosecute conspiracies meant to deprive persons of their right to due process and equal protection under the law. Thus, within a few years of its founding, America's most notorious homegrown terrorist movement would be effectively suppressed—although violence would unfortunately continue from other groups not necessarily linked to the KKK.[8]

Given the original Klan's geographically limited constituency of former slaveholders and secessionists situated mostly in America's southern states, its original iteration also had little appeal, much less acceptance, in other parts of the country. But that would change with the release of D. W. Griffith's landmark feature film *The Birth of a Nation*, fifty years after the Civil War ended.

David Wark Griffith was a product of the South: steeped in the antebellum romanticism of that era and thus inclined to uncritically accept as axiomatic the mythology of the fabled Lost Cause. Kentucky born and bred, Griffith worshipped his father, a celebrated Civil War battlefield commander who had risen to the rank of colonel in the Confederate army. Known as "Roaring Jake" or "Thunder Jake" for his prodigious oratorical skills, the elder Griffith was a state legislator and inveterate gambler who died when David was ten, leaving the family impoverished. Mother and son moved from the family farm to nearby

Louisville, where David found work in a bookstore. Financial difficulties prevented him from finishing high school, but that job nurtured a lifelong love of literature and storytelling. The young Griffith aspired to be a playwright but was more successful as an actor. He moved from St. Louis to San Francisco and eventually to New York. It was there, in 1908, that Griffith directed his first motion picture. Two years later, his peripatetic existence ended when Griffith revolutionized filmmaking by discovering a small village north of Los Angeles. Directed by Griffith, *In Old California* is widely credited as the first movie shot entirely in Hollywood.[9]

Griffith's ticket to fame and fortune, however, would be his adaptation of Thomas Dixon Jr.'s 1905 novel *The Clansman: A Historical Romance of the Ku Klux Klan*. Described by the renowned University of Kentucky historian Thomas D. Clark as a work bereft of "artistic conception or literary craftsmanship," *The Clansman* nevertheless "opened wider a vein of racial hatred which was to poison further an age already in social and political upheaval. Dixon had in fact given voice in his novel to one of the most powerful latent forces in the social and political mind of the South."[10] The book was catnip for a transplanted southerner like Griffith who longed as much for his bucolic childhood home as for what he regarded as a halcyon, bygone era. Griffith wrote, produced, and directed the groundbreaking three-hour-and-ten-minute feature film. It presented a gripping narrative of southern womanhood subjected to the depredations of licentious freed slaves before being rescued and ultimately avenged by the brave night riders of the post–Civil War South.[11]

The Birth of a Nation was the longest and the most expensive film production to date—at a cost of $112,000. It went on to earn a staggering $10 million.[12] Griffith's innovative staging, photography, and cohesive story line changed cinema forever. Pauline Kael, the doyenne of twentieth-century American film criticism, has argued that "almost every major tradition and most of the genres, and even many of the metaphors, in movies" had their origins in *The Birth of a Nation*.[13] It became the first moving picture to be shown at the White House. President Woodrow Wilson, a friend and classmate of Dixon's from their time as graduate students at Johns Hopkins University, reportedly described the film as "like writing history with lightning"—although a 2013 biography could find no evidence to support that assertion.[14]

The Birth of a Nation premiered in February 1915, just as one of the country's most iniquitous and shameful legal cases was lurching toward its final, tragic denouement. Two years earlier, Leo Max Frank, the Jewish superintendent of an Atlanta pencil factory and president of the Atlanta chapter of the prominent Jewish organization B'nai B'rith International, had been convicted of the murder of one of his employees, a thirteen-year-old girl named Mary Phagan.[15] Entrenched antisemitism combined with popular depictions of lascivious Jewish men lusting after young Christian girls had produced a unanimous jury verdict. Frank was sentenced to death and embarked on a series of appeals that finally came before the U.S. Supreme Court in April 1915. In a seven-to-two vote, the court denied Frank's petition. However, two months later, Governor John Slaton of Georgia commuted Frank's murder conviction to life imprisonment. Outrage over the commutation immediately surfaced and continued to intensify as the second anniversary of Frank's conviction approached.[16]

On August 16, 1915, an eight-car convoy carrying the "Knights of Mary Phagan," also known as the "Vigilance Committee," departed Marietta, Georgia, for the state prison in Milledgeville, over a hundred miles away. Its passengers included some of that city's most prominent citizens—a former superior court judge, a former sheriff, and a clergyman. They abducted Frank from the prison hospital, where he was recovering from a near-fatal attack by a knife-wielding fellow prisoner, and brought him to Marietta—Phagan's birth place. As an excited crowd gathered, the men hanged Frank from a tree. His body, already bloodied from the knife wounds to his neck that the noose had reopened, was then taken down and stomped and kicked. Photographs of the gruesome scene, clearly showing the faces of Frank's murderers, could be purchased locally as souvenir postcards for years afterward. A grand jury investigating the killing returned no indictments. Tom Watson, a popular Georgia politician and newspaper and magazine publisher who had already served in the U.S. House of Representatives and would subsequently be elected to the U.S. Senate, had repeatedly called for precisely this kind of vigilante action.[17] Described by the *Georgia Encyclopedia* as a "force for white supremacy and anti-Catholic rhetoric,"[18] Watson captured the prevailing sentiment in his subsequent justification of the lynching. "All over this broad land," he proclaimed, "there are millions of good people, not doped by Jew money, and lies, that enthusiastically greet the triumph of law in Georgia.

Womanhood is made safer, everywhere."[19] Others reacted differently: the Frank murder would inspire a group of prominent Jews to form a new organization dedicated to ending the defamation of the Jewish people— the Anti-Defamation League of B'nai B'rith would grow into a leading civil rights organization speaking out against hate in all its forms.[20]

Meanwhile, an Atlanta resident named William James Simmons watched these developments with increasing interest. A native Alabamian and veteran of the Spanish-American War, the self-appointed "Colonel" Simmons had a uniquely undistinguished career as soldier, itinerant Methodist minister, garter salesman, history teacher, and paid organizer for a variety of fraternal orders. A compulsive networker and opportunist, Simmons belonged to over a dozen fraternal and Masonic orders. While preaching the gospel in rural Alabama fourteen years earlier, he claimed to have had a vision of the white-robed night riders of the past galloping across the sky against the backdrop of a map of the United States.[21] Simmons would later testify before Congress that *The Birth of a Nation* had cemented his decision to engineer the Klan's resurrection and thus fulfill the vision that had appeared to him years before.[22]

The intense passions aroused by the Frank trial and lynching provided Simmons with the perfect proof of concept. Accordingly, on October 16, 1915, he gathered thirty-three men who signed an application to the state of Georgia for the granting of a charter for a new organization to be called the Knights of the Ku Klux Klan. Among the signatories were three members of the original KKK—to which Simmons's father had also belonged.[23] The timing was propitious. *The Birth of a Nation* was scheduled to open in Atlanta the following week. Simmons announced the appearance of his new iteration of the Klan in newspaper advertisements strategically placed alongside movie showtimes at theaters screening the film. He and fellow Klansmen attended the premiere.[24] Five weeks later, on Thanksgiving night, Simmons and fourteen followers climbed to the summit of nearby Stone Mountain. Beneath a tall wooden cross was an altar consisting of the U.S. flag, an unsheathed sword, and the Bible. The cross was set aflame. "The angels that have anxiously watched the Reformation from its beginnings, must have hovered about Stone Mountain [that night] and shouted hosanas to the highest heavens," Simmons recalled.[25] Soon, Klan-sponsored showings of Griffith's compelling film would be used to attract more members.[26] Its purpose was described by Simmons as nostalgic and cultural.

"To keep alive the memory of the original Klan and the principles, traditions and institutions which they risked their lives to preserve for themselves and for posterity," he explained in a 1916 recruiting pamphlet,

> the men of today, who appreciate their patriotic and chivalric work, have established a living, lasting memorial to them by the organization of the Invisible Empire, Knights of the Ku Klux Klan, as a national standard fraternal order composed of real American manhood of the nation who uncompromisingly believe in perpetual preservation of the fundamental principles, ideals and institutions of the pure Anglo-Saxon civilization and all the fruits thereof.[27]

This reincarnated Klan differed significantly from its previous manifestation. While Simmons's reenvisioned KKK retained the familiar racist, white supremacist essence of its predecessor, he also sought new recruits beyond the regional niche occupied by the original Klan. To do this, Simmons adopted the stridently anti-immigrant, anti-Catholic, and antisemitic tropes expressed by Tom Watson, among others.[28] "We exclude Jews because they do not believe in the Christian religion," Simmons explained. "We exclude Catholics because they owe allegiance to an institution that is foreign to the Government of the United States. To assure the supremacy of the white race, we believe in the exclusion of the yellow race and in the disenfranchisement of the Negro."[29]

Simmons's Klan thus shared many of the traits associated with present-day violent, far-right extremist movements. It championed an idiosyncratic and exclusionist conception of patriotism, was profoundly antielitist and anti-intellectual, disdained science, regarded most elected politicians and civil servants as corrupt and self-serving, and thought cities incorrigible cesspits of depravity—despite the Klan's popularity in many of the nation's urban centers.[30] New York City, he predicted, would eventually self-destruct—leaving nothing but "dust and desolation."[31] Simmons always maintained that the Klan was a patriotic, law-abiding movement comprised of "a high class order for men of intelligence and character."[32] "Our robes are not worn for the purpose of terrorizing people," he also claimed. "They are as innocent as the breath of an angel."[33] Simmons's leadership of the revived movement, however, was always tenuous. More a dreamer than a doer, he was removed from his "emperorship" and position as Imperial Wizard in 1924 for incompetence and inefficiency. A toxic combination of internecine rivalries and power struggles, corruption, criminal embezzlement, and scandal involving Simmons's successor subsequently paralyzed the organization and led to this second Klan's demise.[34]

The KKK struggled to survive throughout the Depression and war years. It was forced to officially disband in 1944 because of an IRS lien being levied for back taxes, but various state and local chapters remained active.[35] The historic *Brown v. Topeka Board of Education* Supreme Court decision in 1954, however, breathed new life into the movement. The fusion of religion and bigotry—Protestantism with white supremacy—had of course always been a core Klan belief. But, more critically, it reflected the dominant mindset of the American South since the end of Reconstruction. Maintaining that status quo and the Jim Crow laws that preserved it thus assumed new urgency with the court's desegregation ruling—at this critical turning point, when the Jim Crow–era laws of post-Reconstruction were eroding.[36] By the 1960s, these responses had exploded into some of the most infamous acts of violence of the period. The bombing of the Sixteenth Street Baptist Church in Birmingham—a city that sustained so many bombings during the civil rights era it earned the macabre nickname "Bombingham"[37]—and the murder of the NAACP state field secretary for Mississippi, the World War II veteran Medgar Evers, both occurred in 1963. In 1964, three civil rights activists registering voters—Michael Schwerner, James Chaney, and Andrew Goodman—were kidnapped, tortured, and killed in Mississippi as well. The following year, a Michigan civil rights worker named Viola Liuzzo was shot to death in Selma, Alabama. And in 1966, Vernon Dahmer, another NAACP leader in Mississippi, was also murdered. The KKK was responsible for each.

The enhanced civil rights and voting rights legislation championed by President Lyndon Johnson infused the Klan with additional momentum. In 1966, for instance, it had over 25,000 members organized in some five hundred chapters across the South—small compared to the previous iteration but still a consequential force.[38] However, by the 1970s, the Klan was a fading enterprise—weakened by the attention focused on it by the

FBI. Violence became more spasmodic, as seen at Greensboro, North Carolina, in 1979, when KKK and American Nazi Party members opened fire at a "Death to the Klan" rally planned by the Communist Workers Party, killing five demonstrators. Membership had tanked to five thousand people in 1973, and although it had roughly doubled by the end of the decade,[39] the KKK by the early 1980s had been overtaken by new and even more extreme, violent, and sedition-minded white supremacist groups. Louis Beam, Frazier Glenn Miller, and Robert Miles were all former Klan leaders who would play a pivotal role in the reinvention—and longevity—of the white power movement in America.

. . .

The search for new issues in order to appeal to an expanding base and thus attract new sources of recruits and support had transformed the KKK in the early twentieth century from an isolated and regional to a truly nationwide phenomenon. In the aftermath of the Fort Smith trial acquittals, the Klan's contemporary counterparts embarked on a similar quest to infuse the movement with new momentum and enthusiasts. This same imperative had in fact long animated William Potter Gale's efforts to broaden American white supremacism's ambit.

In the early 1980s, Gale articulated his vision of an "unorganized militia" supporting a modern-day version of the post–Revolutionary War Committee of the States (COS).[40] Under the Articles of Confederation, the short-lived original committee performed various executive functions regarding trade, commerce, and education during such times when Congress was in session. To Gale's mind, this meant that the twentieth-century iteration was a perfectly legal, constitutionally protected version of its eighteenth- and early-nineteenth-century predecessors—with a modern-day remit to defend against government tyranny and the suppression of citizens' fundamental rights.[41] In practice, Gale's COS harassed IRS agents, intimidated judges, and adhered to core Christian Identity beliefs.[42] Its membership, according to a confidential FBI memorandum, included members of the now defunct Minutemen (a 1960s-era "paramilitary secret society dedicated to protecting America from communist invasion from abroad and communist subversion at home"),[43] Klansmen, and "other adherents of extreme right wing anti-black, anti-Jewish, anti-Federal Government organizations."[44]

Gale appointed himself the "chief of staff" of the COS's militia and began to offer two-day paramilitary training at his Mannassah Ranch in Mariposa, California.[45] Among the topics covered, the FBI reported, were ambush techniques, the placement of mines, and use of tripwire explosive devices.[46] "It's exploding," Gale bragged in 1987, describing the intentions and trajectory of his "unorganized militia." "It's right under the surface. But the shot at Concord Bridge hasn't been fired yet," he explained. "It will be shortly fired. And when it is fired, the King's magistrates better head for England, or they're gonna be hung by the neck. The same as occurred in 1776 and 1778 by your ancestors. Is that a threat? Oh no. I predict it. That's coming, and it's coming soon."[47]

Gale died before his dream of a national "unorganized militia" could be realized. But as he had predicted, the concept was gaining traction among the die-hard survivors of a movement that had few tangible accomplishments to show despite a decade of intensifying efforts. Below suggests that the first groups to use the militia label appeared in the Pacific Northwest around 1989.[48] However, as far back as 1963, according to the FBI, a group calling itself the Alabama Militia Volunteers had existed. Composed of active Klansmen, it was publicly known as the Volunteers for Alabama and Wallace—in reference to the state's segregationist governor, George Wallace. Indeed, supporting Wallace in preventing the integration of Alabama's public schools was the group's purpose. Given that this discussion of the Alabama militia appears in a file on Gale, he was presumably aware of—and perhaps inspired or reminded of—its then uncommon moniker.[49]

Militias, however, were still not a distinctly prominent dimension of the white supremacist movement until two incidents in 1992 and 1993 changed everything. For those already deeply suspicious of a tyrannical federal government intent on violating the Second Amendment and constraining other constitutional rights, the botched attempt by federal authorities to arrest a survivalist and former U.S. Army Green Beret living off the grid in Idaho and the siege and then brutal assault of a religious sect's rural Texas compound confirmed their worst fears. Both Ruby Ridge and Waco would infuse the movement with newfound purpose and momentum and become rallying cries for those who flocked to militias in the years that followed.

• • •

The rugged individualist who rejects conventional, modern society, thumbs his nose at authority, and heads West in search of peace and tranquility amid the country's most spectacular natural splendor is enshrined in American mythology. Thus in the summer of 1983 did Randy Weaver, his wife, Vicki, and three children pack up and move from Cedar Falls, Iowa, to the northernmost tip of the Idaho panhandle, just south of the Canadian border. They settled in Boundary County,[50] which, according to the 1980 census, had just over seven thousand residents. Then, as now, the population was almost entirely white[51]—which suited the Weavers perfectly, given their strict interpretation of scripture that established the societal preeminence of white Anglo-Saxon Protestantism and its adherents. As hardcore Christian survivalists, Randy and Vicki were intent on escaping the coming apocalypse by fleeing to the isolated safety of the Rocky Mountains. "The Bible teaches us," Randy had told a local reporter before leaving Iowa, "that somewhere near, during the reign of the One World Leader, God will free the hands of Satan to wreak havoc with the peoples of the Earth." He was intent, therefore, to create a "kill zone"—a three-hundred-yard defensive perimeter—around their future home to protect him and his family.[52] As a Vietnam War–era veteran of the U.S. Army who had trained as a combat engineer and Special Forces Green Beret, Weaver had acquired the requisite knowledge and skills to do so.[53]

It was Vicki who, through intense Bible study, had in 1978 discovered the end-of-times theology rooted in Old Testament prophecy. It was all both so simple and now so clear to Vicki what was occurring. A global conspiracy orchestrated by Free Masons and the eighteenth-century secret society known as the Illuminati, allied with the Council on Foreign Relations, the Trilateral Commission, and other "New World Order"–advocacy institutions—manipulated and controlled by "evil, money-grubbing Jews"—was at the root of the globe's tribulations and coming apocalypse. As God's genuine "chosen people," it was incumbent on the Weavers to survive. Such beliefs thus led Vicki and Randy to Christian Identity.[54] Their path to the kind of divinely justified antisemitism and racism embedded in that theology may have been facilitated by the representative from Butler's Aryan Nations who reportedly visited the John Deere farm machinery plant in Waterloo, Iowa, where Randy worked.[55] Regardless, the modest mountainside cabin that Randy and Vicki built themselves on Ruby Ridge was only an hour's drive north of Butler's compound in Hayden Lake. And it was Weaver's presence at the 1986 annual Aryan Nations Congress that set in motion the chain of events that culminated in tragedy six years later.[56]

Within two years of relocating to Idaho, Weaver found himself the subject of a federal investigation. U.S. Secret Service agents interviewed him in February 1985 after learning about threats Weaver had allegedly made against President Ronald Reagan, Governor John Evans of Idaho, and law enforcement officers. Weaver was also questioned about his relationship with people belonging to the Aryan Nations and the number of weapons and amount of ammunition he had stockpiled at the cabin. Although no charges were brought against him, Weaver's remarks about "the world ending in two years," when his home would "be under siege and assaulted," caught the agents' attention.[57] But it was not Weaver's political beliefs that got him into trouble with the feds. It was his and his family's perennial financial woes.[58]

Given Weaver's specialized military training and known extremist beliefs, his name came up the following summer as a result of a Bureau of Alcohol, Tobacco, and Firearms (ATF) investigation into a string of bombings in Coeur d'Alene that would eventually be linked to the Brüder Schweigen Strike Force II. Once more, no charges were filed against Weaver, but in the meantime the ATF had tasked an informant named Kenneth Fadeley to gather information about attendees at the 1986 Aryan Nations Congress. It was there that he was introduced to Weaver. Fadeley presented himself as an arms dealer who supplied weapons to motorcycle gangs. They met again at the 1987 event—to which Weaver, for the first time, had brought along Vicki and the children. The ATF agents saw an opening to try to enlist Weaver as a confidential informant when he complained to Fadeley about money problems. It was not until two years later that any kind of transaction that might criminally implicate Weaver would occur.[59]

Despite his increasingly extremist views, Weaver had never actually joined the Aryan Nations. Moreover, he was openly critical of the group's senior leadership and especially of Butler. But Weaver was indisputably adopting views that aligned him closely with its ideology. He competed unsuccessfully in the Republican Party primary for county sheriff on a platform promising to enforce only those laws that the local people wanted. Weaver also had progressed from a mere attendee at Aryan Nations congresses to a speaker at the 1989 gathering. It was there, the DOJ Ruby Ridge Task Force explains, that Weaver told Fadeley of his interest in "forming a group to fight the 'Zionist Organized Government.'" Apparently, to raise funds both for the new group and to provide for his family, Weaver had offered to sell Fadeley illegally modified, sawed-off shotguns. In October 1989, Fadeley purchased an initial consignment of two such weapons. With that sale, Weaver had now broken the law and therefore had furnished the ATF with the leverage they sought to turn him. In June 1990, agents offered Weaver a proposition that would spare the former Green Beret from going to prison on illegal weapons sales charges in return for his cooperation "in their investigation of Aryan Nations members." Weaver replied that he was not willing to become a "snitch." To underscore that point and highlight what Vicki claimed were the federal government's efforts to entrap her husband, two weeks later she sent an impassioned letter to the "Aryan Nations & all our brethren of the Anglo Saxon Race." Vicki emphasized that "we cannot make deals with the enemy. This is a war against the sons of Isaac. Yahweh [God] our Yashua [Jesus] is our Savior and King. . . . If we are not free to obey the laws of Yahweh, we may as well be dead! Let Yah-Yashua's perfect will be done. If its [sic] our time, we'll go home. If it is not we will praise his Separated name."[60]

On December 13, 1990, a federal grand jury indicted Weaver. Having concluded that "it would be too dangerous to the arresting agents and to the Weaver children for BATF to arrest Weaver at his residence," the DOJ Task Force report recounts, ATF agents "decided to carry out a ruse to arrest Weaver by surprise away from his home." He was apprehended on January 17, 1991, and arraigned the following day. Weaver was represented by Everett Hofmeister, who had represented Butler at the Fort Smith trial. He pleaded not guilty and was released on bond. Weaver's trial date was set for late February.[61] Vicki then sent two letters to the U.S. Attorney's Office responsible for her husband's prosecution. They were addressed to "the servants of the Queen of Babylon" and warned that the blood of "tyrants . . . will flow." Whether she and Randy "live or whether we die, we will not bow to your evil commandments."[62] After Randy failed to appear for trial, another indictment and arrest warrant were issued.[63]

For the next nearly year and a half, the U.S. Marshals Service attempted to persuade Weaver to surrender. In addition to marshals observing that he and other family members went about armed at all times, they also noted that Weaver had reached out to the local sheriff. Couched in the apocalyptic argot that had shaped and molded Vicki and Randy's beliefs for over a decade, he threatened to shoot anyone who tried to arrest him. According to the DOJ Task Force report, surveillance done by the marshals had revealed that

> Weaver and his children responded to approaching persons and vehicles by taking armed positions over the driveway leading to the Weaver cabin. During this period, Weaver continued to make statements that he would not surrender peacefully and that his family was prepared to defend him.
>
> The Director of the Marshals Service ordered that no action be taken that could endanger the Weaver children. In the Spring of 1992, the marshals developed an undercover plan to arrest Weaver away from his cabin and family.[64]

It was another such reconnaissance mission undertaken by marshals of the Weaver residence on August 21, 1992, that went tragically awry.

A team of six marshals was just leaving when one of the Weavers' dogs began to chase three of them. Kevin Harris, a family friend; thirteen-year-old Sammy Weaver; and his sisters followed. They were all armed. Hearing the commotion, Randy rushed over as well. What happened next has always been disputed. According to the marshals, they identified themselves and told Randy to halt. Gunfire erupted. Within seconds, Deputy Marshal William Degan, Sammy Weaver, and the dog were dead. Randy and Harris, however, have always claimed that a marshal fired the first shot—killing the dog. An enraged Sammy then opened fire on the marshal but was himself cut down in a hail of bullets from the marshals. Harris would later argue that the marshals had not identified themselves and that he had killed one of them while trying to protect Sammy. In any event, Harris and the surviving Weavers retreated to their cabin, and the standoff on Ruby Ridge began.[65]

Upon learning of the shootout, the deaths, and a dangerous situation with five of the marshals still pinned down on the hillside, the Marshals Service requested assistance from the FBI and its elite Hostage Rescue Team (HRT). A team of Idaho state police managed to extract the trapped marshals just before midnight—about twelve hours after the shooting started. The HRT arrived and quickly formulated a plan that involved the use of snipers and armored personnel carriers.[66] Coulson, the HRT commander, was back in Washington manning the FBI Strategic Information and Operations Center (SIOC) when he received a fax requesting approval. His first reaction was to think to himself: *"These dumb shits. Have they got their heads up their ass or what?* What I had in my hand didn't resemble anything that the HRT or any law enforcement agency should do. It was a military assault plan."[67]

The HRT on-the-scene commander had proposed to use one of the carriers to deliver a telephone to the cabin and thus initiate negotiations. The snipers were meant to defend against the possibility of people sympathetic to the Weavers lying in wait on the hillside or an attempt by the Weavers themselves to ambush an assault team. Snipers from both the HRT and the Marshal's Special Operations Group were briefed on the special rules of engagement that would govern any use of deadly force and had settled into position around 5:45 PM on the evening of August 22. An HRT helicopter was circling overhead when Lon Horiuchi, an HRT sniper, observed a man he thought was Harris emerge from the cabin with a rifle. Believing that he was preparing to shoot at the helicopter, Horiuchi opened fire—slightly wounding the armed individual, who turned out to be Weaver, not Harris. He fired a second shot as Weaver entered the cabin. It missed but went through the curtained window of the open door, striking and killing Vicki before lodging in Harris's arm.[68]

From the moment that news of the botched arrest and massive law enforcement response reached the nearby towns of Bonner's Ferry and Naples, neighbors and supporters had rushed to the end of Molar Creek Road, where police barricades blocked access to the Weavers' cabin on Ruby Ridge. The initial two dozen or so protestors had gathered peacefully, waving signs reading "Tell the Truth," "Freedom of Religion," and "Your Home Could Be Next." But as word spread, the crowd swelled with the likes of appreciably more bellicose neo-Nazi skinheads, Aryan Nations zealots, and Christian Identity adherents, among others. They hailed from Colorado, Idaho, Montana, Nevada, Oregon, Utah, and even Canada.[69] An estimated two hundred men, women, and children now maintained a twenty-four-hour vigil. They jeered and taunted the police and federal agents manning the cordon surrounding the Weavers' abode and held aloft signs declaring: "Death to ZOG," "F.B.I. Burn in Hell," "The Weavers Today! Our Families Tomorrow," "Remember Kent State. Red Square. Tiananmen Square. My Lai. Ruby Ridge," "Government Lies/Patriot Dies," "Your home could be next," "We're Fed UP with the Feds," "Christians Against Tyranny," "Leave the Family Alone, Go Home," "Let's Stop This Abuse of Our Freedom," "30.06 Go Thru Your Vest Easy Fed Dogs," and "Zionist Murderers."[70] The names of the movement's iconic martyrs— Gordon Kahl and Robert Mathews—were mournfully recalled in speeches depicting a legacy of government persecution that had now culminated in the deaths of a devoted mother and her beloved son.[71] Mathews's widow, Debbie, now a white supremacist celebrity, was there, too. Beside her stood their ten-year-old son, Clint, who clutched his own sign with the words "Baby Killers!"[72] It was hard in some cases to tell the difference between some of the protestors and law enforcement officers, who both wore the same tactical gear. Five skinheads, for instance, were arrested by identically attired federal agents on August 25 as they attempted to smuggle an assortment of weapons to the Weavers.[73]

Unaware of Vicki's death and Harris's wounding, the FBI attempted to initiate negotiations. As the DOJ Task Force report tersely notes, "There was no response." Indeed, nearly a week would pass before Weaver agreed on Friday, August 28, to speak with retired U.S. Army Special Forces colonel James "Bo" Gritz.[74] Gritz, a highly decorated Vietnam War veteran who had subsequently led covert missions to South East Asia in search of missing American prisoners of war—the "Rambo" films starring Sylvester Stallone were reportedly modeled on Gritz—was well-known in American extremist circles.[75] According to the FBI's Wayne Manis, he was the leader of a group of "anti-government sympathizers" living in the mountains about four hours south in Kamiah, Idaho.[76] Gritz was also a candidate in 1988 for vice president on the Populist Party ticket and was quoted as having declared at a 1991 Bible camp run by the Reverend Pete Peters, a prominent exponent of Identity theology, that "the enemy you face today is a satanic overthrow [*sic*] where he would change the United States of America, a nation under God, into USA, Incorporated. . . . And a Zionist that would rule over us as long as satan might be upon this earth, that is your enemy."[77] The following day, Weaver allowed Gritz; a retired Phoenix police officer active in Patriot and antigovernment extremist circles named Jack McLamb; Jackie Brown, a friend of Vicki's; and a local pastor to enter the cabin and discuss resolving the standoff. Negotiations resumed on August 30. The seriously injured Harris surrendered first. Gritz and Jackie Brown followed him out of the cabin with Vicki's lifeless body in their arms. Randy gave himself up the following day, ending the eleven-day-long siege of Ruby Ridge.[78]

Both Harris and Weaver were arrested and charged with first-degree murder in the death of Deputy Marshal Degan as well as assaulting and resisting federal officers and conspiracy to provoke a violent confrontation. Their trial began on April 13, 1993. After deliberating for nearly a month, the jury acquitted both men of all charges. In a separate trial, Weaver was subsequently convicted of failing to appear for trial and committing an offense while on bail. He was acquitted on the prior charges of manufacturing illegal firearms, using a firearm to commit a violent crime, and harboring a fugitive. Weaver was sentenced to eighteen months in prison, fined $10,000, and placed on three years' probation. The presiding judge also criticized and fined the FBI for failing to produce discovery materials and respond to court directives as well as for "its indifference to the rights of the defendant and to the administration of justice."[79] In an editorial titled "Another Federal Fiasco," the *New York Times* censoriously observed:

> Randy Weaver was a white supremacist. He lived as a heavily armed recluse in a cabin on a ridge in rural Idaho. Neither of those things is against the law in the United States. . . .
>
> Last week Mr. Weaver and Mr. Harris were acquitted of murder in the death of the marshal. During the trial the F.B.I., the lead agency, admitted that it had tampered with evidence.
>
> There are a lot of lunatics out there in the woods. But it is not the job of Federal law enforcement agencies to behave in a way that seems designed to confirm their paranoia—especially when there is no proof they have violated any laws.[80]

In August 1995, the DOJ settled a lawsuit brought by Weaver and his three daughters. He received a cash settlement of $100,000, and each of the girls was paid $1 million.[81] Harris received $380,000 in a separate lawsuit.[82] The payouts provided additional confirmation of what the crowd that had gathered down the road from the Weavers' cabin during the siege had already concluded: an aggressive, predatory government was waging war on its own citizens. And the tragedy that had befallen the Weavers had become a rallying—if not a battle—cry for people who were formerly concerned about the loss of their constitutional rights but now feared for their lives.[83]

• • •

The spontaneous grassroots gathering at the edge of that paved road in rural Idaho would reinvigorate and reinvent late-twentieth-century white supremacism, much as had occurred in Georgia with the Klan seventy years earlier. Like many concepts that suddenly garner increased notoriety and popularity, no lone individual can be credited as their sole progenitor. But a handful of movement notables quickly recognized the opportunity that the federal debacle at Ruby Ridge presented—and ran with it.

Bo Gritz could at least claim to have been there and witnessed the overwhelming force massed by the U.S. government against a man, his family, and a friend of theirs. "The lesson for America is this could happen to anybody," he observed. "We've got to change the bureaucracy."[84] Returning to the campaign stump after successfully negotiating Weaver's surrender, Gritz went further: calling for the formation of people's militias to defend against the predatory federal government and the repressive "New World Order" (NWO) it was inextricably entwined with.[85] At a campaign stop in Montana he delighted the crowd by tearing to shreds a United Nations flag symbolic of the NWO; in Idaho he advised his supporters that if his campaign bid was unsuccessful that year, in four years "we may be required to defend our rights with bullets."[86] President Trump would say something similar to his followers before they attacked the U.S. Capitol building almost thirty years later.[87]

An Identity theology pastor from LaPorte, Colorado—just outside of Fort Collins—named Peter J. "Pete" Peters was thinking along similar lines. Formerly employed by the U.S. Department of Agriculture, Peters had achieved some notoriety after Bob Mathews had attended two meetings at his church in 1984.[88] He moved quickly to position himself at the vanguard of the diverse constituencies that had converged on Ruby Ridge in protest, but once it had ended, he lacked both direction and cohesion. Within days of Weaver's and Harris's surrender, invitations from Peters to a conference that would "confront the injustice and tyranny manifested in the killings of Vicki Weaver and her son Samuel"[89] were en route to a "Scriptures for America" mailing list and other interested parties across the country.[90]

On October 22, 1992, about 150 people from some thirty states convened at a YMCA conference center in Estes Park, Colorado. Among the attendees were dyed-in-the-wool racists like Butler and Beam but also zealous Second Amendment advocates like Larry Pratt, the executive director of Gun Owners of America, who would subsequently prove critical in the emergence of the Christian Patriot movement in the United States.[91] "Men came together," Peters later boasted,

> who in the past would normally not be caught together under the same roof, who greatly disagree with each other on many theological and philosophical points, whose teachings contradict each other in many ways. Yet, not only did they come together, they worked together for they all agreed what was done to the Weaver family was wrong and could not, and should not, be ignored by Christian men.[92]

Indeed, for the next three days, neo-Nazis, Klansmen, Identity adherents, militant opponents of taxation, and "concerned citizens" representing various grassroots organizations rubbed shoulders as they debated next steps in light of the patent threat posed by an aggressively predatory federal government.[93] Beam delivered the keynote. He movingly described how "the attack on the Weaver family by federal assassins was an attack upon every family in the United States. This time the federal terrorists, masquerading as officers, came for Randy Weaver. Next time they may come for you. . . . They may also come again for me." It was also only the beginning, Beam warned. "If federal terrorism goes unchallenged, then no one in this nation is safe. Government terrorism, if ignored, does not go away, but gets worse. Like a lion having tasted the blood of human victims, they will come for more, new victims."[94]

Beam went on to invoke the words "New World Order" to describe the vast conspiracy being engineered by global elites through the United Nations to undermine the independence of the United States and subject its citizens to a tyrannical rule. Mobilizing against this threat would shortly become a rallying cry for the American far right and its embryonic militia movement.[95] Once again fusing religion and resistance, Beam told his audience:

> Those in government who have labored over the years to build the road that leads to a new world order are beside [themselves] with joy, excitement, and anticipation for they are almost there. . . .
>
> Ah, but those last few miles will be rough ones. For in the name of Yahweh . . . we pledge that those last few miles will not just be paved with the bones, blood, and broken hearts of patriots. We will pave that road with tyrant's blood, tyrants' bones, and you shall know the broken heart. . . .
>
> We will not yield this country to the forces of darkness[,] oppression, and tyranny. . . . It is the enemies of Christ that we wage our struggle against, and there are no bounds to their evil. There are no limits to their lust for power. . . .
>
> I and many others in this country, many in this room tonight, will not roll over and play dead for your New World Order.[96]

Beam's stirring battle cry might have gone unnoticed by violently inclined extremists who had missed what Peters had dubbed the "Rocky Mountain Rendezvous" had the entrepreneurial cleric not enshrined it in a "special report" titled "A Battle Plan for Future Conflicts." Peters very helpfully included the entire text of Beam's decade-old leaderless resistance treatise—thus ensuring its accessibility to a new generation of antigovernment militants.[97]

The activist and author David Neiwert has described how the incident at Ruby Ridge was therefore "a stone thrown into a pond whose ripples have since grown into a tidal wave." He cites Beam's declamation and Peters's promulgation of this strategy as "in essence, a blueprint for patriots to begin a 'militia movement.'"[98] Indeed, the centrality of the Estes Park gathering to the subsequent emergence of a militant, aggressive, antigovernment, nationwide militia movement has long been debated by scholars and others. Schlachter, for instance, downplays its significance. Citing the ADL's Mark Pitcavage, among the leading scholars of the American far right, she notes that the most prominent figures of what was already an emerging phenomenon did not attend Peters's much-publicized rendezvous. To her mind, it was retrospectively seized upon by the media as the "birthplace" of a movement that subsequently proliferated and gained increasing momentum.[99] Both Kenneth Stern and Leonard Zeskind, two prominent American human rights activists with long experience of studying American far-right extremism, similarly warn against exaggerating the conference's importance—although Stern notes that within a couple of years "Beam's principles for white supremacist response to the Randy Weaver siege would become the model structure for many militia groups."[100] And, as the historian Kathleen Belew argues, militias had emerged in the Pacific Northwest at least three years earlier and were already actively "shar[ing] personnel, funds, images, and ideologies with the established white power movement."[101]

But, at the same time, the Estes Park gathering was notable for the absence of the speeches, proclamations, and discussions of all the classic white supremacist themes and catchphrases that were fixtures of previous such gatherings. Indeed, one of the unusual features of the conference was reportedly that none of the blatantly racist, antisemitic, and xenophobic rhetoric typical of other events that many of the same participants would have attended in the past was openly voiced. Instead, rhetoric about the critical role of "patriots"—locked and loaded white Anglo-Saxon Christians organized in self-defense militias—was fed to a receptive audience. The conference's overriding theme was that the enemy was now in plain sight: It was a patently aggressive and predatory federal government controlled by a conspiratorial cabal of bankers and other elites allied with the United Nations determined to impose a "New World Order" on that unsuspecting demographic of patriotic, white, Anglo-Saxon Americans, of which Gale had long warned.[102] And, if they needed any further proof of the U.S. government's malevolent intentions toward its own citizens, especially when exercising their Second Amendment constitutional rights, the tragic chain of events that unfolded just months later at the Waco, Texas, compound of a religious cult calling itself the Branch Davidians delivered it.[103]

The Branch Davidians, led by the self-proclaimed prophet David Koresh, had fallen under federal investigation for stockpiling illegal weapons at their remote Mount Carmel Center (while newspaper reporting also alleged Koresh was committing widespread statutory rape and taking child brides).[104] But a raid planned for February 28 went disastrously awry, resulting in a chaotic firefight in which six Davidians and four ATF agents were killed. The subject of numerous books, documentaries, commentaries, and even a six-part Netflix mini-series,[105] a subsequent fifty-one-day standoff ended dramatically on April 19, 1993, when two specially equipped M-60 tanks breached the walls of the compound's main building and began to pump tear gas into the structure in hopes of flushing the Davidians out. After that failed to produce the desired result, the FBI deployed four U.S. Army Bradley fighting vehicles. Over the next six hours, they repeatedly fired 40 mm. canisters of CS (tear) gas into the structure through its windows. Then, around noon, three separate fires broke out in different parts of the building and spread rapidly. Only nine survived the ensuing inferno, which killed seventy-six people and whose cause remains a matter of intense debate.[106]

The tragic climax to the weeks-long confrontation that once again seemingly pitted ordinary citizens accused of weapons violations against the militarized might of the same two federal law enforcement agencies responsible for the Ruby Ridge debacle could hardly have come at a less propitious time for the U.S. government. Just as the FBI was readying its final assault plan, Randy Weaver's trial was beginning in Boise, Idaho. Five days in, the judge had to instruct the jurors to ignore the tragic news occurring two thousand miles away in Waco.[107] The televised images of the assault and its fiery denouement thus fed the paranoia, fears of government overreach, and calls to violent resistance that were already gathering momentum as a result of the Ruby Ridge siege and the Fort Estes conference that had followed.[108] "Ruby Ridge—like the even more deadly confrontation at the Branch Davidian compound near Waco, Tex., in 1993, which left more than 80 people dead," the *Los Angeles Times* lamented a couple of years later, "has become a symbol to anti-government conservatives of federal law enforcement run amok."[109] At least two historians of the U.S. far right make the same argument.[110] "Randy Weaver and Waco would become key symbols of murderous federal power menacing the freedom of innocent American citizens," the Syracuse University professor David H. Bennett wrote in 1995. "Militia activists continually have used these incidents as examples of government tyranny."[111] Similarly, the historian Catherine McNicol Stock explains in her 1996 book how "the Ruby Ridge incident galvanized thousands of Americans who had distrusted the government but until then had not believed that FBI agents might actually invade their homes or kill their wives and children."[112]

A Montanan named John Trochmann was among those who needed no further proof of the U.S. government's malevolent intentions toward its own citizens. The fifty-year-old U.S. Navy veteran had been born and raised on a farm in northwestern Minnesota. In 1988, he followed his brother, David, and settled in Noxon, Montana. Located less than a two-hour drive from Hayden Lake, Idaho, Trochmann became a regular visitor to the Aryan Nations headquarters and was a featured speaker at the 1990 Annual Congress.[113] At an Aryan Nations "family day," he and his wife, Carolyn, befriended Randy and Vicki Weaver. The two families became increasingly intertwined. Carolyn often brought food to the impoverished Weavers and assisted as midwife in baby Elishaba's birth. Caleb, the Trochmann's son, was Sara Weaver's boyfriend, and throughout the Ruby Ridge siege the Trochmann clan could be seen among the group of protestors down the road from the Weavers' cabin.[114] John Trochmann allegedly was among the people trafficking in illegal weapons that the ATF had sought Weaver's help in implicating.[115] Trochmann had also founded the United Citizens for Justice (UCJ) to support the Weavers in the aftermath of the Ruby Ridge incident and served as its co-chair alongside Louis Beam.[116] The close friendship of the Trochmanns and Weavers further substantiates the point Belew makes in her book about how the social relationships within the white supremacist community of the 1980s and 1990s "undergirded political ones within the movement."[117]

Trochmann also attended the Estes Park conference—where his beliefs about the need to arm and prepare for any future confrontation with the U.S. government as well as to resist the imposition of a "New World Order" appear to have been cemented.[118] An exponent of Christian Identity, Trochmann was able to tap into a network of like-minded adherents along with people on the UCJ's mailing list whose support he needed to launch a new kind of far-right paramilitary group called the Militia of Montana

(MOM). MOM debuted in February 1994. Trochmann, assisted by his brother, David, and nephew, Randy, positioned the militia first and foremost as an organization dedicated to protecting Second Amendment rights.[119] The enactment of the Brady Bill the previous November, which mandated a five-day waiting period for all handgun purchases and transfers, and later in 1994 the federal ban on semiautomatic long guns that were defined as assault weapons as well as on large-capacity ammunition magazines,[120] resonated with many ordinary people who were outside the far-right extremist milieu but were deeply concerned about any infringement of their constitutional rights.[121] "From the beginning, the militias pointed to gun-control measures as precursors to overarching federal tyranny," Thomas Halpern, then director of the ADL's Fact Finding Department, explained. "From the militia's standpoint, the necessary response to federal tyranny is to stockpile weapons and engage in paramilitary training for what they regard as an impending showdown."[122]

For militia groups like MOM, concerns about the preservation of Second Amendment rights proved an effective magnet to attract diverse constituencies. According to Stern, "truck drivers, housewives, lawyers, doctors, dentists, barbers, accountants, [and] grocers" were among those who flocked to MOM events and subscribed to Trochmann's view that "gun control is for only one thing; people control."[123] Once in the MOM's orbit, these people were introduced to Identity theology, paranoiac fantasies about the coming "New World Order," and vast conspiracies orchestrated by the U.S. government, Jews, bankers, globalists, and others.[124] MOM's eight-page pamphlet provided a compelling introduction to the organization's core purpose:

> To balance the military power of the nation with the might of the militia will put at odds any scheme by government officials to use the force of the government against the people. Therefore, when the codes and statutes are unjust for the majority of the people, the people will rightly revolt and the government will have to acquiesce without a shot being fired, because the militia stands vigilant in carrying out the will of the people in defense of rights, liberty and freedom.[125]

Trochmann was unabashed in describing the impending conflict between American patriots and their government. "The battle lines are drawn," he repeatedly warned.[126] To this end the sales tables at MOM events sold U.S. Army manuals on the construction of booby traps, guerrilla warfare techniques, hand-to-hand combat, sniper training, small-arms defense against air attacks, and survival, escape, and evasion. They competed with tomes about the many conspiracies afoot to subjugate Americans and deprive them of their constitutional rights and civil liberties.[127] "Men in stetsons and lumberjack shirts thumbed through videos on *America in Peril* and *Battle Preparations Now*," a 1994 article in a British newspaper reported, while their "wives had a look at the sachets of freeze-dried food, ideal for surviving in the wilderness when the Feds come to get you."[128]

But Trochmann's most important and consequential contribution to the revival of violent, far-right extremism then occurring was not just in showcasing militias as the latest organizational innovation to attain the movement's most cherished goals but in peddling ever more widely Beam's leaderless resistance strategy. The two-hundred-page manual (sold for $75) bearing the MOM imprimatur was explicit in its advocacy of Beam's so-called phantom cell concept. MOM members were thus encouraged to independently form their own seven-person cells to protect against informants and penetration by federal law enforcement agencies. Communication between cells was discouraged and operational security emphasized in service to this strategy, which was designed to inspire dozens of small brushfires started by individual cells that would eventually become a giant, seditious conflagration—as depicted in *The Turner Diaries*.[129]

Before an audience of members of the Washington State Militia in 1996, Trochmann unpacked MOM's strategy. "If the enemy forces have no idea what's . . . in store for them if they come to our backyard . . . leave the element of surprise on your side," he explained. "Not everyone has to stand up publicly. Go with the cell structure in some of your areas—have a ball. Let them guess what's going on for a change, instead of us."[130] Not surprisingly, among the many militia organizations that surfaced across the country in the early and mid-1990s, MOM has been cited as "the most active"—and indeed most effective—"disseminator of militia propaganda."[131] Most significantly, however, was that the militias were proving to be an idea whose time had finally come. As Stock notes, "By early April 1995 there were militias on guard in thirty-six states across America. As many as fifteen thousand men trained, gathered arms, and distributed literature that explained the international conspiracy and the constitutional right to bear arms."[132] Members of this new movement adhered to the following core principles:

- First, the people should always fear the federal government; despite its electoral accountability, it could always become corrupt, pursuing its own interests rather than those of the people.
- Second, to counteract the threat of a corrupt and tyrannical central government, the people should be armed to overawe the government or, in extremis, to stage a revolution.
- Third, for the people to be able to make a revolution, they must be organized into militias.
- Finally, when government wishes to oppress the people, it begins by disarming them, so they cannot resist. Militia groups would add that the federal government has already become corrupt and tyrannical and the time for revolution is fast approaching.[133]

Dan Shoemaker's *U.S. Militiaman's Handbook*, published in 1994, was unambiguous in its message of violent resistance and rebellion. The title of its third chapter was "Who Is the Enemy" and described how "the greatest threat to the U.S. Constitution and the U.S. Militia comes from domestic government. Federal, state, and local governments are now attempting to circumvent or abrogate the U.S. Constitution and to eliminate the existence of the U.S. Militia."[134] Or, as another militia newsletter bluntly warned: "THE U.S. GOVERNMENT HAS DECLARED OPEN WARFARE ON THE AMERICAN PEOPLE."[135]

The moment to respond was drawing near.

5

LEADERLESS RESISTANCE

For one thing our efforts against the System gained immeasurably in credibility. More important, though, is what we taught the politicians and the bureaucrats. They learned this afternoon that not one of them is beyond our reach. They can huddle behind barbed wire and tanks in the city, or they can hide behind the concrete walls and alarm systems of their country estates, but we can still find them and kill them. All the armed guards and bulletproof limousines in America cannot guarantee their safety. That is a lesson they will not forget.

—EARL TURNER, IN *THE TURNER DIARIES*

t is difficult today to recall a time in recent American history where terrorism was not a significant concern. The early 1990s were thus exceptional. A succession of official FBI reports repeatedly heralded its successes in countering threats from foreign and domestic terrorists. In the preface to an eleven-year retrospective of FBI counterterrorism achievements released in 1993, Director William S. Sessions wrote that "when this publication was being prepared, the United States had been relatively free of terrorism. Since the end of 1983, there had been only one act of international terrorism inside the United States and the level of domestic terrorism has been reduced significantly."[1] Among the achievements cited was the diminishment of violence from far-right extremists.

"Right-wing groups reached their zenith in the mid-1980s," the report stated, before explaining that they had been in a free-fall since.[2] The continuation of this decline was cited in the FBI's annual report on domestic terrorism for 1994 as well. That year was noteworthy for the complete absence of any reported domestic terrorist incidents.[3] Indeed, the only mention of any kind of threat from the far right were two nonlethal bombings of the NAACP office in Tacoma, Washington, perpetrated by an otherwise inconsequential skinhead gang.[4]

The attention of the FBI—and indeed all other law enforcement and national intelligence agencies for that matter—was thus fixated on organized groups and not lone individuals or two- or three-person cells operating independently of any existing or identifiable terrorist organization or command-and-control structure. The intense concern about threats from so-called lone wolves or lone actors was still a couple decades away and would emerge mostly in the context of the terrorist strategies pursued by al-Qaeda and the Islamic State. Accordingly, the lethally destructive potential of a real-life Earl Turner did not appear in any official domestic terrorism assessment of that era. A twenty-seven-year-old decorated combat veteran of the 1991 Gulf War named Timothy McVeigh would change all that in April 1995.[5]

• • •

"It is impossible to overstate the significance of the bombing of the Alfred P. Murrah Federal Building in downtown Oklahoma City—to America and Americans," begins the introduction to *April 19, 1995, 9:02 a.m.: The Historical Record of the Oklahoma City Bombing*, compiled by *Oklahoma Today* magazine.[6] It claimed the lives of 168 people—including nineteen children—and injured 850 others. The FBI has described the incident as "the worst act of homegrown terrorism in the nation's history,"[7] with a death toll eclipsed only by that of the attacks on September 11, 2001. A Ryder rental truck packed with 5,400 pounds of ammonium nitrate, mixed with racing fuel (nitromethane) and ignited by Tovex high-explosive gelatin "sausages,"[8] was, in the words of an engineering assessment, "hurled broadside into three of four two-story exposed columns," thus initiating the successive collapse of half of the nine-story structure.[9] It took two more weeks to recover the last of the bodies from beneath the rubble where the seventy-foot-tall, seven-hundred-foot-long Murrah Building had stood.[10]

McVeigh's odyssey from an unremarkable boyhood in northern New York State to Oklahoma City is well known and told in remarkable detail by the journalists Lou Michel and Dan Herbeck in their 2001 book *American Terrorist: Timothy McVeigh and the Oklahoma City Bombing*. It is worthwhile, though, to put in sharper focus the absolutely seminal role that *The Turner Diaries* played throughout McVeigh's adult life and his terrorist trajectory. The commander of the FBI's HRT unit, Danny O. Coulson, had surmised even before the identity of the Oklahoma City bomber was confirmed that whoever had done it likely "took *The Turner Diaries* as gospel." This was because of

the loving detail with which the book described how to make a truck bomb using only common ingredients, ammonium nitrate fertilizer and fuel oil, boosted with stolen dynamite and hidden inside a stolen delivery truck. If you followed author William Pierce's recipe, you'd end up with a bomb that could take down the Murrah building. . . ."Turner" and his pals had bombed the fictional FBI building at 9:15 A.M., just after the start of business, to maximize the number of casualties. The Murrah building had been blown up at 9:02 A.M.[11]

McVeigh appears to have learned of the book shortly after graduating from high school and then a few months later dropping out of a local two-year business college in the fall of 1986. He had embarked on an all-consuming project of self-education centered mostly around gun magazines and subsequently the various books he found advertised in them. In addition to books advocating a "combat mindset" and others detailing various survivalist techniques, McVeigh also discovered Pierce's dystopian novel. He would later claim that the book's championing of Second Amendment rights and the teaser on its back cover, often repeated in the ads—"What will you do when they [the U.S. government] come to take your guns?"—is what caught his eye.[12] More than a decade later, McVeigh's sister, Jennifer, would testify in a Denver federal court that her brother had urged her to read the book and had specifically drawn her attention to those same words on the back cover.[13]

The next big turning point in McVeigh's life came in May 1988, when he joined the U.S. Army. One of the other men in his basic training unit was an older recruit from rural Michigan named Terry Nichols. He and McVeigh shared the same obsession with safeguarding Second Amendment rights, and despite a thirteen-year age gap they became close friends. After completing basic training at Fort Benning, Georgia, McVeigh and Nichols were assigned to the First Infantry Division—the famed "Big Red One"—and were ordered to report for specialized training at Fort Riley, Kansas. Among the other soldiers who received the same assignment was an Arizonan named Michael Fortier. The three men comprised a third of the eight-man squad and shared a mutual interest in target shooting that solidified their friendship. Fortier would later recall how McVeigh both praised *The Turner Diaries* and gave him a copy to read.[14] Apparently, McVeigh recommended the book and pressed copies onto other soldiers serving with him at Fort Riley—despite being warned by at least two superiors about even having it in the barracks, much less distributing copies of racist literature.[15]

This incident apart, McVeigh thrived in the army. He was promoted to sergeant and given the responsibility as gunner atop one of the new Bradley Fighting Vehicles that had arrived at Fort Riley. As one of his army buddies recalled, "Any captain or lieutenant would gladly take a hundred Tim McVeighs in their platoon."[16] In January 1991, McVeigh deployed to Saudi Arabia as part of the invasion force preparing to liberate Kuwait. Six weeks after fighting commenced, the First Gulf War was over. Distinguishing himself in combat, McVeigh was awarded the Bronze Star, Army Commendation Medal, and the coveted Combat Infantry Badge, among other decorations. In fact, he was on the verge of realizing his dream of joining the army's elite Special Forces. Orders arrived for McVeigh to return to the United States and report to Fort Bragg to undergo the rigorous Green Beret selection process. Exhausted from combat and the lightning thrust that brought the war to its rapid conclusion, McVeigh couldn't hack the intense physical and mental testing regimen. He dropped out and returned to Fort Riley.[17]

McVeigh was a different person than when he first arrived on base two years earlier. Gone was the enthusiasm and gung-ho attitude that had previously sustained him. Dejected and embittered, McVeigh was also reportedly more noticeably racist than before. In his spare time, he had also begun selling *The Turner Diaries* at local gun shows.[18] This presumably landed him on a Ku Klux Klan mailing list and an invitation to join for a one-year trial membership. McVeigh paid twenty dollars and would later claim that he had joined in part to obtain a free "WHITE POWER" T-shirt. He told Michel and Herbeck that he never wore it and was less interested in the Klan's racist obsessions than with the preservation of individual liberties, especially those pertaining to the Second Amendment. Accordingly, McVeigh did not renew his membership.[19] But around this time his occasional use of the N-word was noted—along with his penchant for assigning African American soldiers to menial duties.[20] From their jailhouse interviews with McVeigh, Michel and Herbeck had concluded that his "enemies weren't blacks; they were politicians who were pushing more gun laws."[21] However, in a 2020 article published to mark the bombing's twenty-fifth anniversary, the two *Buffalo News* journalists changed their minds. Despite McVeigh's repeated denials that he had ever been a racist, Michel and Herbeck concluded that "his words and actions belied that claim."[22]

McVeigh's disillusionment with the army only deepened during the ensuing months. It bled into his feelings about the United States and the government on whose behalf he had fought. His killing of Iraqi soldiers clearly troubled him. So did what McVeigh saw as a growing politically correct culture that devalued individual freedom, as evidenced by the alleged diminution of Second Amendment rights. He consequently left the service at the end of 1991 and returned to his hometown of Pendleton, New York. McVeigh's high hopes that his time in the military would significantly enhance his employment prospects were another profound disappointment. He intermittently found work, at one point working as a security guard at the Buffalo Zoo. A letter to the editor he sent to the *Lockport Union Sun & Journal*, his local paper, in February 1992 sheds light on his increasingly dyspeptic mindset. Echoing some of the arguments found in *The Turner Diaries* and eerily hinting at the tragic events he would engineer three years later, McVeigh explained that "crime is so out of control. Criminals have no fear of punishment"; "Taxes are a joke"; "Politicians are out of control"; "America is in serious decline"; "Is a civil war imminent?"; and "Do we have to shed blood to reform the current system? I hope it doesn't come to that, but it might."[23]

Life back in upstate New York for McVeigh became one setback or triggering event after another. When a woman was arrested for carrying a can of Mace, he sounded off in a letter to his congressman about federal laws restricting the carrying of firearms now being extended to nonlethal self-defense implements. He ascribed his failure to get a job with the New York State Thruway Authority to "equal-opportunity shit" after putting down on his application that he would accept assignment to anywhere but New York City. McVeigh's disappointment at not being hired as a U.S. Marshal was similarly attributed to minority hiring preferences. He was now regularly consuming antigovernment books and magazines and, as previously noted, sharing them with his sister, Jennifer. McVeigh would often helpfully highlight what he thought were the most important passages for Jennifer. Testifying at his 1997 trial, she explained how the standoff at Ruby Ridge had confirmed her brother's worst fears about the erosion of Second Amendment rights.[24] McVeigh's growing extremism was further evidenced by his decision not to renew his membership in the National Rifle Association—which he considered too moderate on protecting Second Amendment guarantees. Meanwhile, he continued to circulate antigovernment, tax resistance, and racist literature. He also gave a supervisor at the security company where he worked a copy of *The White Patriot: Worldwide Voice of the Aryan People—This Is the Klan!*[25]

McVeigh was also becoming fed up with New York State's high taxation rate. Proclaiming that he wanted to live under "God's law, natural law" and less government regulation, he hit the road in February 1993, searching for a state that didn't tax its citizens at every opportunity and make them pay tolls to drive anywhere. While in Florida, his father told McVeigh about a letter that had arrived for him from the Department of Defense. They were demanding that he refund the $1,058 overpayment that McVeigh had received while still in the service. In a letter sent in reply, he railed against both the government and taxes. "Feel good as you grow fat and rich at my expense," McVeigh wrote, "sucking my tax dollars and property, tax dollars which justify your existence and pay your federal salary. Do you get it? By doing your evil job, you put me out of work."[26] As if to prove everything that McVeigh had been reading and publicizing, the fifty-one-day-long standoff between federal law enforcement officers and the followers of David Koresh at the Branch Davidian compound in Waco, Texas, commenced only days later.[27]

Hitherto directionless, there was now only one place to be for McVeigh. He loaded his car with antigovernment literature, bumper stickers, and other paraphernalia and drove to Waco. McVeigh only got as far as a checkpoint about three miles from the Branch Davidian compound. The well-armed federal agents, attired in tactical gear, reminded McVeigh more of preparations for the type of military assault he had participated in overseas than a domestic law enforcement operation. Michelle Rauch was a journalism student at Southern Methodist University who spent her spring break that year covering the siege for the school paper. She happened upon McVeigh near the ATF checkpoint, and he agreed to an interview.[28] At his trial, she testified that the bumper stickers McVeigh was selling had caught her eye. They contained statements such as "Fear the Government That Fears Your Gun," "Make the Streets Safe for a Government Takeover" and "A Man with a Gun Is a citizen, A Man Without a Gun Is a Subject." McVeigh's comments, which were published in Rauch's article, reflected these same views. "The government is afraid of the guns people have," he explained, "because they have to have control of the people at all times. Once you take away the guns, you can do anything to the people." In McVeigh's opinion, America was "slowly turning into a socialist government. The government is continually growing bigger and more powerful, and the people need to prepare to defend themselves against government control."[29]

As McVeigh's sister would later testify, from this point forward his obsession with "gun control, Ruby Ridge, Waco, constitutional things" was total.[30] It was reinforced almost daily by McVeigh's peripatetic life, which now revolved around traveling to the gun shows where he hawked *The Turner Diaries* along with other antigovernment, survivalist, and Second Amendment literature and bumper stickers. He regularly rubbed shoulders with likeminded conspiracists and fervent Second Amendment exponents. Evenings spent listening to the paranoid antigovernment rants on various Patriot radio talk shows further cemented McVeigh's darkening worldview.[31] The final, tragic climax to the Branch Davidian siege was still a couple of weeks away when McVeigh arrived in Tulsa to attend the event billed as Wanenmacher's World's Largest Gun and Knife Show in April 1993. A gun dealer who had frequently interacted with McVeigh at previous shows recounted how deeply immersed in New World Order delusions his acquaintance had become. The planet, McVeigh argued, would soon be under supranational rule with a single global currency enforced by a single, worldwide police force.[32]

At the time, McVeigh had been living with Michael and Lori Fortier in Kingman, Arizona. Michael, his friend from Fort Riley, would later describe their shared fears of this New World Order in testimony at McVeigh's trial. "We both believed that the United Nations was actively trying to form a one-world government," he later testified. "To do this, they had to meet certain ends, one of them being they needed to disarm the American public, take away our weapons. We were calling this the New World Order. We spoke quite a bit about that."[33] Lori would similarly testify that McVeigh was convinced that the United Nations had a plan to "take over America."[34]

McVeigh's next stop was the farm in rural Michigan owned by his former army buddy Terry Nichols.[35] Since his discharge from the service in 1989, Terry and his older brother James had drifted further into the antigovernment milieu of the common-law movement that held that U.S. currency was worthless, the country's legal system was invalid, and any taxation was a violation of governmental authority. It was there that McVeigh first learned about fabricating improvised explosives from farm workers amusing themselves through experimenting with homemade bombs. And that's when news broke about the fiery denouement in Waco. He and Nichols had been getting ready to depart for Texas to monitor the ongoing siege that same day—April 19, 1993. McVeigh now returned to the Fortiers' home in Kingman.[36] Michael would later testify that both he and McVeigh were convinced that "the federal government had intentionally attacked those people and maybe not intentionally started the fire, but they were certainly the cause of the fire and potentially they murdered those people in Waco."[37] Fortier's recollection dovetailed with that of Lori Fortier[38] and Jennifer McVeigh. She described her brother as being "very angry. I think he thought the government murdered the people there, basically gassed and burned them." He specifically blamed the ATF and FBI for the deaths and was adamant that "someone should be held accountable."[39]

McVeigh stayed in Kingman for the next five months. He again found work as a security guard and supplemented his pay by manning his table at the region's gun shows. At one show he bought a videotape titled *Waco, the Big Lie*,[40] made by the militia advocate Linda Thompson, whose assertions confirmed McVeigh's worst suspicions about governmental lies and aggression.[41] At another he purchased a T-shirt for fourteen dollars that encapsulated his thinking. On the front was a photograph of Abraham Lincoln with the words "SIC SEMPER TYRANNIS"—the words John Wilkes Booth shouted after assassinating the president.[42] On the back was a facsimile of the Liberty Tree shedding tears of blood and Thomas Jefferson's well-known statement that "THE TREE OF LIBERTY MUST BE REFRESHED FROM TIME TO TIME WITH THE BLOOD OF PATRIOTS AND TYRANTS." He also spotted a baseball cap with the ATF logo and what was meant to appear as two bullet holes in it. McVeigh was so taken with the hat that he started selling it himself. He also began to hand out business cards with the name and address of the FBI sniper responsible for Vicki Weaver's death on it. According to Michel and Herbeck, McVeigh hoped to inspire someone to kill the sniper or, for that matter, any other federal agent present at either Ruby Ridge or Waco.[43]

It was now clear that McVeigh's trajectory had progressed from extremism to violent activism. The "U.S. Government had declared war on the American public," he told Fortier, and "were actively taking our rights away." McVeigh cited the fates of Gordon Kahl and Randy Weaver and was therefore prepared for the day when the government came looking for him. He kept guns hidden around his house and had built a defensive barrier in his backyard that he said was designed to "block bullets in case there was ever any type of Waco-style raid on his home."[44] As the 1993 July Fourth holiday approached, he and Fortier discussed the idea of forming a militia to resist the impending New World Order. McVeigh drove up to Las Vegas to have flyers printed up soliciting members that he distributed at gun shows.[45] Within months, McVeigh was building improvised explosive devices—including pipe bombs capable of splitting a large boulder in two.[46]

On September 13, 1994, President Bill Clinton signed into law Title XI of the Federal Violent Crime Control and Law Enforcement Act. A subsection of the omnibus bill, the Public Safety and Recreational Firearms Use Protection Act, more commonly known as the federal assault weapons ban, outlawed the manufacture, sale, transfer, and possession of certain semiautomatic firearms with large-capacity magazines and eight other specified features (including flash suppressors, folding stocks, and silencer-equipped barrels).[47] This was the last straw for McVeigh. To his mind history was repeating itself. Just as the British had suppressed the colonists' freedom in pre–Revolutionary War America, the U.S. government was now doing the same. Indeed, less than a year before, Congress had passed the Brady Handgun Violence Prevention Act (the so-called Brady Bill was named after President Ronald Reagan's press secretary, James Brady, who was grievously wounded in the 1981 attempt on the president's life). The new law amended the Gun Control Act of 1968 by requiring mandatory federal background checks for firearms purchases and, at the time, a five-day waiting period for handgun purchases.[48] McVeigh now fully subscribed to the message on one of the bumper stickers: "WHEN GUNS ARE OUTLAWED, I WILL BECOME AN OUTLAW."[49] Indeed, while awaiting execution six years later, McVeigh directed a British journalist to a letter he sent to Bob Papovich, a friend from his time in Michigan who had visited McVeigh on death row. In it, McVeigh specifically cites the legislation as "the final piece missing from the 'why' equation." Describing the correspondence as the "why I bombed the Murrah building," he explained:

> It was at this time, after waiting for non-violent checks and balances to correct ongoing federal abuses and seeing no such results, that the assault weapons ban was passed and rumours subsequently surfaced of nationwide, Waco-style raids scheduled for the spring of 1995 to confiscate firearms. . . . For those who dismiss such concerns as paranoia you need to look at the facts as they existed at the time and further reflect that the Waco raid was not imaginary—it was a real event.
>
> It was in this climate then, that I reached the decision to go on the offensive—to put a check on government abuse of power where others had failed in stopping the federal juggernaut run amok.[50]

McVeigh lost no time in communicating his decision "to take action against the government" in a letter to Fortier. He showed up at Fortier's house a couple of weeks later. Sitting in their living room, McVeigh calmly told Michael and Lori of his plans "to blow up . . . a federal building."[51] Terry Nichols had agreed to participate. McVeigh asked Michael to join them. Fortier demurred, explaining that it would take "a UN tank sitting in my front yard" before he would be driven to commit such an act.[52] McVeigh, however, was unconvinced and thought that his friend would eventually change his mind.[53] Fortier never did. But he also never turned on McVeigh and continued to help his former army buddy whenever possible.

Meanwhile, McVeigh pressed ahead with his plans. Later that month he and Nichols broke into the padlocked locker at a quarry in Marion, Kansas. They stole seven boxes of high-explosive Tovex "sausages" along with five hundred electric blasting caps and eighty spools of detonating cord. In addition, they separately began to purchase large quantities of ammonium nitrate from local feed stores. By mid-October, Nichols and McVeigh had amassed four thousand pounds of the ordinary fertilizer that would constitute the bomb's main explosive charge.[54] At the end of October, McVeigh described the final details of his and Nichols's plot to Fortier. In some of the most riveting testimony heard at McVeigh's trial two years later, Fortier explained how his two army buddies had revealed to him both the target they planned to attack and their reasoning—"a federal building in Oklahoma City . . . because that was where the orders for the attack on Waco came from."[55] McVeigh doubled down on this justification in a letter sent to Fox News in April 2001, less than two months before his execution. "Knowledge of these multiple and ever-more aggressive raids across the country constituted an identifiable pattern of conduct within and by the federal government and amongst its various agencies," McVeigh declared.

> For all intents and purposes, federal agents had become "soldiers" (using military training, tactics, techniques, equipment, language, dress, organization, and mindset) and they were escalating their behavior. Therefore, this bombing was also meant as a pre-emptive (or pro-active) strike against these forces and their command and control centers within the federal building. When an aggressor force continually launches attacks from a particular base of operation, it is sound military strategy to take the fight to the enemy.[56]

McVeigh and Nichols were likely unaware that the Alfred P. Murrah Federal Building had figured prominently in a previous antigovernment extremist plot. In November 1983, three members of the Covenant, the Sword, and the Arm of the Lord—including its leader, James Ellison—had traveled from their Arkansas survivalist compound to Oklahoma City to reconnoiter the same building. Their plan was to launch a devastating rocket attack on the facility from a truck parked some distance away. Like McVeigh, *The Turner Diaries* was the inspiration behind Ellison's grandiose scheme. And the motive was the same: revenge and igniting a revolution. Ellison had sought simultaneously to avenge the killing of Gordon Kahl the previous June and also incite what he boasted would be "the Second American Revolution." "We need something with a large body count to make the government sit up and take notice," Ellison had told his followers. But like all of Ellison's mad schemes to foment a second American Revolution, this one never came to fruition.[57]

McVeigh had reportedly offered a nearly identical explanation when asked by his attorney whether he could not have achieved the same effect of drawing attention to his grievances against the U.S. government without killing anyone. "That would not have gotten the point across," McVeigh allegedly replied, directly mimicking language used in *The Turner Diaries*.[58] "We needed a body count to make our point." This assertion, from confidential summaries of lawyer-client interviews that the *Dallas Morning News* publicized just a month before McVeigh's trial was set to begin in 1997,[59] dovetailed with how McVeigh had described to Fortier in late October 1994 his plan to destroy the Murrah Building. Fortier testified that McVeigh had drawn a diagram "in the shape of a triangle" to depict how he would arrange the fifty-five-gallon drums containing the explosives into a "shape charge" that would take down the building. "He explained to me," Fortier stated, that "the base of the triangle would be pointing towards the building because that is the direction the blast would travel." McVeigh's intention—just like Ellison's twelve years previously—was that the attack would "cause a general uprising in America hopefully that would knock some people off the fence . . . and urge them into taking action against the federal government." Accordingly, McVeigh planned to detonate the bomb at 11:00 AM. Fortier asked why McVeigh had selected that time. "Because everybody would be getting ready for lunch," he replied. McVeigh justified the loss of life by citing the Star Wars films. "He explained to me," Fortier said, "that he considered all those people to be as if they were the storm troopers in the movie. . . . They may be individually innocent; but because they are part of the—the evil empire, they were—they were guilty by association."[60]

During that same October meeting with Fortier, McVeigh announced that he had chosen the date. "He told me that he wanted to bomb the building on the anniversary of Waco," Fortier later testified.[61] The fact that April 19, 1995, also marked the 220th anniversary of the opening shots fired in the American Revolution at Lexington and Concord also appealed to McVeigh. His fascination with that period in American history—as well as with the Declaration of Independence and brave patriots like Patrick Henry—had been well known around the barracks at Fort Riley during McVeigh's time in the army. Indeed, McVeigh saw himself as the modern-day embodiment of the famed Minutemen, who had unstintingly taken up arms to defend their inalienable rights against a tyrannical government.[62] While awaiting execution, McVeigh cited this analogy in an interview with a British journalist. "Any able-bodied adult male, any patriot," he explained, "is responsible for defending his liberty. Just like the Minutemen of the revolution."[63] And just like the Minutemen were willing to die for freedom, so was McVeigh. In December 1994, he told Fortier that "he was thinking that he would have to stay inside the vehicle to make sure that it was going to go off." After further discussion, Fortier convinced his friend to abandon the idea of a suicide attack and instead continue to be a part of the revolution that McVeigh sought to inspire.[64]

In mid-December, McVeigh and Fortier drove from Kingman to Kansas via Oklahoma City. Passing a Ryder rental truck on their journey, McVeigh casually mentioned that he planned to rent a larger version with a different storage configuration for the bombing.[65] They passed by the Murrah Building in Oklahoma City. It was McVeigh's second visit. He had identified an eleven-foot indented loading space on the sidewalk outside the facility and asked Fortier if he thought the space was sufficient to accommodate a truck the size McVeigh had in mind. Fortier replied that he thought "you could probably fit three trucks in the front there." McVeigh always maintained that he never noticed the daycare center on the second floor, overlooking that spot. He also showed Fortier the place down the street where he would position the car he would later use to flee the scene in the brief interval between setting the timer and the explosion.[66]

That same month McVeigh had enigmatically advised his sister that he was no longer "in the propaganda stage." On the witness stand at his trial she explained that that meant her brother was beyond "passing out papers . . . he was now in the action stage." A few weeks later McVeigh sent her another letter with instructions to be careful: the government may be monitoring her phone. McVeigh urged his sister to "read back cover of Turner Diaries." A final letter arrived shortly afterward. "Won't be back . . . ever."[67]

McVeigh returned to Oklahoma City on April 16, 1995. He parked his nondescript getaway car, a rusted yellow 1977 Mercury Marquis, down the street from the Murrah Building and phoned Nichols to come collect him. The following day, McVeigh picked up the twenty-foot cargo truck from a Ryder Rental Company dealer in Junction City, Kansas. He spent April 18 loading the 108 bags of ammonium nitrate by himself into the cargo bay. With Nichols's help, later that day they maneuvered the vats of easily acquired nitromethane racing fuel into place followed by the Tovex and other explosive materials.[68] They then drove to nearby Geary County State Park to mix the ingredients and ready the bomb. The barrels were arranged in the shape of the letter *T*. As Michel and Herbeck recount, McVeigh figured out a way to create a devastatingly effective shaped-charge improvised explosive device that—with the addition of seventeen bags of ammonium nitrate soaked in fuel oil—would direct the force of the blast with even greater power toward the government building. McVeigh then connected the dual-fuse detonation system that he had devised. Meticulous to a fault, McVeigh created a third redundancy that would turn the vehicle into a suicide bomb, should worse come to worst. "The blast thundering into the Oklahoma City morning would certainly devour him, but it didn't matter to McVeigh," the *Buffalo News* journalists explain. "To him life was a small price to pay for the lesson he intended to teach."[69]

Around 8:40 AM on April 19, an Oklahoma City parking enforcement officer recalled seeing a Ryder truck driving slowly down NW Fifth Street a few blocks from the Murrah Building. Seventeen minutes later, McVeigh pulled over and using a disposable lighter lit the five-minute fuse to the bomb. At 9:00 he stopped at a red light a block away from his target and lit the second, two-minute fuse. McVeigh parked the truck in the indented loading zone alongside the federal building, hopped out, locked the door, and calmly walked away. He had just turned down an alley on NW Sixth Street when he heard the blast. It impacted a sixteen-block section of downtown Oklahoma City around the Murrah Building. Many of the surrounding structures were so severely damaged that they would have to be demolished. The bomb left a crater more than six-and-a-half feet deep and twenty-eight feet in length.[70]

McVeigh had driven about seventy-five miles from Oklahoma City when a state trooper pulled him over for driving with a missing rear license plate. He was wearing a thin, windbreaker-style jacket above his "SIC SEMPER TYRANNIS" T-shirt.[71] Charles J. Hanger had over twenty years service; as McVeigh reached to remove his wallet from the back pocket of his trousers, Hanger spotted a bulge under his left arm. "I instructed him to take both hands," the Oklahoma state trooper later testified, "unzip his jacket, and to very slowly move his jacket back." At the time, it was illegal to transport a loaded firearm in Oklahoma. In a second, Hanger had his hand on the bulge and had ordered McVeigh to raise his hands and turn around. Hanger kept his own pistol pressed tightly against McVeigh's head. He cuffed McVeigh and removed a Glock .45 caliber semiautomatic pistol from the shoulder holster McVeigh was wearing. It would later transpire that McVeigh's gun had been loaded with powerful, hollow-point Black Talon ammunition. Hanger took McVeigh to the Noble County jail in Perry, Oklahoma, where he was booked on illegal weapons possession charges and failure to display a current license plate and comply with liability insurance laws.[72]

Only hours after the blast, investigators got their first significant break when they recovered a piece of the Ryder truck's axle with the vehicle identification number on it and a bit later the rear bumper and its Florida state license plate. They traced it to the dealer in Junction City and began to unravel the trail of aliases McVeigh had used across multiple states in hopes of eluding detection. McVeigh was about to appear before a judge in the Noble County Courthouse on the morning of April 21 to answer to the misdemeanor weapons and license tag charges lodged against him and have bail set when the local sheriff received a phone call informing him that a federal magistrate had signed an arrest warrant for McVeigh and that FBI agents were en route to Perry to take him into custody. Special Agent Floyd Zimms asked McVeigh if he knew why the FBI wanted to speak with him. "That thing in Oklahoma City, I guess," was how McVeigh replied.[73]

On August 10, 1995, McVeigh was charged with eleven federal offenses, including conspiracy "to use a weapon of mass destruction to kill persons and destroy federal property, for using a truck bomb to kill people, and for malicious destruction of federal property resulting in death." The remaining eight counts pertained to the first-degree murder in the deaths of federal law enforcement officers who perished in the blast—one count for each of the eight officers.[74] His attorney's request for a change of trial venue to Denver was granted, and on April 24, 1997, McVeigh's trial began. At least half of the jurors broke down in tears that first day while listening to testimony from parents whose children had perished in the blast that detonated just below their second-story daycare center.[75] McVeigh was found guilty of all counts on June 2, 1997, and eleven days later the jury recommended that McVeigh receive the death penalty. He was sentenced to death on August 14, 1997, and, following the denial of his appeal, McVeigh was executed at the Federal Correctional Complex in Terre Haute, Indiana, on June 11, 2001.[76] Nichols was sentenced to life imprisonment; Michael Fortier was released in 2006 after serving ten years of a twelve-year sentence.[77]

The Turner Diaries figured prominently in the trial. The government's opening statement zeroed in on the seminal influence that the book had on McVeigh. Assistant U.S. Attorney Joseph Hartzler described how McVeigh "read and believed in it like the Bible" and had used the novel as "a blueprint . . . for his planning and execution of the bombing in Oklahoma City."[78] Both McVeigh's sister and best friend, among other witnesses, detailed his obsession with it.[79] The prosecution's closing statement twice referred to McVeigh's fascination with a work of fiction that he nonetheless truly "believed in."[80] Indeed, an envelope that McVeigh had left on the front seat of his getaway car contained pages from the book that had especially resonated with him, which he had carefully removed. Among them was the page containing the accelerationist instruction "to create unrest by destroying the population's sense of security and their belief in the invincibility of the government."[81]

McVeigh epitomized the leaderless resistance warrior that Louis Beam had summoned when he addressed the Estes Park conference three years earlier. McVeigh belonged to no organization, was not part of any kind of command and control structure, and followed no one's orders. Instead he had conceived and executed an attack plan of his own devising, abetted actively by Nichols and less so by Fortier. Beam had promised his audience at Estes Park that the final miles on the road to revolution would "not just be paved with the bones, blood, and broken hearts of patriots . . . [but] with tyrant's blood, tyrants' bones" and that America would inevitably come to "know the broken heart."[82] With the Murrah Building bombing, McVeigh had likely surpassed even Beam's expectations of what one individual with the help of one or two other people could accomplish. It certainly achieved the "body count" that McVeigh had sought and that leading movement figures like Beam and Pierce, *The Turner Diaries*' author, had long advocated. And McVeigh had done so with an improvised explosive device that had cost him no more than five thousand dollars to construct.[83] In an interview just days after the blast, Pierce denied that the book could have served as blueprint for McVeigh but readily admitted that it was intended to inspire just such an attack. "I don't have the time to write just for entertainment," he remarked. "It's to explain things to people."[84] Pierce's explanation had clearly resonated with McVeigh[85]—although the revolution that each sought failed to materialize.[86]

Beam understood better than most the implications of the Oklahoma City bombing for the white power movement that his treatises and innovations had nourished over the previous fifteen years. Writing in the May–June 1995 issue of *Jubilee*—a California-based Christian Identity newspaper[87]—Beam denounced the "horrendous explosion and senseless loss of life" that his own strategy of leaderless resistance had spawned. This throat-clearing imparted, he got to the point. The authorities, Beam warned, would eagerly exploit the bombing to unleash a concerted effort to curtail Second Amendment freedoms and suppress the militias and other Christian Patriot groups.[88] Although his concerns were proven correct, Beam had grossly overestimated the FBI's current knowledge, much less understanding, of the extent to which this parallel universe of antigovernment extremism had evolved to produce a monster like McVeigh.

A combination of the rosy threat assessments detailed at the beginning of this chapter plus the strict legal regulations imposed following revelations of widespread domestic spying on civil rights and antiwar groups during the 1960s and 1970s were the main reasons for the FBI's shallow understanding of this threat. The serial successes that the FBI had achieved throughout the 1980s against these violent militants and their seditious intentions had arguably bred a false confidence that the bureau was still on top of the threat. The Oklahoma City bombing, however, had now completely shattered that assumption. The FBI was perhaps slow to recognize that the white power movement had changed—precisely because of the bureau's effectiveness in identifying and uprooting the dominant, hierarchically organized groups of the past. The movement's incorporation of Beam's leaderless resistance–type of lone wolf approach did not mean that the threat from larger collections of individuals belonging to traditional command-and-control-driven structures had disappeared. The FBI, though, believed that its ability to gather information on this latest manifestation of a movement whose ability to reinvent itself was at the core of its survival was being impeded by guidelines on domestic intelligence collection.[89] "Many of these militia groups freely advocate violence, make direct and indirect threats against individuals and government officials," the FBI Associate Deputy Director Oliver "Buck" Revell complained in the aftermath of the bombing, "and yet they are not subject to scrutiny to see if their advocacy of violence is about to be acted upon. Their hateful rhetoric is everywhere," he continued, "yet the FBI isn't allowed to even collect this public information and place it in a file." In other words, the FBI could not collect information on such serious threats in the absence of a specific criminal predicate—that is, when an act of violence has either already been committed or is believed to be imminent. Accordingly, twice in as many days Revell had to publicly correct White House Chief of Staff Leon Panetta's assurances that the FBI was keeping close watch over the militias and that there was no reason for worry. "I happened to know that was not true," Revell recalled, "and . . . I said as much."[90] The gravity of this admission was striking, given that by 1996 militias had spread to virtually every state of the union.[91] The SPLC had identified at least 441 such groups—with claims of upward of twelve million members,[92] though fifty thousand was thought to be a more realistic number.[93]

At the same time, there could be no doubt that the FBI had learned from its previous mistakes. A potential repetition of the disastrous Ruby Ridge and Waco sieges was successfully defused exactly a year later in rural Montana. The so-called Freemen group seemed to combine all the elements of 1990s American violent, far-right extremism. Its members believed in Identity theology, were survivalists awaiting an impending apocalypse, and were militantly opposed to any government other than that of their own devising. They therefore saw themselves as "sovereign citizens"—which, the FBI explains, are "anti-government extremists who believe that even though they physically reside in this country, they are separate or 'sovereign' from the United States. As a result, they believe that they don't have to answer to any government authority, including courts, taxing entities, motor vehicle departments or law enforcement."[94]

"Sovereign citizens" like Freemen thus are bound only by common law: invented legal statutes meant to facilitate a range of fraudulent practices and intimidate any persons or any authority that challenges or interferes with them and their illicit activities. The FBI has termed this "paper terrorism." Hence, judges, court officers, local officials, and law enforcement officers, among others, were subjected to frivolous lawsuits and other dubious legal proceedings that never succeeded but served their intended aims of annoyance, harassment, and disruption of normal judicial and governmental processes.[95]

In March 1996, the FBI arrested two Freemen who were wanted on a variety of federal offenses—including mail and bank fraud and possession of firearms during the commission of a violent crime. The remaining dozen or so members of the group barricaded themselves in the ranch house on the property they called "Justus Township"—a biblical reference to the name of one of Jesus Christ's more obscure followers. In response, the FBI adopted a deliberately nonconfrontational response. There were none of the roadblocks, snipers, armored vehicles, or bright lights and loudspeakers blaring music arrayed around the ranch house that had characterized previous confrontations. Instead, the FBI relied on its negotiators and behavioral science experts. And, after eighty-one days, the standoff was resolved peacefully when the sixteen individuals surrendered. The subsequent trial, conviction, and imprisonment of its founder and leader, LeRoy M. Schweitzer, and seven others on a variety of federal charges effectively ended the group's existence.[96] The following year, the FBI was able to defuse a similar standoff with members of another group of sovereign citizens calling themselves the independent Republic of Texas—although a person who refused to surrender and fled was subsequently killed in a gunfight with the agents pursuing him. The killing elicited none of the outrage that had occurred either at Ruby Ridge or Waco, and, crippled by arrests and imprisonment, the group disappeared.[97]

The fate of both these militias evidenced the overall decline in membership and fervor of the movement that followed the Murrah Building bombing.[98] "After Oklahoma, a lot of people seemed to sit back and say,

'Is this really what we want?'" Robert Blitzer, the chief of the FBI's domestic terrorism and counterterrorism planning section, observed in a 1998 interview. "It's one thing to defend your country—and a lot of these militia groups believe they are defending their country—but it's another to be tainted by the murder of your own citizens. So there is a smaller number of groups."[99] But if the militias were receding as a threat, McVeigh's example of the damage and impact that a couple of people—or even someone acting entirely on their own—could accomplish was already inspiring tragic emulation.

. . .

The 1996 Summer Olympics were intended to be a triumphal celebration of the games' history, American entrepreneurship, and the undisputed status of the United States not only as the leader of the free world but as the globe's sole, reigning superpower. Billed as the "Centennial Olympics," in recognition of the hundredth anniversary of the international sporting event's modern reincarnation, Atlanta had surprisingly surged ahead of Athens, Greece, its actual birthplace, to be selected as host city. Eschewing the governmental subventions that had been required of all previous games, this Olympics was entirely privately funded. Corporate sponsors like Coca-Cola, the city's longstanding economic powerhouse, contributed nearly $1.7 billion to ensure the most lavish event to date. The city came away with a brand-new baseball stadium, and its many universities and historically Black colleges benefited from new housing units and dormitories, athletic complexes, and other sporting facilities. But, as one retrospective appreciation noted, the jewel in this crown of Olympic largesse was Atlanta's Centennial Park. "What had been a 21-acre blighted eyesore on the edge of downtown was transformed into a dazzling central gathering spot for entertainment and mingling during the Olympics."[100] Conceived as a "town square" for the games, the park was also the site of a cruel bombing that claimed the life of a Georgia woman celebrating the festivities and led to the death of a Turkish cameraman who suffered a fatal heart attack while rushing to the blast scene.

The American soul and R&B band Jack Mack and the Heart Attack was on stage an hour past midnight on Saturday, July 27, playing to a large crowd of 15,000 people enjoying the free concert and festive atmosphere.

Around 1:00 AM an anonymous caller telephoned 911 and warned that a bomb had been left at Centennial Park and would explode in thirty minutes. A hastily mounted search discovered a military-style backpack containing three pipe bombs that had been left beneath a bench near a sound tower. Minutes later, as the area was still being cleared of concertgoers, the device exploded. In addition to the two people who died, over a hundred were injured. The local security guard who found the bomb, Richard Jewell, would later famously be accused—but then cleared—of planting the bomb in order to attract attention to himself as a hero and further his ambitions for a career in law enforcement.[101] With tragically misplaced certitude, the FBI derisively dubbed the incident the "Bubba Bomb."[102] It would take agents another eighteen months before they identified the real bomber—a twenty-nine-year-old Christian Identity and antiabortion militant named Eric Rudolph.[103] In the meantime, Rudolph carried out three more bombings: of a clinic performing abortions outside Atlanta in January 1997 that injured over fifty people; a month later, an Atlanta nightclub frequented by LGBTQ patrons where five people were injured; and a Birmingham, Alabama, family-planning clinic on January 29, 1998. A police officer was killed in the latest incident and a nurse critically injured.[104] In each of those attacks, credit was claimed in the name of the "Army of God." But federal investigators in 1997 were able to match components from the Centennial Park device with those used in the abortion clinic and LGBTQ nightclub bombings earlier that year, confirming that the bomber in each was the same person. A witness reported seeing a man walking quickly from the Birmingham clinic who then drove off in a gray Nissan pickup truck with North Carolina license plates. The vehicle was registered to Rudolph, and the FBI got their first genuine break in the case.[105] Armed with a name and an address, law enforcement officers converged on Rudolph's residence and associated property. In a trailer storage unit that Rudolph had rented, they found materials linking Rudolph to each of the bombings.[106]

Rudolph, like McVeigh, had served in the U.S. Army—but was cut of an entirely different cloth and had a markedly dissimilar background. Whereas McVeigh was raised Catholic in upstate New York and had started as a patriotic enlistee with a highly creditable military record who gradually became disillusioned before turning against the government he had once proudly served, Rudolph hailed from Florida and had grown up

in North Carolina, was a racist and antisemite, a homophobe, an Identity theology adherent, and zealously opposed legalized abortion; he had
joined the army to enhance his killing and destructive skills. From childhood, Rudolph had been steeped in Christian Identity and white supremacist ideology. A ninth-grade term paper, for instance, had argued that the
Holocaust never occurred. When he was still a teenager, Rudolph's mother
had brought him and one of his brothers to Reverend Dan Gayman's
Church of Israel in Schell City, Missouri, to study Identity theology. Gayman, as mentioned in chapter 2, had been the recipient of some of the cash
obtained by Robert Mathews from the Order's heists. Eric had even
dated Gayman's daughter, Julie.[107] Shortly afterward, he enlisted in the
U.S. Army and was eventually assigned to the elite 101st Airborne Division
in Fort Campbell, Kentucky. As Rudolph recounts in his prison-authored
memoir, his service had a treasonous ulterior motive. "At the age of 20, I
dedicated my life to the national resistance," Rudolph recalled.

> Being young and naïve, I thought I could best serve the Cause in a mili
> tant capacity. Surely, I thought, the American people would rise up to
> reclaim their country. I wasn't content with waiting around for the "Col
> lapse," or the UN to take over and "round-up all the guns." I asked
> myself what would George Washington do? He would fight! I saw a war
> coming on the horizon, and I wanted to be ready for it. So, in the spring
> of 1987, I walked into a recruiter's office in Franklin, North Carolina and
> joined the U.S. Army.
>
> Needless to say, I harbored no illusions about whose orders I'd be serv
> ing under. As far as I was concerned, the Constitution had been over
> thrown decades earlier and the central government was in the hands of
> traitors. Those who issued the orders at the political level were not my
> leaders. The plan was to acquire knowledge about weapons and small
> unit tactics—get as much training in as short an amount of time as
> possible—and then get out. When the real war came, I'd be ready.[108]

He had aspired to join the army's elite Ranger unit, but just as McVeigh
washed out of Special Forces selection, Rudolph also did not make the cut.
Deprived of learning the additional skills he had hoped to take from the
army, Rudolph found a willing teacher in his commanding officer, a former Ranger. From him, Rudolph learned how to construct improvised

explosive devices using ordinary materials such as nails as shrapnel.[109] His Olympics bomb would utilize six pounds of 2.5-inch $4 flooring nails packed tightly into Tupperware containers.[110] While serving in the 101st, Rudolph also received SERE training (Survival, Evasion, Resistance, Escape) that he would later make excellent use of—in addition to already being an accomplished outdoorsman.[111]

By 1988, Rudolph had had enough. He was counseled multiple times for poor attitude and insubordination, using disrespectful language to a superior, dereliction of duty, violation of post security procedures, and finally for using marijuana. Rudolph was discharged in January 1989.[112] The army in fact had confirmed all that Rudolph had come to loathe in America. To his mind, the army rejected excellence in favor of the affirmative action policies that he believed were corroding American society. "Because the Army was an institution built for war, I'd always thought that the officers would have the authority to cull the weak and the incompetent," he later explained. "Not so. Washington's Army, I discovered, was infected with the same egalitarianism that was sickening the rest of the country."[113]

The license plate match made by the FBI following the Birmingham bombing identified Rudolph as the vehicle's owner, and days later a criminal complaint was filed seeking his arrest. In April 1998 five counts of malicious use of an explosive in violation of federal law were added to the original complaint—covering the Olympics, abortion clinics, and gay nightclub bombings as well.[114] These charges landed Rudolph on the FBI's "Ten Most Wanted" fugitive list and set off a five-year manhunt. He was finally apprehended in rural Murphy, North Carolina, on May 31, 2003. A rookie local police officer had spotted an individual rummaging through trash bins behind a grocery store. The dumpster diver was Rudolph.[115] The now thirty-eight-year-old fugitive pleaded guilty on April 13, 2005, to the Atlanta and Birmingham bombings and agreed to waive all rights to appeal. He was sentenced to multiple life terms without the possibility of parole and was incarcerated in Colorado on ADX Florence Supermax's infamous "Bomber Row" alongside Terry Nichols and numerous other notorious domestic and international terrorists.[116]

Rudolph, like McVeigh, was unrepentant about the death and destruction his actions had caused.[117] He excoriated the U.S. government for allowing legalized abortion, for tolerating and indeed protecting the rights of LGBTQ persons, and for its own intrinsic corruption and debasement. Invoking the patriotic example of America's Founding Fathers, Rudolph explained that "at various times in history men and women of good conscience have had to decide when the lawfully constituted authorities have overstepped their moral bounds and forfeited their right to rule." The Supreme Court's 1973 landmark decision legalizing abortion constituted just such a moment. "Because I believe that abortion is murder," he declared, "I also believe that force is justified in an attempt to stop it." Rudolph also railed at "the concerted effort to legitimize the practice of homosexuality" and the "'in your face' attempt to force society to accept and recognize this behavior as being just as legitimate and normal as the natural man/woman relationship." According to Rudolph, "every effort should be made, including force if necessary, to halt this effort." Finally, he detailed the motive and rationale behind the Olympic bombing. "For many years I thought long and hard on these issues and then in 1996 I decided to act," Rudolph recounted.

> In the summer of 1996, the world converged upon Atlanta for the Olympic Games. Under the protection and auspices of the regime in Washington millions of people came out to celebrate the ideals of global socialism . . . though the purpose of the Olympics is to promote these despicable ideals, the purpose of the attack on July 27th was to confound, anger and embarrass the Washington government in the eyes of the world for its abominable sanctioning of abortion on demand.
>
> The plan was to force the cancellation of the Games, or at least create a state of insecurity to empty the streets around the venues and thereby eat into the vast amounts of money invested.[118]

Rudolph achieved none of his objectives—except for the infliction of death, injury, destruction, and misery on those unfortunate enough to have been caught in the path of his rage against America and Americans. But like McVeigh, Rudolph had clearly demonstrated the violence that even a single individual could unleash, the suffering he could cause, and the impact of such traumatic events on the American psyche.[119] As McVeigh later said, "Isn't it scary that one man could reap this kind of hell?"[120] Neither McVeigh nor Rudolph belonged to any identifiable organization, nor were they fulfilling the orders of a hierarchical command structure. They were unaffiliated, lone individuals who acted independently but situated their violence firmly within a broader, increasingly expansive ideological context that at the end of the twentieth century remained deeply rooted in an extreme nativist mindset.[121] The SPLC would record nearly sixty domestic terrorist plots during the decade following the Oklahoma City attack, a handful of which were lethal.[122] Just as McVeigh's hoped-for revolution never came to pass and Rudolph's deranged attempt to derail the Olympic Games or end legalized abortion in the United States failed, none of these isolated spasms of violence fulfilled their perpetrators' grandiose aims. But neither did they slake the movement's thirst for more violence.

Overshadowed by the epochal September 11, 2001, attacks and the wars in Afghanistan and Iraq, domestic terrorism from the American violent far right mostly abated. The election of the first person of color to the presidency in 2008 along with that year's economic recession, however, would soon galvanize an entirely new generation of sedition, upheaval, and violence.

6

RACISM REKINDLED

We are no longer trying to destroy the System directly, but are now con-
centrating on undermining the general public's support for the System.

—EARL TURNER, IN *THE TURNER DIARIES*

On January 20, 2009, America's newly inaugurated first African American president stood in front of a record crowd of some 1.8 million people on the National Mall.[1] The culmination of a campaign founded on iconic images of hope and change, President Barack Obama's first inauguration speech sought to promote unity, to appeal to an American identity over party affiliation. "On this day," the president declared, "we gather because we have chosen hope over fear, unity of purpose over conflict and discord."[2]

Obama's 2008 victory shattered voting records in the United States—which he would break again four years later. But for the country's racists and bigots, this outcome underscored everything that was wrong in America. The election of America's first Black president—who some of his detractors wrongfully claimed was not a Christian but a Muslim and moreover had in fact not even been born in the United States—provided fresh evidence that tyranny and electoral malfeasance had again taken root. "There are a lot of angry White people out there looking for answers," Don Black, founder of the white supremacist message board Stormfront, wrote the day after the election. "Let's show them. We will not be defeated." The former KKK leader, elected Louisiana state legislator, and longstanding racist David Duke issued a similar call to arms. "We as European Americans have got to rally for our own heritage, our own freedom, our own survival as a people," he argued. "And if we don't do that—and if we don't begin now to build a real movement, a dedicated movement for our rights and our heritage—we're going to lose everything that's important to us and vital to us."[3]

The so-called birther theories that predated and persisted even after Obama's election represented perhaps the most conspicuously racist response. As early as Obama's Senate run in 2004, internet conspiracy theorists had attempted to smear the candidate for allegedly concealing a religious affiliation. Then, two years later, similarly unsubstantiated theories claimed that even Obama's birth certificate was faked and that he had not been born in the United States, as the Constitution requires, but in fact hailed from Kenya and was therefore ineligible to run for president. These slanderous aspersions were fanned by the increasingly influential Fox News network and by the New York real estate mogul and reality television star Donald J. Trump.[4] The effect was unprecedented, rapidly mounting threats against the biracial candidate. Accordingly, on May 3, 2007, Michael Chertoff, secretary of homeland security under President George W. Bush, approved Secret Service protection for Obama—codename "Renegade"—nine months before the Democratic primaries and earlier than any other presidential candidate had ever been assigned a government-provided security detail.[5]

Until a Black man became a serious contender for his party's presidential nomination, the far-right terrorism threat had laid largely dormant over the previous decade. The United States had turned its counterterrorism attention fully against the Salafi jihadist threat that had so devastatingly materialized on September 11, 2001. For the next eighteen years this intense focus on foreign threats to America's national security kept the homeland safe. Indeed, the first successful foreign-orchestrated plot against the American homeland since 9/11 would not take place until December 6, 2019, with the attack at the Naval Air Station in Pensacola, Florida, when a sleeper agent recruited by al-Qaeda's Arabian Peninsula franchise infiltrated and killed three people and wounded eight others. In the years that followed 9/11, the threat of domestic terrorism—as exemplified by the 1995 Oklahoma City bombing and the attack the following year at Atlanta's Centennial Olympic Park—was widely thought to be a relic of the distant past.

Obama's election victory, though, inspired a new eruption of hate and vilification. In the weeks following the election, the SPLC documented "hundreds of incidents of abuse or intimidation apparently motivated by racial hatred . . . though most have not involved violence."[6] Militias and other antigovernment organizations proliferated following the election—rebuilding what they had lost in the immediate aftermath of the McVeigh bombing. By the end of Obama's first term in office, for example, the number of antigovernment militias and other so-called Patriot groups active in the United States surpassed the previous peak of 858 in 1996 to reach a new high of 1,360.[7] Most notably, 2009 saw the formation of the Oath Keepers, a nationwide militia dedicated to defending its own distorted interpretation of the U.S. Constitution, as well as the Three Percenters, whose name evokes the spurious claim that only 3 percent of American colonists fought in the American Revolutionary War.[8]

Like the 1980s and 1990s, veterans of the U.S. military could be found in the ranks of many of these militia and Patriot groups. The Oath Keepers, an organization composed mostly of current and former military and law enforcement personnel, was founded by a former U.S. Army paratrooper and Yale Law School graduate named Elmer Stewart Rhodes. As the group's website explains, the Oath Keepers pledge

> to fulfill the oath all military and police take to "defend the Constitution against all enemies, foreign and domestic." That oath, mandated by Article VI of the Constitution itself, is to the Constitution, not to the politicians, and Oath Keepers declare that they will not obey unconstitutional orders, such as orders to disarm the American people, to conduct warrantless searches, or to detain Americans as "enemy combatants" in violation of their ancient right to jury trial.[9]

By prioritizing the recruitment of active duty, reservist, and National Guard personnel and others with prior military service, the Oath Keepers sought to position themselves as the "tip of the spear" should the U.S. government ever deploy the country's bona fide military to curtail individual civil liberties in violation of the 1878 Posse Comitatus Act.[10]

Reminiscent of many of the antigovernment movements that emerged in the decades following America's withdrawal from Vietnam, these new militia organizations grew both in number and threat as a result of the influx of individuals with recent combat and relevant communications and logistical experience acquired in Afghanistan and Iraq. As the journalist and activist David Neiwert observed about the newly formed Oath Keepers, "suddenly, as more veterans and people with serious training in the handling of arms came on board, these militia training exercises transformed from the often-bumbling comedies of errors that typified pre–Tea Party militia activities to serious training sessions with deadly intent."[11] The Oath Keepers' efforts to establish themselves as a protective force against perceived tyranny were reminiscent of al-Qaeda's own attempts to create an elite vanguard of Muslims to defend the global *ummah* against the West.

Obama's early years coincided with two successive developments that would greatly complicate his first term in office as well as challenge the nation's cohesion. The first was the financial crisis that preceded Obama's presidency—and likely propelled his victory—which generated widespread insecurity and, much as had occurred during earlier economic downturns, fed conspiracy theories that undermined trust and confidence in core governmental institutions and processes. And the second was the related emergence and popularity of the Tea Party movement within the Republican Party. The Tea Party's platform of fiscal conservatism, reducing the national debt, and small government accentuated doubts about the federal government's competence, and in some circles its populist, antifederalist messaging created new fears over unwarranted governmental overreach and the imposition of liberal cultural norms. Both developments fed a new populism that argued that Washington, DC, no longer cared about the ordinary American worker and especially the white middle and lower-middle classes. These sentiments unsurprisingly accelerated deepening polarization and proved fertile ground for a popular backlash.[12] It was grist for the mill for those already disturbed by the election of a Black man to the nation's highest office, which increasingly included political officeholders and candidates in the political mainstream. "I believe personally, we're at a crossroads," an Indiana Republican Senate candidate and Tea Party supporter proclaimed in 2009. "We have one last opportunity. And I believe 2010 is it. All right?

And we can do it with our vote. And we can get new faces in, whether it's my face or not, I pray to God that I see new faces. And if we don't see new faces, I'm cleaning my guns and getting ready for the big show. And I'm serious about that, and I bet you are, too."[13]

Only three months into Obama's first term, the Department of Homeland Security issued an intelligence assessment warning of a dangerous increase of far-right recruitment and violence. The report compared the situation with that of the early 1990s, when the unimpeded growth of homegrown militias and antigovernment sentiment fed the terrorist violence visited on Oklahoma City and Atlanta, among other places. The "combination of environmental factors that echo the 1990s," the DHS cautioned,

> including heightened interest in legislation for tighter firearms restrictions and returning military veterans, as well as several new trends, including an uncertain economy and a perceived rising influence of other countries, may be invigorating rightwing extremist activity, specifically the white supremacist and militia movements. To the extent that these factors persist, rightwing extremism is likely to grow in strength.[14]

The assessment also presciently warned that the internet would likely fuel violence and subversion. In addition to facilitating communication among likeminded hate-mongers and antigovernment extremists, as Louis Beam had promised, bomb-making manuals and other instructional material would become more accessible and readily available to those intent on harming their fellow citizens.

The leaked DHS report was attacked by conservative commentators and lawmakers who decried its alleged ideological bias and identification of military personnel and veterans as potential threats.[15] DHS Secretary Janet Napolitano was consequently pressured into rescinding the report and issuing a public apology to veterans.[16] Two years later, the report's lead author, the DHS analyst Daryl Johnson, lamented in an interview how the department and the Obama administration had caved to political pressure and thus forfeited a timely opportunity to better understand and counter a serious, emerging threat. Not only did DHS repudiate its own report, but the analytical unit that Johnson headed was disbanded, he and his team were reassigned elsewhere, and the briefings and training they were scheduled to provide were cancelled.[17] "What worries me," Johnson later explained,

> is the fact that our country is under attack from within, from our own radical citizenry. There have been a lot of small-scale attacks lately. . . . These incidents are starting to add up. Yet our legislators, politicians and national leaders don't appear too concerned about this. So, my greatest fear is that domestic extremists in this country will somehow become emboldened to the point of carrying out a mass-casualty attack, because they perceive that no one is being vigilant about the threat from within. That is what keeps me up at night.[18]

On July 22, 2011, a thirty-two-year-old white supremacist calmly stepped off a ferry at Utøya Island on Lake Tyrifjorden in Norway. Utøya was home to an annual summer camp hosted by the Workers' Youth League, the youth wing of Norway's Labour Party. That afternoon, the children, some as young as eleven, had heard news of an explosion in Oslo, the country's capital city.[19] The city's government quarter had been targeted. "We're not safe here," Simon Sæbø, an eighteen-year-old from Salangen in the country's north, warned. "I'm only saying that it's no coincidence they went for the government quarter. That means this is an attack on the Labour Party, and we're part of the Labour Party."[20] He was correct. Two hours after the bombing, Sæbø and the children were under attack, a hail of bullets piercing the quiet landscape. There was nowhere to escape. Sæbø, whom friends had nicknamed "JFK" for his charisma, valiantly helped others hide beneath a cliff. Rescuers would later discover his body slumped over a rock at the water's edge, killed by a bullet through the heart.[21]

Anders Behring Breivik stalked the island for an hour before police finally arrived at the scene of the carnage and arrested him. By then, sixty-nine people lay dead. Some were found floating in the lake—having desperately tried to swim away from the island. Others had clustered together, trying to shield and comfort one other as the gunman approached. Most died from execution-style, point-blank shots to the head. A further eight people had perished as a result of the downtown bombing, which the authorities learned had been intended to kill Prime Minister Jens Stoltenberg. Just before the attacks, Breivik had emailed to a list of contacts an

extensive, rambling manifesto. It explained his motivations and preparations and was named 2083, after the year Breivik hoped "the third wave
of Jihad will have been repelled and the cultural Marxist/multicultural-
ist hegemony in Western Europe will be shattered and lying in ruin." His
tedious and frequently-plagiarized 1,500-page manifesto articulated a
patently xenophobic, racist, and white supremacist ideology. "If they [what
Breivik called 'the cultural Marxists,' including Europe's political lead-
ers] continue to defy the will of Europeans for decades to come and force
Europe to the brink of catastrophe, they will be shown no mercy," Breivik
declared. "It will be an extremely bloody reckoning and thousands of them
will most likely be executed."[22]

But Breivik's path toward the violence that would shake Norway and
the Western world on July 22, 2011, began years earlier. In fact, the killer
claims—probably spuriously—to have begun his manifesto in 2002, nine
years before the act.[23] Tracing Breivik's life through the years leading
up to his devastating twin attack in Oslo and on Utøya reveals many
familiar patterns in the radicalization, trials and tribulations, and mobilization of an eventual terrorist. "It was a parallel life he maintained
meticulously in recent years," the New York Times wrote of the killer in
the days after the attack. "Former classmates and colleagues described
him as unremarkable and easy to forget, qualities, perhaps inborn, that
he cultivated—consciously, he would say—to mask his dedication to what
he called his 'martyrdom operation.'"[24] Breivik, reflecting on the challenges posed by his "double life," declared, "My goal is obviously to prevent my closest network from asking specific questions, and it has worked
perfectly so far."[25]

Anders Behring Breivik did not have an easy childhood. His parents
divorced, and a psychologist found his mother abusive and unfit to care
for Anders and his sister. "The whole family is affected by the mother's
poor psychological functioning," the report stated. "Anders is the victim
of his mother's projections of paranoid aggressive and sexual fear of men
generally."[26] Social services recommended removing the boy from his
mother, but the case stalled in court. Breivik's mental health struggles
likely contributed to his sense of isolation—a profound loneliness that
plagued his life since his childhood. "He does not take the initiative in
making contact with other children," the evaluation noted. "He partici-
pates mechanically in activities without showing any pleasure or

enthusiasm. Often looks sad."[27] Adolescence brought a struggle to fit in—
both in the graffiti scene he had sought out, as well as with the Norwegian Progress Party, a right-wing party known for strict immigration policies. His father then disowned him at age fifteen, after his third arrest for
graffiti tagging. In early adulthood, Breivik's inability to fit in only com-
pounded—he struggled to find good, legal work; a relationship with an
online girlfriend from Belarus fell through; and he yearned for ideological and political belonging. At twenty-seven, Breivik moved back home,
needing to save money. He stopped seeing old friends, preferring instead
to play video games online. When he did leave the sanctity of his computer, he most enjoyed discussing political topics. "The Muslims will take
power in Europe because they have so many bloody children," he told
friends. "They pretend to be subordinating themselves, but they'll soon
be in the majority. Look at the statistics."[28] His radicalization had started,
and mobilization to violence would quickly follow.

In early 2011, Breivik withdrew to the countryside—perhaps the Scandinavian equivalent of Robert Mathews's flight to the American
northwest—finding a farm near the Swedish border where solitude would
allow him to finalize preparations. His almost three months spent there
were a classic case study of life as a subversive radical. The farm, located
on the eastern bank of the Glomma river, near Åsta in eastern Norway,
played an essential role in Breivik's attack planning, a secluded haven
where he perfected his fabrication of improvised explosives, worked to
render the ammunition he was stockpiling even more lethal, worked out,
and polished the manifesto that would accompany his attack. It was here
in idyllic Åsta that a political mass murderer put the finishing touches on
his plans to declare war—on his country, his political enemies, and, most
importantly, on their children.[29]

Breivik was thirty-two—single, unemployed, a drug user with no university education, and with multiple arrests on his record. His mental state
has been the subject of much debate as well as competing diagnoses. In
the weeks and months after the attack, Breivik was visited by multiple
teams of psychiatrists. The first two court-appointed psychiatrists spent
thirty-six hours with the killer, and "based on Breivik's symptomatology,
in particular the presence of bizarre grandiose delusions, the psychiatrists
concluded that he had schizophrenia, paranoid type." A second pair of
appointed psychiatrists disagreed, concluding instead "that Breivik's

symptoms were due to a severe narcissistic personality disorder combined with pseudologia fantastica (pathological lying), and that he was psychotic neither during their interviews nor at the time of his crimes, thus being legally accountable."[30] Breivik himself was desperate to prove his sanity, to provide legitimacy for his plea—not guilty on account of self-defense against a perceived invasion. The court agreed and sentenced him to a maximum penalty of twenty-one years' imprisonment, which can be extended in five-year increments, indefinitely.[31]

A spectacularly horrific display of the barbarity and brutality of terrorism, Breivik's twin attacks fundamentally changed the counterterrorism landscape. For the previous decade, the focus of Western intelligence and law enforcement had been almost entirely on the threat from Islamist extremists. But now, a lone terrorist, who was white, Christian, and Norwegian, had emerged from obscurity to claim more lives than any terrorist in Europe since the Madrid bombings, which seven years before had targeted commuter trains and killed 193. Oslo and Utøya were in fact the opening salvo in a campaign by a newly energized and more violent far right in the United States and elsewhere that would similarly pursue an accelerationist strategy in hope of igniting a race war in their own countries.

• • •

On a sunny morning in Oak Creek, Wisconsin, on August 5, 2012, a forty-year-old white power rock-'n'-roll enthusiast and U.S. Army veteran entered the Sikh Temple of Wisconsin and opened fire. Six worshippers were killed and four wounded—one of whom years later succumbed to his injuries—before the gunman, Wade Michael Page, took his own life.[32] At the time, Page's shooting rampage was the deadliest far-right attack in the United States since the Oklahoma City bombing, over fifteen years earlier. Neither his motive nor why Page chose a Sikh place of worship is known. He did not provide a manifesto, and there was no trail of online messages or posts to be parsed and dissected for clues.[33]

Page was a neo-Nazi skinhead who had played in bands with deliberately menacing names such as Definite Hate and Intimidation One. He worked as a truck driver during the years preceding the attack, but Page had spent most of the 1990s in the army, partly in a psychological operations unit. Page was radicalized in the military, during his training at Fort Bragg, North Carolina.[34] In 1995, when he reported to the base, open expression of neo-Nazism was common. Swastikas hung in the barracks, and a nearby recruitment billboard, erected by an active-duty Fort Bragg soldier, encouraged soldiers to join William Luther Pierce's National Alliance, then the country's leading white supremacist and neo-Nazi political organization. That year, two members of the army's elite Eighty-Second Airborne Division had murdered a Black couple in nearby Fayetteville. The soldiers were part of a group of some two dozen neo-Nazis at Fort Bragg. One of the killers, Pvt. James Norman Burmeister II, had a Nazi flag displayed above his bed.[35]

By this stage, the U.S. military was wary of extremists in its midst. In 1986, for example, Secretary of Defense Caspar Weinberger responded to reports of active-duty soldiers providing training to civilian Ku Klux Klan members (part of a group led by army veteran Frazier Glenn Miller) by declaring that "military personnel must reject participation in white supremacy, neo-Nazi and other such groups which espouse or attempt to create overt discrimination. Active participation, including public demonstrations, recruiting and training members, and organizing or leading such organizations is utterly incompatible with military service."[36] But 1995, the year of both the Fayetteville killings and McVeigh's bloody assault on Oklahoma City, led the military to view the infiltrations far more urgently. Both Fayetteville killers were convicted and sentenced to life in prison. But perhaps just as importantly, nineteen other soldiers in the same unit were subsequently dishonorably discharged after investigators discovered that they belonged to the same neo-Nazi gang.[37]

In response to both these developments, the DoD reiterated its policy regarding membership in extremist organizations espousing racially, religiously, and ethnically motivated violence: "Engaging in activities in relation to [extremist] organizations, or in furtherance of the objectives of such organizations that are viewed by command to be detrimental to the good order of the unit," the directive read, "is incompatible with Military Service, and is, therefore, prohibited."[38] Congressional hearings were also held and a U.S. Army task force to counter hate and intolerance within the service was created.[39] In 1998, however, an unrelated DoD report revealed another alarming trend. It found that "adult leaders of far-right extremist groups encouraged young men and women to enlist in the

military to gain access to weapons, military training and other personnel prior to returning to civilian life."[40] It appears that recruiting quotas
for the all-volunteer military took priority over the careful vetting of
inductees for membership in groups espousing, or adhering to, violent,
white supremacist ideologies.[41]

With the advent of the war on terror, the issue was largely forgotten.
In fact, as the Southern Poverty Law Center reported, two overseas wars
meant that, again, "due to recruiting shortages, the military [was] relax-
ing bans on extremists joining the armed forces."[42] Aryan Nations graffiti surfaced in Baghdad, and a Department of Defense gang investigator
told the SPLC that "there's plenty of evidence we're talking numbers well
into the thousands, just in the Army."[43] The question resurfaced in 2008
with an FBI report titled "White Supremacist Recruitment of Military Personnel Since 9/11." The FBI warned that "the prestige which the extremist
movement bestows upon members with military experience grants them
the potential for influence beyond their numbers. Many members of
domestic violent extremist groups have served in the U.S. military, and
those with this experience often hold positions of authority within the
groups to which they belong."[44] Daryl Johnson's unit then doubled down
early the following year.

Despite claiming that joining the army was "the best thing he ever did,"
Page was discharged in 1998 for "patterns of misconduct," which included
being drunk on duty and going AWOL.[45] By then, he was already wearing his extremist beliefs proudly. As a fellow soldier who served with Page
recalled, "it didn't matter if they were Black, Indian, Native American,
Latin—he hated them all."[46] Page himself had told the sociologist Pete
Simi, "If you don't go into the military as a racist, you definitely leave as
one."[47] Page's radicalization during his time in the army thus again brought
to light the long and discomforting connection between the U.S. military,
the Confederacy's fabled "Lost Cause," and the origins of the Ku Klux
Klan from the embers of the Confederate Army.[48] Indeed, Fort Bragg is
infelicitously named for a Civil War–era Confederate general, Braxton
Bragg, and is in the process of being renamed.[49]

The Sikh temple massacre was praised on far-right extremist social
media channels. "We White realists know that a low to medium grade
racial war has been waged against Whites by mexicans [sic], central [sic]
Americans, and [N-word] for several decades," a member of these forums

posted after the attack. "Those acts against us are most often not explicitly political," the post continued,

> but rather, are perpetrated because those beings intuitively, reptilian
> know they are our competing enemies. Their logical skills aren't usually
> shining, but their brawn and quicknesses with knives are. So we have
> been losing the racial war. More frequently lately, a few of ours have
> begun to heroically sacrifice themselves for their people. Score: we're a
> few tens of thousands down and a few dozen up.[50]

But mass-casualty attacks also can expose divisions within a
movement—especially concerning timing and tactics and even the overall utility of violence. Echoing these often-repeated debates within terrorist movements, one message posted on Stormfront—a forum also
frequented by Breivik and Page—declared, "I fully expect Jewish, Black,
Latino, Muslim and Gay special interest groups and or activists railing
against our right to guns and they will be ordering Obama to do something. He will wilt and they will finally score the near impossible victory of
disarming White folks. We are sitting ducks. All because of some mental
case or buffoon nitwit." On the same thread, another extremist seethed,
"These are the people I hate most. They are too stupid to realize the harm
they are doing to us. We must absolutely shun anyone on this site who so
much as hints at causing injury to other races. They are poison."[51]
Obama's reelection just three months later reignited the same intense
racist animus that had characterized his previous electoral victory—with a
new round of calls for his assassination. The University of Mississippi had
recently marked the fifty-year anniversary of riots that had been prompted
by the university's desegregation, when a student protest against Obama's
reelection grew unruly. Students made deeply offensive, racist insults of
the president, and two people were in fact arrested for disorderly conduct.[52]
The reaction to Obama's return to office was even more vituperative on
the internet. An incoherent rant posted on the Crew 38 Hammerskin
forum was typical. "i show my daughter that electing fucked up [N-word]
will get us what weve gotten over the past 5yrs," it explained.

> I tell her that there is no way that ppl can be that stupid again . . . guess
> what . . . these dumb asses elected him again!!!! I hate that i have no control

over the future that is being left for her to live in . . . instead what i saw today was a bumch of dumb uneducated [*N-word*] putting this moron in office again!!! shouldn't there be some kind of requirement to vote? I am so frustrated that i cant stand it!!! My husband is on the east coast working fema and busting his ass for a country that has no common sense. . . . wish hurricane sandy had wiped every last dumb ass out to sea!!![53]

Two years elapsed between the Sikh temple shooting and the next significant attack. The perpetrator this time was a prominent figure in the white power movement and another U.S. Army veteran—Frazier Glenn Miller. He struck on Passover eve, on April 13, 2014. Miller first murdered a fourteen-year-old boy with his grandfather outside a Jewish community center in Overland Park, Kansas. He then attacked a nearby Jewish retirement home, where he shot to death a woman who was visiting her mother. None of his victims were Jewish.[54] Miller, whose activities during the 1980s are documented in previous chapters, was a longtime neo-Nazi and KKK activist and an eager participant on the Vanguard News Network forum—having written over 12,600 posts since joining it back in early 2004.[55] As television news crews recorded his arrest, Miller shouted "Heil Hitler!"[56]

In the days after the attack, Vanguard News Network was awash in comments lauding the killings. "Thank God people are finally fighting back against these vicious demonic parasites," one post said. "The jews are so evil. It is shocking that most people still don't have a clue despite the fact that the Internet has given total transparency to their incredible and innumerable crimes."[57] Another post weighed in, "The only legitimate criticism might be his score"—a reference to the disappointingly low body count from the perspective of the Vanguard News Network's users, who may or may not have known about Miller's efforts in the 1980s to establish a point system by which to grade the success of far-right terrorist attacks.[58] One skinhead forum, however, was explicit in denigrating the attack both for failing to kill any Jews and because its perpetrator had been a government witness at Fort Smith. "I don't see how it was a good job," this person posted. "It appears that the 14 year old child and his grandfather were not even Jewish and were only there as the boy was attending some theatre group. Glenn Miller is nothing but a rat who cut a deal with the feds in the late 80's and testified against the Order to save his own ass."[59] Indeed, as a result of Miller's testimony for the prosecution during the 1988 Fort Smith seditious conspiracy trial, he had received a reduced prison sentence and thereafter had changed his name to Frazier Glenn Cross—the name by which the media had initially referred to him following the shootings.[60]

Miller's attack provided fresh evidence of Breivik's continuing impact and influence. Three years before, Miller had praised Breivik's homicidal rampage. "I mean, if some enterprising American fellow, went to a youth camp in the Catskills, Camp David, or Martha's Vineyard, and 'sprayed' some young'uns belonging to our immigrant-loving JOG," he wrote in reference to the "Jewish Occupation Government," a derivation of the more common ZOG, "I dare say I might not lose a whole lot of sleep on account of it. In fact, as much as it 'pains' me to say it, I just might sleep even better than my norm, possibly with a wide grin on my face."[61]

The American militia community was another beneficiary of the populist sentiment and growing antigovernment extremism that had resurfaced in opposition to Obama's time in office. Only weeks before Miller's killing spree, an armed confrontation had erupted between Bureau of Land Management (BLM) agents and a family of ranchers backed by a growing number of supporters linked to the broader militia movement, including an Oath Keepers contingent led by Stewart Rhodes.[62] The Bundy family, led by patriarch Cliven, had been grazing their cattle on government land for twenty years without obtaining and paying for the required permits. The BLM obtained a court order directing Bundy to pay the government $1 million. Bundy refused, and the BLM began a roundup of Bundy's cattle in March 2014, precipitating the standoff. Responding to the family's plea for assistance, members of a variety of militias from across the American west converged on the Bundy farm outside Bunkerville, Nevada, in support of the defiant ranchers. "If they are going to be out in the hills stealing our property, we will put measures of defense," Ryan, one of Cliven's sons, declared. "And they have always asked us, 'What will you do, what will you do?' and our stance has always been we will do whatever it takes. Open-ended. And because of that, that's why they are scared, because they don't know to what level we will go to protect, but we will protect."[63] On Stormfront, extremists recalled the many standoffs and tragic outcomes of the 1990s, fearing a similar outcome but anticipating the boost in membership and support that would follow.

"Burn the federal government to the ground," a typical post urged. "I swear if they try murdering those people like at Waco and Ruby Ridge, the murderers will get theirs. I gurantee [*sic*] it will set off a domino effect."[64] The confrontation with the Bundys seemed to encapsulate the profound gulf separating America's often fiercely independent ranchers and farmers from the federal government but also the growing chasm separating the country's two preeminent political parties. Both Nevada's senators, for instance, disagreed profoundly in their assessments of the standoff. Junior senator Dean Heller, a Republican, praised the Bundys and their supporters as "patriots"; his Democratic Party counterpart, Senate Majority Leader Harry Reid, dismissed them all as "domestic terrorists."[65]

The incident ended the following month after the BLM relented and allowed the Bundys to continue grazing cattle on federal land without the required permits. This decision may have defused the confrontation and averted imminent bloodshed, but the BLM's decision inadvertently fanned extremist antigovernment sentiment while infusing the militia movement with newfound confidence and bravado. The resurrection of the myth of the laconic, independent Westerner bravely standing up to overly intrusive, even predatory federal government continued breathing new life into the antigovernment universe and militia movement, which had largely been moribund for almost two decades.[66] As the former DHS analyst Daryl Johnson noted, "The whole event, including partisan political coverage and an embrace of illegal and anti-government rhetoric by elected officials, was becoming distressingly normal."[67]

Among those who rallied to the Bundys' defense was a thirty-one-year-old ex-con and unemployed construction worker and his wife. Jerad and Amanda Miller had traveled in April 2014 from Indiana to participate in the standoff. They already "had a reputation for spouting racist, antigovernment views [and] bragging about their gun collection" on Facebook and YouTube.[68] Jerad proved irresistible to the television reporters and other journalists covering the standoff. He gave numerous interviews while attired in full combat gear—including a Kevlar vest—lambasting the federal government, citing the bloody outcomes at both Ruby Ridge and Waco, and proclaiming his willingness to violently defy the authorities even at the risk of death. "So, you know, I feel sorry for any federal agents that want to come in here and try to push us around, or anything like that," Miller told one reporter. "I really don't want violence toward them, but if they're gonna come bring violence to us, well, if that's the language they want to speak, we'll learn it." He was even more specific with another. "I'm not afraid of death," he asserted. "I'm afraid of being a slave. I'm afraid of living under tyranny."[69] Jerad, ironically, was deemed too extreme and unstable by the protest's organizers, who asked him to leave. He reportedly took the request poorly and departed crying hysterically. "He wanted to do the right thing, but he didn't know how to do that," one fellow protestor recalled.[70]

Jerad took his antigovernment animus and frustrations to the internet, posting messages on Facebook and videos on YouTube under the username "USATruePatriot." A self-made YouTube video highlights his discontent because of "the New World Order and shit." In one Facebook post on June 2, 2014, Miller averred that "to stop this oppression, I fear, can only be accomplished with bloodshed." Then, five days later, in what would be Jerad's final message, he cryptically wrote, "May all of our coming sacrifices be worth it."[71] On June 8, he and Amanda gunned down two Las Vegas police officers, Igor Soldo and Alyn Beck, as they ate lunch at a Cici's Pizza parlor. The couple draped a Gadsden flag over one officer's body along with a swastika and left a note on the other corpse that proclaimed, "This is the beginning of the revolution."[72] The Millers continued to the nearby Walmart, where they shot to death a shopper before being killed in a shootout with police. Their odyssey from the Midwest to the Nevada high desert to a Las Vegas strip mall underscored the growing power of the internet to radicalize, inspire, and animate Americans across the country—a process facilitated by the ease, ubiquity, and modest costs of social media.

· · ·

Terrorism, as a renowned book from the 1980s was titled, is violence as communication.[73] Historically, the most consequential attacks for terrorists are the ones that are remembered by the resonance of the attack's message—strategically successful terrorist attacks may change the course of political history; less successful ones may be little remembered outside the victims' families' grief and suffering.[74] Media coverage, then, is a perennial desideratum of every terrorist attack that aspires to have some long-term impact—as well as every group seeking attention, recruits, and other support. That criticality was most dramatically realized by a group of organized militants who descended on Munich in the summer of 1972 and proceeded to take the Israeli Olympic delegation hostage. Indeed, as the pioneering terrorism scholar Brian Michael Jenkins famously observed: "Terrorism is theater."[75]

America's violent, far-right extremists have long understood the importance of messaging and have therefore sought to spread their ideology through the media and the entertainment industry. The Ku Klux Klan's revival in the early twentieth century was partly attributable to the popularity of the film *The Birth of a Nation*. Decades later, the emergence of digital technology and desktop computing was enthusiastically welcomed by racist, antigovernment extremists as an especially promising, cheap, and effective means by which to reach a wider constituency.[76] In the twenty-first century, Beam's trailblazing Aryan Nations Liberty Net would evolve into powerful internet sites like Stormfront and Vanguard News Network. In contrast to the text-only capacity of the Aryan Nations Liberty Net's slow dial-up modems, these platforms made instantaneous communication possible along with the sharing of enormous digital files containing photographs, video clips, memes, animation, and other graphics.

The internet subsequently then spawned another new innovation—social media, which offered an immediacy and intimacy that allowed friends, family, and strangers to connect virtually, inexpensively, and in real time. Beyond its social impacts, the use of these platforms for political organizational purposes proved transformational. Social media played a pivotal role in the so-called Arab Spring protests in 2010 and 2011 that challenged the Middle East's and North Africa's entrenched authoritarian governments and upended the political status quo across the region. Mass civil disobedience and outright revolution, for instance, were organized via virtual platforms that overcame even the most repressive—but technologically clueless—regimes in the region. This newfound power was not lost on violent extremists elsewhere, who also eagerly adopted the new technology for their own villainous purposes.

Breivik was perhaps the first major far-right terrorist for whom social media played a central role in his radicalization. Unemployed, single, and exhibiting several risk factors—including possible mental illness and a history of substance abuse and loneliness—Breivik's entry into the world of political extremism was facilitated by gaming websites. In 2006, the twenty-seven-year-old moved into his mother's home—a "sabbatical," in his words.[77] From his small room in Skøyen, an Oslo neighborhood, Breivik spent increasingly more time in front of his computer screen, eventually up to seventeen hours a day. In *World of Warcraft*, his favorite game, there was no obvious end—gameplay just continued, hour upon hour, day after day, with new tasks to complete, alliances to form, wars to fight. For Breivik, the world of gaming was an easy conduit to political extremism and racism. Other users Breivik regularly encountered espoused blatant prejudices wrapped in highly charged language. Breivik both admired—and then emulated—them. Curiosity, joined with his own innate conservatism, introduced Breivik to still more extreme sites. During the five years he spent glued to his computer—"hibernating," one friend had called it—Breivik's fascination with *World of Warcraft* was replaced by neo-Nazi websites like Stormfront and Gates of Vienna, which celebrated the Christian victory of the Habsburgs over the invading Muslim Ottomans in 1683.[78]

In hidden corners of the internet, Breivik found a world where he belonged. As a white European man, he was celebrated simply for being Caucasian and Christian. "The websites had a strong sense of solidarity, of 'us,'" the Norwegian journalist Åsne Seierstad explains in *One of Us*, the definitive story of Breivik's life and attack. "It's us against the interlopers. Us as a group under threat. Us as the chosen people. Us against them. Us against your lot."[79] This appealed to Breivik's personal desire for respect and fed his ego. His increasing radicalization propelled him deeper into a parallel digital universe of racism, conspiracy theories, and exultant white pride and power. Breivik now began to castigate others whom he encountered online who did not share his vehemence and extremism. "If these writers are too scared to propagate a conservative revolution and armed resistance, then other writers will have to," Breivik exclaimed in frustration, dismissing those who did not share his commitment to action over words.[80]

By the mid-2010s, terrorists from across the ideological spectrum were utilizing social media: radicalizing at will on platforms that were either unaware of their malignant presence or too engrossed with skyrocketing profits to even notice or care. One Stormfront thread published in April 2013, for example, heralded "Facebook—An Effective Way to Awaken White

People!"[81] In 2014, the legendary former CIA psychiatrist Dr. Jerrold Post wrote an important, coauthored article published in the scholarly journal *Behavioral Sciences and the Law* that warned unequivocally of the rising danger of what he and his coauthors termed a "virtual community of hatred." Online radicalization, via social media, was transforming terrorism by weaponizing the threat in previously unimagined ways. "In this age of the Internet, these lonely isolated individuals who so wish to belong and be accepted are driven to spend an inordinate amount of time online," Post and his coauthors argued. "Far from being isolated loners, they are now members of a group dedicated to a cause larger than themselves."[82]

The malicious influence of social media was revealed clearly with the so-called Gamergate scandal. A vicious online harassment campaign targeted a female game designer. Her personal details were publicly posted online in a phenomenon known as "doxxing" (or "doxing"), alongside accusations that she had used sexual favors to advance her career in the male-dominated gaming world. This incident laid bare how easily personal disputes and attendant attacks by one party on another could quickly go "viral" and how readily misogynistic and racist language could turn an entire network against one person. "A campaign that began as revenge against an allegedly cheating girlfriend," the social media expert Talia Lavin explained, "morphed into a retrograde wave that encompassed racial minorities, women, and progressive ideology more generally. The young men energized by reactionary politics, radicalized by participation in harassment campaigns, and ready and able to engage in nimble, hard-to-foil propaganda operations were ripe for recruitment by America's organized racist movements."[83] Suddenly, both personal spats as well as major global events were first being reported, digested, and discussed online, in real time, with no editing, little to no moderation, and often no authoritative voice of reason. Three near-simultaneous developments would also unfold in the middle of the decade to reveal the reach and power of social media.

First, in August 2014, protests erupted in Ferguson, Missouri, over the police shooting of Michael Brown, an eighteen-year-old Black teen. Brown was the latest young person of color killed by police under highly dubious circumstances. His death fed into the longstanding racial grievances of African Americans and others that had already resurfaced two years before as a result of the lethal shooting by a self-proclaimed security guard of another African American youth, Trayvon Martin. Videos of protests, unrest, rioting, and looting were posted on Twitter and Facebook feeds across the country. For America's racists and white supremacists, this was heralded as the start of a race war: "Please, please, just unleash the [N-word] storm," a white supremacist gushed over social media. "This guy is committing a grave error; he's attempting to reason with the negro. All the negro really wants is the green light to start destroying everything. GET ON WITH IT."[84]

Second, much of Europe was engulfed that same year in the political and social chaos resulting from an unprecedented influx of migrants desperately seeking refuge from the civil wars and attendant unrest then raging across the Mediterranean in the wake of the Arab Spring. Tens of thousands of immigrants had fled their embattled homelands to create a continent-wide refugee crisis. Xenophobes and others seized on the flow of migrants into their countries to push the notion of a "crisis" in order to capitalize politically on the fraught humanitarian situation.[85] Fears of being overrun by migrants were stoked by conservative reporting and media commentary both in Europe and the United States. Britain's right-wing tabloids, for instance, published a steady stream of fear-mongering copy. The *Daily Express* front page on July 30, 2015, read, "Send in Army to Halt Migrant Invasion"; while on August 28, the lead headline in the *Daily Mail* asked, "Migrants: How Many More Can We Take?"

The political fallout from the migrant "crisis" transformed European politics. Radical right parties gained new, unprecedented levels of support across the continent, including in France, Germany, and Sweden. In Britain, 2016 brought to vote a referendum on that country's continued membership in the European Union, in what was popularly known as "Brexit." Less than a week before the referendum, a violent, far-right extremist assassinated a Labour member of parliament, Jo Cox, declaring that "This is for Britain!"[86] Despite the killing, the Leave campaign triumphed. On far-right chatrooms, Chancellor Angela Merkel of Germany was subjected to especially vitriolic criticism. "The length of time that Time Magazine's 'Person of the Year' remains on planet earth, walking and talking and defiling and genociding," one Stormfront denizen pontificated, "is a measure of the courage and understanding and dedication and patriotism of White European men."[87] Meanwhile, another commenter on the same site suggested that the chancellor's "head should roll for what she has done to Europe."[88]

Nor were the political ramifications of the migrant crisis confined to Europe. In yet another example of the growing transnational spread of far-right extremism, fears of increased migration from the Middle East and North Africa became intertwined with longstanding frustrations over illegal immigration from Latin America via the United States' porous southern border with Mexico to become a major preoccupation in this country. One Facebook thread discussing the arrival of Syrian refugees into Idaho in July 2015 prompted the exhortation to "shoot the towel heads on their way into the state." A response read, "They will make good fertilizer for the fields. I hope that they do not ruin the taste of the potatoes."[89] On Stormfront, one post argued that "we should be there when the planes arrive, and greet them with bricks and bats. This is the only way the government will understand: NO MORE FOREIGN INVADERS!"[90]

Finally, the rising threat posed by the Islamic State of Iraq and Syria (ISIS) in 2014 and its lightning conquest of western Iraq and eastern Syria was displayed across social media throughout the world. ISIS's unimpeded expansion was widely communicated through hashtags—most notably the #AllEyesonISIS tag, which allowed the world to follow their successes in real time—and similar innovations.[91] ISIS's enthusiastic and dexterous use of social media revolutionized terrorist radicalization and recruitment. It completely caught all its enemies off guard: not only publicizing its rise to prominence but inspiring Westerners, many of whom had little connection to Islam or the Muslim world beyond their parents' heritage, to heed the group's clarion call to journey to the Middle East and help build the caliphate. In a process that the terrorism analyst Peter Bergen has called the "crowdsourcing of jihad," ISIS's reach extended across the globe: an estimated forty thousand foreign fighters from approximately 120 countries joined its ranks.[92] Through its deft exploitation of digital communications, ISIS was able to connect directly with angry and/or alienated young Muslims across the world and thus "convert personal grievances into what they believe is a righteous holy war."[93] At least five thousand Europeans answered ISIS's summons; others stayed home to wage holy war in their countries of origin.

ISIS propaganda was a departure from the more sober, heavily historical and theological messaging of al-Qaeda. ISIS's appeal to what the scholars Jessica Stern and J. M. Berger term "ultraviolence"—the exultation in graphic depictions of executions, suicide bombings, and torture— was at once devastatingly simple and stunningly effective.[94] With social media, jihadis no longer needed to deploy fighters from terrorist bases to metropolises in their enemy nations: they just had to inspire and animate alienated sympathizers already living in those countries to commit acts of violence on ISIS's behalf and in support of its goals. The first major Western terrorist incident of this type linked to the group occurred in May 2014, when a Frenchman, of Algerian descent and who had spent time in Syria, attacked the Jewish Museum of Belgium in Brussels, shooting four people to death. A joint DHS and FBI intelligence bulletin subsequently warned that "many of the recent calls by ISIL and its supporters on violent extremist web forums and social media for violence in the Homeland are being made in retaliation for ongoing U.S. airstrikes in Iraq and Syria. These calls could motivate homegrown violent extremists (HVEs) to conduct Homeland attacks, particularly against law enforcement personnel."[95] It was indeed not long before ISIS's propaganda efforts resulted in terrorist attacks within the United States. A husband and wife carried out a lethal gun attack in San Bernardino, California. Then, a gunman attacked a gay nightclub in Orlando, Florida, killing forty-nine. And a native of Uzbekistan legally residing in the United States killed eight pedestrians in a van-ramming attack in lower Manhattan. ISIS's successful manipulation of social media to inspire this series of troubling terrorist incidents was not lost on America's violent, far-right extremists, who turned to many of the same communications platforms and social media techniques to disseminate their own incitements to violence.

ISIS's rapid rise diverted whatever U.S. government resources might have been allocated to counter the rise of domestic far-right extremism and violence. But equally significantly, this trio of simultaneous social media–related developments provided a new and powerful boost to an emerging ideological battle-cry known as the "Great Replacement" theory. The Great Replacement theory contends that the global white race is being steadily eroded and replaced by people of color. In its more antisemitic American variant, the "white genocide" theory, a key additional dimension to the replacement trope holds that this process is being actively orchestrated by Jews aligned with other similarly dark, conspiratorial forces.[96] The Great Replacement theory has thus infused far-right violent extremism with a profound sense of urgency. The backlash in parts of the United States to the Black Lives Matter movement, combined with long-existent fears about a wave of nonwhite immigrants submerging historically white societies and the string of attacks in Western countries by homegrown Muslim extremists, all fed into this narrative at an especially critical time. These nativist fears and anxieties were effectively weaponized by far-right politicians in Europe and then in the United States—most especially during the 2016 presidential primaries following the San Bernardino shootings. For the first time in over a decade, the threat of terrorism again became a key campaign issue. And it all was dramatically splayed across social media, in full view of anyone with an internet connection.

Indeed, the rise of American domestic terrorism in the twenty-first century cannot be understood without also understanding the revolutionary impact of the social media echo chamber that ISIS had employed. Social media allowed individuals to curate their own community, where dissenting views were dismissed not with erudite and fact-based argumentation but by a single click of an "unfollow" or "unfriend" button. The result, whether achieved by the most violent radical or most innocent teenager—was the creation of a digital universe where only one's own worldview is legitimate, with any debate or discourse suppressed, excluded, and thus silenced. "Attacks can now be against anyone; and for any cause," the University of St Andrews scholar Tim Wilson explains. "The dark progress of western political violence has taken the form of a relentless and irresistible diffusion: from assassination to massacre: from hazard of social rank to rank social hazard; from the classes to the masses; from feud to fad—an ever widening gyre."[97]

The tragedy that unfolded at a historic African American church in Charleston, South Carolina, in June 2015 would clearly reveal the lethal consequences of hate fueled by digital media.

• • •

The terrorist moved methodically around the basement prayer room. Victim by victim, gunshot after gunshot, a procession of lives was claimed in the name of that most abhorrent and pernicious of ideologies: racism. In perhaps the most chilling indication of the killer's callous disregard for human life, the eldest victim, eighty-seven-year-old Susie Jackson, was also shot the most times, suffering eleven hollow-point bullet wounds.[98] Once nine bodies lay dying beneath him, the gunman stopped. "We need someone to survive, because I'm gonna shoot myself, and you'll be the only survivor," he told Polly Sheppard, a retired nurse.[99] She was spared. The killer then turned his gun on himself—but discovered that it was out of ammunition.[100] He turned, and walked out of the "Mother" Emanuel African Methodist Episcopal Church in Charleston, South Carolina, and into the evening air.

A manifesto explaining the attack surfaced shortly afterward. Posted on a website titled *The Last Rhodesian*, its author, twenty-one-year-old Dylann Roof, a devotee of the fabled "Lost Cause" of the South's short-lived Confederate States of America and unabashed white supremacist, gave full voice to his litany of grievances. "I have no choice," he wrote, echoing in identical terms the proclamation issued by his ideological forefather, the Order's founder and leader Robert Mathews, thirty years earlier. "I am not in the position to, alone, go into the ghetto and fight. I chose Charleston because it is [the] most historic city in my state, and at one time had the highest ratio of blacks to Whites in the country. We have no skinheads, no real KKK, no one doing anything but talking on the internet. Well someone has to have the bravery to take it to the real world, and I guess that has to be me."[101] Roof styled himself as the latest white martyr in a history of racial warfare—an enlightened, altruistic vanguard for whiteness in a depressingly changing world. He was, as the title of Rachel Kaadzi Ghansah's Pulitzer Prize–winning profile of Roof and the community he terrorized explains, "A Most American Terrorist."[102]

Roof's radicalization and decision to commit this heinous crime reflected many of the ideological and tactical themes that have long characterized American far-right extremism. His attack targeted a historically important African American church known for hosting many civil rights icons, including the Reverend Martin Luther King Jr. Roof was particularly inspired by the news coverage of the 2012 shooting death of Trayvon Martin, a seventeen-year-old African American killed by a community watch coordinator named George Zimmerman, who had then been acquitted of murder and manslaughter charges. Roof claimed to have been inspired by the incident to search the internet for Black-on-white crime, which, he later said, opened his eyes to the violent reality of race relations in America. "I have to do it," Roof told the worshippers during the rampage. "You rape our women, and you're taking over our country. And you have to go."[103] Roof thus invoked one of the venomous shibboleths of the American South, which has inspired both violence and the worst miscarriages of justice: the defense of protecting innocent white women from the depredations of nonwhites.[104]

An aspersion prominently profiled in *The Birth of a Nation*, the preservation of "white purity" has historically been cited to justify the lynching murder of slaves, freed men, and ordinary, law-abiding African American males in the South. Indeed, precisely this justification is reflected in the lesser-known of David Lane's "14 Words" slogans: "Because the beauty of the White Aryan woman must not perish from the Earth." The 1921 Tulsa race massacre, which the Oklahoma Historical Society has called "the single worst incident of racial violence in American history," was sparked by a nineteen-year-old African American accidentally stepping on the toe of a seventeen-year-old white female elevator operator.[105] In the 1931 Scottsboro Boys case, nine African American boys, one just twelve years old, were falsely accused of raping two white women on a train. All but one were initially sentenced to death, before their sentences were reconsidered and reduced. In August 1955, Emmitt Till, at age fourteen, was lynched in Mississippi after being accused of flirting with an older white woman. "When a [N-word] gets close to mentioning sex with a white woman, he's tired o' livin'. I'm likely to kill him," J. W. Milam, one of the confessed killers, raged. Milam was acquitted.[106] Roof used this justification to explain his violent act. "I have noticed a great disdain for race mixing White women within the White nationalists community, bordering on insanity," Roof wrote. "These women are victims, and they can be saved. Stop."[107] And yet, as the antilynching crusader Ida B. Wells explained in *A Red Record*, "In numerous instances where colored men have been lynched on the charge of rape, it was positively known at the time of lynching, and indisputably proven after the victim's death, that the relationship sustained between the man and woman was voluntary and clandestine, and that in no court of law could even the charge of assault have been successfully maintained."[108]

Few twenty-first-century terrorists more emphatically embodied accelerationism—and its American roots—than Roof. He hoped to spark a race war. Instead, some in Charleston's African American religious community chose to heal their wounds with mercy and forgiveness. "I forgive you," Nadine Collier, the daughter of seventy-year-old victim Ethel Lance, told Roof over video conference at his bond hearing. "You took something very precious from me. I will never talk to her again. I will never, ever hold her again. But I forgive you. And have mercy on your soul."[109] Roof's savage June 2015 act was a shock to the American system, a catastrophic return of racist, white supremacist violence and painful reminder of deeply held racial resentment in a country that nearly seven years earlier had elected its first Black president. But hindsight paints an even bleaker picture: Roof was not, as some hoped, the final, violent spasm of a dying ideology. He was a foreshadowing of even darker days to come.

Meanwhile, in the far West, another antigovernment confrontation was unfolding. Emboldened by their triumph over the Bureau of Land Management in Nevada two years earlier, the Bundys in January 2016 turned their attention to Oregon. Led by Ammon Bundy, son of Cliven, a band of militia members, including people belonging to the "sovereign citizens" movement, occupied a building at the Malheur National Wildlife Refuge—where the local headquarters of the federal agencies responsible for land use, forest service, and fish and wildlife are located. Once again, the protest centered on whether the federal government had the authority to determine access and use of public lands—the specific grievance this time being the pending incarceration of Dwight and Steven Hammond. The Hammonds had been sentenced to five years in prison for setting fire to federal lands in protest of government control over access to public spaces.[110] The standoff continued for forty days and ended only after federal law enforcement agencies forcibly resolved it. At a police roadblock in snowy Harney County, in which the reserve is located, one of the protestors and spokesmen, LaVoy Finicum, resisted arrest and attempted to draw his personal firearm. Officers from the Oregon State Police and FBI agents opened fire, and Finicum was killed. He was immediately lauded as a hero and another martyr to the cause of resisting governmental overreach. "I would not be surprised if Mr. Finicum was rubbed out, in other words assassinated," a message left on Stormfront read. "Whether or not he was assassinated or killed by police in self-defense, he is now a martyr for our race."[111] The confrontation was once more trumpeted by antigovernment extremists as the latest skirmish in its longstanding battle with the federal authorities. "I want to emphasize that the American people are wondering why they can't seem to get ahead or why everything is costing more and you are getting less," Ammon Bundy told CNN, "and that is because the federal government is taking and using the land and resources."[112] A lawyer for the Hammonds, however, explained that they had neither solicited nor welcomed Bundy's assistance.[113]

The standoff was noteworthy for the presence of several veterans of the U.S. military. They included Jon Ritzheimer, a former Marine twice deployed to Iraq, and Ryan Payne, a former army infantryman who also served in Iraq.[114] "We had counter-sniper positions on their sniper positions," Payne boasted. "We had at least one guy—sometimes two guys—per BLM agent in there. If they made one wrong move, every single BLM agent in that camp would have died . . . in most states you have the lawful authority to kill a police officer that is unlawfully trying to arrest you."[115] Matt Shea was a veteran who had served in Iraq with both the army and the Washington State National Guard. Elected as a Republican to the Washington State House of Representatives, Shea became the subject of an investigation by the legislature because of his involvement in the standoff. A report of Shea's activities, released in 2019, concluded that the representative had "participated in an act of domestic terrorism against the United States" at Malheur.[116] Shea was specifically found to have "planned, engaged in, and promoted a total of three armed conflicts of political violence against the United States," according to the state investigation. It also found that Shea had participated in training exercises that provided instruction on how to wage "holy war" and was responsible for a pamphlet titled "Biblical Basis for War." Shea had argued that a Christian theocracy should replace America's democratic system and called for "the killing of all males who do not agree."[117] Although no criminal charges were ever brought against Shea, he was dismissed from the state's House Republican Caucus.[118]

This second confrontation with the federal government engineered by the Bundys not surprisingly resonated throughout the American militia underground. Preparations were made for new standoffs with federal officials—egged on by increasingly confrontational online fulminations. "I'm furious. Absolutely enraged," one person fumed on Stormfront, citing especially the killing of Finicum. "This is a direct, frontal assault on White America by the hostile, occupation government in Washington, D.C."[119] Another warned, "There's a lot of simmering anger out there.

Little brush fires can grow into raging forest fires."[120] The seeds for out-right resistance and rebellion had also been planted. Reflecting the accel-erationists' end goal of full-scale civil war and revolt, a member of a mili-tant skinhead group observed that "the revolution is lying just beneath the surface right now boiling and ready to explode. I can't wait."[121]

7

THE MOVEMENT GOES GLOBAL

This little episode taught me something about political terror. Its very arbitrariness and unpredictability are important aspects of its effectiveness.

—EARL TURNER, IN *THE TURNER DIARIES*

On the surface, there was very little remarkable about Alexandre Bissonnette. A university student and former cadet in the Royal Canadian Army, Bissonnette had no police record and a normal family life. His father repeats a sentiment often heard in the wake of mass murders: "Alexandre is the very last person that we, and all those who know him, could ever fathom doing something so out of character."[1] In hindsight, it was perhaps his ordinariness that made him so dangerous. Throughout his life, Bissonnette suffered unrelenting bullying and also had untreated mental health issues. He had previously attempted suicide. Bissonnette dreamed of exacting revenge. "He had fantasies to do something big so that people would not laugh at him after his death, so that people would remember him," a psychologist who interviewed him recalled.[2] He was particularly fascinated by murderers who had suffered bullying during their childhood and who then had killed themselves as part of their attacks.[3]

Notwithstanding his personal predisposition toward terroristic violence, Bissonnette is arguably the first mass murderer inspired by both a

U.S. presidential campaign and an election that some commentators would uniquely characterize as "threatening," "extraordinary," and as embodying "a kind of white racial backlash."[4] In the month leading up to the attack, Bissonnette searched for Donald Trump over eight hundred times on Twitter, Google, YouTube, and Facebook.[5] More specifically, Bissonnette was motivated by the response of Prime Minister Justin Trudeau of Canada to the Trump administration's immigration policies. On January 27, 2017, the newly inaugurated president signed an executive order banning travel to the United States from several Muslim-majority countries. Trudeau responded on Twitter the following day, writing, "To those fleeing persecution, terror & war, Canadians will welcome you, regardless of your faith. Diversity is our strength #WelcomeToCanada."[6] Then, on January 29, Bissonnette walked into the Islamic Cultural Centre of Quebec City and opened fire, killing six worshippers using a 9mm Glock. Several of those killed were executed by point-blank shots to the head after previously being felled by bullets. "The tragic events for which Alexandre Bissonnette has admitted criminal responsibility have not only saddened and distressed the residents of Québec, our province and the entire country, but have also torn the fabric of our society," a Canadian Superior Court sentencing document read two years later, noting the profound social impacts such attacks inflict on communities. "From one day to the next, fear and mistrust took hold of a good part of our population. Québec, a welcoming city, open to the world, wrapped itself in a shroud and for a time sank into shame, fear and suspicion." On the day of the killings, Bissonnette was drunk and on leave from work because of anxiety.[7]

From the moment that Trump had descended the gilded escalator at his namesake tower on Manhattan's Fifth Avenue to declare his candidacy for the Republican Party's nomination for president on June 16, 2015, he had employed blatant nativist rhetoric. Trump variously used pejorative and xenophobic language to describe persons of color and those from outside the Christian faith. They all were also deliberately caricatured as threats to U.S. national security and indeed to Americans themselves. Trump's much-heralded announcement had specifically singled out Mexican immigrants for vilification. "They're bringing drugs. They're bringing crime. They're rapists," the famed New York real estate mogul declared. "And some, I assume, are good people."[8] Following the ISIS-inspired shooting in San Bernardino that killed fourteen people six months later,

Trump called for a Muslim travel ban. "Donald J. Trump is calling for a total and complete shut down of Muslims entering the United States until our country's representatives can figure out what the hell is going on," he proclaimed.[9] "We have no choice," the Republican frontrunner added— employing the alarmist language reminiscent of extremists embracing nativist positions. Following another ISIS-inspired mass shooting that targeted an Orlando, Florida, gay nightclub in June 2016, resulting in the deaths of forty-nine people, Trump tweeted: "Appreciate the congrats for being right on radical Islamic terrorism, I don't want congrats, I want toughness & vigilance. We must be smart!"[10]

The Republican Party candidate's statements struck a chord with America's far-right extremists. The longtime white supremacist writer and editor Jared Taylor gushed that "there will never be another campaign like this one" on his *American Renaissance* website. In an article titled "Is Trump Our Last Chance?" Taylor warned, "If Mr. Trump loses, this could be the last chance whites have to vote for a president who could actually do something useful for them and for their country." To many white supremacists, Trump was helping shift the Overton Window—the spectrum of policy deemed acceptable for debate and consideration by the political mainstream at any given moment—feeding their ideas and policies, which previously had been considered too fringe or too extremist, into the center of American political discourse and debate.[11] As one white supremacist writer presciently noted shortly after Trump declared his candidacy, "If he can mobilize Republicans behind him and make a credible run for the Presidency, he can create a whole new media environment for patriots to openly speak their mind without fear of losing their jobs."[12] Stormfront's online community also chimed in, with one person observing in connection with the San Bernardino attack, "At this point, if you still don't support Trump I'm seriously questioning whether or not you're [white nationalist]."[13] Another Stormfront post opined how easy it would be for the presidential aspirant to inspire racist violence. "Trump gets them so riled up," this post explained, in reference to more violently inclined Trump supporters. "They would charge and attack if he told them too. They love Trump. He is almost like a Fuhrer."[14]

Trump's surprise electoral victory in November 2016 brought joy to the far-right extremist universe. On election night, Stormfront was filled with exultant posts like "Michelle [Obama] better get her bitch to sanitizing the

White House for the next, authentic family. Ah! It's now a White house once again" and "You can be white again without the requirement to express shame."[15] James Mason, the longstanding neo-Nazi writer who channeled his admiration of both Hitler and the murderer and cult leader Charles Manson into an especially virulent interpretation of acceleration known as *Siege*,[16] told *ProPublica*: "With Trump winning that election by surprise—and it was a surprise—I now believe anything could be possible."[17] The *Daily Stormer*'s high-profile editor, Andrew Anglin, who named his publication after the Nazi tabloid *Der Stürmer*, could barely contain his joy. "Our Glorious Leader has ascended to God Emperor," he enthused. "Make no mistake about it: we did this. If it were not for us, it wouldn't have been possible. . . . The White race is back in the game. And if we're playing, no one can beat us. The winning is not going to stop."[18] Within weeks, white supremacists were offering Nazi salutes in celebration of Trump's electoral victory. "Hail Trump! Hail our people! Hail victory!" the white supremacist Richard Spencer declared at an alt-right conference held in Washington, DC, at the end of November 2016. The attendees responded with Sieg Heil salutes.[19] And after Trump named Stephen Bannon, the former executive chairman of Breitbart News, as White House chief strategist and senior counselor to the president, the antisemitic far right was especially jubilant. "Stephen Bannon: racist, anti-homo, anti-immigrant, anti-jewish, anti-establishment. Declared war on (((Paul Ryan))) Sounds perfect. Muhahahaha," Stormfront rhapsodized. "The man who will have Trump's ear more than anyone else. Being anti-jewish is not illegal. Nothing you dirty stinking jews can do to keep him out."[20]

As the boasting and threats multiplied into calls for decisive action, those early days also proved that words matter—especially now in the digital age, given the powerful echo-chamber effect of social media. "Extirpate," one militia blogger wrote on December 9. "It is what is for breakfast. And you'd better understand—this is the last chance Liberty has in America. If we fail to move now and Go Hard, under the supporting fire from on-high that the Trumpening 'may' offer, we lose."[21] Indeed, much like after Obama's election, hate crimes began to rise across the nation—driven less by previous "great replacement" fears than by the opportunities that Trump's election was seen to present. The Southern Poverty Law Center documented 867 reports of harassment and intimidation in the ten days after the election, and the Anti-Defamation League reported "a massive increase in the amount of harassment of American Jews" during the first three months of 2017.[22] The norms of civility were noticeably fraying—as the incident aboard a Portland, Oregon, commuter train demonstrated in May, just months into the administration. After two young Black girls were taunted with racial and Islamophobic epithets, two white men who intervened were stabbed to death by the assailant, and a third was gravely wounded. The perpetrator, a white power advocate named Jeremy Joseph Christian, had been active on Facebook, where he pondered whether Trump might be "the Next Hitler" and posted declarations such as "Death to Hillary Rodham Clinton and all her supporters!" He had also celebrated the anniversary of April 19 by declaring Timothy McVeigh "a TRUE PATRIOT!!!"[23]

Meanwhile, the very nature of truth and falsehood were being repeatedly challenged—both by Americans and the country's foreign adversaries. Throughout the 2016 presidential campaign and immediately after, online posts of questionable accuracy were disseminated by overseas entities—including the Internet Research Agency, based in Saint Petersburg, Russia. Over 30 million American social media users, most unwittingly, spread disinformation about hot-button political and social issues.[24] This intense traffic raised suspicions that Russian government interference had helped secure Trump's victory. Such so-called troll farms were but one arm of a massive Russian influence operation, commandeering Western social media platforms to promote Trump and his most radical policies. Russia's objective appears to have been to sow national discord and to undermine Hillary Clinton, the Democratic Party's candidate. The success of this strategy may be seen in the doubt cast on the veracity of America's own intelligence community after it had confirmed that Russia interfered in the election. Trump astonishingly rejected the community's assessments—preferring to trust the word of President Vladimir Putin of Russia instead. "Every time he sees me, he says, 'I didn't do that,'" Trump said of Putin. "And I believe, I really believe, that when he tells me that, he means it."[25] Russia's electoral disinformation efforts were definitively confirmed in the report issued by special counsel and former FBI director Robert Mueller in 2019. "The Russian government," the *Report on the Investigation Into Russian Interference in the 2016 Presidential*

Election concluded, "interfered in the 2016 presidential election in sweeping and systematic fashion."[26] But the damage had already been done. If the president himself was questioning U.S. intelligence conclusions, then who could be believed?

Indeed, the concept of truth or fact was no longer unassailable; truth could now be manipulated depending on whatever narrative one chose to believe. And from the time Trump entered the White House, he and his administration would continually blur the boundary between truth and fiction. Senior Counselor to the President Kellyanne Conway's quip about the existence of "alternative facts" in response to claims that the president had lied about the size of his inaugural crowd, in addition to the president's persistent use of the term "fake news" (roughly two thousand times during his term in office) to dismiss coverage he considered critical of his leadership, corrosively entered the national psyche.[27] As the disinformation specialists P. W. Singer and Emerson Brooking lamented, "Even the term used to describe untruths went from an objective measure of accuracy to a subjective statement of opinion."[28]

Accordingly, by the summer of 2017, this confluence of developments had set the stage for some kind of tragic confrontation. The nativist grievances that had catapulted Trump into office—notably rising fears of both legal as well as illegal immigration intertwined with the polarizing power of "great replacement" arguments—were simultaneously gathering momentum as they spilled into mainstream American politics. The violence-prone extremist fringe of this populist groundswell was also growing increasingly restive and becoming more emboldened, with the string of attacks that had succeeded one another over the past six years in Oslo, Charleston, and Quebec City touted by racists, antisemites, xenophobes, and other militants as exemplars of what was required. And the serial exploitation and manipulation of social media—whether by ISIS or Russia—guided new imitators and admirers in the homeland seeking to harness and exploit this divisive potential. "The xenophobia of the Trump campaign unleashed a whirlwind of hate across America," Heidi Beirich, then director of the Southern Poverty Law Center's Intelligence Project and a leading expert on the American far right, warned on August 4, 2017. "It's only a matter of time until terror strikes again."[29]

Fewer than ten days would pass before Beirich's fears materialized in Charlottesville, Virginia.

• • •

On an otherwise quiet, hot weekend in August 2017, America's most outspoken, committed, and violent far-right extremists arrived in the city of Charlottesville, the home of Thomas Jefferson's fabled University of Virginia. The two-day Unite the Right Rally had been deliberately conceived to bring together a unique cross-section of neo-Nazis, white supremacists, Ku Klux Klansmen, Christian Identity adherents, Three Percenters, and neo-Confederates to protest the city's planned removal of a statue of Confederate General Robert E. Lee.[30]

A tiki torch–lit parade—in keeping with the alt-right leader Richard Spencer's dictum "Let's party like it's 1933"[31]—wound its way through the campus of the University of Virginia on the evening of August 11. Although in some ways the march was reminiscent of the Nazi parades made famous in such propaganda classics as Leni Riefenstahl's film *Triumph of the Will*,[32] the marchers were clad in preppy-looking polo shirts and chinos, not brown shirts and jackboots. But their message was unmistakable as they variously chanted "Jews will not replace us," the Nazi cry of "blood and soil," and "into the ovens."[33] Both the procession and the fist fights and worse that erupted drew national media attention, and the following morning, Governor Terry McAuliffe declared a state of emergency, and shortly afterward the Virginia State Police designated the rally an unlawful assembly. The protests, counterprotests, and confrontations continued. Then early that afternoon, a 2010 Dodge Challenger sped down Charlottesville's Fourth Street and deliberately plowed into a crowd of demonstrators who had gathered to oppose the far-right rally. Nineteen people were wounded, and one, Heather Heyer, was killed.[34] A dramatic image of the attack was captured by the photographer Ryan Kelly of the *Daily Progress*, showing some victims tossed upside down in mid-air as the car plunged through the crowd. It won the Pulitzer Prize for Breaking News Photography[35]—underscoring how gravely America was beginning to view the far-right militant threat and how susceptible any community was to the centrifugal forces polarizing America. The two-day ordeal was described by the city's mayor, Michael Signer, as "a coordinated invasion of the city by white nationalist paramilitary groups." He termed Heyer's death an "act of terrorism."[36] Her murderer, James Alex Fields, was a vehement neo-Nazi who had come to Charlottesville intent on violence. When his mother had texted him to be careful just before the rally commenced, Fields replied with a photograph of Adolf Hitler and the boast that "We're not the one [sic] who need to be careful."[37] He had served briefly in the U.S. Army in 2015 before being discharged, in the words of an army spokeswoman, for "a failure to meet training standards." Fields was by then an ardent neo-Nazi.[38]

In the days that followed the shocking images of neo-Nazis in torchlight procession in one of the country's leading college towns, the incessant brawling between demonstrators and counterprotestors, and Heyer's death and the injuries to many others caused by Fields, media attention turned to the White House for a call for national unity and a condemnation of the tragic events. Trump, however, seemed incapable of condemning the attack. In the aftermath of Saturday's events, the president decried the "hatred, bigotry, and violence, on many sides."[39] A few days later, Trump doubled down on his refusal to place sole blame on the extremists who had descended on the city, averring that there were "very bad people in that group, but you also had very fine people on both sides."[40]

Trump's apparent inability to condemn the racist and antisemitic extremism that had convulsed Charlottesville provided an enormous boost to the movement. "Thank you President Trump for your honesty & courage," David Duke, the former Klansman turned Louisiana legislator and early proponent of the cleaned-up alt-right tweeted.[41] He had previously described amid the melee at Lee Park on Saturday morning that "we are determined to take our country back. We are going to fulfill the promises of Donald Trump. That's what we believed in. That's why we voted for Donald Trump, because he said he's going to take our country back."[42] One Stormfront denizen could not contain his enthusiasm: "As I have said from the start, President Trump is only the beginning, not the end. Yet he continues to ring true. I have never abandoned him or criticized him and I never will. Meine Ehre heißt Treue," he concluded, repeating the motto of Adolf Hitler's SS—My Honor Is Loyalty. "It is wonderful having this man as President," another interlocutor swooned. "Moreover, it is high time someone stands up to the socialist, multicultural morons who want to destroy our culture and dumb down and adulterate the most intelligent, creative and productive race of people the World has ever known. I think everyone who wants to rebuild our European culture should feel emboldened by our President's courageous actions."[43]

Years later, Richard Spencer would recall the galvanizing effect that the president's comments had on the white nationalist movement. "There is no question that Charlottesville wouldn't have occurred without Trump," he observed. "It really was because of his campaign and this new potential for a nationalist candidate who was resonating with the public in a very intense way. The alt-right found something in Trump. He changed the paradigm and made this kind of public presence of the alt-right possible."[44] The events, however, also provided a political boost to the Democratic Party and the left: twenty months later, former vice president Joe Biden would use the Charlottesville rally as the opening message of his presidential campaign, a video announcement decrying the rally as "a defining moment for this nation in the last few years" and lamenting the president's words as having "assigned a moral equivalence between those spreading hate and those with the courage to stand against it."[45]

Charlottesville marked the advent of a new far right, one characterized by its youthfulness, viciousness, mobilization and free rein online, and vehement, passionate support for President Trump. Styling itself as the "alt-right," the movement was noteworthy for its makeover and self-constructed veneer of respectability. It represented the apogee of the long-standing efforts to "mainstream" and make more acceptable odious racism, antisemitism, and xenophobia. Gone was the stereotype of the loud and aggressive skinhead, hate-spewing brownshirt, or hooded Klansman. Spencer was the embodiment of the well-kempt, respectably dressed, model next-door-neighbor. Charlottesville, then, marked the completion of a transition advocated for by Duke nearly four decades before: it's time to "get out of the cow pasture and into hotel meeting rooms."[46] Breivik had offered similar advice to millennials growing up in the digital age: "Appear politically correct or at least moderate, dress normally. Try to limit your rhetorical activities. Avoid excessive forum posting. Excessive forum activity might get you 'flagged' by your national government."[47] As the extremism expert Julia Ebner, who had infiltrated the movement, explains, "The far-right's obsession with aesthetics stems from the desire to look legitimate and appealing to more mainstream audiences. Fashion and lifestyle serve extremist movements as a gateway to their political ideologies."[48] Or, as another observer commented after Charlottesville, "The uniform of white hate is now average, mundane, the stuff of everyday American life."[49] But more consequential was the new attitude permeating the violent, far-right extremist universe. The events in Charlottesville had convinced many that they could get away with their activism and occasional violence—that political leaders would shield them. That message was also delivered to the American rural militia movement, when, maintaining the antiestablishment veneer that propelled him to election, Trump in July 2018 pardoned Dwight and Steven Hammond, the ranchers whose arson attacks on federal land and subsequent imprisonment had triggered the 2016 Malheur occupation described in chapter 6.[50]

During protests that broke out in reaction to the hate on display at Charlottesville, one Holocaust survivor from New York stood defiant. "I escaped the Nazis once," her sign read. "You will not defeat me now."[51] But darker days were ahead. As Heather Heyer had warned in her final Facebook post, "If you're not outraged, you're not paying attention."[52]

• • •

The rising danger from the far right was perhaps most keenly felt in a blizzard of violence in the ten days leading up to the November 2018 U.S. midterm election, dragging media attention away from the peaceful exercise of democracy and toward those who preferred to kill than vote. On October 22, an improvised explosive device was found in a New York postbox belonging to George Soros, the wealthy, Jewish financier and perennially popular target of antisemites and far-right conspiracists. Over the course of the next week, postal authorities discovered additional package bombs addressed to senior Democratic Party leaders, including former president Barack Obama, former vice president Joe Biden, former secretary of state Hillary Clinton, senators Kamala Harris and Cory Booker, representative Maxine Waters, former attorney general Eric Holder, former director of national intelligence James Clapper, and former CIA director John Brennan, as well as the actor Robert De Niro, billionaire Tom Steyer, and CNN.[53] The person responsible for building and mailing the bombs, a Florida man named Cesar Sayoc, would later claim that his "intention was to only intimidate & scare." Most definitions of terrorism include this intimidation element.[54] Regardless of his claimed nonlethal objective and, for that matter, whether the bombs would have actually detonated, no other twenty-first-century far-right terrorist had yet been as ambitious in plotting to potentially kill most of the Democratic Party leadership and others reflecting contemporary left-of-center or liberal politics in America.

Eventually captured in Florida, Sayoc was a pitiable, broken man who had found a purpose in worshipping Trump. The victim of sexual abuse, with attendant mental health issues, Sayoc, his defense attorneys would later explain, had emerged from a life of darkness to find "light in Donald J. Trump."[55] The day that the bomber—who had previously described Trump rallies as "like a new found drug"—was arrested, the subject of his adulation had cast doubt on the mail bombs, suggesting in a tweet that they were a canard designed to influence the 2018 electoral outcome. "Republicans are doing so well in early voting, and at the polls," Trump claimed, "and now this 'Bomb' stuff happens and the momentum greatly slows—news not talking politics. Very unfortunate, what is going on. Republicans, go out and vote!" The statement followed an earlier tweet where Trump had abrogated any responsibility for the acute partisanship polarizing the country, blaming instead the news media. "A very big part of the Anger we see today in our society is caused by the purposely false and inaccurate reporting of the Mainstream Media that I refer to as Fake News," he opined. "It has gotten so bad and hateful that it is beyond description. Mainstream Media must clean up its act, FAST!"[56]

The mail bombs revealed the proclivity of the far right to deflect blame away from actual violence committed by its exponents as part and parcel of some grandiose "false flag" designed to discredit their president and party. On Stormfront, one extremist went even further, invoking the persistent myth of Jewish machination and manipulation in reference to the targeting of Soros. "I am wondering who found the so called device? How big was it? Could it have actually done anything to that old monster? Let's just say I reserve judgement. The Jews have pulled that poor little me I am being persecuted crap before. I am not buying it. Someone does need to get rid of that old fool." Another responded, "I think this was a staged event. More incidents right before the midterms to show how radical the right is now. Soros likely planted it himself." Others were just simply celebratory: "Someone's finally taking the fight to the enemy."[57]

The violence continued to escalate. On October 24, two Black shoppers were killed at a Kroger grocery store in Jeffersontown, Kentucky. The gunman, fifty-one-year-old Gregory Bush, had initially attempted to gain entry to the town's predominantly Black First Baptist Church but found the doors locked. He murdered a man shopping inside with his grandson before gunning down a woman in the parking lot.[58] Bush reportedly told a bystander, "Don't shoot me. I won't shoot you. Whites don't shoot whites."[59] Bush suffered from serious mental illness. "On the day of this tragedy, Mr. Bush's schizophrenia was not medicated, so he was tortured by voices that threatened to kill him and his family," his lawyer said. "He acted out of his psychosis and his illness."[60] But even this tragic spasm of violence was but a harbinger for still worse to come.

On October 27, a terrorist walked into the Tree of Life synagogue in the Squirrel Hill neighborhood of Pittsburgh, Pennsylvania. That morning, three separate Sabbath services were underway in three different sanctuaries. Robert Bowers was armed with a Colt AR-15 assault rifle as well as with three semiautomatic handguns. At 9:50 AM he opened fire. Declaring his desire to "kill Jews," Bowers killed eleven mostly elderly worshippers and critically wounded two others.[61] He appears to have been motivated as much by a profound animus against immigrants as by antisemitism. In particular, news about "caravans" of migrants headed to the United States' southern border and the role of a Jewish charity that provides assistance to all newcomers to the country in need had prompted the attack, appealing to Bowers's conspiratorial "white genocide" fears. A post from Bowers on the far-right social media site Gab shortly before he burst into the synagogue revealed his motivation: "HIAS [Hebrew Immigrant Aid Society] likes to bring invaders in that kill our people. I can't sit by and watch my people get slaughtered. Screw your optics, I'm going in."[62] The attack at Tree of Life was the deadliest act of antisemitic violence in American history. Bowers's "screw your optics" declamation was his retort to the efforts of Richard Spencer and David Duke, among others, to present a more socially acceptable face of violent, far-right extremism to the American public—arguing, as accelerationists before him, that such efforts had plainly failed and that violence was now the only option. The terrorism analyst Rita Katz of the SITE Intelligence Group explained, "Bowers's act was to many in the far right the only way to 'fight back' against the changing world; they saw an existential threat to their race, something the old guard of the movement didn't have the stomach to take on."[63]

The violence that election season finally ended on November 2, when two women were killed in a shooting at a Tallahassee, Florida, yoga studio. Although motivated primarily by so-called incel ideology,[64] the killer, Scott Beierle, had also displayed a history of violent rhetoric against minorities and Jews and was an admirer of the Aryan Nations. One old social group that Beierle belonged to had dubbed him "Nazi Scott." According to someone who knew Beierle, "He'd walk up and just start talking about weapons and killing people in the military and how Hitler was right to clear the human race of gays and Jews and blacks." Beierle had been kicked out of the army, albeit with an honorable discharge, for "unacceptable conduct" after being investigated over his behavior toward female soldiers. A Secret Service investigation conducted years later found Beierle had showed signs of profound misogynist extremism since his teenage years and that his parents had even slept with their door locked out of fear of their son.[65]

Trump's implicit encouragement of violent, far-right extremists was perhaps best depicted by the exculpatory statements offered near the end of October by the lawyers for three Kansas militia members convicted earlier that year for plotting to bomb the homes of Somali immigrants. In a plea for leniency, the defense attorney for one of the convicted claimed, "The court cannot ignore the circumstances of one of the most rhetorically mold-breaking, violent, awful, hateful and contentious presidential elections in modern history, driven in large measure by the rhetorical China shop bull who is now our president."[66]

The 2018 midterm elections, held on November 6, saw Democrats win back the House of Representatives, with a net gain of forty-one seats—a popular rejection of sorts of the nation's rising militant activism. But those who believed the violence that fall to be an aberration would soon learn how mistaken they were.

• • •

In 1992, in his landmark essay on leaderless resistance, Louis Beam had laid out the only white power strategy he felt still stood a chance of success. "Let the coming night be filled with a thousand points of resistance," he wrote. "Like the fog which forms when conditions are right and disappears when they are not, so must the resistance to tyranny be."[67] With the 1995 Oklahoma City bombing, McVeigh had sought to position himself at the vanguard of the revolution that Beam had hoped his strategy would inspire. Despite its failure then, the promise of leaderless resistance continued to burn bright in the minds of more violently inclined contemporary far-right extremists. And, in 2019, it would again dramatically resurface.

An ambitious assassination plot came to light that February. The authorities learned of it only because of the poor operational security of the would-be perpetrator, a former Marine, Army reservist, and member of the Virginia National Guard who was then serving in the U.S. Coast Guard. Lieutenant Christopher Paul Hasson had used his work computer to compile a hit list of prominent Democratic Party officials and perceived liberal media figures as well as to compose his manifesto explaining the reasons behind the attacks. Hasson had assembled a small arsenal of weapons—including fifteen firearms, two silencers, and over a thousand rounds of ammunition[68]—with which he planned to assassinate Speaker of the House of Representatives Nancy Pelosi and Representative Alexandria Ocasio-Cortez, Senate Minority Leader Chuck Schumer, media figures including CNN hosts Chris Cuomo and Don Lemon, and others.[69] He was serving as an acquisitions officer at the Coast Guard's National Security Cutter program, and the on-the-job skills he acquired in that position may have facilitated Hasson's plans as he amassed his armory. Hasson was another in a succession of far-right extremists directly inspired by Breivik. He had studied Breivik's manifesto for tactical tips and operational advice.[70] Hasson would be arrested at his workplace, the U.S. Coast Guard headquarters in Washington, DC.

Like Sayoc, Hasson was also prepared to use what prosecutors termed "focused violence" to target his high-profile list of political enemies. His plot reflected both longstanding white supremacist accelerationist and leaderless resistance strategies in his twisted bid to create a "white homeland" in the United States—another longstanding white nationalist ambition. His plans, however, were far broader: "I am dreaming of a way to kill almost every last person on the earth," Hasson had mused. "I think a plague would be most successful but how do I acquire the needed /

Spanish flu, botulism, anthrax not sure yet but will find something."[71] Hasson's hope was that the wave of assassinations would set in motion the core accelerationist goal of widespread societal violence, chaos, and disorder, eventually leading to the establishment of an authoritarian white supremacist state. "Look up tactics used during Ukrainian civil war," he had written. "During unrest target both sides to increase tension. In other words provoke gov/police to over react which should help to escalate violence. BLM protests or other left crap would be ideal to incite to violence." The detention motion submitted by the government prosecutors was blunt in its assessment: "The defendant intends to murder innocent civilians on a scale rarely seen in this country."[72] Hasson had been motivated in part by his anger over congressional efforts to impeach Trump because of the latter's alleged attempts to pressure Ukraine by suspending arms transfers into cooperating with an investigation of the son of Joe Biden, Trump's likely 2020 general election opponent. Among the search terms used by Hasson on the internet were phrases such as "what if trump illegally impeached," "best place in dc to see congress people," "where in dc to congress live," and "civil war if trump impeached."[73]

The federal charges ultimately brought against Hasson underscored the challenges of indicting and prosecuting violent extremists in the United States in the absence of specific domestic terrorism statutes, particularly with the seditious conspiracy charges having failed so spectacularly at Fort Smith. Salafi jihadist adherents of the Islamic State and al-Qaeda, for example, can be charged with providing "material support to a foreign terrorist organization" under 18 U.S. Code § 2339B. This includes not only support in the planning and execution of terrorist attacks but conspiracy to commit these acts of violence, procuring materiel and finances for U.S. State Department–designated foreign terrorist organizations (FTOs), and recruitment and radicalization of individuals (including oneself) on behalf of terrorist groups. No such legal framework, however, exists to prosecute domestic extremists planning and plotting identical acts of violence or providing material support to violently inclined domestic organizations or ideologies.[74] Hasson was therefore charged with—and convicted of—an assortment of weapons and substance abuse charges. Although he was sentenced to more than thirteen years in federal prison,[75] Hasson's ideological intent to engage in mass murder targeting politicians, journalists, and civilians in the service of accelerationist aims designed to overthrow the U.S. government was astonishingly peripheral to the charges on which he was convicted.

On March 15, 2019, a twenty-eight-year-old white supremacist attired in military fatigues approached the Al Noor mosque in Christchurch, New Zealand. Like Hasson, he had amassed a small arsenal of firearms, including assault rifles and shotguns.[76] He first encountered Haji-Daoud Nabi, an elderly man who had emigrated from Afghanistan in the late 1970s. "Hello, brother," Nabi welcomed the visitor. Moments later, Nabi, beloved father of four, grandfather of nine, and "father and an uncle to people who had none," became the first of the fifty-one people Brenton Tarrant would murder over the next twenty minutes.[77]

Tarrant, an Australian national, was a self-proclaimed "eco-fascist" and a creature of the far-right extremist online world. The report of the Royal Commission of Inquiry Into the Terrorist Attack on Christchurch Mosques on 15 March 2019, convened by the New Zealand government and released almost two years later, provided a chilling portrait of Tarrant's radicalization trajectory. He discovered 4chan, an online anonymous image board site notorious for its radical discourse, at age fourteen. Tarrant was also an avid gamer and regularly expressed extremist views to his online friends.[78] Tarrant expressed growing anger over political opinions different from his own on a Facebook page belonging to the United Patriots Front, an Australian far-right extremist group that railed against immigration, multiculturalism, and the Islamic religion.[79] "Communists will get what communists get," one of Tarrant's posts read. "I would love to be there holding one end of the rope when you get yours traitor."[80] Trips to Europe further propelled his radicalization, confirming to Tarrant the societal changes affecting whites that he had previously read about online.[81]

Just moments before his attack, Tarrant left a final message on 8chan (a platform similar to 4chan): "Well lads, it's time to stop shitposting and time to make a real life effort post. I will carry out and attack the invaders, and will even live stream the attack via facebook. . . . I have provided links to my writings below, please do your part by spreading my message, making memes and shitposting as you usually do."[82] The "writings" that Tarrant referred to were his own seventy-four-page manifesto, which, like

Roof and Breivik before him, Tarrant had posted online in advance of his attack. It laid out in chilling detail both his plans and the twisted justification behind the violence shortly to be visited on the two mosques. The text was a panegyric to accelerationism, arguing that nonviolent political activism had failed. It was time for action. "True change and the change we need to enact only arises in the great crucible of crisis," Tarrant wrote. "A gradual change is never going to achieve victory. Stability and comfort are the enemies of revolutionary change. Therefore we must destabilize and discomfort society where ever possible." Tarrant's manifesto repeated many age-old motifs of the far-right's ideological lineage. "Goodbye, god bless you all and I will see you in Valhalla," Tarrant concluded, echoing a promise reminiscent of the one made by the Order's Robert Mathews as he prepared to face his death on Whidbey Island thirty-five years earlier, as well as one by Louis Beam at the Aryan Nations Congress in 1983. Again, Trump's influence was clear: although dismissing his support for the U.S. president, Brenton Tarrant's rant also specifically praised Trump, describing the president "as a symbol of renewed white identity and common purpose."[83]

With this attack Tarrant revolutionized terrorism. The entire incident was livestreamed on Facebook for seventeen minutes, where an audience of at least four thousand watched the slaughter before the video was removed. Over the next twenty-four hours, Facebook removed 1.5 million copies from its website. During that time period there was also one upload of the livestreamed video per second over YouTube.[84] According to the Royal Commission's report: "Those who watched the video included survivors of the terrorist attack as they lay in hospital, [family] of the [martyrs], witnesses of the attack and ordinary people in Christchurch and around the world—adults and children alike." It autoplayed, meaning some people saw it without even clicking on the video link. Gaming featured prominently, with Tarrant beginning his livestream by invoking the name of PewDiePie, a Swedish YouTube gamer. Though Tarrant's intention appears to have been deliberately to deceive and confuse law enforcement and analysts, contained within his rant were dog-whistles for the broader far-right community from which he emerged—memes and phrases recognizable only to those as deeply immersed in the movement as Tarrant was. In the hours that followed, the *New York Times* technology reporter Kevin Roose wrote that "In some ways, it felt like a first—an internet-native mass shooting, conceived and produced entirely within the irony-soaked discourse of modern extremism."[85]

The far right could now achieve a reach and have an impact that would have been unimaginable to twentieth-century white supremacist ideologues and accelerationism advocates like Pierce and Beam. In a highly networked and globalized world, far-right extremists of all stripes were now able to share strategies, tactics, and calls to arms in real time with fellow hate-mongers scattered across the globe. Significantly, it also signaled the erosion of any distinction between domestic and international terrorism. Identical ideologies and shared strategies and tactics were now inspiring terrorists from America to Europe to Oceania. Tarrant in fact specifically cited Breivik's inspiration. "I have read the writings of Dylan [sic] Roof and many others, but only really took true inspiration from Knight Justiciar Breivik," he explained, acceding to Breivik's desire to portray himself as a modern answer to the Knights Templar, which had fought Muslims in the Holy Land during the Crusades. The common dream of a whites-only homeland was uniting extremists throughout the world and producing a global ideology of hate, intolerance, and violence. Tarrant's call for others to emulate his attack—and, indeed, to escalate further by assassinating European politicians, including Chancellor Angela Merkel of Germany, President Recep Tayyip Erdoğan of Turkey, and Mayor Sadiq Khan of London—was meant to reinforce the transnational bonds and interconnectivity of contemporary violent, far-right extremism. "Merkel, the mother of all things anti-white and anti-germanic, is top of the list," Tarrant declared. "Few have done more to damage and racially cleanse Europe of its people."[86]

Tarrant's battle cry echoed those of other terrorists before him. Osama bin Laden's 1998 fatwa, for instance, had asserted that "the ruling to kill the Americans and their allies—civilians and military—is an individual duty for every Muslim who can do it in any country in which it is possible to do it." Tarrant aped bin Laden when he wrote, "Make your plans, get training, form alliances, get equipped and then act. The time for meekness has long since passed, the time for a political solution has long since passed. Men of the West must be men once more." And, just as bin Laden's appeal resonated far beyond his base in Afghanistan, this hitherto unknown Australian ecofascist struck responsive chords elsewhere. Like

Breivik's twin attacks eight years before, the armed assault against wor-shippers at two mosques in Christchurch animated white supremacists across the Pacific in the United States and further afield in Europe. Tar-rant's theatrical template for violent action—the posting of statements pre-saging, explaining, and publicizing the violence to come that was then accompanied by livestreamed terror—was subsequently repeated in Cal-ifornia, Texas, Norway, and Germany.[87]

Only a few weeks had passed before another lone gunman attacked another place of worship. On April 27, John Earnest opened fire inside the Chabad of Poway near San Diego, California. An accomplished pianist, volunteer tutor, dean's list student at the California state college where he was studying nursing, and white supremacist murderer, Earnest brought an AR-15 assault rifle into Sabbath services. Four persons were hit before the gun jammed—including the sixty-year-old congregant Lori Gilbert-Kaye, who heroically shielded the rabbi and in turn became the only per-son to die in the attack.[88] Like Breivik and Tarrant before him, Earnest had also previously posted a manifesto explaining the attack, in this case depicting his intense hatred of Jews. "To the Jew. Your crimes—innumerable. Your deeds—unacceptable. Your lies—everywhere. The European man will rise up," Earnest proclaimed, "and strike your squalid and parasitic race into the dust. And this time there will be nowhere for you to run." Reviving his many predecessors' proclivity to couch their vio-lence in religious justification, Earnest declared, "You cannot love God if you do not hate Satan. You cannot love righteousness if you do not also hate sin." He also listed Jesus Christ as his primary inspiration—above Adolf Hitler, Brenton Tarrant, the Pittsburgh gunman Robert Bowers, and an array of other figures.

Like Tarrant, the Poway gunman also dispensed tactical advice designed to inspire imitation. "It is so easy to log on to Minecraft and get away with burning a synagogue (or mosque) to the ground if you're smart about it," Earnest advised, employing a commonly used tactic of specify-ing a threat within a video game context to evade legal culpability by mak-ing slightly veiled threats. "You can even shoot up a mosque, synagogue, immigration center, traitorous politicians, wealthy Jews in gated commu-nities, Jewish-owned company buildings, etc. and get away with it as well," he continued. "If your goal is strictly carnage and the highest score—I'd highly recommend you look into flamethrowers (remember kids, napalm is more effective than gasoline if you want Jews to really light up like a menorah).” As part of his attack, Earnest also launched an accelerationist appeal to *The Turner Diaries* acolytes: “Some of you have been waiting for The Day of the Rope for years. Well, The Day of the Rope is here right now—that is if you have the gnads [*sic*] to keep the ball rolling.”[89] Accordingly, he deliberately copied Tarrant by using firearms as a means to achieve dramatic political effects. “I used a gun for the same reason that Brenton Tarrant used a gun,” Earnest explained. “In case you haven’t noticed we are running out of time. If this revolution doesn’t happen soon, we won’t have the numbers to win it. The goal is for the US government to start confiscating guns. People will defend their right to own a firearm—civil war has just started.” A technical malfunction scuttled Earnest’s hope to emulate Tarrant by livestreaming his attack.

Earnest’s attack had followed what would soon become a familiar template: lone actor, radicalized online, committing a mass shooting at a place of worship. But the shooting at Poway was in fact Earnest’s second terrorist act. A month earlier, he had set fire to a mosque in Escondido, California. The worshippers inside were unharmed, and the fire was quickly extinguished.[90] Earnest claimed to have also spray-painted a pledge of allegiance to the Christchurch murderer and the 8chan forum that had inspired them outside the mosque: “For Brenton Tarrant -t. /pol/,” he wrote, referencing the shorthand nickname of 8chan’s vehemently racist and violent “Politically Incorrect” forum.

The next attack occurred on August 3, at a Walmart store in El Paso frequented by Latino immigrants. Claiming in a preattack manifesto to have been inspired by Tarrant’s example, the twenty-one-year-old gunman, Patrick Crusius, described his hatred of people of Latin American heritage. Its opening sentences told the whole story: “In general, I support the Christchurch shooter and his manifesto,” Crusius declared. “This attack is a response to the Hispanic invasion of Texas.” Twenty-three people were killed, in the deadliest act of domestic terrorism on U.S. soil since Oklahoma City. Through Earnest and now Crusius, the international white supremacist terrorist chain reaction that had started eight years earlier in Norway had now traveled through New Zealand before reaching the United States.[91]

Europe was next. That same month, a neo-Nazi in Bærum, Norway, shot to death his Asian stepsister before attacking a nearby mosque. Philip

Manshaus, the twenty-one-year-old Norwegian murderer, was subdued by worshippers before he could inflict any harm. There was no written manifesto this time, although Manshaus had attempted to livestream his assault on the mosque via Facebook.[92] Instead he posted a brief message on 8chan: "well cobbers [Australian slang for 'good buddy'] it's my time, I was elected by saint tarrant after all[.] we can't let this go on, you gotta bump the race war thread irl [in real life] and if you're reading this you have been elected by me[.]"[93] "Valhalla awaits," he concluded in Norwegian, echoing several of his predecessors. In a prison interview, Manshaus recalled that, like Tarrant, the internet had played the main role in his radicalization.

> There are a lot of different ways to get the views I have, which are quite different from the normal. Some people for example read books, for example *Mein Kampf*, or another fascist literary work, and then in a period of maybe 5–15 years come to a conclusion that things may not be as they were brought up to believe. Going through the process I did goes significantly faster. I only spent a year, maybe one and a half years, to get my view on society. And it really represents the impact the internet has. The internet is like a super-highway for ideas, in which ideas and opinions can be shared so fast, as we have never seen before. . . . I can safely say that the main actor in my political upheaval was the internet.[94]

Tarrant and Manshaus had another life story in common—both had a parent commit suicide in their youth, Manshaus having lost his mother when he was just four.[95]

The final attack in 2019 that Tarrant's twin assaults on the mosques had triggered occurred on the Jewish high holiday of Yom Kippur ("Day of Atonement") in Halle, Germany. On October 9, a German national named Stephan Balliet attempted to enter a synagogue during morning services, armed with homemade, 3D-printed weapons and several improvised explosive devices he had also built.[96] Balliet also livestreamed the entire incident. He is shown swearing at the locked synagogue door and then gunning down a passerby. Balliet then murdered a patron at a nearby kebab shop before fleeing in his automobile. Despite the attack's multiple failures (both in gaining entrance to the synagogue and, similarly to Frazier Glenn Miller, in his only victims being ethnic Germans and not Jews or immigrants), the incident was significant in several respects. First, he had deliberately chosen the date, when he knew the synagogue would be packed, to maximize casualties. "The best day of action should be Jom [*sic*] Kippur," Balliet had explained, "because even 'non-religious' Jews are often visiting the synagogue on this date." Second, he deliberately sought to highlight the homemade, 3D-printed murder weapons he had created as a way to inspire other Europeans from "no fun countries"—where strict national firearms laws restrict access to weapons—to emulate his example by fabricating their own means of attack. Balliet admitted in fact that his primary purpose was to "prove the viability of improvised weapons" as a means to inspire and encourage more far-right attacks both in Germany and elsewhere.[97] Finally, Balliet, like Breivik, Tarrant, Earnest, Crusius, and Manshaus before him, survived. They each sought veneration and imitation—not martyrdom.

Tarrant's attack was among the first perpetrated by a far-right extremist to effortlessly straddle the divide between the real and virtual worlds. With his first-person livestream and references to the gaming world, Tarrant succeeded in transforming the mass murder of fifty-one innocent worshippers into a real-world reality show of carnage and mayhem deliberately choreographed and executed to appeal specifically to his fellow inhabitants of extremist online forums. Exactly as Tarrant had hoped, it went on to inspire imitation and emulation, as the four consecutive white supremacist terrorist attacks that followed throughout 2019 demonstrated. Tarrant had transformed terrorism into a real-world video game where subsequent attackers encouraged the next to top previous "high scores" in terms of dead and wounded—a perverse manifestation of what the former FBI agent Clint Watts calls "cascading terrorism."[98] Balliet, in fact, ended his manifesto with a list of "achievements" he hoped others would unlock. According to the priorities that Balliet defined, "points" could be achieved for the killing of Jews, Muslims, Christians, Blacks, children, and communists, as well as through different tactics and technologies, including with 3D-printed guns, grenades, swords, nail bombs, and a "secret weapon," which likely involved the use of a vehicle. Balliet doubtless intended that others would be inspired to top his and one another's "high score" and thereby set in motion a macabre contest to outdo the body count of each previous attack.[99] Balliet's idea, however, was also far from novel. The past was once again prologue, this time in adapting the idea of a "point system" that the Order as well as Frazier Glenn Miller had suggested years earlier as a means to similarly encourage and demystify the murder of political and racial enemies. To drive home the gaming point, Balliet livestreamed his attack on Twitch, a video game livestreaming service owned by Amazon.[100]

This series of shootings had also focused new attention on a fringe online forum called 8chan, which hosted the preattack posts of several of the attackers. "Shut the site down," Fredrick Brennan, the founder of 8chan, said after the El Paso attack. "It's not doing the world any good. It's a complete negative to everybody except the users that are there. And you know what? It's a negative to them, too. They just don't realize it."[101] The site was dropped by its web security provider, Cloudflare, only to quickly reemerge under a new moniker, 8kun.[102] Sites like 8chan and 8kun abetted the continuing internationalization of the far right, a trend that is reflected in the symmetry of ideologies that inspired each of these terrorists. The more local factors that inspired Dylann Roof in 2015—including civil rights and gun rights—had become less salient, replaced by transnational grievances like immigration and attendant concerns over the "Islamization" of one's country and high "birthrates" among immigrants and nonwhite citizens—all allegedly orchestrated by a shadowy global conspiracy led and directed by Jewish elites.

This was also a time in which accelerationism entrenched itself as a distinct, publicly recognized political ideology and strategy. In 2019, Zack Beauchamp, a leading journalist covering domestic terrorism in the United States, described accelerationism as "the idea that Western governments are irreparably corrupt. As a result, the best thing white supremacists can do is accelerate their demise by sowing chaos and creating political tension."[103] This strategy was embraced by a new generation of tech-savvy neo-Nazis in the group they formed and named the Atomwaffen Division—German for "Nuclear Weapons." An offshoot of an online forum called Iron March, the group had been founded by a Bahamian-American National Guardsman called Brandon Russell in 2015. Seeking to pursue more violent offline activism, Russell's main goal was to "build a Fourth Reich," according to a Florida cell member named Devon Arthurs. Atomwaffen would eventually inspire an international network linking likeminded groups from Canada, Germany, and the Baltic countries.[104] Their stated targets included a range of minority groups but also power lines and other infrastructure, as *The Turner Diaries* had advocated and the Order had planned to attack. Another group that surfaced around this time, the Base, similarly sought to inspire destabilizing acts of violence in order to create disorder and accelerate the inevitable coming race war.

Although accelerationism is distinct enough to be considered a contemporary strategy followed by far-right extremists, as has been discussed throughout this book it is in fact an organizing principle for violence adopted decades ago by movement icons such as Robert Mathews, Timothy McVeigh, and James Mason. The short-lived Atomwaffen Division and its successor terrorist groups, accordingly, lauded these individuals as pioneering figures who understood accelerationism's power and promise potentially to succeed where other movement strategies had foundered.[105] Atomwaffen's first incarnation fell apart after Arthurs murdered his two roommates, who were also group members. When law enforcement officers searched the apartment they found a framed photo of Timothy McVeigh in addition to a variety of explosive materials. The Base, meanwhile, was hoping to pick up where the Order had left off three decades previously. An account using the pseudonymous moniker frequently employed by the Base's leader left a tribute on the far-right social media app Gab dedicated to the imprisoned Order member Gary Lee Yarbrough after his death. "Your sacrifice & those of other Order members shall not be in vain. Hail Victory!"[106]

During 2019, accelerationism was most clearly evidenced both by Tarrant's attack and in Hasson's thwarted plot. But mercifully, some of the more organized groups that had most energetically propagated the accelerationist doctrine, including Atomwaffen and the Base, were mostly unsuccessful in implementing their sanguinary plans as a result of the timely, preemptive actions of U.S. federal law enforcement agencies.[107] In fact, given the overall diffusion of the domestic terrorism threat in recent years, where lone individuals emerged as the main challenge confronting law enforcement and intelligence agencies, the tracking of actual organized entities like Atomwaffen and the Base was comparatively easier and more straightforward. Susceptible to infiltration and the cultivation of confidential informants, Atomwaffen, for instance, was swept up after it undertook an extensive "SWAT-ing" campaign against journalists and other political enemies. This entailed calling in phony reports of armed barricade-and-hostage situations at residences that result in aggressive responses from police special weapons and tactics (SWAT) units. Members of the Base were also identified and arrested after the authorities learned of several plots, the most serious of which entailed a false-flag operation planned for January 2020 that would have targeted Trump supporters attending a Second Amendment rally in Richmond, Virginia—in the hope that a gunfight would erupt between police and militia members, setting off a broader conflagration. The attackers' intention reflected a clear accelerationist mindset: foment chaos and deepen polarization and suspicion, thereby encouraging more violence. That cell had fabricated an assault rifle for the attack so powerful that one of them remarked, "Oh oops, it looks like I accidentally made a machine gun."[108] The Base was dismantled in no small part thanks to an FBI undercover operative, "Scott," who had slipped through the group's operational security defenses and embedded with the Base's Georgia cell.[109] Despite nominal efforts to separate the group into independent, networked cells, its demise as a result of FBI penetration proved Beam correct in his warning that pyramid organizations were vulnerable to infiltration. As Beam had cautioned two decades earlier: "This has been seen repeatedly in the United States where pro-government infiltrators or agent provocateurs weasel their way into patriotic groups and destroy them from within."[110]

Despite these failures, both Atomwaffen and the Base were successful in their efforts to resurrect another longstanding trend among American domestic terrorist groups. In recent years, newer, younger, more tech-savvy far-right groups have again sought out and benefited from the combat and related logistical and communications knowledge acquired from military service. The Atomwaffen Division's founding leader, Brandon Russell, for example, joined the Florida National Guard in January 2016 —"specifically for the knowledge and the training, and he wants to use that training against the government," his fellow AWD member Devon Arthurs explained. "These people join the military specially to get training. To get access to equipment." By that time, Russell was already sporting a distinctive tattoo on his upper arm, a radiation symbol inside a shield—Atomwaffen's notorious but then unknown logo.[111] He was one of at least nine AWD members who had served in the U.S. military. The group included active-duty personnel and veterans from the U.S. Marines, Navy, Army, Air Force, and National Guard.[112] One of them,

Joshua Beckett, an Army veteran who served in Afghanistan and who went on to train members of the group, recounted both how invaluable his combat experience was and more generally the role that the war on terror against al-Qaeda and its allies had played in his radicalization. "The army itself woke me up to race and the war woke me up to the Jews. The US military gives great training," Beckett explained, "you learn how to fight, and survive."[113] Another U.S. far-right group, Identity Evropa, reportedly had eleven active or former military service personnel in its ranks.[114] And Vanguard America was formed by a marine who had deployed to both Iraq and Afghanistan.[115]

However, perhaps no group captures the reverence that military experience holds within the movement better than the Base. The group's leader, Rinaldo Nazzaro, had been a Pentagon contractor working with U.S. Special Operations Command as late as 2014—just four years before he founded this neo-Nazi group. Nazzaro (aka "Norman Spear" and "Roman Wolf") consulted on counterterrorism and military targeting, held a top secret security clearance, and claimed to have deployed on "multiple tours in Iraq and Afghanistan."[116] Nazzaro had also worked as an analyst for the FBI.[117] One of the group's foremost recruiters was a Canadian Army reservist named Patrik Mathews.[118] Mathews entered the United States illegally in August 2019 to link up with other members of the Base, and on at least one known occasion, he provided combat training to members of the Base in Georgia.[119] Mathews was eventually apprehended in Maryland and charged with planning the previously mentioned attack on a January 2020 gun rights rally in Richmond, Virginia. Among the two other members of Mathews's own terrorist cell was a U.S. Army veteran trained in combat reconnaissance operations.[120] Like their predecessors, Atomwaffen and the Base actively sought recruits with military experience for both the credibility and skills they brought to the group.

Data compiled by the FBI reveals the connection between people with prior military service and mass violence, including terrorism. Among adult active shooters in the United States from 2000 to 2013, for instance, nearly a quarter had some level of military experience, almost half of whom had served in the army.[121] And in an assessment of fifty-two "lone offender" terrorists in the United States between 1972 and 2015, the FBI concluded that over a third had served in the military.[122] These percentages are considerably noteworthy, given that only an estimated 7 percent of living Americans have served in the military.[123] This alarming trend has led to redoubled education efforts and other measures to counter it. In 2019, the U.S. House of Representatives, at the urging of the Maryland congressman and retired army colonel Anthony Brown, inserted language in the House version of the National Defense Authorization Act for FY2020 that required the DoD to track white nationalist activity via Pentagon personnel surveys. Republican senators, however, removed the words "white nationalists" from the bill.[124] And in February 2020, a House Armed Services subcommittee held a hearing titled "Alarming Incidents of White Supremacy in the Military—How to Stop It?" In his opening remarks, Republican congressman Trent Kelly of Mississippi, himself a major general in the Mississippi National Guard who survived the June 2017 attack on GOP representatives training for the annual charity baseball game against their Democratic counterparts, stated that "extremist activities of any kind are unacceptable, and cannot be tolerated in the military."[125] Kelly's was a lone voice among his fellow Republican committee members.

There are many reasons why a veteran might be drawn to extremism on return from deployment, including a sense of alienation from the civilian world; an inability to break from the militarily essential "us versus them" mentality toward both perceived and actual enemies; a desire for belonging or brotherhood among likeminded, objective-oriented individuals; post-traumatic stress conditions; addictions to drugs or alcohol; or an inability to find civilian employment.[126] And, in many instances they are deliberately targeted for recruitment by extremist groups and cells who wish to make use of these veterans' combat as well as communications and logistical skills. As the German scholar Daniel Koehler, who has conducted one of the most in-depth studies of far-right extremism in the military in North America and Europe, has noted, the size of the military means that it will naturally attract a cross-section of society, representing significant social, economic, and political diversity, and therefore inevitably including extremists. "Hence," Koehler notes, "the question is not whether or not right-wing extremists are able to enter the military but rather if they are identified in time and if the military reacts adequately to the case (e.g., disciplinary action or removal from service)."[127]

The infiltration of extremist ideologies into the U.S. military and deliberate cultivation for recruitment of service personnel and veterans is now receiving increased scrutiny. "Far-right nationalism in the U.S. military and veteran community has a destructive effect on civil-military relations and how the American people view the armed forces," the retired U.S. Army colonel Jeff McCausland has observed. "It is corrosive to morale and security among military personnel. Even non-violent activism from soldiers, sailors, airmen, or Marines with extremist views has a negative effect on good order and discipline as well as readiness and cohesion."[128] Against arguments that this threat has been exaggerated, Carter F. Smith, an army criminal investigator for thirty years, counters that the Pentagon and senior military commanders "always say the numbers are small, and because of that, it is not a priority. Well, the numbers might be small, but they are like a drop of cyanide in your drink. They can do a lot of damage."[129]

The importance of the issue, particularly to the future of the military, was best summarized by Congressman Kelly. Speaking during the House Armed Services subcommittee hearing in 2020, he argued that "no group is more diverse or culturally integrated than our United States military. None, anywhere. We must keep it that way."[130] A ready and representative U.S. military is essential to the country's foreign policy and to international security. It is undermined by the extremists in its midst.

• • •

Reviving tactics pioneered by the American far right in the 1970s and 1980s, today's white supremacist and neo-Nazi terrorists continue to rely on digital spaces to communicate and recruit while also calling for lone wolf attacks against a historically continuous set of defined targets.[131] The cellular organizational structures of the Atomwaffen Division and the Base have mostly been eschewed as operationally insecure and vulnerable to penetration or informants. The repeated resurrection of Beam's twentieth-century leaderless resistance strategy via twenty-first-century social media, accordingly, has endowed even the most amateurish, isolated individuals with opportunities to quickly radicalize and commit violent acts in furtherance of a common political agenda. Tarrant eagerly exploited the munificent benefits of contemporary communications to become the archetypal twenty-first-century terrorist—broadcasting his attack and message across the globe and in real time. He emerged from an eclectic and radical online space with existent extremist ideas about race and immigration, combined with fears over environmental degradation, and fed himself back into an endless loop among the denizens of these networks by livestreaming his attack and providing a lengthy manifesto. Yet the conceptualization, planning, preparation, and execution of his attack were accomplished by Tarrant acting completely on his own. "No group ordered my attack," Tarrant boasted. "I make the decision myself."[132]

In the first couple of decades of the twenty-first century, lone-actor terrorists have arguably displayed, to devastating effect and across multiple continents, an agency and power that rivals that of actual, existing organizations seeking the same ends. Since 9/11, the two most deadly terrorist attacks that took place in the West were ordered and coordinated by foreign terrorist organizations—al-Qaeda, in the 2004 Madrid commuter train bombings, and the Islamic State, with its simultaneous 2015 suicide attacks in Paris. But apart from those two incidents, the deadliest terrorist violence over the past two-plus decades has been perpetrated by individuals and not organized groups:

- the Norwegian neo-Nazi who claimed seventy-seven lives in his twin attacks;
- the homophobic American ISIS supporter who murdered forty-nine in Orlando;
- the Tunisian immigrant whose vehicular attack a month later in Nice, France, killed eighty-six; and,
- the Australian Islamophobe, white supremacist, and ecofascist whose killings in New Zealand resulted in fifty-one deaths.

The internet played a key role in each story.[133]

Lone-actor terrorism presents an especially formidable challenge to those charged with countering this threat. First, there is limited intelligence value in the capture of a lone actor, who likely has little information to share, given that there are often few connections to a broader network or group or anything similar to a traditional terrorist organization's hierarchy. Second, in a social media world, lone actors have the technology and expertise to create their own propaganda platform. As previously noted, Tarrant's livestream was shared on Facebook 1.5 million times during the first twenty-four hours after the attack, depriving government and media organizations of the ability to contain this unimpeded broadcasting of wanton death and injury.[134] And finally, and most importantly, lone-actor terrorism turns counterterrorism into a needle-in-the-haystack exercise of identifying one individual intent on violence amid a vast digital universe of voices. That challenge has been made more difficult by modern internet culture. Extremists hide behind a façade of "shitposting," the practice of sharing increasingly inflammatory, extreme, violent, and often humorous material online. Those who take offence or flag concerns are mocked as "liberal snowflakes" or "social justice warriors."[135] But through that smokescreen, bonds inside the in-group are strengthened, and distrust and hatred of the out-group crystallizes, as connections solidify between geographically vast and diverse extremist networks. Through humor and mockery, radicalization intensifies and violence is desensitized—leaving those seeking to prevent carnage and mayhem having to wade through a staggering multiplicity of bloviating, albeit graphic, threats in order to identify those who are not merely shitposting but actually planning to commit violence.

The violent far right has been absorbing the concept of leaderless resistance since Beam first articulated the strategy in the early 1980s. But contemporary social media has empowered extremists to propagate Beam's message to an array of lone actors seeking agency and influence by turning their blood-drenched fantasies into real-life violence. Today, even the more organized far-right networks usually prefer the leaderless resistance strategy to the traditional top-down/command-and-control model of terrorism. "The man that is strongest alone is the prime recruit!" Atomwaffen Division's German offshoot asserted in its internal "AWD Program"—the group's action plan, which was posted onto open Telegram channels in early 2020. Indeed, all the acts of violence linked to the AWD's once extensive network—most notably the stabbing murder of a gay Jewish University of Pennsylvania student in California in January 2018—were perpetrated by lone actors, without any known coordination by or direction from the group's leaders.[136] "We are dedicated to promoting radical autonomy while fomenting a revolutionary atmosphere," Atomwaffen's successor group, National Socialist Order (NSO), reiterated in July 2020.[137] In addition to its adherence to James Mason's idiosyncratic

Siege philosophy promoting violence and chaos as part of an acceleration-ist strategy, NSO's statement was reminiscent of Charles Manson's "Helter Skelter" prophecy, which called for random acts of violence as a necessary prerequisite to the national race war Manson hoped to trigger. "Is it a conspiracy that the music is telling the youth to rise up against the establishment because the establishment is rapidly destroying things?" Manson had explained while on trial. "The music speaks to you every day, but you are too deaf, dumb, and blind to even listen to the music. . . . It is not my conspiracy. It is not my music. I hear what it relates. It says 'Rise.' It says 'Kill.'"[138] Not unlike the Islamic State, the violent far right often revels in chaotic "ultra-violence."[139]

The open promulgation of extremism via social media platforms has thus fueled terrorism in the twenty-first century. Whatever guardrails once existed that someone would have to surmount as part of their vio-lent trajectory no longer exist. In the far-right universe, this trend has been especially prominent among teenagers on the internet and especially on gaming and social media platforms. In these online milieus, young people—particularly those who lack a sense of belonging, community, or mentorship in their offline lives—are often groomed by older extrem-ists with the ideological legitimacy to impart compelling tales of the adventure and excitement of life underground. Youngsters also have inde-pendently banded together to create their own extremist forums. The phe-nomenon has led to all-youth white power groups such as the British Hand, a neo-Nazi group led by a fifteen-year-old.[140] Perhaps the most shocking example of youth radicalization was provided by Feuerkrieg ("Fire War") Division, an offshoot of Atomwaffen located in the Baltics. When the authorities arrested the leader of the group in Estonia, he was found to be thirteen years old.[141]

Social media is also providing extremists with a means to speak directly to the psychologically vulnerable and lonely—especially those going through a difficult adolescence. During its short-lived reign, the Atom-waffen Division, for instance, was responsible for five murders, perpe-trated by three killers. News reporting surrounding the individual cases confirms that each of the group's killers—Devon Arthurs, Nicholas Giampa, and Sam Woodward—as well as the group's founding leader, Brandon Russell, all suffered from an array of mental health issues, includ-ing varying levels of autism in every case, in addition to schizophrenia, attention deficit disorder, and depression.[142] During Russell's trial, his mother tearfully explained that "he was always looking for something to belong to."[143] In another Atomwaffen case, the defense attorney described her client as "susceptible to radicalization" because "he has never felt like he fit in."[144] Christian Picciolini, a former white power rock musician now involved in efforts to turn youngsters away from violence and extremism, claims that almost three of every four far-right extremists he has worked with suffered from autism spectrum–related disorders. The connection is so strong that Picciolini encourages all new cases to see a psychologist or counselor.[145] With social media and extremist forums now pervasive, vulnerable young people are more easily exposed to radical rhetoric and a variety of radical communities. And with terrorism no longer the domain of organized groups with coherent ideologies, mentally ill lone actors have come to play a larger role in domestic terrorism everywhere.

The lowered barriers to terrorism also have tactical implications: the bombings that characterized an earlier wave of far-right accelerationist terrorism—such as those perpetrated by McVeigh and Rudolph—have been superseded by another tactic: the mass shooting. The mass shooting has sadly become a regular occurrence in America today and an occasional one in other countries. But the United States is a special case, where firearms are widely and readily available and armed attackers can create havoc and bloodshed on a scale completely divorced from their training or expertise, in turn making terrorism more accessible to violently inclined people with a political axe to grind. Consider the Poway Chabad shooting, in April 2019. The gunman, John Earnest, was at least on the surface an all-American teenager, having grown up in the idyllic suburb of Rancho Peñasquitos, California—or "Commiefornia," as he called it. Earnest radicalized rapidly—as he noted in his own manifesto. "If you told me even 6 months ago that I would do this I would have been surprised," he wrote. Earnest admitted to having only limited firearms training when he decided to launch his attack. This piano prodigy's lack of technological expertise with firearms likely contributed to his gun's jamming, but he was still able claim one life, injure three more, devastate a community he hated, and broadcast his ideology to an audience far beyond his San Diego suburb. Earnest used the firearm now almost synonymous with the American mass shooting: the AR-15 semiautomatic rifle, the civilian version of the U.S. Army's standard M-4 carbine and its predecessor, the M-16.

For the would-be accelerationist, mass shootings with a demonstrable political motive have the additional benefit of further tearing at the fabric of American society, ripping communities into polarized camps based on an individual's support or rejection of the Second Amendment. Tarrant actually planned his attack with an eye on the effect it would have on opinion in the United States. "I chose firearms for the affect [sic] it would have on social discourse, the extra media coverage they would provide and the affect it could have on the politics of United states and thereby the political situation of the world," he wrote. "This attempted abolishment of rights by the left will result in a dramatic polarization of the people in the United States and eventually a fracturing of the US along cultural and racial lines."[146]

Of course, not all terrorists choose the tactic of mass shooting. Arson is a popular tactic among both far-left and far-right extremists. Although the tactic has been less common in the United States—although, as previously noted, Earnest preceded his synagogue shooting by deliberately setting fire to a mosque in Escondido—it has been used more widely in Europe. Arson has devastated refugee centers and mosques from Bingen, Germany, to Eskilstuna, Sweden.[147] Stabbings are also more common in Europe, where firearms are difficult to acquire. In October 2015, for instance, a Swedish neo-Nazi used a sword to stab multiple victims to death in a school in Trollhättan. The twenty-one-year-old perpetrator had deliberately chosen that particular target because of its large proportion of immigrant students and teachers.[148] In the United States, however, mass shootings are most common. The FBI's November 2019 study of fifty-two "lone offender terrorism" acts in the United States between 1972 and 2015 found that more than two-thirds used firearms—and that the guns were legally purchased by the perpetrator in nearly three-quarters of cases.[149]

The persistence of the mass shooting as America's preferred domestic terrorist tactic has produced significant changes in the targets—and victims—of this violence. In previous terrorism waves, government facilities were often targeted particularly for their symbolism as representing the alleged repression that was at the heart of extremist grievances. Courthouses, IRS offices, and buildings housing government agencies were attacked.[150] McVeigh's preoccupation with the Alfred P. Murrah Federal Building is the most notable case in point: it contained an office of the Bureau of Alcohol, Firearms, and Tobacco (ATF), one of the leading organizations involved in the federal responses at Ruby Ridge and Waco. McVeigh, accordingly, fastened on an improvised explosive device as the best means for inflicting maximum damage to the government and making his point. As security was tightened at government buildings throughout the country in the aftermath of the Oklahoma City bombing, these facilities became harder targets to access and therefore attack. Eric Rudolph, for instance, targeted nongovernmental facilities with his bombs: a public concert venue in a park just outside the Atlanta Olympics compound, abortion clinics, and a gay bar.

In recent years, however, American far-right terrorists have continued to focus almost exclusively on the same type of publicly accessible soft targets: places of worship. In a recurring trend spanning the religious spectrum, Christian churches, Jewish synagogues, Islamic mosques, and Sikh gurdwaras, as well as community centers linked with these faiths, have been repeatedly targeted. Those who forgo places of worship might look for other locations where their target community typically gathers. Patrick Crusius, for instance, drove ten hours from his home in the Dallas–Fort Worth area to commit his attack at an El Paso Walmart that he believed would be full with Latino shoppers.[151] It is unclear whether Crusius considered other targets, although he did write in his manifesto that "the Hispanic community was not my target before I read the Great Replacement"—Tarrant's manifesto.[152] The key to effective targeting had been laid out years before by James Mason in his white supremacist newsletter *Siege*: "His greatest concern must be to pick his target well so that his act may speak so clearly for itself that no member of White America can mistake its message."[153]

Accordingly, often far-right terrorist targeting is no more complex than the offensive presence of a "foreigner" or a person of color or different religion or appearance in a particular locality. In February 2017, an Indian immigrant was killed in a shooting at a restaurant in Olathe, Kansas, by a gunman who thought he was targeting people from Iran.[154] And the previously cited stabbing on a Portland train in 2017 began with the attacker screaming abuse at two young Black girls, a seventeen-year-old Muslim Somali and her non-Muslim friend, alongside the demand that they should "go back to Saudi Arabia."[155] The seamless transition between targeting a place of worship and the broader minority community is best exemplified by Gregory Bush, the 2018 murderer of two African American shoppers in Jeffersontown, Kentucky. Surveillance video footage had showed Bush first trying to enter the predominantly Black First Baptist Church of Jeffersontown—an attempt that, had he succeeded, would have put him on the long list of American terrorists to target a minority group in their place of prayer. When that did not work, he focused on a nearby supermarket frequented by African American patrons—the next best target for his terroristic intentions.

Elsewhere, mixed-race couples, as has long been the case, remain firmly in the cross-hairs of white supremacists. James Harris Jackson, who stabbed a Black man to death with a sword in New York City in March 2017, had intended to continue his rampage by attacking mixed-race couples in Times Square. Jackson, however, surrendered to authorities instead—later regretting that decision, castigating himself during his taped police interview: "Could have been the champion. The champ."[156] In June 2019, two members of the neo-Nazi Sonnenkrieg Division, a British group later banned under British antiterror laws, were jailed in part for plotting to assassinate Prince Harry—a "race traitor," they argued, for his marriage to the mixed-race actress Meghan Markle.[157] White supremacists have also established at least one website dedicated to doxxing mixed-race couples—"the website names, shames, and effectively promotes violence against interracial couples and families," according to the journalist Tess Owen. This publicly posted personal information has often proven difficult to remove completely from the internet.[158] The mass murder of interracial couples was also the topic of a second, lesser-known book penned by William Luther Pierce under his Andrew Macdonald pseudonym. The book, titled *Hunter*, was "dedicated" to Joseph Paul Franklin, a white supremacist serial killer who killed up to twenty people in the 1970s and 1980s.[159] These measures continue a longstanding tradition among the far right, as seen in Nazi Germany's *rassenschande* policies, to prevent the apparent dilution of the white bloodline through interracial relations.[160]

Medical centers performing legalized abortions have also remained a persistent target of far-right terrorists. These facilities have been attacked with both bombs and guns. The most lethal incident in recent years was perpetrated in November 2015 by Robert Lewis Dear in Colorado Springs,

Colorado. Dear killed three people at a Planned Parenthood clinic and during his trial described himself as "a warrior for the babies."[161] Dear's assault was the latest manifestation of the violence directed against providers of legalized abortion encouraged and perpetrated by a religious fringe of the American far right. The early 2000s, for instance, had produced a website calling itself the "Nuremberg Files"; it posted personal information of abortion providers, including home addresses, and kept a tally of those killed. This early form of doxxing displayed names that would be struck through after they were killed—a macabre "mission accomplished" imperative.

Accelerationists know, however, that to achieve their aims—fomenting chaos and disorder in order to precipitate the collapse of society and existing governance—they need to think bigger. Mass shootings at places of worship, abortion clinics, or targeting people of color are unlikely to precipitate the chain reaction of cataclysmic events required to bring everything crashing down. "It's a war of attrition," one extremist complained on Telegram in a jeremiad over the far right's penchant for mass shootings. "When we compare the number of White men willing to kill and die for their people to the raw mass of invaders that stink up our homeland, we lose more proportionally than they do in each attack."[162] That might explain why, despite the changes in terrorist targeting just described, replicating the Oklahoma City bombing and its record death toll remains the aspiration of many far-right terrorists. Breivik sought to emulate the carnage and destruction at the Murrah Building by detonating a large truck bomb in front of an Oslo government facility that he considered the nerve center of Norway's government. Fortunately, he fell far short of the death toll achieved by McVeigh—at least during that phase of his attack.

• • •

The El Paso shooting resulted in a dramatic reassessment of the threat of domestic terrorism. At the Department of Homeland Security, a new strategy was fast-tracked. Less than a month later the department released its new *Strategic Framework for Countering Terrorism and Targeted Violence*. The document provided "an extended assessment of the dangers posed by domestic terrorists, including racially- and ethnically-motivated violent extremists, particularly white supremacist violent extremists." It prioritized strengthening federal government support of locally based prevention and countering violent extremism (CVE) programs, engaging with private sector stakeholders in countering online extremism, working to reduce recidivism among those convicted of hate crimes, and enhancing cyber defenses, including against emerging technologies.[163]

Nevertheless, the new strategy lacked the urgency and White House prioritization that some senior DHS officials thought was needed. At a congressional committee hearing in February 2020, Elizabeth Neumann, the principal architect of the DHS Strategic Framework, observed that it "feels like we are at the doorstep of another 9/11—maybe not something that catastrophic in terms of the visual or the numbers—but that we can see it building, and we don't quite know how to stop it."[164]

8

AMERICAN CARNAGE

Actually, it has been true all through history that only small portions of a population are either good or evil. The great bulk are morally neutral—incapable of distinguishing absolute right from absolute wrong—and they take their cue from whoever is on top at the moment.

—EARL TURNER, IN *THE TURNER DIARIES*

What makes the perfect conspiracy theory? In their seminal work on conspiracism, Russell Muirhead and Nancy L. Rosenblum argue that "classic conspiracism tries to make sense of a disorderly and complicated world by insisting that powerful people control the course of events." It gives meaning to events that cannot otherwise be easily explained and thereby "makes sense of things by imposing a version of proportionality: world-changing events cannot happen because of the actions of a single obscure person or a string of senseless accidents."[1]

In other words, conspiracy theories allow those who are confused, overwhelmed with too much information, fearful, or distrustful of current events to make sense of it all by inventing simpler explanations of their own or adopting those of others. Casting blame on different ethnic, religious, or racial groups; on specific government officials or private individuals; or on governmental or private institutions—whether corporations, think tanks, or philanthropies—at once provides both comfort and epiphany. As explanations for otherwise highly complex phenomena become clear to them, to their minds, it all suddenly makes sense. In the words of the British journalist Peter Pomerantsev: "If all the world is a conspiracy, then your own failures are no longer your fault. The fact that you achieved less than you hoped for, that your life is a mess—it's all the fault of the conspiracy."[2] The problem is that if even merely a small number of people decides that the conspiracy must be countered with violence, civil society itself can be undermined.

The mysterious virus that spread from the Chinese city of Wuhan and resulted in March 2020 in a global pandemic and government-enforced lockdowns in many countries, including the United States, infused conspiratorial extremists across the far-right spectrum with new purpose and focus. The fears of contagion, lockdowns, and overall uncertainty accordingly handed antisemites, racists, xenophobes, and antigovernment extremists a new rallying cry. For example, government-mandated initiatives to control the pandemic—including business closures and stay-at-home orders—were met with complaints that such measures violated fundamental constitutional guarantees and civil liberties and sparked major protests across the nation. Masking requirements alongside concerns about mandatory vaccinations to protect against the virus stoked widespread fear and suspicion within extremist circles that quickly resurrected age-old antisemitic conspiracy theories blaming Jews for profiting from the pandemic or using it to tighten their control over commerce and governance. David Duke, the former KKK leader, for instance, blamed Jewish banking interests for the pandemic: "The Wall Street bankers, and the biggest international bankers, which are overwhelmingly, very, very powerfully Jewish . . . they all made a mint," Duke declared on his podcast in February 2021.[3] This web of conspiracies quickly expanded to include other religious, ethnic, and racial groups, including through the resurrection of the age-old canard of disease transmission by immigrants, as Asian persons were blamed for the disease's spread. As one observer noted, "pandemics are the perfect environment for conspiracy theories to flourish."[4]

While some extremists exploited the pandemic to embellish their pet conspiracy theories, others saw an opportunity to deploy the virus as a crude bioweapon. Social media posts quickly surfaced encouraging fellow extremists to deliberately infect themselves with the coronavirus and then in turn infect politicians and law enforcement officers, Jews, Asians, people of color, and Muslims. Public transportation, supermarkets, places of worship, street corners—virtually any public venue—were cited as examples where the virus could be intentionally spread. Early in the pandemic, to cite one especially notorious example, a self-identified neo-Nazi posted on Telegram a checklist of how to exploit the pandemic for accelerationist ends. "List of things to do if you are unlucky and get Coronavirus," the post read.

- spit on every doorknob or doorbar or handle or whatever you touch
- lick fruit and vegetables in the local grocery store and put it back
- spit into a super soaker and start blasting people
- cough in people's faces
- go to your local town hall and start spitting in politicians faces and shooting them with the super soaker
- when you get arrested, spit and cough all over the car and cops
- don't wash your hands (i forgot to mention this earlier)
- try to infect as many police officers as you can
- if they bring you to a hospital if your symptoms worsen, infect the doctors as well; rip off their facemasks and spit at them
  . . . just go to synigog [sic] and do the same . . . Spray the jews with coronavirus super soaker[5]

By late March, this form of incitement, often accompanied by practical suggestions, had grown so common that the U.S. Department of Justice issued a warning that such acts would be treated as biological terrorism and prosecuted accordingly.[6] That same month, a New Jersey man was charged with making terrorist threats by coughing on supermarket workers.[7] The virus and its tactical weaponization fit neatly into the accelerationist mindset, and many saw the virus as the perfect trigger for the dreamed-of societal collapse.

Typical of views expressed across multiple platforms and forums was a Telegram post on March 24, 2020, that argued the coronavirus was being used by Jews to advance their longstanding goals of replacing white people. "I think it's real, however zog [the Zionist Occupation Government] is using it as an excuse to destroy our people," a U.S. Navy veteran named

Timothy Wilson wrote. "They scare people and have society break down."⁸ Later that evening, Wilson would die in a gunfight with the FBI. He had been planning to use a truck bomb to attack a hospital in Belton, Missouri.⁹ According to the FBI, Wilson sought to inflict casualties on a massive scale—hoping that the force of the explosion would shatter the hospital's windows, producing lethal shards of glass that would increase the death toll.¹⁰ Wilson had brought forward the attack's timeline, fearing that the COVID-related government-ordered lockdowns might derail it. He had ominously previously contemplated attacking a school attended by African American children as well as a mosque and a synagogue.¹¹

The FBI had learned of the plot through a confidential informant who was in contact with an active-duty U.S. Army soldier stationed at Fort Riley, a base that is about a two-hour drive from Kansas City. The criminal complaint filed in the U.S. District Court for the District of Kansas alleged that Private First Class Jarrett William Smith had "disseminated guidance on how to construct Improvised Explosive Devices (IEDs)" to Wilson and had also "spoken about his desire to travel to Ukraine to fight with" a violent far-right paramilitary group in that country. Smith was also a member of the Feuerkrieg Division, a far-right terrorist group and Atomwaffen Division offshoot. He and Wilson had been in regular contact through an encrypted social media platform.¹² Smith was convicted in August 2020 and sentenced to thirty months in prison.¹³

Meanwhile, the government-imposed pandemic lockdowns were also generating more militant popular dissent. By mid-April, rolling protests against the federal and state mandates had surfaced across the country, demanding an end to the restrictions, which were allegedly harming the country's economy. President Trump joined the cacophony, posting a series of tweets calling on his followers to "liberate" several states whose Democratic Party governors and/or legislatures had imposed public health mandates and to reverse these restrictions. "LIBERATE VIRGINIA," the president tweeted. Seizing an opportunity to amplify other causes dear to his supporters, Trump added, "and save your great 2nd Amendment. It is under siege!"¹⁴ His other tweets singled out Michigan and Minnesota. Trump's words were interpreted by some of the more militant protestors as a green light for more aggressive resistance to the mandates than the hitherto mostly peaceful antilockdown and antivaccination protests.¹⁵ Chatrooms on social media drew exactly this conclusion. On Telegram, for example, a poster highlighted Trump's tweets to argue that the president "did just say you can start shooting and hanging your state politicians."[16]

An especially disquieting manifestation of Trump's repeated summons to "liberate" state capitols was the series of events that unfolded in Lansing, Michigan, on April 30, 2020. Protestors there broke into the state's capitol building. Many openly carried assault rifles and sidearms and wore military tactical gear. Outside, on the statehouse's lawn, a sign prominently proclaimed: "Tyrants get the rope"[17]—likely a deliberate reference to the infamous "Day of the Rope" depicted in *The Turner Diaries*. Andrew Anglin, a well-known neo-Nazi propagandist, used his *Daily Stormer* website to publicize the need for even more, intensified violence. Embracing a core accelerationist precept, Anglin explained that what happened in Lansing "was not a riot."

> But riots are coming. All kinds of riots are coming. Food riots, lockdown riots, race riots. Pick your riot genre, and you've got it coming up. The people are angry now just because they're being locked in their houses and lost their jobs. Imagine how angry they're going to be when they realize that there is no going back from this, and we've fallen into a permanent state of total poverty.[18]

Then, in the midst of the turmoil and upheaval already generated by the pandemic, lockdown, and mask-mandate controversies, an unarmed Black man, George Floyd, was killed by police in Minneapolis, Minnesota, on May 25 during a routine arrest. Video of a police officer pinning Floyd to the ground, with his knee on Floyd's neck for nearly nine minutes, went viral. Demonstrations, some of which degenerated into rioting and violence, erupted. Peaceful protestors, Black Lives Matter activists, and other demonstrators were increasingly joined by more militant anti-fascist and anarchist agitators, who reveled in the opportunities for arson and vandalism. In Washington, DC, the AFL-CIO union headquarters and historical St. John's Episcopal Church just across Lafayette Square from the White House were set on fire—acts of terrorism that shook the city's and indeed the country's foundations. Like the outcry in previous years to the killings of unarmed young Black men like Trayvon Martin and Michael Brown, the riots and more widespread peaceful protests that followed Floyd's killing fed a longstanding white supremacist narrative that the white-dominated status quo was being systematically undermined by radical leftists and anarchists.

Some far-right extremists took advantage of the unrest to opportunistically embed themselves among protestors in hopes of inciting more violence and further spreading disorder and upheaval.[19] One particularly bellicose rioter in Minneapolis, dubbed the "Umbrella Man," was in fact found to be linked to the white supremacist Aryan Cowboy Brotherhood prison gang. "This was the first fire that set off a string of fires and looting throughout the precinct and the rest of the city," Sergeant Erika Christensen wrote of the Umbrella Man's incitement strategy, which included vandalism and other actions designed to enflame the mob. "Until the actions of the . . .'Umbrella Man,' the protests had been relatively peaceful," Christensen argued in an affidavit. "The actions of this person created an atmosphere of hostility and tension. Your affiant believes that this individual's sole aim was to incite violence."[20] On the Telegram channel associated with the neo-Nazi Vorherrschaft [Supremacy] Division, one extremist sought to take advantage of the unrest to commit accelerationist acts of violence: exhorting others to "find a lawless area, look for a small group of [N-word], fire on them from a concealed position in GTA [Grand Theft Auto, another video game analogy often used to evade legal culpability] then run."[21] The president's response to this highly charged situation was to tweet that "The United States of America will be designating ANTIFA as a Terrorist Organization"—disregarding both the evidence that this radical left-wing collective was in fact not the sole driving force behind the violence and unrest[22] and the legal complexity involved in rendering such a designation.[23]

The ongoing protests coincided with the growing popularity of a progun, antigovernment movement calling itself the "boogaloo." Derived from the 1984 movie *Breakin' 2: Electric Boogaloo*, the "boogaloo" moniker was adopted as a trope to refer to a coming second civil war. "Boogaloo bois"—a play on the word "boys"—became a regular feature at protests across the country. Incongruously attired in brightly colored Hawaiian Aloha shirts with combat webbing, ammunition pouches, and assault weapons, these radicals await or actively plan for what they call the coming "big luau" or "big igloo"—both code names for the "boogaloo" used to evade online content-moderation algorithms. Between February and

April 2020, there was a 60 percent growth of Facebook pages and groups advocating such sedition. Their number peaked at 125 such groups with over 73,000 followers before Facebook removed and then banned these pages.[24] Although the ideology first surfaced around 2012, until recently the boogaloo movement lurked around the fringes of the internet and was not popularly known.[25] That changed during 2020 as a growing number of boogaloo adherents responded to government-enforced coronavirus lockdowns in some states and municipalities and protests over George Floyd's killing. Crucially, the boogaloo bois frequently mobilized on both sides of that summer's divide—often supporting police and opposing racial justice activists but sometimes protecting Black Lives Matter protesters from threats and harassment by police.[26]

Contrary to reporting from the conservative media and attendant rhetoric from elected officials and others, the lethal violence linked to the protests that summer was almost exclusively perpetrated by antigovernment and far-right extremists.[27] On May 29, 2020, a DHS advisory cautioned state and local authorities to be aware of the possibility of "incidents of domestic terrorists exploiting First Amendment protected events." Channels on Telegram, they warned, were intent on fomenting chaos and disorder and triggering the "boogaloo."[28] That same day, a noncommissioned officer stationed at Travis Air Base murdered a Federal Protective Service security officer standing guard outside a federal office building in Oakland, California—less than an hour's drive away. The perpetrator, U.S. Air Force Sergeant Steven Carrillo, had adopted the accelerationist strategy of inflicting random acts of lethal violence to incite civil unrest. "Use their anger to fuel our fire," Carrillo had explained in a Facebook post he wrote just before this murder. "We have mobs of angry people to use to our advantage."[29] Carrillo was apprehended eight days later, after he killed a sheriff's deputy in nearby Ben Lomond. Wounded in an exchange of gunfire with California Highway Patrol officers and Santa Cruz County deputy sheriffs, Carrillo had scrawled the word "boog" using his own blood on the hood of a car. According to the ATF, he had used "a privately made firearm, with no markings or serial number. This firearm is a machine gun, which had a silencer attached to its barrel." Carrillo, it should be noted, was a team leader of a specially trained unit known as Phoenix Raven,[30] whose mission the U.S. Air

Force describes as "providing security for Air Mobility Command aircraft transiting high terrorist and criminal threat areas."[31]

A second incident linked to the boogaloo movement took place in Denver, also on May 29. Police in that city intercepted a vehicle of boogaloo bois armed with assault weapons who were driving to a "Reopen Colorado" demonstration.[32] And on June 2, in Las Vegas, three men were arrested on state terrorism charges for a plot to use Molotov cocktails in a "false flag" attack at a Black Lives Matter rally, designed to provoke more violence.[33] The plotters all had U.S. military experience—with the navy, air force, and the army reserve.[34] They had reportedly modeled their cell and tactics on the Irish Republican Army.[35] This series of incidents generated concern that Washington, DC, would be targeted next. In June 2020, the National Capital Region Threat Intelligence Consortium, a DHS fusion center, disseminated a threat assessment of boogaloo-inspired violence, warning that Washington, DC, was "an attractive target for violent adherents of the boogaloo ideology due to the significant presence of US law enforcement entities, and the wide range of First Amendment-Protected events hosted here."[36]

Arguably, no dimension of the American violent far-right evokes the accelerationist mindset as stridently and openly as the boogaloo movement—given its goal of engineering the federal government's collapse by fomenting widespread societal disorder. In fact, the entire boogaloo raison d'être is neatly summarized in a three-word Facebook post left by one of the Las Vegas plotters: "Start. Fomenting. Insurrection."[37] In this respect, the boogaloo movement in its targeting of law enforcement personnel is reminiscent of the ongoing antiauthoritarian threat posed by "sovereign citizens." Although bogus liens and frivolous lawsuits brought against public officials are sovereign citizens' preferred weapons (sometimes referred to as "paper terrorism") and not guns and bombs,[38] people claiming membership in the movement have committed crimes involving murder and physical assault; threatened judges, public officials, and law enforcement personnel with physical violence; impersonated police officers and diplomats; used fake currency, passports, license plates, and drivers' licenses; and perpetrated a variety of mortgage fraud and so-called redemption schemes.[39] In 2003, for instance, three people claiming to be sovereign citizens killed two South Carolina police officers after a fourteen-hour standoff over a land dispute with the state erupted in violence. Seven years later, two Arkansas officers were gunned down during a routine traffic stop, and a Florida deputy sheriff was murdered. For this reason, the FBI has regarded the more extreme and violent members of the movement "as comprising a domestic terrorist movement."[40] Elements of the contemporary boogaloo movement have adopted the same longstanding animus against law enforcement. "When a bloody uprising in the west comes, the police should be the first to target," declared one post;[41] another recommended mailing radioactive material "to your local federal agent to make him glow for real."[42]

Inflammatory reports from established news sources heightened societal tensions and deepened existing polarization. One Fox News item in June 2020, for instance, cited a lone, anonymous "government intelligence source" as claiming that "agitators behind the rioting that has paralyzed the country over the past week want to move into more suburban areas."[43] No other evidence was provided, and although the threat did not come to pass, that same month the FBI reported conducting a record-high number of firearm background checks.[44] Intensifying fears and tensions did lead to terroristic violence—again almost exclusively tied to the far right.

That same June also brought to light new evidence of extremism's penetration of the U.S. military. Ethan Melzer, a U.S. Army private, was arrested and charged with leaking U.S. military troop movements to a British neo-Nazi group, the Order of the Nine Angles (O9A). Melzer had plotted to orchestrate an attack on his own unit by O9A in league with al-Qaeda. O9A is an example of the emergent phenomenon of different, though similarly violently oriented ideologies converging to present new threats based on the combination of World War II–era national socialism with contemporary Salafi jihadism. Members of O9A, for instance, venerate both Hitler and bin Laden and regard the U.S. government as their preeminent enemy.[45] According to Department of Justice prosecutors, Melzer provided the group with intelligence on the unit's location, strength, and weapons. Melzer claimed to not care about his own safety; if he died in the attack, he said, he "would've died successfully"— comfortable in the knowledge his final act had damaged the United States and other soldiers.[46] Melzer pleaded guilty in June 2022. The DOJ's press release announcing his plea was noteworthy for the attention it paid to the accelerationist strategy advocated by the O9A. U.S. Attorney

Damian Williams was quoted explaining that Melzer "believed he could force the U.S. into prolonged armed conflict while causing the deaths of as many soldiers as possible." It further revealed how "O9A members are instructed to fulfill 'sinister' deeds, including 'insight roles,' where they attempt to infiltrate various organizations, including the military, to gain training and experience, commit acts of violence, identify like-minded individuals, and ultimately subvert those groups from within."[47]

With the rise of the boogaloo bois and associated plots and violence throughout 2020, this pernicious issue again began to garner widespread attention, with pressure growing for the military to act decisively to eliminate extremism within its ranks. Perhaps the senior-most critic was James L. Jones, a retired four-star general who served as Commandant of the Marine Corps and as President Barack Obama's first national security advisor: "When the military succeeds in promoting meritocracy and banishing prejudice, the benefits accrue to American society as a whole."[48] Far-right accelerationist tendencies were also evident among law enforcement officers. In June 2020, at the height of protests against police brutality, the Wilmington (North Carolina) Police Department fired three of its officers who were recorded on camera inciting racial violence. One of the officers declared he was "ready" for an upcoming civil war, promising that "we are just gonna go out and start slaughtering fucking [N-word]. I can't wait. God I can't wait." The coming uprising, he boasted, would "wipe 'em off the fucking map. That'll put 'em back about four or five generations."[49] And a National Guardsman who was part of a boogaloo chat on the gaming platform Discord publicly flagged his upcoming deployment to Philadelphia on riot control duties in response to protests for racial justice to brag about the opportunities to inflict violence on the people he was assigned to protect.[50]

In August, a Black man in Kenosha, Wisconsin, was shot multiple times by a police officer in a flash of violence again caught on camera. Again, protestors, infiltrated by riotous anarchists, descended on that city—this time joined by armed militants on the right who had deployed themselves allegedly to protect businesses from looting. Tragedy followed when Kyle Rittenhouse, a seventeen-year-old armed with an assault rifle who had traveled from Antioch, Illinois, to Kenosha on this self-appointed mission, shot to death two demonstrators. The gunman was quickly labeled a hero across extremist social media channels—"This man is epic," one person gushed on Telegram[51]—embodying the stated dreams of other militants to take decisive action against their disparaged enemy.[52]

Although these lethal incidents involving firearms received the most attention that summer, there was also a rise in the use of ordinary motor vehicles in attacks—a tactic already demonstrated by James Alex Fields at Charlottesville. According to a study by the Center for Strategic and International Studies: "From January to August 2020, vehicles were used in 11 violent far-right attacks—27 percent of all far-right terrorist incidents—narrowly making them the weapons most frequently used in far-right attacks. This marked a significant increase from 2015 to 2019, during which a vehicle was used in only one violent far-right attack."[53] The deployment of the tactic against Black Lives Matter activists was memorialized in a taunting meme, shared widely on social media, including by American law enforcement officials. "All Lives Splatter—Nobody Cares About Your Protest," it read.[54]

By the fall of 2020, then, America was beset with deep suspicion, proliferating mutually reinforcing conspiracy theories, and repeated calls for violence—a dangerous cocktail that would intensify in the run-up to that November's presidential election. "Civil war is here, right now," the Oath Keepers' founder Stewart Rhodes declared after a Trump supporter was murdered by an Antifa activist in Portland in August—at the time of writing, the only murder conclusively attributed to Antifa. The call to arms prompted Twitter to ban the Oath Keepers from its online platform.[55]

• • •

Two other significant trends in domestic terrorism were also gathering momentum: the popularization of the political assassination and convergence of extremist ideologies.

Political assassination has of course long been embraced by terrorists seeking rapid political change—as the plots respectively by Sayoc and Hasson in 2018 and 2019 evidenced. Exactly that point was made by a person on a neo-Nazi Telegram channel who criticized the growing incidence of mass shootings in the United States as an effective tactic. "So, if a complete madlad grabbed his gun and [REDACTED] high-profile targets one at a time over a longer stretch of time," the anonymous post argued, "he'd sow more terror into their soulless hearts than any mass shooter, and he'd shake up the System where it's more vulnerable. Imagine the headlines!"[56] This fit a pattern of extremist online discourse where even those who killed en masse at public venues were criticized for not setting their sights on higher-profile targets. In one August 2019 Telegram post, a commenter criticized Patrick Crusius for attacking a Walmart store. "Kill powerful people," they implored. "Kill important people. Kill the political opposition. Kill people at the headquarters of literally any far-left/anti-White organization, and kill every motherfucker inside. Wal-Mart, although a shithole, is not where High-Value Targets (HVT's) congregate. We need to kill the HVT's. When a popular HVT is gunned down, it inspires hope and dreams."[57]

Until the fall of 2020, that plea to likeminded extremists to mount more ambitious and even more directly consequential attacks against elected leaders and prominent national figures had fortunately gone mostly unheeded. The Democratic congresswoman Gabrielle Giffords was nearly killed by a mentally unstable would-be assassin in 2011. Despite lacking an ostensible political motive, the shooting was nonetheless widely praised in extremist circles—not least since Giffords was both a Democrat and half-Jewish. "Maybe this will begin what we have all been waiting for, having more political turmoil in general sounds good," a message on Stormfront read, echoing the age-old accelerationist narrative. "In the end it may take us down the road to new civil war." Another opined, "If you can't beat them at the polls, Assassinate them!"[58] Though Giffords survived, a federal judge, Chief Judge John Roll of the U.S. District Court for the District of Arizona, was killed in the attack. In July 2020, an assassin failed to kill Esther Salas, a Latina New Jersey judge. A radical antifeminist and ardent Trump supporter, the murderer had accused Salas of working "to convince America that whites, especially white males, were barbarians, and all those of a darker skin complexion were victims."[59] Salas was not harmed, but her twenty-year-old son was murdered, and her husband suffered critical injuries. And the South Carolina state senator Clementa C. Pinckney was the first victim of Dylann Roof's rampage at Charleston—although it is unclear whether or not he was the specific target of the attack.

The coronavirus pandemic was reviving discussion of this high-profile tactic among violently inclined far-right extremists. In March, for example, a man angry at government-imposed lockdowns was arrested after he sent online death threats to several Democratic politicians. "If youre a dem or apart of the establishment in the democrats side," he had written in one post, "I view you as a criminal and a terrorist and I advise everyone to Go SOS and use live rounds."[60] Dr. Anthony Fauci, the head of the National Institute of Allergy and Infectious Diseases and a key figure in framing the federal government's response to the pandemic, was provided with a personal protection security detail after receiving repeated threats.[61] In April 2020, New York police arrested a weeping woman who had traveled to the city intent on assassinating Joe Biden, then a presidential candidate. She had written on Facebook that "Hillary Clinton and her assistant, Joe Biden and Tony Podesta need to be taken out in the name of Babylon!"[62]

The months when the coronavirus pandemic was at its height seemed also to encourage the mixing and matching of different ideologies, as evident in Melzer's idiosyncratic affinities for both Hitler and bin Laden. And the boogaloo bois' sudden popularity exemplified the ideological fluidity of a movement that variously made common cause with elements on both the far left as well as far right. "Boogaloo retards have been working together WITH antifa and BLM, the only reason they're called rightwing is because of their obsession with guns and second amendment," a post on 4chan raged. "But they're libertarian civnat pieces of shit who express solidarity with BLM and left wing extremists."[63] The amorphous ideological contours of the boogaloo movement, however, paled in comparison to the "big tent" approach of the conspiracy theory–driven QAnon phenomenon.

Although "Q," the supposedly omniscient government insider behind the eponymous online posts, first surfaced in October 2017, it was not until the pandemic that the movement truly gained momentum. Indeed, by the time of the 2020 presidential election, QAnon had become a major player on the American—and increasingly European—political stage. After emerging as an online community, QAnon amassed a cult-like following who eagerly accepted the fantastical conspiracy theory that the Democratic Party and the Los Angeles–based entertainment industry, as well as banks and the media, were being run by Satan-worshipping pedophiles—and that Trump had somehow been divinely chosen to fight this treacherous cabal. Its preoccupation with shadowy, nefarious forces secretly conspiring to dominate and control the world seemed to resurrect the early-twentieth-century Russian Tsarist hoax *The Protocols of the Learned Elders of Zion* and transpose it to the context of contemporary U.S. politics.

The convergence of multiple, sometimes contradictory, ideologies into an incoherent, highly decentralized movement appealed to American far-right extremists who had long sought to appeal to a broader constituency by embracing an array of racist, antisemitic, xenophobic, antigovernment, tax-resistance, antiabortion, and white nationalist and white supremacist causes.[64] The calls for violence that emerged from this mélange of far-ranging and far-fetched beliefs not surprisingly led to a less predictable, almost illogical range of targets for attack. In November 2016, for instance, Edgar Welch, an adherent of the "Pizzagate" variant of the QAnon theory, drove from North Carolina to Washington, DC, on a self-appointed mission to free children he was convinced were being held captive by Democratic Party leadership in a family-oriented restaurant in DC's fashionable—and mostly liberal—Chevy Chase neighborhood. Armed with an assault rifle, Welch attempted to shoot the lock off a door of a supply closet that he was convinced led downstairs to the nonexistent basement, where children were supposedly imprisoned and subjected to sexual assault. The Pizzagate conspiracy theory of pedophiles and politicians working in tandem has continually inspired subsequent QAnon adherents to mount their own operations to free enslaved children, protest government-mandated public health measures because of the coronavirus, and attempt to assassinate elected officials both in Canada and the United States.[65] One of the more bizarre incidents was the 2019 murder of Francesco Cali, a boss of the Gambino crime family, in Staten Island by a QAnon devotee who believed Cali was part of the "deep state" working to undermine President Trump. The targets of QAnon-inspired attacks have been so erratic that researchers at the University of Maryland have argued that traditional counterterrorism means may be irrelevant and that mental health counseling and intervention might be more effective.[66] Indeed, Cali's killer was deemed mentally unfit for trial.[67]

Ecofascism, an ideological convergence between old forms of Nazi and fascist ideologies with contemporary environmental extremism, also raises the prospect of additional new and hard-to-predict combinations of extremists and targets of attacks. In Sweden, for instance, an arson attack committed against a mink farm by an ecofascist, neo-Nazi group linked to the Base highlighted the difficulty in predicting the targets such combinations would focus on. Neo-Nazis, partly inspired by environmental and animal rights grievances, had selected a target and a tactic more commonly associated with far-left extremists.[68] At the same time, it should be noted that both Tarrant and Crusius were immersed in ecofascist ideology but attacked more predictable locations.

The emergence of distinctively twenty-first-century extremist movements such as QAnon, the boogaloo bois, and ecofascism presents a dangerous new challenge for law enforcement: U.S. federal agencies and their state, local, and tribal counterparts often lack the knowledge, training, and human resources to cover every possible target of a conspiracy theory. The coronavirus pandemic has breathed new life into or given added momentum to these trends. This was especially evident in the immediate aftermath of the nationwide lockdown and the violent responses it triggered.[69] A hospital was the planned target of a foiled Kansas City plot, as previously mentioned. In addition, the USNS *Mercy*, a hospital ship docked in Long Beach, California, was the reason for a deliberate train derailment meant to disrupt the ship's operations. According to federal prosecutors, the train's engineer believed the ship "had an alternate purpose related to covid-19 or a government takeover."[70] Inspired by their European counterparts, North American neo-Luddites also began targeting 5G technology, including cell towers, claiming that they were the cause of a variety of illnesses. And as a result of the pandemic combined with infelicitous comments by President Trump and other elected officials insisting on calling the pandemic the "Chinese virus," Asian Americans increasingly became the targets of hate crimes in the United States.[71] Stop AAPI Hate, a newly founded organization dedicated to preventing hate crimes against the Asian-American and Pacific Islander communities, reported nearly four thousand incidents during the pandemic's first year.[72]

This mixing of ideologies and issues—what the FBI has termed the "salad bar" approach to choosing ideologies[73] but also known as "fluidity of the fringes"[74]—is facilitated by social media, which lends itself to more personal radicalization processes. A wider range of people can therefore be inspired by more idiosyncratic ideologies that appeal to more personal grievances. This also contributes to the increasing prevalence of teenagers involved with terrorism.[75] Unlike in the past, where a potential young recruit had to conform to an extremist ideology, they can now plot their own path forward, channeling their own frustrations into a violent political or quasi-political agenda more easily.

If the pandemic had any kind of a silver lining for counterterrorism, it was that the soft targets generally preferred by terrorists were depopulated or closed. Data show a high number of domestic terror attacks and plots in 2020, with a 69 percent increase from the previous year, but lower fatalities, with an 86 percent drop from the 2019 level.[76] In other words, the figures suggested a fraught political environment, perhaps coupled with frustration over COVID-related restrictions, led to high levels of violence, but fatalities were unintentionally modest thanks to stay-at-home orders, which drained would-be targets of possible victims.

• • •

The conspiratorial inclinations that both the pandemic and coinciding racial protests had fostered also affected the November 2020 presidential race. At least seven months before Americans cast their votes, Trump tweeted that the coming vote was already "RAMPANT WITH FRAUD."[77] Copying from a playbook used in 2016, when Trump and others claimed electoral fraud long before polls even opened in order to undermine an expected Hillary Clinton victory,[78] the president warned about the impending stolen election again in June, declaring that "This will be the Election disaster of our time. Mail-In Ballots will lead to a RIGGED Election."[79] And in August he doubled down on this claim, telling a Wisconsin rally that "the only way we're going to lose this election is if the election is rigged."[80] Trump specifically would repeatedly cite concerns of widespread electoral fraud involving mail-in voting—an option offered in many states because of pandemic-related health concerns over voters congregating at the polls—despite the president himself having voted by mail in the primaries.[81] Other Republicans, the president's core support base, and far-right extremists perpetuated this falsehood—thus laying the groundwork to delegitimize the election should Trump lose.[82] QAnon's propaganda machine, for instance, kicked into gear, rallying to its supposedly beleaguered commander-in-chief's side by describing any possibility of Trump's defeat as an almost existential threat.[83] Muirhead and Rosenblum draw a distinction between classic conspiracism and the new conspiracism. What distinguishes the latter, they write, is that "there is no punctilious demand for proofs, no exhaustive amassing of evidence, no dots revealed to form a pattern, no close examination of operators plotting in the shadows. . . . What validates the new conspiracism is not evidence but repetition." Within this new conspiratorial atmosphere, where evidence could be drowned out by conviction, Trump repeatedly cast doubt on the legitimacy of the 2020 presidential election—both before and after the voting on November 3.[84]

The president also stubbornly refused to condemn, much less distance himself from, his most extreme and violent supporters. When asked about this during the first 2020 presidential debate that September, Trump first claimed that he'd be "willing" to condemn white supremacists and militia groups. But, then, seeming to address a group classified as bigots and "Western chauvinists" by the SPLC[85] and as a "right-wing extremist group with a violent agenda" by the ADL,[86] the president declared, "Proud Boys, stand back and stand by, but I'll tell you what, I'll tell you what, somebody's got to do something about Antifa and the left, because this is not a right-wing problem."[87] On Telegram, Proud Boys members were exultant. "Leftist fags are seething right now lol," read one triumphal post. "It's glorious."[88] Other messages struck a more menacing tone. "Standing down and standing by sir."[89] On Parler, a right-wing social media app, the Proud Boys leader Joe Biggs enthused, "Trump basically said to go fuck them up! this makes me so happy," as the group starting selling shirts emblazoned with Trump's words.[90] Another member later testified that the group size "tripled" after the comment.[91] The president had previously also refused to condemn QAnon. "I don't know much about the movement, other than I understand they like me very much. Which I appreciate," Trump stated at an August 2020 press conference, thus embracing the support of a movement that continually demonizes his political opponents as satanic pedophiles.[92] At a town hall two months later, he basically endorsed the movement. "Let me just tell you what I do hear about it is they [QAnon] are very strongly against pedophilia and I agree with that. And I agree with it very strongly."[93] "This was the biggest pitch for QANON I've ever seen," one reaction read on 4chan.[94]

In October 2020, the potentially lethal consequences of growing anti-government extremism were laid bare when the Department of Justice announced indictments against thirteen men accused of plotting to kidnap Gretchen Whitmer, governor of Michigan. Evidence subsequently came to light that the group had also considered kidnapping Governor Ralph Northam of Virginia and the Republican Governor Henry McMaster of South Carolina as well. Two of those three governors led states mentioned in Trump's April 2020 "liberate" tweets. The plot was partially inspired by boogaloo militancy but also demonstrated the often-scattered focus of the antigovernment right's vitriol.[95] Even President Trump was mentioned in the group's plans, one member writing, "I say we hang everything currently governing us, they're all guilty!!!" and more narrowly about Trump, "True colors shining through, wanna hang this mf'er too!!!"[96] "I'm going to do some of the most nasty, disgusting things that you have ever read about in the history of your life," the same defendant promised.[97] Adding to this mix of radical causes and ideological beliefs, several of the would-be kidnappers had protected protestors at a May 2020 Black Lives Matter rally in Detroit.[98] The contradictory contours of the Michigan plot provided a timely reminder of how deep the violent far right's hatred of government and elected officials runs. As far as some extremists are concerned, there is no difference between Republicans and Democrats but only between "us" and "them"—patriots and tyrants—thus evoking the accelerationist mindset found in *The Turner Diaries* and its infamous "Day of the Rope" trope.

As the vote approached and the Democratic candidate Joe Biden gained momentum, a new fear consequently now arose: that violent extremists, emboldened by the cover provided by a sitting president coupled with his claims of electoral fraud, would rally to prevent an orderly transfer of power. "A nightmare scenario," Richard Haass, president of the Council on Foreign Relations, tweeted on September 1, envisioning a situation where "Election nite shows Trump leading elec college b/c of in-person votes; Biden gains lead over weeks w mail ballots. Trump says fraud; 2 victory/no concession speeches. The question arises as to whether US democracy up to the challenge."[99] We foresaw this same possibility. On November 1, 2020, two days before Election Day, we warned that

several . . . groups, including QAnon adherents, are highly motivated by President Trump; any appearance of voting irregularities that favor the Biden campaign against Trump, whether legitimate or not, may spark widespread violence—especially if the president chooses to amplify such concerns. But predicting which of these groups is most likely to attack and what targets would be most in danger is not possible. In the absence of a clear, comprehensive national strategy, fear and anxiety is increasingly fueled by uncertainty and discord.[100]

On November 7, 2020, the days of uncertainty and vote tallying finally concluded. CNN was the first major network to call the election in favor of the former vice president and Democratic candidate Joe Biden. Trump immediately escalated his torrent of claims about electoral fraud—styling himself as the victim of a massive conspiracy to oust him from office. "For years the Dems have been preaching how unsafe and rigged our elections have been," he tweeted on November 13. "Now they are saying what a wonderful job the Trump Administration did in making 2020 the most secure election ever. Actually this is true, except for what the Democrats did. Rigged Election!"[101] Trump's allies and apologists were even more forthright and blunt in both their defense of the president and allegations of a stolen election—and what should be done about it. Twitter banned the former Trump chief strategist Stephen Bannon from the platform after he suggested that Trump, once he duly assumed office for his second term, should behead Anthony Fauci and FBI Director Christopher Wray and put their heads on spikes outside the White House "as a warning to federal bureaucrats, you either get with the program, or you're gone."[102] After Christopher Krebs, the director of the Cybersecurity and Infrastructure Security Agency within DHS, was fired for refuting Trump's claims of voter fraud, Joseph DiGenova, an attorney with the Trump campaign, declared that Krebs "should be drawn and quartered. Taken out at dawn and shot."[103] And Lin Wood, a conspiratorial lawyer who litigated several election cases on the president's behalf, predicted that Vice President Mike Pence would be "executed by firing squad."[104] Several rallies in Washington, DC, billed as "Stop the Steal" protests, drew Trump supporters increasingly enraged at alleged voter fraud and their inability to undo the election results. On December 12, the white nationalist commentator Nick Fuentes led a MAGA hat–wearing crowd in DC in chants of "Destroy the GOP."[105]

A rally and march in support of President Trump and to protest the stolen election were planned to occur in Washington, DC, on January 6, 2021—the day that Congress would meet to legally certify the electoral college vote. Another "Stop the Steal" rally, the gathering promised to bring together Trump supporters from across the country to expose the electoral fraud and reinstate Trump as president. Trump had enthusiastically encouraged his supporters in a tweet on December 19. "Be there, will be wild!" he promised.[106] The messaging on extremist social media channels was more menacing. "We should march into the capital building and make them quake in their shoes," read one Telegram post on December 28.[107] Trump's allies in Congress declared their intention to nullify the election results and warned of revolution, the newly seated Georgia congresswoman Marjorie Taylor Greene telling Newsmax, "I'll echo the words of many of my colleagues as we were just meeting together in our GOP conference meeting this morning: this is our 1776 moment."[108] On January 5, the FBI's office in Norfolk, Virginia, issued the most unambiguous warning of potential violence to date. Its analysts monitoring online messaging reported that people arriving in the city were boasting of the weapons they had brought amid calls for the use of violence and outright sedition. "Be ready to fight," one online thread implored. "Congress needs to hear glass breaking, doors being kicked in, and blood from their BLM and Pantifa slave soldiers being spilled. Get violent. Stop calling this a march, or rally, or a protest. Go there ready for war. We get our President or we die. NOTHING else will achieve this goal," read another.[109] Alarmingly, many of these messages were explicitly welcoming the opportunity to clash with police and wrest control of government as a means to derail this final, critical denouement of the 2020 presidential electoral process. "Cops don't have 'standing' if they are laying on the ground in a pool of their own blood," someone posted on the TheDonald.win website.[110] The final report of the U.S. House of Representatives Select Committee to Investigate the January 6th Attack on the United States Capitol revealed that a tip emailed to the Secret Service concerning the Proud Boys detailed a similar intent: "Their plan is to literally kill people. . . . Please please take this tip seriously and investigate further."[111]

The planned protest appealed to all the variegated elements that comprised Trump's constituents—from ordinary supporters intent on displaying their fealty to their president and who accepted unquestionably his claims of voter fraud to hardened militants, some with military training and combat experience, belonging to extremist organizations like the Oath Keepers and Three Percenters who had come to Washington looking for trouble. They were united by their unstinting allegiance to Trump fused with a powerful, albeit misguided, belief that a historic moment beckoned. As David Neiwert writes:

> The key to understanding people who have become drawn into the Alt-America universe is the role that the hero myth plays in framing their worldview. Dedicated patriots and white nationalists, just like the hate criminals they inspire, genuinely envision themselves as heroes. They are saving the country, or perhaps the white race, or perhaps just their local community. And so anything, *anything* they might do in that act of defense is excusable, even laudable.[112]

One late-December fundraising appeal sent by the stopthesteal.us organizer Ali Alexander captured the mood on the far right as the New Year approached: *"Let's make history—the right way!"*[113]

• • •

January 6, 2021, was a cold and cloudy day in the nation's capital. Passengers on buses carrying Trump supporters to DC recited the pledge of allegiance. The excitement of the crowd gathering on the Ellipse, just south of the White House, and on the National Mall that morning was palpable: they were there to save the country and keep Trump in office. "It's gonna be a great day, it's gonna be wild, as Trump says," one demonstrator predicted.[114] Angered by the smaller-than-expected crowd on the Ellipse, Trump had instructed the Secret Service to stop screening for weapons. "Take the fucking [magnetometers] away," Trump had reportedly said. "They're not here to hurt me."[115] DC Metropolitan Police radio transmissions, meanwhile, documented numerous firearms in the crowd gathering beyond the metal detectors—including an AR-15 being held by a man who had climbed a tree.[116] The president addressed the crowd from behind a thick screen of protective glass. "Because you'll never take back our country with weakness," he implored, "you have to show strength and you have to be strong." He said that they had to fight—and never give up. "We fight like Hell and if you don't fight like Hell," he declared, "you're not going to have a country anymore." Trump then dispensed their marching orders. "We're going to walk down Pennsylvania Avenue, I love

Pennsylvania Avenue, and we're going to the Capitol and we're going to try and give . . . our Republicans, the weak ones, because the strong ones don't need any of our help, we're going to try and give them the kind of pride and boldness that they need to take back our country. So let's walk down Pennsylvania Avenue."[117] Trump's own efforts to join the crowd marching toward the Capitol were stopped by the Secret Service, who, breaking protocol, repeatedly ignored his commands. One aide's testimony at a House of Representatives January 6 committee hearing suggested Trump had even tried to grab the steering wheel of the presidential limousine when agents refused to take him to the Hill.[118]

At 2:24 PM Eastern Time, Donald J. Trump sent one of his final tweets as president. "Mike Pence didn't have the courage to do what should have been done to protect our Country and our Constitution, giving States a chance to certify a corrected set of facts, not the fraudulent or inaccurate ones which they were asked to previously certify," it read. "USA demands the truth!" At that moment, less than two miles away from the White House, a group of marchers had broken through police lines and forcibly approached the U.S. Capitol, where lawmakers in their respective chambers were meeting to certify the electoral vote. Intense fighting broke out at several entrances, as retreating police officers fought to hold the line as they were attacked with fists, hockey sticks, and American flags. Less protected doors and windows were punched through. "Hang Mike Pence!" the crowd chanted, as the vice president and his family were rushed out of the Senate chamber, just steps ahead of the advancing mob. Members of Congress were shepherded toward the building's basement floors; others were left stranded in the House chamber as members of Congress from both parties joined together to barricade the door. For the first time since 1814, when the British burned Washington, DC, the U.S. Capitol had been breached.[119]

Some protestors had come prepared to take members of Congress prisoner. In the Senate chamber, cameras captured invaders wielding zipties with which to cuff hostages. As members of the Oath Keepers moved through the Rotunda, they communicated with one another over walkie-talkies. On one recorded transmission, reported by the House of Representatives committee investigating the attack, an Oath Keeper boasted that members of Congress were hunted prey: "There is no safe place in the United States for any of these motherfuckers right now."[120] Another member of that group—a navy veteran who had held a top secret security clearance since 1979—would later confirm, "If we'd had guns I guarantee we would have killed 100 politicians. They ran off and were spirited away through their tunnels like the rats they are."[121] The guns were nearby, ready to be called into action if required: Oath Keepers had established a "quick reaction force" in a hotel across the river in Virginia, and one member would later testify that he had "not seen that many weapons in one location since [he] was in the military."[122] Both members of Congress and police officers who were people of color were especially vilified by many of the attackers. They were subjected to racial epithets and threats of violence,[123] and over 150 years after the American Civil War ended, a Confederate flag—a banner still associated with white supremacism, secession, and treason—was proudly paraded through the halls of Congress. And a makeshift gallows was erected outside—an unmistakable evocation of *The Turner Diaries*' summons to "hold accountable" America's elected representatives. The appearance of the scaffold conforms to the terrorism scholars Andrew Kydd and Barbara Walter's observation about the intimidation element of terrorist strategy. Such images are meant to show that "terrorists have the power to punish whoever disobeys them, and that the government is powerless to stop them."[124] The mob encapsulated the diversity of diehard Trump supporters: from trained and armed militia members to lifelong white supremacists to mothers who had fallen into QAnon's orbit along with other ordinary citizens.

It took several hours for the police, now belatedly supported by the Washington, Maryland, and Virginia National Guards, to regain control of the seat of the U.S. government. The rioters departed only after President Trump released a video calling for an end to the violence and occupation of the building. "Go home, we love you, you're very special," he said. Reluctantly, they left—with some already warning of renewed violent attacks. "If we gotta come back here and start a revolution and take all these traitors out, which is what should be done, then we will," one intruder told a journalist covering the mayhem.[125] They left behind a trail of wanton vandalism and destruction: shattered windows, broken furniture, ransacked offices, and walls smeared with human feces and stained by urine. In addition to the defilement of this citadel of American democracy, there were four deaths: A QAnon supporter was shot by police as she attempted to climb through the broken glass of an entrance to the Speaker's Lobby; a second person died of a drug overdose while being trampled by her fellow Trump supporters during one particularly violent skirmish with police, as advancing rioters sarcastically chanted a Black Lives Matter slogan, "I can't breathe!";[126] and a third and fourth person died from heart conditions.[127] In the days that followed, three police officers also perished—one from a stroke likely caused by bear repellant sprayed in his face by rioters and two from self-inflicted gunshot wounds. At least 150 other officers were wounded.[128]

Hours after the attack ended, as members of Congress returned to the House and Senate chambers to complete the certification process and analysts began the postmortem, Trump was back on Twitter. "These are the things and events that happen when a sacred landslide election victory is so unceremoniously & viciously stripped away from great patriots who have been badly & unfairly treated for so long," he unabashedly tweeted. "Go home with love & in peace," the president continued, before concluding, "Remember this day forever!" Barely an hour later, Twitter removed Trump from the platform—a ban subsequently made permanent until new ownership reinstated the former president in November 2022.[129] Facebook followed suit, announcing after removing several Trump posts, "We made the decision that on balance these posts contribute to, rather than diminish, the risk of ongoing violence."[130]

In the hours and days that followed, extremists promised more violence and made preparations for a new assault on the nation's capital.[131] "I'm proud as fuck what we accomplished yesterday," one Proud Boys member texted on January 7, 2021, "but we need to start planning and we are starting planning, for a Biden presidency." Another member betrayed his group's fundamental disagreement with mainstream conservatives' historical support for law enforcement, declaring, "if you feel bad for the police, you are part of the problem."[132] And, in private messaging channels, Stewart Rhodes, the leader of the Oath Keepers militia, likened the storming of the Capitol to the opening salvos of the American Revolutionary War. "The founding generation Sons of Liberty stormed the mansion of the corrupt Royal Governor of Massachusetts, and trashed the place," he wrote—a call to arms issued in similar terms to William Potter Gale's exhortations nearly thirty-five years earlier.

They also jumped on board a ship carrying East India Tea, and dumped it in the harbor. We are actually in a far more deadly situation given the FACT that enemies foreign and domestic have subverted, infiltrated, and taken over near every single office and level of power in this nation. We have one FINAL chance to get Trump to do his job and his duty. Patriots entering their own Capitol to send a message to the traitors is NOTHING compared to what's coming if Trump doesn't take decisive action right now. It helped to send that message to HIM. He was the most important audience today. I hope he got the message.[133]

It later emerged that the Proud Boys had used similar revolutionary rhetoric in their planning. A document circulated among the group in the days before the attack was titled "1776 Returns." "These are OUR buildings, they are just renting space," the document declared. "We must show our politicians We the People are in charge."[134] The leaders of the Oath Keepers and Proud Boys, Stewart Rhodes and Enrique Tarrio, had met in a parking garage in Washington, DC, the day before the riot.[135]

"The Battle of Capitol Hill," as the terrorism expert Brian Michael Jenkins termed it, was over—but its legacy changed both the stakes and contours of the government's effort to counter extremism that crossed First Amendment boundaries into violence and insurrection. Polling conducted later that month indicated that, astonishingly, over a third of Republicans agreed that "if elected leaders will not protect America, the people must do it themselves even if it requires taking violent actions."[136] The rioter who was shot dead, an air force veteran named Ashli Babbitt, was quickly elevated into the violent far right's pantheon of heroes, joining figureheads such as Gordon Kahl and Robert Mathews and the Ruby Ridge and Waco dead as martyrs who had fallen at the hands of an overreaching government. America's foreign adversaries, meanwhile, eagerly celebrated the developments. Al-Qaeda, among America's preeminent foreign terrorist enemies, rejoiced. A writer for its *One Ummah* online magazine celebrated the events of January 6, 2021, as having made up for errors made on 9/11, declaring, "I realized the wisdom of God almighty in not guiding the fourth plane to its target, for their [the American rioters'] destroying the citadel of their democracy by their own hands . . . is more damaging to them & more soothing to the hearts of the believers."[137] In al-Qaeda's eyes, Osama bin Laden's attrition strategy against the West was made all the more effective by the United States wounding itself.

Two cabinet officials resigned after the attack, along with several senior national security officials. Minority Leader Kevin McCarthy, an unflinching Trump defender in the House, reacted angrily to the president's suggestion that Antifa had caused the riot, telling him, "It's not Antifa, it's MAGA. I know. I was there."[138] Others placed the blame squarely on the president. "Would anybody have marched on the Capitol, and tried to overrun the Capitol, without the president's speech?" Chris Miller, acting secretary of defense for the last months of the administration, asked. "I think it's pretty much definitive that wouldn't have happened."[139]

Many of the insurrectionists arrested after that day themselves blamed Trump. The lawyer for one Proud Boy—a marine veteran who, at 2:13 PM, had used a stolen police riot shield to break open a window on the Capitol's west side and was the first rioter to breach the building—cited the president's encouragement as the reason his client had come to Washington that day.[140] "The boss of the country said, 'People of the country, come on down, let people know what you think.' The logical thinking was, 'He invited us down.'"[141] A video uploaded to Parler on January 6 similarly depicted one insurrectionist screaming at the police, "We were invited here. We were invited by the President of the United States."[142] In another exchange, one rioter berated a group of police officers: "You're outnumbered! There's a fucking million of us out there! And we are listening to Trump! Your boss!"[143] Many therefore asked for presidential pardons in the remaining two weeks before the inauguration—and were outraged when they were not provided. "I feel like I was basically following my president," one attacker who had traveled from Texas argued. "I was following what we were called to do. He asked us to fly there. He asked us to be there. So I was doing what he asked us to do. I think we all deserve a pardon. I'm facing a prison sentence. I think I do not deserve that."[144]

The defendants' own words illuminated perhaps the most important and painful lesson of January 6: the singular influence wielded by Trump and his veneration by far-right extremists in this country. Trump basked in their adulation and praised and celebrated the insurrectionists. "It was zero threat. Right from the start, it was zero threat," Trump told Fox News two months later. "Look, they went in—they shouldn't have done it—some of them went in, and they're hugging and kissing the police and the guards, you know? They had great relationships. A lot of the people were waved in, and then they walked in, and they walked out."[145] Three U.S. Capitol police officers were dead and at least 150 others had been injured on January 6.

The events of that day were perhaps the inevitable outcome of four years of patent falsehoods and dissembling.[146] "The attack on the Capitol was the culmination of four years of conspiracies and lies that Trump and his allies had fed to his supporters on social media platforms, in speeches, and on television," Dr. Fiona Hill, the former National Security Council senior director for Europe and Russia during the Trump administration, later reflected. "The 'Big Lie' that Trump had won the election was built on the backs of the thousands of little lies that Trump uttered nearly every time he spoke and that were then nurtured within the dense ecosystem of Trumpist media outlets."[147] Crucially, among these false claims was Trump's repeated redirection of America's federal law enforcement and homeland security resources away from increasingly violent far-right threats to focus instead on the far left.[148] Trump's efforts to skewer domestic threat reporting resulted in the former chief of DHS intelligence, Brian Murphy, filing a twenty-four page whistleblower complaint over the manipulation of intelligence reports to diminish threat assessments warning of increasing far-right violence to reflect the president's citing of the greater threat posed by far-left extremists.[149] The two threats in fact were barely comparable. Although a far-left terrorist attack early in the administration very nearly resulted in the devastating mass murder of several Republican members of Congress—if not for then–House Majority Whip Steve Scalise's heroic Capitol Police detail, it "would have been a massacre," according to Rep. Rodney Davis—Trump's preoccupation with Antifa was misplaced given its comparatively limited potential for violence.[150] Data gathered by the Anti-Defamation League, for instance, has repeatedly demonstrated that for more than a decade violent, far-right extremists have accounted for far more homicides in the United States than their radical left-wing counterparts.[151] And ongoing research and analysis conducted by New America's leading researchers on terrorism, Peter Bergen and David Sterman, similarly shows that in the twenty years after 9/11, far-right extremists have been responsible for over one hundred killings in America; far left extremists are responsible for just one.[152] Antifa is a loosely organized militant movement that has committed acts of terrorism—but these have rarely killed anyone and mostly involved crimes like looting and rioting rather than more typical terrorist tactics like bombing, shooting, and kidnapping.

But as this historical analysis of the past forty years has revealed, Trump is just one factor in the more recent rise of far-right extremism in the United States. The conditions dividing and polarizing America today have been building for a long time, and as previous chapters have demonstrated, one cannot understand accelerationism and its grip on a growing segment of the country today without a careful assessment of how past developments have brought us to this current juncture in American politics. By the time each essential cog had rotated into place, it was arguably already too late to avert the chain of events that led to January 6, 2021.

No single structure symbolized the generational threat to American democracy that emerged that day than the seven-foot wall erected around the U.S. Capitol building in the days following the riots—a countermeasure reminiscent of dramatic changes in airport security screening after 9/11 and the implementation of Jersey barriers to protect government buildings after the 1995 Oklahoma City bombing. Washington, DC, in January 2021, moreover, looked like Baghdad in January 2005, when Iraq's first-ever democratic elections were held. As in Baghdad eighteen years earlier, troops lined the streets. Some 25,000 National Guard soldiers were mobilized to ensure the security of President-elect Biden's inauguration—over twenty thousand more troops than were then stationed in Afghanistan, another powerful symbol of how far the terrorism threat had shifted from foreign to domestic enemies.[153]

In his inaugural address in 2017, President Trump had promised, "This American carnage stops right here and stops right now." Although no one quite understood what "carnage" he meant, the next four years would catalyze a kaleidoscope of extremist violence that brought death and harm to Americans as well as those in other Western countries. In just four years, America's formidable counterterrorism bureaucracy would pivot almost a full 180 degrees away from the Salafi jihadist threats that had dominated national security for nearly two decades and toward entirely domestic terrorist threats. "It's going to take decades to undo the damage," Elizabeth Neumann, a former senior DHS official during Trump's time in office, observed weeks after the events of January 6.[154]

• • •

On January 20, 2021, Joe Biden was sworn in as the forty-sixth president of the United States. He immediately signaled that countering domestic terrorist threats would be a focus of his administration—and that the country would have to come together to fight it. In the days after the inauguration, various absurd conspiracy theories circulated among Trump's more extremist supporters—while some were convinced that the election would eventually be overturned, others argued that Trump had shape-shifted into Biden's body and that Biden's characteristic, occasionally slurred voice (caused by a stutter) was actually Trump learning how to speak like the former vice president.[155] By the time the Biden administration was two months old, over three hundred people who had participated in the January 6 insurrection had been charged with federal crimes ranging from trespassing to conspiracy to injure officers.[156]

The new administration had an immediate effect. "One of the most important changes is one of the easiest—ending the sense that white supremacy is tolerated from on high," the terrorism analysts Daniel Byman and Mark Pitcavage argued. To their minds,

> though the FBI has been aggressive in recent years in investigating white supremacist violence, the Trump administration sent ambiguous signals toward the broader movement, at times seemingly reluctantly condemning it but also defending causes it champions, like the preservation of Confederate statues and military bases named after Confederate generals, and promoting conspiracy theories related to immigrants. It has also rhetorically labeled enemies of the movement, such as Black Lives Matter and Antifa, as terrorist organizations, creating confusion and false equivalence. High-level support for cracking down on white supremacist violence will ensure that resources are in place to fight white supremacists, that agencies know their roles, and that more mainstream groups that are critical of immigration or otherwise share some concerns of white supremacists know they must reject the violent haters in their ranks.[157]

Trump became the only president to be impeached twice. Yet thirty-eight days after the riot, Trump—this time impeached for "incitement of insurrection"—was acquitted, albeit in the most bipartisan impeachment vote of all time. Seven Republicans joined fifty Democrats in voting to convict, including senators from deep-red states such as Louisiana, Nebraska, and Utah.[158] "Former President Trump's actions that preceded the riot were a disgraceful, disgraceful dereliction of duty," Republican Senate Minority Leader Mitch McConnell seethed, despite voting to acquit. "Trump is practically and morally responsible for provoking the events of the day."[159] The Monday following the impeachment acquittal, February 15, Speaker of the House Nancy Pelosi announced a 9/11-style commission to investigate the events of January 6.

On March 17, the Office of the Director of National Intelligence unclassified the U.S. intelligence community's assessments of the shifting terrorism threat. "The IC assesses that domestic violent extremists (DVEs) who are motivated by a range of ideologies and galvanized by recent political and societal events in the United States pose an elevated threat to the Homeland in 2021," it began. "Enduring DVE motivations pertaining to biases against minority populations and perceived government overreach will almost certainly continue to drive DVE radicalization and mobilization to violence. Newer sociopolitical developments—such as narratives of fraud in the recent general election, the emboldening impact of the violent breach of the US Capitol, conditions related to the COVID-19 pandemic, and conspiracy theories promoting violence will almost certainly spur some DVEs to try to engage in violence this year."[160] More specifically, the report went on to add that "racially or ethnically motivated violent extremists (RMVEs) and militia violent extremists (MVEs) present the most lethal DVE threats, with RMVEs most likely to conduct mass-casualty attacks against civilians and MVEs typically targeting law enforcement and government personnel and facilities."

Meanwhile, the threats from many of those who had participated in or supported the January 6 insurrection continued. "So that everyone knows I go to see the FBI and a judge tomorrow," one rioter from Utah wrote on Facebook on April 28. "I guess peacefully protesting at the Capitol is now illegal and they are trying to hunt us all down to try and teach us a lesson. Unfortunately, only one option remains when we return. We bring guns and take the Capitol building without intention of being peaceful. This ends with the government bombing their own people. I had hopes it wouldn't. But here we are."[161]

The remainder of 2021 was relatively peaceful, but the tensions and divisions continued, and several times the familiar calls to violence and sedition were again issued. After George Floyd's killer, Derek Chauvin, was convicted on murder charges on April 20, for example, adherents on social media forums repeated their calls for a race war: "This was a huge win for white america. Now we are free to assassinate all [N-word] we see. Cops aren't going to police [N-word] anymore. [N-word] Slaughter 2021. Let the fun begin."[162] The implication was that it was now a public duty to protect communities from Black criminality. After the Kenosha killer Kyle Rittenhouse was acquitted that November, extremists rejoiced and called for more violence. "Don't let this one victory lull you back to sleep," a White Lives Matter movement supporter implored on Telegram.

> That's what they want. They know small "victories" can placate the angry masses more than anything else. Instead let this win fuel your rage. Never forget the simple fact that this clear-cut self-defense should have never gone to trial in the first place. Muslim, Hispanic, and African invaders have raped millions of our women, WHTIE [sic] women. Their time of terrorizing our people with 0 consequences is coming to an end. The Rittenhouse verdict was a single tick in the scoreboard on our side. Our enemy doesn't have a scoreboard big enough for their victories. Fight harder, stronger, fiercer, and with the same remorse they show us. None.
> Get going, White man.[163]

In June 2021, the White House released its National Strategy for Countering Domestic Terrorism. The document was the first formal strategy ever released by the White House regarding domestic terrorist threats—yet another indication of the extent to which terrorism had shifted homeward. The administration's approach was based on four pillars:

- understand and share domestic terrorism–related information;
- prevent domestic terrorism recruitment and mobilization to violence;
- disrupt and deter domestic terrorism activity; and,
- confront long-term contributors to domestic terrorism.[164]

The American political system's divergent views on the events of January 6 nonetheless grew even wider as 2021 turned into 2022. In December, Trump again insisted that the election was stolen. "Anybody that doesn't think there wasn't massive Election Fraud in the 2020 Presidential Election is either very stupid, or very corrupt!" he wrote in a statement on an aide's Twitter account because he himself was suspended, the accidental use of a double negative inadvertently insulting his supporters. The Republican National Committee, meanwhile, voted to censure the two Republican representatives serving on the House committee investigating the January 6 insurrection—Liz Cheney of Wyoming and Adam Kinzinger of Illinois. The resolution also described the January 6 attack on the Capitol as a form of "legitimate political discourse"—defying both logic and evidence.[165]

On January 12, the DOJ indicted eleven January 6 attackers on the same "seditious conspiracy" charge that had been leveled against the Fort Smith defendants in 1988.[166] Among the defendants was the Oath Keepers' founder, Stewart Rhodes. On March 2, one of his followers, Joshua James, pleaded guilty. "In taking such actions, James intended to influence or affect the conduct of the United States government or to retaliate against the United States government," a DOJ statement of offense explained. "He accomplished this by intimidating and coercing government personnel who were participating in or supporting the Congressional proceeding, including Members of Congress, Congressional staff, and law enforcement officers with the Capitol Police and Metropolitan Police Department."[167] The DOJ thus succeeded where its 1988 predecessors had failed: proving that America's violent, antigovernment extremists and their terrorist acts constituted a seditious conspiracy.

In March 2022, the Southern Poverty Law Center released its latest "The Year in Hate & Extremism" report. This iteration offered a particularly sobering assessment of the continuing threat of far-right extremism. "Rather than demonstrating a decline in the power of the far right," the report argued, "the dropping numbers of organized hate and antigovernment groups suggest that the extremist ideas that mobilize them now operate more openly in the political mainstream."[168] Although the SPLC's conclusions pointed to the far right's pernicious infiltrations of the political process, a reminder of the lethal potential of the leaderless resistance threat occurred on May 14 when eighteen-year-old Payton Gendron, of Conklin, New York, opened fire at a Tops Friendly Markets store in Buffalo, killing ten Black shoppers and employees. After several years of extremism primarily driven by COVID and election grievances against the government, Gendron revived the Tarrant model—attacking a soft target frequented by a minority group and publishing a manifesto that heavily plagiarized the Christchurch gunman's but redirected its venom toward America's Black community. Like Tarrant, Gendron also livestreamed the attack. "In conclusion from all of this," Gendron's twisted manifesto declared, "blacks are pre dispositioned to have weaker brain ability due to genetics. This is important because it leads to the question if blacks should live in a western world built by Whites. The answer to this question is no, they simply are not built to live in the White world. This advanced human civilization that we have today can only be built by Whites, blacks simply hold us down."[169] Sparking the usual banter on far-right chatrooms—with some posts celebrating a new "Saint," others deriding his targeting of African Americans instead of Jews—Gendron also inspired a new theme for neo-Nazi chatrooms.[170] Dubbed the "14th Day Initiative"—a reference both to the date of Gendron's attack as well as the "14 Words"—the plan aimed to make the fourteenth day of every month "OUR day" to "Make the news. Make the enemy afraid. Hold the guilty to account. Drive out the invaders."[171]

Throughout the spring of 2022, observers of online extreme chatrooms noticed a further intensification of the calls for violence against specific public figures, a worrying trend that had originated in the conspiratorial cocktail created by COVID lockdowns and the rise of QAnon. In fact, on many channels, violence against public figures was becoming the answer to virtually every political grievance. Many online forums were deluged with death threats targeting politicians and other leaders, relentlessly blaming them for every imaginable sleight.[172] These threats often targeted Republicans deemed insufficiently hardline—so-called "RINOS," or "Republicans In Name Only," one of Trump's preferred insults—thus highlighting the far right's animus against not just Democratic politicians but to the entire concept of the Western, liberal-democratic nation-state. Extremists that March, for instance, threatened Maine's Republican senator Susan Collins for voting affirmatively for Ketanji Brown Jackson's nomination to the U.S. Supreme Court—the first Black female justice. "Ballot box isn't working, time to use the bullet box," one threat read, with another more simply stating "Hang her."[173] In May, the pro-Trump Arizona attorney general Mark Brnovich came under attack after a state election fraud report was released, despite the report alleging "concerns" with the vote, with one person declaring, "He should be run through his ass to his mouth with a spear, raised up on display in front of the voting precinct." Others posted threats targeting his family: "Don't forget his wife and kids. Being a traitor to your country needs to have consequences that go beyond one's own neck."[174] And in June, a group of ten Republican senators came under fire for helping advance moderate gun control laws after the previous month's deadly school shooting in Uvalde, Texas. "Blindfolds. Brick wall. Now," a thread warned on the far-right forum "The Donald." "Ammo is expensive, but the gallows is free," another user responded.[175]

The FBI's search of Trump's Mar-a-Lago Florida residence on August 8, 2022, for classified documents allegedly retained by the former president emerged as yet another flashpoint. Authorized by Attorney General Merrick Garland after the DOJ was convinced there was sufficient evidence, the raid produced a new wellspring of violent rhetoric. As the SPLC had warned, this time the calls to arms were also issued by politicians, including both high-profile GOP figureheads and fringe hopefuls. "If they try to prosecute President Trump for mishandling classified information after Hillary Clinton set up a server in her basement, there literally will be riots in the street. I worry about our country," Senator Lindsey Graham of South Carolina warned on Fox News before later walking back his apparent incitement after an outcry, saying, "I reject violence."[176] Others were more confrontational. Ronny Jackson, a congressman from Texas, declared: "Tonight the FBI officially became the enemy of the people!!!"[177] A candidate for the Florida State House of Representatives was banned from Twitter after declaring: "Under my plan, all Floridians will have permission to shoot FBI, IRS, ATF and all other feds on sight! Let freedom ring!"[178] And Steven Crowder, a prominent conservative commentator, warned on Twitter, "Tomorrow is war. Sleep well."[179] Later that month on Truth Social, a social media platform developed by a Trump-owned business, the former president shared voluminous QAnon content—as well as photographs of Joe Biden, Kamala Harris, Nancy Pelosi, Barack Obama,

Hillary Clinton, and George Soros, with the ominous tagline "Your enemy is not in Russia."[180]

Genuine threats were also directed against FBI agents and their families.[181] In Cincinnati, an armed assailant tried to shoot his way into the FBI's office before being killed in a shootout. A Navy veteran and January 6 attendee who had been on the bureau's radar, the would-be killer had posted on Truth Social two days before the attack, "People, this is it. I hope a call to arms comes from someone better qualified, but if not, this is your call to arms from me. Leave work tomorrow as soon as the gun shop/Army-Navy store/pawn shop opens, get whatever you need to be ready for combat. We must not tolerate this one."[182] It was an unfortunate coincidence, too, that the judge who approved the warrant to search Trump's home was Jewish. His synagogue in Florida was forced to cancel services because of threats against the judge and his family.[183] In a *Politico* op-ed ominously titled "The Real Fallout from the Mar-a-Lago Search," Steven Simon and Jonathan Stevenson warned, "Watching agents search Mar-a-Lago could turn a large enough portion of Trump's far-right base decisively against federal authority that its defiance could shift from episodic to systemic, eventually leading to regular armed resistance to federal law enforcement on the order of Ruby Ridge and potentially even Waco." Only law enforcement activity that is "both strategically aggressive and tactically restrained," they argued, can thread the needle between combating the far-right extremist threat without inciting further violence.[184]

The most serious incident, though, in the weeks leading up to the 2022 midterm elections was the home invasion of and violent assault on Paul Pelosi, husband of Speaker of the House Nancy Pelosi. On October 28, just after 2 AM, David DePape, a Canadian illegal immigrant steeped in conspiracy theories, broke through the back door of the Pelosis' San Francisco home. DePape was looking for the speaker, who was on his "target list" and whom he viewed as the "leader of the pack" of the Democratic Party's alleged peddling of lies and deceptions. DePape intended to break the speaker's kneecaps, according to the criminal indictment filed against him. His intent was that the speaker would therefore "have to be wheeled into Congress, which would show other Members of Congress that there were consequences to their actions."[185] Paul Pelosi had managed to call police during the break-in, and when they arrived, officers confronted

DePape and asked him to drop a hammer he was holding and that Pelosi was trying to wrestle away. "Um, nope," DePape said, before bludgeoning the octogenarian Pelosi, who was seriously injured. DePape would later call a journalist for the Bay Area's KTVU television station from prison and state, "I have an important message for everyone in America. You're welcome. Freedom and liberty isn't dying, it's being killed, systematically and deliberately. The people killing it have names and addresses." Regretting that he could not target more of his perceived enemies, DePape added, "I should've come better prepared."[186] Aside from the plot against Pelosi, the midterms otherwise passed relatively peacefully and were marked by the defeats of several Trump-backed Republican candidates, who chose to forgo the former president's playbook of refusing to accept defeat. Their grace provided hope that the national temperature was at last dropping.[187]

On November 29, in a stunning development, a jury sitting in Washington, DC, federal court found Stewart Rhodes—a former army paratrooper, Yale Law School graduate, and leader of one of the country's most well-known and dangerous militia groups, the Oath Keepers—guilty of seditious conspiracy. Unlike in Fort Smith, Arkansas, thirty-four years earlier, Department of Justice prosecutors had proven that Rhodes had plotted to overthrow the U.S. government. Although it followed Joshua James's earlier guilty plea, Rhodes's conviction, alongside that of one co-conspirator and four more found guilty the following month, demonstrated clearly that leaders of politically extreme organizations bent on violence and revolution would be held accountable for their subversive plans and preparations. Speaking to the *Washington Post*, Tasha Adams, Rhodes's ex-wife and a frequent critic of her former spouse, captured the significance of the verdict and its broader implications. "For the first time," Adams said, "he is facing the consequence of his own actions and, barring any pardon after the 2024 election, he can now disappear into obscurity where he belongs."[188]

On December 22, 2022, the U.S. House Select Committee on the January 6th Attack released its final report after a wide-ranging investigation and several primetime televised hearings. Leaving little doubt regarding the committee's findings on the former president's role, the report stated that "the central cause of January 6th was one man, former President Donald Trump, whom many others followed. None of the events of

January 6th would have happened without him."[189] The committee issued a non–legally binding referral to the Department of Justice, recommending that Trump be prosecuted on four charges, including supporting insurrection.[190] Although the committee's exhaustive research accurately portrayed Trump's galvanizing role in the days and hours before the riot, it arguably failed to capture the forty years of violent farright organizing, plotting, and scheming that had preceded the attack.

9

COUNTERING FAR-RIGHT TERRORISM

Freedom is a fragile thing and it's never more than one generation away from extinction. It is not ours by way of inheritance; it must be fought for and defended constantly by each generation, for it comes only once to people. And those in world history who have known freedom and then lost it have never known it again.

—RONALD REAGAN, JANUARY 5, 1967

The chain of events that led to the assault on the U.S. Capitol Building on January 6, 2021, did not begin with President Trump's baseless "stop the steal" declamations. Nor did they commence during the first presidential debate the previous September when Trump instructed the Proud Boys to "stand back and stand by." They were not triggered by his assertion that the neo-Nazis, Klansmen, neo-Confederates, racists, antisemites, and xenophobes who attended the 2017 "Unite the Right" rally in Charlottesville, Virginia, and were responsible for the death of a counterprotestor were "very fine people" or by Trump's 2016 election victory over Hillary Clinton. Even the historical milestone of the first African American elected president in 2008 did not set in motion the process that culminated in that attack on this citadel of American democracy. Their origin, as this book has shown, instead dates back over four decades. Then, a longstanding ideology of hate and intolerance was revitalized and infused with new vigor by calls for outright sedition from a new generation of white supremacists now allied with militant, antigovernment extremists. The gallows erected on the Mall in front of the Capitol Building that fateful day thus embodied the hopes and dreams of these zealots who in an age before digital platforms and social media could not have envisioned a scenario in which democracy nearly died.[1]

At that time, the threat from these extremists was mostly isolated and effectively contained by vigorous government action. Louis Beam's leaderless resistance strategy advocating individual acts of violence by lone wolves in hopes of provoking a wider conflagration never gained a significant following. It admittedly led to the tragic 1995 Oklahoma City bombing. But Timothy McVeigh's spectacularly lethal act of violence did not ignite, as he had intended and the leaderless resistance strategy promised, a nationwide uprising against the U.S. government. Not only was no group or person inspired to follow in McVeigh's footsteps but—with the notable exception of the 1996 Atlanta Olympics bombing and the series of similar attacks on abortion clinics and a gay bar by the same perpetrator—all other inclinations to violent insurrection were suppressed by landmark antiterrorism legislation enacted by Congress in 1996 and signal action by the FBI and other law enforcement agencies.[2]

Today, however, such extremist and radical beliefs are both more prevalent and more pervasive. Social media has propagated poisonous ideologies and spread them wider and faster than Beam and his fellow hate-mongers could ever have imagined. They have crossed into and become embedded in mainstream politics and public discourse and are shared and advocated by more Americans than ever before. As previously noted, a disturbingly large number of Americans agree that violence against their government could be justified in certain circumstances, more than at any time since this survey question was first posed over two decades ago. It is therefore not surprising that fully nine out of ten Americans also believe that the intensification of political divisiveness and polarization has made politically motivated violence in this country more likely. In a country awash with privately owned firearms and where, according to the American University scholar Cynthia Miller-Idriss's "best estimate" at least 75,000 to 100,000 individuals are actively involved with white supremacist extremist groups,[3] in addition to the 15,000 to 20,000 people who belong to armed militia organizations comprising some three hundred different groups,[4] the threat of wide-spread acts of domestic terrorism—perhaps leading to a sustained insurgency campaign and even civil war—is not hyperbolic.

The United States today is thus confronted by a serious domestic terrorist threat in addition to the foreign ones that have commanded our attention for the past two decades. Whether because of distraction, indifference, or complacency, violent extremism has woven itself into the fabric of national, state, and local politics. And, historically, terrorism has thrived in environments torn by division and disagreement that in turn are consumed by polarization and enmity. A combination of apathy and inaction will only encourage further polarization, greater extremism, and more violence. Whether this will lead to the civil war that scholars, policy analysts, journalists, and pundits have warned of is by no means certain. But even if this unfathomable, worst-case-scenario is avoided, the current trajectory of domestic unrest and potential upheaval presents as grave a threat to our country and its democratic values and institutions as any since the civil war that consumed the nation 180 years ago.

Countering domestic terrorism will likely prove far more challenging than combating the overseas Salafi jihadist threats that have persisted since the epochal September 11, 2001, attacks. The formidable instruments of military power successfully employed against al-Qaeda and ISIS and their various affiliates and branches—most prominently the targeted killings achieved by drone strikes and the lethally effective raids conducted by special operations forces—are completely irrelevant to countering domestic terrorism for the obvious reasons that they cannot and should never be deployed against our fellow citizens. Without being able to rely on these proven and effective military counterterrorism measures, the United States will have to build almost from scratch nonlethal, flexible, and innovative measures both to counter violent extremists and address new and emerging, entirely homegrown terrorist threats.

But much as military strategists urge targeting an adversary's "center of gravity" to achieve lasting, decisive results, the most vulnerable pressure points of a violent political movement's weaknesses must similarly be the focus of government efforts to counter subversive and seditious domestic threats.[5] The centers of gravity of the violent extremist right in the United States today are evident in themes explored by this book: an obsessive conspiratorial mindset; the exploitation of social media for radicalization, recruitment, and encouragement of violence; and the insidious injection of ideologies promoting hate, intolerance, and conspiracy into mainstream American politics, our military, and law enforcement communities. These are the centers of gravity that a domestic counterextremism and counterterrorism strategy must focus on.

The United States today thus requires a comprehensive, wide-ranging, institutionalized strategy to effectively counter these threats—including measures to strengthen American civil society as well as those that specifically target violent extremist groups, their activists and supporters, their propagandists and sympathizers, and their recruiters and financiers. The policy recommendations that emerge from this examination and exegesis of the far-right terrorist threat in the United States fit into three categories:

- short-term measures to create a stronger regulatory framework, with relatively immediate effects;
- medium-term measures to strengthen civil society, with impacts over the next five to ten years; and,
- long-term measures to build national unity, which will break the cycle of recruitment and regeneration that has sustained this movement across multiple decades and therefore build resilience that will benefit future generations and inoculate them against the allure of extremist ideologies.

All these efforts need to commence immediately and not unfold sequentially. They should be undertaken without delay but with the expectation that, while some can have more immediate effects, others will take years, if not decades, to achieve the desired impact. This range of measures, it should be emphasized, is applicable to both extremes of the political spectrum—left as well as right—and include, as the preeminent goal, restoring the integrity of and respect for the American political system. To implement this admittedly optimistic but nonetheless crucial goal, a series of equally critical additional steps is required, such as enacting legislation designed to address all manifestations of extremist violence, whether from the right or the left or any other section, and effectively counter the ideological and social appeal of extremism and conspiracy theories more generally. By taking decisive action today, the United States can begin to make meaningful inroads against these highly corrosive and insidious threats to our democratic values and ensure the safety and security of our fellow citizens in a more secure and inclusive environment than currently exists.

· · ·

January 6 showed to devastating effect that conspiracy theories that demonize government and reject the authority of its institutions and processes pose a clear and pressing danger to law, order, and the stability of the American political system. Restoring popular faith in our government and reinforcing the democratic principles for which this country was conceived is therefore the highest priority. But such a reckoning cannot be achieved either organically or quickly. Accordingly, a series of remedial legislative steps must first occur to jumpstart the revitalization of a common national identity. Among these, depriving extremists of the free rein they have long enjoyed on social media is imperative. Legislation is needed to ensure greater clarity between First Amendment rights to free and open expression and the planning and plotting of violent acts of domestic terrorism.[6]

Hence, first and foremost, rebuilding and strengthening American democracy will require addressing the pervasive and pernicious impact of social media. Digital communication has contributed in hitherto unprecedented ways to the rise of lone-actor terrorism. It has in particular amplified and accelerated Beam's leaderless resistance strategy. In the past, exponents of leaderless resistance were constrained by the limited reach of their message through traditional media and generally stymied in their efforts to achieve any kind of mass following. But social media has facilitated the emergence of a loosely connected global far-right terrorist movement whose grievances and motivations transcend borders and national contexts but are linked by a shared belief in the efficacy of violence. The posited trope entailing the replacement of the European white male through immigration of other races and religions, for instance, has become a compelling contemporary battle cry of the violent far right. Exaggerated fears of soaring nonwhite birthrates coupled with the alleged role that Jewish and associated villainous global and liberal elites play in deliberately pushing and exploiting this trend play into conspiracy theories that become increasingly common and accepted as political dogma. This online echo chamber's most significant real-world impact has been the erosion of the previously defined demarcation between "international" and "domestic" terrorism along with the facilitation of the convergence of multiple hitherto divergent ideologies into a combustible mélange of new justifications for collective violence. In extremist social media bubbles, adherents arguably have more in common with ideological brethren an ocean away than with their physical real-world neighbors. The result today is an international succession of lone-actor terrorists who revel in their use of social media both to presage and advertise their violent acts and then post their unhinged rants in hopes of inspiring imitation and emulation.[7]

In their 2018 book *The Future of Terrorism*, the historians Walter Laqueur and Christopher Wall argue that "terrorism is not an exogenous feature of the modern nation-state but rather a symptom of bad governance."[8] Their analysis referred to failed states around the world that have allowed extremists to thrive in power vacuums. But, in a contemporaneous twist, their analysis can also be applied to social media. For over a decade, an ever-growing array of zealots advocating violence and sedition has been given free rein on social media platforms. With sometimes tragic consequences, they easily acquire access to some of society's most vulnerable individuals. The social media titans who have repeatedly watched as their products are used and exploited by dangerous actors but who have refused to intervene have facilitated and encouraged this process. They must do more to moderate extreme speech on their platforms, both to prevent new radicalization and protect vulnerable communities from being targeted by hate speech online. Examples include removing content altogether or affixing particularly controversial posts with disclaimers or contextual explainers. Greater efforts must also be directed toward helping smaller sites, which might be more willing to push back against extremism but lack the resources to police their platform, better ensure their sites are safe from extremist recruiters and radicalizers. Sites that refuse to comply should be considered for expulsion from various internet hosting providers. International efforts like the Christchurch Call and Delhi Declaration should be multiplied and deepened, while organizations like the

Global Internet Forum to Counter Terrorism need more encouragement and funding.

But responsibility both wittingly and unwittingly for this malignancy increasingly lies with governments, too. First Amendment champions maintain that social media cannot be restrained because it would violate American citizens' constitutional rights to freedom of speech. Yet in recent years, social media has evolved to a point where an extremist's right to spew abuse online appears to take precedence over their target's rights to be safe from fear and online abuse. This development has to be addressed if we are to control this poisonous dimension of social media and check its unimpeded incitements to violence. As an example, we can look to Great Britain's efforts to clamp down on online hate through white papers and legislation, which has showcased both the challenges and potential legal remedies.[9] According to the 2019 British government white paper detailing its "online harms" initiative, this policy is designed to counter "the most serious illegal harms which threaten our national security and the physical safety of children." In the context of terrorism, the white paper is explicit about the continuing threats of online radicalization and recruitment. It also commendably provides a practical framework within which government and industry can work together "to prevent exploitation of the internet for terrorist purposes."[10] Measures to moderate online dialogue are easier to implement in Europe, where they do not have the stringent free speech laws made sacred in the United States by the First Amendment. But, conversely, the social media companies that host hateful rhetoric are private companies and therefore are not constrained by the First Amendment. They should not be allowed to hide behind inapplicable constitutional protections as an excuse for inaction.

Government efforts to contain the endless spiral of extremism online should include encouraging algorithm reform. Social media algorithms on major platforms are specifically meant to maximize engagement and attract new audiences, thus enabling social media companies to maximize advertising revenue from users deliberately drawn into spending more time on their sites. Their algorithms thus frequently push users toward more shocking or upsetting material, in order to keep them riveted to a particular platform's content. Social media companies should be disincentivized from driving users toward ever more polarizing and radicalizing content. Banning violent extremists from monetizing their content would be the most critical positive step in this respect, as would prohibiting the advertising of material advocating especially hate-filled, violently inclined content.[11] Our executive, judicial, and legislative branches might also join forces to collectively reform Section 230, the Title 47 provision that protects social media companies from being held legally liable for material posted on their platforms. The safety of social media titans from responsibility for content their platforms disseminate removes any incentive for those companies to create a healthier experience for users—a deficit that ultimately encourages everything from extremism to teen suicide.[12] "We expect that companies shouldn't be allowed to pollute the air and water in ways that might hurt us," Safiya Noble, a communications expert at the University of Southern California whose research focuses on how digital media platforms affect society, argues. "We should also expect a high-quality media environment not polluted with disinformation, lies, propaganda. We need for democracy to work. Those are fair things for people to expect and require policymakers to start talking about."[13]

Demanding accountability from social media companies would perhaps also have the critical ancillary benefit of helping curb the rising menace of propaganda from authoritarian states seeking to undermine core Western democratic values. Social media in this age of mass online communication has arguably become the most intersectional factor in national security today. Through social media, the lines between war and peace, diplomacy and competition, and information and disinformation have blurred. In creating division and, in select cases, actively supporting violent domestic extremist movements in the United States and allied countries, America's rivals have succeeded in undermining U.S. national security.[14] Russia's repeated, malignant interference in the 2016 presidential election, for instance, is a well-documented tactical achievement. But since that time the Kremlin's continued manipulation of Western democracies has delivered to Russia a potential strategic victory: succeeding where decades of Soviet-era subversion during the Cold War had failed by undermining public trust and confidence in the Western state system and the democratic process.[15] Whether wittingly or not, Russia's efforts have been abetted and emboldened by repeated claims of electoral fraud. As the former FBI agent and information operations expert Clint Watts observed: "The American electorate remains divided, government operations are severely disrupted, and faith in elected leaders continues to fall. Americans still don't grasp the information war Russia perpetrated against the West, why it works, and why it continues."[16] Russia therefore achieved what the Soviet Union could not accomplish despite decades of trying—eroding the remarkable bipartisan support for core U.S. foreign policy objectives that existed throughout the Cold War. The threat of falsehoods spreading online can thus be even more corrosive to democracy than terrorism.[17] Social media is now one of the defining battlefields of twenty-first-century conflict, from domestic terrorism to international great power competition—and Western liberal democracy is in danger of losing ground there.

Part of the challenge in fashioning an effective response to the more pernicious effects of social media is that these platforms have also shed greater light than ever onto processes of terrorist radicalization, mobilization, and planning. The exploitation of social media as a key law enforcement tool was most clearly evidenced by the arrests of hundreds of people who occupied the U.S. Capitol on January 6, 2021, based on their own social media posts.[18] The ease that governments have in amassing and utilizing for prosecution intelligence gathered online has even led some terrorist groups to eschew social media altogether—maintaining that the risks now outweigh the benefits. An offshoot of the terrorist group Atomwaffen, for instance, has a declared "NO social media" policy. Members are also instructed that "this also means keeping friends/family in check: making sure that they don't put your photos on social media." Instead, the group preaches the importance of "keeping your communications and electronics encrypted and secure."[19] The New Zealand commission investigating the Christchurch attacks concluded that Tarrant took a similar approach to his social media interactions. "The individual took a number of steps intended to minimise his digital footprint so as to reduce the chances of relevant Public sector agencies, following the terrorist attack, being able to obtain a full understanding of his internet activity," the commission's report explained.[20] "In a world of secret sources, analysts could be separated from intelligence collectors," the former chair of the National Intelligence Council, Dr. Gregory Treverton, presciently wrote in his 2009 book *Intelligence for an Age of Terror*. "In the world of the Web, analysts are also their own collectors."[21] We have thus reached a point where social media is both arsonist and firefighter. A delicate approach, where social media companies better moderate their sites without necessarily incinerating all intelligence, would be ideal.

In addition to putting more pressure on social media companies to police their content, policy makers should consider more targeted legal measures to counter the rise of violent extremist movements and their ability to both radicalize and recruit newcomers and incite violence. This entails enhancing both America's instruments of foreign policy and our domestic laws to more effectively contain and deter the spread of violent extremism.

First, Congress should consider the establishment of a high-threshold domestic terrorism law to formally criminalize plots and violence targeting individuals based on race, ethnicity, religion, national identity, sexuality, gender, political affiliation, and other protected categories. The absence of domestic terrorism laws has led to an inequity of sentencing depending on whether the crimes were committed on behalf of designated foreign terrorist organizations or a domestic violent extremist group. There is a substantial sentencing gap today between violent far-right extremists convicted of violent offenses in this country compared with others convicted of similar crimes for foreign groups. According to the Program on Extremism at George Washington University, the average sentence for those convicted in the United States of providing material support to the Islamic State is 13.5 years.[22] Violent, entirely domestic extremists, however, currently cannot be charged for providing material in support of patently violent domestic organizations or for planning and plotting what would otherwise be classified as terrorist attacks were a foreign terrorist entity involved. Christopher Hasson, a former U.S. Coast Guard officer, is a case in point. Violent extremists like Hasson, who amassed a small arsenal with which to assassinate elected Democratic Party representatives and media figures, are typically prosecuted for other nonterrorist offenses, such as drug and gun charges, in order to ensure convictions. Hasson was sentenced to over thirteen years in prison but was never tried for his terroristic plans themselves. To get around this gap in our laws, in some situations federal authorities have resorted to using the name of a designated foreign terrorist organization to secure material support to terrorism charges and thus obtain longer sentences for those convicted of these offenses. This was evident in the FBI sting operation that resulted in the 2020 arrest and conviction of two Booga-loo adherents who were apprehended after discussing violence against government targets to an undercover agent purporting to represent Hamas.[23]

The comparatively shorter sentences handed to convicted domestic ter-rorists are damaging for at least two reasons. First, they reinforce a per-ception that "foreign" terrorists, often distinguishable from "domestic" terrorists only by the color of their skin and religion, are treated more harshly by an allegedly racist judicial system. This "sows confusion," according to Thomas Brzozowski, Department of Justice counsel for domestic terrorism, and also leads to assumptions that international ter-rorism perpetrated by Muslims, for instance, is a more serious threat to the homeland than far-right terrorism—which has been statistically untrue in the post-9/11 era.[24] As Helen Taylor, whose scholarly work focuses on terrorism and hate crimes, writes: "Labelling an act as terror-ism serves as an official statement about the severity of the crime. While hate crime statutes carry significant penalties, they nevertheless do not carry the symbolic weight of a terrorism charge."[25]

But second, and even more importantly, domestic terrorists are often released after remarkably short prison terms. The founder of the Atom-waffen Division, Brandon Russell, was sentenced in 2018 to five years' imprisonment on charges of "possessing an unregistered destructive device and for unlawful storage of explosive material"—despite arresting law enforcement officers believing they had successfully thwarted his plans to perpetrate a mass casualty attack.[26] Similarly, in 2020 another Atomwaffen member, Andrew Thomasberg, was sentenced to a year and a day in prison on charges of possessing firearms while a drug user. He had participated in the infamous 2017 Charlottesville "Unite the Right" rally and when arrested had over a dozen firearms in his home, along with fifty loaded magazines. He had previously been arrested as a juvenile for firing a weapon at a moving car during a botched drug deal.[27] And in 2021, two members of the Base, Patrik Mathews and Brian Lemley, pleaded guilty to various firearms and immigration charges related to planned attacks that entailed "crippling such infrastructure as roads and power plants to provoke a White uprising," assassinating elected representatives, killing police officers, and overthrowing the U.S. government. Prosecu-tors had requested twenty-five-year prison terms. Mathews and Lemley were sentenced to nine years' imprisonment—and only after the presiding judge invoked special "terrorist enhancement" provisions that extended their time in prison to three times that of federal sentencing guidelines.[28] By comparison, Nicholas Young, a former suburban Virginia police officer, was sentenced in 2018 to fifteen years in prison on charges of attempting to provide material support to ISIS.[29] And in 2022, Jonathan Guerra Blanco of Miami, Florida, was sentenced to sixteen years in prison after he was similarly convicted of attempting to provide material support to ISIS.[30] With such disparity, recidivism becomes a serious concern when it comes to countering far-right terrorism. In February 2023, Brandon Russell was again arrested and charged with an accomplice for plotting to attack five electrical power substations in Maryland and thereby "completely destroy" Baltimore.[31] The Atomwaffen leader had been released from his previous sentence on explosives charges in August 2021.

However, endowing the U.S. attorney general and the DOJ with the ability to designate violent extremist groups and individuals as domestic terrorists is both controversial and challenging. Several critics of this proposal—including the RAND Corporation's longstanding terrorism expert Brian M. Jenkins and the former FBI agent and now Brennan Center analyst Michael German—have argued that the designation of domestic violent extremist groups as terrorist organizations would inevitably become dangerously politicized and partisan. They fear that, using such a law, a future authoritarian president could simply designate any group or movement that protested, demonstrated against, or otherwise disagreed with that leader's policies as terrorists.[32] Ensuring that only the perpetrators of lethal violence—or plots to commit lethal violence—are charged could help ensure that the law was never used against peaceful protestors or extremists who nonetheless eschew violence. And should a far-left extremist then murder somebody in furtherance of their ideology, they would be indeed eligible to be charged with the domestic terrorism statute. Those fearing overbearing legal remedies should remember that in 1870 President Ulysses S. Grant created the Department of Justice specifically to counter far-right terrorism from the Ku Klux Klan and other violent groups active in post–Civil War southern states.[33] A new domestic terrorism law seems a small step in comparison and would send a resounding societal message of opprobrium that there is no place for political violence in a democracy. Legislation establishing a domestic terrorism legal category would also contain provisions that would ensure the improved collection, collation, and analysis of data across states and localities throughout the United States, which does not exist in any uniform fashion now.

Efforts also need to be directed internationally against violent foreign groups that provide operational guidance and ideological encouragement to cells or individuals who carry out terrorist attacks whether independently or at the direct behest of these organizations. The White House should therefore direct the State Department to designate foreign neo-Nazi and white supremacist groups whose activities make them candidates for inclusion in its list of foreign terrorist organizations (FTOs). At present, of the seventy-three foreign terrorist organizations on the list, no relevant neo-Nazi or white supremacist groups are included. This is surprising in view of the fact that the latest iteration of the *National Strategy for Counterterrorism of the United States of America*, released in October 2018, described two violent, far-right extremist organizations—the Nordic Resistance Movement in Scandinavian countries and the National Action Group in the United Kingdom—as groups "whose use of violence and intent to destabilize societies often puts American lives at risk."[34] In April 2020 the State Department did designate the Russian Imperial Movement—a transnational, violent far-right extremist group—as a Specially Designated Global Terrorist, imposing a variety of restrictive financial counterterrorism measures.[35] The Treasury Department in January 2023 additionally listed the Wagner Group, a Russian paramilitary group with far-right elements, as a "significant transnational criminal organization" for its activities in Ukraine and beyond.[36] But these categories are a step below FTO designation, and the logic behind the decision to use the lesser classifications was never fully explicated. The FTO designation would prove particularly useful should the potentiality of white supremacist foreign fighters migrating from one conflict to another emerge. The Base, an international neo-Nazi organization run from Saint Petersburg, Russia, and responsible for several violent plots in the United States, is an obvious candidate for FTO designation.[37] Additional candidates include the Feuerkrieg Division in the Baltics and, as noted, the National Action Group in Britain and Nordic Resistance Movement in Scandinavia. This would send a powerful message from the United States to other countries that, much as America was in the lead in the Global War on Terror against transnational Salafi jihadist terrorist groups threatening world security, the United States will again be in the lead regarding global efforts to counter the rise of transnational far-right terrorism.

In addition to FTO designations and a domestic terrorism law, lawmakers should also consider measures to enhance the enforcement of existing gun laws as well as additional steps that make mass shootings more difficult to execute and armed insurrection less likely. Mass shootings, abetted by the widespread commercial availability of firearms, have in recent years become a favored tactic of domestic terrorists—but debates over gun control have too often devolved into black-and-white, all-or-nothing shouting matches. Instead, the U.S. government should take a more nuanced approach, one focused on both preventing and thwarting acts of mass casualty violence using firearms while protecting law-abiding individual gun owners' rights to self-defense and guaranteeing Second Amendment freedoms. A more exhaustive and better-enforced gun licensing system, including enhanced and more rigorously conducted background checks; prohibitions against unregistered sales and transfers of firearms; and stronger bans on straw purchases need to be considered. Legislation to restrict the sale of the most lethal, so-called cop-killer ammunition, which can pierce even reinforced ceramic plates, could provide a sensible starting point for broader discussions about how to discourage or disincentivize ownership of other extraordinarily lethal weaponry. Sensible firearms laws that better protect society but preserve Second Amendment rights need to be bipartisan and delicately framed so as to assuage the concerns that coalesced to produce national tragedies like the 1995 Oklahoma City bombing. They also need to be designed in a way that deprives violent extremist groups of a powerful emotional argument with which to rally support and attract recruits. The Biden administration's bipartisan gun control legislation, which was signed into law in June 2022 and promised enhanced background checks for young gun buyers and also expanded mental health services, was an important first step in this direction.[38]

In addition to these measures to curb overall gun violence, U.S. lawmakers should act to end the production and trade of 3D-printed firearms and other lethal homemade weapons. Fearing the future enactment of new gun control legislation in Germany, for instance, the Halle synagogue shooter Stephan Balliet claimed in his manifesto, which included details on how he had fabricated his homemade weapons, to be providing invaluable information to would-be violent extremists in other countries—which he termed "no-fun countries." Balliet, like Breivik, Tarrant, and others, deliberately sought to inspire imitation and emulation through his attack—in this case with the additional intention of providing guidance to others about how to manufacture their own firearms and thus commit their own acts of terrorism. Many violent extremists, particularly in Europe, already see homemade firearms as an attractive option both to undermine and frustrate gun regulation.[39] The prevalence of commercially produced firearms in the United States should not deflect attention to this issue or obfuscate the need for proactive legislative responses in the United States regarding "ghost" guns and 3D-manufactured firearms. Gun control has been among the more effective counterterrorism measures employed by European governments. Adapting this lesson to the American context—while also protecting against homemade circumvention—thus remains a pressing need.

Finally, Congress might also consider more aggressive steps to identify, root out, and perhaps criminalize personnel espousing and adhering to violent extremism in the U.S. military and law enforcement. The services have grappled with spasmodic outbursts of racism and violent manifestations of hate within the ranks for decades. These efforts, while mostly successful, need to be enforced and reemphasized. Following the January 6, 2021, attack on the U.S. Capitol, the new secretary of defense, retired U.S. Army General Lloyd Austin, the first African American to occupy that office, ordered a one-day military-wide stand-down devoted to discussing hate and intolerance across the entire military. He also appointed a Pentagon task force that was charged with recommending measures to raise awareness of and mitigate extremism within the ranks. Austin drew on his own experience fighting extremism in the military, having served as a lieutenant colonel in the 82nd Airborne when the 1995 Fayetteville racially motivated killings took place. "We woke up one day and discovered that we had extremist elements in our ranks, and they did bad things that we certainly held them accountable for," the secretary explained in his confirmation hearing. "But we discovered that the signs for that activity were there all along. We just didn't know what to look for or what to pay attention to—but we learned from that."[40] The Defense Department issued revised guidance in December 2021 that imposed harsher measures for soldiers actively participating in such groups. Military personnel simply "liking" certain social media posts could now face disciplinary action.[41]

Recruitment of U.S. military veterans into violent extremist organizations should also be a major concern for the Department of Veterans Affairs (VA), as it now is for the DoD. Congressional pressure and oversight would ensure that both the DoD and VA continue to focus on countering hatred and intolerance and implement policies designed to address the vulnerability of veterans to recruitment by extremists from both ends of the ideological spectrum. The VA in particular needs to pay ongoing attention to veterans recovering from psychological and physical wounds caused by their time in service to protect them from the appeal of extremist groups advocating violence.[42] Additional efforts to address suicide among military veterans could have the ancillary benefit of dampening the appeal of violent political extremists who prey on vulnerable former servicemen and women. But the military, too, must remain vigilant to infiltration by violent, political extremists and the inadvertent recruitment of extremists, treating it as both a self-defense and readiness priority. Maintaining recruitment and retention standards along with both initial and ongoing screening of enlistees would help keep out those who seek to infiltrate the services, while counterintelligence efforts focused specifically on violent, political extremism would highlight the threat that hatred and intolerance poses to military readiness and performance. America's armed services rightly take pride in being one of the country's most successfully diverse and integrated institutions. Accordingly, any measures to root out hatred and intolerance within the ranks should take care to protect and celebrate the vast majority of servicemembers and veterans who serve honorably and bravely and do not embrace violent political extremism and its attendant seditious ideologies.

The problem of extremist infiltration of law enforcement agencies and departments across the country presents another significant challenge to countering violent extremism in the United States. At least nineteen current or former police officers, for instance, have been charged with violent offences during the January 6, 2021, storming of the U.S. Capitol—including assaulting U.S. Capitol Police and District of Columbia

Metropolitan Police deployed to protect the building.[43] A 2022 report by the Anti-Defamation League analyzed leaked membership information that the Distributed Denial of Secrets collective, a nonprofit journalist entity, obtained from the Oath Keepers. Of the 38,000 names and personal details in the membership database, the ADL was able to identify at least 373 Oath Keepers currently serving in law enforcement agencies and departments throughout the United States (there were additionally "117 individuals who . . . currently serve in the U.S. military, an additional 11 people who serve in the reserves, and 31 individuals who hold civilian positions or are military contractors"). They range from patrol officers to individuals in senior command positions; among them are detectives, sergeants, lieutenants, and captains. Some of these officers are alleged to have provided information and training derived from their experiences in law enforcement to fellow Oath Keepers. In addition, the ADL determined that 1,100 former law enforcement officers have similarly provided training and assistance to Oath Keeper members. Officers knowledgeable of police intelligence-gathering techniques, undercover investigations, forensics, communications, and other law enforcement tasks are able to enhance, improve, and better secure the operations of violent extremist organizations and thereby enable them to obviate and frustrate real law enforcement.[44]

Considering that the Oath Keepers organization has reportedly claimed to have tens of thousands of members who are either current or former law enforcement officers, the ADL's figures may be far smaller than the actual extent of infiltration.[45] A first order of business for federal authorities should be to determine the number of officers actively involved with violent extremist organizations such as the Oath Keepers, among others. Then, once that determination is made and active membership in a violent and/or seditious movement is defined and determined, legal processes, such as decertification of law enforcement officers and that individual's employment termination, should be considered as appropriate. A second needed step would be both to require and strengthen instruction and training of law enforcement about far-right terrorism, including hate crimes—along with threats from the far left as well. Many police departments across the United States still lack comprehensive national standard training for hate crimes, which are in fact no different from domestic terrorism.[46] Only eighteen states have statutes requiring training for law enforcement to identify, respond to, and collect data about hate crimes.[47] Setting nationwide training standards for law enforcement to recognize and report incidents of violent extremism along with the additional training of victim witness advocates who deal with the targets of such violence are essential measures both to understand the dimensions and patterns of these crimes and to provide effective assistance to those who have experienced them, whether as victims or witnesses. Ensuring that law enforcement takes the threat of infiltration and collusion seriously is especially important considering that most domestic terrorist killings of police officers are committed by extremists on the violent far right of the ideological spectrum and not, as is frequently assumed, by anarchists or others associated with far left extremism.[48]

• • •

Social media regulation and laws criminalizing terrorist plotting and other manifestations of extremist violence, though, are wholly defensive. Although these measures can hamper recruitment and radicalization in the short term, they are unable to achieve tangible, lasting results in countering violent extremism. They therefore need to be complemented and strengthened with more medium-term, active efforts to strengthen civil society, including by combating radicalization and extremist ideology. While these efforts, it should be emphasized, are unlikely to achieve immediate results, they are essential in reducing over time the attractiveness of these movements and their violently oriented ideologies.

Countering violent extremism (CVE) addresses the "demand side" (or "push factors") of extremist radicalization—targeting the conditions and circumstances that make some people more vulnerable to radicalization and recruitment. CVE programs can encompass a range of measures, from interventions led by former extremists seeking to deradicalize their former comrades to counternarratives shared online and in local communities to undermine extremist messaging and arguments favoring violence. Community-based initiatives are also a critical component to strengthen and encourage positive engagement in civil society. They are typically supported by government grants but organized and implemented by nongovernment organizations, often at the grassroots, local level.

Greater government resources should therefore be devoted to expand and deepen these critical CVE efforts. They should aim as well to proactively address potential community vulnerabilities and thus penetrate deeper into the extremist ecosystem that encourages, justifies, and celebrates violence.

Effective CVE would better address the mental health issues or past traumas of those attracted to and by violent ideologies. The roles that personal histories involving loneliness and isolation as well as bullying and harassment play in radicalization remain both poorly understood and unaddressed. Terrorist organizations like the Atomwaffen Division, for instance, have long prioritized recruitment of loners and other people isolated from mainstream society. James Mason, one of the most important proponents of neo-Nazi ideology in the United States, wrote in *Siege* that "to be outside this society is a marked badge of honor"[49]—and makes it easier for these movements to harness frustration and anger and convert them into violence and revenge. Radicalization today is not just caused by longstanding prejudices or hatred and viciousness; it can also arise from individual pain and suffering. In the words of the former white supremacist Arno Michaelis: "hurt people hurt people."[50] Whenever a violent extremist movement successfully recruits someone with a history of developmental mental health issues or who was a victim of bullying, the threat to our society consequently also increases.

Improving domestic CVE efforts will require deeper research into the violent extremist offline universe. The 2020s have seen the growth of so-called free spaces, both online and offline, that have crossed into the gaming world and have now entrenched themselves on social media.[51] A number of questions with critical counterterrorism implications, however, mostly remain unanswered, such as:

- How does far-right culture, including music and sport, facilitate radicalization into the movement and lead to violence?
- How do drugs and alcohol as well as mental health vulnerabilities encourage one's self-destructive spiral into increasingly violent extremist company?
- How does the gaming world and the camaraderie and friendship it provides introduce violent ideas to new recruits? And,

- What makes a life in the shadows, underground, more attractive than a productive life in society?

The importance of studying life and culture among violent far-right extremists is exemplified by the former neo-Nazi, skinhead rocker Christian Picciolini's own recollections of how he drifted into the movement—as well as how he got out. "Music," he says, "was the common link allowing us all to see we were not lost and alone. In it we found each other, and through it we collectively directed our teen angst at a grown-up society we saw as intolerant of us."[52] Picciolini eventually discovered the white nationalist punk rock band Skrewdriver, led by a neo-Nazi named Ian Stuart Donaldson, and was further radicalized by the lyrics of the band's songs. But music also helped him leave years later. Opening his own record store forced Picciolini to interact with an increasingly diverse clientele, which slowly made him more tolerant of people of other sexual orientations, races, and religions, and this eventually challenged his extremist views and commitment to violence. "I'd spent so many years immersing myself in the movement that the diversity of my customer base continued to fascinate me," Picciolini writes.

> I began to meet gay and Jewish customers. Our conversations were brief, guarded at first, but slowly we got to know each other through our shared interest in music. And they kept coming back. I was indebted to their business, and I found myself thinking clearly, "These are good people. I don't want to hurt them." . . . I'd started opening up to people who looked different from me, and life had become interesting in a way I never would have guessed it could.[53]

There is an understandable proclivity among counterterrorism experts and practitioners to focus on ideology, processes of radicalization, and terrorist tactics and strategy. But by ignoring the world behind the violence, the lived experiences enjoyed and suffered by the movement's denizens, and the cultural touchstones that cement a sense of community among an otherwise geographically and ideologically diverse mass, there is an equally great risk of misidentifying the key factors that sustain the movement, drawing in those looking for belonging and a purpose and cementing their membership in such groups. In the words of the terrorist scholar

Alessandro Orsini, who successfully infiltrated Italian neofascist groups, "the parallel world isn't a sudden, momentary eruption of violence but a symbolic universe that is built up day after day."[54] And while terrorism scholars have devoted significant time and resources to studying radicalization and to analyzing how and why individuals join extremist movements and groups, insufficient attention has been dedicated to understanding how and why individuals *stay* in a violent movement. The keys to entrenchment might unlock more effective approaches to deradicalization and provide a clearer picture of the attraction of living life underground, or at least what makes it difficult to abandon it. This research could help clarify the narratives that the counterterrorism community needs to employ to disincentivize the drift into violent extremism. Studying stories like Picciolini's is thus essential in understanding what might encourage somebody to exit the movement—and may help shed light on how those qualities can therefore be brought to extremists in order to encourage their disengagement.

Toward the end of his 1,500-page manifesto, Anders Behring Breivik offers an extract from *In Praise of the New Knighthood*, written by Bernard of Clairvaux in the twelfth century. Eulogizing the lifestyle of the Knights Templar, Bernard writes, "Thus in a wondrous and unique manner they appear gentler than lambs, yet fiercer than lions. I do not know if it would be more appropriate to refer to them as monks or as soldiers, unless perhaps it would be better to recognize them as being both. Indeed they lack neither monastic meekness nor military might."[55] The romance with which Breivik saw his act stands in stark contrast to the wanton bloodshed that took place on Utøya Island, where sixty-nine people, the majority of whom were children, were murdered on July 22, 2011. But the counterterrorism implications of Breivik's allegory should not be dismissed or ignored. In every lion, there is perhaps potentially a lamb. In every soldier, there may also be a monk. How these nonviolent tendencies within people prone to or already enmeshed in violence could reveal new pathways to identify the lamb and the monk and deflect their misguided altruism to nonviolent means of change before they turn to terrorism is thus an important consideration.

Crucially, CVE is best done by nongovernmental organizations. Two of the key lessons of this book's historical analysis of far-right terrorism in America are the intense distrust that the U.S. government generates among precisely the target audience of these efforts and the fact that the U.S. government alone cannot make lasting inroads against these violently inclined extremists. Rather, a truly effective public-private partnership is needed to more fully undermine the threat. To maximize credibility in the prevention realm, government should arguably play a more passive role by encouraging both the private and nonprofit sectors to build strong programs, along with metrics that can measure the programs' successes and failures, while managing and ensuring that effective programming is both well funded and sustainable. Social impact bonds, which tie additional funding to tangible programmatic success, may provide an encouraging model for ensuring effective organizations and programs retain their funding over the long term.[56]

We must note that CVE efforts have historically also been controversial. Criticism has focused on failures to find viable interlocutors who are politically moderate but still have credibility with extremists. Respected members of targeted communities have also found themselves in the unenviable position of having to explain and justify both programmatic failures and the targeted community's inability to police its own. Finally, critics have condemned CVE programs for securitizing teachers and guidance and mental health counselors by turning them into government informants or blaming them for failing to identify a budding extremist at the earliest possible stage.[57] Lessons need to be studied and learned from some of the excesses that involved Muslim communities in the years following the September 11, 2001, attacks. This responsibility is best managed by nongovernmental organizations, who are better placed to identify credible, local moderates and interlocutors who can effectively engage and communicate with people likely to be attracted to violent ideologies.

Both the government and private sector are needed to explore the potential for instituting media (also known as digital) literacy training into educational programs at all age levels. This would enhance the ability of citizens to identify false or malicious online information and hopefully impart skills with which to better navigate the digital world—what some term "cyber citizenship."[58] Efforts to improve media literacy were specifically cited in the Biden administration's 2021 domestic terrorism strategy. "Today's digital age requires an American population that can utilize essential aspects of Internet-based communications platforms," the document states, "while avoiding vulnerability to domestic terrorist recruitment and other harmful content deliberately disseminated by malicious actors online, such as international terrorist groups like al-Qa'ida trying to incite imminent violence or hostile foreign powers seeking to undermine American democracy." In implementing the strategy, the White House pledged to "pursue innovative ways to foster and cultivate digital literacy and related programs, including educational materials and interactive online resources such as skills-enhancing online games. This can prove a useful component," it concluded, "to forging the resilience that may help to stem domestic terrorism recruitment and mobilization to violence."[59] Various branches of the U.S. government have begun to create and fund media literacy programming,[60] and efforts are also being undertaken at community levels to strengthen resilience as early as the elementary-school age group.[61] Several European countries have also pioneered media literacy programming—including the United Kingdom, through its RESIST disinformation toolkit.[62] Meaningful progress in this critical area, however, remains uncertain both in this country and abroad.

Strengthening media literacy is admittedly designed more to prevent the next generation from radicalizing and being drawn to violent extremism, but it is also perhaps the only way to effectively counter widespread conspiracy theories such as those propagated by QAnon. The movement rose to prominence through an imploration to its followers to "do your own research"—which resulted in millions of Americans seemingly without the skills to discern fact from fiction uncritically swallowing the pervasive disinformation linking the Democratic Party to pedophilia. The effects of this conspiratorial mindset were highlighted in a post-arrest interview of a QAnon supporter from Iowa who was taped chasing the Capitol Police officer Eugene Goodman up the stairs and through the corridors of the U.S. Senate on January 6. This person had entered the building in the expectation that he would witness the mass arrests of elected officials who refused to invalidate the presidential electoral results.[63] "Am I being duped?" he asked an FBI agent, a seeming glimmer of realization at last reaching him. "Can you guys let me in on that if you know those arrests are real?"[64]

A potential countermeasure to such disinformation and its pernicious effects is perhaps to embrace QAnon's suggestion to "do your own research"—but by providing guidance and encouragement on how to acquire one's information from accurate and reliable sources. By imparting both education and better skills to identify disinformation and patent falsehoods, citizens would be able to make judgments and reach conclusions based on accurate and reliable information sources. Government should act as the convener and funder of such efforts but not direct or oversee them, as any attempt by federal authorities, for instance, to either "teach" or "train" Americans in social media best practices will immediately be dismissed by precisely the people most in need of this education as indoctrination and propaganda—and therefore lose all credibility. Initiatives such as media literacy need to be pursued, encouraged, and implemented through grassroots initiatives—including at schools, places of worship, community groups, business associations, and other civic institutions. They should also be implemented at home with respect to families with children who are increasingly targeted for radicalization and recruitment by violent extremists.[65] Our educational system, however, neither prioritizes instruction on these vital tools nor provides guidance to teachers on how to educate our students. Social studies curricula, for instance, could provide students with skills that are currently rarely taught in schools but would greatly enhance their critical thinking and research skills, such as:

- How to identify credible information sources and understand the reasons that they are reliable;
- How to determine if someone is indeed an expert on a subject and is therefore imparting accurate and authoritative information; and,
- How to identify trusted information sources and find reliable information, ideally from multiple sources, on especially contentious issues.[66]

Media literacy training, in concert with steps to moderate social media, would also have the benefit of better inculcating U.S. citizens against the disinformation promulgated by foreign state adversaries and more generally in countering the dangerous embrace toward authoritarianism now challenging many democratic states.

Beyond countering extremism through the public health and educational lenses that CVE encourages, socioeconomic and development initiatives can also help build resilience against radicalization and counter the appeal of antigovernment and antiestablishment conspiracy theories. Bringing improved access to broadband in America's rural communities would not only help enhance digital literacy on a truly national basis; it would also bring economic growth, better health care, and additional benefits to neglected or forgotten corners of the country.[67] According to a 2018 Federal Communications Commission report, 25 percent of rural Americans did not have access to high-speed internet connections, compared with 1.5 percent of Americans living in cities.[68] This disparity has fueled the resentment already permeating America's rural areas among impoverished communities that feel neglected and forgotten by an uncaring federal government. Such sentiments are grist for the antigovernment milieu that generates violent extremism. As the policy analysts Mark Dornauer and Robert Bryce argue: "The lack of broadband in rural areas is one of the most striking inequalities in US society."[69]

The Infrastructure Investment and Jobs Act (IIJA), passed by Congress in 2022, is an important step in remedying this urban-rural disparity of connectivity. Nonetheless, concerns remain that even this important legislation will still "leave millions of Americans disconnected, especially those already restricted in their economic and social mobilities."[70] A concerted effort to improve communication access across the country would have significant symbolic and tangible economic and societal benefits. It could prove as transformative for America's rural areas today as President Franklin Roosevelt's New Deal initiatives for the same regions were nearly a century ago. In 1930, for instance, nine out of ten rural farms and ranches lacked electricity. Both the Public Utility Holding Company Act of 1935 and the Rural Electrification Act of 1936 began to connect these localities to the electric grid. Within twenty years electricity was brought to nine out of ten rural farms and ranches. Today, nearly all rural areas that want access to electricity can obtain it.[71] A similar investment is needed today to expand broadband and cell phone coverage nationwide; this could pay vast dividends in fostering greater economic opportunity, enhancing digital literacy, and bringing improved access to reliable and trustworthy information sources. More widespread broadband of course poses a risk, too, as it could provide easier access for many to the vast quantities of online extremist material. This only reinforces why pushing social media companies to create more healthy platforms is the first and most essential step. Such an initiative could also tangibly help heal the divisions in education, medical care, wealth, and attitudes that separate rural from urban America. Improved access to the communications capabilities enjoyed by the vast majority of the country's population mostly concentrated in and around cities could also mitigate the "have" and "have not" mentality that generates resentment toward "bi-coastal elites" and fosters great polarization and new corrosive forms of populist sentiment.[72]

. . .

While a healthier social media ecosystem, new laws more harshly punishing domestic terrorist plotting, a range of countering violent extremism programming, and development measures to bring greater opportunities and perhaps prosperity to America's forgotten communities would all help incrementally push back against violent far-right extremism, the most critical imperative in fact transcends counterterrorism and is instead essential to the broader health of our nation. In the long term, the United States needs to restore, reenergize, and strengthen its democratic norms and institutions, rebuilding faith in the system and encouraging politicians and public alike to once again place country above party. The wanton assault on the federal electoral system in the wake of the 2020 presidential election sought to undermine trust and faith in American democracy—an objective that this book has shown has been building for decades. Spreading doubts about election integrity for partisan gain without regard to tangible evidence of malfeasance, should it continue unimpeded, will systematically erode the foundational values of our republic. We now live in a climate of crippling political polarization, where anger and distrust are the primary currency—and where votes and support are not always won through cooperation and promises of a better world but often by opposition to the opposition. Terrorism is, fundamentally, also an ineluctably political process—a strategic decision made by violent extremists who no longer believe in the existence of peaceful political solutions to address their grievances.[73] Overheated language that feeds an increasingly polarized, absolutist mindset thus only serves to encourage violent mobilization and terrorist-imposed solutions.

One salient challenge in fighting domestic terrorism today has been the inability of many of the former president's supporters to admit a problem actually exists. Over one hundred Republican members of the House of Representatives, for instance, responded to the January 6 insurrection by nonetheless voting to invalidate the 2020 presidential election results. A year later, former Speaker of the House Newt Gingrich declared on Fox News that, following a Republican victory in the next election, those working on the January 6, 2021, congressional committee would be arrested.[74] The persistence of these beliefs is vitiated by the facts, given that elected officials of both parties were targeted for assassination on January 6—including Vice President Mike Pence. These political divisions and the partisan credulousness they have produced with respect to the events on January 6 make any hopes of achieving national unity difficult. They are also a dangerous departure from our collective ability to recover from past incidents of national trauma. And, there is of course every likelihood that America's foreign enemies will take advantage of domestic divisiveness and disunity to advance their own malignant national interests and totalitarian aims.

Restoring national unity and the common sense of purpose that once existed in American politics will likely prove the most effective means to counter domestic terrorism and blunt foreign efforts to undermine the power and stature of the United States. There was once an arguably more halcyon time, when despite political differences and disagreement, a bipartisan spirit of cooperation mostly prevailed—as exemplified by the surgeon treating President Ronald Reagan following the attempt on his life in 1981, who declared, "Today, Mr. President, we are all Republicans."[75] And there was the moment not so long ago when members of Congress from both parties gathered together on the steps of the U.S. Capitol on the evening of September 11, 2001, to sing "God Bless America." Another example of bipartisan comity and national unity worth noting occurred in New Zealand in connection with that country's response to the tragic terrorist attacks on two mosques in 2019. The Christchurch Commission report, chaired by a Supreme Court justice and presented to the government the following year, was titled *Ko tō tātou kāinga tēnei*—Maori for "This is our home"—an ironclad statement of unity across party, race,

252 COUNTERING FAR-RIGHT TERRORISM

culture, and language.[76] Such grace has rarely been seen in America after acts of far-right terrorism. Lawmakers across the aisle in this country should emulate their New Zealand counterparts and need to reestablish norms that reject the use of divisive language and violence, to ensure that those who spread hate are once again marginalized to the fringes of the political spectrum.

These bromides might appear excessively idealistic. But at a time when fear of civil war has again surfaced, it bears remembering that this country has faced profound internal strife and division before—and emerged intact. The fabric of the nation was stitched back together despite hundreds of thousands of deaths during the Civil War, with many on the losing side putting aside their loss and resentment to build a more promising future by working to reunite the country. As Amos T. Akerman, a former colonel in the Confederate Army, reflected regarding his decision to join the Grant administration as attorney general of the newly formed Department of Justice, "Some of us who had adhered to the Confederacy felt it to be our duty when we were to participate in the politics of the Union, to let Confederate ideas rule us no longer. . . . Regarding the subjugation of one race by the other as an appurtenance of slavery, we were content that it should go to the grave in which slavery had been buried."[77] And the assassinations of leading political and civil rights figures during the 1960s, against the backdrop of widespread antiwar and civil rights demonstrations, also failed to undermine the country's march toward a more just future. Precedent suggests that America will rise again, its internal wounds insufficient to diminish the luster of what Ronald Reagan called a "shining city on a hill." For that to happen again, the dangerous slide toward the normalization of political violence as a legitimate form of activism and the undermining of this country's hallowed democratic processes must end, through a bipartisan commitment from both parties and its leaders to a renewed faith in America's fundamental values of democracy, its system of governance, and the rule of law.

• • •

Many of the initiatives outlined in this chapter will not produce immediate results—some may take decades to mature and prove effective. But by initiating them now, we will begin the groundwork to ensure that future generations are not subjected to the same threats of domestic political violence we face today. By combining short-term measures to better regulate social media and create a stronger legal response to violent acts that are in fact domestic terrorism, medium-term steps to strengthen the resilience of the American public against extremism and radicalization, and a long-term commitment to restoring the faith of the American people in their government and elected officials, the United States can build a society that is far more resistant to the centrifugal forces of fear, hate, and intolerance. Terrorism will still occur. But, even if terrorism cannot ever be completely eliminated, America can strive toward a future where politically motivated violence is not tolerated nor excused—and where those who choose the violent option are shunned, shamed, and incarcerated for the terrorist crimes they commit and do not provide a heroic example for others to follow.

Finally, contrary to the conventional wisdom, terrorism and the prominence of leaderless resistance strategies should be seen not as an indication of weakness of the Western, liberal state but of its strength. In the words of the University of St Andrews historian Dr. Tim Wilson, the resort to lone-actor attacks should actually be seen as "an unwilling tribute to the power of the state at the dawn of the internet age."[78] The renowned terrorism expert Martha Crenshaw similarly argues that "an organization or faction of an organization may choose terrorism because other methods are not expected to work or are considered too time-consuming, given the urgency of the situation and the government's superior resources."[79] Terrorism is thus embraced by violent extremists who believe they have no other viable alternatives to implement their fringe agenda. As has always been the case, stressing the availability of peaceful political alternatives in a democracy is thus an educational and civics priority of the highest imperative.

Terrorism is also a strategy of provocation; it is meant to provoke governments to react in ways that play into the terrorists' narrative of reluctant warriors cast on the defensive against an allegedly predatory, aggressive state.[80] "Terrorism has prevailed in the past, but not because terrorists vanquished their foes with car bombs or with assassinations," the historians Laqueur and Wall note. "They succeeded when governments overreacted."[81] Accordingly, less lethal and physically destructive terrorist acts than on September, 11, 2001, such as the Oslo attacks of July 22, 2011, and the January 6, 2021, assault on the U.S. Capitol building, may pose greater long-term threats to Western liberal democracy. They force domestic audiences to pick sides, to organize against fellow compatriots and their homegrown ideologies, complicating cooperation and a nuanced government response, and slowly corroding democracies from within. Maintaining national cohesiveness when confronting individuals who seek to divide societies—a goal that today has become increasingly difficult—is thus absolutely vital.

NOTES

PREFACE

1. Bruce Hoffman, *Right-Wing Terrorism in Europe*, N-1856-AF (Santa Monica, CA: RAND Corporation, March 1982); Hoffman, "Right-Wing Terrorism in Europe Since 1980," *Orbis* no. 1 (Spring 1984); Hoffman, "Right-Wing Terrorism in Europe," *Conflict* 5, no. 3 (Fall 1984); Hoffman, *Right-Wing Terrorism in Germany*, Research Report No. 13, Institute of Jewish Affairs, London, England, December 1986; Hoffman, "Right-Wing Terrorism in Europe," in *European Terrorism*, ed. Edward Moxon-Browne (New York: G. K. Hall, 1994); and Hoffman, "American Right-Wing Extremism," *Jane's Intelligence Review* 7, no. 7 (July 1995).

2. For example, the long-since-closed Rocky Flats Environmental Technology Site in Colorado along with the still active ones such as the Hanford Site in Washington state; the Idaho National Laboratory in Idaho Falls, Idaho; the Pantex Ordnance Plant in Amarillo, Texas; the Los Alamos National Laboratory in New Mexico; and the Nevada National Security Site outside Las Vegas.

3. Bruce Hoffman, *Terrorism in the United States and the Potential Threat to Nuclear Weapons Facilities*, R-3351-DOE (Santa Monica, CA: RAND Corporation, January 1986); Hoffman, *A Reassessment of Potential Adversaries to U.S. Nuclear Programs*, R-3363-DOE (Santa Monica, CA: RAND Corporation, March 1986); Hoffman, *The Threat of Nuclear Terrorism: A Reassessment*, N-2706 (Santa Monica, CA: RAND Corporation, January 1988); Hoffman, *Insider Crimes: The Threat to Nuclear Facilities and Programs*, R-3782-DOE (Santa Monica, CA: RAND Corporation, February 1990); and Hoffman, *Force-on-Force Attacks: Their Implications for the Defense of U.S. Nuclear Facilities*, N-3638-DOE (Santa Monica, CA: RAND Corporation, 1993).

4. Hoffman, *Recent Trends and Future Prospects of Terrorism in the United States*, R-3618 (Santa Monica, CA: RAND Corporation, May 1988).

5. Kevin Jack Riley and Bruce Hoffman. *Domestic Terrorism: A National Assessment of State and Local Preparedness*, MR-505-NIJ (Santa Monica, CA: RAND Corporation, 1995).

6. Jacob Ware, "Siege: The Atomwaffen Division and Rising Far-Right Terrorism in the United States," International Centre for Counter-Terrorism–The Hague, July 2019, https://icct.nl/publication/siege-the-atomwaffen-division-and-rising-far-right -terrorism-in-the-united-states/.

1. ACCELERATIONISM REBORN

1. See, for instance, Daniel Byman, "Riots, White Supremacy, and Accelerationism," Brookings Institution, June 2, 2020, https://www.brookings.edu/blog/order-from-chaos /2020/06/02/riots-white-supremacy-and-accelerationism/; Daveed Gartenstein-Ross, Samuel Hodgson, and Colin P. Clarke, "The Growing Threat Posed by Acceleration- ism and Accelerationist Groups Worldwide," Foreign Policy Research Institute, April 20, 2020, https://www.fpri.org/article/2020/04/the-growing-threat-posed-by -accelerationism-and-accelerationist-groups-worldwide/; "Intelbrief: White Suprema- cists and the Weaponization of the Coronavirus (COVID-19)," Soufan Center, March 25, 2020, https://thesoufancenter.org/intelbrief-white-supremacists-and-the -weaponization-of-the-coronavirus-covid-19/; and Cassie Miller, "White Supremacists See Coronavirus as an Opportunity," Southern Poverty Law Center, March 26, 2020, https://www.splcenter.org/hatewatch/2020/03/26/white-supremacists-see-coronavirus -opportunity.

2. Donald J. Trump (@realDonaldTrump), Twitter, April 17, 2020, 11:25 AM, https://twitter .com/realdonaldtrump/status/1251169987110330372; Hannah Allam, " 'Boogaloo' Is the New Far-Right Slang for Civil War," *All Things Considered*, National Public Radio, Jan- uary 10, 2020, https://www.npr.org/2020/01/10/795366630/boogaloo-is-the-new-far -right-slang-for-civil-war; "COVID-19 Disinformation Briefing No. 2: Far-Right Mobil- isation," Institute for Strategic Dialogue, April 9, 2020, https://www.isdglobal.org/wp -content/uploads/2020/04/Covid-19-Briefing-PDF.pdf.

3. Screenshot, April 25, 2020, 4:30:07 PM, taken by one of the authors.

4. Campaign for Accountability, "Broken Promises: Extremists Are Using Facebook to Organize for Civil War Amid Coronavirus," Tech Transparency Project, April 22, 2020, https://www.techtransparencyproject.org/articles/extremists-are-using-facebook-to -organize-for-civil-war-amid-coronavirus. According to Facebook, "Groups are a place to communicate about shared interests with certain people. You can create a group for anything—your family reunion, your after-work sports team or your book club." Face- book, "About Groups," https://www.facebook.com/help/1629740080681586; "Join and Interact with Groups," Facebook Help Center, https://www.facebook.com/help /1210322209008185.

5. Screenshots, April 25, 2020, 4:22:04 PM; April 26, 2020, 8:56:22 AM; April 25, 2020, 4:32:52 PM, taken by one of the authors.

6. Quoted in "Accelerationist Neo-Nazis Threaten Journalists Following Media Reports of Health Organization Data Leak," SITE Intelligence Group, April 22, 2020, https://ent .siteintelgroup.com/Far-Right-/-Far-Left-Threat/accelerationist-neo-nazis-threaten -journalists-following-media-reports-of-health-organization-data-leak.html.

7. Quoted in "Praising Accelerationism, Neo-Nazis Call For Sniper Attacks Targeting 'Elites,'" SITE Intelligence Group, April 24, 2020, https://ent.siteintelgroup.com/Far -Right-Far-Left-Threat/praising-accelerationism-neo-nazis-call-for-sniper-attacks -targeting-elites.html.

8. Quoted in "Neo-Nazi Venues Suggest Followers Avoid Lockdown Protests, Encourage Alternative Methods Of 'Stoking Tensions,'" SITE Intelligence Group, May 5, 2020, https://ent.siteintelgroup.com/Far-Right-Far-Left-Threat/neo-nazi-venues-suggest -followers-avoid-lockdown-protests-encourage-alternative-methods-of-stoking-ten sions.html.

9. Quoted in "Exploiting Chaos of Riots, Prominent Neo-Nazi Group Calls For Attacks Against Black Protestors," SITE Intelligence Group, June 2, 2020, https://ent.sitein telgroup.com/Far-Right-Far-Left-Threat/exploiting-chaos-of-riots-prominent-neo -nazi-group-calls-for-attacks-against-black-protesters.html.

10. Quoted in United States District Court, Western District of Michigan, Southern Divi sion, United States of America v. Adam Dean Fox, Case No. 1:20-cr-00183-RJJ, Decem ber 17, 2020, https://www.documentcloud.org/documents/7225185-Adam-Fox-affidavit, 8–9.

11. United States of America v. Adam Dean Fox, 1–15; and Jonathan Oosting, "FBI Infor mant: Facebook Led Me to Infiltrate Plot to Kidnap Gretchen Whitmer," The Bridge (Michigan), March 5, 2021, https://www.bridgemi.com/michigan-government/fbi -informant-facebook-led-me-infiltrate-plot-kidnap-gretchen-whitmer. See also Nich olas Bogel-Burroughs, "What We Know About the Alleged Plot to Kidnap Michigan's Governor," New York Times, October 9, 2020; and Neil MacFarquhar, "Defendant in Plot to Kidnap Michigan Governor Is Sentenced to Six Years," New York Times, August 25, 2021.

12. Quoted in United States of America v. Adam Dean Fox, 8–9; See also Kim Bellware, Alex Horton, Devlin Barrett, and Matt Zapotosky, "Accused Leader of Plot to Kidnap Michigan Governor Was Struggling Financially, Living in Basement Storage Space," Washington Post, October 9, 2020; Bogel-Burroughs, "What We Know About the Alleged Plot to Kidnap Michigan's Governor,"; MacFarquhar, "Defendant in Plot to Kid nap Michigan Governor Is Sentenced to Six Years,"; and Oosting, "FBI Informant."

13. "Continuation of a Criminal Complaint," Case 1:20-mj-00416-SJB ECF No. 1-1, filed October 6, 2020, 13, http://www.seditionists.com/michigankidnap1.pdf. See also Bogel-Burroughs, "What We Know About the Alleged Plot to Kidnap Michigan's Governor."

14. Devlin Barrett, Spencer S. Hsu, and Matt Zapotosky, "FBI Focuses on Whether Some Capitol Rioters Intended to Harm Lawmakers," Washington Post, January 8, 2021; Dan Kois, "They Were Out for Blood," Slate, January 8, 2021, https://slate.com/news-and -politics/2021/01/was-there-a-plan-for-hostages-or-killings-at-the-capitol.html.

15. Photograph by Shay Horse/Nur Photo, via Getty Images, https://www.nytimes.com /2021/01/12/books/turner-diaries-white-supremacists.html.

16. Anti-Defamation League (ADL), "Day of the Rope," https://www.adl.org/education /references/hate-symbols/day-of-the-rope; Andrew Macdonald [William L. Pierce], *The Turner Diaries*, 2nd ed. (Arlington, VA: National Vanguard, 1985), 160–62.

17. United States Attorney's Office, Northern District of Texas, United States Department of Justice, "Texas Man Sentenced to 10 Years for Plotting to Attack Data Centers," October 1, 2021, https://www.justice.gov/usao-ndtx/pr/texas-man-sentenced-10-years-plotting -attack-data-centers.

18. United States District Court for the Northern District of Texas, Forth Worth Division, United States of America v. Seth Aaron Pendley, Criminal Complaint, No. 4:21-MJ-240-BJ, April 9, 2021, https://www.texomashomepage.com/wp-content /uploads/sites/41/2021/04/Pendley-Complaint.pdf.

19. "All that is solid melts into air, all that is holy is profaned, and man is at least compelled to face with sober senses, his real conditions of life, and his relations with his kind." See Karl Marx and Frederick Engels, *Manifesto of the Communist Party* (1848; Chicago: Charles H. Kerr & Company, 1906), 17.

20. James Mason, *Siege*, digital ed., Revision 1 (n.p.: ironmarch.org, June 2, 2015), 13, 199.

21. See Zack Beauchamp, "Accelerationism: The Obscure Idea Inspiring White Supremacist Killers Round the World," *Vox*, November 18, 2019, https://www.vox.com/the -highlight/2019/11/11/20882005/accelerationism-white-supremacy-christchurch.

22. Gartenstein-Ross, Hodgson, and Clarke, "The Growing Threat Posed by Accelerationism."

23. Brenton Tarrant, *The Great Replacement*, March 15, 2019, https://nex24.news/2019/03/ the-great-replacement-by-brenton-tarrant/.

24. John Earnest, "An Open Letter," April 2019.

25. Marc Fisher and Phil McCombs, "The Book of Hate," *Washington Post*, April 25, 1995.

26. Barbara F. Walter, *How Civil Wars Start—and How to Stop Them* (New York: Crown, 2022), 159, 175.

27. Steven Simon and Jonathan Stevenson, "These Disunited States," *New York Review of Books*, September 22, 2022, https://www.nybooks.com/articles/2022/09/22/these -disunited-states-steven-simon-jonathan-stevenson/.

28. Stephen Marche, *The Next Civil War: Dispatches from the American Future* (New York: Avid, 2022), 1.

29. "Dec. 17–19, 2021, Washington Post-University of Maryland Poll," *Washington Post*, January 1, 2022, https://www.washingtonpost.com/context/dec-17-19-2021-washington -post-university-of-maryland-poll/2960c330-4bbd-4b3a-af9d-72de946d7281/.

30. Walter, *How Civil Wars Start*, 156.

31. Dan Balz, Scott Clement, and Emily Guskin, "Republicans and Democrats Divided Over Jan. 6 Insurrection and Trump's Culpability, Post-UMD Poll Finds," *Washington Post*, January 1, 2022, https://www.washingtonpost.com/politics/2022/01/01/post -poll-january-6/.

32. Luke Broadwater, "Jan. 6 Committee Refers Former President Trump for Criminal Prosecution," *New York Times*, December 19, 2022.

33. Emily Guskin, "A Wide Majority of Americans Are Concerned About Politically Motivated Violence," *Washington Post*, November 4, 2022, https://www.washingtonpost.com/politics/2022/11/04/poll-americans-concern-political-violence/.

34. "Global Firearms Holdings: Interactive Map—United States of America," Small Arms Survey, March 29, 2020, https://www.smallarmssurvey.org/database/global-firearms-holdings; "Small Arms Survey Reveals: More Than One Billion Firearms in the World," Small Arms Survey, June 18, 2018, https://www.smallarmssurvey.org/sites/default/files/resources/SAS-Press-release-global-firearms-holdings.pdf.

35. Lois Beckett, "Americans Have Bought Record 17M Guns in Year of Unrest, Analysis Finds," *Guardian*, October 30, 2020, https://www.theguardian.com/us-news/2020/oct/29/coronavirus-pandemic-americans-gun-sales.

36. Steven Simon and Jonathan Stevenson, "How Can We Neutralize the Militias?," *New York Review of Books,* August 19, 2021, https://www.nybooks.com/articles/2021/08/19/how-can-we-neutralize-militias/.

37. See Lois Beckett, "Virginia Democrats Won an Election. Gun Owners Are Talking Civil War," *Guardian*, January 10, 2020, https://www.theguardian.com/us-news/2020/jan/09/virginia-gun-control-second-amendment-civil-war.

38. Walter, *How Civil Wars Start*, 192, 159; Central Intelligence Agency, *Guide to the Analysis of Insurgency* (Washington, DC: Central Intelligence Agency, 2012), 13–16.

39. Richard Haass, *The Bill of Obligations: The Ten Habits of Good Citizens* (New York: Penguin, 2023), 22.

40. See "Experts: Richard Haass, President, Council on Foreign Relations," https://www.cfr.org/expert/richard-haass.

41. ADL, *Computerized Networks of Hate: An ADL Fact Finding Report* (New York: Anti-Defamation League of B'nai B'rith, 1984), 12, https://archive.org/details/ComputerizedNetworksOfHate/mode/2up.

42. See Bruce Hoffman, *Inside Terrorism* (New York: Columbia University Press, 2017), 1–4; and Anders Ravik Jupskås and Eviane Leidig, eds., "Knowing What's (Far) Right: A Compendium," *C-REX*, 2020, https://www.sv.uio.no/c-rex/english/groups/compendium/c-rex-compendium-print-version.pdf.

43. Madison Hall et al., "At Least 1,003 People Have Been Charged in the Capitol Insurrection So Far. This Searchable Table Shows Them All," *Insider*, December 7, 2022, https://www.insider.com/all-the-us-capitol-pro-trump-riot-arrests-charges-names-2021-1; Madison Hall et al., "465 Rioters Have Pleaded Guilty for Their Role in the Capitol Insurrection So Far. This Table Is Tracking Them All," *Insider*, January 5, 2023, https://www.insider.com/all-the-us-capitol-pro-trump-riot-arrests-charges-names-2021-1.

2. BATTLE PLAN

1. Southern Poverty Law Center, "Fighting Hate," https://www.splcenter.org/fighting-hate. See also George Michael, *Confronting Right-Wing Extremism and Terrorism in the USA* (London: Routledge, 2003), 21–25.

2. Southern Poverty Law Center, "William Pierce," https://www.splcenter.org/fighting -hate/extremist-files/individual/william-pierce.

3. Southern Poverty Law Center, "William Pierce"; Southern Poverty Law Center, "William Pierce: A Political History," https://www.splcenter.org/fighting-hate/intelligence -report/2015/william-pierce-political-history; Anti-Defamation League of B'nai B'rith, *Hate Groups in America: A Record of Bigotry and Violence* (New York: Anti-Defamation League, 1982), 32–33; Anti-Defamation League, *Extremism on the Right: A Handbook* (New York: Anti-Defamation League, 1983), 120–21; Thomas Martinez with John Guinther, *Brotherhood of Murder: How One Man's Journey Through Fear Brought the Order—The Most Dangerous Racist Gang in America—to Justice* (New York: McGraw-Hill, 1988), 32–33; George Michael, "Blueprints and Fantasies: A Review and Analysis of Extremist Fiction," *Studies in Conflict & Terrorism* 33, no. 2 (February 2010): 153; Leonard Zeskind, *Blood and Politics: The History of the White Nationalist Movement from the Margins to the Mainstream* (New York: Farrar Straus Giroux, 2009), 17–25.

4. "What Is The National Alliance? National Alliance Goals," https://natall.com/about /what-is-the-national-alliance/. See Morris Dees with James Corcoran, *Gathering Storm: America's Militia Threat* (New York: HarperCollins, 1996), 138.

5. See Anti-Defamation League, "Our Mission," https://www.adl.org/who-we-are/our -mission. The ADL has been described in one scholarly work as "the most important watchdog group involved in countering right-wing extremism." See also Michael, *Confronting Right-Wing Extremism*, 15–17.

6. Anti-Defamation League, *Explosion of Hate: The Growing Danger of the National Alliance* (New York: Anti-Defamation League, 2000), https://www.adl.org/sites/default /files/documents/assets/pdf/combating-hate/Explosion-of-Hate.pdf. See also Michael, *Confronting Right-Wing Extremism*, 17.

7. Jerome Walters, *One Aryan Nation Under God: How Religious Extremists Use the Bible to Justify Their Actions* (Naperville, IL: Sourcebooks, 2001), 46, 49–55.

8. Quoted in Wayne King, "Links of Anti-Semitic Band Provoke 6-State Parley," *New York Times*, December 27, 1984.

9. Quoted on the back cover of Macdonald, *The Turner Diaries*, 2nd ed., 1985.

10. The authors could find no open-source official records (e.g., public testimony, press releases, and published FBI/DOJ reports) of either the U.S. Department of Justice or the FBI having ever described *The Turner Diaries* in this way. In addition, the Southern Poverty Law Center was contacted on June 5, 2020, regarding the quote, which appears in their discussion "The Turner Diaries, Other Racist Novels, Inspire Extremist Violence," *Intelligence Report*, Fall 2004, https://www.splcenter.org/fighting-hate /intelligence-report/2004/turner-diaries-other-racist-novels-inspire-extremist -violence. The SPLC was unable to provide any additional information, clarification, or sourcing regarding the quote's origin. The FBI allegedly stated this, but the quote could not be substantiated through open-source means. For other instances where this quote appears see ADL, "The Turner Diaries," https://www.adl.org

/education/resources/backgrounders/turner-diaries; John Sutherland, "Goodbye, Good Riddance," *Guardian*, July 29, 2002, https://www.theguardian.com/books /2002/jul/29/comment.news.

11. AIRTEL, SAC, San Antonio to Director, FBI, August 20, 1991, http://intelfiles.egoplex .com/91-08-20-airtel-turner-diaries2.pdf.

12. OKC Bombing Trial Transcript—04/24/1997, Opening Statement by Prosecutor Joseph Hartzler, 10, 12, 13, 14, 22, 27, 31, https://oklahoman.com/article/1074825/okc-bombing -trial-transcript-04241997-1139-cdtcst; "Closing Argument for the Prosecution in the Trial of Timothy McVeigh (Argument by Larry D. Mackey), May 29, 1997, http://law2 .umkc.edu/faculty/projects/ftrials/mcveigh/mcveighclosing.html.

13. The lower figure is cited in OKC Bombing Trial Transcript—04/24/1997, Opening Statement by Stephen Jones, 44; and the higher in Kathleen Belew, *Bring the War Home: The White Power Movement and Paramilitary America* (Cambridge, MA: Harvard University Press, 2018), 110; Sutherland, "Goodbye, Good Riddance"; and Zeskind, *Blood and Politics*, 31. David Segal, "The Pied Piper of Racism: William Pierce Wants Young People to March to His Hate Records," *Washington Post*, January 12, 2000, reported sales at 350,000 copies; David H. Bennett, *The Party of Fear: The American Far Right from Nativism to the Militia Movement* (New York: Vintage, 1995), 437, stated that there were 185,000 copies in print.

14. The title page of the copy in the possession of one author has a gold sticker attached to it listing National Vanguard Books and a post office box in Arlington, Virginia, that is identical to the National Alliance's official address. The sticker reads: "Write for free catalog of books on science and sociology of race; history of European man; White folkways, legends, sagas, and archaeology; Communism, Zionism, and World War II; racist ideology, philosophy, and politics; survival and self-defense—and a selection of consciousness-raising books for White children and young people."

15. Opening statement by Stephen Jones, April 24, 1997.

16. One of the authors purchased his copy at the Soldier of Fortune Convention on September 20, 1986. See also Belew, *Bring the War Home*, 1; Lou Michel and Dan Herbeck, *American Terrorist: Timothy McVeigh and the Oklahoma City Bombing* (New York: ReganBooks, 2001) 88, 124–25; Segal, "The Pied Piper of Racism"; and Zeskind, *Blood and Politics*, 31.

17. Macdonald, *The Turner Diaries*, 162.

18. Macdonald, *The Turner Diaries*, 42.

19. Macdonald, *The Turner Diaries*, 190–211.

20. Interview with William Pierce, quoted in Michael, "Blueprints and Fantasies," 155. See, for instance, J. M. Berger, "Alt History: How a Self-Published, Racist Novel Changed White Nationalism and Inspired Decades of Violence," *Atlantic*, September 16, 2016, https://www.theatlantic.com/politics/archive/2016/09/how-the-turner-diaries -changed-white-nationalism/500039/; J. M. Berger, "The Turner Legacy: The Storied Origins and Enduring Impact of White Nationalism's Deadly Bible," ICCT, International Centre for Counter-Terrorism—The Hague, September 2016, https://icct.nl

/publication/the-turner-legacy-the-storied-origins-and-enduring-impact-of-white
-nationalisms-deadly-bible/; James Corcoran, *Bitter Harvest: The Birth of Paramilitary
Terrorism in the Heartland* (New York: Penguin, 1995), 37; Anti-Defamation League,
"Day of the Rope: Hate Slogans/Slang Terms," https://www.adl.org/resources/hate
-symbol/day-rope; Robert Jimson, "How the FBI Smashed White Supremacist Group
The Order," CNN, August 21, 2018; Michael, "Blueprints and Fantasies," 154; Michael,
Confronting Right-Wing Extremism and Terrorism, 68, 98; Segal, "The Pied Piper of
Racism."

21.   Kevin Flynn and Gary Gerhardt, *The Silent Brotherhood: Inside America's Racist Under-
ground* (New York: Free Press, 1989), 32–38; Mattias Gardell, "Robert J. Mathews," in
Encyclopedia of White Power: A Sourcebook on the Radical Racist Right, ed. Jeffrey
Kaplan (Walnut Creek, CA: AltaMira, 2000), 199; Robert S. Griffin, *The Fame of a
Dead Man's Deeds: An Up-Close Portrait of White Nationalist William Pierce* (n.p,
2001; rev. ed., 2018), chap. 15, "Bob Mathews," https://archive.org/stream/FameOfA
DeadMansDeedsRobertS.Griffin/Fame%20of%20a%20Dead%20Man%27s%20
Deeds%20-%20Robert%20S.%20Griffin_djvu.txt; Mark S. Hamm, *Terrorism as Crime:
From Oklahoma City to Al-Qaeda and Beyond* (New York: New York University Press,
2007), 116–19; Martinez, *Brotherhood of Murder,* 16–17; David A. Neiwert, *In God's
Country: The Patriot Movement and the Pacific Northwest* (Pullman: Washington
State University Press, 2019), 55–56; Jeffrey Ian Ross, ed., *Religion and Violence: An
Encyclopedia of Faith and Conflict from Antiquity to the Present* (London: Routledge,
2015), 451; Evelyn A. Schlatter, *Aryan Cowboys: White Supremacists and the Search for
a New Frontier, 1970–2000* (Austin: University of Texas Press, 2006), 9, 76; Stephen
Singular, *Talked to Death: The Life and Murder of Alan Berg* (New York: Beech Tree,
1987), 125.

22.   Gardell, "Robert J. Mathews," 199.

23.   Gardell, "Robert J. Mathews," 199; Flynn and Gerhardt, *The Silent Brotherhood,* 38–40;
Daniel Levitas, *The Terrorist Next Door: The Militia Movement and the Radical Right*
(New York: Thomas Dunne, 2002), 105–6; Martinez, *Brotherhood of Murder,* 17; Neiwert, *In God's Country,* 56; Ross, ed., *Religion and Violence,* 451–52; Schlatter, *Aryan Cowboys,* 76–77.

24.   "Robert Jay Mathews' Last Letter," http://www.mourningtheancient.com/mathews3bb
.htm. See also Danny O. Coulson and Elaine Shannon, *No Heroes: Inside the FBI's Secret
Counter-Terror Force* (New York: Pocket, 199), 189; Flynn and Gerhardt, *The Silent
Brotherhood,* 42; Hamm, *Terrorism as Crime,* 122; Levitas, *The Terrorist Next Door,* 106;
Neiwert, *In God's Country,* 56; Schlatter, *Aryan Cowboys,* 77.

25.   Martinez, *Brotherhood of Murder,* 17, 82; Ross, ed., *Religion and Violence,* 452.

26.   "Robert Jay Mathews' Last Letter." See also Coulson and Shannon, *No Heroes,* 189; Martinez, *Brotherhood of Murder,* 17–18; Neiwert, *In God's Country,* 56; Schlatter, *Aryan
Cowboys,* 77; Singular, *Talked to Death,* 126–27.

27.   See William Gayley Simpson, *Which Way Western Man?,* https://booksrun.com
/9780937944165-which-way-western-man-2nd-edition.

28. Griffin, *The Fame of a Dead Man's Deeds*. See also the excerpt at http://www.racialre-alism.wordpress.com; James Coates, *Armed and Dangerous: The Rise of the Survivalist Right* (New York: Hill & Wang, 1987), 215; and, Neiwert, *In God's Country*, 56. See also Singular, *Talked to Death*, 127.

29. "Robert Jay Mathews' Last Letter." See also Singular, *Talked to Death*, 130.

30. Coulson and Shannon, *No Heroes*, 189; Martinez, *Brotherhood of Murder*, 16–17; Ross, ed., *Religion and Violence*, 452; Singular, *Talked to Death*, 125–27.

31. James A. Aho, *The Politics of Righteousness: Idaho Christian Patriotism* (Seattle: University of Washington Press, 1995), 56; Singular, *Talked to Death*, 126–27.

32. Flynn and Gerhardt, *The Silent Brotherhood*, 53; Ross, ed., *Religion and Violence*, 452; Schlatter, *Aryan Cowboys*, 64–65, 77.

33. Elaine Woo, "Richard Butler, 86; Supremacist Founded the Aryan Nations," *Los Angeles Times*, September 9, 2004.

34. Flynn and Gerhardt, *The Silent Brotherhood*, 49–50. See also Anti-Defamation League, *Extremism on the Right*, 86–87; Martinez, *Brotherhood of Murder*, 29; Schlatter, *Aryan Cowboys*, 64.

35. Anti-Defamation League, *Extremism on the Right*, 8–87; Anti-Defamation League, *Hate Groups in America*, 96–97; Belew, *Bring the War Home*, 171; Coates, *Armed and Dangerous*, 96–97, 104–5; Bennett, *The Party of Fear*, 352; Corcoran, *Bitter Harvest*, 31; Dees, *Gathering Storm*, 23; Flynn and Gerhardt, *The Silent Brotherhood*, 49–50; Levitas, *The Terrorist Next Door*, 3, 4, 8–9; Schlatter, *Aryan Cowboys*, 105–6; Walters, *One Aryan Nation Under God*; Stuart A. Wright, *Patriots, Politics, and the Oklahoma City Bombing* (Cambridge: Cambridge University Press, 2007), 58, 62–64.

36. David Audsley, "Posse Comitatus: An Extremist Tax Protest Group," *TVI: Terrorism, Violence Insurgency Journal* 6, no. 1 (Summer 1985): 13–14; Belew, *Bring the War Home*, 119; Kerry Noble, *Tabernacle of Hate* (Prescott, Ontario: Voyageur, 1998), 130; Schlatter, *Aryan Cowboys*, 8, 77; Catherine McNicol Stock, *Rural Radicals: Righteous Rage in the American Grain* (Ithaca, NY: Cornell University Press, 1996), 171; Wright, *Patriots, Politics, and the Oklahoma City Bombing*, 20.

37. "Church of Jesus Christ-Christian—The Ministry of Dr. Wesley A. Swift," http://www.kingidentity.com/cjc.html.

38. Michael Barkun, *Religion and the Racist Right* (Chapel Hill: University of North Carolina Press, 1997), ix–x; Arnold Forster and Benjamin Epstein, *The Trouble-Makers: An Anti-Defamation League Report on Intolerance in the United States* (Garden City, NY: Doubleday, 1952), 22, 27, 30, 80, 204–5, 246–47.

39. Flynn and Gerhardt, *The Silent Brotherhood*, 50–51.

40. See Aryan Nations, "Yesterday: the Tribes of Israel; Today: the Aryan Nations," n.d.; Aryan Nations, "Why Are Jews Persecuted for Their Religion?," n.d.; Anti-Defamation League, "Christian Identity," https://www.adl.org/resources/backgrounders/christian-identity; Sean Anderson and Stephen Sloan, *Historical Dictionary of Terrorism* (Metuchen, NJ: Scarecrow, 1995), 139–41; Chip Berlet, "Christian Identity: The Apocalyptic Style, Political Religion, Palingesis and Neo-Fascism," *Totalitarian Movements*

and Political Religions 5, no. 3 (Winter 2004): 471; Coulson and Shannon, *No Heroes*, 190–91; Kaplan, *Encyclopedia of White Power*, 50–53; Kaplan, "Right-Wing Violence in North America," in *Terror from the Extreme Right*, ed. Tore Bjorgo (London: Frank Cass, 1995), 50–51; Wayne F. Manis, *The Street Agent: After Taking on the Mob, the Klan, and the Aryan Nations, He Walks Softly and Carries a .357 Magnum—The True Story* (Palisades, NY: History Publishing, 2014), 277–79; Noble, *Tabernacle of Hate*, 88–89; Stock, *Rural Radicals*, 173.

41. Anti-Defamation League, "Aryan Nations/Church of Jesus Christ Christian," https://www.adl.org/education/resources/profiles/aryan-nations; Flynn and Gerhardt, *The Silent Brotherhood*, 53; Kaplan "Right-Wing Violence in North America," 53; Kenneth S. Stern, *A Force Upon the Plain: The American Militia Movement and the Politics of Hate* (New York: Simon & Schuster, 1996), 47; Irwin Suall and David Lowe, "The Hate Movement Today: A Chronicle of Violence and Disarray," *Terrorism* 10, no. 4 (1987): 352.

42. See Dan Gayman, *The Two Seeds of Genesis 3:15* (n.p., 1977; rev. ed., 1994), 310–13; author's notes of Peter Lake, "Neo-Nazi Terrorism in the United States," presented at the RAND Corporation, Santa Monica, CA, September 8, 1986; and email correspondence with Dr. David Brannan, Naval Postgraduate School, Monterey, CA, June 9, 2020. Dr. Brannan has interviewed and studied the teachings of Dan Gayman. See also Hamm, *Terrorism as Crime*, 92–93.

43. International Association of Chiefs of Police (IACP), *Terrorist Trends: The Quarterly Intelligence Reporter* (Alexandria, VA: International Association of Chiefs of Police, 1985), 13.

44. Aryan Nations, *Calling Our Nation* 53 (n.d.): 2, http://www.stormfront.org/aryan_nations/platform.html.

45. Aryan Nations, *This Is Aryan Nations* (n.d.), http://www.stormfront.org/aryan_nations/platform.html.

46. Flynn and Gerhardt, *The Silent Brotherhood*, 53, 66; Tanya Telfair Sharpe, "The Identity Christian Movement: Ideology of Domestic Terrorism," *Journal of Black Studies* 30, no. 4 (March 2000): 613; Association of Chiefs of Police (IACP), *Terrorist Trends*, 13.

47. Sharpe, "The Identity Christian Movement," 619.

48. Coulson and Shannon, *No Heroes*, 191.

49. Quoted in Lake, "Neo-Nazi Terrorism in the United States."

50. Photograph in the author's possession.

51. "To Our New People," open letter from Reverend Richard G. Butler, *Aryan Nations* (n.d.); "To Our Kinsmen," open letter from Reverend Richard G. Butler, *Aryan Nations* (n.d.).

52. *This Is Aryan Nations* brochure.

53. Roy B. Masker, "An All White Nation? Why Not?" *Calling Our Nation* 53 (n.d.).

54. Jeremy Noakes, "Hitler and 'Lebensraum' in the East," BBC, March 30, 2011, https://www.bbc.co.uk/history/worldwars/wwtwo/hitler_lebensraum_01.shtml.

55. Schlatter, *Aryan Cowboys*, 64–65.

56. Stock, *Rural Radicals*, 173.

57. Different accounts state that the Aryan Nations compound was situated on either twenty or forty acres. See, respectively, Meagan Day, "Welcome to Hayden Lake, Where White Supremacists Tried to Build Their Homeland," *Timeline*, November 4, 2016, https://timeline.com/white-supremacist-rural-paradise-fb62b74b29e0; Schlatter, *Aryan Cowboys*, 70; Martinez, *Brotherhood of Murder*, 29; and Daniel J. Wakin, "Richard G. Butler, 86, Founder of the Aryan Nations, Dies," *New York Times*, September 9, 2004; John W. Philips, *Sign of the Cross: The Prosecutor's True Story of a Landmark Trial Against the Klan* (Louisville, KY: Westminster John Knox, 2000), 85.

58. Quoted in Anti-Defamation League, "Aryan Nations/Church of Jesus Christ Christian," https://www.adl.org/education/resources/profiles/aryan-nations; Schlatter, *Aryan Cowboys*, 66.

59. Belew, *Bring the War Home*, 105; Flynn and Gerhardt, *The Silent Brotherhood*, 53–54, 67–68; Manis, *The Street Agent*, 307; Martinez, *Brotherhood of Murder*, 29; Philips, *Sign of the Cross*, 85; Pete Simi and Robert Futrell, *American Swastika: Inside the White Power Movement's Hidden Spaces of Hate* (Lanham, MD: Rowman & Littlefield, 2015), 112; Andrew Zahler, "Aryan Nations: Summary," *Spokesman-Review* (Spokane, WA), n.d.

60. Photograph in the author's possession.

61. Schlatter, *Aryan Cowboys*, 66.

62. James Aho, "Christian Fundamentalism and Militia Movements in the United States," in *The Making of a Terrorist: Recruitment, Training, and Root Causes*, vol. 1: *Recruitment*, ed. James J. F. Forest (Westport, CT: Praeger, 2006), 228–29; James Aho, *The Politics of Righteousness*, 230; Hamm, *Terrorism as Crime*, 100.

63. Noble, *Tabernacle of Hate*, 131. See also Flynn and Gerhardt, *The Silent Brotherhood*, 89.

64. Belew, *Bring the War Home*, 105.

65. Corcoran, *Bitter Harvest*, 41–42; Simi and Futrell, *American Swastika*, 114; Flynn and Gerhardt, *The Silent Brotherhood*, 67; Schlatter, *Aryan Cowboys*, 66. See also Southern Poverty Law Center, "Aryan Nations," https://www.splcenter.org/fighting-hate/extremist-files/group/aryan-nations.

66. Quoted in Coates, *Armed and Dangerous*, 41. See also Martinez, *Brotherhood of Murder*, 29.

67. "1996 ARYAN NATIONAL CONGRESS, JULY 19, 20 & 21ST, 1996" handbill, https://www.amazon.com/NEWSLETTER-LITERATURE-COLLECTION-NEWSLETTERS-OUTREACH/dp/B008EAWLLY. See also Simi and Futrell, *American Swastika*, 114–15, 119; and Eckard Toy, "'Promised Land' or Armageddon? History, Survivalists, and the Aryan Nations in the Pacific Northwest," *Montana: The Magazine of Western History* 36, no. 3 (Summer 1986): 82.

68. Anti-Defamation League, "Burning Cross: General Hate Symbols: Ku Klux Klan Symbols," https://www.adl.org/education/references/hate-symbols/burning-cross; Rian Dundon, "Why Does the Ku Klux Klan Burn Crosses? They Got the Idea from a Movie," *Timeline*, March 16, 2017, https://timeline.com/why-does-the-ku-klux-klan-burn-crosses-they-got-the-idea-from-a-movie-75a70f7ab135; Linda Gordon, *The Second*

Coming of the KKK: The Ku Klux Klan of the 1920s and the American Political Tradition (New York: Liveright, 2018), 84; Patsy Sims, *The Klan* (New York: Dorset, 1978), 18.

69. Quoted in Flynn and Gerhardt, *The Silent Brotherhood*, 68.

70. Belew, *Bring the War Home*, 119; Coulson and Shannon, *No Heroes*, 192.

71. Anti-Defamation League, *Extremism on the Right*, 43; Corcoran, *Bitter Harvest*, 43; Coulson and Shannon, *No Heroes*, 192, 195; Lake, "Neo-Nazi Terrorism in the United States"; Michael, *Confronting Right-Wing Extremism and Terrorism in the USA*, 102; Schlatter, *Aryan Cowboys*, 83.

72. Corcoran, *Bitter Harvest*, 45–51; Coulson and Shannon, *No Heroes*, 192; Neiwert, *In God's Country*, 236. For Kahl's antisemitic beliefs, see Levitas, *The Terrorist Next Door*, 5, 174, 192, 215; Noble, *Tabernacle of Hate*, 130; Coates, *Armed and Dangerous*, 107–10.

73. Quoted in Corcoran, *Bitter Harvest*, 52.

74. See United States v. Kahl, 583 F. 2d 1351—Court of Appeals, 5th Circuit 1978, https://scholar.google.com/scholar_case?q=%22583+F.2d+1351%22&as_sdt=3,44&case=898117 8823130363349&scilh=0.

75. Coates, *Armed and Dangerous*, 104; Corcoran, *Bitter Harvest*, 43–64; Levitas, *The Terrorist Next Door*, 193–94, 205, 217; Noble, *Tabernacle of Hate*, 130; Wright, *Patriots, Politics, and the Oklahoma City Bombing*, 84.

76. Audsley, "Posse Comitatus," 13–14; Coates, *Armed and Dangerous*, 106.

77. Coates, *Armed and Dangerous*, 109; Noble, *Tabernacle of Hate*, 130.

78. For a full text of the letter, see "Gordon Kahl Letter," http://www.outpost-of-freedom.com/kahl01.htm; and Corcoran, *Bitter Harvest*, 149–51. Excerpts can be found in Coates, *Armed and Dangerous*, 107. See also Noble, *Tabernacle of Hate*, 131.

79. Corcoran, *Bitter Harvest*, 75–114, 170–71; Tony Spilde, "Changing Lives—in 15 Seconds," *Bismarck Tribune*, February 9, 2003, https://bismarcktribune.com/news/local/changing-lives-in-15-seconds/article_d1e97691-ea36-5a7a-978b-cc529942b019.html; Tony Spilde, "From Mild to Madness," *Bismarck Tribune*, February 9, 2003, excerpted at https://murderpedia.org/male.K/k/kahl-gordon.htm; Mike Albrecht, "Neighbors Remember Events of Shoot-out," *Bismarck Tribune*, February 9, 2003, https://bismarcktribune.com/news/local/neighbors-remember-events-of-shoot-out/article_e0ab237e-d51f-521c-b0c6-365a438310e4.html. See also Coates, *Armed and Dangerous*, 107–8; Levitas, *The Terrorist Next Door*, 194–97; Noble, *Tabernacle of Hate*, 130–31; Stern, *A Force Upon the Plain*, 52; Wright, *Patriots, Politics, and the Oklahoma City Bombing*, 85–86.

80. "Gordon Kahl Letter." See also excerpts quoted in Corcoran, *Bitter Harvest*, 152–54; Levitas, *The Terrorist Next Door*, 198–99; and, "Kahl Defense Fund Circular, 1983," quoted in Belew, *Bring the War Home*, 119.

81. Quoted in Art Harris, "Evader's End," *Washington Post*, June 5, 1983.

82. For the most detailed account of Kahl's death, see Corcoran, *Bitter Harvest*, 233–46. See also Coulson and Shannon, *No Heroes*, 192–93; Flynn and Gerhardt, *The Silent Brotherhood*, 87–88; Levitas, *The Terrorist Next Door*, 219–20.

83. Coates, *Armed and Dangerous*, 15–16, 140; Corcoran, *Bitter Harvest*, 248–49; Flynn and Gerhardt, *The Silent Brotherhood*, 88; Kaplan, "Right-Wing Violence in North America," 87; Levitas, *The Terrorist Next Door*, 5, 223; Manis, *The Street Agent*, 304; Michael,

Confronting Right-Wing Extremism, 46; Neiwert, *In God's Country*, 237–38; Noble, *Tabernacle of Hate*, 131; Schlatter, *Aryan Cowboys*, 121; Simi and Futrell, *American Swastika*, 27; Stern, *A Force Upon the Plain*, 53, 57; Wright, *Patriots, Politics, and the Oklahoma City Bombing*, 98. A made-for-TV movie was eventually made about Kahl, *In the Line of Duty: Manhunt in the Dakotas* (1991), starring Rod Steiger as Kahl and Michael Gross as the fictional Agent Richard Mayberly, https://www.imdb.com/title /tt0102112/fullcredits/.

84. Noble, *Tabernacle of Hate*, 131. See also Coulson and Shannon, *No Heroes*, 192; Hamm, *Terrorism as Crime*, 100; Jessica Stern, *Terror in the Name of God: Why Religious Militants Kills* (New York: HarperCollins, 2003), 26.

85. Hamm, *Terrorism as Crime*, 100.

86. FBI, Freedom of Information/Privacy Acts Section, "Subject: The Covenant, The Sword, The Arm of The Lord," File 100-HQ-487200, Kansas City, MO, July 2, 1982, 1, https:// vault.fbi.gov/The%20Covenant%20The%20Sword%20The%20Arm%20of%20the%20 Lord%20/The%20Covenant%20The%20Sword%20The%20Arm%20of%20the%20 Lord%20Part%201%20of%202 and https://archive.org/details/CovenantTheSwordAnd TheArmOfTheLord/page/n1/mode/2up. See also Jessica Stern, "The Covenant, the Sword, and the Arm of the Lord" (1985), in *Toxic Terror: Assessing Terrorist Use of Chemical and Biological Weapons*, ed. J. B. Tucker (Cambridge, MA: MIT Press, 2000), 140.

87. FBI, "Covenant; Sword and The Arm of The Lord; Domestic Security," Kansas City, MO, July 2, 1982, https://archive.org/details/CovenantTheSwordAndTheArmOfTheL ord/page/n1/mode/2up; Hamm, *Terrorism as Crime*, 90; Levitas, *The Terrorist Next Door*, 205; Stern, "The Covenant, the Sword, and the Arm of the Lord," 140.

88. FBI, "Covenant; Sword and The Arm of The Lord; Domestic Security," See also Belew, *Bring the War Home*, 218; Flynn and Gerhardt, *The Silent Brotherhood*, 90; Hamm, *Terrorism as Crime*, 99; Levitas, *The Terrorist Next Door*, 205; Stern, "The Covenant, the Sword, and the Arm of the Lord," 145.

89. Noble, *Tabernacle of Hate*, 10, 26–28; and the interview with Noble in Stern, *Terror in the Name of God*, 14–15. See also Levitas, *The Terrorist Next Door*, 205.

90. Quoted in Noble, *Tabernacle of Hate*, 30–31. See also Noble quoted in Stern, *Terror in the Name of God*, 11. See also Stern, "The Covenant, the Sword, and the Arm of the Lord," 145–46.

91. FBI, "Subject: The Covenant, The Sword, The Arm of The Lord," File 100-HQ-487200, Kansas City, Missouri July 2, 1982, 1.

92. Noble, *Tabernacle of Hate*, 73. See also Hamm, *Terrorism as Crime*, 91.

93. Coulson quoted in Noble, *Tabernacle of Hate*, 22.

94. FBI, "Subject: The Covenant, The Sword, The Arm of The Lord," 1.

95. Quoted in Anti-Defamation League, *Hate Groups in America*, 52.

96. Noble, *Tabernacle of Hate*, 101. See also the quote in Anti-Defamation League, *Hate Groups in America*, 51. See also Belew, *Bring the War Home*, 139.

97. Quoted in Noble, *Tabernacle of Hate*, 100. Ellison also designed a special military patch for the rebranded group featuring a flaming sword and rainbow. See also Stern, "The Covenant, the Sword, and the Arm of the Lord," 144–45.

98. Noble, *Tabernacle of Hate*, 88–94. See also Hamm, *Terrorism as Crime*, 92–93; Stern, "The Covenant, the Sword, and the Arm of the Lord," 141–44.

99. "This government—not my government, not your government—this Jewish-controlled government, is transporting large armies of foreign mercenaries to complete the works of death, desolation, and tyranny," Ellison preached. "It has excited [*sic*] domestic insurrections amongst us, and has endeavored to bring on the inhabitants of a white America, the merciless [n-word] savages, trained to kill in the government-created ghettos and in prison! The Jews have declared war on our race, promoting race-mixing and thereby polluting the pure seed of God. This ZOG, this Zionist Occupied Government, is killing our white babies through abortion!" Quoted in Noble, *Tabernacle of Hate*, 87.

100. Noble, *Tabernacle of Hate*, 91. See also Noble quoted in Stern, *Terror in the Name of God*, 18.

101. Hamm, *Terrorism as Crime*, 94; Stern, "The Covenant, the Sword, and the Arm of the Lord," 141; Stern, *Terror in the Name of God*, 22.

102. Noble, *Tabernacle of Hate*, 97. See also Noble quoted in Stern, *Terror in the Name of God*, 20–21; Hamm, *Terrorism as Crime*, 92–96; Levitas, *The Terrorist Next Door*, 205.

103. See FBI News, "Hogan's Alley Turns 30: The Evolution of the FBI's Mock Training Ground," May 12, 2017, http://www.fbi.gov/news/stories/hogans-alley-turns-30; FBI Services/Training Academy, "Tactical/Hogan's Alley," https://www.fbi.gov/services/training-academy/hogans-alley; Hamm, *Terrorism as Crime*, 95.

104. Noble, *Tabernacle of Hate*, 35. See also Corcoran, *Bitter Harvest*, 238; Hamm, *Terrorism as Crime*, 95.

105. FBI, "Subject: The Covenant, The Sword, The Arm of The Lord," 1–2. See also Corcoran, *Bitter Harvest*, 35, 238; Stern, *Terror in the Name of God*, 21.

106. Corcoran, *Bitter Harvest*, 64, 35; Levitas, *The Terrorist Next Door*, 205–6; Wright, *Patriots, Politics, and the Oklahoma City Bombing*, 84; Hamm, *Terrorism as Crime*, 96; Stern, *Terror in the Name of God*, 21.

107. Quoted in Noble, *Tabernacle of Hate*, 131–32. See also Noble quoted in Stern, *Terror in the Name of God*, 27.

108. Flynn and Gerhardt, *The Silent Brotherhood*, 90–91.

109. Flynn and Gerhardt, *The Silent Brotherhood*, 88–89; Griffin, *The Fame of a Dead Man's Deeds*; Hamm, *Terrorism as Crime*, 123; Levitas, *The Terrorist Next Door*, 206; Neiwert, *In God's Country*, 56; Schlatter, *Aryan Cowboys*, 79; Singular, *Talked to Death*, 130.

110. Lake, "Neo-Nazi Terrorism in the United States." See also Belew, *Bring the War Home*, 26; Hamm, *Terrorism as Crime*, 134.

111. Anti-Defamation League, *Extremism on the Right*, 54; Belew, *Bring the War Home*, 26; Laura Smith, "Armed Resistance, Lone Wolves, and Media Messaging: Meet the Godfather of the 'Alt-Right,'" *Timeline*, November 6, 2017, https://timeline.com/louis-beam-white-supremacy-history-20d028315d; Southern Poverty Law Center, "Louis Beam," https://www.splcenter.org/fighting-hate/extremist-files/individual/louis-beam.

112. Smith, "Armed Resistance, Lone Wolves, and Media Messaging."

113. Smith, "Armed Resistance, Lone Wolves, and Media Messaging,"; Belew, *Bring the War Home*, 30–32; Southern Poverty Law Center, "Louis Beam."

114. Louis Beam, "Forget? Hell No!," in *Essays of a Klansman*, 1983.

115. Smith, "Armed Resistance, Lone Wolves, and Media Messaging"; Southern Poverty Law Center, "Louis Beam."

116. Belew, *Bring the War Home*, 33.

117. Belew, *Bring the War Home*, 32–40. See also Anti-Defamation League, *Extremism on the Right*, 54; Smith, "Armed Resistance, Lone Wolves, and Media Messaging"; Southern Poverty Law Center, "Louis Beam."

118. Belew, *Bring the War Home*, 35–36; Southern Poverty Law Center, "David Duke," https://www.splcenter.org/fighting-hate/extremist-files/individual/david-duke.

119. See Gavin Haynes, "The White Polo Shirt: How the Alt-Right Co-opted a Modern Classic," *Guardian*, August 30, 2017, https://www.theguardian.com/fashion/2017/aug/30/the-white-polo-shirt-how-the-alt-right-co-opted-a-modern-classic; Booth Moore, "White Nationalist Uniform of Polo Shirts Takes Center Stage in Charlottesville," *Hollywood Reporter*, August 14, 2017, https://www.hollywoodreporter.com/news/white-nationalist-uniform-polo-shirts-takes-center-stage-charlottsville-1029184; Cam Wolf, "The New Uniform of White Supremacy," *GQ*, August 17, 2017, https://www.gq.com/story/uniform-of-white-supremacy.

120. Quoted in Smith, "Armed Resistance, Lone Wolves, and Media Messaging." See also Belew, *Bring the War Home*, 40–53; Southern Poverty Law Center, "Louis Beam."

121. Belew, *Bring the War Home*, 53–54, 107. See also Anti-Defamation League, *Extremism on the Right*, 55; Dees, *Gathering Storm*, 39; Levitas, *The Terrorist Next Door*, 290; Martinez, *Brotherhood of Murder*, 57; Smith, "Armed Resistance, Lone Wolves, and Media Messaging"; Southern Poverty Law Center, "Louis Beam."

122. Dees, *Gathering Storm*, 39.

123. Anti-Defamation League, *Extremism on the Right*, 55; Southern Poverty Law Center, "Louis Beam." See also Louis Beam, "Address to the Aryan Nations," in "Patriotism, the Pacific Northwest and the Ku Klux Klan," Contents of Case 2, Foley Library, Gonzaga University, Spokane, WA, https://researchguides.gonzaga.edu/c.php?g=1023670&p=7447531; Smith, "Armed Resistance, Lone Wolves, and Media Messaging."

124. Louis Beam, "Leaderless Resistance," *Inter-Klan Newsletter and Survival Alert* (c. Spring/Summer 1983, probably May), https://simson.net/ref/leaderless/1983.inter-klan_newsletter.pdf.

125. Quoted in Chip Berlet, "Leaderless Resistance Publishing History—The Amoss Version—1953 & 1962," *Chip Berlet's Home on the Internet*, https://www.chipberlet.us/leaderless-resistance-publishing-history/. For details on Amoss's wartime exploits and postwar career, see also "Ulius L. Amoss papers, 1941–1963," the "Summary" and "Historical Note," http://archiveswest.orbiscascade.org/ark:/80444/xv35579; Anthony Cave Brown, *Wild Bill Donovan: The Last Hero* (New York: Times, 1982), 597; and Douglas Waller, *Wild Bill Donovan: The Spymaster Who Created the OSS and Modern American Espionage* (New York: Free Press, 2011), 154–55.

126. Beam, "Leaderless Resistance," 12–13. See also Stern, *A Force Upon the Plain*, 36.

127. Louis R. Beam Jr., "An Ode to Gordon Kahl," in *Inter-Klan Newsletter and Survival Alert* (c. Spring/Summer 1983), 10. See also Schlatter, *Aryan Cowboys*, 121.

128. Louis Beam, "ADDRESS TO THE ARYAN NATIONS CONGRESS" (1983), 7, in Collected Materials on White Nationalism, courtesy of Dr. Emily Clark, Gonzaga University, https://researchguides.gonzaga.edu/c.php?g=1023670&p=7447531. See also Coulson and Shannon, *No Heroes*, 193; Neiwert, *In God's Country*, 57.

129. Flynn and Gerhardt, *The Silent Brotherhood*, 89.

130. Southern Poverty Law Center, "Louis Beam—In His Own Words: Speech at the 1983 Aryan World Congress," n.d., https://www.splcenter.org/fighting-hate/extremist-files /individual/louis-beam.

131. Quoted in Flynn and Gerhardt, *The Silent Brotherhood*, 90. See also Below, *Bring the War Home*, 105; Coulson and Shannon, *No Heroes*, 193.

132. Anti-Defamation League, *Computerized Networks of Hate: An ADL Fact Finding Report* (New York: Anti-Defamation League of B'nai B'rith, January 1984), 1, https://archive .org/details/ComputerizedNetworksOfHate/mode/2up; Below, *Bring the War Home*, 120. David Lowe, "Computerized Networks of Hate," *USA Today*, July 1985, https:// archive.org/details/ComputerizedNetworksOfHate/page/n11/mode/2up.

133. Below, *Bring the War Home*, 105–6. See also Anti-Defamation League, *Computerized Networks of Hate*, 5; Chip Berlet, "When Hate Went Online," *Chip Berlet's Home on the Internet*, April 28, 2001, rev. July 4, 2008, http://www.researchforprogress.us/topic /34691/when-hate-went-online/; see also the scanned version of the original paper, http://simson.net/ref/leaderless/berlet_when_hate_went_online.pdf; Lowe, "Computerized Networks of Hate"; Stern, "The Covenant, the Sword, and the Arm of the Lord," 147.

134. Yoshihito Sakurai, Atsushi Oikawa, and Norihisa Hatakeyama, "IEEE Milestone Dedication Ceremony for International Standardization of G3 Facsimile," *NTT Technical Review* 10, no. 8 (2012), https://www.ntt-review.jp/archive/ntttechnical.php?contents =ntr201208in2.html.

135. The equivalent of $3,315 today. "Apple II and ///—UK pricelist from 1983," https:// jesperalsed.com/vintageapple/product/apple-ii-and-uk-pricelist-from-1983/; In2013Dollars, https://www.in2013dollars.com/us/inflation/1983?amount=12https://jesperalsed .com/vintageapple/product/apple-ii-and-uk-pricelist-from-1983/81.

136. James Grahame, "Getting Online: The Hayes Smartmodem," *Retro Thing: Vintage Gadgets & Technology*, https://www.retrothing.com/2009/03/hayes-smartmodem .html.

137. "Nazi BBS a Challenge to Hackers," *2600: The Monthly Journal of the American Hacker* 2, no. 3 (March 1985): 1, http://www.vtda.org/pubs/2600/2600_2-3.pdf. See also Berlet, "When Hate Went Online," 1, 4.

138. "Nazi BBS a Challenge to Hackers," 1. See also Anti-Defamation League, *Computerized Networks of Hate*, 1; Berlet, "When Hate Went Online," 3; Wayne King, "Link by Computer Used by Rightists," *New York Times*, February 15, 1985; Lowe, "Computerized Networks of Hate."

139. Grahame, "Getting Online." See also N. Z. Bear, "When 300 Baud Was the Bomb," *Salon*, May 31, 2002, https://www.salon.com/2002/05/31/back_in_the_day/.

140. Beam, "Leaderless Resistance." See also Louis Beam, "LEADERLESS RESISTANCE," *The Seditionist* 12 (February 1992, final ed.), http://www.louisbeam.com/leaderless.htm, for a more expansive and detailed version of this concept.

141. Louis Beam, "COMPUTER AND THE AMERICAN PATRIOT," *Inter-Klan Newsletter & Survival Alert*, c. April/May 1984, https://simson.net/ref/leaderless/1984.inter-klan_newsletter.pdf.

142. Quoted in Anti-Defamation League, *Computerized Networks of Hate*, 2. See also Berlet, "When Hate Went Online," 4–5; Coates, *Armed and Dangerous*, 206–7; Dees, *Gathering Storm*, 40; King, "Link by Computer Used by Rightists"; Lowe, "Computerized Networks of Hate"; Martinez, *Brotherhood of Murder*, 57.

143. Lowe, "Computerized Networks of Hate."

144. Belew, *Bring the War Home*, 105; Coulson and Shannon, *No Heroes*, 193; Manis, *The Street Agent*, 282; Schlatter, *Aryan Cowboys*, 79.

145. Singular, *Talked to Death*, 130–32. See also Coulson and Shannon, *No Heroes*, 193.

146. "Robert Jay Mathews' Last Letter."

147. Lake, "Neo-Nazi Terrorism in the United States." The same point is made in Corcoran, *Bitter Harvest*, 37. See also Suall and Lowe, "The Hate Movement Today," 353.

148. Quoted in Griffin, *The Fame of a Dead Man's Deeds*. See also Coulson and Shannon, *No Heroes*, 193; Martinez, *Brotherhood of Murder*, 40–41; Michael, *Confronting Right-Wing Extremism and Terrorism in the USA*, 101.

149. Coulson and Shannon, *No Heroes*, 193; Manis, *The Street Agent*, 279; Martinez, *Brotherhood of Murder*, 25–26; Schlatter, *Aryan Cowboys*, 79.

150. Coulson and Shannon, *No Heroes*, 193; Hamm, *Terrorism as Crime*, 125; Martinez, *Brotherhood of Murder*, 41; Singular, *Talked to Death*, 134–35.

151. Quoted in Manis, *The Street Agent*, 280. See also Belew, *Bring the War Home*, 114; Coulson and Shannon, *No Heroes*, 193; Hamm, *Terrorism as Crime*, 125–26.

152. Manis, *The Street Agent*, 281–82.

153. Flynn and Gerhardt, *The Silent Brotherhood*, xii–xiii, 86–87, 112, 139–40; Hamm, *Terrorism as Crime*, 119–22, 124–25.

154. Coates, *Armed and Dangerous*, 45.

155. Coates, *Armed and Dangerous*, 43–44; Corcoran, *Bitter Harvest*, 32; Flynn and Gerhardt, *The Silent Brotherhood*, xii–xiii, 58–59, 177, 214–15; Hamm, *Terrorism as Crime*, 125; Wayne King, "Right-Wing Extremists Seek to Recruit Farmers," *New York Times*, September 20, 1985; Schlatter, *Aryan Cowboys*, 82. "A Letter from Richard Scutari, The Unbroken Warrior, dated 12 December 2014," Facebook post on Richard Scutari, the Unbroken Warrior Facebook page, January 17, 2015, https://www.facebook.com/theunbrokenwarrior/posts/892506194133622:0.

156. Belew, *Bring the War Home*, 115; Coates, *Armed and Dangerous*, 43–44; Flynn and Gerhardt, *The Silent Brotherhood*, xiii, 184–89; Hamm, *Terrorism as Crime*, 125.

157. Belew, *Bring the War Home*, 115; Corcoran, *Bitter Harvest*, 32; Flynn and Gerhardt, *The Silent Brotherhood*, xii, 214–15; Hamm, *Terrorism as Crime*, 124, 133–34; Levitas, *The*

Terrorist Next Door, 225–28; King, "Right-Wing Extremists Seek to Recruit Farmers";
Singular, *Talked to Death*, 177–88.

158. Anti-Defamation League, "14 Words," https://www.adl.org/education/references/hate
-symbols/14-words; Southern Poverty Law Center, "David Lane," https://www.splcenter
.org/fighting-hate/extremist-files/individual/david-lane. See also Meagan Day, "Welcome to Hayden Lake, Where White Supremacists Tried to Build Their Homeland: The
Troubling Rise of the Aryan Nations Compound," *Timeline*, November 4, 2016, https://
timeline.com/white-supremacist-rural-paradise-fb62b74b29e0; George Michael, "David
Lane and the Fourteen Words," *Totalitarian Movements and Political Religions* 10,
no. 1 (July 2009): 43–61.

159. Belew, *Bring the War Home*, 113–15; Flynn and Gerhardt, *The Silent Brotherhood*, xiii,
60–61; Hamm, *Terrorism as Crime*, 123; Schlatter, *Aryan Cowboys*, 82; Chad Sokol,
"Gary Lee Yarbrough, Onetime Bodyguard of Aryan Nations Founder, Dies in Prison,"
Spokesman-Review, April 6, 2018, https://www.spokesman.com/stories/2018/apr/06
/gary-lee-yarbrough-onetime-bodyguard-of-aryan-nati/.

160. Belew, *Bring the War Home*, 20–32, 117, 128. See also Schlatter, *Aryan Cowboys*, 83.

161. Hamm, *Terrorism as Crime*, 123.

162. Belew, *Bring the War Home*, 116; Dees, *Gathering Storm*, 139; Hamm, *Terrorism as Crime*,
116; Neiwert, *In God's Country*, 57, 121; Levitas, *The Terrorist Next Door*, 336; Martinez,
Brotherhood of Murder, 37; Michael, *Confronting Right-Wing Extremism and Terrorism
in the USA*, 98, 100; Noble, *Tabernacle of Hate*, 155; Schlatter, *Aryan Cowboys*, 77–79,
81; Stern, "The Covenant, the Sword, and the Arm of the Lord," 147; Stern, *A Force Upon
the Plain*, 20; Stock, *Rural Radicals*, 173–74; Wright, *Patriots, Politics, and the Oklahoma
City Bombing*, 88.

163. Singular, *Talked to Death*, 134.

164. Flynn and Gerhardt, *The Silent Brotherhood*, 294–95; Manis, *The Street Agent*, 299;
Hamm, *Terrorism as Crime*, 129, 146.

165. Martinez, *Brotherhood of Murder*, 18; Coates, *Armed and Dangerous*, 49; Coulson and
Shannon, *No Heroes*, 197, 188; Manis, *The Street Agent*, 286, 275–76.

166. Coates, *Armed and Dangerous*, 50; Dees, *Gathering Storm*, 142; Manis, *The Street Agent*,
286; Singular, *Talked to Death*, 135; Stern, *A Force Upon the Plain*, 16, 53, 138.

167. Manis, *The Street Agent*, 281.

168. Noble, *Tabernacle of Hate*, 155.

169. Suall and Lowe, "The Hate Movement Today," 354. See also Flynn and Gerhardt, *The
Silent Brotherhood*, 268–69; "Former KKK Leader Robert Miles Dead at 67," UPI,
August 18, 1992, https://www.upi.com/Archives/1992/08/18/Former-KKK-leader-Robert
-Miles-dead-at-67/7854714110400/; Singular, *Talked to Death*, 208.

170. Anti-Defamation League, *Hate Groups in America*, 113.

171. Quoted in Flynn and Gerhardt, *The Silent Brotherhood*, 90–91. See also Singular, *Talked
to Death*, 232–33.

172. Noble, *Tabernacle of Hate*, 155.

173. Associated Press, "10 Members of The Order Convicted: Neo-Nazis Guilty of Racketeering, Armored-Car Robberies," *Los Angeles Times*, December 31. 1985; Bennett, *The*

Party of Fear, 349; Manis, *The Street Agent*, 363–67; Neiwert, *In God's Country*, 59; Stern, *A Force Upon the Plain*, 56.

174. Belew, *Bring the War Home*, 123–24; James Coates, "Writer's Exposé Left Him Exposed," *Chicago Tribune*, September 19, 1985, https://www.chicagotribune.com/news/ct-xpm-1985-09-19-8503030757-story.html; Flynn and Gerhardt, *The Silent Brotherhood*, 144–45, 192–93, 195, 203–7, 221, 338–39; Dees, *Gathering Storm*, 144; Coulson and Shannon, *No Heroes*, 195–96; Hamm, *Terrorism as Crime*, 133–35; Martinez, *Brotherhood of Murder*, 92–93; Michael, *Confronting Right-Wing Extremism and Terrorism in the USA*, 100; Neiwert, *In God's Country*, 58–59; Stern, *A Force Upon the Plain*, 55; "Death List Names Given to U.S. Jury," *New York Times*, September 17, 1985; Schlatter, *Aryan Cowboys*, 80; Singular, *Talked to Death*, 216–17, 224–27, 230; Wright, *Patriots, Politics, and the Oklahoma City Bombing*, 89.

175. Belew, *Bring the War Home*, 132.

176. Coates, "Writer's Exposé Left Him Exposed"; Flynn and Gerhardt, *The Silent Brotherhood*, 145; Hamm, *Terrorism as Crime*, 133–34, 145; Levitas, *The Terrorist Next Door*, 294–95.

177. Belew, *Bring the War Home*, 118–19; Dees, *Gathering Storm*, 142; Hamm, *Terrorism as Crime*, 127; Neiwert, *In God's Country*, 57; Stern, *A Force Upon the Plain*, 55.

178. Flynn and Gerhardt, *The Silent Brotherhood*, 123–25.

179. Belew, *Bring the War Home*, 122; Dees, *Gathering Storm*, 143; Manis, *The Street Agent*, 295, 363–64; Stern, "The Covenant, the Sword, and the Arm of the Lord," 148.

180. Belew, *Bring the War Home*, 126, 131–32; Flynn and Gerhardt, *The Silent Brotherhood*, 217–18, 225–43; Manis, *The Street Agent*, 320–25; Singular, *Talked to Death*, 238–39; United Press International, "6 Gunmen Hold Up Brink's Truck and Escape with Sacks of Loot," *New York Times*, July 20, 1984.

181. Flynn and Gerhardt, *The Silent Brotherhood*, 249; Hamm, *Terrorism as Crime*, 140; Singular, *Talked to Death*, 239.

182. Belew, *Bring the War Home*, 122, 126, 134, 143; Dees, *Gathering Storm*, 143; Flynn and Gerhardt, *The Silent Brotherhood*, 53, 249, 271–72; Hamm, *Terrorism as Crime*, 139–40; Manis, *The Street Agent*, 249, 285–86, 298; Michael, *Confronting Right-Wing Extremism and Terrorism in the USA*, 100–1; MSNBC, "The Rachel Maddow Show, Transcript 8/14/17: White America Has a Chronic Nazi Problem," http://www.msnbc.com/transcripts/rachel-maddow-show/2017-08-14; Neiwert, *In God's Country*, 58; Schlatter, *Aryan Cowboys*, 80, 189n97; Singular, *Talked to Death*, 207–8; Southern Poverty Law Center, "Frazier Glenn Miller," https://www.splcenter.org/fighting-hate/extremist-files/individual/frazier-glenn-miller; Stern, *A Force Upon the Plain*, 55.

183. Belew, *Bring the War Home*, 133–34; Dees, *Gathering Storm*, 143.

184. Belew, *Bring the War Home*, 134.

185. Belew, *Bring the War Home*, 126, 134, 143.

186. Hamm, *Terrorism as Crime*, 140.

187. Belew, *Bring the War Home*, 122; Manis, *The Street Agent*, 285–86, 298; Hamm, *Terrorism as Crime*, 128–29; Michael, *Confronting Right-Wing Extremism and Terrorism in the USA*, 100–1; Neiwert, *In God's Country*, 57; Stern, *A Force Upon the Plain*, 55.

188. Flynn and Gerhardt, *The Silent Brotherhood*, 261; Hamm, *Terrorism as Crime*, 131, 142–43; Manis, *The Street Agent*, 326; Schlatter, *Aryan Cowboys*, 80, 189n97.

189. Manis, *The Street Agent*, 331–32; Hamm, *Terrorism as Crime*, 145.

190. "Robert Jay Mathews' Last Letter"; Coulson and Shannon, *No Heroes*, 197–207; Hamm, *Terrorism as Crime*, 145–48; Manis, *The Street Agent*, 326–37.

191. Belew, *Bring the War Home*, 124, 128; Coulson and Shannon, *No Heroes*, 199; Dees, *Gathering Storm*, 144; Hamm, *Terrorism as Crime*, 148–49; Manis, *The Street Agent*, 330, 345–49; Flynn and Gerhardt, *The Silent Brotherhood*, 221–24, 302, 303, 330–31, 333–47; interview with William Pierce in Michael, *Confronting Right-Wing Extremism and Terrorism in the USA*, 102; Neiwert, *In God's Country*, 58; Singular, *Talked to Death*, 230–31, 242–43; Stern, *A Force Upon the Plain*, 55–56.

192. Belew, *Bring the War Home*, 128, 134; Coulson and Shannon, *No Heroes*, 199; Hamm, *Terrorism as Crime*, 149–50; Manis, *The Street Agent*, 342–49; Singular, *Talked to Death*, 282.

193. Singular, *Talked to Death*, 252.

194. Quoted in Singular, *Talked to Death*, 251–56. See also Noble, *Tabernacle of Hate*, 157–62; and the excerpts in Manis, *The Street Agent*, 349–51. See also Belew, *Bring the War Home*, 129; Coulson and Shannon, *No Heroes*, 200–1; Hamm, *Terror as Crime*, 150–51.

195. Coulson and Shannon, *No Heroes*, 201–7; Manis, *The Street Agent*, 352–61; Oliver "Buck" Revell and Dwight Williams, *A G-Man's Journal* (New York: Pocket, 1998), 218. See also Belew, *Bring the War Home*, 128; Hamm, *Terrorism as Crime*, 152–53; Schlatter, *Aryan Cowboys*, 80.

196. Noble, *Tabernacle of Hate*, 162. See also Simi and Futrell, *American Swastika*, 27.

3. RACE WAR

1. Wayne King, "Links of Anti-Semitic Band Provoke 6-State Parley," *New York Times*, December 27, 1984; Robert L. Jackson and Ronald J. Ostrow, "Law in War on Far-Right Sect: White Supremacists Tied to Western Crime Spree," *Los Angeles Times*, January 21, 1985; Mary Thornton and T. R. Reid, "Aryan Group, Jail Gangs Linked: FBI Reports on White Supremacist Organization," *Washington Post*, December 18, 1984.

2. U.S. District Court, Western Division of Washington at Seattle, United States of America v. Bruce Carroll Pierce, et al., No. CR85-001M, July 18, 1985.

3. Quoted in Jackson and Ostrow, "Law in War on Far-Right Sect."

4. Sgt. Allen D. Hines, "Trooper Jimmie E. 'Jim' Linegar, Badge #865, EOW . . . April 15, 1985," (no date), https://www.mshp.dps.missouri.gov/MSHPWeb/UltimateSacrifice/OfficerPages/documents/Linegar.pdf. See also "Slaying Suspect Tate Seized in Missouri Hills," *Los Angeles Times*, April 21, 1995; Kathleen Belew, *Bring the War Home: The White Power Movement and Paramilitary America* (Cambridge, MA: Harvard University Press, 2018), 131–32; James Coates, *Armed and Dangerous: The Rise of the Survivalist Right* (New York: Hill & Wang, 1987), 140–41; James Coates, "Neo-Nazis Indicted

in Bizarre Crime Spree," *Chicago Tribune*, April 16, 1985; Kevin Flynn and Gary Ger-
hardt, *The Silent Brotherhood: Inside America's Racist Underground* (New York: Free
Press, 1989), 286, 398; Mark S. Hamm, *Terrorism as Crime: From Oklahoma City to
Al-Qaeda and Beyond* (New York: New York University Press, 2007), 109; Jessica Stern,
"The Covenant, the Sword, and the Arm of the Lord" (1985), in *Toxic Terror: Assessing
Terrorist Use of Chemical and Biological Weapons*, ed. J. B. Tucker (Cambridge, MA:
MIT Press, 2000), 149–50; and United Press International, "Neo-Nazi David Tate, who
is serving a life prison . . .," March 3, 1986, https://www.upi.com/Archives/1986/03/03
/Neo-Nazi-David-Tate-who-is-serving-a-life-prison/2514510210000/.

5. Flynn and Gerhardt, *The Silent Brotherhood*, xiii, 108–9.

6. Flynn and Gerhardt, *The Silent Brotherhood*, 108–9; "David Tate | Gary Yarbrough's
    Blog, "MORE INFIGHTING? WHAT'S WRONG WITH YOU?! Another Scolding by
    David C. Tate," December 18, 2019, https://susan1219.wordpress.com/tag/david-tate/;
    Coates, *Armed and Dangerous*, 140–41; and Kerry Noble, *Tabernacle of Hate* (Prescott,
    Ontario: Voyageur, 1998), 17.

7. "Slaying Suspect Tate Seized in Missouri Hills"; Belew, *Bring the War Home*, 131; Coates,
    Armed and Dangerous, 140–41; Danny O. Coulson and Elaine Shannon, *No Heroes:
    Inside the FBI's Secret Counter-Terror Force* (New York: Pocket, 199), 252; Hamm,
    Terrorism as Crime, 109.

8. "Slaying Suspect Tate Seized in Missouri Hills"; Coates, *Armed and Dangerous*, 141–
    42; Flynn and Gerhardt, *The Silent Brotherhood*, 287, 386, 398; Hamm, *Terrorism as
    Crime*, 109–10; Hines, "Trooper Jimmie E. "Jim" Linegar"; Stern, "Covenant, Sword, and
    Arm of the Lord," 150; Noble, *Tabernacle of Hate*, 17.

9. FBI Records: The Vault, Memorandum, from SAC, Little Rick, to Director, FBI Sub-
    ject: The Covenant, Sword, And Arm of The Lord (CSA), Domestic Security, August 8,
    1983; Memorandum, Supervisor [name redacted] to SAC (100A-4858), Subject: The
    Covenant, The Sword, And The Arm of The Lord; DS/T, March 29, 1985; Memoran-
    dum, from J. W. Hicks to Mr. Geer, Re: The Covenant, The Sword, And The Arm of The
    Lord; Domestic Security—Terrorism OO: Little Rock, May 2, 1985; Memorandum,
    from ASAC Danny O. Coulson to SAC, Washington Field, Subject: Covenant, Sword,
    And The Arm of The Lord (CSA); Domestic Terrorism, May 8, 1985; Memorandum,
    from ASAC Danny O. Coulson to SAC, Washington Field, The Covenant, The Sword,
    The Arm of The Lord; Domestic Security/Terrorism, May 20, 1985; Little Rock Field
    Office, Memorandum, Subject: The Covenant, The Sword, And The Arm of The Lord;
    Domestic Security—Terrorism, July 29, 1985; Part I, https://vault.fbi.gov/The%20Cov-
    enant%20The%20Sword%20The%20Arm%20of%20the%20Lord%20/The%20Cove-
    nant%20The%20Sword%20The%20Arm%20of%20the%20Lord%20Part%201%20
    of%202/view; Little Rock Field Office, Memorandum, Subject: The Covenant, The
    Sword, And The Arm of The Lord; Domestic Security/Terrorism, July 2, 1985; Little
    Rock Field Office, December 29, 1987; Little Rock Field Office, Memorandum [sender
    and recipient redacted], Subject: The Covenant, The Sword, And The Arm of The Lord
    (DS/T), January 12, 1988 Part II, https://vault.fbi.gov/The%20Covenant%20The%20

Sword%20The%20Arm%20of%20the%20Lord%20/The%20Covenant%20The%20
Sword%20The%20Arm%20of%20the%20Lord%20Part%202%20of%202/view. See also
Hamm, *Terrorism as Crime*, 110; Belew, *Bring the War Home*, 132; Coulson and
Shannon, *No Heroes*, 252; Morris Dees with James Corcoran, *Gathering Storm:
America's Militia Threat* (New York: HarperCollins, 1996), 24; Noble, *Tabernacle of
Hate*, 17–18, 165; Oliver "Buck" Revell and Dwight Williams, *A G-Man's Journal: A
Legendary Career Inside the FBI—from the Kennedy Assassination to the Oklahoma
City Bombing* (New York: Pocket, 1998), 218–219; United Press International, "Neo-
Nazi David Tate."

10. FBI Records: The Vault, Little Rock Field Office, Memorandum, Subject: The Covenant, The
Sword, And The Arm of The Lord; Domestic Security/Terrorism, September 7, 1984; FBI
Records: The Vault, Little Rock Field Office, Memorandum, Subject: The Covenant, The
Sword, And The Arm of The Lord; Domestic Security/Terrorism, May 20, 1985; FBI
Records: The Vault, Little Rock Field Office, Memorandum, Subject: The Covenant, The
Sword, And The Arm of The Lord; Domestic Security/Terrorism, July 2, 1985; and FBI
Records: The Vault, Little Rock Field Office, Memorandum, Subject: The Covenant, The
Sword, And The Arm of The Lord; Domestic Security/Terrorism, December 29, 1987,
Part I, https://vault.fbi.gov/The%20Covenant%20The%20Sword%20The%20Arm%20
of%20the%20Lord%20/The%20Covenant%20The%20Sword%20The%20Arm%20of%20
the%20Lord%20Part%201%20of%202/view; July 2, 1987, Part II, https://vault.fbi.gov
/The%20Covenant%20The%20Sword%20The%20Arm%20of%20the%20Lord%20
/The%20Covenant%20The%20Sword%20The%20Arm%20of%20the%20Lord%20
Part%202%20of%202/view. See also Coulson and Shannon, *No Heroes*, 312; Noble, *Tabernacle of Hate*, 22; Revell and Williams, *A G-Man's Journal*, 219; Stern, "Covenant, Sword,
and Arm of the Lord," 150.

11. FBI Records: The Vault, Memorandum, Supervisor [name redacted] to SAC (100A-
4858), Subject: The Covenant, The Sword, And The Arm of The Lord; DS/T, March 29,
1985.

12. Noble, *Tabernacle of Hate*, 17, 163, 166. See also Hamm, *Terrorism as Crime*, 110–11.

13. Coulson and Shannon, *No Heroes*, 257, 264; Noble, *Tabernacle of Hate*, 22.

14. Quoted in Hamm, *Terrorism as Crime*, 111. See also Noble, *Tabernacle of Hate*, 22.

15. Noble, *Tabernacle of Hate*, 14–15, 163–65.

16. See CBC (Canada), "The Survivalists; Shopping for Doomsday," *The Fifth Estate* (1981),
https://www.youtube.com/watch?v=0YHUiL9HI5g.

17. Noble, *Tabernacle of Hate*, 23, 163; Revell and Williams, *A G-Man's Journal*, 219; Stern,
"Covenant, Sword, and Arm of the Lord," 139, 155.

18. FBI Records: The Vault, FBI Laboratory Division, May 1, 1985, attachment The Cove-
nant, The Sword, The Arm Of The Lord; Domestic Security/Terrorism, May 20, 1985;
FBI Records: The Vault, Memorandum, from ASAC Danny O. Coulson to SAC, Wash-
ington Field, Subject: Covenant, Sword, And The Arm of The Lord (CSA); Domestic
Terrorism, May 8, 1985; FBI Records: The Vault, Memorandum, From J. W. Hicks to
Mr. Geer, Re: The Covenant, The Sword, And The Arm of The Lord; Domestic

Security—Terrorism OO: Little Rock, May 2, 1985, https://vault.fbi.gov/The%20Cove-nant%20The%20Sword%20The%20Arm%20of%20the%20Lord%20/The%20Cove-nant%20The%20Sword%20The%20Arm%20of%20the%20Lord%20Part%201%20 of%202/view; ibid., Little Rock Field Office, The Covenant, The Sword, And The Arm of The Lord; Domestic Security/Terrorism, December 29, 1987;, Part II, https://vault .fbi.gov/The%20Covenant%20The%20Sword%20The%20Arm%20of%20the%20 Lord%20/The%20Covenant%20The%20Sword%20The%20Arm%20of%20the%20 Lord%20Part%202%20of%202/view; Coulson and Shannon, *No Heroes*, 263–313, 111–14; George Michael, *Confronting Right-Wing Extremism and Terrorism in the USA* (London: Routledge, 2003), 143; Noble, *Tabernacle of Hate*, 169; Revell and Williams, *A G-Man's Journal*, 219–21.

19.   Quoted in Coulson and Shannon, *No Heroes*, 311.

20.   Coulson and Shannon, *No Heroes*, 312; FBI Records: The Vault, Little Rock Field Office, Memorandum, Subject: The Covenant, The Sword, And The Arm of The Lord; Domestic Security/Terrorism, July 2, 1987, Part II, https://vault.fbi.gov/The%20Covenant%20 The%20Sword%20The%20Arm%20of%20the%20Lord%20/The%20Covenant%20 The%20Sword%20The%20Arm%20of%20the%20Lord%20Part%202%20of%202/view; "Ellison Trial Begins Monday," Associated Press, July 14, 1985, https://apnews.com/article /5abfc20488f8935f3757d0545addo1ec; Katherine Bishop, "Plot Against U.S. Described In Court," *New York Times*, February 28, 1988; Hamm, *Terrorism as Crime*, 100; Noble, *Tab-ernacle of Hate*, 103, 173; Stern, "Covenant, Sword, and Arm of the Lord," 139, 150–56. Note that in an interview with Stern, Noble denied that any specific cities had been selected. Stern, "Covenant, Sword, and Arm of the Lord," 151.

21.   Coulson and Shannon, *No Heroes*, 312.

22.   Email correspondence with Dr. Seth Carus, an expert on biological and chemical weap-ons, at the National Defense University, Washington, DC, October 5, 2020; Richard C. Dart, "Hydroxocabalamin for Acute Poisoning: New Data from Preclinical and Clinical Studies; New Results from the Prehospital Emergency Setting," *Clinical Toxi-cology* 44, suppl. 1, nos. 1–3 (2006): 1–3; Stern, "Covenant, Sword, and Arm of the Lord," 153–54, 156. All these contradict the assertion in Belew, *Bring the War Home*, 179.

23.   Quoted in Stern, "Covenant, Sword, and Arm of the Lord," 151.

24.   Coulson and Shannon, *No Heroes*, 313.

25.   Belew, *Bring the War Home*, 171; James Coates and Stephen Franklin, "'Underground' of Racist Leaders Coordinated Crimes, FBI Tapes Show," *Washington Post*, Decem-ber 28, 1987; Wayne King, "20 Held in 7 States in Sweep of Nazis Arming for 'War' on U.S.," *New York Times*, March 3, 1985.

26.   Belew, *Bring the War Home*, 171.

27.   Belew, *Bring the War Home*; James Coates, "U.S. Aims to Break Neo-Nazis," *Chicago Tribune*, April 26, 1987.

28.   Iver Peterson, "White Supremacists Meet in Quest for Homeland," *New York Times*, July 14, 1986, https://www.nytimes.com/1986/07/14/us/white-supremacists-meet-in -quest-for-homeland.html.

29.   Metzger's recent obituary described him "one of the most influential leaders of the white supremacist movement." Concepción de León, "Tom Metzger, Notorious White Supremacist, Dies at 82," *New York Times*, November 12, 2020, https://www.nytimes.com/2020/11/12/us/tom-metzger-dead.html.

30.   Withrow left the movement and renounced white supremacism the following year and thereafter spoke out against racism and antisemitism. James Alfred Aho, *The Politics of Righteousness: Idaho Christian Patriotism* (Seattle: University of Washington Press, 2014), 33; Jim Mulvaney, " 'Skinheads' Founder Now 'Sorry for What I've Done,' " *Chicago Sun-Times*, July 27, 1993, https://web.archive.org/web/20140921122235/http://www.highbeam.com/doc/1P2-4181798.html.

31.   Steve Green, "White Supremacists Meet in Idaho," United Press International, July 12, 1986, https://www.upi.com/Archives/1986/07/12/White-supremacists-meet-in-Idaho/9315521524800/.

32.   Quoted in Peterson, "White Supremacists Meet in Quest for Homeland."

33.   Quoted in Flynn and Gerhardt, *The Silent Brotherhood*, 388.

34.   State v. Dorr, 120 Idaho 441, 816 P.2d 998 (1991), July 1, 1991, 441–45, https://cite.case.law/idaho/120/441/; Coates, *Armed and Dangerous*, 261; Flynn and Gerhardt, *The Silent Brotherhood*, 388; Charles W. Hall, "Former Neo-Nazi Had Troubled MD. Past," *Washington Post*, February 26, 1987, https://www.washingtonpost.com/archive/local/1987/02/26/former-neo-nazi-had-troubled-md-past/5e801fd0-94f9-4dce-8901-0d52ba25c95b/; Edward B. Havens, "One Neo-Nazi Guilty of Murder, Two of Counterfeiting," United Press International, February 5, 1987, https://www.upi.com/Archives/1987/02/05/One-neo-Nazi-guilty-of-murder-two-of-counterfeiting/3730539499600/; David A. Neiwert, *In God's Country: The Patriot Movement and the Pacific Northwest* (Pullman: Washington State University Press, 2019), 60–61; Eric Scigliano, "He Was Not Following Orders," *Seattle Weekly*, October 9, 2006, https://www.seattleweekly.com/news/he-was-not-following-orders/; Brent L. Smith, *Terrorism in America: Pipe Bombs and Pipe Dreams* (Albany: State University of New York Press, 1994), 77–79; Wallace Turner, "3 in Racist Group Held on Counterfeiting Charges," *New York Times*, October 4, 1986, https://www.nytimes.com/1986/10/04/us/3-in-racist-group-held-on-counterfeiting-charges.html; Stuart A. Wright, *Patriots, Politics, and the Oklahoma City Bombing* (Cambridge: Cambridge University Press, 2007), 93–94; Glen Warchol, "Coeur d'Alene Bombing Suspects Arraigned," United Press International, October 1, 1987, https://www.upi.com/Archives/1987/10/01/Coeur-dAlene-bombing-suspects-arraigned/1813560059200/; Bernie Wilson, "URGENT—3 Linked to Aryan Nations Arrested," *Associated Press*, October 3, 1986, https://apnews.com/article/db0830b9459db28bf3fbb815cda29976.

35.   State v. Dorr, 442–43; Smith, *Terrorism in America*, 78–79; Warchol, "Coeur d'Alene Bombing Suspects Arraigned."

36.   Sam Meddis, "Neo-Nazis Weakened, FBI Says," *USA Today*, February 18, 1985.

37.   "Wanted by FBI: Thomas George Harrelson," Identification Order 5023, November 8, 1986, https://www.ebay.com/itm/ARYAN-NATION-LEADER-NEO-NAZI-THOMAS

-HARRELSON-FBI-WANTED-POSTER-PLS-OFFER-/224135654820 ; "Most Wanted: Thomas George Harrelson—Former Ten Most Wanted Fugitive #407," https://www.fbi .gov/wanted/topten/topten-history/hires_images/FBI-407-ThomasGeorgeHarrelson .jpg/view; "Thomas Harrelson," *Unsolved Mysteries*, https://unsolvedmysteries.fandom .com/wiki/Thomas_Harrelson; "Suspect in Bank Robberies One of FBI's Most Wanted," *Los Angeles Times*, November 30, 1986; "Man Arrested for Bank Robbery on FBI Fugitives List," Associated Press, February 20, 1987; Coates, "U.S. Aims To Break Neo-Nazis"; Wayne King, "Neo-Nazi Is Focus of Searching by F.B.I.," *New York Times*, August 18, 1986; and Gerald Kopplin, "Suspected White Supremacist to Face Bank Robbery Charges," United Press International, February 24, 1987.

38.   David H. Bennett, *The Party of Fear: The American Far Right from Nativism to the Militia Movement* (New York: Vintage, 1995), 448; "Eight Suspects Have Been Arrested in a White Supremacist Plot," United Press International, December 16, 1986, https://www .upi.com/Archives/1986/12/16/Eight-suspects-have-been-arrested-in-a-white-supre macist/5811535093200/; Flynn and Gerhardt, *The Silent Brotherhood*, 389; Andy Hall, "Secret War: 'Patriots' Have Loose Ties to Rightists Nationwide," *Arizona Republic*, December 21, 1986; Thomas J. Knudson, "Right-Wing Group Accused of Bank Robbery Plot," *New York Times*, December 17, 1986; Daniel Levitas, *The Terrorist Next Door: The Militia Movement and the Radical Right* (New York: Thomas Dunne, 2002), 289–90; Brent L. Smith, Kelly R. Damphousse, and Paxton Roberts, *Pre-Incident Indicators of Terrorist Incidents: The Identification of Behavioral, Geographic, and Temporary Patterns of Preparatory Conduct* (Washington, DC: Department of Justice, May 2006), appendix C, "Case Study Narratives: 1.1 Arizona Patriots," 1; Kenneth S. Stern, *A Force Upon the Plain: The American Militia Movement and the Politics of Hate* (New York: Simon & Schuster, 1996), 185, 191; Wright, *Patriots, Politics, and the Oklahoma City Bombing*, 94–95.

39.   "Ty Hardin: Biography," *IMDb*, https://www.imdb.com/name/nm0362249/bio; Levitas, *The Terrorist Next Door*, 289. See also Bennett, *The Party of Fear*, 448; "Eight Suspects Have Been Arrested in a White Supremacist Plot"; Smith et al., *Pre-Incident Indicators of Terrorist Incidents*, 1; Smith, *Terrorism in America*, 80; Wright, *Patriots, Politics, and the Oklahoma City Bombing*, 94.

40.   Quoted in "Ty Hardin: Biography."

41.   Hall, "Secret War: 'Patriots' Have Loose Ties to Rightists Nationwide"; Levitas, *The Terrorist Next Door*, 289; Wright, *Patriots, Politics, and the Oklahoma City Bombing*, 92.

42.   Wayne F. Manis, *The Street Agent: After Taking on the Mob, the Klan, and the Aryan Nations, He Walks Softly and Carries a .357 Magnum—The True Story* (Palisades, NY: History Publishing, 2014), 394, 315; Wright, *Patriots, Politics, and the Oklahoma City Bombing*, 92.

43.   Belew, *Bring the War Home*, 214; Levitas, *The Terrorist Next Door*, 289; Smith, *Terrorism in America*, 80; Wright, *Patriots, Politics, and the Oklahoma City Bombing*, 94–95.

44.   Belew, *Bring the War Home*, 171; Flynn and Gerhardt, *The Silent Brotherhood*, 389; Hall, ""Secret War: 'Patriots' Have Loose Ties to Rightists Nationwide"; Levitas, *The*

Terrorist Next Door, 289; Neiwert, *In God's Country*, 134; Smith, *Terrorism in America*, 80–81; Wright, *Patriots, Politics, and the Oklahoma City Bombing*, 94–95.

45. Quoted in Belew, *Bring the War Home*, 171, 214.

46. Evelyn A. Schlatter, *Aryan Cowboys: White Supremacists and the Search for a New Frontier, 1970–2000* (Austin: University of Texas Press, 2006), 41. See also Hall, "Secret War: 'Patriots' Have Loose Ties to Rightists Nationwide."

47. Smith et al., *Pre-Incident Indicators of Terrorist Incidents*, 3–4.

48. Stern, *A Force Upon the Plain*, 191; Klanwatch, *False Patriots: The Threat of Antigovernment Extremists* (Montgomery, AL: Southern Poverty Law Center, 1996), 21.

49. James Coates and Stephen Franklin, "Court Records Detail Neo-Nazis' Network," *Chicago Tribune*, December 27, 1987. See also Anti-Defamation League, *Extremism on the Right: A Handbook* (New York: Anti-Defamation League, 1983), 116–17; Belew, *Bring the War Home*, 171–72; "Covenant (CSA)—the Rock Star," GlobalSecurity.org, https://www.globalsecurity.org/military/world/para/csa-1.htm.

50. District Court for the Western District of Arkansas, Fort Smith Division: United States of America v. Robert Edward Miles, Louis Ray Beam, Jr., Richard Girnt Butler, Richard Joseph Scutari, Bruce Carroll Pierce, Andrew Virgil Barnhill, Ardie McBrearty, David Eden Lane, Lambert Miller, Robert Neil Smalley, Ivan Ray Wade, William H. Wade, Richard Wayne Snell, David Michael McGuire: Trial Testimony of Robert E. Miles, 1988, no. 87-20008-01-14; Belew, *Bring the War Home*, 171–72; Coates and Franklin, "'Underground' of Racist Leaders Coordinated Crimes"; Bill Morlin, "Former Butler Associate, Klan Leader Remain at Large," *Spokesman-Review Spokane Chronicle*, April 25, 1987; Risks International, *Weekly Risk Assessment* 4, no. 18 (May 1, 1987): 1.

51. "18 U.S.C. § 2384—U.S. Code—Unannotated Title 18. Crimes and Criminal Procedure § 2384. Seditious Conspiracy," *FindLaw*, https://codes.findlaw.com/us/title-18-crimes-and-criminal-procedure/18-usc-sect-2384.html; Richard Perez-Pena, "The Terror Conspiracy: The Charges; A Gamble Pays Off as the Prosecution Uses an Obscure 19th-Century Law," *New York Times*, October 2, 1995.

52. United States of America v. Robert Edward Miles et al.; Stephen E. Atkins, *Encyclopedia of Right-Wing Extremism in Modern American History* (Santa Barbara, CA: ABC-CLIO, 2011), 215; Belew, *Bring the War Home*, 172–73; Bishop, "Conspiracy Trial of 14 White Supremacists Begins"; Coulson and Shannon, *No Heroes*, 533; "Fort Smith Sedition Trial of 1988," *Encyclopedia of Arkansas*, https://encyclopediaofarkansas.net/entries/fort-smith-sedition-trial-of-1988-13802/; and Morlin, "Former Butler Associate, Klan Leader Remain at Large."

53. "Fort Smith Sedition Trial of 1988," *Encyclopedia of Arkansas*; Bill Simmons, "Defendants All Acquitted in Sedition Trial," *Journal News* (White Plains, NY), April 8, 1988.

54. Atkins, *Encyclopedia of Right-Wing Extremism*, 215; Belew, *Bring the War Home*, 181; Chip Berlet, "Were Feds Duped by White Supremacist and Alleged Killer Frazier Glenn Miller?," *American Prospect*, May 21, 2014, https://prospect.org/justice/feds-duped-white-supremacist-alleged-killer-frazier-glenn-miller/; "Fort Smith Sedition Trial of

1988," *Encyclopedia of Arkansas*; "Juror Falls in Love With Ex-defendant," *The Oklahoman* (Oklahoma City), September 13, 1988; Simmons, "Defendants All Acquitted in Sedition Trial"; "Embedded: The Terrorist," National Public Radio, October 30, 2019, https://podcasts.google.com/feed/aHRocHM6Ly9mZWVkcy5ucHIub3JnLzUxMDM xMS9wb2RjYXNoLnhtbA/episode/ZmU3ZGYxOTktY2VkZS00NmY1LThhYjAtOW UxMzZlOGY5NjBi?sa=X&ved=0CAUQkfYCahcKEwjgmvuqqrn_AhUAAAAAHQA AAAAQQQ.

55. Associated Press, "13 Supremacists Are Not Guilty of Conspiracies," *New York Times*, April 8, 1988; Atkins, *Encyclopedia of Right-Wing Extremism*, 215; Belew, *Bring the War Home*, 173–79; Berlet, "Were Feds Duped by White Supremacist and Alleged Killer Frazier Glenn Miller?"; Coulson and Shannon, *No Heroes*, 533.

56. Belew, *Bring the War Home*, 179; Coulson and Shannon, *No Heroes*, 533; Simmons, "Defendants All Acquitted in Sedition Trial."

57. Anti-Defamation League, "ADL Releases Backgrounder on White Supremacist Kansas Shooter Frazier Glenn Miller," April 14, 2014, https://www.adl.org/news/press -releases/adl-releases-backgrounder-on-white-supremacist-kansas-jewish-commun ity-shooter; Coates, "U.S. Aims To Break Neo-Nazis"; Southern Poverty Law Center, "Frazier Glenn Miller," https://www.splcenter.org/fighting-hate/extremist-files/indiv idual/frazier-glenn-miller; "Embedded: The Terrorist," National Public Radio; Morlin, "Former Butler Associate, Klan Leader Remain at Large."

58. "Archive: April 6, 1987 letter from Frazier Glenn Miller, 'Declaration of War, April 6, 1987,'" *Springfield News Leader* (Springfield, MO), April 14, 2014, https://www.news -leader.com/story/news/local/ozarks/2014/04/14/archive-april-6-1987-letter-from -frazier-glenn-miller/7708641/.

59. Glenn Miller, *A White Man Speaks Out: The Former Leader of the Largest Active White Rights Group in the United States, Speaks Out for White America* (1999), 61–64, 100–101, https://heavy.com/wp-content/uploads/2014/04/awmso.pdf.

60. Mark Berman, "White Supremacist Sentenced to Death for Killing Three People Near Jewish Facilities," *Washington Post*, November 10, 2015; Berlet, "Were Feds Duped by White Supremacist and Alleged Killer Frazier Glenn Miller?"; David Helling, Judy Thomas, and Mark Morris, "Records Suggest That F. Glenn Miller Jr. Was Once in Witness Protection Program," *Wichita Eagle* (Kansas), April 15, 2014.

61. Stephen E. Atkins, *Encyclopedia of Right-Wing Extremism in Modern American History* (Santa Barbara, CA: ABC-CLLIO, 2011), 215; Katherine Bishop, "Conspiracy Trial of 14 White Supremacists Begins," *New York Times*, February 18, 1988; Noble, *Tabernacle of Hate*, 132.

62. Quoted in Bishop, "Conspiracy Trial of 14 White Supremacists Begins." See also "Fort Smith Sedition Trial of 1988," *Encyclopedia of Arkansas*.

63. Coulson and Shannon, *No Heroes*, 533.

64. Atkins, *Encyclopedia of Right-Wing Extremism*, 215; "Fort Smith Sedition Trial of 1988," *Encyclopedia of Arkansas*.

65. Belew, *Bring the War Home*, 179; Noble, *Tabernacle of Hate*, 197.

66. Quoted in AP, "13 Supremacists Are Not Guilty of Conspiracies."

67. Quoted in Simmons, "Defendants All Acquitted in Sedition Trial."

68. Bruce Hoffman, *Recent Trends and Future Prospects of Terrorism in the United States* (Santa Monica, CA: RAND Corporation, May 1988, R-3618), 48.

69. Belew, *Bring the War Home*, 191.

70. Associated Press, "Utah Radio Station Cancels 'Aryan Nations Hour,'" *New York Times*, December 17, 1987; Howard Rosenberg, "Neo-Nazis Cloud the Utah Air: 'Aryan Nations' to Debut Over Tiny Salt Lake City Station," *Los Angeles Times*, November 24, 1987. United Press International, September 23, 1987, quoted in Hoffman, *Recent Trends*, 52.

71. Arie Perliger, *American Zealots: Inside Right-Wing Domestic Terrorism* (New York: Columbia University Press, 2020), 48–49, 51–53; Irwin Suall et al., *ADL Special Report: Shaved for Battle: Skinheads Target America's Youth* (New York: Anti-Defamation League of B'nai B'rith, November 1987), 2–4; Belew, *Bring the War Home*, 194–95; Bennett, *The Party of Fear*, 433–34; Smith, *Terrorism in America*, 91; Cheryl Sullivan, "White Supremacists. Neo-Nazi Drive to Recruit US Youth Has Some Success Among 'Skinheads,'" *Christian Science Monitor*, August 14, 1987.

72. Bennett, *The Party of Fear*, 434; Bill Buford, *Among the Thugs* (New York: Vintage, 1993), 141–52; Robert Forbes and Eddie Stampton, *The White Nationalist Skinhead Movement: UK & USA, 1979–1993* (Minneapolis, MN: Feral House, 2015), 9–41; Suall et al., *ADL Special Report: Shaved for Battle*, 2.

73. Michael Connelly, "Arrests of Teen Members of 'Skinhead' Faction Spell End of Spree of 'Hate Crimes,' Police Say," *Los Angeles Times*, November 1, 1987; "Extremist Admits Gang's Racial Attack," *Los Angeles Times*, July 30, 1987; George Hackett and Pamela Abramson, "Skinheads on the Rampage," *Newsweek*, September 7, 1987; Dennis McLellan, "Ganging Up: 'Skinhead' Groups of White Youths Appear on Rise," *Los Angeles Times*, November 30, 1987; Perliger, *American Zealots*, 50–51; Suall et al., *ADL Special Report: Shaved for Battle*, 1–22; Sullivan, "White Supremacists"; "Terrorism Charges Dropped Against Reputed Skinhead Leader," United Press International, December 1, 1987; "Seven Reputed 'Skinheads' Indicted," United Press International, February 19, 1988.

74. "Man Arrested in Vandalism of Jewish Businesses," Associated Press, November 14, 1987, https://apnews.com/article/b389ba1466e19803a9e8a229dff5bda7; Christian Picciolini, *White American Youth: My Descent Into America's Most Violent Hate Movement—and How I Got Out* (New York: Hachette, 2017), 57–58.

75. Suall et al., *ADL Special Report: Shaved for Battle*, 4–6; Sullivan, "White Supremacists."

76. Quoted in Suall and Lowe, *The Hate Movement Today*, 360.

77. Church of Jesus Christ Christian, *The Way: A Prison Outreach Newsletter by the Church of Jesus Christ Christian* 1 (June 1987): 1. Smith, *Terrorism in America*, 90–91.

78. Church of Jesus Christ Christian, *The Way: A Prison Outreach Newsletter by the Church of Jesus Christ Christian* 2 (September–October 1987).

79. See Louis Beam, "Leaderless Resistance," *The Seditionist* 12 (final ed., February 1992), http://www.louisbeam.com/leaderless.htm. See also Klanwatch/Militia Task Force,

False Patriots: The Threat of Antigovernment Extremists (Montgomery, AL: Southern Poverty Law Center, 1996), 40.

80. FBI Counterterrorism Division Intelligence Assessment, *State of the Domestic White Nationalist Extremist Movement in the United States* (Washington, DC: Federal Bureau of Investigation, December 13, 2006), 5, https://archive.org/details/foia_FBI_Monograph -State_of_Domestic_White_Nationalist_Extremist_Movement_in_the_U.S./mode /2up.

81. Levitas, *The Terrorist Next Door*, 72. See also Anti-Defamation League, *Extremism on the Right*, 86; Wright, *Patriots, Politics, and the Oklahoma City Bombing*, 58, 62.

82. See Ernie Lazar FOIA Collection, "GALE, William Potter HQ 1," https://archive.org /details/GaleWilliamP.HQ1/page/n1/mode/2up; "GALE, William Potter—San Diego 100-13121," https://archive.org/details/GALEWilliamPotterSanDiego01001312175pp; GALE, William Potter = HQ 62-05253, Misc Serials, tps://archive.org/details/galewilli ampotterhq62105253miscserials/page/n17/mode/2up; "GALE, William Potter— Committee of the States-San Francisco 100-63097 and 100A-80325," December 22, 1984, https://archive.org/details/galewilliampottercommitteeofthestatessanfrancisco1 0063097and100a80325/page/n1/mode/2up," "GALE, William Potter—Ministry of Christ Church=HQ157-289, April 3, 1975, https://archive.org/details/galewilliampotter ministryofchristchurchhq15728219/page/n1/mode/2up; "GALE, William Potter— Ministry of Christ Church = Los Angeles 157-7775," May 1, 1973, https://archive.org /details/galewilliampotterministryofchristchurchlosangeles1577775/page/n5/mode /2up.

83. Ernie Lazar FOIA Collection, "Gale, William Potter HQ 1," Letter, From: Director, FBI (Hoover) To: Kenneth O'Donnell, Special Assistant to the President, June 7, 1963, 29– 30, https://archive.org/details/GaleWilliamP.HQ1/page/n27/mode/2up.

84. Quoted in Ernie Lazar FOIA Collection, "GALE, William Potter HQ 1," "Interview with Mrs. William Potter Gale," Los Angeles FBI Field Office, January 13, 1964, https:// archive.org/details/GaleWilliamP.HQ1/page/n90/mode/1up. See also Ernie Lazar FOIA Collection, "GALE, William Potter HQ 1," "William Potter Gale: Racial Matters," Report by SA Harry L. Griffin, Los Angeles Field Office, July 24, 1963, https://archive .org/details/GaleWilliamP.HQ1/page/n90/mode/1up.

85. Ernie Lazar FOIA Collection, "Gale, William Potter HQ 1," FBI AIRTEL communica- tion, From: SAC, San Diego To: Director, FBI, December 23, 1958, https://archive.org /details/GaleWilliamP.HQ1/page/n1/mode/2up.

86. Ernie Lazar FOIA Collection, "GALE, William Potter HQ 1," "Christian Defense League," FBI date-stamped January 12, 1959, https://archive.org/details/GaleWilliamP .HQ1/page/n5/mode/2up.

87. Ernie Lazar FOIA Collection, "Gale, William Potter HQ 1," "William Potter Gale: Racial Matters," Report by SA Harry L. Griffin, Los Angeles Field Office, July 24, 1963, https:// archive.org/details/GaleWilliamP.HQ1/page/n62/mode/1up. See also Ernie Lazar FOIA Collection, "GALE, William Potter HQ 1," "WILLIAM POTTER GALE," Los Angeles Field Office, January 13, 1964, https://archive.org/details/GaleWilliamP.HQ1

/page/n150/mode/1up; Ernie Lazar FOIA Collection, "GALE, William Potter HQ 1," Report by SA Harry L. Griffin, Los Angeles Field Office, May 25, 1964.

88. Quoted in Ernie Lazar FOIA Collection, "Gale, William Potter HQ 1," Letter, From: Director, FBI (Hoover) To: Kenneth O'Donnell, Special Assistant to the President, June 7, 1963, https://archive.org/details/GaleWilliamP.HQ1/page/n41/mode/2up.

89. Ernie Lazar FOIA Collection, "GALE, William Potter HQ 1," "GALE, William Potter— Ministry of Christ Church—HQ 157-28219," containing AIRTEL Communication, From: Special Agent-in-Charge, Los Angeles To: FBI DIRECTOR (J. Edgar Hoover), September 24, 1963, https://archive.org/details/galewilliampotterministryofchristchur chhq15728219/page/n69/mode/2.

90. Ernie Lazar FOIA Collection, "GALE, William Potter HQ 1," Letter, From: Director, FBI (Hoover) To: Kenneth O'Donnell, Special Assistant to the President, June 7, 1963.

91. Ernie Lazar FOIA Collection, "GALE, William Potter HQ 1," "GALE, William Potter— Ministry of Christ Church—HQ 157-28219," AIRTEL Communication, From: Special Agent-in-Charge, Los Angeles To: FBI DIRECTOR (J. Edgar Hoover), September 24, 1963.

92. "Baptist Street Church Bombing," FBI—History: Famous Cases and Criminals (no date), https://www.fbi.gov/history/famous-cases/baptist-street-church-bombing. See also FBI, Freedom of Information and Privacy Acts, Subject: Birmingham, Alabama, Sixteenth Street Baptist Church Bombing/September 15, 1963, part 9 of 11, "Sixteenth (16th Street Church Bombing," FBI Records: The Vault (no date) Urgent Teletype from SAC, Atlanta to SACS, El Paso and Birmingham, September 21, 1963, https://vault.fbi .gov/16th%20Street%20Church%20Bombing%20/16th%20Street%20Church%20 Bombing%20Part%2037%20of%2051.

93. Ernie Lazar FOIA Collection, "GALE, William Potter HQ 1," https://archive.org/details /GALEWilliamPotterSanDiego1001312175pp/page/n7/mode/2up, "William Potter Gale: Racial Matters," Report by SA Harry L. Griffin, Los Angeles Field Office, July 24, 1963, https://archive.org/details/GaleWilliamP.HQ1/page/n104/mode/1up.

94. Ernie Lazar FOIA Collection, "GALE, William Potter HQ 1," "GALE, William Potter— Ministry of Christ Church—HQ 157-28219," AIRTEL Communication, From: Special Agent-in-Charge, Los Angeles To: FBI DIR (J. Edgar Hoover), September 24, 1963, https://archive.org/details/galewilliampotterministrychurchhq15728219/page /n69/mode/2.

95. Ernie Lazar FOIA Collection, "GALE, William Potter HQ 1," "William Potter Gale: Racial Matters," Report by SA Harry L. Griffin, Los Angeles Field Office, July 24, 1963, https://archive.org/details/GaleWilliamP.HQ1/page/n107/mode/1up; Ernie Lazar FOIA Collection, "GALE, William Potter HQ 1," Memorandum From: SAC, Los Angeles Field Office To: Director, FBI (Hoover), June 16, 1964; Ernie Lazar FOIA Collection, "GALE, William Potter HQ 1," Memorandum, SA John C. O'Neill to U.S. Secret Service, Los Angeles; 115th INTC, Region II, Pasadena; FIO, Los Angeles; OSI, District 18, Maywood, October 6, 1964.

96. Ernie Lazar FOIA Collection, "GALE, William Potter HQ 1," "William Potter Gale: Racial Matters," Report by SA Harry L. Griffin, Los Angeles Field Office, July 24, 1963; Ernie Lazar FOIA Collection, "GALE, William Potter HQ 1," "GALE, William Potter— San Diego 100-13121," WILLIAM POTTER GALE—RACIAL MATTERS, July 24, 1963.

97. Ernie Lazar FOIA Collection, "GALE, William Potter HQ 1," "Gale, William Potter HQ 1," Letter, From: Director, FBI (Hoover) To: Kenneth O'Donnell, Special Assistant to the President, June 7, 1963.

98. Ernie Lazar FOIA Collection, "GALE, William Potter HQ 1," https://archive.org/details /galewilliampotterhq62105253miscserials/page/n17/mode/2up, Memorandum, Los Angeles Field Office, Subject: WILLIAM POTTER GALE, January 22, 1964.

99. Ernie Lazar FOIA Collection, "GALE, William Potter HQ 1," Memorandum, Re: Christian Defense League, Federal Bureau of Investigation, Miami, Florida, February 3, 1964. See also, ADL, "Christian Identity," (no date), https://www.adl.org/resources /backgrounders/christian-identity

100. Ernie Lazar FOIA Collection, "GALE, William Potter HQ 1, https://archive.org/details /GaleWilliamP.HQ1/page/n1/mode/2up, HQ1 Memorandum, Miami Field Office, FBI February 3, 1964; and, Letter, from Richard Girnt Butler, National Director to Dear Christian, January 23, 1964.

101. Ernie Lazar FOIA Collection, "GALE, William Potter HQ 1," Memorandum: WILLIAM POTTER GALE," Los Angeles Field Office, July 25, 1963.

102. Ernie Lazar FOIA Collection, "GALE, William Potter HQ 1," Attachment, SAC, Miami Field Office to Director, FBI (Hoover), February 26, 1964 National Headquarters, Christian Defense League, Membership Application Pledge (no date).

103. Ernie Lazar FOIA Collection, "GALE, William Potter HQ 1," AIRTEL, SAC, Los Angeles Field Office to Director, FBI (Hoover), January 14, 1964.

104. Ernie Lazar FOIA Collection, "GALE, William Potter HQ 1," Memorandum: WILLIAM POTTER GALE," Los Angeles Field Office, March 5, 1964.

105. Ernie Lazar FOIA Collection, "GALE, William Potter HQ 1," IDENTITY GROUP, aka Ministry of Christ Church, Memorandum, FBI Los Angeles Field Office, March 5, 1975 Appendix: Identify Group: Characterization Of Subversive Organization; Extremist Matter—White Hate Group (revised August 16, 1974).

106. Ernie Lazar FOIA Collection, "GALE, William Potter HQ 1," Ministry of Christ Church, Sacramento Field Office "William Potter Gale," May 16, 1973.

107. Ernie Lazar FOIA Collection, "GALE, William Potter HQ 1," Ministry of Christ Church, Sacramento Field Office "William Potter Gale," August 24, 1973.

108. Ernie Lazar FOIA Collection, "GALE, William Potter HQ 1," Sacramento Field Office "William Potter Gale," "Sheriffs Posse Comitatus—Detroit 157–10687," quoted in "Law of the Land" (n.d.), https://archive.org/details/SheriffsPosseComitatusDetroit1571068 7. See also "Posse Comitatus," Federal Bureau of Investigation, Sheriff's Posse Comitatus, Detroit File Number: 100A-43113, June 6, 1974; and "The Posse Comitatus by the authority of The Constitution Of The United States" (n.d.), 1.

109. Quoted in Ernie Lazar FOIA Collection, "GALE, William Potter HQ 1," Memorandum, FBI Portland [Oregon] Field Office to U.S. Attorney, Portland, et al. June 6, 1974; 4. See also, Ernie Lazar FOIA Collection, "GALE, William Potter HQ 1," Ministry of Christ Church, Sacramento Field Office "William Potter Gale," GALE, William Potter—Ministry of Christ Church = Los Angeles 157–7775, "Manual of Christian Common Law for Christians . . . and their Posses (no date), https://archive.org /details/galewilliampotterministryofchristchurchlosangeles1577775/page/n3/mode /2up.

110. Ernie Lazar FOIA Collection, "GALE, William Potter HQ 1," IDENTITY GROUP, aka Ministry of Christ Church, Memorandum, FBI Los Angeles Field Office, March 5, 1975, Appendix: Identify Group: Characterization Of Subversive Organization; Extremist Matter—White Hate Group (revised August 16, 1974).

111. Ernie Lazar FOIA Collection, "GALE, William Potter HQ 1," William Potter Gale, "How To Protect Yourself From The Internal Revenue Service (on your income tax)," (no date).

112. Levitas, *The Terrorist Next Door*, 3–4.

113. James Corcoran, *Bitter Harvest: The Birth of Paramilitary Terrorism in the Heartland* (New York: Penguin, 1995), 30; Christopher Hewitt, *Understanding Terrorism in America: From the Klan to Al Qaeda* (London: Routledge, 2003), 73.

114. Paul de Armond, "The Law Applied," *Albion Monitor/Features*, April 15, 1996 at: www .albionmonitor.com/freemen/ci-view.html.

115. Wright, *Patriots, Politics, and the Oklahoma City Bombing*, 64.

116. Levitas, *The Terrorist Next Door*, 120. See also Sean Anderson and Stephen Sloan, *Historical Dictionary of Terrorism* (Metuchen, NJ: Scarecrow, 1995), 290; Perliger, *American Zealots*, 64.

117. Wright, *Patriots, Politics, and the Oklahoma City Bombing*, 64.

118. Corcoran, *Bitter Harvest*, 5–23.

119. Quoted in Megan Rosenfeld, "Dodge City Showdown Racist, Anti-Semitic Radio Broadcasts Alleged," *Washington Post*, May 7, 1983. See also "Obituaries: William Gale; Led Several Racist Groups," *Los Angeles Times*, May 4, 1988.

120. Quoted in Corcoran, *Bitter Harvest*, 31.

121. Quoted in Anti-Defamation League, *Extremism on the Right*, 87. See also Bennett, *The Party of Fear*, 447–48.

122. Levitas, *The Terrorist Next Door*, 284; "Obituaries: William Gale"; "Posse Comitatus Leader, Six Associates, Held Without Bond," Associated Press, October 30, 1986.

123. Quoted in Levitas, *The Terrorist Next Door*, 286.

124. Levitas, *The Terrorist Next Door*, 284; "Obituaries: William Gale"; "Posse Comitatus Leader, Six Associates, Held Without Bond."

125. Levitas, *The Terrorist Next Door*, 3.

126. Schlatter, *Aryan Cowboys*, 105–6.

127. Levitas, *The Terrorist Next Door*, 2–3.

128. Levitas, *The Terrorist Next Door*, 10–21, 63–65, 298.

4. ARMED AND DANGEROUS

1. David Cunningham, *Klansville, U.S.A.: The Rise and Fall of the Civil Rights–Era Ku Klux Klan* (Oxford: Oxford University Press, 2013), 24; Arnold Forster and Benjamin Epstein, *The Troublemakers: An Anti-Defamation League Report* (Garden City, NY: Doubleday, 1952), 112; Linda Gordon, *The Second Coming of the KKK: The Ku Klux Klan of the 1920s and the American Political Tradition* (New York: Liveright, 2017), 2, 217n4; Patsy Sims, *The Klan* (New York: Dorset, 1978), 2; "William Simmons of Ku Klux Klan; First Imperial Wizard of the Organization Dies—Left It in 20's After a Row Responsible for Founding Law-Abiding, He Claimed," *New York Times*, May 22, 1945.

2. Sims, *The Klan*, 2–3, 12. See also Cas Mudde, *The Far Right Today* (Cambridge: Polity, 2019), 46.

3. Gordon, *The Second Coming of the KKK*, 3.

4. Gordon, *The Second Coming of the KKK*, 195; Anna Diamond, "The 1924 Law That Slammed the Door on Immigrants and the Politicians Who Pushed It Back Open," *Smithsonian Magazine*, May 19, 2020, https://www.smithsonianmag.com/history/1924 -law-slammed-door-immigrants-and-politicians-who-pushed-it-back-open -180974910/; Office of the Historian, "The Immigration Act of 1924 (The Johnson-Reed Act)," U.S. Department of State, https://history.state.gov/milestones/1921–1936 /immigration-act.

5. British Pathé, "40,000 Ku Klux (1925)," April 13, 2014, https://www.youtube.com/watch ?v=BnI8SUQPB4k; Terence McArdle, "The Day 30,000 White Supremacists in KKK Robes Marched in the Nation's Capital," *Washington Post*, August 11, 2018; Sims, *The Klan*, 2.

6. Daniel Byman, "White Supremacy, Terrorism, and the Failure of Reconstruction in the United States," *International Security* 46, no. 1 (Summer 2021): 53–103.

7. Bryan Greene, "Created 150 Years Ago, the Justice Department's First Mission Was to Protect Black Rights," *Smithsonian Magazine*, July 1, 2020, https://www.smithsonianmag .com/history/created-150-years-ago-justice-departments-first-mission-was-protect -black-rights-180975232/; https://www.justice.gov/opa/speech/attorney-general-merrick -b-garland-delivers-remarks-civil-rights-division-s-virtual.

8. Ron Chernow, *Grant* (New York: Penguin, 2017), 705–10; Cunningham, *Klansville, U.S.A.*, 19–22; Eric Foner, *The Second Founding: How the Civil War and Reconstruction Remade the Constitution* (New York: Norton, 2019), 119–21; National Security Council, *National Strategy for Countering Domestic Terrorism* (Washington, DC: White House, June 2021), 5, https://www.whitehouse.gov/wp-content/uploads/2021/06/National -Strategy-for-Countering-Domestic-Terrorism.pdf; Office of the Historian, Office of Art & Archives, "The Ku Klux Klan Act of 1871," United States House of Representatives, History, Art & Archives, https://history.house.gov/Historical-Highlights/1851 -1900/hh_1871_04_20_KKK_Act/; Sims, *The Klan*, 4; Leonard Zeskind, *Blood and Politics: The History of the White Nationalist Movement from the Margins to the Mainstream* (New York: Farrar Straus Giroux, 2009), 37.

9. "In Old California (1910)," *Silent Era*, January 21, 2007, http://www.silentera.com/PSFL /data/I/InOldCalifornia1910.html; American Mutoscope & Biograph Co., *Light Cone: Distribution, Exhibition and Conservation of Experimental Film*, https://lightcone.org /en/group-4-american-mutoscope-biograph-co.

10. Thomas D. Clark, introduction to Thomas Dixon Jr., *The Clansman: A Historical Romance of the Ku Klux Klan* (Lexington: University Press of Kentucky, 1970), 1–2.

11. A. Scott Berg, *Wilson* (New York: G. P. Putnam's Sons, 2013), 347–48; Roger Ebert, "The Birth of a Nation," RogerEbert.com, March 30, 2003, https://www.rogerebert.com /reviews/great-movie-the-birth-of-a-nation-1915.

12. Berg, *Wilson*, 348; Scott Kirsner, *Inventing the Movies: Hollywood's Epic Battle Between Innovation and the Status Quo, from Thomas Edison to Steve Jobs* (CinemaTech, 2008), 13.

13. Pauline Kael, *For Keeps* (New York: Plume/Penguin, 1996), 172–73. See also the similar points made by Ebert, "The Birth of a Nation."

14. Berg, *Wilson*, 94, 308, 349. See also Ebert, "The Birth of a Nation"; Gordon, *The Second Coming of the KKK*, 11; Sims, *The Klan*, 12; Zeskind, *Blood and Politics*, 38.

15. Steve Oney, *And the Dead Shall Rise: The Murder of Mary Phagan and the Lynching of Leo Frank* (New York: Pantheon, 2003).

16. Albert S. Lindemann, *The Jew Accused: Three Anti-Semitic Affairs (Dreyfus, Beilis, Frank), 1894–1915* (Cambridge: Cambridge University Press, 1993), 235–71. See also Anti-Defamation League, "Remembering Leo Frank," August 12, 2015, https://www.adl.org /resources/backgrounders/remembering-leo-frank.

17. Lindemann, *The Jew Accused*, 271–72; Anti-Defamation League, "Remembering Leo Frank"; Jacob Bogage, "Leo Frank Was Lynched for a Murder He Didn't Commit. Now Neo-Nazis Are Trying to Rewrite History," *Washington Post*, May 22, 2017.

18. C. Vann Woodward, *Tom Watson: Agrarian Rebel* (Oxford: Oxford University Press, 1963), 431–50; Carol Pierannunzi, "Thomas E. Watson (1856–1922)," in *Georgia Encyclopedia: History & Archeology, Late Nineteenth Century, 1877–1900*, July 14, 2020, https://www.georgiaencyclopedia.org/articles/history-archaeology/thomas-e-watson -1856-1922.

19. Quoted in Woodward, *Tom Watson*, 445.

20. *The People v. Leo Frank Teacher's Guide* (New York: Anti-Defamation League, 2009), https://www.adl.org/sites/default/files/people-v-leo-frank-teachers-guide-the.pdf.

21. Charles O. Jackson, "William J. Simmons: A Career in Ku Kluxism," *Georgia Historical Quarterly* 50, no. 4 (December 1966): 351–52. See also DeNeen L. Brown, "The Preacher Who Used Christianity to Revive the Ku Klux Klan," *Washington Post*, April 10, 2018; Gordon, *The Second Coming of the KKK*, 12; "The 20th Century Ku Klux Klan in Alabama," *Alabama Moments in American History*, http://www .alabamamoments.alabama.gov/sec46det.html; Keith S. Hébert, "Ku Klux Klan in Alabama from 1915–1930," *Encyclopedia of Alabama*, March 30, 2023, https://encyclopedia ofalabama.org/article/ku-klux-klan-in-alabama-from-1915-1930/; "William Simmons of Ku Klux Klan."

22. Brown, "The Preacher Who Used Christianity to Revive the Ku Klux Klan." See also Cunningham, *Klansville, U.S.A.*, 24; Gordon, *The Second Coming of the KKK*, 12.

23. Jackson, "William J. Simmons," 353.

24. Desmond Ang, "Birth of a Nation: Media and Racial Hate," Faculty Research Working Paper Series, Harvard Kennedy School, Cambridge, MA, November 2020, RWP20-038, 10, https://scholar.harvard.edu/ang/publications/birth-nation-media-and-racial-hate. See also Claire Haley, "Stone Mountain: Carving Fact from Fiction," Atlanta History Center, November 18, 2022, https://www.atlantahistorycenter.com/blog/stone-mou ntain-a-brief-history/; Sims, *The Klan*, 4.

25. Quoted in Jackson, "William J. Simmons," 351. See also "The 20th Century Ku Klux Klan in Alabama"; "William Simmons of Ku Klux Klan."

26. Gordon, *The Second Coming of the KKK*, 40, 97, 141; Sims, *The Klan*.

27. National Museum of African American History & Culture, Smithsonian; Colonel William Joseph Simmons, Imperial Wizard, *The Ku Klux Klan: Yesterday Today and Forever* (c. 1916), 1.

28. Forster and Epstein, *The Troublemakers*, 111; Mudde, *The Far Right Today*, 46.

29. Quoted in Forster and Epstein, *The Troublemakers*, 111.

30. Ang, "Birth of a Nation: Media and Racial Hate," 4–5, 15, 23; Gordon, *The Second Coming of the KKK*, 2–4, 40–42, 96; Katherine Lennard, "Old Purpose, 'New Body': *The Birth Of A Nation* and the Revival of the Ku Klux Klan," *Journal of the Gilded Age and Progressive Era* 14, no. 4 (October 2015): 616; Sims, *The Klan*, 4.

31. Quoted in "William Simmons of Ku Klux Klan."

32. "William Simmons of Ku Klux Klan"; quoted in Ang, "Birth of a Nation: Media and Racial Hate," 10.

33. Quoted in "William Simmons of Ku Klux Klan."

34. Cunningham, *Klansville, U.S.A.*, 26; Gordon, *The Second Coming of the KKK*, 15–16, 191–94.

35. Cunningham, *Klansville, U.S.A.*, 26–32; Sims, *The Klan*, 3.

36. Cunningham, *Klansville, U.S.A.*, 32; Zeskind, *Blood and Politics*, 39.

37. Debbie Elliott, "Remembering Birmingham's 'Dynamite Hill' Neighborhood," National Public Radio: Code Sw!tch, July 6, 2013, https://www.npr.org/sections /codeswitch/2013/07/06/197342590/remembering-birminghams-dynamite-hill -neighborhood.

38. Cunningham, *Klansville, U.S.A.*, 4.

39. Anti-Defamation League of B'nai B'rith, *Hate Groups in America: A Record of Bigotry and Violence*, rev. ed. (New York: Anti-Defamation League of B'nai B'rith), 4.

40. Cheri Seymour, *Committee of the States: Inside the Radical Right* (Mariposa, CA: Camden Place Communications, 1987). See also Anti-Defamation League, *The Militia Movement* (2001), https://www.adl.org/education/resources/backgrounders/militia -movement, 4–5.

41. Anti-Defamation League, *The Militia Movement*, 4.

42. Daniel Levitas, *The Terrorist Next Door: The Militia Movement and the Radical Right* (New York: Thomas Dunne, 2002), 284–85.

43. David H. Bennett, *The Party of Fear: The American Far Right from Nativism to the Militia Movement* (New York: Vintage, 1995), 325.

44. Ernie Lazar FOIA Collection, "Gale CSA 2 Memorandum," SAC, Sacramento to SAC, Indianapolis, September 12, 1986, https://archive.org/details/galewilliampottercommi tteeofthestatessanfrancisco10063097and100a80325/page/n63/mode/2up.

45. Anti-Defamation League, *The Militia Movement*, 4.

46. Ernie Lazar FOIA Collection, "Gale CSA 2 Memorandum," SAC, Sacramento to SAC, Indianapolis, September 12, 1986.

47. Quoted in Seymour, *Committee of the States*, 288.

48. Kathleen Belew, *Bring the War Home: The White Power Movement and Paramilitary America* (Cambridge, MA: Harvard University Press, 2018), 191.

49. "Appendix; Volunteers for Alabama and Wallace, Also Known as Alabama Militia Volunteers," 41, in Gale HQ1 Report by Harry L. Griffin, Los Angeles Field Office, Subject; William Potter Gale/Racial Matters, July 24, 1963.

50. U.S. Department of Justice, *Report of the Ruby Ridge Task Force to the Office of Professional Responsibility of Investigation of Allegations of Improper Governmental Conduct in the Investigation, Apprehension and Prosecution of Randall C. Weaver and Kevin L. Harris*, June 10, 1994, 22–24, https://www.justice.gov/sites/default/files/opr/legacy/2006 /11/09/rubyreportcover_39.pdf. See also Douglas O. Linder, "The Ruby Ridge (Randy Weaver) Trial: An Account," University of Missouri Kansas City School of Law, https:// www.famous-trials.com/rubyridge/1152-home; Wayne F. Manis, *The Street Agent: After Taking on the Mob, the Klan, and the Aryan Nations, He Walks Softly and Carries a .357 Magnum—The True Story* (Palisades, NY: History Publishing, 2014), 414–15; David A. Neiwert, *In God's Country: The Patriot Movement and the Pacific Northwest* (Pullman: Washington State University Press, 2019), 63; Evelyn A. Schlatter, *Aryan Cowboys: White Supremacists and the Search for a New Frontier, 1970–2000* (Austin: University of Texas Press, 2006), 134–36; Kenneth S. Stern, *A Force Upon the Plain: The American Militia Movement and the Politics of Hate* (New York: Simon & Schuster, 1996), 19; Jess Walter, *Ruby Ridge: The Truth and Tragedy of the Randy Weaver Family* (New York: Harper Perennial, 2002); Stuart A. Wright, *Patriots, Politics, and the Oklahoma City Bombing* (Cambridge: Cambridge University Press, 2007), 140–41; Zeskind, *Blood and Politics*, 301.

51. "Boundary County, Idaho Population, 2023," https://worldpopulationreview.com/us -counties/id/boundary-county-population.

52. Quoted in Walter, *Ruby Ridge*, 45; see also 22–24. Belew, *Bring the War Home*, 186; Morris Dees with James Corcoran, *Gathering Storm: America's Militia Threat* (New York: HarperCollins, 1996), 10–13; Linder, "The Ruby Ridge (Randy Weaver) Trial"; Neiwert, *In God's Country*, 63; Naomi E. Pearson, "Fringe Religion and the Far-Right: Dangerous Behavior Patterns Among Christian Millennialists," *Inquiries Journal* 11, no. 3 (Fall 2019): 1, http://www.inquiriesjournal.com/articles/1761/fringe-religion-and-the-far -right-dangerous-behavior-patterns-among-christian-millennialists; U.S. Department of Justice, *Report of the Ruby Ridge Task Force*, 23.

53. Walter, *Ruby Ridge*, 45; see also 22–24. Belew, *Bring the War Home*, 24, 196; Pearson, "Fringe Religion and the Far-Right," 1; Schlatter, *Aryan Cowboys*, 135; Stern, *A Force Upon the Plain*, 19; Zeskind, *Blood and Politics*, 301.

54. Walter, *Ruby Ridge*, 43; see also 4, 13, 28–29. Belew, *Bring the War Home*, 196; Danny O. Coulson and Elaine Shannon, *No Heroes: Inside the FBI's Secret Counter-Terror Force* (New York: Pocket, 199), 393; Dees, *Gathering Storm*, 9–12; Levitas, *The Terrorist Next Door*, 302; Manis, *The Street Agent*, 415; Pearson, "Fringe Religion and the Far-Right," 1, 5–7; Stern, *A Force Upon the Plain*, 21; Catherine McNicol Stock, *Rural Radicals: Righteous Rage in the American Grain* (Ithaca, NY: Cornell, 1996), 143–44; Zeskind, *Blood and Politics*, 301.

55. Zeskind, *Blood and Politics*, 301.

56. Neiwert, *In God's Country*, 63; Schlatter, *Aryan Cowboys*, 136–37; Stern, *A Force Upon the Plain*, 21–22; Stock, *Rural Radicals*, 145; Walter, *Ruby Ridge*, 2, 65, 70, 74–75, 80, 95–97; Wright, *Patriots, Politics, and the Oklahoma City Bombing*, 140–41; Zeskind, *Blood and Politics*, 302.

57. Quoted in U.S. Department of Justice, *Report of the Ruby Ridge Task Force*, 13, 21, 23, 25–26. See also Linder, "The Ruby Ridge (Randy Weaver) Trial"; Manis, *The Street Agent*, 415–16; and Walter, *Ruby Ridge*, 64–65.

58. Walter, *Ruby Ridge*, 53–54, 57–58, 60, 92–96.

59. U.S. Department of Justice, *Report of the Ruby Ridge Task Force*, 13, 21–30. See also Linder, "The Ruby Ridge (Randy Weaver) Trial."

60. Quoted in U.S. Department of Justice, *Report of the Ruby Ridge Task Force*, 25–26, 29–30, n51; see also 37. Belew, *Bring the War Home*, 96–97; Anne Hull, "Randy Weaver's Return from Ruby Ridge," *Washington Post*, April 30, 2001; Levitas, *The Terrorist Next Door*, 302; Linder, "The Ruby Ridge (Randy Weaver) Trial"; Manis, *The Street Agent*, 415–16; Neiwert, *In God's Country*, 63–64; Pearson, "Fringe Religion and the Far-Right," 5–8; Schlatter, *Aryan Cowboys*, 137; Stern, *A Force Upon the Plain*, 21–22; Stock, *Rural Radicals*, 144; Walter, *Ruby Ridge*, 64–65; Zeskind, *Blood and Politics*, 301–2.

61. U.S. Department of Justice, *Report of the Ruby Ridge Task Force*, 13, 31, 36–37. See also Bishop, "Conspiracy Trial of 14 White Supremacists Begins"; Manis, *The Street Agent*, 415; Neiwert, *In God's Country*, 64.

62. Quoted in U.S. Department of Justice, *Report of the Ruby Ridge Task Force*, 13. See also Neiwert, *In God's Country*, 64–65; Pearson, "Fringe Religion and the Far-Right," 7; Stern, *A Force Upon the Plain*, 22; Stock, *Rural Radicals*, 145.

63. U.S. Department of Justice, *Report of the Ruby Ridge Task Force*, 2, 36. See also Neiwert, *In God's Country*, 64–65; Pearson, "Fringe Religion and the Far-Right," 7; Stern, *A Force Upon the Plain*, 22; Stock, *Rural Radicals*, 145.

64. U.S. Department of Justice, *Report of the Ruby Ridge Task Force*, 14. See also Linder, "The Ruby Ridge (Randy Weaver) Trial"; Neiwert, *In God's Country*, 65.

65. U.S. Department of Justice, *Report of the Ruby Ridge Task Force*, 14–15. See also Belew, *Bring the War Home*, 197–98; Linder, "The Ruby Ridge (Randy Weaver) Trial"; Manis, *The Street Agent*, 416–17; Neiwert, *In God's Country*, 65; Pearson, "Fringe Religion and the Far-Right," 8; Stern, *A Force Upon the Plain*, 23–24, 31–32; Wright, *Patriots, Politics, and the Oklahoma City Bombing*, 144–45; Zeskind, *Blood and Politics*, 303.

66. U.S. Department of Justice, *Report of the Ruby Ridge Task Force*, 16–17, italics in original. See also Pearson, "Fringe Religion and the Far-Right," 8; Stern, *A Force Upon the Plain*, 24.

67. Coulson and Shannon, *No Heroes*, 405. See also Wright, *Patriots, Politics, and the Oklahoma City Bombing*, 146.

68. U.S. Department of Justice, *Report of the Ruby Ridge Task Force*, 17–18. See also Manis, *The Street Agent*, 417–19; Neiwert, *In God's Country*, 65–66; Wright, *Patriots, Politics, and the Oklahoma City Bombing*, 147.

69. Stock, *Rural Radicals*, 146; Walter, *Ruby Ridge*, 246; Zeskind, *Blood and Politics*, 304.

70. Zeskind, *Blood and Politics*, 304; Stock, *Rural Radicals*, 145; Stern, *A Force Upon the Plain*, 24–25; Wright, *Patriots, Politics and the Oklahoma City Bombing*, 146.

71. Zeskind, *Blood and Politics*, 304.

72. Belew, *Bring the War Home*, 198; Stern, *A Force Upon the Plain*, 25.

73. Belew, *Bring the War Home*, 198; Stern, *A Force Upon the Plain*, 25.

74. U.S. Department of Justice, *Report of the Ruby Ridge Task Force*, 19.

75. Belew, *Bring the War Home*, 199; Briana Erickson, "War Hero 'Bo' Gritz Reflects on Ruby Ridge Siege 28 Years Later," *Las Vegas Review-Journal*, September 21, 2020; Dees, *Gathering Storm*, 24; Philip Oltermann, "Erase and Forget: New Documentary Reveals Life Story of the Real Rambo," *Guardian*, February 13, 2017; Neiwert, *In God's Country*, 66; Pearson, "Fringe Religion and the Far-Right," 8; Schlatter, *Aryan Cowboys*, 137–39; Stern, *A Force Upon the Plain*, 29. The Rambo films include *First Blood* (1982), *Rambo: First Blood Part II* (1985), *Rambo III* (1988), *Rambo* (2008), and *Rambo: Last Blood* (2019).

76. Manis, *The Street Agent*, 419.

77. Quoted in Stern, *A Force Upon the Plain*, 30.

78. Walter, *Ruby Ridge*, 136, 233–45. See also "A Timeline of the Ruby Ridge Standoff and Its fallout," Associated Press, August 22, 1997, https://apnews.com/article/9d100cbcc4b5202ff1de0810ce4b1869; "Fugitive's Friend Gives Up in Idaho," *New York Times*, August 31, 1992; Dees, *Gathering Storm*, 25; Manis, *The Street Agent*, 419–20; Neiwert, *In God's Country*, 66; Hatewatch Staff, " 'Patriot' Conspiracy Theorist Jack McLamb Dies," Southern Poverty Law Center, January 13, 2014, https://www.splcenter.org/hatewatch/2014/01/13/patriot-conspiracy-theorist-jack-mclamb-dies; Stern, *A Force Upon the Plain*, 30–33; Stock, *Rural Radicals*, 146;, Zeskind, *Blood and Politics*, 305–6.

79. U.S. Department of Justice, *Report of the Ruby Ridge Task Force*, 20. See also "18 Months in Jail for Supremacist," *New York Times*, October 19, 1993; Belew, *Bring the War Home*, 196, 199–200; "Opening Statement of Louis J. Freeh, Director, Federal Bureau of Investigation Before the Subcommittee on Terrorism, Technology, and Government Information, Committee on the Judiciary, United States Senate, Washington, D.C.," Ruby Ridge Hearing, October 19, 1995, https://fas.org/irp/congress/1995_hr/s951019f.htm#reforms%20subsequent; Oliver "Buck" Revell and Dwight Williams, *A G-Man's Journal: A Legendary Career Inside the FBI—from the Kennedy Assassination to the Oklahoma City Bombing* (New York: Pocket, 1998), 467–68; Stern, *A Force Upon the Plain*, 39–41; Wright, *Patriots, Politics, and the Oklahoma City Bombing*, 148.

80. "Another Federal Fiasco," *New York Times*, July 12, 1993.

81. Douglas O. Linder, "Charges and the Defense Strategy in the Ruby Ridge (Weaver and Harris) Trial," *Famous Trials*, https://www.famous-trials.com/rubyridge/1146 -weaverdefense; Douglas O. Linder, "The Ruby Ridge (Randy Weaver) Trial"; "The Ruby Ridge (Weaver and Harris) Trial: Selected Excerpts from the Trial Transcript," *Famous Trials*, https://www.famous-trials.com/rubyridge/1146-weaverdefense; "A Timeline of the Ruby Ridge Standoff and Its Fallout"; Pearson, "Fringe Religion and the Far-Right," 8–9; Schlatter, *Aryan Cowboys*, 139; Sam Howe Verhovek, "F.B.I. Agent to Be Spared Prosecution in Shooting," *New York Times*, June 15, 2001.

82. Levitas, *The Terrorist Next Door*, 303.

83. Bennett, *The Party of Fear*, 449; Robert L. Jackson, "Militant Relives Idaho Tragedy for Senators," *Los Angeles Times*, September 7, 1995; Schlatter, *Aryan Cowboys*, 140; Stock, *Rural Radicals*, 145; David C. Williams, "The Militia Movement and Second Amendment Revolution: Conjuring with the People," *Digital Repository @ Maurer Law*, Law Library, University of Indiana, 1996, 880, 891, 903, 928, 938, https://www.repository.law .indiana.edu/facpub/633; Zeskind, *Blood and Politics*, 301, 304, 310.

84. Quoted in Stern, *A Force Upon the Plain*, 34.

85. Stern, *A Force Upon the Plain*, 27; Zeskind, *Blood and Politics*, 306–7.

86. Quoted in Zeskind, *Blood and Politics*, 306.

87. "We fight like hell. And if you don't fight like hell, you're not going to have a country anymore." See Brian Naylor, "Read Trump's Jan. 6 Speech, a Key Part of Impeachment Trial," National Public Radio: WAMU 88.5, February 10, 2021, https://www.npr.org/2021 /02/10/966396848/read-trumps-jan-6-speech-a-key-part-of-impeachment-trial.

88. Anti-Defamation League of B'nai B'rith, *Extremism on the Right: A Handbook*, new red. ed. (New York: Anti-Defamation League of B'nai B'rith, 1988), 143; Neiwert, *In God's Country*, 67. Mathews was there to hear Jack Mohr speak. Mohr, a highly decorated Korean War veteran, had been a member of the John Birch Society before drifting into the Identity movement and becoming one of its prominent figures. See Anti-Defamation League, *Extremism on the Right*, 137–38; Southern Poverty Law Center, "Remaking the Right," *Intelligence Report*, November 12, 2003, https://www.splcenter.org/fighting-hate /intelligence-report/2003/remaking-right.

89. Quoted in Newiert, *In God's Country*, 67.

90. Zeskind, *Blood and Politics*, 310.

91. Anti-Defamation League, *Armed and Dangerous: Militias Take Aim at the Federal Government* (New York: Anti-Defamation League, 2001), 17; Dees, *Gathering Storm*, 49; Newiert, *In God's Country*, 67; Southern Poverty Law Center, "Larry Pratt," https://www .splcenter.org/fighting-hate/extremist-files/individual/larry-pratt; Schlatter, *Aryan Cowboys*, 140; Zeskind, *Blood and Politics*, 314–17.

92. Quoted in Dees, *Gathering Storm*, 50.

93. Anti-Defamation League, *The Militia Movement* (New York: Anti-Defamation League, 2001), 5–6; Dees, *Gathering Storm*, 49–50; Levitas, *The Terrorist Next Door*, 303; Newiert, *In God's Country*, 67; Southern Poverty Law Center, "Larry Pratt."

94. Louis Beam, "Louis Beam's Estes Park, Colorado Speech," http://www.louisbeam.com /estes.htm, http://video.google.com/videosearch?q=louis+beam&emb=0&aq=f#; Dees, *Gathering Storm*, 50–52. See also Morris Dees with James Corcoran, "The Nazi Link with Militias: White Racists Play Down Their Politics to Recruit from the Middle Class," *Baltimore Sun*, June 16, 1996; Levitas, *The Terrorist Next Door*, 303; Schlatter, *Aryan Cowboys*, 140; Southern Poverty Law Center, "Louis Beam: In His Own Words— Speech at Estes Park, Colo., 1992"; "Louis Beam: In His Own Words," *Intelligence Report*, 2015 https://www.splcenter.org/fighting-hate/intelligence-report/2015/louis -beam-his-own-words; Stern, *A Force Upon the Plain*, 35.

95. Chip Berlet and Matthew N. Lyons, *Right-Wing Populism in America: Too Close for Comfort* (New York: Guilford, 2000), 13, 15.

96. Louis Beam, "Louis Beam's Estes Park, Colorado Speech"; Dees, *Gathering Storm*, 50–52.

97. Dees, *Gathering Storm*, 49, 50. Newiert, *In God's Country*, 68; Schlatter, *Aryan Cowboys*, 140–41; Stern, *A Force Upon the Plain*, 35.

98. Neiwert, *In God's Country*, 66.

99. Schlatter, *Aryan Cowboys*, 140.

100. Stern, *A Force Upon the Plain*, 37; Zeskind, *Blood and Politics*, 318.

101. Belew, *Bring the War Home*, 191.

102. Dees, *Gathering Storm*, 58; Arie Perliger, *Challengers from the Sidelines: Understanding America's Violent Far-Right* (West Point, NY: Combating Terrorism Center, November 2012), 65–68, 81–82; Zeskind, *Blood and Politics*, 310, 315–19.

103. Anti-Defamation League, *The Militia Movement*, 6–7.

104. U.S. Treasury Enforcement, *Report of the Department of the Treasury on the Bureau of Alcohol, Tobacco, and Firearms Investigation of Vernon Wayne Howell Also Known as David Koresh* (Washington, DC: U.S. Government Printing Office, 1993), https://ia800209.us.archive.org/17/items/reportofdepartmeoounit/reportofdepart meoounit.pdf. See also Kevin Cook, *Waco Rising: David Koresh, the FBI, and the Birth of America's Modern Militias* (New York: Henry Holt, 2023), 16, 20–21, 34–36, 42–44, 62, 129–30; Jeff Guinn, *Waco: David Koresh, the Branch Davidians, and a Legacy of Rage* (New York: Simon & Schuster, 2023), 108–9, 117–18, 122–23, 140, 211–12.

105. See, for instance, the more than 1.3 million "hits" and over two dozen books that a Google search generates as well as the many documentaries, such as *David Koresh: The Final 24*, *Waco Siege: Days That Shaped America*, *Waco: The Inside Story*, *Waco: The Rules of Engagement*, *Waco: A New Revelation*, and *Witness to Waco*, among others, and the Netflix series *Waco*, https://www.imdb.com/title/tt6040674/.

106. Department of Justice Archives, *Report to the Deputy Attorney General on the Events at Waco, Texas: The Aftermath of the April 19 Fire* (Washington, DC: U.S. Department of Justice, updated February 14, 2018), https://www.justice.gov/archives/publications /waco/report-deputy-attorney-general-events-waco-texas-aftermath-april-19-fire. See also Cook, *Waco Rising*, 1–2, 170–87; Jeff Guinn, *Waco*, 1–10, 203–7; James D. Tabor and

Eugene V. Gallagher, *Why Waco? Cults and the Battle for Religious Freedom in America* (Berkeley: University of California Press, 1995), 2–3.

107. Walter, *Ruby Ridge*, 299.

108. Henry Schuster with Charles Stone, *Hunting Eric Rudolph: An Insider's Account of the Five-Year Search for the Olympic Bombing Suspect* (New York: Berkley, 2005), 168–69.

109. Robert L. Jackson, "Militant Relives Idaho Tragedy for Senators," *Los Angeles Times*, September 7, 1995.

110. See also Anti-Defamation League, "ADL Report Focused on Militia Movement Six Months Before Oklahoma," *ADL on the Frontline: A Monthly Newsletter*, May/June 1995, 1, 4, https://www.adl.org/sites/default/files/on-the-frontline-may-june-1995.pdf.

111. Bennett, *The Party of Fear*, 449.

112. Stock, *Rural Radicals*, 146.

113. Anti-Defamation League, *Armed and Dangerous*, 17; Steven E. Atkins, *Encyclopedia of Right-Wing Extremism in Modern American History* (Santa Barbara, CA: ABC-CLIO, 2011), 228; Barry J. Balleck, *Modern American Extremism and Domestic Terrorism: An Encyclopedia of Extremist Groups* (Santa Barbara, CA: ABC-CLIO, 2018), 364; Bennett, *The Party of Fear*, 450–51; Immanuel Ness, *Encyclopedia of American Social Movements* (London: Routledge, 2015), 4:1445.

114. Stern, *A Force Upon the Plain*, 26. See also Belew, *Bring the War Home*, 197–98; Stock, *Rural Radicals*, 146.

115. Wright, *Patriots, Politics, and the Oklahoma City Bombing*, 170.

116. Stern, *A Force Upon the Plain*, 37; Wright, *Patriots, Politics, and the Oklahoma City Bombing*, 170.

117. Belew, *Bring the War Home*, 197. See also Stern, *A Force Upon the Plain*, 26; Walter, *Ruby Ridge*, 147, 247.

118. Neiwert, *In God's Country*, 52–55, 68; Schlatter, *Aryan Cowboys*, 140.

119. Bennett, *The Party of Fear*, 450; Wright, *Patriots, Politics, and the Oklahoma City Bombing*, 170.

120. See Bureau of Alcohol, Tobacco, Firearms, and Explosives, "Brady Law," July 15, 2021, https://www.atf.gov/rules-and-regulations/brady-law; Jeffrey A. Roth and Christopher S. Koper, "Impacts of the 1994 Assault Weapons Ban: 1994–96," *National Institute of Justice: Research in Brief* (Washington, DC: U.S. Department of Justice, March 1999), 11.

121. Anti-Defamation League, "ADL Report Focused on Militia Movement Six Months Before Oklahoma," 1; Anti-Defamation League, *Armed and Dangerous*, 1; Williams, "The Militia Movement and Second Amendment Revolution," 880.

122. Quoted in Anti-Defamation League, "Stand Off Against the Government—New Book Examines the Defiance of Armed Citizens," press release, June 10, 1996, https://www.adl.org/sites/default/files/press-releases-1995-1998-re-okc-bombing-militia-mvt.pdf.

123. Quoted in Stern, *A Force Upon the Plain*, 72. See also Jonathan Freedland, "Adolf's US Army: Neo-Fascist Militia Groups Are on the March in the US, and Washington Is Their Target," *Guardian*, December 15, 1994.

124. Stern, *A Force Upon the Plain*, 72–74. See also Williams, "The Militia Movement and Second Amendment Revolution," 931–33; Wright, *Patriots, Politics, and the Oklahoma City Bombing*, 170.

125. Quoted in Anti-Defamation League, *Armed and Dangerous*, 1.

126. Quoted in Freedland, "Adolf's US Army"; Stern, *A Force Upon the Plain*, 74.

127. Freedland, "Adolf's US Army"; Ness, *Encyclopedia of American Social Movements*, 1445; Wright, *Patriots, Politics, and the Oklahoma City Bombing*, 170–71.

128. Freedland, "Adolf's US Army."

129. Atkins, *Encyclopedia of Right-Wing Extremism in Modern American History*, 228; Bennett, *The Party of Fear*, 450; Stern, *A Force Upon the Plain*, 76.

130. Quoted in Paul de Armond, "Leaderless Resistance: The Two-Pronged Movement Consolidates Under Identity," *Public Good*, June 1997, http://www.nwcitizen.com /publicgood.

131. Stern, *A Force Upon the Plain*, 45, 75. See also Anti-Defamation League, *The Militia Movement*, 8.

132. Stock, *Rural Radicals*, 146–47. See also Anti-Defamation League, *The Militia Movement*, 1.

133. Williams, "The Militia Movement and Second Amendment Revolution," 881.

134. Quoted in Anti-Defamation League, "ADL Cites Extremist Literature as a 'Paper Trail of Violence,'" press release, May 15, 1996. See also Anti-Defamation League, Civil Rights Division, Research and Evaluation Department, *The Literature of Apocalypse: Far-Right Voices of Violence* (New York: ADL, 1996), 6–7.

135. Quoted in Williams, "The Militia Movement and Second Amendment Revolution," 915.

5. LEADERLESS RESISTANCE

1. "Message from the Director," in Terrorist Research and Analytical Center, *Counterterrorism Section, Intelligence Division, Terrorism in the United States 1982–1992* (Washington, DC: U.S. Department of Justice, Federal Bureau of Investigation, 1993), 2.

2. "Message from the Director," 13.

3. Terrorist Research and Analytical Center, Counterterrorism Section National Security Division, *Terrorism in the United States 1994* (Washington, DC: U.S. Department of Justice, Federal Bureau of Investigation, 1995), 2.

4. Terrorist Research and Analytical Center, *Terrorism in the United States 1994*, 26. See also "N.A.A.C.P. Bombings Linked to a Wider Plot, F.B.I. Says," *New York Times*, July 30, 1993.

5. Dale Russakoff and Serge F. Kovaleski, "An Ordinary Boy's Extraordinary Rage," *Washington Post*, July 2, 1995.

6. "The Fork In The Road," in *April 19, 1995 9:02 a.m.: The Historical Record of the Oklahoma City Bombing Compiled by Oklahoma Today* 46, no. 1 (Winter 1996): 7.

7. "Oklahoma City Bombing," FBI History: Famous Cases & Criminals, https://www.fbi .gov/history/famous-cases/oklahoma-city-bombing; Rick Bragg, "Terror in Oklahoma:

The Children; Tender Memories of Day Care Center Are All That Remain After the Bomb," *New York Times*, May 3, 1995; Sue Mallonee, Sheryll Shariat, Gail Stennies et al., "Physical Injuries and Fatalities Resulting from the Oklahoma City Bombing," *JAMA: Journal of the American Medical Association* 276, no. 5 (August 7, 1996), https://jamanetwork.com/journals/jama/article-abstract/406032.

8. Lou Michel and Dan Herbeck, *American Terrorist: Timothy McVeigh and the Oklahoma City Bombing* (New York: HarperCollins, 2001), 163–65, 171. See also "McVeigh Admits Planting Okla. City Bomb," Reuters, February 28, 1997.

9. Nancy Gibbs, "The Blood of Innocents: In the Bomb's Aftermath, Tales of Horror and Heroism," *Time*, May 1, 1995; Rob McManamy, "Oklahoma Blast Forces Unsettling Design Questions," *Engineering News Record* 234, no. 17 (May 1, 1995): 10–13. The building housed a variety of U.S. government departments and agencies, including the Social Security Administration, Health and Human Services, General Services Administration, General Accounting Office, Defense Investigative Service, Federal Credit Union, Department of Transportation, Federal Highway Administration, U.S. Army, U.S. Customs Service, Department of Labor, Department of Agriculture, Veterans Administration, U.S. Marine Corps, Housing and Urban Development, Small Business Administration, Drug Enforcement Administration, U.S. Secret Service, Bureau of Alcohol, Tobacco, and Firearms, and, of course, a daycare center. These were obliterated by the blast—which also damaged seventy-five other buildings in the immediate vicinity.

10. Jane H. Lii, "After 15 Days, Search for Bodies Is Coming to an End," *New York Times*, May 4, 1995.

11. Danny O. Coulson and Elaine Shannon, *No Heroes: Inside the FBI's Secret Counter-Terror Force* (New York: Pocket, 199), 497, 507, 527.

12. Michel and Herbeck, *American Terrorist*, 36–40; John Kifner, "McVeigh's Mind," *New York Times*, December 31, 1995; Andrew Macdonald [William L. Pierce], *The Turner Diaries*, 2nd ed. (Arlington, VA: National Vanguard, 1985), back cover.

13. Testimony of Jennifer McVeigh, May 5, 1997, in Douglas O. Linder, *Oklahoma City Bombing Trial (1997)*, 34–35, https://famous-trials.com/oklacity/723-jennifertestimony.

14. Testimony of Michael Fortier in the Timothy McVeigh Trial, May 12, 1997, in Douglas O. Linder, *Oklahoma City Bombing Trial (1997)*, 3–4, https://www.famous-trials.com/oklacity/712-fortiertestimony. See also See also "Closing Argument for the Prosecution in the Trial of Timothy McVeigh (Argument by Larry D. Mackey)," May 29, 1997, in Douglas O. Linder, *Oklahoma City Bombing Trial (1997)*, https://www.famous-trials.com/oklacity/725-mcveighclosing, 12; Michel and Herbeck, *American Terrorist*, 58–69.

15. John Kifner, "The Gun Network: McVeigh's World—a Special Report. Bomb Suspect Felt at Home Riding the Gun-Show Circuit," *New York Times*, July 5, 1995; Michel and Herbeck, *American Terrorist*, 56–69; Lou Michel and Dan Herbeck, "Could the Oklahoma City Bombing Have Been Prevented?," *Buffalo News*, April 13, 2020.

16. Quoted in Michel and Herbeck, *American Terrorist*, 61.

17. Michel and Herbeck, *American Terrorist*, 75–86; Sally Jacobs, "The Radicalization of Timothy McVeigh," *Tulsa World*, June 10, 1995; Russakoff and Kovaleski, "An Ordinary Boy's Extraordinary Rage."

18. Kifner, "Bomb Suspect Felt at Home Riding the Gun-Show Circuit"; Michel and Herbeck, *American Terrorist*, 88–89; Michel and Herbeck, "Could the Oklahoma City Bombing Have Been Prevented?"

19. Michel and Herbeck, *American Terrorist*, 87–89; Tom Rhodes, "Man Charged with Oklahoma Bombing 'Had Klan Links,'" *Times* (London), March 21, 1997.

20. Michel and Herbeck, *American Terrorist*, 87–89; Mark Hamm, "Tragic Irony: State Malfeasance and the Oklahoma City Bombing Conspiracy," *Critical Criminologist*, 1998, 4, http://sun.soci/niu/~critcrim/CC/hamm98.htm; Rhodes, "Man Charged with Oklahoma Bombing 'Had Klan Links.'"

21. Michel and Herbeck, *American Terrorist*, 88–89.

22. Lou Michel and Dan Herbeck, "How Oklahoma City Bomber Timothy McVeigh Changed the Fringe Right," *Buffalo News*, April 19, 2020.

23. Quoted from "Letter from Timothy McVeigh to the Union-Sun & Journal," February 11, 1992, CNN Interactive: Oklahoma City Tragedy, https://web.archive.org/web/20080119111020/http://www.cnn.com/US/OKC/faces/Suspects/McVeigh/1st-letter6–15/index.html; See also Coulson and Shannon, *No Heroes*, 508; Michel and Herbeck, *American Terrorist*, 91–92, 95–97, 98–99; Michel and Herbeck, "Could the Oklahoma City Bombing Have Been Prevented?"; Michel and Herbeck, "How Oklahoma City Bomber Timothy McVeigh Changed the Fringe Right"; Rick Pfeiffer, "Oklahoma City Bombing Quickly Linked to Timothy McVeigh 25 Years Ago," *Lockport Union Sun & Journal,* April 19, 2020.

24. Testimony of Jennifer McVeigh, May 5, 1997, 33–35; Michel and Herbeck, *American Terrorist*, 99–108.

25. Michel and Herbeck, *American Terrorist*, 111–13. See also, *White Patriot: Worldwide Voice of the Aryan People—This Is the Klan!* (Tuscumbia, AL: Patriot Press, no date), https://www.biblio.com/book/white-patriot-worldwide-voice-aryan-people/d/1360232328.

26. Quoted in Michel and Herbeck, *American Terrorist*, 116–18.

27. Michel and Herbeck, *American Terrorist*, 118–19.

28. Testimony of Michelle Rauch in the Timothy McVeigh Trial, June 10, 1997, in Douglas O. Linder, *Oklahoma City Bombing Trial (1997)*, 2, 8–9; Michel and Herbeck, *American Terrorist*, 119–20. See also "Spotlight: Timothy McVeigh: Rise to Extremism," *Counterterrorism Digest* 11 (n.d.).

29. Testimony of Michelle Rauch, 5–6, 12–13. See also "Closing Argument for the Prosecution in the Trial of Timothy McVeigh (Argument by Larry D. Mackey)," May 29, 1997, 13–14, https://www.famous-trials.com/oklacity/725-mcveighclosing.

30. Testimony of Jennifer McVeigh, May 5, 1997, 33.

31. Testimony of Jennifer McVeigh, May 5, 1997, 35; Hamm, "Tragic Irony: State Malfeasance and the Oklahoma City Bombing Conspiracy," 5; Kifner, "Bomb Suspect

Felt at Home Riding the Gun-Show Circuit"; Michel and Herbeck, *American Terrorist*, 121–23.

32.   Michel and Herbeck, *American Terrorist*, 124–25.

33.   Testimony of Michael Fortier in the Timothy McVeigh Trial, May 12, 1997, 9.

34.   Testimony of Lori Fortier in the Timothy McVeigh Trial, April 29, 1997, 25, https://www
.famous-trials.com/oklacity/724-loritestimony.

35.   Testimony of Lori Fortier in the Timothy McVeigh Trial, April 29, 1997, 7.

36.   Testimony of Lori Fortier in the Timothy McVeigh Trial, April 29, 1997, 7; Michel and
Herbeck, *American Terrorist*, 129–35.

37.   Testimony of Michael Fortier in the Timothy McVeigh Trial, May 12, 1997, 6.

38.   Testimony of Lori Fortier in the Timothy McVeigh Trial, April 29, 1997, 11, 25.

39.   Testimony of Jennifer McVeigh, May 5, 1997, 38–39.

40.   *Waco, the Big Lie*, https://www.imdb.com/title/tt3385784/. See also Tom Kenworthy,
"FBI Agents Testify About Guns, Fertilizer at Home of Nichols," *Washington Post*,
November 18, 1997; Jo Thomas, "Political Ideas of McVeigh Are Subject at Bomb Trial,"
New York Times, June 11, 1997.

41.   Testimony of Michael Fortier in the Timothy McVeigh Trial, May 12, 1997, 6; Testimony
of Lori Fortier in the Timothy McVeigh Trial, April 29, 1997, 84.

42.   Timothy S. Good, *We Saw Lincoln Shot: One Hundred Eyewitness Accounts* (Jackson:
University of Mississippi Press, 1995).

43.   Michel and Herbeck, *American Terrorist*, 137. See also Michel and Herbeck, "Could the
Oklahoma City Bombing Have Been Prevented?"; Testimony of Lori Fortier in the Timothy McVeigh Trial, April 29, 1997, 25–26.

44.   Testimony of Michael Fortier in the Timothy McVeigh Trial, May 12, 1997, 11–12; Testimony of Lori Fortier in the Timothy McVeigh Trial, April 29, 1997, 27. See also OKC
Bombing Trial Transcript-04/24/1997 11:39 CDT/CST, Criminal Action no. 96-CR-68,
United States of America, Plaintiff vs. Timothy James McVeigh, Defendant, Reporter's
Transcript (Trial to Jury, Volume 60), Joseph H. Hartzler, Special Attorney to the U.S.
Attorney General, 32, https://www.oklahoman.com/article/1074825/okc-bombing-trial
-transcript-04241997-1139-cdtcst.

45.   Testimony of Lori Fortier in the Timothy McVeigh Trial, April 29, 1997, 26–27; Michel
and Herbeck, *American Terrorist*, 141–42.

46.   Testimony of Lori Fortier in the Timothy McVeigh Trial, April 29, 1997, 24–25; Michel
and Herbeck, *American Terrorist*, 152.

47.   Jeffrey A. Roth and Christopher S. Koper, "Impacts of the 1994 Assault Weapons Ban:
1994–96, *National Institute of Justice: Research in Brief* (Washington, DC: U.S. Department of Justice, March 1999), 1–11, https://www.ojp.gov/pdffiles1/173405.pdf.

48.   Bureau of Alcohol, Tobacco, Firearms and Explosives, "Brady Law," https://www.atf.gov
/rules-and-regulations/brady-law.

49.   Michel and Herbeck, *American Terrorist*, 159–61.

50.   Letter, McVeigh to Papovich (n.d.), quoted in Tracy McVeigh, "The McVeigh Letters:
Why I Bombed Oklahoma," *Observer Life*, May 3, 2001. See also "'Dear Tracy'—by Mass

Killer Timothy McVeigh," *Guardian*, May 5, 2001; "US McVeigh Lawyer: Interview with Stephen Jones, McVeigh Former Lawyer," Associated Press, May 6, 2001. See also, "Interview with "Stephen Jones, McVeigh former lawyer," Associated Press Archive, June 10, 2001, https://www.youtube.com/watch?v=PBN1aOrhxi8.

51. Testimony of Lori Fortier in the Timothy McVeigh Trial, April 29, 1997, 28–30; OKC Bombing Trial Transcript-04/24/1997 11:39 CDT/CST 19; and, United States of America, Plaintiff-Appellee, v. Timothy James McVeigh, Defendant-appellant, Appeal from the United States District Court for the District of Colorado, in Decision of the Tenth Circuit Court of Appeals, Affirming the Conviction of Timothy McVeigh (n.d.), 3, http://law2.umkc.edu/faculty/projects/ftrials/mcveigh/mcveigh10thcircuit.html.

52. Testimony of Michael Fortier in the Timothy McVeigh Trial, May 12, 1997, 15.

53. Michel and Herbeck, *American Terrorist*, 162.

54. Testimony of Michael Fortier in the Timothy McVeigh Trial, May 12, 1997, 21; Appeal from the United States District Court, 3; Michel and Herbeck, *American Terrorist*, 162–65.

55. Testimony of Michael Fortier in the Timothy McVeigh Trial, May 12, 1997, 20. See also Tim Kelsey, "The Oklahoma Suspect Awaits Day of Reckoning," *Sunday Times* (London), April 21, 1996.

56. "McVeigh's Apr. 26 Letter to Fox News," *Fox News*, January 13, 2015, https://www.foxnews.com/story/mcveighs-apr-26-letter-to-fox-news.

57. Kerry Noble, *Tabernacle of Hate* (Prescott, Ontario: Voyageur, 1998), 134–35. See also Coulson and Shannon, *No Heroes*, 533–35; Jessica Stern, "The Covenant, the Sword, and the Arm of the Lord" (1985), in *Toxic Terror: Assessing Terrorist Use of Chemical and Biological Weapons*, ed. J. B. Tucker (Cambridge, MA: MIT Press, 2000), 27; Jessica Stern, *Terror in the Name of God: Why Religious Militants Kills* (New York: Harper-Collins, 2003), 27–29; Jo Thomas and Ronald Smothers, "Oklahoma City Building Was Target of Plot as Early as '83, Official Says," *New York Times*, May 20, 1995; Stuart A. Wright, *Patriots, Politics, and the Oklahoma City Bombing* (Cambridge: Cambridge University Press, 2007), 90–91.

58. Michel and Herbeck, *American Terrorist*, 38–39, 59–60, 88, 124–25, 167, 288, 329–30.

59. Quoted in James Brooke, "Newspaper Says McVeigh Described Role in Bombing," *New York Times*, March 1, 1997. McVeigh "voiced the identical response" to the academician Stuart A. Wright, who was retained as an expert witness by McVeigh's attorneys and met with McVeigh both while he was awaiting trial and during the trial. Wright, *Patriots, Politics, and the Oklahoma City Bombing*, xiii–xiv, 91. See also Jerrold Post, "Psychological and Motivational Factors in Terrorist Decision-Making: Implications for CBW Terrorism," in *Toxic Terror: Assessing Terrorist Use of Chemical and Biological Weapons*, ed. J. B. Tucker (Cambridge, MA: MIT Press, 2000), 285. See also Tom Kenworthy, "McVeigh 'Confession' Clouds Bombing Trial," *Washington Post*, March 3, 1997.

60. Testimony of Michael Fortier in the Timothy McVeigh Trial, May 12, 1997, 20; Testimony of Lori Fortier in the Timothy McVeigh Trial, April 29, 1997, 41. See also Appeal from the United States District Court for the District of Colorado, 3; OKC Bombing

Trial Transcript-04/24/1997 11:39 CDT/CST, 31; "McVeigh Aimed to Spark Revolt, Ex-Buddy Says," *International Herald Tribune*, May 13, 1997; Michel and Herbeck, *American Terrorist*, 168–69, 223–25; Jo Thomas, "For First Time, Woman Says McVeigh Told of Bomb Plan," *New York Times*, April 30, 1997; Jo Thomas, "Friend Says McVeigh Wanted Bombing to Start an 'Uprising,'" *New York Times*, May 13, 1997.

61. Testimony of Michael Fortier in the Timothy McVeigh Trial, May 12, 1997, 20; OKC Bombing Trial Transcript-04/24/1997 11:39 CDT/CST, 14.

62. Michel and Herbeck, *American Terrorist*, 59, 226–28.

63. Quoted in Kelsey, "The Oklahoma Suspect Awaits Day of Reckoning."

64. Testimony of Michael Fortier in the Timothy McVeigh Trial, May 12, 1997, 28. See also Michel and Herbeck, *American Terrorist*, 226.

65. Testimony of Michael Fortier in the Timothy McVeigh Trial, May 12, 1997, 28. See also Michel and Herbeck, *American Terrorist*, 186–87.

66. Testimony of Michael Fortier in the Timothy McVeigh Trial, May 12, 1997, 19–20, 27–28. See also Bob Ricks's comments in "Crimes of the Century: Oklahoma City," CNN Transcripts, August 11, 2013, http://www.cnn.com/TRANSCRIPTS/1308/11/cotc.01.html; "Chronology: Following a Trail of Aliases and Other Clues," *New York Times*, August 13, 1995; Michel and Herbeck, *American Terrorist*, 186–88.

67. Testimony of Jennifer McVeigh in the Timothy McVeigh Trial, May 5, 1997, 46, 51, 53. See also Appeal from the United States District Court for the District of Colorado, 4; "Closing Argument for the Prosecution in the Trial of Timothy McVeigh (argument by Larry D. Mackey)," May 29, 1997, 13; OKC Bombing Trial Transcript-04/24/1997 11:39 CDT/CST, 19; Michel and Herbeck, *American Terrorist*, 197–98, 203–4; Jo Thomas, "In a Letter, McVeigh Told of Shifting to 'Animal,'" *New York Times*, May 9, 1997; Jo Thomas, "McVeigh Letters Before Blast Show the Depth of His Anger," *New York Times*, July 1, 1998.

68. See Nitro 50-50, "Drag Racing," https://vpracingfuels.com/product/nitro-50-50/.

69. Michel and Herbeck, *American Terrorist*, 212–19. See also "Chronology: Following a Trail of Aliases and Other Clues"; Neil MacFarquhar, "Oklahoma City Marks 25 Years Since America's Deadliest Homegrown Attack," *New York Times*, April 19, 2020.

70. James H. Anderson, Hans Butzer, and Charles Robert Goins, "Bombing of the Alfred P. Murrah Federal Building, 1995" in *Historical Atlas of Oklahoma*, ed. Danney Goble (Norman: University of Oklahoma Press, 2006), 222; "Chronology: Following a Trail of Aliases and Other Clues"; Michel and Herbeck, *American Terrorist*, 229–32; "McVeigh Chronology," *Frontline*, PBS, https://www.pbs.org/wgbh/pages/frontline/documents/mcveigh/mcveigh3.html.

71. T-shirt worn by McVeigh on April 19, 1995, with accompanying mug shot (#95 057), on display at the Oklahoma City Memorial & Museum, 620 N Harvey Avenue, Oklahoma City, OK, visited by and photograph taken by one of the authors on August 14, 2016.

72. "Testimony of Oklahoma State Trooper Charles J. Hangar Concerning His Arrest of Timothy McVeigh on April 19, 1995 (Nichols Trial–Nov. 5, 1997)," 5–7, 13, 18–20, http://law2.umkc.edu/faculty/projects/ftrials/mcveigh/mcveigharrest.html. See also "Closing

Argument for the Prosecution in the Trial of Timothy McVeigh (argument by Larry D. Mackey)," May 29, 1997, 5–7; OKC Bombing Trial Transcript-04/24/1997 11:39 CDT/CST, 10; Coulson and Shannon, *No Heroes*, 496; Tom Kenworthy, "Anti-Government Writings in McVeigh's Car, Agent Says," *Washington Post*, April 29, 1997; Michel and Herbeck, *American Terrorist*, 226–27, 238–46; Jo Thomas, "Officer Describes His Arrest of a Suspect in the Oklahoma City Bombing," *New York Times*, April 29, 1997.

73. Quoted in "Jim Norman, Case Agent, Oklahoma City Bombing Investigation: Video Transcript," FBI, https://www.fbi.gov/video-repository/newss-jim-norman-case-agent-oklahoma-city-bombing-investigation/view. See also Appeal from the United States District Court for the District of Colorado, 4; "Closing Argument for the Prosecution in the Trial of Timothy McVeigh (argument by Larry D. Mackey)," May 29, 1997, 8; OKC Bombing Trial Transcript-04/24/1997 11:39 CDT/CST, 30; Coulson and Shannon, *No Heroes*, 492–502; Michel and Herbeck, *American Terrorist*, 247–55.

74. U.S. Department of Justice, "#439 Oklahoma Bombing Indictment Statement: Attorney General's Statement," August 10, 1995, https://www.justice.gov/archive/opa/pr/Pre_96/August95/439.txt.html.

75. "Witness, Jurors Weep at Bomb Trial," *Orange County Register*, April 26, 1997; Jo Thomas, "At Bomb Trial, Tearful Stories of Terrible Day," *New York Times*, April 26, 1997.

76. United States District Court for the District of Colorado, the Honorable Richard P. Matsch, Criminal Action No. 96-CR-68-M, United States of America, Plaintiff, v. Timothy J. McVeigh, Defendant, Brief of the United States Opposed Stay of Execution, Sean Connelly, Special Attorney to the U.S. District Attorney, United States Department of Justice Archives, https://www.justice.gov/archives/opa/brief-united-states-opposing-stay-execution; Appeal from the United States District Court for the District of Colorado, 4. See also "The McVeigh Jury Speaks," *New York Times*, June 3, 1997; Jo Thomas, "McVeigh Jury Decides on Sentence of Death in Oklahoma Bombing," *New York Times*, June 14, 1997.

77. "The Oklahoma Bombing Conspirators," http://law2.umkc.edu/faculty/projects/ftrials/mcveigh/conspirators.html; MacFarquhar, "Oklahoma City Marks 25 Years Since America's Deadliest Homegrown Attack."

78. OKC Bombing Trial Transcript-04/24/1997 11:39 CDT/CST, 4, 6; see also 7–8, 17, 24, 28–29.

79. Testimony of Jennifer McVeigh, May 5, 1997, 34, 51; Testimony of Michael Fortier in the Timothy McVeigh Trial, May 12, 1997, 4, 41.

80. "Closing Argument for the Prosecution in the Trial of Timothy McVeigh (argument by Larry D. Mackey)," May 29, 1997, 12–13.

81. OKC Bombing Trial Transcript-04/24/1997 11:39 CDT/CST, 11; "Closing Argument for the Prosecution in the Trial of Timothy McVeigh (argument by Larry D. Mackey)," May 29, 1997, 6. See also Coulson and Shannon, *No Heroes*, 507; Kenworthy, "Anti-Government Writings In McVeigh's Car, Agent Says"; Thomas, "Officer Describes His Arrest of a Suspect in the Oklahoma City Bombing."

82. Louis Beam, "Louis Beam's Estes Park, Colorado Speech," http://www.louisbeam.com /estes.htm, http://video.google.com/videosearch?q=louis+beam&emb=0&aq=f#.

83. Michel and Herbeck, *American Terrorist*, 176.

84. Quoted in Marc Fisher and Phil McCombs, "The Book of Hate," *Washington Post*, April 25, 1995.

85. People who had encountered McVeigh at gun shows recalled that McVeigh "carried that book all the time. He sold it at the shows. He'd have a few copies in the cargo pocket of his cammies. They were supposed to be $10, but he'd sell them for $5. It was like he was looking for converts." Quoted in Kifner, "Bomb Suspect Felt at Home Riding the Gun-Show Circuit."

86. Kifner, "Bomb Suspect Felt at Home Riding the Gun-Show Circuit"; Beam, "Louis Beam's Estes Park, Colorado Speech"; "Closing Argument for the Prosecution in the Trial of Timothy McVeigh (argument by Larry D. Mackey)," May 29, 1997, 12–13; OKC Bombing Trial Transcript-04/24/1997 11:39 CDT/CST, 7, 8, 12, 33; MacFarquhar, "Oklahoma City Marks 25 Years Since America's Deadliest Homegrown Attack."

87. Anti-Defamation League, "Louis Beam," 5, https://www.adl.org/sites/default/files /documents/assets/pdf/combating-hate/Louis-Beam.pdf; Heidi Beirich and Mark Potok, "40 to Watch: Leaders of the Radical Right," *SPLC Intelligence Report*, November 12, 2003, https://www.splcenter.org/fighting-hate/intelligence-report/2003/40 -watch-leaders-radical-right.

88. Quoted in Kathleen Belew, *Bring the War Home: The White Power Movement and Paramilitary America* (Cambridge, MA: Harvard University Press, 2018), 231; see also 210, 212, 234; Daniel Levitas, *The Terrorist Next Door: The Militia Movement and the Radical Right* (New York: Thomas Dunne, 2002), 324–25; Leonard Zeskind, *Blood and Politics: The History of the White Nationalist Movement from the Margins to the Mainstream* (New York: Farrar Straus Giroux, 2009), 413–16.

89. Kevin Jack Riley and Bruce Hoffman, *Domestic Terrorism: A National Assessment of State and Local Preparedness* (Santa Monica, CA: RAND Corporation, MR-505J, 1995), x, 16–17. See also Brian Michael Jenkins, Sorrel Wildhorn, and Marvin M. Lavin, *Intelligence Constraints of the 1970s and Domestic Terrorism: Executive Summary* (Santa Monica, CA: RAND Corporation, R-29239-DOJ, December 1982), iii, 1–2, 21–22; Brian Michael Jenkins, Sorrel Wildhorn, and Marvin M. Lavin, *Intelligence Constraints of the 1970s and Domestic Terrorism*, vol. 1: *Effects on the Incidence, Investigation, and Prosecution of Terrorist Activity* (Santa Monica, CA: RAND Corporation, N-1901-DOJ, December 1982), v, 106–8; Oliver "Buck" Revell and Dwight Williams, *A G-Man's Journal: A Legendary Career Inside the FBI—from the Kennedy Assassination to the Oklahoma City Bombing* (New York: Pocket, 1998), 444–46.

90. Revell and Williams, *A G-Man's Journal*, 445–46.

91. Anti-Defamation League, *The Militia Movement* (2001), https://www.adl.org/education /resources/backgrounders/militia-movement, 9.

92. Klanwatch, *False Patriots: The Threat of Antigovernment Extremists* (Montgomery, AL: Southern Poverty Law Center, 1996), 5; see also 34–35, 58–68; Morris Dees with James

Corcoran, *Gathering Storm: America's Militia Threat* (New York: HarperCollins, 1996), 199.

93. Bruce Hoffman, "American Right-Wing Extremism," *Jane's Intelligence Review* 7, no. 7 (July 1995): 329.

94. Federal Bureau of Investigation, "Domestic Terrorism: The Sovereign Citizen Movement," April 13, 2010, https://www.fbi.gov/news/stories/2010/april/sovereigncitizens _041310/domestic-terrorism-the-sovereign-citizen-movement.

95. Counterterrorism Threat Assessment and Warning Unit, National Security Division, *Terrorism in the United States 1996* (Washington, DC: U.S. Department of Justice, Federal Bureau of Investigation, 1997), 7–8, 13–14; Counterterrorism Threat Assessment and Warning Unit, National Security Division, *Terrorism in the United States 1997* (Washington, DC: U.S. Department of Justice, Federal Bureau of Investigation, 1998), 11–12; James Brooke, "Officials Say Montana 'Freemen' Collected $1.8 Million in Scheme," *New York Times*, March 29, 1996; Lori Linzer and David Rosenberg, *Vigilante Justice* (New York: Anti-Defamation League, 1997), iii–iv, 1–6; Zeskind, *Blood and Politics*, 361–62.

96. Counterterrorism Threat Assessment and Warning Unit, *Terrorism in the United States 1996*, 6–8, 13–14; Counterterrorism Threat Assessment and Warning Unit, *Terrorism in the United States 1997*, 8; "Freemen, FBI Standoff Drags On," CNN, March 28, 1996, http://www.cnn.com/US/9603/montana_freemen/28/index.html; Levitas, *The Terrorist Next Door*, 325; David A. Neiwert, *Alt-America: The Rise of the Radical Right in the Age of Trump* (New York: Verso, 2017), 61–62; Schlatter, *Aryan Cowboys: White Supremacists and the Search for a New Frontier*, 146–58; Lorna Thackeray, "The Freeman Standoff," *Billings Gazette*, March 25, 2006; Zeskind, *Blood and Politics*, 408–12.

97. Levitas, *The Terrorist Next Door*, 324–25; Schlatter, *Aryan Cowboys*, 153–58.

98. Anti-Defamation League, *The Militia Movement* (2001), 8, 12; "Cover Story: Hate Thy Neighbor: Local Author Daniel Levitas Exposes the History and Hypocrisy of the Militant White Supremacist Movement," *Creative Loafing*, November 27, 2002, https:// creativeloafing.com/content-184623-cover-story-hate-thy-neighbor; Nella Van Dyke and Sarah A. Soule, "Structural Social Change and the Mobilizing Effect of Threat: Explaining Levels of Patriot and Militia Organizing in the United States," *Social Problems* 49, no. 4 (November 2002): 500, https://www.jstor.org/stable/10.1525/sp.2002.49.4 .497; Wright, *Patriots, Politics, and the Oklahoma City Bombing*, 211–14.

99. "FBI Point Man Robert Blitzer Discusses Agency's Work with Extremist Groups," *Intelligence Report* (SPLC), December 15, 1998, 5.

100. Dahleen Glanton and *Tribune* reporter, "Atlanta Debates How Golden It Was," *Chicago Tribune*, September 21, 2009. See also Peter Applebome, "So, You Want to Hold an Olympics," *New York Times*, August 4, 1996; "Atlanta 1996 Olympic Games," *Encyclopedia Britannica*, https://www.britannica.com/event/Atlanta-1996-Olympic-Games.

101. Marie Brenner, "American Nightmare: The Ballad of Richard Jewell," *Vanity Fair*, February 1997, 100–7, 151–65, https://archive.vanityfair.com/article/share/1fd2d7ae-10d8 -474b-9bf1-d1558af697be; Scott Freeman, "Fallout: An Oral History of the Olympic Park Bombing," *Atlanta Magazine*, July 1, 2011, https://www.atlantamagazine.com/great

-reads/olympic-park-bombing-oral-history/; "Olympic Park Bombing," Clinton Digital Library, Clinton Presidential Library & Museum, https://clinton.presidentiallibraries.us/olympic-park.

102. Telephone discussion with then *Los Angeles Times* reporter Robin Wright, July 1996.

103. "Eric Rudolph: A Profile," *Washington Post*, December 12, 1998; Freeman, "Fallout: An Oral History of the Olympic Park Bombing."

104. Federal Bureau of Investigation, U.S. Department of Justice, "Eric Rudolph Charged in Centennial Olympic Park Bombing," October 14, 1998, https://www.justice.gov/archive/opa/pr/1998/October/477crm.htm; U.S. Department of Justice, "Eric Robert Rudolph to Plead Guilty to Serial Bombing Attacks in Atlanta and Birmingham; Will Receive Life Sentences," April 8, 2005, https://web.archive.org/web/20130414003813/http://www.justice.gov/opa/pr/2005/April/05_crm_176.htm.

105. Terrorist Threat Assessment and Warning Unit, National Security Division, *Terrorism in the United States 1998* (Washington, DC: U.S. Department of Justice, Federal Bureau of Investigation, 1999), 3.

106. Henry Schuster with Charles Stone, *Hunting Eric Rudolph: An Insider's Account of the Five-Year Search for the Olympic Bombing Suspect* (New York: Berkley, 2005), 58–61, 334.

107. Schuster with Stone, *Hunting Eric Rudolph*, 112–13, 120, 191–92, 199–200, 203–7, 297. See also Anti-Defamation League, "Backgrounder: Eric Robert Rudolph," June 5, 2003, https://www.adl.org/resources/backgrounders/backgrounder-eric-robert-rudolph.

108. Eric Rudolph, *Between the Lines of Drift: The Memoirs of a Militant*, 3rd ed. (Army of God, 2015), 145, http://www.armyofgod.com/EricLinesOfDrift1_18_15.pdf. See also Jon Elliston, "Bomber Eric Rudolph's Memoir Published by Virginia-Based Army of God," *Carolina Public Press*, December 18, 2013, https://carolinapublicpress.org/17293/bomber-eric-rudolphs-memoir-published-by-virginia-based-army-of-god/.

109. Schuster with Stone, *Hunting Eric Rudolph*, 110–42.

110. Schuster with Stone, *Hunting Eric Rudolph*, 253, 259; Freeman, "Fallout: An Oral History of the Olympic Park Bombing."

111. Schuster with Stone, *Hunting Eric Rudolph*, 143.

112. Schuster with Stone, *Hunting Eric Rudolph*, 113; Jeffrey Gettleman with David M. Halbfinger, "Suspect in '96 Olympic Bombing and 3 Other Attacks Is Caught," *New York Times*, June 1, 2003.

113. Rudolph, *Between the Lines of Drift*, 177.

114. Federal Bureau of Investigation, "Eric Rudolph Charged in Centennial Olympic Park Bombing," October 14, 1998.

115. Federal Bureau of Investigation, "Eric Rudolph: FBI Ten Most Wanted Fugitive," History: Famous Cases & Criminals, https://www.fbi.gov/history/famous-cases/eric-rudolph. See also Sue Anne Pressley, "Bomb Suspect Is Outfoxing His Pursuers," *Washington Post*, July 22, 1998.

116. U.S. Department of Justice, "Eric Robert Rudolph to Plead Guilty to Serial Bombing Attacks in Atlanta and Birmingham; Will Receive Life Sentences," April 8, 2005; Maryanne Vollers, "Inside Bomber Row," *Time*, November 5, 2006, http://content.time.com/time/subscriber/article/0,33009,1555145,00.html.

117. Jay Reeves, "Rudolph Gets 2 Life Terms in Abortion Clinic Attack," *Washington Post*, July 19, 2005.

118. "Law: Full Text of Eric Rudolph's Confession," National Public Radio, April 14, 2005, 3, 6–7, https://www.npr.org/templates/story/story.php?storyId=4600480.

119. See Michael German, "Behind the Lone Terrorists, a Pack Mentality," *Washington Post*, June 5, 2005; Henry Schuster, "Lone Wolves: Solitary Threats Harder to Hunt," CNN, February 1, 2005, http://www.cnn.com/2005/US/02/01/schuster.column/index.html.

120. Jeffrey Simon, *Lone Wolf Terrorism: Understanding the Growing Threat* (Amherst, MA: Prometheus, 2016), 256–57.

121. See Henry Schuster, "Why Did Rudolph Do It? Question Lingers After Plea Deal Reached," CNN, http://www.cnn.com/2005/US/04/11/schuster.column/index.html; Shaila Dewan, "Bomber Offers Guilty Pleas, and Defiance," *New York Times*, April 14, 2005.

122. Andrew Blejwas, Anthony Griggs, and Mark Potok, "Almost 60 Terrorist Plots Uncovered in the U.S. Since the Oklahoma City Bombing," *SPLC Intelligence Report*, 2005 Summer Issue/July 27, 2005, https://www.splcenter.org/fighting-hate/intelligence-report/2005/almost-60-terrorist-plots-uncovered-us-oklahoma-city-bombing. See also Bruce Hoffman, *Inside Terrorism* (New York: Columbia University Press, 2017), 112–14.

6. RACISM REKINDLED

1. Morgan Winsor, "2009 vs. 2017: Comparing Trump's and Obama's Inauguration Crowds," *ABC News*, January 25, 2017, https://abcnews.go.com/Politics/2009-2017-comparing-trumps-obamas-inauguration-crowds/story?id=44927217.

2. "President Barack Obama's Inaugural Address," White House, January 21, 2009, https://obamawhitehouse.archives.gov/blog/2009/01/21/president-barack-obamas-inaugural-address.

3. Sonia Scherr, "Hate Groups Claim Obama Win Is Sparking Recruitment Surge," Southern Poverty Law Center, November 6, 2008, https://www.splcenter.org/hatewatch/2008/11/06/hate-groups-claim-obama-win-sparking-recruitment-surge.

4. See, for instance, Tommy De Seno, "Obama's to Blame for the Birther Movement," *Fox News*, July 29, 2009, https://www.foxnews.com/opinion/obamas-to-blame-for-the-birther-movement; and Gregory Krieg, "14 of Trump's Most Outrageous 'Birther' Claims—Half from After 2011," CNN, September 16, 2016, https://www.cnn.com/2016/09/09/politics/donald-trump-birther.

5. Jeff Zeleny, "Secret Service Guards Obama, Taking Unusually Early Step," *New York Times*, May 4, 2007, https://www.nytimes.com/2007/05/04/us/politics/04obama.html; Barack Obama, *A Promised Land* (New York: Viking, 2020), 137.

6. Matthew Bigg, "Election of Obama Provokes Rise in U.S. Hate Crimes," Reuters, November 24, 2008, https://www.reuters.com/article/us-usa-obama-hatecrimes/election-of-obama-provokes-rise-in-u-s-hate-crimes-idUSTRE4AN81U20081124.

7. Mark Potok, "The Year in Hate and Extremism," *Intelligence Report*, Spring 2013, March 4, 2013, https://www.splcenter.org/fighting-hate/intelligence-report/2013/year-hate-and-extremism.

8. "Antigovernment Movement," Southern Poverty Law Center, https://www.splcenter.org/fighting-hate/extremist-files/ideology/antigovernment.

9. VAOK, https://virginiaoathkeepers.org/.

10. Sam Jackson, *Oath Keepers: Patriotism and the Edge of Violence in a Right-Wing Antigovernment Group* (New York: Columbia University Press, 2020), 31. The Posse Comitatus Act, originally enacted in 1878, applied only to the U.S. Army. An amendment in 1956 broadened it to include the U.S. Air Force. It therefore "outlaws the willful use of any part of the Army or Air Force to execute the law unless expressly authorized by the Constitution or an act of Congress. . . . The express statutory exceptions include the legislation that allows the President to use military force to suppress insurrection or to enforce federal authority . . . and laws that permit the Department of Defense to provide federal, state and local police with information, equipment, and personnel." See Jennifer K. Elsea, *The Posse Comitatus Act and Related Matters: The Use of the Military to Execute Civilian Law* (Washington, DC: Congressional Research Service, R42659, November 6, 2018), iii. See also Joseph Nunn, "The Posse Comitatus Act Explained," Brennan Center for Justice, October 14, 2021, https://www.brennancenter.org/our-work/research-reports/posse-comitatus-act-explained.

11. David Neiwert, *Alt-America: The Rise of the Radical Right in the Age of Trump* (New York: Verso, 2017), 152.

12. See, for example, Jacqueline Best, "How the 2008 Financial Crisis Helped Fuel Today's Right-Wing Populism," *Conversation*, October 1, 2018, https://theconversation.com/how-the-2008-financial-crisis-helped-fuel-todays-right-wing-populism-103979; Ben McGrath, "The Movement: The Rise of Tea Party Activism," *New Yorker*, January 24, 2010, https://www.newyorker.com/magazine/2010/02/01/the-movement; Liz Halloran, "What's Behind the New Populism?," National Public Radio, The Tea Party in America, February 5, 2010, https://www.npr.org/templates/story/story.php?storyId=123137382; David Barstow, "Tea Party Lights Fuse for Rebellion on Right," *New York Times*, February 15, 2010, https://www.nytimes.com/2010/02/16/us/politics/16teaparty.html.

13. Eric Kleefeld, "Tea Party Activist and Senate Candidate: 'If We Don't See New Faces, I'm Cleaning My Guns and Getting Ready for the Big Show' (VIDEO)," *Talking Points Memo*, January 26, 2010, https://talkingpointsmemo.com/dc/tea-party-activist-and-senate-candidate-if-we-don-t-see-new-faces-i-m-cleaning-my-guns-and-getting-ready-for-the-big-show-video.

14. Office of Intelligence and Analysis Assessment (U//FOUO), *Rightwing Extremism: Current Economic and Political Climate Fueling Resurgence in Radicalization and Recruitment* (Washington, DC: Department of Homeland Security, IA-0257-09, April 7, 2009), 8, https://fas.org/irp/eprint/rightwing.pdf.

15. Office of Intelligence and Analysis Assessment (U//FOUO), *Rightwing Extremism*, 3, 7–9.

16.   "It turns out the report was right, and it was prescient, and we see today increasing incidents of right-wing or white nationalist activity across the country," Janet Napolitano said years later. Zolan Kanno-Youngs and Nicole Hong, "Biden Steps Up Federal Efforts to Combat Domestic Extremism," *New York Times*, April 4, 2021, https://www.nytimes.com/2021/04/04/us/politics/domestic-terrorism-biden.html. See also Daryl Johnson, "I Warned of Right-Wing Violence in 2009. Republicans Objected. I Was Right," *Washington Post*, August 21, 2017; Matt Kennard, *Irregular Army: How the US Military Recruited Neo-Nazis, Gang Members, and Criminals to Fight the War on Terror* (London: Verso, 2015), 39; Brett Murphy, Will Carless, Marisa Kwiatkowski, and Tricia L. Nadolny, "A 2009 Warning About Right-Wing Extremism Was Engulfed by Politics. There Are Signs It's Happening Again," *USA Today*, January 27, 2021.

17.   See "Former DHS Analyst Daryl Johnson on How He Was Silenced for Warning of Far-Right Militants in U.S.," *Democracy Now!*, August 9, 2012, https://www.democracynow.org/2012/8/9/former_dhs_analyst_daryl_johnson_on; Ben Wofford, "The GOP Shut Down a Program That Might Have Prevented Dallas and Baton Rouge," *Politico*, July 24, 2016, https://www.politico.com/magazine/story/2016/07/gop-veteran-radicalization-dhs-dallas-baton-rouge-214089/.

18.   Heidi Beirich, "Inside the DHS: Former Top Analyst Says Agency Bowed to Political Pressure," Southern Poverty Law Center, June 17, 2011, https://www.splcenter.org/fighting-hate/intelligence-report/2011/inside-dhs-former-top-analyst-says-agency-bowed-political-pressure. See also Neiwert, *Alt-America*, 15.

19.   Kirsti Haga Honningsøy and Kristine Ramberg Aasen, " 'Du har allerede drept pappaen min, jeg er for ung til å dø,' " *NRK*, July 24, 2011, https://www.nrk.no/norge/_jeg-er-for-ung-til-a-do_-1.7725593.

20.   Åsne Seierstad, *One of Us: The Story of Anders Breivik and the Massacre in Norway* (New York: FSG, 2015), 294.

21.   Seierstad, *One of Us*, 370; Anna Doble, "Norway's Lost Leaders," Channel 4, July 26, 2011, https://www.channel4.com/news/norways-lost-leaders.

22.   Andrew Berwick [pseud.], "2083: A European Declaration of Independence," 2011.

23.   Berwick, "2083," 15.

24.   Michael Schwirtz and Matthew Saltmarsh, "Oslo Suspect Cultivated Parallel Life to Disguise 'Martyrdom Operation,' " *New York Times*, July 24, 2011, https://www.nytimes.com/2011/07/25/world/europe/25breivik.html.

25.   Berwick, "2083," 1382.

26.   Seierstad, *One of Us*, 27.

27.   Seierstad, *One of Us*, 26.

28.   Seierstad, *One of Us*, 154.

29.   Seierstad, *One of Us*, 221.

30.   Ingrid Melle, "The Breivik Case and What Psychiatrists Can Learn from It," *World Psychiatry* 12, no. 1 (2013): 16–21.

31.   Mark Lewis and Sarah Lyall, "Norway Mass Killer Gets the Maximum: 21 Years," *New York Times*, August 24, 2012; "Norway Killer Breivik Tests Limits of Lenient Justice

System," *Voice of America*, January 22, 2022, https://www.voanews.com/a/norway
-killer-breivik-tests-limits-of-lenient-justice-system/6407441.html.

32. Pete Simi and Robert Futrell, *American Swastika: Inside the White Power Movement's Hidden Spaces of Hate* (Boulder, CO: Rowman & Littlefield, 2015), 1; Caroline Porter, Ben Kesling, and Nathan Koppel, "Shooter Linked to Hate Group," *Wall Street Journal*, August 6, 2012.

33. Marilyn Elias, "Sikh Temple Killer Wade Michael Page Radicalized in Army," Southern Poverty Law Center, November 11, 2012, https://www.splcenter.org/fighting -hate/intelligence-report/2012/sikh-temple-killer-wade-michael-page-radicalized -army.

34. Elias, "Sikh Temple Killer Wade Michael Page Radicalized in Army"; Simi and Futrell, *American Swastika*, iii.

35. Kennard, *Irregular Army*, 18, 22, 39, 180; William Branigin and Dana Priest, "3 White Soldiers Held in Slaying of Black Couple," *Washington Post*, December 9, 1995, https:// www.washingtonpost.com/archive/politics/1995/12/09/3-white-soldiers-held-in-slay ing-of-black-couple/1f11ca9f-9fe2-4e28-a637-a635007deeaf/.

36. David Holthouse, "Several High Profile Racist Extremists Serve in the U.S. Military," Southern Poverty Law Center, August, 11 2006, https://www.splcenter.org /fighting-hate/intelligence-report/2006/several-high-profile-racist-extremists-serve -us-military.

37. Holthouse, "Several High Profile Racist Extremists Serve in the U.S. Military."

38. Holthouse, "Several High Profile Racist Extremists Serve in the U.S. Military."

39. Mark Potok, "Extremism and the Military," Southern Poverty Law Center, August 11, 2006, https://www.splcenter.org/fighting-hate/intelligence-report/2006/extremism -and-military.

40. Jeff McCausland, "Inside the U.S. Military's Battle with White Supremacy and Far-Right Extremism," *NBC News*, May 25, 2019, https://www.nbcnews.com/think/opinion /inside-u-s-military-s-battle-white-supremacy-far-right-ncna1010221.

41. Kennard, *Irregular Army*, 24–29.

42. Potok, "Extremism and the Military."

43. Holthouse, "Several High Profile Racist Extremists Serve in the U.S. Military."

44. FBI Counterterrorism Division, "White Supremacist Recruitment of Military Personnel Since 9/11," *Federal Bureau of Investigation Intelligence Assessment*, July 7, 2008, https://documents.law.yale.edu/sites/default/files/White%20Supremacist%20Recruit-ment%20of%20Military%20Personnel%20Since%209–11-ocr.pdf.

45. Porter et al., "Shooter Linked to Hate Group"; Leo Shane III and Megan McCloskey, "Sikh Temple Shooter Was Army Veteran, White Supremacist," *Stars and Stripes*, August 6, 2012, https://www.stripes.com/news/us/sikh-temple-shooter-was-army -veteran-white-supremacist-1.184975.

46. Rick Romell, "Shooter's Odd Behavior Did Not Go Unnoticed," *Milwaukee Journal Sentinel*, August 6, 2012, http://archive.jsonline.com/news/crime/shooter-wade-page-was -army-vet-white-supremacist-856cn28–165123946.html/.

47. Brian Levin, "Exclusive: Interview with Professor Who Extensively Studied Alleged Wisconsin Mass Killer," *Huffington Post*, August 7, 2012, https://www.huffpost.com /entry/exclusive-interview-with_b_1751181.

48. Daniel Koehler, "A Threat from Within? Exploring the Link Between the Extreme Right and the Military," International Centre for Counter-Terrorism–The Hague, September 2019, https://www.icct.nl/sites/default/files/import/publication/ICCT-Koehler-A -Threat-from-Within-Exploring-the-Link-between-the-Extreme-Right-and-the -Military.pdf.

49. James McPherson, *Battle Cry of Freedom: The Civil War Era* (New York: Oxford University Press, 1988), 406, 458.

50. "Prominent Neo-Nazi Proclaims Wade Michael Page Was Heroic," *SITE Intelligence Group*, August 8, 2012, https://ent.siteintelgroup.com/Far-Right-/-Far-Left-Threat /prominent-neo-nazi-proclaims-wade-michael-page-was-heroic.html.

51. "White Supremacists Concerned Sikh Temple Massacre Looks Badly on Them," *SITE Intelligence Group*, August 6, 2012, https://ent.siteintelgroup.com/Far-Right-/-Far-Left-Threat /white-supremacists-concerned-sikh-temple-massacre-looks-badly-on-them.html.

52. Robbie Brown, "Anti-Obama Protest at Ole Miss Turns Unruly," *New York Times*, November 7, 2012.

53. "Hammerskins Denigrate President Obama, Lament His Re-election," *SITE Intelligence Group*, November 7, 2012, https://ent.siteintelgroup.com/Jihadist-News/hammerskins -denigrate-president-obama-lament-his-re-election.html.

54. Laura Bauer, Dave Helling, and Brian Burnes, "Man with History of Anti-Semitism Jailed in Fatal Shooting of Three at Johnson County Jewish Centers," *Kansas City Star*, May 16, 2014; Heidi Beirich, "Frazier Glenn Miller, Longtime Anti-Semite, Arrested in Center Murders," Southern Poverty Law Center, April 13, 2014, https://www.splcenter .org/news/2014/04/13/frazier-glenn-miller-longtime-anti-semite-arrested-kansas -jewish-community-center-murders; Tony Rizzo, "Federal Hate-Crime Charges, State Charges Likely in Overland Park Shootings," *Kansas City Star*, May 16, 2014.

55. "Glenn Miller: Prominent Member of Neo-Nazi Forum," *SITE Intelligence Group*, April 14, 2014, https://ent.siteintelgroup.com/Far-Right-Far-Left-Threat/glenn-miller -prominent-member-of-neo-nazi-forum.html.

56. Quoted in Steven Yaccino and Dan Barry, "Bullets, Blood and Then Cry of 'Heil Hitler,'" *New York Times*, April 14, 2014.

57. "Neo-Nazis Celebrate JCC Shooting in Kansas," *SITE Intelligence Group*, April 14, 2014, https://ent.siteintelgroup.com/Far-Right-Far-Left-Threat/neo-nazis-celebrate-jcc -shooting-respond-to-claims-that-forum-member-is-responsible.html.

58. "InSITE: Violence on Forum Linked to JCC Shooter," *SITE Intelligence Group*, April 18, 2014, https://ent.siteintelgroup.com/Far-Right-/-Far-Left-Threat/insite-violence-on -forum-linked-to-jcc-shooter.html.

59. "Skinhead Forum Responds to Overland Parks Shooting," *SITE Intelligence Group*, April 16, 2014, https://ent.siteintelgroup.com/Far-Right-/-Far-Left-Threat/skinhead -forum-responds-to-overland-parks-shooting.html.

60.   Elle Moxley, "Why KCUR Refers to the Accused JCC Shooter as Frazier Glenn Cross," KCUR: NPR in Kansas City, March 4, 2015, https://www.kcur.org/community/2015-03 -04/why-kcur-refers-to-the-accused-jcc-shooter-as-frazier-glenn-cross. See also David Helling, Judy Thomas, and Mark Morris, "Records Suggest That F. Glenn Miller Jr. Was Once in Witness Protection Program," *Wichita Eagle* (Kansas), April 15, 2014, https:// www.kansas.com/news/article1140256.html.

61.   "Overland Park Shooter A Supporter of Anders Breivik and Utoya Massacre," *SITE Intelligence Group*, April 14, 2014, https://ent.siteintelgroup.com/Far-Right-Far-Left -Threat/overland-park-shooter-a-supporter-of-anders-breivik-and-utoya-massacre .html.

62.   Anthony McCann, *Shadowlands: Fear and Freedom at the Oregon Standoff—A Western Tale of America in Crisis* (New York: Bloomsbury, 2019), 42, *passim*. See also Neiwert, *Alt-America*, 161–77; "Elmer Stewart Rhodes," Southern Poverty Law Center, https://www.splcenter.org/fighting-hate/extremist-files/individual/elmer-stewart -rhodes.

63.   McCann, *Shadowlands*; Barry J. Balleck, *Modern American Extremism and Domestic Terrorism: An Encyclopedia of Extremists and Extremist Groups* (Santa Barbara: ABC-CLIO, 2018), 55.

64.   "Forum Members Brace for Confrontation at Bundy Ranch," *SITE Intelligence Group*, April 11, 2014, https://ent.siteintelgroup.com/Far-Right-Far-Left-Threat/forum -members-brace-for-confrontation-at-bundy-ranch.html.

65.   Adam Nagourney, "A Defiant Rancher Savors the Audience That Rallied to His Side," *New York Times*, April 23, 2014, https://www.nytimes.com/2014/04/24/us/politics /rancher-proudly-breaks-the-law-becoming-a-hero-in-the-west.html.

66.   Neiwert, *Alt-America*, 167.

67.   Daryl Johnson, *Hateland: A Long, Hard Look at America's Extremist Heart* (Amherst, MA: Prometheus, 2019), 160.

68.   Dana Liebelson, "Inside the Unraveling of Las Vegas Shooting Spree Suspect Jerad Miller," *Mother Jones*, June 9, 2014, https://www.motherjones.com/politics/2014/06/las -vegas-jerad-miller-unraveling-infowars-alex-jones/; "A Look Inside the Lives of Shooters Jerad Miller, Amanda Miller," *Las Vegas Sun*, June 9, 2014.

69.   Quoted in Neiwert, *Alt-America*, 177–78. See also "Las Vegas Shooting Couple Had Been Booted from Bundy Ranch as 'Too Radical,'" *ABC News*, June 10, 2014, https://abcnews .go.com/US/rampaging-couple-booted-bundy-ranch-radical/story?id=24067414.

70.   Quoted in Neiwert, *Alt-America*, 179.

71.   Quoted in and also see the video clip embedded in "A Look Inside the Lives of Shooters Jerad Miller, Amanda Miller."

72.   "'Anti-Government' Killers Put Swastika, Flag on Metro Police Officer's Body," *Las Vegas Sun*, June 9, 2014, https://lasvegassun.com/news/2014/jun/09/police-describe -bloodbath-created-neo-nazi-couple-/.

73.   Alex Schmid and Janny De Graaf, *Violence as Communication: Insurgent Terrorism and the Western News Media* (Beverly Hills, CA: Sage, 1982).

74. See, for example, Bruce Hoffman and Jacob Ware, "July 22: A Pivotal Day in Terrorism History," *War on the Rocks*, July 22, 2021, https://warontherocks.com/2021/07/july-22-a-pivotal-day-in-terrorism-history/.

75. Brian M. Jenkins, "International Terrorism: A New Mode of Conflict," in *International Terrorism and World Security*, ed. David Carlton and Carlo Schaerf (London: Croom Helm, 1975), 16.

76. Kathleen Belew, *Bring the War Home: The White Power Movement and Paramilitary America* (Cambridge, MA: Harvard University Press, 2018), 120.

77. Helen Pidd, "Anders Breivik 'Trained' for Shooting Attacks by Playing *Call of Duty*," *Guardian*, April 19, 2012, https://www.theguardian.com/world/2012/apr/19/anders-breivik-call-of-duty.

78. Seierstad, *One of Us*, 130, 153, 155.

79. Quoted in Seierstad, *One of Us*, 155.

80. Seierstad, *One of Us*, 169.

81. "White Supremacists Urge to Use Facebook to 'Awaken' Whites," *SITE Intelligence Group*, April 8, 2013, https://ent.siteintelgroup.com/Far-Right-Far-Left-Threat/white-supremacists-urge-to-use-facebook-to-awaken-whites.html.

82. Jerrold Post, Cody McGinnis, and Kristen Moody, "The Changing Face of Terrorism in the 21st Century: The Communications Revolution and the Virtual Community of Hatred," *Behavioral Sciences & the Law* 32, no. 3 (2014): 330.

83. Talia Lavin, *Culture Warlords: My Journey into the Dark Web of White Supremacy* (New York: Hachette, 2020), 105

84. "White Supremacists & Neo-Nazis Offer Initial Reactions to Lack of Indictment and Unrest in Ferguson," *SITE Intelligence Group*, November 25, 2014, https://ent.siteintelgroup.com/Far-Right-Far-Left-Threat/white-supremacists-neo-nazis-offer-initial-reactions-to-lack-of-indictment-and-unrest-in-ferguson.html.

85. Cas Mudde, *The Far Right Today* (Cambridge: Polity, 2019), 4.

86. Ian Cobain and Matthew Taylor, "Far-Right Terrorist Thomas Mair Jailed for Life for Jo Cox Murder," *Guardian*, November 23, 2016, https://www.theguardian.com/uk-news/2016/nov/23/thomas-mair-found-guilty-of-jo-cox-murder.

87. "White Supremacists: Merkel 'Should be Hung' Following Reiteration of Refugee Stance," *SITE Intelligence Group*, December 14, 2015, https://ent.siteintelgroup.com/Far-Right-Far-Left-Threat/white-supremacists-merkel-should-be-hung-following-reiteration-of-refugee-stance.html.

88. "White Supremacists Wish for Deaths of Chancellor Merkel and German Politicians," *SITE Intelligence Group*, November 25, 2015, https://ent.siteintelgroup.com/Far-Right-Far-Left-Threat/white-supremacists-wish-for-deaths-of-chancellor-merkel-and-german-politicians.html.

89. "Syrian Refugees Being Sent to Idaho Angers White Supremacists," *SITE Intelligence Group*, July 31, 2015, https://ent.siteintelgroup.com/Far-Right-/-Far-Left-Threat/syrian-refugees-being-sent-to-idaho-angers-white-supremacists.html.

90. "Announcement That US Will Accept More Refugees Infuriates White Supremacists," *SITE Intelligence Group*, September 21, 2015, https://ent.siteintelgroup.com/Far-Right

-Far-Left-Threat/announcement-that-us-will-accept-more-refugees-infuriates-white
-supremacists.html.

91. J. M. Berger, "How ISIS Games Twitter," *Atlantic*, June 16, 2014, https://www.the
atlantic.com/international/archive/2014/06/isis-iraq-twitter-social-media-strategy
/372856/.

92. UN Office on Drugs and Crime, "Foreign Terrorist Fighters," https://www.unodc.org
/unodc/en/terrorism/expertise/foreign-terrorist-fighters.html; Ryan Browne and Barbara Starr, "US Military Official: 50 ISIS Foreign Fighters Captured Since November,"
CNN Politics, December 12, 2017, https://www.cnn.com/2017/12/12/politics/isis-foreign
-fighters-captured-syria-iraq/index.html.

93. Peter Bergen, *United States of Jihad: Investigating America's Homegrown Terrorists* (New
York: Broadway, 2016), 287.

94. Jessica Stern and J. M. Berger, *ISIS: The State of Terror* (New York: HarperCollins, 2015);
Jessica Stern and J. M. Berger, "Smart Mobs, Ultraviolence, and Civil Society: ISIS Innovations," *Lawfare*, March 23, 2015, https://www.lawfareblog.com/smart-mobs-ultrav
iolence-and-civil-society-isis-innovations.

95. "Islamic State of Iraq and the Levant and Its Supporters Encouraging Attacks Against
Law Enforcement and Government Personnel," *U.S. Department of Homeland Security
and Department of Justice Federal Bureau of Investigation Joint Intelligence Bulletin*,
October 11, 2014, https://www.aclu.org/sites/default/files/field_document/Email-re-JIB
-ISIL-and-Its-Supporters-Encouraging-Attacks-1660–1665.pdf.

96. Jacob Davey and Julia Ebner, "'The Great Replacement': The Violent Consequences of
Mainstreamed Extremism," Institute for Strategic Dialogue, July 2019, https://www
.isdglobal.org/wp-content/uploads/2019/07/The-Great-Replacement-The-Violent
-Consequences-of-Mainstreamed-Extremism-by-ISD.pdf.

97. T. K. Wilson, *Killing Strangers: How Political Violence Became Modern* (Oxford: Oxford
University Press, 2020), 215.

98. Rachel Kaadzi Ghansah, "A Most American Terrorist: The Making of Dylann Roof,"
GQ, August 21, 2017, https://www.gq.com/story/dylann-roof-making-of-an-american
-terrorist.

99. Neiwert, *Alt-America*, 20.

100. Timothy M. Phelps, "Dylann Roof Tried to Kill Himself During Attack, Victim's Son
Says," *Los Angeles Times*, June 20, 2015, https://www.latimes.com/nation/nationnow/la
-na-dylann-roof-suicide-attempt-20150620-story.html.

101. Dylann Roof, "rtf88," June 2015.

102. Ghansah, "A Most American Terrorist."

103. Lenny Bernstein, Sari Horwitz, and Peter Holley, "Dylann Roof's Racist Manifesto: 'I
Have No Choice,'" *Washington Post*, June 20, 2015, https://www.washingtonpost.com
/national/health-science/authorities-investigate-whether-racist-manifesto-was
-written-by-sc-gunman/2015/06/20/f0bd3052-1762-11e5-9ddc-e3353542100c_story
.html.

104. See, for example, Jamelle Bouie, "The Deadly History of 'They're Raping Our Women,'"
Slate, June 18, 2015, https://slate.com/news-and-politics/2015/06/the-deadly-history-of

-theyre-raping-our-women-racists-have-long-defended-their-worst-crimes-in-the
-name-of-defending-white-womens-honor.html.

105. Scott Ellsworth, "Tulsa Race Massacre," Oklahoma Historical Society, https://www
.okhistory.org/publications/enc/entry.php?entry=TU013.

106. "Getting Away with Murder," *American Experience*, https://www.pbs.org/wgbh
/americanexperience/features/emmett-biography-roy-carolyn-bryant-and-jw-milam/.
See also, William Bradford Huie, "The Shocking Story of Approved Killing in Mississippi," *Look*, January 1956, http://www.shoppbs.pbs.org/wgbh/amex/till/sfeature/sf_look
_confession.html.

107. Roof, "rtf88."

108. Ida B. Wells, *Southern Horrors and Other Writings: The Anti-Lynching Campaign of
Ida B. Wells, 1892–1900*, 2nd ed., ed. Jacqueline Jones Royster (Boston: Bedford/St. Martin's, 2016), 74.

109. Mark Berman, "'I Forgive You.' Relatives of Charleston Church Shooting Victims
Address Dylann Roof," *Washington Post*, June 19, 2015, https://www.washingtonpost
.com/news/post-nation/wp/2015/06/19/i-forgive-you-relatives-of-charleston-church
-victims-address-dylann-roof/.

110. Maxine Bernstein, "Ammon Bundy to Challenge Authority of Feds to Prosecute Oregon Standoff Defendants," *The Oregonian*, April 25, 2016.

111. "White Supremacists Hail Finicum as Hero, Speculate Assassination," *SITE Intelligence
Group*, January 27, 2016, https://ent.siteintelgroup.com/Far-Right-Far-Left-Threat/white
-supremacists-hail-finnicum-as-hero-speculate-assassination.html.

112. Ashley Fantz, Joe Sutton, and Holly Yan, "Armed Group's Leader in Federal Building:
'We Will Be Here as Long as It Takes,'" CNN, January 4, 2016, https://www.cnn.com
/2016/01/03/us/oregon-wildlife-refuge-protest/.

113. Liam Stack, "Wildlife Refuge Occupied in Protest of Oregon Ranchers' Prison Terms,"
New York Times, January 2, 2016, https://www.nytimes.com/2016/01/03/us/oregon
-ranchers-will-return-to-prison-angering-far-right-activists.html.

114. McCann, *Shadowlands*, 28; Thomas Gibbons-Neff, "Meet the Veterans Who Have
Joined the Oregon Militiamen," *Washington Post*, January 4, 2016, https://www
.washingtonpost.com/news/checkpoint/wp/2016/01/04/meet-the-motley-crew-of
-veteran-militiamen-in-harney-country-oregon/.

115. United States of America, Plaintiff, v. Ryan W. Payne, Defendant, Case
No. 2:16-CR-00046-GMN-PAL, Order Re: Motion to Reopen Detention Hearing
(ECF No. 1208), December 29, 2016, 4, https://casetext.com/case/united-states-v
-payne-99.

116. Washington State Legislature, House of Representatives, House of Representatives
Investigation Report Regarding Re. Matt Shea, December 1, 2019, https://leg.wa.gov
/House/InvestigationReport/Pages/default.aspx; see also Jason Wilson, "Republican
Matt Shea 'Participated in Act of Domestic Terrorism,' Says Report," *Guardian*, Decem-
ber 20, 2019, https://www.theguardian.com/us-news/2019/dec/20/matt-shea-domestic
-terrorism-washington-state-report.

117. Quoted in Vanessa Romo, "Washington Legislator Matt Shea Accused of 'Domestic Terrorism,' Report Finds," National Public Radio—WAMU 88.5, December 20, 2019,

https://www.npr.org/2019/12/20/790192972/washington-legislator-matt-shea-accused
-of-domestic-terrorism-report-finds.

118. Jim Camden and Chad Sokol, "Rep. Matt Shea Expelled from GOP Caucus After Investigation Finds He Engaged in Domestic Terrorism," *Spokesman-Review*, December 19,
2019, https://www.spokesman.com/stories/2019/dec/19/rep-matt-shea-engaged-in-dom
estic-terrorism-during/.

119. "White Supremacists Hail Finicum as Hero, Speculate Assassination."

120. "White Supremacists Support Standoff in Burns, Oregon," *SITE Intelligence Group*, January 3, 2016, https://ent.siteintelgroup.com/Far-Right-Far-Left-Threat/white-suprem
acists-support-standoff-in-burns-oregon.html.

121. "Skinheads Discuss Second American Revolution," *SITE Intelligence Group*, April 8,
2016, https://ent.siteintelgroup.com/Far-Right-Far-Left-Threat/skinheads-discuss-sec
ond-american-revolution.html.

7. THE MOVEMENT GOES GLOBAL

1. Marie-Hélène Hétu, "How Alexandre Bissonnette—and Other Mass Shooters—Could
Be Stopped Before they Kill," CBC, October 19, 2019, https://www.cbc.ca/news/canada
/alexandre-bissonnette-mass-shooters-1.5326201.

2. Dan Bilefsky, "Quebec Mosque Shooter Was Consumed by Refugees, Trump and Far
Right," *New York Times*, May 5, 2018, https://www.nytimes.com/2018/05/05/world
/canada/quebec-mosque-attack-alexandre-bissonnette.html.

3. "R. c. Bissonnette, 2019 QCCS 354 (CanLII)," *CanLII*, February 8, 2019, https://www
.canlii.org/en/qc/qccs/doc/2019/2019qccs354/2019qccs354.html.

4. Shelley Hepworth, Vanessa Gezari, Kyle Pope, Cory Schouten, Carlett Spike, David
Uberti, and Pete Vernon, "Covering Trump: An Oral History of an Unforgettable Campaign," *Columbia Journalism Review*, November 22, 2016, https://www.cjr.org/special
_report/trump_media_press_journalists.php.

5. "Alexandre Bissonnette Searched Online for Trump More Than 800 Times Before Killing Six Men at Mosque," *National Observer*, April 16, 2018, https://www.national
observer.com/2018/04/16/news/alexandre-bissonnette-searched-online-trump-more
-800-times-killing-six-men-mosque.

6. Justin Trudeau (@JustinTrudeau), Twitter, January 28, 2017, 3:20 PM, https://twitter.com
/justintrudeau/status/825438460265762816.

7. "R. c. Bissonnette, 2019 QCCS 354 (CanLII)."

8. CNN, "Donald Trump Doubles Down on Calling Mexicans 'Rapists,'" YouTube video,
June 25, 2015, https://www.youtube.com/watch?v=Jaz1Jos-cL4&ab_channel=CNN.

9. BBC News, "Donald Trump Wants 'Total' Halt to Muslims Coming to US," YouTube
video, December 8, 2015, https://www.youtube.com/watch?v=mo_nYQ6ItWM&ab
_channel=BBCNews.

10. James Fallows, "Trump Time Capsule #19: 'Appreciate the Congrats,'" *Atlantic*, June 12,
2016, https://www.theatlantic.com/politics/archive/2016/06/trump-time-capsule-19
-appreciate-the-congrats/623785/.

11.   Derek Robertson, "How an Obscure Conservative Theory Became the Trump Era's Go-to Nerd Phrase," *Politico*, February 25, 2018, https://www.politico.com/magazine/story/2018/02/25/overton-window-explained-definition-meaning-217010/.

12.   David Neiwert, *Alt-America: The Rise of the Radical Right in the Age of Trump* (New York: Verso, 2017), 271. See also Jared Taylor, "Is Trump Our Last Chance?," *American Resistance*, August 21, 2015, https://www.amren.com/features/2015/08/is-trump-our-last-chance/.

13.   "White Supremacists Support Trump's Call to Ban Muslims, Split on Candidacy," *SITE Intelligence Group*, December 8, 2015, https://ent.siteintelgroup.com/Far-Right-Far-Left-Threat/white-supremacists-support-trump-s-call-to-ban-muslims-split-on-candidacy.html.

14.   "White Supremacists and Neo-Nazis Celebrate Violence at Trump Rally," *SITE Intelligence Group*, November 23, 2015, https://ent.siteintelgroup.com/Far-Right-Far-Left-Threat/white-supremacists-and-neo-nazis-celebrate-violence-at-trump-rally.html.

15.   "White Supremacists Applaud Trump Presidential Victory, Call It a Win for 'Nationalism,'" *SITE Intelligence Group*, November 9, 2016, https://ent.siteintelgroup.com/Far-Right-Far-Left-Threat/white-supremacists-applaud-trump-presidential-victory-call-it-a-win-for-nationalism.html.

16.   See James Mason, *Siege*, digital ed., rev. 1 (ironmarch.org), June 2, 2015; James Mason, *Articles and Interviews*, 3rd ed. (Dark Foreigner, 2018).

17.   "Documenting Hate: New American Nazis," *Frontline*, November 20, 2018, https://www.pbs.org/wgbh/frontline/film/documenting-hate-new-american-nazis/.

18.   Stephen Piggott, "White Nationalists and the So-Called 'Alt-Right' Celebrate Trump's Victory," Southern Poverty Law Center, November 9, 2016, https://www.splcenter.org/hatewatch/2016/11/09/white-nationalists-and-so-called-alt-right-celebrate-trumps-victory.

19.   Eric Bradner, "Alt-Right Leader: 'Hail Trump! Hail Our people! Hail Victory!,'" CNN, November 22, 2016, https://www.cnn.com/2016/11/21/politics/alt-right-gathering-donald-trump/index.html.

20.   "White Supremacists Laud the Presidential Appointments of Reince Priebus and Stephen K. Bannon," *SITE Intelligence Group*, November 14, 2016, https://ent.siteintelgroup.com/Far-Right-/-Far-Left-Threat/white-supremacists-laud-the-presidential-appointments-of-reince-priebus-and-stephen-k-bannon.html.

21.   "Militia Blog Claims That Without Action, 'the Trumpening' Will Be Wasted," *SITE Intelligence Group*, December 9, 2016, https://ent.siteintelgroup.com/Far-Right-Far-Left-Threat/militia-blog-claims-that-without-action-the-trumpening-will-be-wasted.html.

22.   "U.S. Anti-Semitic Incidents Spike 86 Percent So Far in 2017 After Surging Last Year, ADL Finds," Anti-Defamation League, April 24, 2017, https://www.adl.org/news/press-releases/us-anti-semitic-incidents-spike-86-percent-so-far-in-2017; "Ten Days After: Harassment and Intimidation in the Aftermath of the Election," Southern Poverty Law Center, November 29, 2016, https://www.splcenter.org/20161129/ten-days-after-harassment-and-intimidation-aftermath-election.

23. In an odd twist, he also shared a number of posts supportive of candidate Bernie Sanders. "Facebook Profile of Alleged Oregonian Murderer Praises Timothy McVeigh, Wishes Violence on Hillary Clinton," *SITE Intelligence Group*, May 28, 2017, https://ent.siteintelgroup.com/Far-Right-/-Far-Left-Threat/facebook-profile-of-alleged-oregonian-murderer-praises-timothy-mcveigh-wishes-violence-on-hillary-clinton.html.

24. Philip N. Howard, Bharath Ganesh, Dimitra Liotsiou, John Kelly, and Camille François, *The IRA, Social Media and Political Polarization in the United States, 2012–2018* (Oxford: University of Oxford, 2019), https://digitalcommons.unl.edu/cgi/viewcontent.cgi?article=1004&context=senatedocs. For more, see Peter Pomerantsev, *This Is Not Propaganda: Adventures in the War Against Reality* (New York: PublicAffairs, 2019).

25. Office of the Director of National Intelligence and Office of the Director of the National Intelligence Council, "Background to 'Assessing Russian Activities and Intentions in Recent US Elections': The Analytic Process and Cyber Incident Attribution," January 6, 2017, https://www.dni.gov/files/documents/ICA_2017_01.pdf; Marshall Cohen, "Trump Versus US Intelligence on Russian Election Interference," CNN, July 19, 2018, https://www.cnn.com/2018/07/18/politics/trump-versus-us-intelligence-on-russian-election-interference/index.html.

26. Special Counsel Robert S. Mueller, *Report on the Investigation Into Russian Interference in the 2016 Presidential Election*, vol. 1, March 2019, https://www.justice.gov/archives/sco/file/1373816/download.

27. Alex Woodward, " 'Fake News': A Guide to Trump's Favourite Phrase—and the Dangers It Obscures," *Independent*, October 2, 2020, https://www.independent.co.uk/news/world/americas/us-election/trump-fake-news-counter-history-b732873.html.

28. P. W. Singer and Emerson T. Brooking, *Like War: The Weaponization of Social Media* (Boston: Eamon Dolan/Houghton Mifflin Harcourt, 2018), 131.

29. Heidi Beirich, "Domestic Terror Threat Remains Serious Five Years After Sikh Massacre," Southern Poverty Law Center, August 4, 2017, https://www.splcenter.org/news/2017/08/04/domestic-terror-threat-remains-serious-five-years-after-sikh-massacre.

30. Michael Signer, *Cry Havoc: Charlottesville and American Democracy Under Siege* (New York: PublicAffairs, 2020), 3–4, 120–21, 125, 135, 151, 201, 214, 219–20, 231. See also Terry McAuliffe, *Beyond Charlottesville: Taking a Stand Against White Nationalism* (New York: Thomas Dunne, 2019), 1–2, 55–56, 60, 90–91.

31. Quoted in McAuliffe, *Beyond Charlottesville*, 55.

32. *Triumph of the Will*, dir. Leni Riefenstahl (1935; Reichsparteitag-Film), at: https://www.imdb.com/title/tt0025913/.

33. Quoted in McAuliffe, *Beyond Charlottesville*, 79–80; and in Signer, *Cry Havoc*, 205–6.

34. McAuliffe, *Beyond Charlottesville*, 98–100; Signer, *Cry Havoc*, 211–13.

35. "Ryan Kelly of the *Daily Progress*, Charlottesville, Va.," The Pulitzer Prizes, February 24, 2023, https://www.pulitzer.org/winners/ryan-kelly-daily-progress.

36. Signer, *Cry Havoc*, 211, 220.

37. Quoted in McAuliffe, *Beyond Charlottesville*, 99. See also Neal Augenstein, "Prosecutors Use Hitler Image Texted to Mother in James Alex Fields Murder Trial," WTOP,

December 4, 2018, https://wtop.com/virginia/2018/12/prosecutors-seek-to-use-hitler
-image-texted-to-mother-in-james-alex-fields-murder-trial/.

38.   Quoted in James Pilcher, "Charlottesville Suspect's Beliefs Were 'Along the Party Lines
      of the Neo-Nazi Movement,' Ex-teacher Says," *USA Today*, August 13, 2017, https://www
      .usatoday.com/story/news/nation-now/2017/08/13/charlottesville-suspects-views-neo
      -nazi-ex-teacher/563199001/.

39.   Quoted in Signer, *Cry Havoc*, 213. See also Dan Merica, "Trump Condemns 'Hatred,
      Bigotry and Violence on Many Sides' in Charlottesville," CNN, August 13, 2017,
      https://www.cnn.com/2017/08/12/politics/trump-statement-alt-right-protests
      /index.html.

40.   NBC News, "Trump's Full, Heated Press Conference on Race and Violence in Charlot-
      tesville (Full)," YouTube video, August 15, 2017, https://www.youtube.com/watch?v
      =QGKbFA7HW-U&ab_channel=NBCNews.

41.   Z. Byron Wolf, "Trump's Defense of the 'Very Fine People' at Charlottesville White
      Nationalist March has David Duke Gushing," CNN, August 15, 2017, https://www.cnn
      .com/2017/08/15/politics/donald-trump-david-duke-charlottesville.

42.   Libby Nelson, "'Why We Voted for Donald Trump': David Duke Explains the White
      Supremacist Charlottesville Protests," *Vox*, August 12, 2017, https://www.vox.com/2017
      /8/12/16138358/charlottesville-protests-david-duke-kkk.

43.   "White Supremacists Revitalized by President Trump's Additional Comments Regard-
      ing Charlottesville," *SITE Intelligence Group*, August 16, 2017, https://ent.siteintelgroup
      .com/Far-Right-Far-Left-Threat/white-supremacists-revitalized-by-president-trump
      -s-additional-comments-regarding-charlottesville.html.

44.   David A. Graham, Adrienne Green, Cullen Murphy, and Parker Richards, "An Oral
      History of Trump's Bigotry," *Atlantic*, June 2019, https://www.theatlantic.com/magazine
      /archive/2019/06/trump-racism-comments/588067/.

45.   Joe Biden, "Joe Biden for President: America Is an Idea," YouTube video, April 25, 2019,
      https://www.youtube.com/watch?v=VbOU2fTg6cI&ab_channel=JoeBiden.

46.   "David Duke: In His Own Words," Anti-Defamation League, January 3, 2013, https://
      www.adl.org/news/article/david-duke-in-his-own-words.

47.   Andrew Berwick, "2083: A European Declaration of Independence," 2011, 851.

48.   Julia Ebner, *Going Dark: The Secret Social Lives of Extremists* (London: Bloomsbury
      Publishing, 2020), 175–76.

49.   Cam Wolf, "The New Uniform of White Supremacy," *GQ*, August 17, 2017, https://www
      .gq.com/story/uniform-of-white-supremacy.

50.   Bill Chappell, "Trump Pardons Ranchers Dwight and Steven Hammond Over 2012
      Arson Conviction," NPR, July 10, 2018, https://www.npr.org/2018/07/10/627653866
      /president-trump-pardons-ranchers-dwight-and-steven-hammond-over-arson.

51.   Antonia Blumberg, "This Woman Escaped the Nazis Once. Now She's Fighting Nazism
      Again," *HuffPost*, August 14, 2017, https://www.huffpost.com/entry/this-woman
      -escaped-the-nazis-once-now-shes-fighting-nazism-again_n_5991fbe7e4b09096429
      925ce.

52. Hawes Spencer and Richard Pérez-Peña, "Murder Charge Increases in Charlottesville Protest Death," *New York Times*, December 14, 2017, https://www.nytimes.com/2017/12/14/us/charlottesville-fields-white-supremists.html.

53. Richard Gonzales, "Florida Man Who Mailed Bombs to Democrats, Media Gets 20 Years in Prison," NPR-WAMU 88.5, August 5, 2019, https://www.npr.org/2019/08/05/748420957/cesar-sayoc-florida-man-who-mailed-bombs-to-democrats-and-media-gets-20-years.

54. Quoted in Madeline Holcombe, "Pipe Bomb Suspect Writes to Judge That the 16 Devices He Mailed Were Only Meant for Intimidation," CNN, April 3, 2019, https://www.cnn.com/2019/04/03/us/cesar-sayoc-letter-to-judge/index.html.

55. Quoted in Jack Date, "Mail Bomber Cesar Sayoc Obsessed with Trump, Fox News, Chilling New Court Filings Show," *ABC News*, July 23, 2019, https://abcnews.go.com/US/mail-bomber-cesar-sayoc-obsessed-trump-fox-news/story?id=64500598.

56. David Frum, "A President Who Condones Political Violence," *Atlantic*, October 26, 2018, https://www.theatlantic.com/ideas/archive/2018/10/trump-bombs-florida-tweets/574108/.

57. "UPDATE: In Wake of New 'Suspicious Devices' Sent to Targets, White Supremacists Continue Celebrating Attempt on George Soros," *SITE Intelligence Group*, October 24, 2018, https://ent.siteintelgroup.com/Far-Right-Far-Left-Threat/update-in-wake-of-new-suspicious-devices-sent-to-targets-white-supremacists-continue-celebrating-attempt-on-george-soros.html. More deflection can be seen in "UPDATE: As More Suspicious Devices Addressed to Various Figures Appear, White Supremacists Persist in Deflection," *SITE Intelligence Group*, October 25, 2018, https://ent.siteintelgroup.com/Far-Right-/-Far-Left-Threat/update-as-more-suspicious-devices-addressed-to-various-figures-appear-white-supremacists-persist-in-deflection.html.

58. U.S. Department of Justice, "Kroger Shooter Sentenced to Life in Prison for Hate Crime Murders," *Justice News*, June 24, 2021, https://www.justice.gov/opa/pr/kroger-shooter-sentenced-life-prison-hate-crime-murders; Neil Vigdor, "Man Who Killed Two in Racial Attack at Kroger Gets Life," *New York Times*, December 18, 2020.

59. Quoted in Dylan Lovan, " 'Whites Don't Shoot Whites,' Suspected Gunman Told Man After Killing 2 Black Customers at Kentucky Kroger," *Chicago Tribune*, October 25, 2018. See also Vigdor, "Man Who Killed Two in Racial Attack at Kroger Gets Life."

60. Neil Vigdor, "Man Who Killed Two in Racial Attack at Kroger Gets Life."

61. U.S. Department of Justice, "Pennsylvania Man Charged with Federal Hate Crimes for Tree of Life Synagogue Shooting," *Justice News*, October 31, 2018, https://www.justice.gov/opa/pr/pennsylvania-man-charged-federal-hate-crimes-tree-life-synagogue-shooting.

62. Jessica Kwong, "Robert Bowers Gab Before Synagogue Shooting: 'Screw Your Optics, I'm Going In,' " *Newsweek*, October 27, 2018, https://www.newsweek.com/robert-bowers-gab-synagogue-shooting-screw-your-optics-im-going-1190582.

63. Rita Katz, *Saints and Soldiers: Inside Internet-Age Terrorism, from Syria to the Capitol Siege* (New York: Columbia University Press, 2022), 51.

64. See Bruce Hoffman, Jacob Ware, and Ezra Shapiro, "Assessing the Threat of Incel Violence," *Studies in Conflict & Terrorism* 43, no. 7 (April 2020): 565–87.

65. Pete Williams, "Gunman Who Attacked Florida Yoga Studio Gave Off Decades of Warning Signs, Secret Service Finds," *NBC News*, March 15, 2022, https://www.nbcnews .com/politics/politics-news/gunman-attacked-florida-yoga-studio-gave-decades -warning-signs-secret-rcna19883; Steve Hendrix, "He Always Hated Women. Then He Decided to Kill Them," *Washington Post*, June 7, 2019, https://www.washingtonpost .com/graphics/2019/local/yoga-shooting-incel-attack-fueled-by-male-supremacy/.

66. Andrew Hay, "Kansas Militia Men Blame Trump Rhetoric for Mosque Attack Plan," Reuters, October 30, 2018, https://www.reuters.com/article/us-kansas-crime-somalia /kansas-militia-men-blame-trump-rhetoric-for-mosque-attack-plan-idUSKCN1N500O; United States District Court for the District of Kansas, "United States of America v. Patrick Stein," October 29, 2018, https://www.documentcloud.org/documents/5023695 -Patrick-Stein-Sentencing-Memo.

67. Louis Beam, "Leaderless Resistance," *The Seditionist* 12, final ed. (February 1992), http:// www.louisbeam.com/sedition.htm.

68. U.S. Department of Justice, U.S. Attorney's Office, District of Maryland, "Christopher Hasson Facing Federal Indictment for Illegal Possession of Silencers, Possession of Firearms by a Drug Addict and Unlawful User, and Possession of a Controlled Substance," February 27, 2019, https://www.justice.gov/usao-md/pr/christopher-hasson-facing -federal-indictment-illegal-possession-silencers-possession. See also Patricia Kime, "Trial Date Set for Coast Guard Officer Who Allegedly Maintained 'Hit List,' " *Military.com*, August 22, 2019, https://www.military.com/daily-news/2019/08/22/trial-date -set-coast-guard-officer-who-allegedly-maintained-hit-list.html.

69. Tom Cleary, "Christopher Hasson Hit List: Coast Guard LT Targeted Democrats, Media, Feds Say," *Heavy*, February 19, 2019, https://heavy.com/news/2019/02/christopher -hasson-hit-list-targets-democrats-media/. Quoted in Lynh Bui, " 'I Am Dreaming of a Way to Kill Almost Every Last Person on Earth': A Self-Proclaimed White Nationalist Planned a Mass Terrorist Attack, the Government Says," *Washington Post*, February 20, 2019, https://www.washingtonpost.com/local/public-safety/self-proclaimed -white-nationalist-planned-mass-terror-attack-government-says-i-am-dreaming-of -a-way-to-kill-almost-every-last-person-on-earth/2019/02/20/61daf6b8-3544-11e9 -af5b-b51b7ff322e9_story.html/.

70. United States District Court for the District of Maryland, "United States of America v. Christopher Paul Hasson, Motion for Detention Pending Trial," https://int .nyt.com/data/documenthelper/625-us-v-hasson/be7a4841596aba86cce4/optimized/full .pdf.

71. United States District Court for the District of Maryland, "United States of America v. Christopher Paul Hasson, Motion for Detention Pending Trial."

72. United States District Court for the District of Maryland, "United States of America v. Christopher Paul Hasson, Motion for Detention Pending Trial."

73. Bui, " 'I Am Dreaming of a Way to Kill Almost Every Last Person on Earth.' "

74. 18 U.S.C. § 2339B (1996), "Providing material support or resources to designated foreign terrorist organizations," https://www.law.cornell.edu/uscode/text/18/2339B. See also 18 U.S.C. § 2339A, "Providing material support to terrorists," (1994), https://www.law.cornell.edu/uscode/text/18/2339A.

75. U.S. Department of Justice, U.S. Attorney's Office, District of Maryland, "Christopher Hasson Sentenced to More Than 13 Years in Federal Prison on Federal Charges of Illegal Possession of Silencers, Possession of Firearms by an Addict to and Unlawful User of a Controlled Substance, and Possession of a Controlled Substance," January 31, 2020, https://www.justice.gov/usao-md/pr/christopher-hasson-sentenced-more-13-years-federal-prison-federal-charges-illegal.

76. *"Ko tō tātou kāinga tēnei"—Royal Commission of Inquiry Into the Terrorist Attack on Christchurch Masjidain on 15 March 2019*, December 8, 2020, part 4, chap. 5, https://christchurchattack.royalcommission.nz/.

77. Shereena Qazi, "40 Years After Escaping War, Afghan Killed in Christchurch Mosque," *Al Jazeera*, March 16, 2019, https://www.aljazeera.com/news/2019/3/16/40-years-after-escaping-war-afghan-killed-in-christchurch-mosque; Shamim Homayun, "An Ordinary Man with Extraordinary Values: Haji-Daoud, a Victim of the Christchurch Terror Attacks," *Stuff*, March 18, 2019, https://www.stuff.co.nz/national/111364502/an-ordinary-man-with-extraordinary-values-hajidaoud-a-victim-of-the-christchurch-terror-attacks.

78. *"Ko tō tātou kāinga tēnei,"* part 4, chap. 2.

79. See Imogen Richards, "A Dialectical Approach to Online Propaganda: Australia's United Patriots Front, Right-Wing Politics, and Islamic State," *Studies in Conflict & Terrorism* 42, nos. 1–3 (January–March 2019): 46–49, 52–56; Shannon Molloy, "The New Extremist Threat in Australia: Right-Wing Groups Who Have ASIO's Attention," *news.com.au*, January 4, 2019, https://www.news.com.au/national/the-new-extremist-threat-in-australia-rightwing-groups-who-have-asios-attention/news-story/44ae06be0aaa765c862fd6d20426fe9a.

80. *"Ko tō tātou kāinga tēnei,"* part 4, chap. 3.

81. Brenton Tarrant, "The Great Replacement: Towards a New Society," March 2019.

82. *"Ko tō tātou kāinga tēnei,"* part 1, chap. 2, https://christchurchattack.royalcommission.nz/.

83. Tarrant, "The Great Replacement."

84. Jacinda Ardern, "How to Stop the Next Christchurch Massacre," *New York Times*, May 11, 2019; "Facebook: New Zealand Attack Video Viewed 4,000 Times," BBC, March 19, 2019, https://www.bbc.com/news/business-47620519.

85. Kevin Roose, "A Mass Murder of, and for, the Internet," *New York Times*, March 15, 2019, https://www.nytimes.com/2019/03/15/technology/facebook-youtube-christchurch-shooting.html.

86. Tarrant, "The Great Replacement."

87. Jason Burke, "Norway Mosque Attack Suspect 'Inspired by Christchurch and El Paso Shootings,'" *Guardian*, August 11, 2019, https://www.theguardian.com/world/2019/aug

/11/norway-mosque-attack-suspect-may-have-been-inspired-by-christchurch-and-el
-paso-shootings.

88.   Jason Hanna and Darran Simon, "The Suspect in Poway Synagogue Shooting Used an
      Assault Rifle and Had Extra Magazines, Prosecutors Said," CNN, April 30, 2019, https://
      edition.cnn.com/2019/04/30/us/california-synagogue-shooting-investigation/index
      .html; Elliot Spagat and Julie Watson, "John Earnest—Physics Teacher's Son, Celebrated
      Pianist, 8chan User, Synagogue Shooting Suspect," Associated Press, April 30, 2019.

89.   John Earnest, "An Open Letter," April 2019.

90.   Toni McAllister, "Arson and Hate Crime Suspected in Escondido Mosque Fire," *Times
      of San Diego*, March 24, 2019, https://timesofsandiego.com/crime/2019/03/24/arson-and
      -hate-crime-suspected-in-escondido-mosque-fire/.

91.   Graham Macklin, "The El Paso Terrorist Attack: The Chain Reaction of Global Right-
      Wing Terror," *CTC Sentinel* 12, no. 11 (December 2019), https://ctc.usma.edu/el-paso
      -terrorist-attack-chain-reaction-global-right-wing-terror/.

92.   Burke, "Norway Mosque Attack Suspect 'Inspired by Christchurch and El Paso
      Shootings.'"

93.   Lizzie Dearden (@lizziedearden), Twitter, August 11, 2019, 3:07 PM, https://twitter.com
      /lizziedearden/status/1160628753258692608.

94.   Brennpunkt: Philips vei til terror, "Episode 1: 10. august 2019," *NRK TV*, https://tv.nrk
      .no/serie/brennpunkt-philips-vei-til-terror/sesong/1/episode/1/avspiller.

95.   Brennpunkt: Philips vei til terror, "Episode 1: 10. august 2019"; *"Ko tō tātou kāinga tēnei,"*
      part 2, chap. 8.

96.   Bruce Hoffman and Jacob Ware, "Is 3-D Printing the Future of Terrorism?," *Wall Street
      Journal*, October 25, 2019.

97.   Halle manifesto, as seen by authors.

98.   "Expert on the Effect of 'Cascading Terrorism,'" MSNBC, June 29, 2016, https://www
      .msnbc.com/morning-joe/watch/expert-on-the-effect-of-cascading-terrorism
      -715100739718.

99.   The authors thank the International Centre for the Study of Radicalisation and Politi-
      cal Violence at King's College London for providing access to the Halle manifesto.

100. See Sebastian Herrera and Sarah E. Needleman, "Live Stream of Germany Shooting
      Turns Spotlight to Amazon's Twitch," *Wall Street Journal*, October 10, 2019.

101. Kevin Roose, "'Shut the Site Down,' Says the Creator of 8chan, a Megaphone for Gun-
      men," *New York Times*, August 4, 2019, https://www.nytimes.com/2019/08/04
      /technology/8chan-shooting-manifesto.html.

102. Kari Paul, Luke Harding, and Severin Carrell, "Far-Right Website 8kun Again Loses
      Internet Service Protection Following Capitol Attack," *Guardian*, January 15, 2021,
      https://www.theguardian.com/technology/2021/jan/15/8kun-8chan-capitol-breach
      -violence-isp.

103. Zack Beauchamp, "Accelerationism: The Obscure Idea Inspiring White Supremacist
      Killers Around the World," *Vox*, November 18, 2019, https://www.vox.com/the-highlight
      /2019/11/11/20882005/accelerationism-white-supremacy-christchurch.

104. Jason Dearen and Michael Kunzelman, "Deadly Shooting Ends Friendships Forged in Neo-Nazi Group," Associated Press, August 22, 2017, https://apnews.com/article/north-america-shootings-tampa-florida-ap-top-news-222eaf9f330e4cdf812634f0baf3d5ca.

105. For more, see Jacob Ware, "Siege: The Atomwaffen Division and Rising Far-Right Terrorism in the United States," International Centre for Counter-Terrorism–The Hague, July 2019, https://icct.nl/publication/siege-the-atomwaffen-division-and-rising-far-right-terrorism-in-the-united-states/.

106. Brett Barrouquere, "White Separatist Gary Lee Yarbrough, One-Time Security Chief for the Order, Dies in Federal Prison," Southern Poverty Law Center, April 2, 2018, https://www.splcenter.org/hatewatch/2018/04/02/white-separatist-gary-lee-yarbrough-one-time-security-chief-order-dies-federal-prison.

107. For more, see Jacob Ware, "Fighting Back: The Atomwaffen Division, Countering Violent Extremism, and the Evolving Crackdown on Far-Right Terrorism in America," *Journal for Deradicalization* 25 (Winter 2020/21), https://journals.sfu.ca/jd/index.php/jd/article/view/411.

108. "Maryland Neo-Nazis Accused of Discussing Bringing Firearms to Pro-Gun Rally in Virginia," *Fox 5 News*, January 16, 2020, https://www.fox5atlanta.com/news/maryland-neo-nazis-accused-of-discussing-bringing-firearms-to-pro-gun-rally-in-virginia.

109. Eradicate Hate Global Summit, "Undercover in the Far Right," YouTube video, September 21, 2022, https://www.youtube.com/watch?v=2awTHrqByO0&ab_channel=EradicateHateGlobalSummit; Paul Solotaroff, "He Spent 25 Years Infiltrating Nazis, the Klan, and Biker Gangs," *Rolling Stone*, January 30, 2022, https://www.rollingstone.com/culture/culture-features/fbi-infiltrator-nazis-kkk-biker-gangs-1280830/.

110. Louis Beam, "Leaderless Resistance," *The Seditionist* 12, final ed. (February 1992), http://www.louisbeam.com/sedition.htm.

111. Howard Altman, "How to Spot Neo-Nazis in the Military? Brandon Russell Case Shows How Hard It Is," *Tampa Bay Times*, June 4, 2018, https://www.tampabay.com/news/military/How-to-spot-neo-Nazis-in-the-military-Brandon-Russell-case-shows-how-hard-it-is_168714074/. See also A.C. Thompson, "An Atomwaffen Member Sketched a Map to Take the Neo-Nazis Down. What Path Officials Took Is a Mystery," *PBS Frontline*, November 20, 2018, https://www.pbs.org/wgbh/frontline/article/an-atomwaffen-member-sketched-a-map-to-take-the-neo-nazis-down-what-path-officials-took-is-a-mystery/.

112. See A. C. Thompson, Ali Winston, and Jake Hanrahan, "Ranks of Notorious Hate Group Include Active-Duty Military," *ProPublica*, May 3, 2018, https://www.propublica.org/article/atomwaffen-division-hate-group-active-duty-military; Daniel Villarreal, "Navy Kicks Out Alleged Recruiter for Neo-Nazi Group Atomwaffen Division After Investigation," *Newsweek*, April 17, 2020, https://www.newsweek.com/navy-kicks-out-alleged-recruiter-neo-nazi-group-atomwaffen-division-after-investigation-1498704; Tim Lister, "The Nexus Between Far-Right Extremists in the United States and Ukraine," *CTC Sentinel* 13, no. 4 (April 2020), https://ctc.usma.edu/the-nexus-between-far-right-extremists-in-the-united-states-and-ukraine/; "U.S. Army Specialist with

Links to Neo-Nazi Group Pleads Guilty," Anti-Defamation League, February 11, 2020, https://www.adl.org/resources/blog/us-army-specialist-links-neo-nazi-group-pleads-guilty; Janet Reitman, "How Did a Convicted Neo-Nazi Release Propaganda from Prison?" *Rolling Stone*, May 25, 2018, https://www.rollingstone.com/politics/politics-news/how-did-a-convicted-neo-nazi-release-propaganda-from-prison-628437/; Oleksiy Kuzmenko, "'Defend the White Race': American Extremists Being Co-Opted by Ukraine's Far-Right," *BellingCat*, February 15, 2019, https://www.bellingcat.com/news/uk-and-europe/2019/02/15/defend-the-white-race-american-extremists-being-co-opted-by-ukraines-far-right/; Mack Lamoureux and Ben Makuch, "Member of a Neo-Nazi Terror Group Appears to Be Former Canadian Soldier," *Vice*, August 2, 2018, https://www.vice.com/en/article/7xqe8z/member-of-a-neo-nazi-terror-group-appears-to-be-former-canadian-soldier; Christopher Mathias, "Exclusive: Army Investigating Soldier's Alleged Leadership in Neo-Nazi Terror Group," *HuffPost*, May 3, 2019, https://www.huffpost.com/entry/atomwaffen-division-army-soldier-investigation-corwyn-storm-carver_n_5ccb5350e4b0e4d7572fde38; U.S. District Court, District of Nevada, "United States of America v. Conor Climo, Complaint," https://www.documentcloud.org/documents/6318397-Conor-Climo.html.

113.   Thompson et al., "Ranks of Notorious Hate Group Include Active-Duty Military."

114.   Christopher Mathias, "Exposed: Military Investigating 4 More Servicemen for Ties to White Nationalist Group," *HuffPost*, April 27, 2019, https://www.huffpost.com/entry/white-nationalists-military-identity-evropa_n_5cc1a87ee4b0764d31dd839c.

115.   Jeff Schogol, "White Supremacist Group Leader Is Former Marine Corps Recruiter," *Marine Corps Times*, August 15, 2017, https://www.marinecorpstimes.com/news/2017/08/15/white-supremacist-group-leader-is-former-marine-recruiter/.

116.   Ben Makuch and Mack Lamoureux, "Neo-Nazi Terror Leader Said to Have Worked with U.S. Special Forces," *Vice*, September 24, 2020, https://www.vice.com/en/article/k7qdzv/neo-nazi-terror-leader-said-to-have-worked-with-us-special-forces.

117.   Daniel De Simone and Ali Winston, "Neo-Nazi Militant Group Grooms Teenagers," BBC, June 22, 2020, https://www.bbc.com/news/uk-53128169.

118.   Ryan Thorpe, "Homegrown Hate," *Winnipeg Free Press*, August 21, 2019, https://www.winnipegfreepress.com/local/homegrown-hate-547510902.html.

119.   Ben Makuch, Mack Lamoureux, and Zachary Kamel, "Neo-Nazi Terror Group Harbouring Missing Ex-Soldier: Sources," *Vice*, December 5, 2019, https://www.vice.com/en_ca/article/8xwwaa/neo-nazi-terror-group-harbouring-missing-ex-soldier-patrik-mathews-sources; Eradicate Hate Global Summit, "Undercover in the Far Right."

120.   Mike Hellgren, "FBI Arrest U.S. Army Veteran, 2 Other Suspected White Supremacists On Federal Firearms Charges In Maryland," *CBS Baltimore*, January 16, 2020, https://baltimore.cbslocal.com/2020/01/16/alleged-members-racially-motivated-extremist-group-the-base-face-firearms-alien-related-charges/

121.   James Silver, Andre Simons, and Sarah Craun, "A Study of the Pre-Attack Behaviors of Active Shooters in the United States Between 2000–2013," Federal Bureau of Investigation, 2018, https://www.fbi.gov/file-repository/pre-attack-behaviors-of-active-shooters-in-us-2000-2013.pdf/view.

122. Lauren Richards, Peter Molinaro, John Wyman, and Sarah Craun, "Lone Offender: A Study of Lone Offender Terrorism in the United States (1972–2015)," National Center for the Analysis of Violent Crime, Behavioral Analysis Unit, Federal Bureau of Investigation, November 13, 2019, 17, https://www.fbi.gov/news/stories/fbi-releases-lone -offender-terrorism-report-111319.

123. Mona Chalabi, "What Percentage of Americans Have Served in the Military?," *FiveThirtyEight*, March 19, 2015, https://fivethirtyeight.com/features/what-percentage-of-amer icans-have-served-in-the-military/.

124. Christopher Mathias, "Exclusive: Phrase 'White Nationalists' Cut from Measure to Screen Military Enlistees," *HuffPost*, December 19, 2019, https://www.huffpost.com /entry/senate-removes-white-nationalists-from-military-bill-aimed-at-screening-for -extremists_n_5dfab39be4b0eb2264d3a18d.

125. "White Supremacy in the Military," C-SPAN, February 11, 2020, https://www.c-span .org/video/?469238-1/white-supremacy-military.

126. Jeff McCausland, "Inside the U.S. Military's Battle with White Supremacy and Far-Right Extremism," *NBC News*, May 25, 2019, https://www.nbcnews.com/think/opinion /inside-u-s-military-s-battle-white-supremacy-far-right-ncna1010221.

127. Daniel Koehler, "A Threat from Within? Exploring the Link Between the Extreme Right and the Military," International Centre for Counter-Terrorism–The Hague, September 2019, https://www.researchgate.net/publication/336412400_A_Threat_from_Within _Exploring_the_Link_between_the_Extreme_Right_and_the_Military.

128. McCausland, "Inside the U.S. Military's Battle with White Supremacy and Far-Right Extremism."

129. Dave Philipps, "White Supremacism in the U.S. Military, Explained," *New York Times*, February 27, 2019, https://www.nytimes.com/2019/02/27/us/military-white-nationalists -extremists.html.

130. "White Supremacy in the Military."

131. Bruce Hoffman, "Back to the Future: The Return of Violent Far-Right Terrorism in the Age of Lone Wolves," *War on the Rocks*, April 2, 2019, https://warontherocks.com/2019 /04/back-to-the-future-the-return-of-violent-far-right-terrorism-in-the-age-of-lone -wolves/.

132. Tarrant, "The Great Replacement," March 2019.

133. For more, see Mark S. Hamm and Ramón Spaaij, *The Age of Lone Wolf Terrorism* (New York: Columbia University Press, 2017), 60–61.

134. Graham Macklin, "The Christchurch Attacks: Livestream Terror in the Viral Video Age," *CTC Sentinel* 12, no. 6 (July 2019), https://ctc.usma.edu/christchurch-attacks -livestream-terror-viral-video-age/.

135. Cynthia Miller-Idriss, *Hate in the Homeland: The New Global Far Right* (Princeton, NJ: Princeton University Press, 2020), 154.

136. Ware, "Siege."

137. "National Socialist Order Program," seen by authors.

138. Kory Grow, "Charles Manson: How Cult Leader's Twisted Beatles Obsession Inspired Family Murders," *Rolling Stone*, August 9, 2019, https://www.rollingstone.com/feature

/charles-manson-how-cult-leaders-twisted-beatles-obsession-inspired-family
-murders-107176/.

139. Jessica Stern and J. M. Berger, *ISIS: The State of Terror* (New York: HarperCollins, 2015), 72, 114.

140. Patrik Hermansson, "The British Hand: New Extreme Right Terror Cell Exposed," *Hope Not Hate*, September 27, 2020, https://hopenothate.org.uk/2020/09/27/british -hand/.

141. Michael Kunzelman and Jari Tanner, "He Led a Neo-Nazi Group Linked to Bomb Plots. He Was 13," *ABC News*, April 11, 2020, https://abcnews.go.com/US/wireStory/led-neo -nazi-group-linked-bomb-plots-13-70099974.

142. Several doctors testified that Arthurs suffers from both autism and schizophrenia. According to his family, Giampa suffers from autism and depression. According to his lawyer, Sam Woodward has Asperger's syndrome. According to his mother, Brandon Russell is on the autism spectrum and has attention deficit disorder. See Dan Sullivan, "Experts: One-Time Neo-Nazi Charged in Double Murder has Autism, Schizophrenia," *Tampa Bay Times*, December 19, 2019, https://www.tampabay.com/news/crime/2019/12 /19/experts-one-time-neo-nazi-charged-in-double-murder-has-autism -schizophrenia/; Justin Jouvenal, "Va. Teen Accused of Killing Girlfriend's Parents to Be Tried as an Adult," *Washington Post*, September 24, 2019, https://www.washington post.com/local/public-safety/va-teen-accused-of-killing-girlfriends-parents-to-be -tried-as-an-adult/2019/09/24/3e628fae-af13-11e9-a0c9-6d2d7818f3da_story.html; Luke Money, "Newport Man Accused of Murdering Blaze Bernstein Denies Hate Crime," *Daily Pilot*, August 22, 2018, https://www.latimes.com/socal/daily-pilot/news /tn-dpt-me-woodward-hearing-20180822-story.html; "Florida Neo-Nazi Leader Gets 5 Years for Having Explosive Material," *NBC News*, January 9, 2018, https://www .nbcnews.com/news/us-news/florida-neo-nazi-leader-gets-5-years-having-explosive -material-n836246.

143. "Florida Neo-Nazi Leader Gets 5 Years for Having Explosive Material."

144. Rachel Weiner, "After Renouncing White Supremacist Ideology, Virginia Man Sentenced to Year in Prison," *Washington Post*, February 28, 2020, https://www .washingtonpost.com/local/public-safety/after-renouncing-white-supremacist -ideology-virginia-atomwaffen-leader-sentenced-to-year-in-prison/2020/02/28 /9e7c9d28-5975-11ea-9b35-def5a027d47o_story.html.

145. Christian Picciolini, *Breaking Hate: Confronting the New Culture of Extremism* (New York: Hachette, 2020), 75.

146. Tarrant, "The Great Replacement."

147. "Six Hurt in 'Anti-Refugee' Hotel Arson Attack," *The Local*, April 7, 2016, https://www .thelocal.de/20160407/six-hurt-in-anti-refugee-hotel-arson-attack; "Swedish Mosque Hit by Arson in Eskilstuna, Injuring Five," BBC, December 25, 2014, https://www.bbc .com/news/world-europe-30602252.

148. "Killer Spent Two Weeks Planning School Attack," *The Local*, March 8, 2016, https:// www.thelocal.se/20160308/killer-spent-two-weeks-planning-school-attack.

149. Richards et al., "Lone Offender," 47-48.

150. For examples, see Anti-Defamation League, *A Dark & Constant Rage: 25 Years of Right-Wing Terrorism in the United States* (New York: Anti-Defamation League, 2017).

151. Rachel Chason, Annette Nevins, Annie Gowen, and Hailey Fuchs, "As His Environment Changed, Suspect in El Paso Shooting Learned to Hate," *Washington Post*, August 9, 2019, https://www.washingtonpost.com/national/as-his-environment-changed-suspect-in-el-paso-shooting-learned-to-hate/2019/08/09/8ebabf2c-817b-40a3-a79e-e56fbac94cd5_story.html.

152. Patrick Crusius, "The Inconvenient Truth," August 2019.

153. James Mason, *Siege*, rev. 1, June 2, 2015 (ironmarch.org), 92.

154. "Olathe, Kansas, Shooting Suspect 'Said He Killed Iranians,'" BBC, February 28, 2017, https://www.bbc.com/news/world-us-canada-39108060.

155. Maggie Vespa, "'Go Back to Saudi Arabia': Muslim, Black Communities Watching MAX Attack Trial Closely," KGW8, February 18, 2020, https://www.kgw.com/article/news/local/trimet-attack/portland-max-trial-jeremy-christian-black-muslim-communities/283-cd14e46c-f47a-4308-8bd0-239b6f26eb36.

156. Michael E. Miller, "Hunting Black Men to Start a 'Race War,'" *Washington Post*, December 27, 2019, https://www.washingtonpost.com/graphics/2019/local/race-war-murder-hate-crime/.

157. "Teenage Neo-Nazis Jailed Over Terror Offences," BBC, June 18, 2019, https://www.bbc.com/news/uk-48672929.

158. Tess Owen, "White Supremacists Built a Website to Doxx Interracial Couples—and It's Going to Be Hard to Take Down," *Vice*, May 13, 2020, https://www.vice.com/en/article/n7ww4w/white-supremacists-built-a-website-to-doxx-interracial-couples-and-its-going-to-be-hard-to-take-down.

159. Kimball Perry, "Mo. Executes White Supremacist Serial Killer Franklin," *USA Today*, November 20, 2013, https://www.usatoday.com/story/news/nation-now/2013/11/20/joseph-paul-franklin-execution/3648881/. David Cay Johnston, "William Pierce, 69, Neo-Nazi Leader, Dies," *New York Times*, July 24, 2002, https://www.nytimes.com/2002/07/24/us/william-pierce-69-neo-nazi-leader-dies.html.

160. See, for example, "Nazi Court to Try First Foreign Jew for 'Rassenschande,'" *Jewish Telegraphic Agency*, November 3, 1935, https://www.jta.org/archive/nazi-court-to-try-first-foreign-jew-for-rassenschande.

161. Laura Wagner, "Accused Planned Parenthood Shooter: 'I'm A Warrior for the Babies,'" NPR, December 9, 2015, https://www.npr.org/sections/thetwo-way/2015/12/09/459116186/planned-parenthood-shooter-im-a-warrior-for-the-babies.

162. "Neo-Nazi Telegram Channel Offers Alternative to Mass Shooting Strategy, Including Violence Against 'High-Profile' Targets," *SITE Intelligence Group*, March 18, 2020, https://ent.siteintelgroup.com/Far-Right-/-Far-Left-Threat/neo-nazi-telegram-channel-offers-alternative-to-mass-shooting-strategy-including-violence-against-high-profile-targets.html.

163. Department of Homeland Security, *Strategic Framework for Countering Domestic Terrorism and Targeted Violence* (Washington, DC: Department of Homeland Security, September 2019).

164. Homeland Security Committee Events, "Confronting the Rise in Anti-Semitic Domestic Terrorism, Part II," YouTube video, February 26, 2020, https://www.youtube.com/watch?v=BTOW8iWoR2E&ab_channel=HomelandSecurityCommitteeEvents.

8. AMERICAN CARNAGE

1. Russell Muirhead and Nancy L. Rosenblum, *A Lot of People Are Saying: The New Conspiracism and the Assault on Democracy* (Princeton, NJ: Princeton University Press, 2020), 2.

2. Peter Pomerantsev, *This Is Not Propaganda: Adventures in the War Against Reality* (New York: PublicAffairs, 2019), 49.

3. "Dr Duke & Mark Collett of UK Explode the ZioMedia induced Myths of Covid and the Ziostablishment devastating Reponses to False Covid Idol it created!," davidduke .com, February 26, 2021.

4. Nicolas Guilhot, "Why Pandemics Are the Perfect Environment for Conspiracy Theories to Flourish," *The Conversation*, April 6, 2020, https://theconversation.com/why -pandemics-are-the-perfect-environment-for-conspiracy-theories-to-flourish-135475.

5. "Missouri Neo-Nazi Connected to Hospital Bomb Plot Discussed Attacking Infrastructure, Weaponizing Coronavirus in Chat Groups," *SITE Intelligence Group*, March 26, 2020, https://ent.siteintelgroup.com/Far-Right-/-Far-Left-Threat/timothy-wilson-corona virus.html.

6. Matt Zapotosky, "Terrorism Laws May Apply If People Intentionally Spread Coronavirus, Justice Dept. Says," *Washington Post*, March 25, 2020, https://www.washing tonpost.com/national/coronavirus-terrorism-justice-department/2020/03/25/b9a932 30–6e8a-11ea-b148-e4ce3fbd85b5_story.html.

7. Office of the Attorney General, "Man Charged with Terroristic Threats for Allegedly Coughing on Food Store Employee and Telling Her He Has Coronavirus," *The State of New Jersey*, March 24, 2020, https://www.nj.gov/oag/newsreleases20/pr20200324b.html.

8. "Missouri Neo-Nazi Connected to Hospital Bomb Plot Discussed Attacking Infrastructure."

9. Jared Keller, "Navy Vet Allegedly Planned to Bomb Hospital Over Government's COVID-19 Response," *Military.com*, April 16, 2020, https://www.military.com/daily -news/2020/04/16/navy-vet-allegedly-planned-bomb-hospital-over-governments -covid-19-response.html.

10. Nick R. Martin, "Radio Active," *The Informant*, July 29, 2020, https://www.informant. news/p/radio-active.

11. Adam Goldman, "Man Suspected of Planning Attack on Missouri Hospital Is Killed," *New York Times*, March 25, 2020.

12. Quoted in United States District Court for the District of Kansas, United States of America v. Jarrett William Smith, Case No. 19-mj-5105-ADM, August 21, 2019, https://extremism.gwu.edu/sites/g/files/zaxdzs2191/f/Jarrett%20William%20Smith%20Criminal%20Complaint; see also Max McCoy, "Speaking of White Supremacists, Remember These Boys Who Did Not Make Kansas Proud," *Kansas Reflector*, October 4, 2020, https://kansasreflector.com/2020/10/04/speaking-of-white-supremacists-remember-these-boys-who-did-not-make-kansas-proud/; and United States Attorney's Office, District of Kansas, "Guilty Plea: Solider at Fort Riley Described How to Make Explosive Devices," February 10, 2020, https://www.justice.gov/usao-ks/pr/guilty-plea-soldier-fort-riley-described-how-make-explosive-devices.

13. United States Attorney's Office, District of Kansas, "Former Fort Riley Soldier Sentenced for Distributing Info on Napalm, IEDS," August 19, 2020, https://www.justice.gov/usao-ks/pr/former-fort-riley-soldier-sentenced-distributing-info-napalm-ieds.

14. Ben Collins and Brandy Zadrozny, "In Trump's 'LIBERATE' Tweets, Extremists See a Call to Arms," *NBC News*, April 17, 2020, https://www.nbcnews.com/tech/security/trump-s-liberate-tweets-extremists-see-call-arms-n1186561.

15. Collins and Zadrozny, "In Trump's 'LIBERATE' Tweets, Extremists See a Call to Arms."

16. "Neo-Nazi Venue Posits Statements from President as Call for Violent Action, Encourages Attacks on State Politicians," *SITE Intelligence Group*, April 27, 2020, https://ent.siteintelgroup.com/Far-Right-Far-Left-Threat/praising-president-s-support-of-quarantine-protests-as-call-to-action-neo-nazi-venue-encourages-attacks-on-state-politicians.html.

17. Lois Beckett, "Armed Protesters Demonstrate Against Covid-19 Lockdown at Michigan Capitol," *Guardian*, April 30, 2020, https://www.theguardian.com/us-news/2020/apr/30/michigan-protests-coronavirus-lockdown-armed-capitol.

18. "'All Kinds of Riots Are Coming,' Prominent White Nationalist Threatens Amid Michigan Anti-Lockdown Protests," *SITE Intelligence Group*, May 1, 2020, https://ent.siteintelgroup.com/Far-Right-Far-Left-Threat/all-kinds-of-riots-are-coming-prominent-white-nationalist-threatens-amid-michigan-anti-lockdown-protests.html.

19. See, for example, Libor Jany, "Minneapolis Police Say 'Umbrella Man' Was a White Supremacist Trying to Incite George Floyd Rioting," *Star Tribune*, July 28, 2020, https://www.startribune.com/police-umbrella-man-was-a-white-supremacist-trying-to-incite-floyd-rioting/571932272/; "Far-Right Promotes Infiltration Tactics to Subvert BLM Protests," *SITE Intelligence Group*, June 2, 2020, https://ent.siteintelgroup.com/Far-Right-/-Far-Left-Threat/far-right-promotes-infiltration-tactics-to-subvert-blm-protests.html.

20. Jany, "Minneapolis Police Say 'Umbrella Man' Was a White Supremacist."

21. "Exploiting Chaos of Riots, Prominent Neo-Nazi Group Calls for Attacks Against Black Protesters," *SITE Intelligence Group*, June 2, 2020, https://ent.siteintelgroup.com/Far-Right-Far-Left-Threat/exploiting-chaos-of-riots-prominent-neo-nazi-group-calls-for-attacks-against-black-protesters.html.

22. See, for instance, Neil MacFarquhar, Alan Feuer, and Adam Goldman, "Federal Arrests Show No Sign That Antifa Plotted Protests," *New York Times*, June 11, 2020; Meg Kelly and Elyse Samuels, "Who Caused the Violence at Protests? It Wasn't Antifa," *Washington Post*, June 22, 2020.

23. Legally, only the secretary of state can designate a terrorist organization, and then it has to be a foreign and not domestic entity. "Foreign Terrorist Organizations (FTOs) are foreign organizations that are designated by the Secretary of State in accordance with section 219 of the Immigration and Nationality Act (INA), as amended." Bureau of Counterterrorism, "Foreign Terrorist Organizations," U.S. Department of State, https://www.state.gov/foreign-terrorist-organizations/. See also Maggie Haberman and Charlie Savage, "Trump, Lacking Clear Authority, Says U.S. Will Declare Antifa a Terrorist Group," *New York Times*, June 10, 2020.

24. "Extremists Are Using Facebook to Organize for Civil War Amid Coronavirus," *Tech Transparency Project*, April 22, 2020, https://www.techtransparencyproject.org/articles/extremists-are-using-facebook-to-organize-for-civil-war-amid-coronavirus.

25. Cassie Miller, "The 'Boogaloo' Started as a Racist Meme," *SPLC: Hatewatch*, June 5, 2020, https://www.splcenter.org/hatewatch/2020/06/05/boogaloo-started-racist-meme.

26. Jared Thompson, "Examining Extremism: The Boogaloo Movement," Center for Strategic and International Studies, June 30, 2021, https://www.csis.org/blogs/examining-extremism/examining-extremism-boogaloo-movement.

27. Hollie McKay, "Antifa Arrests Coming, Concerns Over Riots Heading to Suburbia, Government Source Says," *Fox News*, June 2, 2020, https://www.foxnews.com/us/antifa-arrests-coming-riots-suburbs.

28. Quoted in Betsy Woodruff Swan and Natasha Bertrand, " 'Domestic Terrorist Actors' Could Exploit Floyd Protests, DHS Memo Warns," *Politico*, June 1, 2020, https://www.politico.com/news/2020/06/01/dhs-domestic-terrorists-protest-294342.

29. Gisela Pérez de Acha, Kathryn Hurd, and Ellie Lightfoot, " 'I Felt Hate More Than Anything': How an Active Duty Airman Tried to Start a Civil War," *Frontline*, April 13, 2021, https://www.pbs.org/wgbh/frontline/article/steven-carrillo-boogaloo-bois-active-duty-airman-incite-civil-war/.

30. Office of Public Affairs, "Two Defendants Charged with Murder and Aiding and Abetting in Slaying of Federal Protective Service Officer at Oakland Courthouse Building," U.S. Department of Justice, June 16, 2020, https://www.justice.gov/opa/pr/two-defendants-charged-murder-and-aiding-and-abetting-slaying-federal-protective-service; Neil MacFarquhar and Thomas Gibbons-Neff, "Air Force Sergeant with Ties to Extremist Group Charged in Federal Officer's Death," *New York Times*, June 16, 2020; Dan Noyes and Amanda del Castillo, "Federal Officer Shooting Suspects Steven Carrillo, Robert Justus 'Came to Oakland to Kill Cops,' FBI Says," ABC 7, June 17, 2020, https://abc7news.com/steven-carrillo-robert-alvin-justus-jr-pat-underwood-killed-oakland/6250277/.

31. "Phoenix Raven," Air Mobility Command, https://www.amc.af.mil/About-Us/Fact-Sheets/Display/Article/144021/phoenix-raven/.

32. Erik Maulbetsch, "Denver Police Seized Assault Rifles from Anti-Government Gun Activists at Friday Night Protest," *Colorado Times Recorder*, May 31, 2020.

33. Andrew Blankstein, Tom Winter, and Brandy Zadrozny, "Three Men Connected to 'Boogaloo' Movement Tried to Provoke Violence at Protests, Feds Say," *NBC News*, June 3, 2020, https://www.nbcnews.com/news/all/three-men-connected-boogaloo -movement-tried-provoke-violence-protests-feds-n1224231.

34. Michelle L. Price and Scott Sonner, "Army Reservist, Navy and Air Force vets Plotted to Terrorize Vegas Protests, Prosecutors Charge," *Military Times*, June 4, 2020, https:// www.militarytimes.com/news/your-military/2020/06/04/army-reservist-navy-and -air-force-vets-plotted-to-terrorize-vegas-protests-prosecutors-charge/.

35. Brett Barrouquere "Three Nevada 'Boogaloo Bois' Arrested by FBI in Plot," Southern Poverty Law Center, June 9, 2020, https://www.splcenter.org/hatewatch/2020/06/09 /three-nevada-boogaloo-bois-arrested-fbi-firebombing-plot; Jack Date, "Feds Charge 3 Self-Identified 'Boogaloo' Adherents Plotting Violence at Black Lives Matter Protest," *ABC News*, June 3, 2020, https://abcnews.go.com/ABCNews/feds-charge-identified -boogaloo-adherents-plotting-violence-black/story?id=71059377.

36. Natasha Bertrand, "Intel Report Warns That Far-Right Extremists May Target Washington, D.C.," *Politico*, June 19, 2020, https://www.politico.com/news/2020/06/19/intel -report-warns-far-right-extremists-target-washington-dc-329771.

37. Andrew Blankstein, Tom Winter, and Brandy Zadrozny, "Three Men Connected to 'Boogaloo' Movement Tried to Provoke Violence at Protests, Feds Say," *NBC News*, June 3, 2020, https://www.nbcnews.com/news/all/three-men-connected-boogaloo -movement-tried-provoke-violence-protests-feds-n1224231.

38. FBI Counterterrorism Analysis Section, "Sovereign Citizens: A Growing Threat to Law Enforcement," *FBI Law Enforcement Bulletin*, https://leb.fbi.gov/2011/september /sovereign-citizens-a-growing-domestic-threat-to-law-enforcement; "Sovereign Citizens Movement," Southern Poverty Law Center, https://www.splcenter.org/fighting -hate/extremist-files/ideology/sovereign-citizens-movement. See also Caitlin Dickson, "Sovereign Citizens Are America's Top Cop-Killers," *Daily Beast*, November 25, 2014, http://www.thedailybeast.com/articles/2014/11/25/sovereign-citizens-are-america-s -top-cop-killers.html.

39. FBI, "Domestic Terrorism: The Sovereign Citizen Movement."

40. FBI Counterterrorism Analysis Section, "Sovereign Citizens: A Growing Threat to Law Enforcement."

41. "Far-Right Forum Suggests First Targeting Police When the Supposed 'Bloody Uprising' Comes," *SITE Intelligence Group*, July 1, 2019, https://ent.siteintelgroup.com/Far -Right-Far-Left-Threat/far-right-forum-suggests-first-targeting-police-when-the -supposed-bloody-uprising-comes.html.

42. "Neo-Nazi Group with History of Violent Incitements Targets Political Enemies, Law Enforcement in Latest Propaganda," *SITE Intelligence Group*, April 27, 2020, https:// ent.siteintelgroup.com/Far-Right-/-Far-Left-Threat/neo-nazi-group-with-history-of -violent-incitements-targets-federal-law-enforcement-in-latest-propaganda.html.

43. McKay, "Antifa Arrests Coming."

44. "NICS Firearm Background Checks: Month/Year," Federal Bureau of Investigation, https://www.fbi.gov/file-repository/nics_firearm_checks_-_month_year.pdf/view.

45. "Anonymous," May 2, 2020, 4Chan discussion thread accessed by the author, June 26, 2020; baeldraca, "Banning the O9A," *Order of 9 Angles*, March 2, 2020, http://www.o9a .org/2020/03/banning-the-o9a/; baeldraca, "The O9A, National Socialism, and Nihil-ism," *Order of 9 Angles*, April 4, 2020, http:www.o9a.org/2020/04/the-o9a-national -socialism-and-nihilism/; baeldraca, "The O9A: Beyond Nihilism and Anarchism," *Order of Nine Angles*, April 20, 2002; "Concerning Propagandists in the Age of the Internet," *Order of 9 Angles*," n.d., http:www.o9a.org/propagandists-on-the-internet; "O9A Ideology at Core of 'RapeWaffen' Group Implicated in Recent Neo-Nazi Terror-ist Plot," *SITE Intelligence Group*, June 24, 2020; "Revealing the Hidden O9A," n.d., http:www.o9a.org/the-hidden-o9A/; Nick Lowles, "Order of Nine Angles," *Hope Not Hate*, February 16, 2019, https://hopenothate.org.uk/2019/02/16/state-of-hate-2019-order -of-nine-angles/; "Two Types of Satanism," *Order of 9 Angles*, n.d., http:www.o9a.org /the-two-types-of-satanism/.

46. Quoted in Office of Public Affairs, "U.S. Army Soldier Charged with Terrorism Offenses for Planning Deadly Ambush on Service Members in His Unit," U.S. Department of Justice, June 22, 2020, https://www.justice.gov/opa/pr/us-army-soldier-charged -terrorism-offenses-planning-deadly-ambush-service-members-his-unit.

47. Quoted in U.S. Attorney's Office, Southern District of New York, "U.S. Army Soldier Pleads Guilty to Attempting to Murder Fellow Service Members in Deadly Ambush," U.S. Department of Justice, June 24, 2022, https://www.justice.gov/usao-sdny/pr/us-army -soldier-pleads-guilty-attempting-murder-fellow-service-members-deadly-ambush.

48. James L. Jones, "Extremists Don't Belong in the Military," *Atlantic*, October 17, 2020, https://www.theatlantic.com/ideas/archive/2020/10/extremists-dont-belong-military /616763/.

49. Wilmington Police Department, "Professional Standards Internal Investigation," June 11, 2020, 2, https://www.wilmingtonnc.gov/home/showdocument?id=12012. See also, Paul Blest, "'Wipe 'Em Off the Fucking Map': 3 Cops Were Caught on Camera Fantasizing About Killing Black People," *Vice*, June 25, 2020, https://www.vice.com/en /article/4ayawq/wipe-em-off-the-fucking-map-3-cops-were-caught-on-camera -fantasizing-about-killing-black-people.

50. Tess Owen, "The U.S. Military Has a Boogaloo Problem," *Vice*, June 24, 2020, https:// www.vice.com/en/article/xg8g87/the-us-military-has-a-boogaloo-problem.

51. "'This Man Is Epic': Far-Right Praises Kenosha Protest Shooter," *SITE Intelligence Group*, August 26, 2020, https://ent.siteintelgroup.com/Far-Right-/-Far-Left-Threat/this -man-is-epic-far-right-praises-kenosha-protest-shooter.html.

52. Rita Katz, "Violent Protests Are a Neo-Nazi Fever Dream Come True," *Daily Beast*, Sep-tember 3, 2020, https://www.thedailybeast.com/violent-protests-are-a-neo-nazi-fever -dream-come-true.

53. Seth G. Jones, Catrina Doxsee, Nicholas Harrington, Grace Hwang, and James Suber, "The War Comes Home: The Evolution of Domestic Terrorism in the United States,"

Center for Strategic and International Studies, October 22, 2020, https://www.csis.org/analysis/war-comes-home-evolution-domestic-terrorism-united-states.

54. Amy B. Wang, "'ALL LIVES SPLATTER': Sheriff's Office Apologizes for Facebook Post of Car Hitting Protesters," *Washington Post*, September 12, 2017.

55. Sam Jackson, "The Long, Dangerous History of Right-Wing Calls for Violence and Civil War," *Washington Post*, September 11, 2020, https://www.washingtonpost.com/politics/2020/09/11/long-dangerous-history-far-rights-calls-violence-civil-war/.

56. "Neo-Nazi Telegram Channel Offers Alternative to Mass Shooting Strategy, Including Violence Against 'High-Profile' Targets," *SITE Intelligence Group*, March 18, 2020, https://ent.siteintelgroup.com/Far-Right-/-Far-Left-Threat/neo-nazi-telegram-channel-offers-alternative-to-mass-shooting-strategy-including-violence-against-high-profile-targets.html.

57. "Far-Right Chat Group Showed Disappointment in El Paso Shooter for Not Killing 'High-Value Targets,'" *SITE Intelligence Group*, August 5, 2019, https://ent.siteintelgroup.com/Far-Right-/-Far-Left-Threat/far-right-chat-group-showed-disappointment-in-el-paso-shooter-for-not-killing-high-value-targets.html.

58. "White Supremacists Encourage Continued Violence Against Officials," *SITE Intelligence Group*, January 20, 2011, https://ent.siteintelgroup.com/Far-Right-Far-Left-Threat/white-supremacists-encourage-continued-violence-against-elected-officals.html.

59. Joshua Benton, "The New Jersey Shooting Suspect Left a Pro-Trump Paper Trail," *The Atlantic*, July 21, 2020, https://www.theatlantic.com/politics/archive/2020/07/judge-esther-salas-shooting-suspect-left-pro-trump-paper-trail/614425/.

60. Neil Vigdor, "Man Charged with Making Death Threats to Nancy Pelosi in Coronavirus Rant," *New York Times*, March 26, 2020, https://www.nytimes.com/2020/03/26/us/texas-man-pelosi-death-threats-virus.html.

61. Kate Bennett and Evan Perez, "Nation's Top Coronavirus Expert Dr. Anthony Fauci Forced to Beef Up Security as Death Threats Increase," CNN, April 2, 2020, https://www.cnn.com/2020/04/01/politics/anthony-fauci-security-detail/index.html.

62. Will Sommer, "A QAnon Devotee Live-Streamed Her Trip to N.Y. to 'Take Out' Joe Biden," *Daily Beast*, April 30, 2020, https://www.thedailybeast.com/a-qanon-devotee-live-streamed-her-trip-to-ny-to-take-out-joe-biden.

63. "Far-Right Users Discuss Article Labeling Far-Right Ideology as Main Threat at Protests," *SITE Intelligence Group*, July 17, 2020, https://ent.siteintelgroup.com/Far-Right-Far-Left-Threat/far-right-users-discuss-article-labeling-far-right-ideology-as-main-threat-at-protests.html.

64. Matthew Alcoke, "The Evolving and Persistent Terrorism Threat to the Homeland," Washington Institute, November 19, 2019, https://www.washingtoninstitute.org/policy-analysis/view/the-evolving-and-persistent-terrorism-threat-to-the-homeland.

65. See Lois Beckett, "QAnon: A Timeline of Violence Linked to the Conspiracy Theory," *Guardian*, October 16, 2020.

66. Michael A. Jensen and Sheehan Kane, "QAnon-Inspired Violence in the United States: An Empirical Assessment of a Misunderstood Threat," in *Behavioral Sciences of Terrorism and Political Aggression* (2021).

67. Frank Donnelly, "The Day QAnon and the NYC Mafia Collided: It's Been 3 Years Since the Murder of Mob Boss Francesco Cali and Uncertainty Surrounds Case." *SI Live*, March 25, 2022, https://www.silive.com/crime-safety/2022/03/the-day-qanon-and-the-nyc-mafia-collided-its-been-3-years-since-the-murder-of-francesco-cali-and-questions-remain.html.

68. Zachary Kamel, Mack Lamoureux, Ben Makuch, "'Eco-Fascist' Arm of Neo-Nazi Terror Group, The Base, Linked to Swedish Arson," *Vice*, January 29, 2020, https://www.vice.com/en/article/qjdvzx/eco-fascist-arm-of-neo-nazi-terror-group-the-base-linked-to-swedish-arson.

69. Samantha Stern, Jacob Ware, and Nicholas Harrington, "Terrorist Targeting in the Age of Coronavirus," *International Counter-Terrorism Review* 1, no. 3 (June 2020).

70. Quoted in Meagan Flynn, "Engineer Intentionally Crashes Train Near Hospital Ship *Mercy*, Believing in Weird Coronavirus Conspiracy, Feds Say," *Washington Post*, April 2, 2020.

71. Jennifer Lee, "Confronting the Invisibility of Anti-Asian Racism," Brookings Institution, May 18, 2022, https://www.brookings.edu/blog/how-we-rise/2022/05/18/confronting-the-invisibility-of-anti-asian-racism/; OCA National Center, "COVID-19 and the Rise in Anti-Asian Hate," *OCA Advocate*, https://www.aapihatecrimes.org/facts; "Two Years and Thousands of Voices: What Community-Generated Data Tells Us About Anti-AAPI Hate," Stop AAPI Hate, July 2022, https://stopaapihate.org/year-2-report/.

72. Aggie J. Yellow Horse et al., "Stop AAPI Hate National Report, 3/19/20–6/30/21," Stop AAPI Hate, https://stopaapihate.org/wp-content/uploads/2021/08/Stop-AAPI-Hate-National-Report-Final.pdf.

73. Alcoke, "The Evolving and Persistent Terrorism Threat to the Homeland."

74. Daveed Gartenstein-Ross and Madeleine Blackman, "Fluidity of the Fringes: Prior Extremist Involvement as a Radicalization Pathway," *Studies in Conflict & Terrorism* 45, no. 7 (2022): 555–78.

75. Farah Pandith and Jacob Ware, "Teen Terrorism Inspired by Social Media Is on the Rise. Here's What We Need to Do," *NBC News*, March 22, 2021, https://www.nbcnews.com/think/opinion/teen-terrorism-inspired-social-media-rise-here-s-what-we-ncna1261307.

76. Seth Jones, Catrina Doxsee, Grace Hwang, and Jared Thompson, "The Military, Police, and the Rise of Terrorism in the United States," Center for Strategic and International Studies, April 12, 2021, https://www.csis.org/analysis/military-police-and-rise-terrorism-united-states.

77. Quoted in Marianna Spring, "'Stop the Steal': The Deep Roots of Trump's 'Voter Fraud' Strategy," *BBC News*, November 23, 2020, https://www.bbc.com/news/blogs-trending-55009950.

78. Atlantic Council's DFRLab, "#StopTheSteal: Timeline of Social Media and Extremist Activities Leading to 1/6 Insurrection," *Just Security*, February 10, 2021, https://www.justsecurity.org/74622/stopthesteal-timeline-of-social-media-and-extremist-activities-leading-to-1-6-insurrection/.

79. Quoted in Marhsall Cohen, "Trump Spreads New Lies About Foreign-Backed Voter Fraud, Stoking Fears of a 'Rigged Election' This November," *CNN Politics*, June 22, 2020, https://www.cnn.com/2020/06/22/politics/trump-voter-fraud-lies-fact-check/index .html.

80. Quoted in Terrance Smith, "Trump Has Longstanding History of Calling Elections 'Rigged' If He Doesn't Like the Results," *ABC News*, November 11, 2020, https://abcnews .go.com/Politics/trump-longstanding-history-calling-elections-rigged-doesnt-results /story?id=74126926.

81. Eugene Kiely and Rem Rieder, "Trump's Repeated False Attacks on Mail-In Ballots," *FactCheck*, September 25, 2020, https://www.factcheck.org/2020/09/trumps-repeated -false-attacks-on-mail-in-ballots/; Amy Sherman, "Fact Check: Did Trump Vote by Mail for the 2020 Election?," *Austin American-Statesman*, January 15, 2022, https://www .statesman.com/story/news/politics/politifact/2022/01/15/fact-check-did-trump-vote -mail-2020-election/6516078001/.

82. Morgan Chalfant, "Trump: 'The Only Way We're Going to Lose This Election Is If the Election Is Rigged,'" *The Hill*, August 17, 2020, https://thehill.com/homenews /administration/512424-trump-the-only-way-we-are-going-to-lose-this-election-is-if -the.

83. Elise Thomas, "Qanon Deploys 'Information Warfare' to Influence the 2020 Election," *Wired*, February 17, 2020, https://www.wired.com/story/qanon-deploys-information -warfare-influence-2020-election/.

84. Muirhead and Rosenblum, *A Lot of People Are Saying*, 3.

85. "The Proud Boys' actions belie their disavowals of bigotry: Rank-and-file Proud Boys and leaders regularly spout white nationalist memes and maintain affiliations with known extremists." "Proud Boys," Southern Poverty Law Center, https://www.splcenter .org/fighting-hate/extremist-files/group/proud-boys.

86. "Backgrounder: Proud Boys," Anti-Defamation League, November 2, 2018, https://www .adl.org/resources/backgrounder/proud-boys-0.

87. CNBC Television, "President Donald Trump: White Supremacist Group Proud Boys Should 'Stand Back and Stand By,'" YouTube video, September 30, 2020, https://www .youtube.com/watch?v=JZk6VzSLe4Y&ab_channel=CNBCTelevision.

88. Author screenshot.

89. Author screenshot.

90. Atlantic Council's DFRLab, "#StopTheSteal."

91. "Deposition of Jeremy Bertino," Select Committee to Investigate the January 6th Attack on the U.S. Capitol, U.S. House of Representatives, April 26, 2022, https://www.govinfo .gov/content/pkg/GPO-J6-TRANSCRIPT-CTRL0000082294/pdf/GPO-J6 -TRANSCRIPT-CTRL0000082294.pdf.

92. "Trump Praises QAnon Supporters: 'I Understand They Like Me Very Much,'" *Axios*, August 19, 2020, https://www.axios.com/trump-praises-qanon-supporters-i-under stand-they-like-me-very-much-42146fb3-bd69-4943-8e80-2f0bcf4b0b17.html.

93. Jessica Guynn, "Trump Believes QAnon Claim It's Fighting Pedophiles, Refuses to Dis- avow Extremist Conspiracy Theory," *USA Today*, October 15, 2020, https://www

.usatoday.com/story/tech/2020/10/15/trump-believes-qanon-claim-fighting-pedophiles/3673377001/.

94. Craig Timberg, "Trump's Comments on Conspiracy Theory Are Celebrated: 'This Was the Biggest Pitch for QAnon I've Ever Seen,'" *Washington Post*, October 16, 2020, https://www.washingtonpost.com/technology/2020/10/16/qanon-trump-conspiracy/.

95. Ben Collins, Brandy Zadrozny, Tom Winter, and Corky Siemaszko, "Whitmer Conspiracy Allegations Tied to 'Boogaloo' Movement," *NBC News*, October 8, 2020, https://www.nbcnews.com/tech/tech-news/whitmer-conspiracy-allegations-tied-boogaloo-movement-n1242670.

96. Andrew Feather, "FBI: Suspect in Whitmer Kidnapping Had History of Violent, Threatening Social Media Posts," WWMT, October 29, 2020, https://wwmt.com/news/local/fbi-suspect-in-whitmer-kidnapping-had-history-of-violent-threatening-social-media-posts.

97. Ken Bensinger and Jessica Garrison, "Watching the Watchmen," *Buzzfeed News*, July 20, 2021, https://www.buzzfeednews.com/article/kenbensinger/michigan-kidnapping-gretchen-whitmer-fbi-informant.

98. Gus Burns, "Accused Whitmer Kidnapping Plotters Attended BLM Rally to Protect Protesters from Police, Attorney Says," *MLive*, March 5, 2021, https://www.mlive.com/public-interest/2021/03/accused-whitmer-kidnapping-plotters-attended-blm-rally-to-protect-protesters-from-police-attorney-says.html.

99. Richard N. Haass (@RichardHaass), September 1, 2020, 8:53 AM, https://twitter.com/RichardHaass/status/1300778731913519104.

100. Bruce Hoffman and Jacob Ware, "The Terrorist Threat from the Fractured Far Right," *Lawfare*, November 1, 2020, https://www.lawfareblog.com/terrorist-threat-fractured-far-right.

101. Jeff Seldin, "Trump Renews 'Rigged Election' Claim Against All Evidence," *Voice of America*, November 13, 2020, https://www.voanews.com/2020-usa-votes/trump-renews-rigged-election-claim-against-all-evidence.

102. Jaclyn Peiser, "Twitter Bans Steve Bannon for Video Suggesting Violence Against Fauci, FBI Director Wray," *Washington Post*, November 6, 2020, https://www.washingtonpost.com/nation/2020/11/06/twitter-bannon-beheaded-fauci-wray/; Frank Figliuzzi (@FrankFigliuzzi1), November 5, 2020, 5:56 PM, https://twitter.com/FrankFigliuzzi1/status/1324485819042705408.

103. Spencer S. Hsu and Dan Morse, "Christopher Krebs Sues Trump Campaign, Lawyer Joe diGenova for Defamation," *Washington Post*, December 8, 2020, https://www.washingtonpost.com/local/legal-issues/chris-krebs-sues-trump-campaign-digenova/2020/12/08/61a68a30-389a-11eb-bc68-96afodaae728_story.html.

104. Joshua Zitser, "Pro-Trump Lawyer Lin Wood Insists He Is Not Insane After Tweeting That Mike Pence Should Face Execution by Firing Squad," *Insider*, January 2, 2021, https://www.businessinsider.com/pro-trump-lawyer-l-lin-wood-tweets-that-pence-executed-2021-1.

105. Atlantic Council's DFRLab, "#StopTheSteal."

106. Dan Barry and Sheera Frenkel, "'Be There. Will Be Wild!': Trump All but Circled the Date," *New York Times*, January 6, 2021, https://www.nytimes.com/2021/01/06/us /politics/capitol-mob-trump-supporters.html.

107. Betsy Woodruff Swan, "'The Intelligence Was There': Law Enforcement Warnings Abounded in the Runup to Jan. 6," *Politico*, October 7, 2021, https://www.politico.com /news/2021/10/07/law-enforcement-warnings-january-6-515531; Ellie Quinlan Houghtaling, "Revealed: Secret Service Knew of Disturbing Neo-Nazi Threats Before Jan. 6," *Daily Beast*, September 22, 2022, https://www.thedailybeast.com/secret-service -knew-of-disturbing-neo-nazi-threats-before-jan-6-capitol-riot.

108. "Hearing on Challenge to Rep. Marjorie Taylor Greene's Candidacy," C-SPAN, April 22, 2022, https://www.c-span.org/video/?519623–101/hearing-challenge-rep-marjorie -taylor-greenes-candidacy.

109. Devlin Barrett and Matt Zapotosky, "FBI Report Warned of 'War' at Capitol, Contra- dicting Claims There Was No Indication of Looming Violence," *Washington Post*, January 12, 2021, https://www.washingtonpost.com/national-security/capitol-riot-fbi -intelligence/2021/01/12/30d12748-546b-11eb-a817-e5e7f8a406d6_story.html.

110. Craig Timberg, "Gallows or Guillotines? The Chilling Debate on TheDonald.win Before the Capitol Siege," *Washington Post*, April 15, 2021, https://www.washingtonpost.com /technology/2021/04/15/thedonald-capitol-attack-advance-democracy/.

111. "Final Report: Select Committee to Investigate the January 6th Attack on the United States Capitol," 117th Congress, Second Session, House Report 117-663, Decem- ber 22, 2022, 61, https://www.govinfo.gov/content/pkg/GPO-J6-REPORT/pdf/GPO -J6-REPORT.pdf.

112. David Neiwert, *Alt-America: The Rise of the Radical Right in the Age of Trump* (New York: Verso, 2017), 373.

113. Atlantic Council's DFRLab, "#StopTheSteal."

114. "Day of Rage: How Trump Supporters Took the U.S. Capitol | Visual Investigation," *New York Times*, YouTube video, July 1, 2021, https://www.youtube.com/watch?v =jWJVMoe7OYo&ab_channel=TheNewYorkTimes.

115. Josh Gerstein, "Aide's Testimony That Trump Was Told of Weapons Could Boost Civil Suits," *Politico*, June 28, 2022, https://www.politico.com/news/2022/06/28/aides-claim -trump-was-told-of-weapons-00042977.

116. Gerstein, "Aide's Testimony That Trump Was Told of Weapons Could Boost Civil Suits."

117. Brian Naylor, "Read Trump's Jan. 6 Speech, a Key Part of Impeachment Trial," NPR, February 10, 2021, https://www.npr.org/2021/02/10/966396848/read-trumps-jan-6 -speech-a-key-part-of-impeachment-trial.

118. "Trump Tried to Grab Steering Wheel to Go to U.S. Capitol Jan 6—Witness," Reuters, June 28, 2022, https://www.reuters.com/world/us/trump-tried-grab-steering-wheel-go -us-capitol-jan-6-witness-2022-06-28/; Margaret Hartmann, "Turns Out the Secret Ser- vice Repeatedly Defied Trump on January 6," *Intelligencer*, October 12, 2022,

https://nymag.com/intelligencer/2022/10/secret-service-repeatedly-defied-trumps
-orders-on-january-6.html.

119. Amanda Holpuch, "US Capitol's Last Breach Was More Than 200 Years Ago," *Guardian*, January 6, 2021, https://www.theguardian.com/us-news/2021/jan/06/us-capitol
-building-washington-history-breach.

120. January 6th Committee (@January6thCmte), September 15, 2022, 5:05 PM, https://
twitter.com/January6thCmte/status/1570519072319709184.

121. Jordan Fischer (@JordanOnRecord), October 6, 2022, 10:57 AM, https://twitter.com
/jordanonrecord/status/1578036716136714241; Kathleen Belew (@kathleen_belew), February 8, 2021, 9:52 PM, https://twitter.com/kathleen_belew/status/1358972035377029123.

122. Holmes Lybrand and Hannah Rabinowitz, "Oath Keeper Testifies About Mass of Guns
Allegedly Stored Near DC on January 6," CNN, October 12, 2022, https://www.cnn.com
/2022/10/12/politics/oath-keeper-guns-dc-january-6.

123. Nicole Austin-Hillery and Victoria Strang, "Racism's Prominent Role in January 6 US
Capitol Attack," Human Rights Watch, January 5, 2022, https://www.hrw.org/news
/2022/01/05/racisms-prominent-role-january-6-us-capitol-attack.

124. Andrew H. Kydd and Barbara F. Walter, "The Strategies of Terrorism," *International
Security* 31, no. 1 (Summer 2006): 66.

125. Ford Fischer (@FordFischer), January 8, 2021, 11:38 AM, https://twitter.com/FordFischer
/status/1347583539865395201.

126. "Day of Rage."

127. "Capitol Rioters' Causes of Death Released; Capitol Officer's Still 'Pending,'" Fox 5
Washington, DC, April 7, 2021, https://www.fox5dc.com/news/capitol-rioters-cause-of
-death-information-released-capitol-officers-cause-of-death-pending.

128. "Day of Rage."

129. "Musk Lifts Donald Trump's Twitter ban," BBC, November 20, 2022, https://www.bbc
.com/news/world-us-canada-63692369.

130. Guy Rosen and Monika Bickert, "Our Response to the Violence in Washington," Facebook, January 6, 2021, https://about.fb.com/news/2021/01/responding-to-the-violence
-in-washington-dc/.

131. See, for example, Julia Ainsley, "Extremists Discussed Plans to 'Remove Democratic
Lawmakers': FBI-Homeland Security Bulletin," *NBC News*, March 3, 2021, https://www
.nbcnews.com/news/us-news/extremists-discussed-plans-remove-democratic
-lawmakers-fbi-homeland-security-bulletin-n1259467.

132. U.S. District Court for the District of Columbia, "United States of America v. Ethan
Nordean, Joseph Biggs, Zachary Rehl, and Charles Donohue, First Superseding Indictment," https://s3.documentcloud.org/documents/20518041/3-10-21-us-v-ethan-nordean
-joseph-biggs-zachary-rehl-charles-donohoe-superseding-indictment.pdf.

133. Alan Feuer (@alanfeuer), March 25, 2021, 6:50 AM, https://twitter.com/alanfeuer/status
/1375037486074892289.

134. Ryan J. Reilly, "Court Document in Proud Boys Case Laid Out Plan to Occupy Capitol
Buildings on Jan. 6," *NBC News*, June 15, 2022, https://www.nbcnews.com/politics

/justice-department/court-document-proud-boys-case-laid-plan-occupy-capitol
-buildings-jan-rcna33755.

135. Spencer S. Hsu, "Video Released of Garage Meeting of Proud Boys, Oath Keepers Leaders," *Washington Post*, May 24, 2022, https://www.washingtonpost.com/dc-md-va/2022/05/24/tarrio-rhodes-video/.

136. Daniel A. Cox, "After the Ballots Are Counted: Conspiracies, Political Violence, and American Exceptionalism," Survey Center on American Life, February 11, 2021, https://www.americansurveycenter.org/research/after-the-ballots-are-counted-conspiracies-political-violence-and-american-exceptionalism/.

137. Cole Bunzel (@colebunzel), April 15, 2021, 1:28 PM, https://twitter.com/colebunzel/status/1382747626521563140.

138. "1 Big Thing: Scoop . . . Trump Blames Antifa for Riot," *Axios*, January 12, 2021, https://www.axios.com/newsletters/axios-sneak-peek-1c44d7d7-d31e-4879-bff1-11965803be69.html.

139. William Cummings, "Chris Miller, Defense Secretary on Jan. 6, Sees 'Cause and Effect' Between Trump's Words and Capitol Riot," *USA Today*, March 12, 2021, https://www.usatoday.com/story/news/politics/2021/03/12/chris-miller-pentagon-chief-trump-caused-capitol-riot/4661721001/.

140. U.S. District Court for the District of Columbia, "United States of America v. Ethan Nordean, Joseph Biggs, Zachary Rehl, and Charles Donohue, First Superseding Indictment"; "Day of Rage"; Jennifer Peltz, "Marine Veteran Among Two Proud Boys Facing Federal Conspiracy Charges in Capitol Riot," *Marine Corps Times*, January 31, 2021, https://www.marinecorpstimes.com/news/pentagon-congress/2021/01/31/marine-veteran-among-two-proud-boys-facing-federal-conspiracy-charges-in-capitol-riot/.

141. Jan Wolfe, " 'He Invited Us': Accused Capitol Rioters Blame Trump in Novel Legal Defense," Reuters, February 2, 2021, https://www.reuters.com/article/us-usa-trump-capitol-defense/he-invited-us-accused-capitol-rioters-blame-trump-in-novel-legal-defense-idUSKBN2A219E.

142. Drew Harwell (@drewharwell), January 13, 2021, 2:22 PM, https://twitter.com/drewharwell/status/1349436733889404928.

143. "How Concerned Is the Military About Insider Threats in the National Guard?," *PBS NewsHour*, January 18, 2021, https://www.pbs.org/newshour/show/how-concerned-is-the-military-about-insider-threats-in-the-national-guard.

144. Jake Bleiberg and Jim Mustian, "Capitol Rioters Hold Out Long-Shot Hope for a Trump Pardon," Associated Press, January 19, 2021, https://apnews.com/article/joe-biden-donald-trump-capitol-siege-riots-32a212d3ac899905be744632d236862c.

145. Colby Itkowitz, "Trump Falsely Claims Jan. 6 Rioters Were 'Hugging and Kissing' Police," *Washington Post*, March 26, 2021, https://www.washingtonpost.com/politics/trump-riot-capitol-police/2021/03/26/0ba7e844-8e40-11eb-9423-04079921c915_story.html.

146. Glenn Kessler, Salvador Rizzo, and Meg Kelly, "Fact Checker: Analysis: In Four Years, President Trump Made 30,573 False or Misleading Claims," *Washington Post*,

January 20, 2021; Glenn Kessler, Salvador Rizzo, and Meg Kelly, *Donald Trump and His Assault on Truth: The President's Falsehoods, Misleading Claims, and Flat-Out Lies* (New York: Scribner, 2020).

147. Fiona Hill, "The Kremlin's Strange Victory," *Foreign Affairs*, November/December 2021, https://www.foreignaffairs.com/articles/united-states/2021-09-27/kremlins-strange-victory.

148. Adam Goldman, Katie Benner, and Zolan Kanno-Youngs, "How Trump's Focus on Antifa Distracted Attention from the Far-Right Threat," *New York Times*, January 30, 2021, https://www.nytimes.com/2021/01/30/us/politics/trump-right-wing-domestic-terrorism.html.

149. Benjamin Siegel, "DHS Whistleblower Testifies Before House Intelligence Committee," *ABC News*, December 11, 2020, https://abcnews.go.com/Politics/dhs-whistleblower-testifies-house-intelligence-committee/story?id=74675983.

150. "Rep. Rodney Davis: 'This Would Have Been a Massacre' If Not for Capitol Police," CBS Chicago, June 14, 2017, https://chicago.cbslocal.com/2017/06/14/rep-rodney-davis-this-would-have-been-a-massacre-if-not-for-police/.

151. See ADL Center for Extremism, "Murder and Extremism in the United States 2021," https://www.adl.org/murder-and-extremism-2021.

152. Peter Bergen and David Sterman, "Terrorism in America After 9/11: What Is the Threat to the United States Today?" *New America*, September 10, 2021, https://www.newamerica.org/international-security/reports/terrorism-in-america/what-is-the-threat-to-the-united-states-today.

153. Luis Martinez, "Inside Look at How 25,000 National Guardsmen Are Arriving in Washington, DC," *ABC News*, January 16, 2021, https://abcnews.go.com/Politics/inside-25000-national-guardsmen-arriving-washington-dc/story?id=75299202.

154. Elizabeth Neumann, "Far-Right Extremists Went Mainstream Under Trump. The Capitol Attack Cements His Legacy," *USA Today*, February 15, 2021, https://www.usatoday.com/story/opinion/2021/02/15/capitol-riots-have-lasting-impact-domestic-terrorism-column/6709778002/.

155. "Did Trump and Biden Swap Bodies???," *Daily Beast*, January 22, 2021, https://www.thedailybeast.com/did-trump-and-biden-swap-bodies.

156. "Capitol Hill Siege," GW Program on Extremism, https://extremism.gwu.edu/Capitol-Hill-Siege; Spencer S. Hsu, Peter Hermann, and Emily Davies, "Two Arrested in Assault on Police Officer Brian D. Sicknick, Who Died After Jan. 6 Capitol Riot," *Washington Post*, March 21, 2021.

157. Daniel L. Byman and Mark Pitcavage, "Identifying and Exploiting the Weaknesses of the White Supremacist Movement," Brookings Institution, April 2021, https://www.brookings.edu/wp-content/uploads/2021/04/Identifying-and-exploiting-the-weaknesses-of-the-white-supremacist-movement.pdf.

158. Barbara Sprunt, "7 GOP Senators Voted to Convict Trump. Only 1 Faces Voters Next Year," NPR, February 15, 2021, https://www.npr.org/sections/trump-impeachment-trial-live-updates/2021/02/15/967878039/7-gop-senators-voted-to-convict-trump-only-1-faces-voters-next-year.

159. Alex Rogers and Manu Raju, "McConnell Blames Trump but Voted Not Guilty Anyway," CNN, February 13, 2021, https://www.cnn.com/2021/02/13/politics/mitch-mcconnell-acquit-trump/index.html; Pilar Menendez, "McConnell Unleashes on 'Shameful' Trump—Moments After Voting 'Not Guilty,'" *Daily Beast*, February 13, 2021, https://www.thedailybeast.com/mitch-mcconnell-unleashes-on-shameful-trump-moments-after-voting-to-acquit-in-impeachment-trial; Ben Leonard, "'Practically and Morally Responsible': McConnell Scorches Trump—but Votes to Acquit," *Politico*, February 13, 2021, https://www.politico.com/news/2021/02/13/mcconnell-condemns-trump-acquitted-469002.

160. "(U) Domestic Violent Extremism Poses Heightened Threat in 2021," Office of the Director of National Intelligence, March 1, 2021, https://www.dni.gov/files/ODNI/documents/assessments/UnclassSummaryofDVEAssessment-17MAR21.pdf.

161. Pilar Menendez, "'Fuck All of You!': Capitol Rioter Raises Hell During Off-the-Rails Court Hearing," *Daily Beast*, May 6, 2021, https://www.thedailybeast.com/landon-kenneth-copeland-utah-man-charged-with-assaulting-police-during-capitol-riots-loses-it-in-court.

162. "'Let the Race War Commence': Far-Right Community Outraged by 'Martyr' Chauvin's Guilty Verdict in Murder of George Floyd," *SITE Intelligence Group*, April 20, 2021, https://ent.siteintelgroup.com/Far-Right-/-Far-Left-Threat/let-the-race-war-commence-far-right-community-outraged-by-martyr-chauvin-s-guilty-verdict-in-murder-of-george-floyd.html.

163. "'Saint Kyle Walks': Emboldened by Rittenhouse Acquittal, Far Right Urges Whites to 'Fight Harder,'" *SITE Intelligence Group*, November 19, 2021, https://ent.siteintelgroup.com/Far-Right-Far-Left-Threat/saint-kyle-walks-emboldened-by-rittenhouse-acquittal-far-right-urges-whites-to-fight-harder.html.

164. National Security Council, *National Strategy for Countering Domestic Terrorism*, June 2021, https://www.whitehouse.gov/wp-content/uploads/2021/06/National-Strategy-for-Countering-Domestic-Terrorism.pdf.

165. Josh Dawsey and Felicia Sonmez, "RNC Votes to Condemn Cheney, Kinzinger for Serving on House Committee Investigating Jan. 6 Attack on the Capitol by Pro-Trump Mob," *Washington Post*, February 3, 2022; Josh Dawsey and Felicia Sonmez, "'Legitimate Political Discourse': Three Words About Jan. 6 Spark Rift Among Republicans," *Washington Post*, February 8, 2022.

166. Office of Public Affairs, U.S. Department of Justice, "Leader of Oath Keepers and 10 Other Individuals Indicted in Federal Court for Seditious Conspiracy and Other Offenses Related to U.S. Capitol Breach," January 13, 2022, https://www.justice.gov/opa/pr/leader-oath-keepers-and-10-other-individuals-indicted-federal-court-seditious-conspiracy-and.

167. U.S. District Court for the District of Columbia, "United States of America v. Joshua James, Statement of Offense," https://www.justice.gov/opa/press-release/file/1479551/download.

168. Southern Poverty Law Center, *The Year in Hate & Extremism 2021*, 2022, https://www.splcenter.org/sites/default/files/splc-2021-year-in-hate-extremism-report.pdf.

169. Payton Gendron, "What You Need to Know," May 2022.
170. "Accelerationist Neo-Nazi Propagandists Celebrate Buffalo Shooter as 'Saint," *SITE Intelligence Group*, May 31, 2022, https://ent.siteintelgroup.com/Far-Right-/-Far-Left -Threat/accelerationist-neo-nazi-propagandists-celebrate-buffalo-shooter-as-saint .html; "Criticizing Buffalo Shooter, Accelerationist Neo-Nazis Incite Attacks on American Jews," *SITE Intelligence Group*, June 2, 2022, https://ent.siteintelgroup.com/Far -Right-/-Far-Left-Threat/criticizing-buffalo-shooter-accelerationist-neo-nazis-incite -attacks-on-american-jews.html.
171. "Neo-Nazi Accelerationists Call for Monthly Attacks on Anniversary of Buffalo Shooting," *SITE Intelligence Group*, May 16, 2022, https://ent.siteintelgroup.com/Far-Right-/ -Far-Left-Threat/neo-nazi-accelerationists-call-for-monthly-attacks-on-anniversary -of-buffalo-shooting.html; "Neo-Nazis Continue Calls for Monthly Violent Attacks on Anniversary of Buffalo Shooting," *SITE Intelligence Group*, June 15, 2022, https://ent .siteintelgroup.com/Far-Right-/-Far-Left-Threat/neo-nazis-continue-calls-for -monthly-violent-attacks-on-anniversary-of-buffalo-shooting.html; "Recent Hate Attacks Celebrated by Neo-Nazis Marking Buffalo Shooting's Month Anniversary," *SITE Intelligence Group*, June 17, 2022, https://ent.siteintelgroup.com/Far-Right-/-Far -Left-Threat/recent-hate-attacks-celebrated-by-neo-nazis-marking-buffalo-shooting -s-month-anniversary.html.
172. For more on the assassination threats, see Bruce Hoffman and Jacob Ware, "The Accelerating Threat of the Political Assassination," *War on the Rocks*, August 24, 2022, https://warontherocks.com/2022/08/the-accelerating-threat-of-the-political -assassination/.
173. "Senator Susan Collins Targeted After Saying She'll Vote to Confirm Ketanji Brown Jackson," *SITE Intelligence Group*, March 30, 2022, https://ent.siteintelgroup.com/Far -Right-/-Far-Left-Threat/senator-susan-collins-targeted-after-saying-she-ll-vote-to -confirm-ketanji-brown-jackson.html.
174. "Violent Threats Made Against Arizona Attorney General After Accusations of Targeting 'Patriots,'" *SITE Intelligence Group*, May 17, 2022, https://ent.siteintelgroup.com /Far-Right-/-Far-Left-Threat/violent-threats-made-against-arizona-attorney-general -after-accusations-of-targeting-patriots.html; Michael McDaniel, "Arizona Attorney General Finds Logistical and Legal 'Concerns' After Election Probe," *Courthouse News Service*, April 6, 2022, https://www.courthousenews.com/arizona-attorney-generals -election-investigation-finds-logistical-and-legal-concerns/.
175. "Announcement of New Gun Legislation Sparks Threats Against Participating Senators," *SITE Intelligence Group*, June 14, 2022, https://ent.siteintelgroup.com/Far-Right -/-Far-Left-Threat/threats-against-traitorous-senators-made-following -announcement-of-new-gun-legislation.html.
176. Alan Feuer and Maggie Haberman, "Hard Right Stokes Outrage After Search of Mar-a-Lago," *New York Times*, August 30, 2022; Kim Bellware, "There Will Be 'Riots in the Street' If Trump Is Prosecuted, Graham Says," *Washington Post*, August 29, 2022, https://www.washingtonpost.com/politics/2022/08/29/lindsey-graham-riots/.

177. Ronny Jackson (@RonnyJacksonTX), August 8, 2022, 10:06 PM, https://twitter.com/RonnyJacksonTX/status/1556824211200647170; Jacob Ware, "The Violent Far-Right Terrorist Threat to American Law Enforcement," CFR.org, January 24, 2023, https://www.cfr.org/blog/violent-far-right-terrorist-threat-american-law-enforcement.

178. Dareh Gregorian and Phil Helsel, "GOP Candidate for Florida House Is Booted from Twitter After Post About Shooting Federal Agents," *NBC News*, August 19, 2022, https://www.nbcnews.com/politics/2022-election/gop-candidate-florida-house-booted-twitter-post-shooting-federal-agent-rcna44020.

179. Alan Feuer, "The F.B.I. Search Ignited the Language of Violence and Civil War on the Far Right," *New York Times*, August 9, 2022, https://www.nytimes.com/2022/08/09/us/fbi-search-violence-civil-war.html.

180. Steve Benen, "Trump Promotes Barrage of QAnon Content via Social Media Platform," *Rachel Maddow Show*, August 30, 2022, https://www.msnbc.com/rachel-maddow-show/maddowblog/trump-promotes-barrage-qanon-content-social-media-platform-rcna45526.

181. FBI National Press Office, "Statement from Director Wray," August 11, 2022, https://www.fbi.gov/news/press-releases/press-releases/statement-from-director-wray.

182. Will Carless, "Suspect in Cincinnati FBI Breach May Have Posted on Trump's Truth Social During Incident," *USA Today*, August 11, 2022, https://www.usatoday.com/story/news/nation/2022/08/11/cincinnati-fbi-trump-truth-social/10304105002/; "Gunman Who Targeted FBI a Radicalized Trump Supporter, Saw Mar-a-Lago Search as Call to Arms," Anti-Defamation League, August 11, 2022, https://www.adl.org/resources/blog/gunman-who-targeted-fbi-radicalized-trump-supporter-saw-mar-lago-search-call-arms.

183. Feuer and Haberman, "Hard Right Stokes Outrage After Search of Mar-a-Lago"; Matt Dixon, "Florida Judge Who Approved FBI Search of Mar-a-Lago Faces Barrage of Anti-semitic Online Attacks," *Politico*, August 12, 2022, https://www.politico.com/news/2022/08/12/florida-judge-fbi-search-of-mar-a-lago-anti-semitic-attacks-00051489.

184. Steven Simon and Jonathan Stevenson, "The Real Fallout from the Mar-a-Lago Search," *Politico*, August 19, 2022, https://www.politico.com/news/magazine/2022/08/19/fallout-mar-a-lago-search-00052799.

185. U.S. District Court for the Northern District of California, "United States v. David DePape, Indictment," https://www.cand.uscourts.gov/wp-content/uploads/cases-of-interest/usa-vs-david-wayne-depape/Dig-Indictment-package-DePape-_003_.pdf.

186. Amber Lee and KTVU Staff, "DePape in Bizarre Phone Call to KTVU Says He Should Have Been 'More Prepared,'" FOX 2 KTVU, January 27, 2023, https://www.ktvu.com/news/depape-in-bizarre-phone-call-to-ktvu-says-he-should-have-been-more-prepared.

187. Alex Seitz-Wald, "Republicans Who Questioned the 2020 Results Are Bringing Back an Old Norm: Admitting Defeat," *NBC News*, November 10, 2022, https://www.nbcnews.com/politics/2022-election/republicans-questioned-2020-results-are-bringing-back-old-norm-admitin-rcna56486; "'We Put Up One Heck of a Fight': Walker Concedes

Senate Runoff to Warnock," Fox 5 Atlanta, December 7, 2022, https://www.fox5atlanta
.com/news/herschel-walker-concession-speech-georgia-senate-runoff-warnock;
Anders Hagstrom and Courtney De George, "Mehmet Oz calls John Fetterman to Officially Concede Pennsylvania Senate Race," *Fox News*, November 9, 2022, https://www
.foxnews.com/politics/mehmet-oz-calls-john-fetterman-officially-concede
-pennsylvania-senate-race.

188. Spencer S. Hsu and Hannah Allam, "Landmark Oath Keepers Verdict Hobbles Group,
but the Movement Lives On," *Washington Post*, December 3, 2022.

189. "Final Report: Select Committee to Investigate the January 6th Attack on the United
States Capitol."

190. Mary Clare Jalonick, "Jan. 6 Panel Shutting Down After Referring Trump for Crimes,"
Associated Press, January 2, 2023, https://apnews.com/article/capitol-siege-politics
-united-states-government-house-of-representatives-us-department-justice-d529c94
071f3ab2bbbca5c520f5f1c48.

9. COUNTERING FAR-RIGHT TERRORISM

1. Catie Edmonson, "'So the Traitors Know the Stakes': The Meaning of the Jan. 6 Gallows," *New York Times*, June 16, 2022.

2. "Antiterrorism And Effective Death Penalty Act Of 1996," https://www.congress.gov
/bill/104th-congress/senate-bill/735; Legal Information Institute, "Antiterrorism and
Effective Death Penalty Act of 1996 (AEDPA)," Cornell Law School, https://www.law
.cornell.edu/wex/antiterrorism_and_effective_death_penalty_act_of_1996_(aedpa).

3. Cynthia Miller-Idriss, *Hate in the Homeland: The New Global Far Right* (Princeton,
NJ: Princeton University Press, 2020), 20.

4. Jennifer Steinhauer, "Veterans Fortify the Ranks of Militias Aligned with Trump's
Views," *New York Times*, September 11, 2021.

5. Carl von Clausewitz, *On War*, ed. Michael Howard and Peter Paret (Princeton, NJ:
Princeton University Press, 1989).

6. Michael Signer, *Cry Havoc: Charlottesville and American Democracy Under Siege* (New
York: PublicAffairs, 2020), 126–30, 141–43, 264–73; James Verini, "The Paradox of Prosecuting Domestic Terrorism," *New York Times Magazine*, February 8, 2023, https://
www.nytimes.com/section/magazine.

7. Mark S. Hamm and Ramón Spaaij, *The Age of Lone Wolf Terrorism* (New York: Columbia University Press, 2017).

8. Walter Laqueur and Christopher Wall, *The Future of Terrorism: ISIS, Al-Qaeda, and
the Alt-Right* (New York: Thomas Dunne, 2018), 242.

9. See, for example, Thomas Seal, "U.K. Is Toughening Up Online Harms Bill, Culture
Secretary Says," *Bloomberg*, November 23, 2021, https://www.bloomberg.com/news
/articles/2021-11-23/u-k-is-toughening-up-online-harms-bill-culture-secretary-says;
Edina Harbinja, "U.K.'s Online Safety Bill: Not That Safe, After All?," *Lawfare*, July 8,

2021, https://www.lawfareblog.com/uks-online-safety-bill-not-safe-after-all; Department for Digital, Culture, Media & Sport and Home Office, *Consultation Outcome: Online Harms White Paper: Full Government Response to the Consultation*, December 15, 2020, https://www.gov.uk/government/consultations/online-harms-white-paper /outcome/online-harms-white-paper-full-government-response.

10. "Executive Summary," in *Consultation Outcome: Online Harms White Paper: Full Government Response to the Consultation*, December 15, 2020, https://www.gov.uk /government/consultations/online-harms-white-paper/outcome/online-harms-white -paper-full-government-response#executive-summary.

11. See, for example, Megan Squire, "Monetizing Propaganda: How Far-Right Extremists Earn Money by Video Streaming," WebSci '21: 13th International ACM Conference on Web Science in 2021, June 21–25, 2021, New York City, https://arxiv.org/pdf/2105.05929 .pdf; Tonya Riley, "Political Extremists Are Using YouTube to Monetize Their Toxic Ideas," *Mother Jones*, September 18, 2018, https://www.motherjones.com/politics/2018 /09/political-extremists-are-using-youtube-to-monetize-their-toxic-ideas/; Rebecca Lewis, "Alternative Influence: Broadcasting the Reactionary Right on YouTube," *Data & Society*, September 18, 2018, https://datasociety.net/library/alternative-influence/; Katherine J. Wu, "Radical Ideas Spread Through Social Media. Are the Algorithms to Blame?" *Nova*, March 28, 2019, https://www.pbs.org/wgbh/nova/article/radical-ideas -social-media-algorithms/.

12. Adam Satariano, "British Ruling Pins Blame on Social Media for Teenager's Suicide," *New York Times*, October 1, 2022.

13. Wu, "Radical Ideas Spread Through Social Media."

14. Elizabeth Grimm Arsenault and Joseph Stabile, "Confronting Russia's Role in Transnational White Supremacist Extremism," *Just Security*, February 6, 2020, https://www .justsecurity.org/68420/confronting-russias-role-in-transnational-white-supremacist -extremism/.

15. For more, see Clint Watts, *Messing with the Enemy: Surviving in a Social Media World of Hackers, Terrorists, Russians, and Fake News* (New York: Harper, 2018), 136.

16. Watts, *Messing with the Enemy*, 156.

17. Yochai Benkler, Robert Faris, and Hal Roberts, *Network Propaganda: Manipulation, Disinformation, and Radicalization in American Politics* (New York: Oxford University Press, 2018), 5.

18. "Capitol Hill Siege," GW Program on Extremism, https://extremism.gwu.edu /Capitol-Hill-Siege; Michael Kunzelman, "Capitol Rioters' Social Media Posts Influencing Sentencings," Associated Press, December 11, 2021, https://apnews.com /article/media-prisons-social-media-capitol-siege-sentencing-0a60a821ce19635b70 681faf86e6526e.

19. AWD Program, seen by authors.

20. *"Ko tō tātou kāinga tēnei"—Royal Commission of Inquiry Into the Terrorist Attack on Christchurch Masjidain on 15 March 2019*, December 8, 2020, part 4, chap. 4, https:// christchurchattack.royalcommission.nz/.

21. Gregory F. Treverton, *Intelligence for an Age of Terror* (New York: Cambridge University Press, 2009), 145.

22. "GW Extremism Tracker," George Washington Program on Extremism, (no date), https://extremism.gwu.edu/sites/g/files/zaxdzs5746/files/DecGWET2022-4.pdf.

23. Office of Public Affairs, U.S. Department of Justice, "Second Member of "Boogaloo Bois" Pleads Guilty to Conspiracy to Provide Material Support to Hamas," May 4, 2021, https://www.justice.gov/opa/pr/second-member-boogaloo-bois-pleads-guilty-conspiracy-provide-material-support-hamas; Christina Carrega, "Two Self-Proclaimed Members of 'Boogaloo Bois' Charged with Attempting to Support Hamas," CNN, September 6, 2020, https://www.cnn.com/2020/09/04/politics/boogaloo-hamas/index.html.

24. Helen Taylor, "Domestic Terrorism and Hate Crimes: Legal Definitions and Media Framing of Mass Shootings in the United States," *Journal of Policing, Intelligence and Counter Terrorism* 14, no. 3 (2019): 230; "What Is the Threat to the United States Today?," *New America*, https://www.newamerica.org/international-security/reports/terrorism-in-america/what-is-the-threat-to-the-united-states-today/.

25. Taylor, "Domestic Terrorism and Hate Crimes," 239.

26. Office of Public Affairs, U.S. Department of Justice, "Neo-Nazi Leader Sentenced to Five Years in Federal Prison for Explosives Charges," January 9, 2018, https://www.justice.gov/opa/pr/neo-nazi-leader-sentenced-five-years-federal-prison-explosives-charges; "Documenting Hate: New American Nazis," *Frontline*, February 4, 2020, https://www.pbs.org/wgbh/frontline/film/documenting-hate-new-american-nazis/.

27. Rachel Weiner, "After Renouncing White Supremacist Ideology, Virginia Man Sentenced to Year in Prison," *Washington Post*, February 28, 2020.

28. Katie Mettler and Paul Duggan, "Two Accused of Plotting Racial 'Civil War' Are Sentenced to 9 Years Each in Federal Prison," *Washington Post*, October 28, 2021; Verini, "The Paradox of Prosecuting Domestic Terrorism."

29. Office of Public Affairs, U.S. Department of Justice, "Former Police Officer Sentenced for Attempting to Support ISIS," February 23, 2018, https://www.justice.gov/opa/pr/former-police-officer-sentenced-attempting-support-isis.

30. U.S. Attorney's Office, Southern District of Florida, United States Department of Justice, "Man Who Attempted to Provide Material Support to ISIS Sentenced to 16 Years in Federal Prison," February 2, 2022, https://www.justice.gov/usao-sdfl/pr/man-who-attempted-provide-material-support-isis-sentenced-16-years-federal-prison.

31. Quoted in U.S. Department of Justice, "Maryland Woman and Florida Man Charged Federally for Conspiring to Destroy Energy Facilities," *Justice News*, February 6, 2023, https://www.justice.gov/opa/pr/maryland-woman-and-florida-man-charged-federally-conspiring-destroy-energy-facilities. See also U.S. Attorney's Office, District of Maryland, "Federal Indictment Returned Charging Maryland Woman and Florida Man for Conspiring to Destroy Energy Facilities," February 14, 2023, https://www.justice.gov/usao-md/pr/federal-indictment-returned-charging-maryland-woman-and-florida-man-conspiring-destroy; Glenn Thrush and Michael Levenson, "Pair Is

Charged with Plotting to 'Destroy Baltimore' by Attacking Electrical Grid," *New York Times*, February 6, 2023; Rachel Weiner, Jasmine Hilton and Dan Morse, "Duo Accused of Neo-Nazi Plot to Target Maryland Power Stations," *Washington Post*, February 6, 2023; Emily Mae Czachor and Nicole Sganga, "2 Suspects Arrested for Conspiring to Attack Baltimore Power Grid, Officials Say," *CBS News*, February 6, 2023, https://www .cbsnews.com/news/baltimore-power-grid-attack-plot-fbi-suspects-arrested-sarah -beth-clendaniel-brandon-russell/.

32. See, for example, Brian Michael Jenkins, "Five Reasons to Be Wary of a New Domestic Terrorism Law," *The Hill*, February 23, 2021, https://thehill.com/opinion/national -security/540096-what-exactly-is-the-definition-of-terrorism-and-four-other -reasons; Nicole Narea, "Why Progressives Are Lining Up Against New Criminal Penalties for Domestic Terrorism," *Vox*, March 22, 2021, https://www.vox.com/22343959 /criminal-law-domestic-terrorism-capitol-riot-congress; Michael German, "Why New Laws Aren't Needed to Take Domestic Terrorism More Seriously," Brennan Center for Justice, December 14, 2018, https://www.brennancenter.org/our-work/analysis-opinion /why-new-laws-arent-needed-take-domestic-terrorism-more-seriously.

33. Ron Chernow, *Grant* (New York: Penguin, 2017), xxi, 708, 786.

34. *National Strategy for Counterterrorism of the United States of America* (Washington, DC: The White House, October 2018), 9, https://www.dni.gov/files/NCTC/documents /news_documents/NSCT.pdf.

35. U.S. Department of State, "Designation of the Russian Imperial Movement: Remarks by Nathan A. Sales, Coordinator for Counterterrorism," April 6, 2020, https://2017-2021 .state.gov/designation-of-the-russian-imperial-movement/index.html.

36. Aamer Madhani, "Treasury to Designate Wagner Transnational Criminal Group," Associated Press, January 20, 2023, https://apnews.com/article/united-states -government-russia-b4a22b4e4ecc7c2b588e5719c05ba871.

37. Daniel De Simone, Andrei Soshnikov, and Ali Winston, "Neo-Nazi Rinaldo Nazzaro Running US Militant Group the Base from Russia," BBC, January 24, 2020, https://www .bbc.com/news/world-51236915.

38. Emily Cochrane and Zolan Kanno-Youngs, "Biden Signs Gun Bill Into Law, Ending Years of Stalemate," *New York Times*, June 25, 2022.

39. See, for instance, "Racialists Begin Discussing Homemade Weaponry," *SITE Intelligence Group*, April 7, 2015, https://ent.siteintelgroup.com/Far-Right-/-Far-Left-Threat /racialists-begin-discussing-homemade-weaponry.html.

40. Paul Sonne and Missy Ryan, "As He Tackles Extremism, Lloyd Austin Draws on Military's Experience Dealing with 1995 Racially Motivated Murders," *Washington Post*, January 31, 2021, https://www.washingtonpost.com/national-security/as-he-tackles -extremism-lloyd-austin-draws-on-militarys-experience-dealing-with-1995-racially -motivated-murders/2021/01/30/64c450ee-5c0d-11eb-aaad-93988621dd28_story.html.

41. Sergio Olmos, "'The Timothy McVeighs Are Still There': Fears Over Extremism in US Military," *Guardian*, January 10, 2022, https://www.theguardian.com/us-news/2022/jan /10/us-military-rightwing-extremism-american-democracy; Helene Cooper, "Pentagon

Updates Its Rules on Extremism in the Military," *New York Times*, December 20, 2021, https://www.nytimes.com/2021/12/20/us/politics/pentagon-military-extremism-rules .html.

42. Chris Buckley, Myrieme Churchill, and Jacob Ware, "Fighting Demons, Healing Hatred, Restoring Hope: How to Defeat Extremism in the US Military," *Air Force Times*, November 28, 2020, https://www.airforcetimes.com/opinion/commentary/2020/11/28 /fighting-demons-healing-hatred-restoring-hope-how-to-defeat-extremism-in-the -us-military/.

43. Bart Jansen, " 'Elephant in the Room': Police Grapple with Charges Against Officers in Jan. 6 Capitol Attack," *USA Today*, May 3, 2022. See also Eric Westervelt, "Off-Duty Police Officers Investigated, Charged with Participating in Capitol Riot," National Public Radio: Criminal Justice Collaborative, January 15, 2021, https://www.npr.org/2021 /01/15/956896923/police-officers-across-nation-face-federal-charges-for-involvement -in-capitol-ri.

44. Anti-Defamation League, *The Oath Keepers Data Leak: Unmasking Extremism in Public Life*, September 6, 2022, https://www.adl.org/resources/report/oath-keepers-data -leak-unmasking-extremism-public-life.

45. Southern Poverty Law Center, *Oath Keepers*, https://www.splcenter.org/fighting-hate /extremist-files/group/oath-keepers; Griffin Connolly and Richard Hall, "America's Largest Militia Says It Will Refuse to Recognize Biden as President and 'Resist' His Administration," *Independent* (London), November 15, 2020.

46. Beatrice Jin, "Biden Signed a New Hate Crimes Law—but There's a Big Flaw," *Politico*, May 20, 2021, https://www.politico.com/interactives/2021/state-hate-crime -laws/.

47. Movement Advancement Project, *Policy Spotlight: Hate Crimes Law* (Boulder, CO: July 2021), 24–28, https://www.lgbtmap.org/file/2021-report-hate-crime-laws.pdf.

48. Jacob Ware, "The Violent Far-Right Terrorist Threat to American Law Enforcement," CFR.org, January 24, 2023, https://www.cfr.org/blog/violent-far-right-terrorist-threat -american-law-enforcement.

49. James Mason, *Siege*, rev. 1, June 2, 2015 (ironmarch.org), 317.

50. "Arno Michaelis on Rejecting His Racist Past, and the Role of Unconditional Forgiveness in Creating a Life After Hate," *Forgiveness Project*, December 22, 2021, https://www .theforgivenessproject.com/arno-michaelis-on-rejecting-his-racist-past-and-the-role -of-unconditional-forgiveness-in-creating-a-life-after-hate/.

51. Simi and Futrell, *American Swastika*.

52. Picciolini, *White American Youth*, 41. See also Jonathan Pieslak, *Radicalism and Music: An Introduction to the Music Cultures of al-Qa'ida, Racist Skinheads, Christian-Affiliated Radicals, and Eco-Animal Rights Militants* (Middletown, CT: Wesleyan University Press, 2015), 45–109.

53. Picciolini, *White American Youth*, 233–34.

54. Alessandro Orsini, *Sacrifice: My Life in a Fascist Militia* (Ithaca, NY: Cornell University Press, 2017), 156.

55. Andrew Berwick, "2083: A European Declaration of Independence," 2011, 1339–40.

56. See, for example, "Public-Private Partnerships for Local P/CVE Position Paper," Strong Cities Network, https://strongcitiesnetwork.org/en/wp-content/uploads/sites/5/2019/03/WG3_position_paper_final.pdf.

57. "Why Countering Violent Extremism Programs Are Bad Policy," Brennan Center for Justice, September 9, 2019, https://www.brennancenter.org/our-work/research-reports/why-countering-violent-extremism-programs-are-bad-policy.

58. P. W. Singer and Michael McConnell, "Want to Stop the Next Crisis? Teaching Cyber Citizenship Must Become a National Priority," *Time*, January 21, 2021, https://time.com/5932134/cyber-citizenship-national-priority/.

59. National Security Council, *National Strategy for Countering Domestic Terrorism* (Washington, DC: The White House, June 2021), https://www.whitehouse.gov/wp-content/uploads/2021/06/National-Strategy-for-Countering-Domestic-Terrorism.pdf.

60. U.S. Department of Homeland Security Center for Prevention Programs and Partnerships, "Media Literacy & Critical Thinking Online," https://www.dhs.gov/sites/default/files/publications/digital_media_literacy_0.pdf; Tina Smith for U.S. Senator for Minnesota, "Klobuchar, Bennet, Slotkin Introduce Bicameral Legislation to Strengthen Media Literacy Education and Improve Personal Cybersecurity," July 8, 2022, https://www.smith.senate.gov/klobuchar-bennet-slotkin-introduce-bicameral-legislation-to-strengthen-media-literacy-education-and-improve-personal-cybersecurity/.

61. "Illinois Now Requires Media Literacy Instruction in Its High School Curriculum," WGLT, September 14, 2022, https://www.wglt.org/2022-09-14/illinois-now-requires-media-literacy-instruction-in-its-high-school-curriculum.

62. Jenny Gross, "How Finland Is Teaching a Generation to Spot Misinformation," *New York Times*, January 10, 2023, https://www.nytimes.com/2023/01/10/world/europe/finland-misinformation-classes.html; "RESIST 2: Counter-Disinformation Toolkit," Government Communication Service, 2021, https://gcs.civilservice.gov.uk/wp-content/uploads/2021/11/RESIST-2-counter-disinformation-toolkit.pdf.

63. David Pitt, "One Iowa Man in Capitol Riot Released, Other Remains in Jail," *U.S. News & World Report*, January 19, 2021, https://www.usnews.com/news/best-states/iowa/articles/2021-01-19/one-iowa-man-in-capitol-riot-released-other-remains-in-jail.

64. Pitt, "One Iowa Man in Capitol Riot Released, Other Remains in Jail."

65. Jesselyn Cook, "'I Miss My Mom': Children of QAnon Believers Are Desperately Trying to Deradicalize Their Own Parents," *Huffington Post*, February 11, 2021, https://www.huffpost.com/entry/children-of-qanon-believers_n_601078e9c5b6c5586aa49077.

66. Andrea Prado Tuma and Alice Huguet, *Engaging Youth with Public Policy: Middle School Lessons to Counter Truth Decay* (Santa Monica, CA: RAND Corporation, TLA387–1, 2022), 17–24, https://www.rand.org/pubs/tools/TLA387-1.html#overcoming-covid19-what-scientists-know-and-what-policy-can-tell-us; Doug Irving, "Lesson Plans for Middle School Teachers to Help Improve Media Literacy Among Students,"

RAND Review, September–October 2022, 16–18, https://www.rand.org/pubs/corporate _pubs/CPA682-13.html.

67.   See Mark E. Dornauer and Robert Bryce, "Too Many Rural Americans Are Living in the Digital Dark. The Problem Demands a New Deal Solution," *Health Affairs*, October 28, 2020, https://www.healthaffairs.org/do/10.1377/forefront.20201026.515764/; Emily A. Vogels, "Some Digital Divides Persist Between Rural, Urban and Suburban America," Pew Research Center, August 19, 2021, https://www.pewresearch.org/fact -tank/2021/08/19/some-digital-divides-persist-between-rural-urban-and-suburban -america/; Nicol Turner Lee, James Seddon, Brooke Tanner, and Samantha Lai, "Why the Federal Government Needs to Step Up Efforts to Close the Rural Broadband Divide," *Brookings*, October 4, 2022, https://www.brookings.edu/research/why-the -federal-government-needs-to-step-up-their-efforts-to-close-the-rural-broadband -divide/.

68.   Federal Communications Commission, *Report*, December 26, 2018, 184, https://docs. fcc.gove/public/attachments/FCC-18-181A1.pdf.

69.   Dornauer and Bryce, "Too Many Rural Americans Are Living in the Digital Dark."

70.   See Lee et al., "Why the Federal Government Needs to Step Up Efforts to Close the Rural Broadband Divide"; White House, "Fact Sheet: The Bipartisan Infrastructure Deal," Briefing Room: Statements and Releases, November 6, 2021, https://www.whitehouse .gov/briefing-room/statements-releases/2021/11/06/fact-sheet-the-bipartisan -infrastructure-deal/.

71.   Dornauer and Bryce, "Too Many Rural Americans Are Living in the Digital Dark."

72.   See, for example, William A. Galston, "'This Is How It Feels to Be Sold Out by Your Country': Economic Hardship and Politics in Indiana," *Brookings*, May 18, 2016, https:// www.brookings.edu/blog/fixgov/2016/05/18/this-is-how-it-feels-to-be-sold-out-by -your-country-economic-hardship-and-politics-in-indiana/; "Victor Davis Hanson: Democrats 'Live Apartheid, Segregated Existences,'" *Fox News*, July 26, 2022, https:// www.foxnews.com/video/6310049745112.

73.   See, for example, Martha Crenshaw, "The Logic of Terrorism: Terrorist Behavior as a Product of Strategic Choice," in *Origins of Terrorism*, ed. Walter Reich (Washington, DC: Woodrow Wilson Center Press, 1998), 7–24.

74.   Chris Cillizza, "Newt Gingrich Thinks Members of the January 6 Committee Should Be Threatened with Jail Time," CNN, January 24, 2022, https://www.cnn.com/2022/01 /24/politics/newt-gingrich-jail-time/index.html.

75.   "President Reagan's Optimism, Courage, and Humility Remembered on 30th Anniversary of Assassination Attempt," Ronald Reagan Presidential Foundation, March 28, 2011, https://www.reaganfoundation.org/media/50862/assassination-press-release .pdf.

76.   *"Ko tō tātou kāinga tēnei."*

77.   Bryan Greene, "Created 150 Years Ago, the Justice Department's First Mission Was to Protect Black Rights," *Smithsonian Magazine*, July 1, 2020, https://www.smithsonianmag .com/history/created-150-years-ago-justice-departments-first-mission-was-protect -black-rights-180975232/.

78. T. K. Wilson, *Killing Strangers: How Political Violence Became Modern* (Oxford: Oxford University Press, 2020), 107.

79. Crenshaw, "The Logic of Terrorism," 7–24.

80. Hoffman, *Inside Terrorism*, 22–23.

81. Laqueur and Wall, *The Future of Terrorism*, 238.

BIBLIOGRAPHY

PRIMARY SOURCES

COURT PROCEEDINGS

"Closing Argument for the Prosecution in the Trial of Timothy McVeigh (Argument by Larry D. Mackey)," May 29, 1997, http://law2.umkc.edu/faculty/projects/ftrials/mcveigh/mcveighclosing.html.

"Continuation of a Criminal Complaint." Case 1:20-mj-00416-SJB ECF No. 1-1, filed 10/06/20 Page ID.2, 15. http://www.seditionists.com/michigankidnap1.pdf.

District Court for the Western District of Arkansas, Fort Smith Division: United States of America v. Robert Edward Miles, Louis Ray Beam Jr., Richard Girnt Butler, Richard Joseph Scutari, Bruce Carroll Pierce, Andrew Virgil Barnhill, Ardie McBrearty, David Eden Lane, Lambert Miller, Robert Neil Smalley, Ivan Ray Wade, William H. Wade, Richard Wayne Snell, David Michael McGuire: Trial Testimony of Robert E. Miles, 1988, no 87-20008-01-14.

"Opening Statement by Prosecutor Joseph Hartzler." OKC Bombing Trial Transcript—04/24/1997, https://oklahoman.com/article/1074825/okc-bombing-trial-transcript-04241997-1139-cdtcst.

"Opening Statement by Stephen Jones," OKC Bombing Trial Transcript—04/24/1997, http://law2.umkc.edu/faculty/projects/ftrials/mcveigh/defenseopen.html.

OKC Bombing Trial Transcript-04/24/1997 11:39 CDT/CST, Criminal Action No. 96-CR-68, United States of America, Plaintiff vs. Timothy James McVeigh, Defendant. Reporter's Transcript (Trial to Jury-Volume 60), Joseph H. Hartzler, Special Attorney to the U.S. Attorney General, https://www.oklahoman.com/article/1074825/okc-bombing-trial-transcript-04241997-1139-cdtcst.

"R. c. Bissonnette, 2019 QCCS 354 (CanLII)," CanLII, February 8, 2019, https://www.canlii.org /en/qc/qccs/doc/2019/2019qccs354/2019qccs354.html.

"The Ruby Ridge (Weaver and Harris) Trial: Selected Excerpts from the Trial Transcript." Famous Trials by Professor Douglas O. Linder. https://www.famous-trials.com/rubyridge /1146-weaverdefense.

State v. Dorr, 120 Idaho 441, 816 P.2d 998 (1991), July 1, 1991.

"Testimony of Jennifer McVeigh May 5, 1997." Famous Trials by Professor Douglas O. Linder. Oklahoma City Bombing Trial, 1997, https://famous-trials.com/oklacity/723-jennifertes timony.

"Testimony of Lori Fortier in the Timothy McVeigh Trial, April 29, 1997." Famous Trials by Professor Douglas O. Linder. Oklahoma City Bombing Trial, 1997, https://www.famous -trials.com/oklacity/724-loritestimony.

"Testimony of Michael Fortier in the Timothy McVeigh Trial, May 12, 1997." Famous Trials by Professor Douglas O. Linder. Oklahoma City Bombing Trial, 1997, https://www.famous -trials.com/oklacity/712-fortiertestimony.

"Testimony of Michelle Rauch in the Timothy McVeigh Trial, June 10, 1997." Famous Trials by Professor Douglas O. Linder. Oklahoma City Bombing Trial, 1997, https://www.famous -trials.com/oklacity/728-rauchtestimony.

"Testimony of Oklahoma State Trooper Charles J. Hangar Concerning His Arrest of Timothy McVeigh on April 19, 1995 (Nichols Trial—Nov. 5, 1997)." http://law2.umkc.edu/faculty /projects/ftrials/mcveigh/mcveigharrest.html.

United States of America, Plaintiff-Appellee, v. Timothy James McVeigh, Defendant-appellant. Appeal from the United States District Court for the District of Colorado, in Decision of the Tenth Circuit Court of Appeals, Affirming the Conviction of Timothy McVeigh (no date). http://law2.umkc.edu/faculty/projects/ftrials/mcveigh/mcveigh10thcircuit.html.

United States of America, Plaintiff, v. Ryan W. Payne, Defendant, Case No. 2:16-CR-00046-GMN-PAL, Order Re: Motion to Reopen Detention Hearing (ECF No. 1208). December 29, 2016. https://casetext.com/case/united-states-v-payne-99.

United States v. Kahl, 583 F. 2d 1351—Court of Appeals, 5th Circuit 1978. https://scholar.google .com/scholar_case?q=%2583+F.2d+1351%22&as_sdt=3,44&case=8981178823130363349&sc ilh=0.

U.S. District Court for the District of Colorado. The Honorable Richard P. Matsch, Criminal Action No. 96-CR-68-M, United States of America, Plaintiff, v. Timothy J. McVeigh, Defendant, Brief of the United States Opposed Stay of Execution, Sean Connelly, Special Attorney to the U.S. District Attorney, United States Department of Justice Archives. https:// www.justice.gov/archives/opa/brief-united-states-opposing-stay-execution.

U.S. District Court for the District of Columbia. "United States of America v. Ethan Nordean, Joseph Biggs, Zachary Rehl, and Charles Donohue, First Superseding Indictment." https://s3 .documentcloud.org/documents/20518041/3-10-21-us-v-ethan-nordean-joseph-biggs-zac hary-rehl-charles-donohoe-superseding-indictment.pdf.

——. "United States of America v. Joshua James, Statement of Offense." https://www.justice .gov/opa/press-release/file/1479551/download.

U.S. District Court for the District of Kansas. United States of America v. Jarrett William Smith, Case No. 19-mj-5105-ADM. August 21, 2019. https://extremism.gwu.edu/sites/g/files/zaxdzs2191/f/Jarrett%20William%20Smith%20Criminal%20Complaint.

——. "United States of America v. Patrick Stein." https://www.documentcloud.org/documents/5023695-Patrick-Stein-Sentencing-Memo.

U.S. District Court for the District of Maryland. "United States of America v. Christopher Paul Hasson, Motion for Detention Pending Trial." https://int.nyt.com/data/documenthelper/625-us-v-hasson/be7a4841596aba86cce4/optimized/full.pdf.

U.S. District Court for the District of Nevada. "United States of America v. Conor Climo, Complaint." https://www.documentcloud.org/documents/6318397-Conor-Climo.html.

U.S. District Court for the Northern District of California. "United States v. David DePape, Indictment." https://www.cand.uscourts.gov/wp-content/uploads/cases-of-interest/usa-vs-david-wayne-depape/Dig-Indictment-package-DePape-_003_.pdf.

U.S. District Court for the Northern District of Texas, Fort Worth Division. United States of America v. Seth Aaron Pendley, Criminal Complaint, No. 4:21-MJ-240-BJ. April 9, 2021. https://www.texomashomepage.com/wp-content/uploads/sites/41/2021/04/Pendley-Complaint.pdf.

U.S. District Court, Western District of Michigan, Southern Division. United States of America v. Adam Dean Fox, Case No. 1:20-cr-00183-RJJ. December 17, 2020. https://www.documentcloud.org/documents/7225185-Adam-Fox-affidavit.

U.S. District Court, Western Division of Washington at Seattle. United States of America v. Bruce Carroll Pierce, et al. No. CR85–001M. July 18, 1985.

FEDERAL BUREAU OF INVESTIGATION ARCHIVAL MATERIALS

FBI. "Domestic Terrorism: The Sovereign Citizen Movement." April 13, 2010. https://www.fbi.gov/news/stories/2010/april/sovereigncitizens_041310/domestic-terrorism-the-sovereign-citizen-movement.

——. "Eric Rudolph Charged in Centennial Olympic Park Bombing." October 14, 1998. https://www.justice.gov/archive/opa/pr/1998/October/477crm.htm.

——. "Eric Rudolph: FBI Ten Most Wanted Fugitive." History: Famous Cases & Criminals. https://www.fbi.gov/history/famous-cases/eric-rudolph.

——. "Thomas George Harrelson—Former Ten Most Wanted Fugitive #407." https://www.fbi.gov/wanted/topten/topten-history/hires_images/FBI-407-ThomasGeorgeHarrelson.jpg/view.

——. "Wanted by FBI: Thomas George Harrelson." Identification Order 5023. November 8, 1986. https://www.ebay.com/itm/ARYAN-NATION-LEADER-NEO-NAZI-THOMAS-HARRELSON-FBI-WANTED-POSTER-PLS-OFFER-/224135654820.

FBI Counterterrorism Analysis Section. "Sovereign Citizens: A Growing Threat to Law Enforcement." FBI Law Enforcement Bulletin. September 2011. https://leb.fbi.gov/2011/september/sovereign-citizens-a-growing-domestic-threat-to-law-enforcement;

FBI Counterterrorism Division. "State of the Domestic White Nationalist Extremist Movement in the United States." Intelligence Assessment. December 13, 2006.

——. "White Supremacist Recruitment of Military Personnel Since 9/11." Intelligence Assessment. July 7, 2008. https://documents.law.yale.edu/sites/default/files/White%20Supremacist%20Recruitment%20of%20Military%20Personnel%20Since%209-11-ocr.pdf.

FBI, Freedom of Information/Privacy Acts Section. "Subject: The Covenant, The Sword, The Arm of The Lord." File 100-HQ-487200, Kansas City, Missouri. July 2, 1982. https://vault.fbi.gov/The%20Covenant%20The%20Sword%20The%20Arm%20of%20the%20Lord%20/The%20Covenant%20The%20Sword%20The%20Arm%20of%20the%20Lord%20Part%201%20of%202 and https://archive.org/details/CovenantTheSwordAndTheArmOfTheLord/page/n1.

FBI National Press Office. "Statement from Director Wray." August 11, 2022. https://www.fbi.gov/news/press-releases/press-releases/statement-from-director-wray.

FBI News. "Hogan's Alley Turns 30: The Evolution of the FBI's Mock Training Ground." May 12, 2017. http://www.fbi.gov/news/stories/hogans-alley-turns-30.

FBI Services/Training Academy. "Tactical/Hogan's Alley." https://www.fbi.gov/services/training-academy/hogans-alley.

FBI RECORDS: THE VAULT

AIRTEL, SAC. San Antonio to Director, FBI, August 20, 1991. http://intelfiles.egoplex.com/91-08-20-airtel-turner-diaries2.pdf.

"Baptist Street Church Bombing." FBI—History: Famous Cases and Criminals. https://www.fbi.gov/history/famous-cases/baptist-street-church-bombing.

FBI Laboratory Division. May 1, 1985 attachment, The Covenant, The Sword, The Arm of the Lord; Domestic Security/Terrorism. May 20, 1985.

Freedom of Information and Privacy Acts. Subject: Birmingham, Alabama Sixteenth Street Baptist Church Bombing/September 15, 1963. Part 9 of 11, "Sixteenth (16th Street Church Bombing." Containing Urgent Teletype from SAC, Atlanta to SACS, El Paso and Birmingham, September 21, 1963. https://vault.fbi.gov/16th%20Street%20Church%20Bombing%20/16th%20Street%20Church%20Bombing%20Part%2037%20of%2051.

Memorandum. From ASAC Danny O. Coulson to SAC, Washington Field Office. Subject: Covenant, Sword, and The Arm of The Lord (CSA); Domestic Terrorism. May 8, 1985.

Memorandum. From ASAC Danny O. Coulson to SAC, Washington Field Office. Subject: The Covenant, The Sword, The Arm of The Lord; Domestic Security/Terrorism. May 20, 1985.

Memorandum. From J. W. Hicks to Mr. Geer. Re: The Covenant, The Sword, and The Arm of The Lord; Domestic Security—Terrorism OO: Little Rock. May 2, 1985.

Memorandum. From SAC, Little Rick to Director. FBI Subject: The Covenant, Sword, and Arm of The Lord (CSA), Domestic Security. August 8, 1983.

Memorandum. Little Rock Field Office. Subject: The Covenant, The Sword, and The Arm of The Lord; Domestic Security/Terrorism. September 7, 1984.

Memorandum. Little Rock Field Office. Subject: The Covenant, The Sword, and The Arm of The Lord; Domestic Security/Terrorism. May 20, 1985.

Memorandum. Little Rock Field Office. Memorandum, Subject: The Covenant, The Sword, and The Arm of The Lord; Domestic Security/Terrorism. July 2, 1985.

Memorandum. Little Rock Field Office. Subject: The Covenant, The Sword, and The Arm of The Lord; Domestic Security/Terrorism. July 29, 1985, part I.

Memorandum, Little Rock Field Office. Subject: The Covenant, The Sword, and The Arm of The Lord; Domestic Security/Terrorism. July 2, 1987, part II.

Memorandum. Little Rock Field Office. Subject: The Covenant, The Sword, and The Arm of The Lord; Domestic Security/Terrorism. December 29, 1987.

Memorandum. Little Rock Field Office. Subject: The Covenant, The Sword, and The Arm of The Lord; Domestic Security/Terrorism. December 29, 1987, part II.

Memorandum. [Sender and Recipient redacted], Subject: The Covenant, The Sword, and The Arm of The Lord (DS/T). January 12, 1988, part II.

Memorandum. Supervisor [name redacted] to SAC (100A-4858). Subject: The Covenant, The Sword, and The Arm of The Lord; DS/T. March 29, 1985.

ERNIE LAZAR FOIA COLLECTION

AIRTEL, SAC. Los Angeles Field Office to Director, FBI (Hoover). January 14, 1964. https://archive.org/details/GaleWilliamP.HQ1/page/n1/mode/2up.

Attachment, SAC. Miami Field Office to Director, FBI (Hoover), February 26, 1964, containing National Headquarters, Christian Defense League, Membership Application Pledge. n.d. https://archive.org/details/GaleWilliamP.HQ1/page/n1/mode/2up.

"Christian Defense League." FBI date-stamped January 12, 1959. https://archive.org/details/GaleWilliamP.HQ1/page/n5/mode/2up.

GALE, William Potter HQ 1. https://archive.org/details/GaleWilliamP.HQ1/page/n1/mode/2up.

GALE, William Potter—San Diego 100-13121. https://archive.org/details/GALEWilliamPotterSanDiego01001312175pp.

GALE, William Potter = HQ 62-105253, Misc Serials. January 22, 1964. https://archive.org/details/galewilliampotterhq62105253miscserials/page/n17/mode/2up.

GALE, William Potter—Committee of the States-San Francisco 100-63097 and 100A-80325. December 22, 1984. https://archive.org/details/galewilliampottercommitteeofthestatessanfrancisco10063097and100a80325/page/n1/mode/2up.

GALE, William Potter—Committee of the States-San Francisco 100-63097 and 100A-80325. "Gale CSA 2 Memorandum." SAC, Sacramento to SAC, Indianapolis, September 12, 1986. https://archive.org/details/galewilliampottercommitteeofthestatessanfrancisco10063097and100a80325/page/n63/mode/2up.

GALE, William Potter—Ministry of Christ Church = HQ 157–28219. April 3, 1975. https://archive.org/details/galewilliampotterministryofchristchurchhq15728219/page/n1/mode/2up.

GALE, William Potter—Ministry of Christ Church = Los Angeles 157–7775. May 1, 1975. https://archive.org/details/galewilliampotterministryofchristchurchlosangeles1577775/page/n5/mode/2up.

GALE, William Potter—Ministry of Christ Church = Los Angeles 157–7775. "Manual of Christian Common Law for Christians . . . and Their Posses." n.d. https://archive.org/details/galewilliampotterministryofchristchurchlosangeles1577775/page/n3/mode/2up.

GALE, William Potter HQ 1, containing Letter, From: Director, FBI (Hoover) To: P. Kenneth O'Donnell, Special Assistant to the President. June 7, 1963. https://archive.org/details/GaleWilliamP.HQ1/page/n27/mode/2up.

GALE, William Potter—Ministry of Christ Church—HQ 157–28219 containing AIRTEL Communication, From: Special Agent-in-Charge, Los Angeles To: FBI DIRECTOR (J. Edgar Hoover). September 24, 1963. https://archive.org/details/galewilliampotterministryofchristchurchhq15728219/page/n69/mode/2.

GALE, William Potter HQ 1, HQ1 Memorandum, Miami Field Office, FBI, February 2, 1964; and, Letter, from Richard Girnt Butler, National Director to Dear Christian, January 23, 1964. https://archive.org/details/GaleWilliamP.HQ1/page/n1/mode/2up.

Gale CSA 2 Memorandum, SAC, Sacramento to SAC, Indianapolis. September 12, 1986. https://archive.org/details/gale-william-potter-hq-100-487547-100-a-80325.

GALE, William Potter HQ 1, containing "Interview with Mrs. William Potter Gale," Los Angeles FBI Field Office. January 13, 1964. https://archive.org/details/GaleWilliamP.HQ1/page/n90/mode/1up.

GALE, William Potter HQ 1. HQ1 Memorandum, Miami Field Office, FBI February 2, 1964; and, Letter, from Richard Girnt Butler, National Director to Dear Christian, January 23, 1964. Memorandum, Re: Christian Defense League, Federal Bureau of Investigation, Miami, Florida. February 3, 1964. https://archive.org/details/GaleWilliamP.HQ1/page/n1/mode/2up.

GALE, William Potter HQ 1. Containing FBI AIRTEL communication, From: SAC, San Diego To: Director, FBI. December 23, 1958. https://archive.org/details/GaleWilliamP.HQ1/page/n1/mode/2up.

HQ1. "Memorandum: WILLIAM POTTER GALE." Los Angeles Field Office. March 5, 1964. https://archive.org/details/GaleWilliamP.HQ1/page/n1/mode/2up.

HQ1. "William Potter Gale: Racial Matters," Report by SA Harry L. Griffin, Los Angeles Field Office. October 21, 1963, https://archive.org/details/GaleWilliamP.HQ1/page/n90/mode/1up.

IDENTITY GROUP, aka Ministry of Christ Church Memorandum. FBI Los Angeles Field Office. March 5, 1975. Containing Appendix: Identify Group: Characterization of Subversive Organization; Extremist Matter—White Hate Group (revised August 16, 1974). https://archive.org/details/GaleWilliamP.HQ1/page/n1/mode/2up.

Memorandum: "WILLIAM POTTER GALE." Los Angeles Field Office. July 25, 1963. https://archive.org/details/GaleWilliamP.HQ1/page/n1/mode/2up.

Memorandum, Los Angeles Field Office. Subject: WILLIAM POTTER GALE. January 22, 1964. https://archive.org/details/galewilliampotterhq62105253miscserials/page/n17/mode/2up.

Memorandum From: SAC, Los Angeles Field Office To: Director, FBI (Hoover). June 16, 1964. https://archive.org/stream/GaleWilliamP.HQ1/Gale%2C%20William%20P.-HQ-1_djvu.txt.

Memorandum, SA John C. O'Neill to U.S. Secret Service, Los Angeles; 115th INTC, Region II, Pasadena; FIO, Los Angeles; and, OSI, District 18, Maywood. October 6, 1964. https://archive.org/stream/GaleWilliamP.HQ1/Gale%2C%20William%20P.-HQ-1_djvu.txt.

"Posse Comitatus," Federal Bureau of Investigation, Sheriff's Posse Comitatus. Detroit File Number: 100A-43113. June 6, 1974. https://archive.org/details/SheriffsPosseComitatusDetroit15710687.

"The Posse Comitatus by the authority of The Constitution Of The United States." n.d. Containing Memorandum, FBI Portland [Oregon] Field Office to U.S. Attorney, Portland, et al. June 6, 1974. https://archive.org/details/SheriffsPosseComitatusDetroit15710687.

Report by SA Harry L. Griffin. Los Angeles Field Office. May 25, 1964. https://archive.org/details/GaleWilliamP.HQ1/page/n1/mode/2up.

"Sheriffs Posse Comitatus—Detroit 157–10687." Quoted in "Law of the Land." n.d. https://archive.org/details/SheriffsPosseComitatusDetroit15710687; https://archive.org/details/GaleWilliamP.HQ1/page/n1/mode/2up.

William Potter Gale, "How To Protect Yourself From The Internal Revenue Service (on your income tax)." n.d. https://archive.org/details/galewilliampotterministryofchristchurchlosangeles1577775/page/n3/mode/2up.

"William Potter Gale: Racial Matters." Report by SA Harry L. Griffin, Los Angeles Field Office. July 24, 1963. https://archive.org/details/GALEWilliamPotterSanDiego01001312175pp/page/n7/mode/2up.

"WILLIAM POTTER GALE." Los Angeles Field Office. January 13, 1964. https://archive.org/details/GaleWilliamP.HQ1/page/n1/mode/2up.

FEDERAL GOVERNMENT DOCUMENTS

18 U.S.C. § 2339A (1994) and 18 U.S.C. § 2339B (1996), https://www.law.cornell.edu/uscode/text/18/2339A.

"18 U.S.C. § 2384—U.S. Code—Unannotated Title 18. Crimes and Criminal Procedure § 2384. Seditious Conspiracy." FindLaw. https://codes.findlaw.com/us/title-18-crimes-and-criminal-procedure/18-usc-sect-2384.html.

Air Mobility Command. "Phoenix Raven." https://www.amc.af.mil/About-Us/Fact-Sheets/Display/Article/144021/phoenix-raven/.

Antiterrorism and Effective Death Penalty Act of 1996. https://www.congress.gov/bill/104th-congress/senate-bill/735.

Bureau of Alcohol, Tobacco, Firearms, and Explosives. "Brady Law." July 15, 2021. https://www.atf.gov/rules-and-regulations/brady-law.

Bureau of Counterterrorism, "Foreign Terrorist Organizations," U.S. Department of State, https://www.state.gov/foreign-terrorist-organizations/.

Central Intelligence Agency. Guide to the Analysis of Insurgency. Washington, DC: Central Intelligence Agency, 2012.

Clinton Presidential Library and Museum. "Olympic Park Bombing." https://clinton.presidentiallibraries.us/olympic-park.

Department for Digital, Culture, Media & Sport, and Home Office. *Consultation Outcome: Online Harms White Paper: Full Government Response to the Consultation*. December 15, 2020. https://www.gov.uk/government/consultations/online-harms-white-paper/outcome /online-harms-white-paper-full-government-response.

"Deposition of Jeremy Bertino." Select Committee to Investigate the January 6th Attack on the U.S. Capitol, U.S. House of Representatives. April 26, 2022. https://www.govinfo.gov /content/pkg/GPO-J6-TRANSCRIPT-CTRL0000082294/pdf/GPO-J6-TRANSCRIPT -CTRL0000082294.pdf.

Elsea, Jennifer K. *The Posse Comitatus Act and Related Matters: The Use of the Military to Execute Civilian Law*. R42659. Washington, DC: Congressional Research Service, November 6, 2018.

Federal Bureau of Investigation. "Jim Norman, Case Agent, Oklahoma City Bombing Investigation: Video Transcript." https://www.fbi.gov/video-repository/newss-jim-norman-case -agent-oklahoma-city-bombing-investigation/view.

——. "NICS Firearm Background Checks: Month/Year." https://www.fbi.gov/file-repository /nics_firearm_checks_-_month_year.pdf/view.

Federal Bureau of Investigation, Counterterrorism Threat Assessment and Warning Unit. *Terrorism in the United States 1997*. 1998.

Federal Bureau of Investigation, National Center for the Analysis of Violent Crime. "Lone Offender: A Study of Lone Offender Terrorism in the United States (1972–2015)." November 13, 2019. https://www.fbi.gov/file-repository/lone-offender-terrorism-report-111319.pdf.

Federal Bureau of Investigation, Terrorist Research and Analytical Center, Counterterrorism Section, National Security Division. *Terrorism in the United States 1994*. 1995.

Federal Bureau of Investigation, Terrorist Threat Assessment and Warning Unit, National Security Division. *Terrorism in the United States 1998*. 1999.

Federal Communications Commission. *Report*. December 26, 2018. https://docs.fcc.gove/public/attachments/FCC-18-181A1.pdf.

"Final Report: Select Committee to Investigate the January 6th Attack on the United States Capitol." 117th Congress, 2nd sess. House Report 117-663. December 22, 2022. https://www .govinfo.gov/content/pkg/GPO-J6-REPORT/pdf/GPO-J6-REPORT.pdf.

Government Communication Service. "RESIST 2: Counter-Disinformation Toolkit." 2021. https://gcs.civilservice.gov.uk/wp-content/uploads/2021/11/RESIST-2-counter-disinform ation-toolkit.pdf.

"Ko tō tātou kāinga tēnei"—Royal Commission of Inquiry Into the Terrorist Attack on Christchurch Masjidain on 15 March 2019. December 8, 2020. https://christchurchattack .royalcommission.nz/.

National Museum of African American History and Culture, Smithsonian. "Colonel William Joseph Simmons, Imperial Wizard." In *The Ku Klux Klan: Yesterday Today and Forever*. c. 1916.

National Security Council. *National Strategy for Countering Domestic Terrorism*. Washington, DC: The White House, June 2021. https://www.whitehouse.gov/wp-content/uploads /2021/06/National-Strategy-for-Countering-Domestic-Terrorism.pdf.

Office of the Director of National Intelligence. "Domestic Violent Extremism Poses Heightened Threat in 2021." March 1, 2021. https://www.dni.gov/files/ODNI/documents/assessments/UnclassSummaryofDVEAssessment-17MAR21.pdf.

Office of the Director of National Intelligence and National Intelligence Council. *Background to "Assessing Russian Activities and Intentions in Recent US Elections": The Analytic Process and Cyber Incident Attribution.* January 6, 2017. https://www.dni.gov/files/documents/ICA_2017_01.pdf.

Office of the Historian, Office of Art and Archives. "The Ku Klux Klan Act of 1871." https://history.house.gov/Historical-Highlights/1851–1900/hh_1871_04_20_KKK_Act/.

"Opening Statement of Louis J. Freeh, Director, Federal Bureau of Investigation Before the Subcommittee on Terrorism, Technology, and Government Information, Committee on the Judiciary, United States Senate, Washington, D.C." Ruby Ridge Hearing, October 19, 1995. https://fas.org/irp/congress/1995_hr/s951019f.htm#reforms%20subsequent.

"Oklahoma City Bombing." FBI History: Famous Cases & Criminals. https://www.fbi.gov/history/famous-cases/oklahoma-city-bombing.

Ronald Reagan Presidential Foundation. "President Reagan's Optimism, Courage, and Humility Remembered on 30th Anniversary of Assassination Attempt." March 28, 2011. https://www.reaganfoundation.org/media/50862/assassination-press-release.pdf.

Roth, Jeffrey A., and Koper, Christopher S. "Impacts of the 1994 Assault Weapons Ban: 1994–96." In *National Institute of Justice: Research in Brief.* Washington, DC: U.S. Department of Justice, March 1999.

Silver, James, Andre Simons, and Sara Craun. "A Study of the Pre-Attack Behaviors of Active Shooters in the United States Between 2000–2013." Federal Bureau of Investigation. 2018. https://www.fbi.gov/file-repository/pre-attack-behaviors-of-active-shooters-in-us-2000-2013.pdf.

Smith, Brent L., Kelly R. Damphousse, and Paxton Roberts. *Pre-Incident Indicators of Terrorist Incidents: The Identification of Behavioral, Geographic, and Temporary Patterns of Preparatory Conduct.* Washington, DC: Department of Justice, May 2006.

State of New Jersey, Office of the Attorney General. "Man Charged with Terroristic Threats for Allegedly Coughing on Food Store Employee and Telling Her He Has Coronavirus." March 24, 2020. https://www.nj.gov/oag/newsreleases20/pr20200324b.html.

Tina Smith for U.S. Senator for Minnesota. "Klobuchar, Bennet, Slotkin Introduce Bicameral Legislation to Strengthen Media Literacy Education and Improve Personal Cybersecurity." July 8, 2022. https://www.smith.senate.gov/klobuchar-bennet-slotkin-introduce-bicameral-legislation-to-strengthen-media-literacy-education-and-improve-personal-cybersecurity/.

U.S. Attorney's Office, District of Kansas. "Former Fort Riley Soldier Sentenced for Distributing Info on Napalm, IEDS." August 19, 2020. https://www.justice.gov/usao-ks/pr/former-fort-riley-soldier-sentenced-distributing-info-napalm-ieds.

——. "Guilty Plea: Solider at Fort Riley Described How to Make Explosive Devices." February 10, 2020. https://www.justice.gov/usao-ks/pr/guilty-plea-soldier-fort-riley-described-how-make-explosive-devices.

U.S. Attorney's Office, District of Maryland. "Christopher Hasson Facing Federal Indictment for Illegal Possession of Silencers, Possession of Firearms by a Drug Addict and Unlawful User, and Possession of a Controlled Substance." February 27, 2019. https://www.justice.gov/usao-md/pr/christopher-hasson-facing-federal-indictment-illegal-possession-silencers-possession.

——. "Federal Indictment Returned Charging Maryland Woman and Florida Man for Conspiring to Destroy Energy Facilities." February 14, 2023. https://www.justice.gov/usao-md/pr/federal-indictment-returned-charging-maryland-woman-and-florida-man-conspiring-destroy.

U.S. Attorney's Office, Northern District of Texas. "Texas Man Sentenced to 10 Years for Plotting to Attack Data Centers." October 1, 2021. https://www.justice.gov/usao-ndtx/pr/texas-man-sentenced-10-years-plotting-attack-data-centers.

U.S. Attorney's Office, Southern District of Florida. "Man Who Attempted to Provide Material Support to ISIS Sentenced to 16 Years in Federal Prison." February 2, 2022. https://www.justice.gov/usao-sdfl/pr/man-who-attempted-provide-material-support-isis-sentenced-16-years-federal-prison.

U.S. Attorney's Office, Southern District of New York. "U.S. Army Soldier Pleads Guilty to Attempting to Murder Fellow Service Members in Deadly Ambush." June 24, 2022. https://www.justice.gov/usao-sdny/pr/us-army-soldier-pleads-guilty-attempting-murder-fellow-service-members-deadly-ambush.

U.S. Department of Homeland Security. "Neo-Nazi Leader Sentenced to Five Years in Federal Prison for Explosives Charges." *Justice News*, January 9, 2018. https://www.justice.gov/opa/pr/neo-nazi-leader-sentenced-five-years-federal-prison-explosives-charges.

U.S. Department of Homeland Security. *Strategic Framework for Countering Domestic Terrorism and Targeted Violence*. Washington, DC: Department of Homeland Security, September 2019.

U.S. Department of Homeland Security and Department of Justice, Federal Bureau of Investigation. "Islamic State of Iraq and the Levant and Its Supporters Encouraging Attacks Against Law Enforcement and Government Personnel." *Joint Intelligence Bulletin*, October 11, 2014. https://www.aclu.org/sites/default/files/field_document/Email-re-JIB-ISIL-and-Its-Supporters-Encouraging-Attacks-1660-1665.pdf.

U.S. Department of Homeland Security, Center for Prevention Programs and Partnerships. "Media Literacy & Critical Thinking Online." https://www.dhs.gov/sites/default/files/publications/digital_media_literacy_0.pdf.

U.S. Department of Homeland Security, Office of Intelligence and Analysis Assessment. *Rightwing Extremism: Current Economic and Political Climate Fueling Resurgence in Radicalization and Recruitment*. IA-0257-09. April 7, 2009. https://fas.org/irp/eprint/rightwing.pdf.

U.S. Department of Justice. "#439 Oklahoma Bombing Indictment Statement: Attorney General's Statement." August 10, 1995. https://www.justice.gov/archive/opa/pr/Pre_96/August95/439.txt.html.

——. "Attorney General Merrick B. Garland Delivers Remarks at the Civil Rights Division's Virtual Program: Celebrating the Life and Legacy of Dr. Martin Luther King Jr." *Justice News*, January 13, 2022. https://www.justice.gov/opa/speech/attorney-general-merrick-b -garland-delivers-remarks-civil-rights-division-s-virtual.

——. "Eric Robert Rudolph to Plead Guilty to Serial Bombing Attacks in Atlanta and Birmingham; Will Receive Life Sentences." April 8, 2005. https://web.archive.org/web /20130414003813/http://www.justice.gov/opa/pr/2005/April/05_crm_176.htm.

——. "Kroger Shooter Sentenced to Life in Prison for Hate Crime Murders." *Justice News*, June 24, 2021. https://www.justice.gov/opa/pr/kroger-shooter-sentenced-life-prison-hate -crime-murders.

——. "Maryland Woman and Florida Man Charged Federally for Conspiring to Destroy Energy Facilities." *Justice News*, February 6, 2023. https://www.justice.gov/opa/pr /maryland-woman-and-florida-man-charged-federally-conspiring-destroy-energy -facilities.

——. "Pennsylvania Man Charged with Federal Hate Crimes for Tree of Life Synagogue Shooting." *Justice News*, October 31, 2018. https://www.justice.gov/opa/pr/pennsylvania -man-charged-federal-hate-crimes-tree-life-synagogue-shooting.

——. *Report of the Ruby Ridge Task Force to the Office of Professional Responsibility of Investigation of Allegations of Improper Governmental Conduct in the Investigation, Apprehension and Prosecution of Randall C. Weaver and Kevin L. Harris.* June 10, 1994. https://www.justice.gov/sites/default/files/opr/legacy/2006/11/09/rubyreportcover_39 .pdf.

——. "Second Member of 'Boogaloo Bois' Pleads Guilty to Conspiracy to Provide Material Support to Hamas." *Justice News*, May 4, 2021. https://www.justice.gov/opa/pr/second -member-boogaloo-bois-pleads-guilty-conspiracy-provide-material-support-hamas.

U.S. Department of Justice Archives. *Report to the Deputy Attorney General on the Events at Waco, Texas: The Aftermath of the April 19 Fire.* Updated February 14, 2018. https://www .justice.gov/archives/publications/waco/report-deputy-attorney-general-events-waco -texas-aftermath-april-19-fire.

U.S. Department of Justice, Office of Public Affairs. "Former Police Officer Sentenced for Attempting to Support ISIS." February 23, 2018. https://www.justice.gov/opa/pr/former -police-officer-sentenced-attempting-support-isis.

——. "Leader of Oath Keepers and 10 Other Individuals Indicted in Federal Court for Seditious Conspiracy and Other Offenses Related to U.S. Capitol Breach." January 13, 2022. https://www.justice.gov/opa/pr/leader-oath-keepers-and-10-other-individuals-indicted -federal-court-seditious-conspiracy-and.

——. "Two Defendants Charged with Murder and Aiding and Abetting in Slaying of Federal Protective Service Officer at Oakland Courthouse Building." June 16, 2020. https://www .justice.gov/opa/pr/two-defendants-charged-murder-and-aiding-and-abetting-slaying -federal-protective-service.

——. "U.S. Army Soldier Charged with Terrorism Offenses for Planning Deadly Ambush on Service Members in His Unit." June 22, 2020. https://www.justice.gov/opa/pr/us-army

-soldier-charged-terrorism-offenses-planning-deadly-ambush-service-members-his
-unit.

U.S. Treasury Enforcement, *Report of the Department of the Treasury on the Bureau of Alcohol, Tobacco, and Firearms Investigation of Vernon Wayne Howell Also Known as David Koresh*. Washington, DC: U.S. Government Printing Office, 1993. https://ia800209.us
.archive.org/17/items/reportofdepartmeoounit/reportofdepartmeoounit.pdf.

U.S. Department of State. "Designation of the Russian Imperial Movement: Remarks by Nathan A. Sales, Coordinator for Counterterrorism." April 6, 2020. https://2017-2021.state
.gov/designation-of-the-russian-imperial-movement/index.html.

U.S. Department of State, Office of the Historian. "The Immigration Act of 1924 (The Johnson-Reed Act)." https://history.state.gov/milestones/1921–1936/immigration-act.

INTERNATIONAL GOVERNMENTAL ORGANIZATIONS

UN Office on Drugs and Crime. "Foreign Terrorist Fighters." https://www.unodc.org/unodc
/en/terrorism/expertise/foreign-terrorist-fighters.html.

MANIFESTOS AND OTHER MATERIALS

"1996 ARYAN NATIONAL CONGRESS, JULY 19, 20 & 21ST, 1996." Handbill. https://www
.amazon.com/NEWSLETTER-LITERATURE-COLLECTION-NEWSLETTERS
-OUTREACH/dp/B008EAWLLY.

Aryan Nations. "Yesterday: the Tribes of Israel; Today: the Aryan Nations." n.d.

Atomwaffen Division (AWD). Program. n.d.

Balliet, Stephan. Manifesto. Provided to the authors by International Centre for the Study of Radicalisation and Political Violence, King's College London.

Beam, Louis. "Forget? Hell No!" Essays of a Klansman. 1983.

——. "Leaderless Resistance." *The Seditionist* 12, final ed. (February 1992). http://www
.louisbeam.com/sedition.htm.

——. "Louis Beam's Estes Park, Colorado Speech." http:www.louisbeam.com/estes.htm.

Berwick, Andrew. "2083: A European Declaration of Independence." 2011. https://www
.researchgate.net/publication/279868578_2083_-_A_European_Declaration_of
Independence-_An_Analysis_of_Discourses_from_the_Extreme.

Church of Jesus Christ Christian. "The Ministry of Dr. Wesley A. Swift." http://www
.kingidentity.com/cjc.html.

——. *The Way: A Prison Outreach Newsletter by the Church of Jesus Christ Christian* 1 (June 1987).

Crusius, Patrick. "The Inconvenient Truth." August 2019.

" 'Dear Tracy'—by Mass Killer Timothy McVeigh." *Guardian*, May 5, 2001.

"Dr Duke & Mark Collett of UK Explode the ZioMedia induced Myths of Covid and the Zio-stablishment devastating Reponses to False Covid Idol it created!" davidduke.com. February 26, 2021.

Earnest, John. "An Open Letter," April 2019.

Gayman, Dan. *The Two Seeds of Genesis 3:15.* n.p., n.d. [1977]. Rev. ed., 1994.

Gendron, Payton. "What You Need to Know." May 2022.

"Gordon Kahl Letter." http://www.outpost-of-freedom.com/kahl01.htm.

"Its a Revolution—My Name Is Elizabeth, I'm from Knoxville Tennessee." YouTube video, https://youtube.com/shorts/H-btEQ9PWWM.

"Letter from Timothy McVeigh to the Union-Sun & Journal. February 11, 1992." CNN Interactive: Oklahoma City Tragedy. https://web.archive.org/web/20080119111020/http://www.cnn.com/US/OKC/faces/Suspects/McVeigh/1st-letter6-15/index.html.

Letter, McVeigh to Papovich, n.d.. Quoted in Tracy McVeigh, "The McVeigh Letters: Why I Bombed Oklahoma," *Observer Life Magazine*, May 3, 2001.

Masker, Roy B. "An All White Nation? Why Not?" *Calling Our Nation* 53 (n.d.): 23.

Mason, James. *Articles and Interviews.* 3rd ed. Dark Foreigner, 2018.

———. *Siege.* Digital ed., rev. 1. ironmarch.org, June 2, 2015.

"McVeigh's Apr. 26 Letter to Fox News." *Fox News*, January 13, 2015. https://www.foxnews.com/story/mcveighs-apr-26-letter-to-fox-news.

Miller, Frazier Glenn. Letter. "Declaration of War, April 6, 1987." *Springfield News Leader*, April 14, 2014. https://www.news-leader.com/story/news/local/ozarks/2014/04/14/archive-april-6-1987-letter-from-frazier-glenn-miller/7708641/.

Miller, Glenn. *A White Man Speaks Out; The former leader of the largest active White Rights Group in the United States, Speaks out for White America.* 1999.

"National Socialist Order Program." n.d.

"Robert Jay Mathews' Last Letter." http://www.mourningtheancient.com/mathews3bb.htm

Rudolph, Eric. *Between the Lines of Drift: The Memoirs of a Militant.* 3rd ed. Army of God, 2015.

Tarrant, Brenton. *The Great Replacement.* March 15, 2019. https://nex24.news/2019/03/the-great-replacement-by-brenton-tarrant/.

Tate, David. "MORE INFIGHTING? WHAT'S WRONG WITH YOU?! Another Scolding by David C. Tate." *Gary Yarbrough's Blog*, December 18, 2019. https://susan1219.wordpress.com/tag/david-tate/.

Taylor, Jared. "Is Trump Our Last Chance?" *American Resistance*, August 21, 2015. https://www.amren.com/features/2015/08/is-trump-our-last-chance/.

"This Is Aryan Nations." Brochure distributed by the Aryan Nations, n.d.

"To Our Kinsmen." Open letter from Reverend Richard G. Butler, Aryan Nations. n.d.

"To Our New People." Open letter from Reverend Richard G. Butler, Aryan Nations. n.d.

Triumph of the Will. Dir. Leni Riefenstahl (1935; Reichsparteitag-Film), https://www.imdb.com/title/tt0025913/.

Virginia Oathkeepers (VAOK). n.d. https://virginiaoathkeepers.org/.

White Patriot: Worldwide Voice of the Aryan People—This Is the Klan! Tuscumbia, AL: Patriot Press, no date. https://www.biblio.com/book/white-patriot-worldwide-voice-aryan-people/d/1360232328.

STATE AND MUNICIPAL ARCHIVES AND OFFICIAL DOCUMENTS

"Boundary County, Idaho Population, 2023." https://worldpopulationreview.com/us-counties /id/boundary-county-population.

Ellsworth, Scott. "Tulsa Race Massacre." Oklahoma Historical Society. https://www.okhistory .org/publications/enc/entry.php?entry=TU013.

"The Fork in the Road." *April 19, 1995 9:02 a.m.: The Historical Record of the Oklahoma City Bombing Compiled by Oklahoma Today.* Vol. 46, no. 1 (Winter 1996).

Hines, Sgt. Allen D. "Trooper Jimmie E. 'Jim' Linegar, Badge #865, EOW . . . April 15, 1985." Missouri State Highway Patrol. https://www.mshp.dps.missouri.gov/MSHPWeb /UltimateSacrifice/OfficerPages/documents/Linegar.pdf.

Missouri State Highway Patrol. "Trooper Jimmie E. Linegar—Badge #865." https://www.mshp .dps.missouri.gov/MSHPWeb/UltimateSacrifice/OfficerPages/trooperJimmieLinegar.html.

T-shirt worn by McVeigh on April 19, 1995, with accompanying mug shot (#95 057). Oklahoma City Memorial and Museum, 620 N Harvey Avenue, Oklahoma City. Photograph taken by one of the authors on August 14, 2016.

"The Twentieth Century Ku Klux Klan in Alabama." Alabama Moments in American History. http://www.alabamamoments.alabama.gov/sec46det.html.

Washington State Legislature, House of Representatives. House of Representatives Investigation Report Regarding Re. Matt Shea. December 1, 2019. https://leg.wa.gov/House /InvestigationReport/Pages/default.aspx.

Wilmington Police Department. "Professional Standards Internal Investigation." June 11, 2020. https://www.wilmingtonnc.gov/home/showdocument?id=12012.

MEMOIRS

"Arno Michaelis on Rejecting His Racist Past, and the Role of Unconditional Forgiveness in Creating a Life After Hate." Forgiveness Project, December 22, 2021. https://www .theforgivenessproject.com/arno-michaelis-on-rejecting-his-racist-past-and-the-role-of -unconditional-forgiveness-in-creating-a-life-after-hate/.

Buford, Bill. *Among The Thugs.* New York: Vintage, 1993.

Coulson, Danny O., and Elaine Shannon. *No Heroes: Inside the FBI's Secret Counter-Terror Force.* New York: Pocket, 1999.

Manis, Wayne F. *The Street Agent: After Taking on the Mob, the Klan, and the Aryan Nations, He Walks Softly and Carries a .357 Magnum—the True Story.* Palisades, NY: History Publishing, 2014.

Martinez, Thomas, with John Guinther. *Brotherhood of Murder: How One Man's Journey Through Fear Brought the Order—the Most Dangerous Racist Gang in America—to Justice.* New York: McGraw-Hill, 1988.

Noble, Kerry. *Tabernacle of Hate.* Prescott, Ontario: Voyageur, 1998.

Orsini, Alessandro. *Sacrifice: My Life in a Fascist Militia.* Ithaca, NY: Cornell University Press, 2017.

Picciolini, Christian. *White American Youth: My Descent Into America's Most Violent Hate Movement—and How I Got Out.* New York: Hachette, 2017.

Revell, Oliver "Buck," and Dwight Williams. *A G-Man's Journal.* New York: Pocket, 1998.

MISCELLANEOUS

Email correspondence with Dr. Seth Carus, an expert on biological and chemical weapons, at the National Defense University, Washington, DC, October 5, 2020.

Lake, Peter. "Neo-Nazi Terrorism in the United States." Notes from a discussion held at the RAND Corporation, Santa Monica, California, September 8, 1986.

SITE INTELLIGENCE GROUP SOCIAL MEDIA DOCUMENTS

"Accelerationist Neo-Nazi Propagandists Celebrate Buffalo Shooter as 'Saint.'" May 31, 2022. https://ent.siteintelgroup.com/Far-Right-/-Far-Left-Threat/accelerationist-neo-nazi -propagandists-celebrate-buffalo-shooter-as-saint.html.

"Accelerationist Neo-Nazis Threaten Journalists Following Media Reports of Health Organization Data Leak." April 22, 2020. https://ent.siteintelgroup.com/Far-Right-/-Far-Left -Threat/accelerationist-neo-nazis-threaten-journalists-following-media-reports-of -health-organization-data-leak.html.

"'All Kinds of Riots Are Coming': Prominent White Nationalist Threatens Amid Michigan Anti-Lockdown Protests." May 1, 2020. https://ent.siteintelgroup.com/Far-Right-Far-Left -Threat/all-kinds-of-riots-are-coming-prominent-white-nationalist-threatens-amid -michigan-anti-lockdown-protests.html.

"Announcement of New Gun Legislation Sparks Threats Against Participating Senators." June 14, 2022. https://ent.siteintelgroup.com/Far-Right-Far-Left-Threat/threats-against -traitorous-senators-made-following-announcement-of-new-gun-legislation.html.

"Announcement That US Will Accept More Refugees Infuriates White Supremacists." September 21, 2015. https://ent.siteintelgroup.com/Far-Right-Far-Left-Threat/announcement -that-us-will-accept-more-refugees-infuriates-white-supremacists.html.

"Criticizing Buffalo Shooter, Accelerationist Neo-Nazis Incite Attacks on American Jews." June 2, 2022. https://ent.siteintelgroup.com/Far-Right-Far-Left-Threat/criticizing-buffalo -shooter-accelerationist-neo-nazis-incite-attacks-on-american-jews.html.

"Exploiting Chaos of Riots, Prominent Neo-Nazi Group Calls for Attacks Against Black Protestors." June 2, 2020. https://ent.siteintelgroup.com/Far-Right-Far-Left-Threat/exploiting -chaos-of-riots-prominent-neo-nazi-group-calls-for-attacks-against-black-protesters .html.

"Facebook Profile of Alleged Oregonian Murderer Praises Timothy McVeigh, Wishes Violence on Hillary Clinton." May 28, 2017. https://ent.siteintelgroup.com/Far-Right-/-Far-Left -Threat/facebook-profile-of-alleged-oregonian-murderer-praises-timothy-mcveigh -wishes-violence-on-hillary-clinton.html.

"Far-Right Chat Group Showed Disappointment in El Paso Shooter for Not Killing 'High-Value Targets.'" August 5, 2019. https://ent.siteintelgroup.com/Far-Right-/-Far-Left-Threat/far -right-chat-group-showed-disappointment-in-el-paso-shooter-for-not-killing-high -value-targets.html.

"Far-Right Forum Suggests First Targeting Police When the Supposed 'Bloody Uprising' Comes." July 1, 2019. https://ent.siteintelgroup.com/Far-Right-Far-Left-Threat/far-right -forum-suggests-first-targeting-police-when-the-supposed-bloody-uprising-comes .html.

"Far-Right Promotes Infiltration Tactics to Subvert BLM Protests." June 2, 2020. https://ent .siteintelgroup.com/Far-Right-Far-Left-Threat/far-right-promotes-infiltration-tactics-to -subvert-blm-protests.html.

"Far-Right Users Discuss Article Labeling Far-Right Ideology as Main Threat at Protests." July 17, 2020. https://ent.siteintelgroup.com/Far-Right-Far-Left-Threat/far-right-users -discuss-article-labeling-far-right-ideology-as-main-threat-at-protests.html.

"Forum Members Brace for Confrontation at Bundy Ranch." April 11, 2014. https://ent .siteintelgroup.com/Far-Right-Far-Left-Threat/forum-members-brace-for-confrontation -at-bundy-ranch.html.

"Glenn Miller: Prominent Member of Neo-Nazi Forum." April 14, 2014. https://ent .siteintelgroup.com/Far-Right-Far-Left-Threat/glenn-miller-prominent-member-of-neo -nazi-forum.html.

"Hammerskins Denigrate President Obama, Lament His Re-election." November 7, 2012. https://ent.siteintelgroup.com/Jihadist-News/hammerskins-denigrate-president-obama -lament-his-re-election.html.

"InSITE: Violence on Forum Linked to JCC Shooter." April 18, 2014. https://ent.siteintelgro up.com/Far-Right-/-Far-Left-Threat/insite-violence-on-forum-linked-to-jcc-shooter .html.

"'Let the Race War Commence': Far-Right Community Outraged by 'Martyr' Chauvin's Guilty Verdict in Murder of George Floyd." April 20, 2021. https://ent.siteintelgroup.com/Far -Right-/-Far-Left-Threat/let-the-race-war-commence-far-right-community-outraged-by -martyr-chauvin-s-guilty-verdict-in-murder-of-george-floyd.html.

"Militia Blog Claims That Without Action, 'The Trumpening' Will Be Wasted." December 9, 2016. https://ent.siteintelgroup.com/Far-Right-Far-Left-Threat/militia-blog-claims-that -without-action-the-trumpening-will-be-wasted.html.

"Missouri Neo-Nazi Connected to Hospital Bomb Plot Discussed Attacking Infrastructure, Weaponizing Coronavirus in Chat Groups." March 26, 2020. https://ent.siteintelgroup.com /Far-Right-/-Far-Left-Threat/timothy-wilson-coronavirus.html.

"Neo-Nazi Accelerationists Call for Monthly Attacks on Anniversary of Buffalo Shooting." May 16, 2022. https://ent.siteintelgroup.com/Far-Right-/-Far-Left-Threat/neo-nazi-ac celerationists-call-for-monthly-attacks-on-anniversary-of-buffalo-shooting.html.

"Neo-Nazi Group with History of Violent Incitements Targets Political Enemies, Law Enforce- ment in Latest Propaganda." April 27, 2020. https://ent.siteintelgroup.com/Far-Right-/ -Far-Left-Threat/neo-nazi-group-with-history-of-violent-incitements-targets-federal -law-enforcement-in-latest-propaganda.html.

"Neo-Nazi Telegram Channel Offers Alternative to Mass Shooting Strategy, Including Violence Against 'High-Profile' Targets." March 18, 2020. https://ent.siteintelgroup.com/Far-Right-/-Far-Left-Threat/neo-nazi-telegram-channel-offers-alternative-to-mass-shooting-strategy-including-violence-against-high-profile-targets.html.

"Neo-Nazi Venue Posits Statements from President as Call for Violent Action, Encourages Attacks on State Politicians." April 27, 2020. https://ent.siteintelgroup.com/Far-Right-Far-Left-Threat/praising-president-s-support-of-quarantine-protests-as-call-to-action-neo-nazi-venue-encourages-attacks-on-state-politicians.html.

"Neo-Nazi Venues Suggest Followers Avoid Lockdown Protests, Encourage Alternative Methods of 'Stoking Tensions.'" May 5, 2020. https://ent.siteintelgroup.com/Far-Right-Far-Left-Threat/neo-nazi-venues-suggest-followers-avoid-lockdown-protests-encourage-alternative-methods-of-stoking-tensions.html

"Neo-Nazis Celebrate JCC Shooting in Kansas." April 14, 2014. https://ent.siteintelgroup.com/Far-Right-Far-Left-Threat/neo-nazis-celebrate-jcc-shooting-respond-to-claims-that-forum-member-is-responsible.html.

"Neo-Nazis Continue Calls for Monthly Violent Attacks on Anniversary of Buffalo Shooting." June 15, 2022. https://ent.siteintelgroup.com/Far-Right-Far-Left-Threat/neo-nazis-continue-calls-for-monthly-violent-attacks-on-anniversary-of-buffalo-shooting.html.

"O9A Ideology at Core of 'RapeWaffen' Group Implicated in Recent Neo-Nazi Terrorist Plot." June 24, 2020. https://ent.siteintelgroup.com/Far-Right-/-Far-Left-Threat/o9a-ideology-at-core-of-rapewaffen-group-implicated-in-recent-neo-nazi-terrorist-plot.html.

"Overland Park Shooter a Supporter of Anders Breivik and Utoya Massacre." April 14, 2014. https://ent.siteintelgroup.com/Far-Right-Far-Left-Threat/overland-park-shooter-a-supporter-of-anders-breivik-and-utoya-massacre.html.

"Praising Accelerationism, Neo-Nazis Call for Sniper Attacks Targeting 'Elites.'" April 24, 2020. https://ent.siteintelgroup.com/Far-Right-Far-Left-Threat/praising-accelerationism-neo-nazis-call-for-sniper-attacks-targeting-elites.html.

"Prominent Neo-Nazi Proclaims Wade Michael Page Was Heroic." August 8, 2012. https://ent.siteintelgroup.com/Far-Right-/-Far-Left-Threat/prominent-neo-nazi-proclaims-wade-michael-page-was-heroic.html.

"Racialists Begin Discussing Homemade Weaponry." April 7, 2015. https://ent.siteintelgroup.com/Far-Right-/-Far-Left-Threat/racialists-begin-discussing-homemade-weaponry.html.

"Recent Hate Attacks Celebrated by Neo-Nazis Marking Buffalo Shooting's Month Anniversary." June 17, 2022. https://ent.siteintelgroup.com/Far-Right-/-Far-Left-Threat/recent-hate-attacks-celebrated-by-neo-nazis-marking-buffalo-shooting-s-month-anniversary.html.

"'Saint Kyle Walks': Emboldened by Rittenhouse Acquittal, Far Right Urges Whites to 'Fight Harder.'" November 19, 2021. https://ent.siteintelgroup.com/Far-Right-Far-Left-Threat/saint-kyle-walks-emboldened-by-rittenhouse-acquittal-far-right-urges-whites-to-fight-harder.html.

"Senator Susan Collins Targeted After Saying She'll Vote to Confirm Ketanji Brown Jackson." March 30, 2022. https://ent.siteintelgroup.com/Far-Right-/-Far-Left-Threat/senator-susan-collins-targeted-after-saying-she-ll-vote-to-confirm-ketanji-brown-jackson.html.

"Skinhead Forum Responds to Overland Parks Shooting." April 16, 2014. https://ent
.siteintelgroup.com/Far-Right-/-Far-Left-Threat/skinhead-forum-responds-to-overland
-parks-shooting.html.

"Skinheads Discuss Second American Revolution." April 8, 2016. https://ent.siteintelgroup.com
/Far-Right-Far-Left-Threat/skinheads-discuss-second-american-revolution.html.

"Syrian Refugees Being Sent to Idaho Angers White Supremacists." July 31, 2015. https://ent
.siteintelgroup.com/Far-Right-/-Far-Left-Threat/syrian-refugees-being-sent-to-idaho
-angers-white-supremacists.html.

"'This Man Is Epic': Far-Right Praises Kenosha Protest Shooter." August 26, 2020. https://ent
.siteintelgroup.com/Far-Right-/-Far-Left-Threat/this-man-is-epic-far-right-praises
-kenosha-protest-shooter.html.

"UPDATE: As More Suspicious Devices Addressed to Various Figures Appear, White Supremacists Persist in Deflection." October 25, 2018. https://ent.siteintelgroup.com/Far-Right-/
-Far-Left-Threat/update-as-more-suspicious-devices-addressed-to-various-figures
-appear-white-supremacists-persist-in-deflection.html.

"UPDATE: In Wake of New 'Suspicious Devices' Sent to Targets, White Supremacists Continue Celebrating Attempt on George Soros." October 24, 2018. https://ent.siteintelgroup
.com/Far-Right-Far-Left-Threat/update-in-wake-of-new-suspicious-devices-sent-to
-targets-white-supremacists-continue-celebrating-attempt-on-george-soros.html.

"Violent Threats Made Against Arizona Attorney General After Accusations of Targeting
'Patriots.'" May 17, 2022. https://ent.siteintelgroup.com/Far-Right-/-Far-Left-Threat/violent
-threats-made-against-arizona-attorney-general-after-accusations-of-targeting-patriots
.html.

"White Supremacists and Neo-Nazis Celebrate Violence at Trump Rally." November 23, 2015.
https://ent.siteintelgroup.com/Far-Right-Far-Left-Threat/white-supremacists-and-neo
-nazis-celebrate-violence-at-trump-rally.html.

"White Supremacists Applaud Trump Presidential Victory, Call It a Win for 'Nationalism.'" November 9, 2016. https://ent.siteintelgroup.com/Far-Right-Far-Left-Threat/wh
ite-supremacists-applaud-trump-presidential-victory-call-it-a-win-for-nationalism
.html.

"White Supremacists Concerned Sikh Temple Massacre Looks Badly on Them." August 6, 2012.
https://ent.siteintelgroup.com/Far-Right-/-Far-Left-Threat/white-supremacists
-concerned-sikh-temple-massacre-looks-badly-on-them.html.

"White Supremacists Encourage Continued Violence Against Officials." January 20, 2011.
https://ent.siteintelgroup.com/Far-Right-/-Far-Left-Threat/white-supremacists-debate
-whether-to-have-a-second-unite-the-right-rally-some-suggesting-shedding-nazi
-imagery.html.

"White Supremacists Hail Finicum as Hero, Speculate Assassination." January 27, 2016. https://
ent.siteintelgroup.com/Far-Right-Far-Left-Threat/white-supremacists-hail-finnicum-as
-hero-speculate-assassination.html.

"White Supremacists Laud the Presidential Appointments of Reince Priebus and Stephen K.
Bannon." November 14, 2016. https://ent.siteintelgroup.com/Far-Right-/-Far-Left-Threat/
white-supremacists-laud-the-presidential-appointments-of-reince-priebus-and-stephen-k-
bannon.html.

"White Supremacists: Merkel 'Should Be Hung' Following Reiteration of Refugee Stance." December 14, 2015. https://ent.siteintelgroup.com/Far-Right-Far-Left-Threat/white -supremacists-merkel-should-be-hung-following-reiteration-of-refugee-stance.html.

"White Supremacists Revitalized by President Trump's Additional Comments Regarding Charlottesville." August 16, 2017. https://ent.siteintelgroup.com/Far-Right-Far-Left-Threat /white-supremacists-revitalized-by-president-trump-s-additional-comments-regarding -charlottesville.html.

"White Supremacists Support Standoff in Burns, Oregon." January 3, 2016. https://ent .siteintelgroup.com/Far-Right-Far-Left-Threat/white-supremacists-support-standoff-in- burns-oregon.html.

"White Supremacists Urge to Use Facebook to 'Awaken' Whites." April 8, 2013. https://ent .siteintelgroup.com/Far-Right-Far-Left-Threat/white-supremacists-urge-to-use -facebook-to-awaken-whites.html.

"White Supremacists Wish for Deaths of Chancellor Merkel and German Politicians." November 25, 2015. https://ent.siteintelgroup.com/Far-Right-Far-Left-Threat/white-supremacists -wish-for-deaths-of-chancellor-merkel-and-german-politicians.html.

SOCIAL MEDIA

"Anonymous." May 2, 2020. 4Chan discussion thread accessed by the author, June 26, 2020.

baeldraca. "Banning the O9A." Order of 9 Angles. March 2, 2020. http:www.o9a.org/http:www .o9a.org/2020/03/banning-the-o9a/.

——. "The O9A: Beyond Nihilism and Anarchism." Order of 9 Angles. April 20, 2002; accessed via "Concerning Propagandists in the Age of the Internet," Order of 9 Angles, n.d., http:www.o9a.org/propagandists-on-the-internet.

——. "The O9A, National Socialism, and Nihilism." Order of 9 Angles. April 4, 2020. http:www .o9a.org/2020/04/the-o9a-national-socialism-and-nihilism/ accessed on May 2, 2020.

"Revealing the Hidden o9A." n.d. http://www.o9a.org/the-hidden-o9A/.

Rosen, Guy, and Monika Bickert. "Our Response to the Violence in Washington." Facebook. January 6, 2021. https://about.fb.com/news/2021/01/responding-to-the-violence-in -washington-dc/.

"Two Types of Satanism." Order of 9 Angles. n.d. http:www.o9a.org/the-two-types-of -satanism/ accessed May 2, 2020.

SECONDARY SOURCES

BOOKS, SCHOLARLY JOURNALS, NEWSPAPERS, MAGAZINES, AND ONLINE PUBLICATIONS

Aho, James. "Christian Fundamentalism and Militia Movements in the United States." In *The Making of a Terrorist: Recruitment, Training, and Root Causes*, vol. 1: *Recruitment*, ed. James Forest. Westport, CT: Praeger, 2006.

——. *The Politics of Righteousness: Idaho Christian Patriotism*. Seattle: University of Washington Press, 2014.

Albrecht, Mike. "Neighbors Remember Events of Shoot-out." *Bismarck Tribune*, February 9, 2003. https://bismarcktribune.com/news/local/neighbors-remember-events-of-shoot-out/article_e0ab237e-d51f-521c-b0c6–365a438310e4.html.

Alcoke, Matthew. "The Evolving and Persistent Terrorism Threat to the Homeland." Washington Institute, November 19, 2019. https://www.washingtoninstitute.org/policy-analysis/view/the-evolving-and-persistent-terrorism-threat-to-the-homeland.

"Alexandre Bissonnette Searched Online for Trump More Than 800 Times Before Killing Six Men at Mosque." *National Observer*, April 16, 2018. https://www.nationalobserver.com/2018/04/16/news/alexandre-bissonnette-searched-online-trump-more-800-times-killing-six-men-mosque.

Altman, Howard. "How to Spot Neo-Nazis in the Military? Brandon Russell Case Shows How Hard It Is." *Tampa Bay Times*, June 4, 2018.

Anderson, James H., Hans Butzer, and Charles Robert Goins. "Bombing of the Alfred P. Murrah Federal Building, 1995." In *Historical Atlas of Oklahoma*, ed. Danney Goble. Norman: University of Oklahoma Press, 2006.

Anderson, Sean, and Stephen Sloan. *Historical Dictionary of Terrorism*. Metuchen, NJ: Scarecrow, 1995.

Ang, Desmond. "Birth of a Nation: Media and Racial Hate." Faculty Research Working Paper Series, RWP20-038, November 2020. Harvard Kennedy School, Cambridge, MA. .https://scholar.harvard.edu/ang/publications/birth-nation-media-and-racial-hate

Anti-Defamation League (ADL). "ADL Releases Backgrounder on White Supremacist Kansas Shooter Frazier Glenn Miller." April 14, 2014. https://www.adl.org/news/press-releases/adl-releases-backgrounder-on-white-supremacist-kansas-jewish-community-shooter.

——. "ADL Report Focused on Militia Movement Six Months Before Oklahoma." *ADL on the Frontline: A Monthly Newsletter*, May/June 1995. https://www.adl.org/sites/default/files/on-the-frontline-may-june-1995.pdf.

——. *Armed and Dangerous: Militias Take Aim at the Federal Government*. New York: Anti-Defamation League, 1994.

——. "Aryan Nations/Church of Jesus Christ Christian." https://www.adl.org/education/resources/profiles/aryan-nations.

——. "Burning Cross." https://www.adl.org/education/references/hate-symbols/burning-cross.

——. *The Literature of Apocalypse: Far-Right Voices of Violence*. New York: ADL, Civil Rights Division, Research and Evaluation Department, 1996.

——. "Backgrounder: Eric Robert Rudolph," June 5, 2003, https://www.adl.org/resources/backgrounders/backgrounder-eric-robert-rudolph.

——. "Christian Identity." n.d. https://www.adl.org/resources/backgrounders/christian-identity.

——. *Computerized Networks of Hate: An ADL Fact Finding Report*. New York: Anti-Defamation League of B'nai B'rith, 1984. https://archive.org/details/Computeri-zedNetworksOfHate/mode/2up.

——. *A Dark and Constant Rage: Twenty-Five Years of Right-Wing Terrorism in the United States*. New York: Anti-Defamation League, 2017.

——. "Day of the Rope." https://www.adl.org/resources/hate-symbol/day-rope.

——. "David Duke: In His Own Words." January 3, 2013, https://www.adl.org/news/article/david-duke-in-his-own-words.

——. *Explosion of Hate: The Growing Danger of the National Alliance*. New York: Anti-Defamation League, 2000. https://www.adl.org/sites/default/files/documents/assets/pdf/combating-hate/Explosion-of-Hate.pdf.

——. *Extremism on the Right: A Handbook*. New York: Anti-Defamation League, 1983.

——. *Extremism on the Right: A Handbook*. New rev. ed. New York: Anti-Defamation League of B'nai B'rith, 1988.

——. "Gunman Who Targeted FBI a Radicalized Trump Supporter, Saw Mar-a-Lago Search as Call to Arms." August 11, 2022, https://www.adl.org/resources/blog/gunman-who-targeted-fbi-radicalized-trump-supporter-saw-mar-lago-search-call-arms.

——. *Hate Groups in America: A Record of Bigotry and Violence*. New York: Anti-Defamation League, 1982.

——. *The Militia Movement*. 2001. https://www.adl.org/education/resources/backgrounders/militia-movement.

——. "Murder and Extremism in the United States, 2021." https://www.adl.org/murder-and-extremism-2021.

——. *The Oath Keepers Data Leak: Unmasking Extremism in Public Life*. September 6, 2022. https://www.adl.org/resources/report/oath-keepers-data-leak-unmasking-extremism-public-life.

——. "Our Mission | ADL: Fighting Hate for Good." https://www.adl.org/who-we-are/our-mission.

——. "Remembering Leo Frank," August 12, 2015. https://www.adl.org/resources/backgrounders/remembering-leo-frank.

——. "Stand Off Against the Government—New Book Examines the Defiance of Armed Citizens." June 10, 1996. https://www.adl.org/sites/default/files/press-releases-1995-1998-re-okc-bombing-militia-mvt.pdf.

——. *The People v. Leo Frank Teacher's Guide*. New York: Anti-Defamation League, 2009. https://www.adl.org/sites/default/files/people-v-leo-frank-teachers-guide-the.pdf.

——. "U.S. Anti-Semitic Incidents Spike 86 Percent So Far in 2017 After Surging Last Year, ADL Finds." April 24, 2017. https://www.adl.org/news/press-releases/us-anti-semitic-incidents-spike-86-percent-so-far-in-2017.

——. "U.S. Army Specialist with Links to Neo-Nazi Group Pleads Guilty." February 11, 2020. https://www.adl.org/resources/blog/us-army-specialist-links-neo-nazi-group-pleads-guilty.

"'Anti-Government' Killers Put Swastika, Flag on Metro Police Officer's Body." *Las Vegas Sun*, June 9, 2014. https://lasvegassun.com/news/2014/jun/09/police-describe-bloodbath-created-neo-nazi-couple-/.

Applebome, Peter. "So, You Want to Hold an Olympics." *New York Times*, August 4, 1996.

Ardern, Jacinda. "How to Stop the Next Christchurch Massacre." *New York Times*, May 11, 2019.

Armond, Paul de. "The Law Applied." *Albion Monitor*, April 15, 1996. http://www.albionmonitor .com/freemen/ci-view.html.

——. "Leaderless Resistance: The Two-Pronged Movement Consolidates Under Identity." *Public Good*, June 1997. http://www.nwcitizen.com/publicgood.

Associated Press. "18 Months in Jail for Supremacist." *New York Times*, October 19, 1993.

——. "Fugitive's Friend Gives Up in Idaho." *New York Times*, August 31, 1992.

——. "Man Arrested for Bank Robbery on FBI Fugitives List." February 20, 1987.

——. "Man Arrested in Vandalism of Jewish Businesses." November 14, 1987.

——. "McVeigh Aimed to Spark Revolt, Ex-Buddy Says." *International Herald Tribune* (Paris), May 13, 1997.

——. "N.A.A.C.P. Bombings Linked to a Wider Plot, F.B.I. Says." *New York Times*, July 30, 1993.

——. "Posse Comitatus Leader, Six Associates, Held Without Bond." October 30, 1986.

——. "Suspect in Bank Robberies One of FBI's Most Wanted." *Los Angeles Times*, November 30, 1986.

——. "Ten Members of the Order Convicted: Neo-Nazis Guilty of Racketeering, Armored-Car Robberies." *Los Angeles Times*, December 31. 1985.

——. "A Timeline of the Ruby Ridge Standoff and Its Fallout." August 22, 1997.

——. "Slaying Suspect Tate Seized in Missouri Hills." *Los Angeles Times*, April 21, 1995.

——. "Thirteen Supremacists Are Not Guilty of Conspiracies." *New York Times*, April 8, 1988.

——. "US McVeigh Lawyer: Interview with Stephen Jones, McVeigh Former Lawyer." May 6, 2001.

——. "Utah Radio Station Cancels 'Aryan Nations Hour.'" *New York Times*, December 17, 1987.

Atkins, Stephen E. *Encyclopedia of Right-Wing Extremism in Modern American History*. Santa Barbara, CA: ABC-CLIO, 2011.

"Atlanta 1996 Olympic Games." *Encyclopedia Britannica*. https://www.britannica.com/event /Atlanta-1996-Olympic-Games.

Atlantic Council's DFRLab. "#StopTheSteal: Timeline of Social Media and Extremist Activities Leading to 1/6 Insurrection." *Just Security*, February 10, 2021. https://www.justsecurity .org/74622/stopthesteal-timeline-of-social-media-and-extremist-activities-leading-to-1 -6-insurrection/.

Audsley, David. "Posse Comitatus: An Extremist Tax Protest Group." *TVI: Terrorism, Violence Insurgency Journal* 6, no. 1 (Summer 1985).

Austin-Hillery, Nicole, and Victoria Strang. "Racism's Prominent Role in January 6 US Capitol Attack." *Human Rights Watch*, January 5, 2022. https://www.hrw.org/news/2022/01/05 /racisms-prominent-role-january-6-us-capitol-attack.

Balleck, Barry J. *Modern American Extremism and Domestic Terrorism: An Encyclopedia of Extremist Groups*. Santa Barbara, CA: ABC-CLIO, 2018.

Balz, Dan, Scott Clement, and Emily Guskin. "Republicans and Democrats Divided Over Jan. 6 Insurrection and Trump's Culpability, Post-UMD Poll Finds." *Washington Post*, January 2, 2022.

Barkun, Michael. *Religion and the Racist Right*. Chapel Hill: University of North Carolina Press, 1997.

Barrett, Devlin, Spencer S. Hsu, and Matt Zapotosky. "FBI Focuses on Whether Some Capitol Rioters Intended to Harm Lawmakers." *Washington Post*, January 8, 2021.

Barrett, Devlin, and Matt Zapotosky. "FBI Report Warned of 'War' at Capitol, Contradicting Claims There Was No Indication of Looming Violence." *Washington Post*, January 12, 2021.

Barrouquere, Brett. "Three Nevada 'Boogaloo Bois' Arrested by FBI in Plot." Southern Poverty Law Center, June 9, 2020. https://www.splcenter.org/hatewatch/2020/06/09/three -nevada-boogaloo-bois-arrested-fbi-firebombing-plot.

——. "White Separatist Gary Lee Yarbrough, One-Time Security Chief for the Order, Dies in Federal Prison." Southern Poverty Law Center, April 2, 2018. https://www.splcenter.org /hatewatch/2018/04/02/white-separatist-gary-lee-yarbrough-one-time-security-chief -order-dies-federal-prison.

Barry, Dan, and Sheera Frenkel. "'Be There. Will Be Wild!': Trump All but Circled the Date." *New York Times*, January 6, 2021.

Barstow, David. "Tea Party Lights Fuse for Rebellion on Right." *New York Times*, February 15, 2010.

Bauer, Laura, Dave Helling, and Brian Burnes. "Man with History of Anti-Semitism Jailed in Fatal Shooting of Three at Johnson County Jewish Centers." *Kansas City Star*, May 16, 2014.

Beauchamp, Zack. "Accelerationism: The Obscure Idea Inspiring White Supremacist Killers Round the World." *Vox*, November 18, 2019. https://www.vox.com/the-highlight/2019/11/11 /20882005/accelerationism-white-supremacy-christchurch.

Beckett, Lois. "Americans Have Bought Record 17M Guns in Year of Unrest, Analysis Finds." *Guardian*, October 30, 2020.

——. "Armed Protesters Demonstrate Against Covid-19 Lockdown at Michigan Capitol." *Guardian*, April 30, 2020.

——. "QAnon: A Timeline of Violence Linked to the Conspiracy Theory." *Guardian*, October 16, 2020.

——. "Virginia Democrats Won an Election. Gun Owners Are Talking Civil War." *Guardian*, January 10, 2020.

Belew, Kathleen. *Bring the War Home: The White Power Movement and Paramilitary America*. Cambridge, MA: Harvard University Press, 2018.

Bellware. Kim, Alex Horton, Devlin Barrett, and Matt Zapotosky. "Accused Leader of Plot to Kidnap Michigan Governor Was Struggling Financially, Living in Basement Storage Space." *Washington Post*, October 9, 2020.

Beirich, Heidi. "Domestic Terror Threat Remains Serious Five Years After Sikh Massacre." Southern Poverty Law Center, August 4, 2017. https://www.splcenter.org/news/2017/08/04 /domestic-terror-threat-remains-serious-five-years-after-sikh-massacre.

——. "Frazier Glenn Miller, Longtime Anti-Semite, Arrested in Center Murders." Southern Poverty Law Center, April 13, 2014. https://www.splcenter.org/news/2014/04/13/frazier -glenn-miller-longtime-anti-semite-arrested-kansas-jewish-community-center -murders.

——. "Inside the DHS: Former Top Analyst Says Agency Bowed to Political Pressure." Southern Poverty Law Center, June 17, 2011. https://www.splcenter.org/fighting-hate/intelligence
-report/2011/inside-dhs-former-top-analyst-says-agency-bowed-political-pressure.

Beirich, Heidi, and Mark Potok. "40 to Watch: Leaders of the Radical Right." *SPLC Intelligence
Report*, November 12, 2003. https://www.splcenter.org/fighting-hate/intelligence-report
/2003/40-watch-leaders-radical-right.

Bellware, Ki. "There Will Be 'Riots in the Street' If Trump Is Prosecuted, Graham Says." *Washington Post*, August 29, 2022.

Benkler, Yochai, Robert Faris, and Hal Roberts. *Network Propaganda: Manipulation, Disinformation, and Radicalization in American Politics.* New York: Oxford University Press, 2018.

Bennett, David H. *The Party of Fear: The American Far Right from Nativism to the Militia
Movement*. New York: Vintage, 1995.

Bensinger, Ken, and Jessica Garrison. "Watching the Watchmen." *Buzzfeed News*, July 20, 2021.
https://www.buzzfeednews.com/article/kenbensinger/michigan-kidnapping-gretchen
-whitmer-fbi-informant.

Benton, Joshua. "The New Jersey Shooting Suspect Left a Pro-Trump Paper Trail." *The Atlantic*, July 21, 2020. https://www.theatlantic.com/politics/archive/2020/07/judge-esther-salas
-shooting-suspect-left-pro-trump-paper-trail/614425/.

Berg, A. Scott. *Wilson.* New York: G. P. Putnam's Sons, 2013.

Bergen, Peter. *United States of Jihad: Investigating America's Homegrown Terrorists.* New York:
Broadway, 2016.

Bergen, Peter, and David Sterman. "Terrorism in America After 9/11: What Is the Threat to
the United States Today?" *New America*, September 10, 2021.9 https://www.newamerica
.org/international-security/reports/terrorism-in-america/what-is-the-threat-to-the
-united-states-today.

Berger, J. M. "Alt History: How a Self-Published, Racist Novel Changed White Nationalism
and Inspired Decades of Violence." *Atlantic*, September 16, 2016. https://www.theatlantic
.com/politics/archive/2016/09/how-the-turner-diaries-changed-white-nationalism
/500039/.

——. "How ISIS Games Twitter." *Atlantic*, June 16, 2014. https://www.theatlantic.com
/international/archive/2014/06/isis-iraq-twitter-social-media-strategy/372856/.

——. "The Turner Legacy: The Storied Origins and Enduring Impact of White Nationalism's
Deadly Bible." International Centre for Counter-Terrorism, The Hague, September 2016.
https://icct.nl/publication/the-turner-legacy-the-storied-origins-and-enduring-impact
-of-white-nationalisms-deadly-bible/.

Berlet, Chip. "Christian Identity: The Apocalyptic Style, Political Religion, Palingesis, and Neo-
Fascism." *Totalitarian Movements and Political Religions* 5, no. 3 (Winter 2004).

——. "Leaderless Resistance Publishing History—the Amoss Version—1953 & 1962." *Chip Berlet's Home on the Internet*, https://www.chipberlet.us/leaderless-resistance-publishing
-history/.

——. "Were Feds Duped by White Supremacist and Alleged Killer Frazier Glenn Miller?"
American Prospect, May 21, 2014. https://prospect.org/justice/feds-duped-white-suprem
acist-alleged-killer-frazier-glenn-miller/.

Berlet, Chip, and Matthew N. Lyons. *Right-Wing Populism in America: Too Close for Comfort.* New York: Guilford, 2000.

Berman, Mark. "White Supremacist Sentenced to Death for Killing Three People Near Jewish Facilities." *Washington Post.* November 10, 2015.

——. "'I Forgive You.' Relatives of Charleston Church Shooting Victims Address Dylann Roof." *Washington Post*, June 19, 2015.

Bernstein, Lenny, Sari Horwitz, and Peter Holley. "Dylann Roof's Racist Manifesto: 'I Have No Choice.'" *Washington Post*, June 20, 2015.

Bernstein, Maxine. "Ammon Bundy to Challenge Authority of Feds to Prosecute Oregon Standoff Defendants." *The Oregonian*, April 25, 2016.

Bertrand, Natasha. "Intel Report Warns That Far-Right Extremists May Target Washington, D.C." *Politico*, June 19, 2020. https://www.politico.com/news/2020/06/19/intel-report-warns -far-right-extremists-target-washington-dc-329771.

Best, Jacqueline. "How the 2008 Financial Crisis Helped Fuel Today's Right-Wing Populism." *Conversation*, October 1, 2018. https://theconversation.com/how-the-2008-financial-crisis -helped-fuel-todays-right-wing-populism-103979.

Bigg, Matthew. "Election of Obama Provokes Rise in U.S. Hate Crimes." Reuters, November 24, 2008. https://www.reuters.com/article/us-usa-obama-hatecrimes/election-of-obama -provokes-rise-in-u-s-hate-crimes-idUSTRE4AN81U20081124.

Bilefsky, Dan. "Quebec Mosque Shooter Was Consumed by Refugees, Trump and Far Right." *New York Times*, May 5, 2018.

Bishop, Katherine. "Conspiracy Trial of 14 White Supremacists Begins." *New York Times*, February 18, 1988.

Bleiberg, Jake, and Jim Mustian. "Capitol Rioters Hold Out Long-Shot Hope for a Trump Pardon." Associated Press, January 19, 2021.

Blejwas, Andrew, Anthony Griggs, and Mark Potok. "Almost 60 Terrorist Plots Uncovered in the U.S. Since the Oklahoma City Bombing." *SPLC Intelligence Report*, 2005 Summer Issue. https://www.splcenter.org/fighting-hate/intelligence-report/2005/almost-60-terrorist -plots-uncovered-us-oklahoma-city-bombing.

Blest, Paul. "'Wipe 'Em Off the Fucking Map': 3 Cops Were Caught on Camera Fantasizing About Killing Black People." *Vice.* June 25, 2020. https://www.vice.com/en/article/4ayawq /wipe-em-off-the-fucking-map-3-cops-were-caught-on-camera-fantasizing-about -killing-black-people.

Blumberg, Antonia. "This Woman Escaped The Nazis Once. Now She's Fighting Nazism Again." *Huffington Post*, August 14, 2017. https://www.huffpost.com/entry/this-woman -escaped-the-nazis-once-now-shes-fighting-nazism-again_n_5991fbe7e4b09096429 925ce.

Bogage, Jacob. "Leo Frank Was Lynched for a Murder He Didn't Commit. Now Neo-Nazis Are Trying to Rewrite History." *Washington Post*, May 22, 2017.

Bogel-Burroughs, Nicholas. "What We Know About the Alleged Plot to Kidnap Michigan's Governor." *New York Times*, October 9, 2020.

Bouie, Jamelle. "The Deadly History of 'They're Raping Our Women.'" *Slate*, June 28, 2015. https://slate.com/news-and-politics/2015/06/the-deadly-history-of-theyre-raping-our

-women-racists-have-long-defended-their-worst-crimes-in-the-name-of-defending
-white-womens-honor.html.

Bragg, Rick. "Terror in Oklahoma: The Children; Tender Memories of Day Care Center Are All That Remain After the Bomb." *New York Times*, May 3, 1995.

Branigin, William, and Dana Priest. "3 White Soldiers Held in Slaying of Black Couple." *Washington Post*, December 9, 1995.

Brenner, Marie. "American Nightmare: The Ballad of Richard Jewell." *Vanity Fair*, February 1997. https://archive.vanityfair.com/article/share/1fd2d7ae-10d8-474b-9bf1-d1558af697be.

Broadwater, Luke. "Jan. 6 Committee Refers Former President Trump for Criminal Prosecution." *New York Times*, December 19, 2022.

Brooke, James. "Newspaper Says McVeigh Described Role in Bombing." *New York Times*, March 1, 1997.

Brown, DeNeen L. "The Preacher Who Used Christianity to Revive the Ku Klux Klan." *Washington Post*, April 10, 2018.

Brown, Robbie. "Anti-Obama Protest at Ole Miss Turns Unruly." *New York Times*, November 7, 2012.

Buckley, Chris, Myrieme Churchill, and Jacob Ware. "Fighting Demons, Healing Hatred, Restoring Hope: How to Defeat Extremism in the US Military." *Air Force Times*, November 28, 2020. https://www.airforcetimes.com/opinion/commentary/2020/11/28/fighting -demons-healing-hatred-restoring-hope-how-to-defeat-extremism-in-the-us-military/.

Bui, Lynh. "'I Am Dreaming of a Way to Kill Almost Every Last Person on Earth': A Self-Proclaimed White Nationalist Planned a Mass Terrorist Attack, the Government Says." *Washington Post*, February 20, 2019.

Burke, Jason. "Norway Mosque Attack Suspect 'Inspired by Christchurch and El Paso shootings.'" *Guardian*, August 11, 2019.

Byman, Daniel. "Riots, White Supremacy, and Accelerationism." Brookings Institution, June 2, 2020. https://www.brookings.edu/blog/order-from-chaos/2020/06/02/riots-white-supremacy-and-accelerationism/.

——. *Spreading Hate*. Oxford: Oxford University Press, 2022.

——. "White Supremacy, Terrorism, and the Failure of Reconstruction in the United States." *International Security* 46, no. 1 (Summer 2021).

Byman, Daniel L., and Mark Pitcavage. "Identifying and Exploiting the Weaknesses of the White Supremacist Movement." Brookings Institution, April 2021. https://www.brookings .edu/wp-content/uploads/2021/04/Identifying-and-exploiting-the-weaknesses-of-the -white-supremacist-movement.pdf.

Camden, Jim, and Chad Sokol. "Rep. Matt Shea Expelled from GOP Caucus After Investigation Finds He Engaged in Domestic Terrorism." *Spokesman-Review*, December 19, 2019.

"Capitol Hill Siege." GW Program on Extremism. https://extremism.gwu.edu/Capitol-Hill -Siege.

Carless, Will. "Suspect in Cincinnati FBI Breach May Have Posted on Trump's Truth Social During Incident." *USA Today*, August 11, 2022.

Chalabi, Mon. "What Percentage of Americans Have Served in the Military?" *FiveThirtyEight*, March 19, 2015. https://fivethirtyeight.com/features/what-percentage-of-americans-have-served-in-the-military/.

Chalfant, Morgan. "Trump: 'The Only Way We're Going to Lose This Election Is If the Election Is Rigged.'" *The Hill*, August 17, 2020. https://thehill.com/homenews/administration/512424-trump-the-only-way-we-are-going-to-lose-this-election-is-if-the.

Chason, Rachel, Annette Nevins, Annie Gowen, and Hailey Fuchs. "As His Environment Changed, Suspect in El Paso Shooting Learned to Hate." *Washington Post*, August 9, 2019.

Chernow, Ron. *Grant*. New York: Penguin, 2017.

"Chronology: Following a Trail of Aliases and Other Clues." *New York Times*, August 13, 1995.

Clark, Thomas D. Introduction to *The Clansman: A Historical Romance of the Ku Klux Klan*, by Thomas Dixon Jr. Lexington: University Press of Kentucky, 1970.

Clausewitz, Carl von. *On War*. Ed. Michael Howard and Peter Paret. Princeton, NJ: Princeton University Press, 1989.

Cleary, Tom. "Christopher Hasson Hit List: Coast Guard LT Targeted Democrats, Media, Feds Say." *Heavy*, February 20, 2019. https://heavy.com/news/2019/02/christopher-hasson-hit-list-targets-democrats-media/.

Coates, James. *Armed and Dangerous: The Rise of the Survivalist Right*. New York: Hill & Wang, 1987.

——. "New-Nazis Indicted in Bizarre Crime Spree." *Chicago Tribune*, April 16, 1985.

——. "U.S. Aims to Break Neo-Nazis." *Chicago Tribune*, April 26, 1987.

——. "Writer's Expose Left Him Exposed." *Chicago Tribune*, September 19, 1985. https://www.chicagotribune.com/news/ct-xpm-1985-09-19-8503030757-story.html.

Coates, James, and Stephen Franklin. "Court Records Detail Neo-Nazis Network." *Chicago Tribune*, December 27, 1987.

——. "'Underground' of Racist Leaders Coordinated Crimes, FBI Tapes Show." *Washington Post*, December 28, 1987.

Cobain, Ian, and Matthew Taylor. "Far-Right Terrorist Thomas Mair Jailed for Life for Jo Cox Murder." *Guardian*, November 23, 2016.

Cochrane, Emily, and Zolan Kanno-Youngs. "Biden Signs Gun Bill Into Law, Ending Years of Stalemate." *New York Times*, June 25, 2022.

Connolly, Griffin, and Richard Hall. "America's Largest Militia Says It Will Refuse to Recognize Biden as President and 'Resist' His Administration." *Independent*, November 15, 2020.

Connelly, Michael. "Arrests of Teen Members of 'Skinhead' Faction Spell End of Spree of 'Hate Crimes,' Police Say." *Los Angeles Times*, November 1, 1987.

Cook, Jesselyn. "'I Miss My Mom': Children of QAnon Believers Are Desperately Trying to Deradicalize Their Own Parents." *Huffington Post*, February 11, 2021. https://www.huffpost.com/entry/children-of-qanon-believers_n_601078e9c5b6c5586aa49077.

Cook, Kevin. *Waco Rising: David Koresh, The FBI, and the Birth of America's Modern Militias*. New York: Henry Holt, 2023.

Cooper, Helene. "Pentagon Updates Its Rules on Extremism in the Military." *New York Times*, December 20, 2021.

Corcoran, James. *Bitter Harvest: The Birth of Paramilitary Terrorism in the Heartland.* New York: Penguin, 1995.

"Covenant (CSA)—The Rock Star." GlobalSecurity.org. https://www.globalsecurity.org/military/world/para/csa-1.htm.

"COVID-19 Disinformation Briefing No. 2: Far-right Mobilisation." Institute for Strategic Dialogue, April 9, 2020. https://www.isdglobal.org/wp-content/uploads/2020/04/Covid-19-Briefing-PDF.pdf.

"Cover Story: Hate Thy Neighbor: Local Author Daniel Levitas Exposes the History and Hypocrisy of the Militant White Supremacist Movement." *Creative Loafing*, November 27, 2002. https://creativeloafing.com/content-184623-cover-story-hate-thy-neighbor.

Cox, Daniel A. "After the Ballots Are Counted: Conspiracies, Political Violence, and American Exceptionalism." Survey Center on American Life, February 11, 2021. https://www.americansurveycenter.org/research/after-the-ballots-are-counted-conspiracies-political-violence-and-american-exceptionalism/.

Crenshaw, Martha. "The Logic of Terrorism: Terrorist Behavior as a Product of Strategic Choice." in *Origins of Terrorism*, ed. Walter Reich. Washington, DC: Woodrow Wilson Center Press, 1998.

Cummings, William. "Chris Miller, Defense Secretary on Jan. 6, Sees 'Cause and Effect' Between Trump's Words and Capitol Riot." *USA Today*, March 12, 2021.

Cunningham, David. *Klansville, U.S.A.: The Rise and Fall of the Civil Rights–Era Ku Klux Klan.* Oxford: Oxford University Press, 2013.

Dart, Richard C. "Hydroxocabalamin for Acute Poisoning: New Data from Preclinical and Clinical Studies; New Results from the Prehospital Emergency Setting." *Clinical Toxicology* 44, suppl. 1, nos. 1–3 (2006).

Davey, Jacob, and Julia Ebner. " 'The Great Replacement': The Violent Consequences of Mainstreamed Extremism." Institute for Strategic Dialogue, July 2019. https://www.isdglobal.org/wp-content/uploads/2019/07/The-Great-Replacement-The-Violent-Consequences-of-Mainstreamed-Extremism-by-ISD.pdf.

Dawsey, Josh, and Felicia Sonmez. " 'Legitimate Political Discourse': Three Words About Jan. 6 Spark Rift Among Republicans." *Washington Post*, February 8, 2022.

——. "RNC Votes to Condemn Cheney, Kinzinger for Serving on House Committee Investigating Jan. 6 Attack on the Capitol by Pro-Trump Mob." *Washington Post*, February 3, 2022.

Day, Meagan. "Welcome to Hayden Lake, Where White Supremacists Tried to Build Their Homeland." *Timeline*, November 4, 2016. https://timeline.com/white-supremacist-rural-paradise-fb62b74b29e0.

"Dec. 17–19, 2021, Washington Post-University of Maryland Poll." *Washington Post*, January 1, 2022. https://www.washingtonpost.com/context/dec-17-19-2021-washington-post-university-of-maryland-poll/2960c330-4bbd-4b3a-af9d-72de946d7281/.

Dearen, Jason, and Michael Kunzelman. "Deadly Shooting Ends Friendships Forged in Neo-Nazi Group." Associated Press, August 22, 2017.

Dees, Morris, with James Corcoran. *Gathering Storm: America's Militia Threat.* New York: HarperCollins, 1996.

———. "The Nazi Link with Militias: White Racists Play Down Their Politics to Recruit from the Middle Class." *Baltimore Sun*, June 16, 1996.

Dewan, Shaila. "Bomber Offers Guilty Pleas, and Defiance." *New York Times*, April 14, 2005.

Diamond, Anna. "The 1924 Law That Slammed the Door on Immigrants and the Politicians Who Pushed It Back Open." *Smithsonian Magazine*, May 19, 2020. https://www.smithsonianmag.com/history/1924-law-slammed-door-immigrants-and-politicians-who-pushed-it-back-open-180974910/.

Dickson, Caitlin. "Sovereign Citizens Are America's Top Cop-Killers." *Daily Beast*, November 25, 2014. http://www.thedailybeast.com/articles/2014/11/25/sovereign-citizens-are-america-s-top-cop-killers.html.

"Did Trump and Biden Swap Bodies???" *Daily Beast*, January 22, 2021. https://www.thedailybeast.com/did-trump-and-biden-swap-bodies.

Dixon, Matt. "Florida Judge Who Approved FBI Search of Mar-a-Lago Faces Barrage of Antisemitic Online Attacks." *Politico*, August 12, 2022. https://www.politico.com/news/2022/08/12/florida-judge-fbi-search-of-mar-a-lago-anti-semitic-attacks-00051489.

Dornauer Mark E., and Robert Bryce. "Too Many Rural Americans Are Living in the Digital Dark. The Problem Demands a New Deal Solution." *Health Affairs*, October 28, 2020. https://www.healthaffairs.org/do/10.1377/forefront.20201026.515764/.

Dundon, Rian. "Why Does the Ku Klux Klan Burn Crosses? They Got the Idea from a Movie." *Timeline*, March 16, 2017. https://timeline.com/why-does-the-ku-klux-klan-burn-crosses-they-got-the-idea-from-a-movie-75a70f7ab135.

Ebert, Roger. "*The Birth of a Nation*." *RogerEbert.com*, March 30, 2003. https://www.rogerebert.com/reviews/great-movie-the-birth-of-a-nation-1915.

Ebner, Julia. *Going Dark: The Secret Social Lives of Extremists*. London: Bloomsbury, 2020.

"Eight suspects Have Been Arrested in a White Supremacist Plot." United Press International, December 16, 1986.

Elias, Marily. "Sikh Temple Killer Wade Michael Page Radicalized in Army." Southern Poverty Law Center, November 11, 2012. https://www.splcenter.org/fighting-hate/intelligence-report/2012/sikh-temple-killer-wade-michael-page-radicalized-army.

Elliston, Jon. "Bomber Eric Rudolph's Memoir Published by Virginia-Based Army of God." *Carolina Public Press*, December 18, 2013.

"Eric Rudolph: A Profile." *Washington Post*, December 12, 1998.

Erickson, Briana. "War Hero 'Bo' Gritz Reflects on Ruby Ridge Siege 28 Years Later." *Las Vegas Review-Journal*, September 21, 2020.

"Experts: Richard Haass, President, Council on Foreign Relations." Council on Foreign Relations. https://www.cfr.org/expert/richard-haass.

"Extremists Are Using Facebook to Organize for Civil War Amid Coronavirus." *Tech Transparency Project*, April 22, 2020. https://www.techtransparencyproject.org/articles/extremists-are-using-facebook-to-organize-for-civil-war-amid-coronavirus.

Fact Checker. "Analysis: In Four Years, President Trump Made 30,573 False or Misleading Claims." *Washington Post*, January 20, 2021.

Fallows, James. "Trump Time Capsule #19: 'Appreciate the Congrats.'" *Atlantic*, June 12, 2016. https://www.theatlantic.com/politics/archive/2016/06/trump-time-capsule-19-appreciate -the-congrats/623785/.

Feuer, Alan. "The F.B.I. Search Ignited the Language of Violence and Civil War on the Far Right." *New York Times*, August 9, 2022.

Feuer, Alan, and Maggie Haberman. "Hard Right Stokes Outrage After Search of Mar-a-Lago." *New York Times*, August 30, 2022.

Fisher, Marc, and Phil McCombs. "The Book of Hate." *Washington Post*, April 25, 1995.

Flynn, Kevin, and Gary Gerhardt. *The Silent Brotherhood: Inside America's Racist Under-ground*. New York: Free Press, 1989.

Flynn, Meagan. "Engineer Intentionally Crashes Train Near Hospital Ship *Mercy*, Believing in Weird Coronavirus Conspiracy, Feds Say." *Washington Post*, April 2, 2020.

Foner, Eric. *The Second Founding: How the Civil War and Reconstruction Remade the Consti-tution*. New York: Norton, 2019.

Forbes, Robert, and Eddie Stampton. *The White Nationalist Skinhead Movement: UK & USA 1979–1993*. Minneapolis, MN: Feral House, 2015.

"Former DHS Analyst Daryl Johnson on How He Was Silenced for Warning of Far-Right Mil-itants in U.S." *Democracy Now!*, August 9, 2012. https://www.democracynow.org/2012/8/9 /former_dhs_analyst_daryl_johnson_on.

"Former KKK Leader Robert Miles Dead at 67." United Press International. August 18, 1992. https://www.upi.com/Archives/1992/08/18/Former-KKK-leader-Robert-Miles-dead-at-67 /7854714110400/.

Forster, Arnold, and Benjamin Epstein. *The Trouble-Makers: An Anti-Defamation League Report on Intolerance in the United States*. Garden City, NY: Doubleday, 1952.

"Fort Smith Sedition Trial of 1988." *Encyclopedia of Arkansas*. https://encyclopediaofarkansas .net/entries/fort-smith-sedition-trial-of-1988-13802/.

Freedland, Jonathan. "Adolf's US Army: Neo-Fascist Militia Groups Are on the March in the US, and Washington Is Their Target." *Guardian*, December 15, 1994.

Freeman, Scott. "Fallout: An Oral History of the Olympic Park Bombing." *Atlanta Magazine*, July 1, 2011. https://www.atlantamagazine.com/great-reads/olympic-park-bombing-oral -history/.

Frum, David. "A President Who Condones Political Violence." *Atlantic*, October 26, 2018. https://www.theatlantic.com/ideas/archive/2018/10/trump-bombs-florida-tweets/574108/.

Galston, William A. "'This Is How It Feels to Be Sold Out by Your Country': Economic Hard-ship and Politics in Indiana." Brookings Institute, May 18, 2016. https://www.brookings.edu /blog/fixgov/2016/05/18/this-is-how-it-feels-to-be-sold-out-by-your-country-economic -hardship-and-politics-in-indiana/.

Gardell, Mattias. "Robert J. Mathews." In *Encyclopedia of White Power: A Sourcebook on the Radical Racist Right*, ed. Jeffrey Kaplan. Walnut Creek, CA: AltaMira, 2000.

Gartenstein-Ross, Daveed, and Madeleine Blackman. "Fluidity of the Fringes: Prior Extrem-ist Involvement as a Radicalization Pathway." *Studies in Conflict & Terrorism* 45, no. 7 (2022).

Gartenstein-Ross, Daveed, Samuel Hodgson, and Colin P. Clarke. "The Growing Threat Posed by Accelerationism and Accelerationist Groups Worldwide." Foreign Policy Research Institute, April 20, 2020. https://www.fpri.org/article/2020/04/the-growing-threat-posed-by-accelerationism-and-accelerationist-groups-worldwide/.

German, Michael. "Behind the Lone Terrorists, a Pack Mentality." Washington Post, June 5, 2005.

——. "Why New Laws Aren't Needed to Take Domestic Terrorism More Seriously." Brennan Center for Justice, December 14, 2018. https://www.brennancenter.org/our-work/analysis-opinion/why-new-laws-arent-needed-take-domestic-terrorism-more-seriously.

Gerstein, Josh. "Aide's Testimony That Trump Was Told of Weapons Could Boost Civil Suits." Politico, June 28, 2022. https://www.politico.com/news/2022/06/28/aides-claim-trump-was-told-of-weapons-00042977.

Gettleman, Jeffrey, with David M. Halbfinger. "Suspect in '96 Olympic Bombing and 3 Other Attacks Is Caught." New York Times, June 1, 2003.

Ghansah, Rachel Kaadzi. "A Most American Terrorist: The Making of Dylann Roof." GQ, August 21, 2017. https://www.gq.com/story/dylann-roof-making-of-an-american-terrorist.

Gibbons-Neff, Thomas. "Meet the Veterans Who Have Joined the Oregon Militiamen." Washington Post, January 4, 2016.

Gibbs, Nancy. "The Blood of Innocents: In the Bomb's Aftermath, Tales of Horror and Heroism." Time, May 1, 1995.

Glanton, Dahleen, and Tribune reporter. "Atlanta Debates How Golden It Was." Chicago Tribune, September 21, 2009.

"Global Firearms Holdings: Interactive Map—United States of America." Small Arms Survey, March 29, 2020. https://www.smallarmssurvey.org/database/global-firearms-holdings.

Goldman, Adam. "Man Suspected of Planning Attack on Missouri Hospital Is Killed." New York Times, March 25, 2020.

Goldman, Adam, Katie Benner, and Zolan Kanno-Youngs. "How Trump's Focus on Antifa Distracted Attention from the Far-Right Threat." New York Times, January 30, 2021.

Good, Timothy S. We Saw Lincoln Shot: One Hundred Eyewitness Accounts. Jackson: University of Mississippi Press, 1995.

Gordon, Linda. The Second Coming of the KKK: The Ku Klux Klan of the 1920s and the American Political Tradition. New York: Liveright, 2018.

Graham, David A., Adrienne Green, Cullen Murphy, and Parker Richards. "An Oral History of Trump's Bigotry." Atlantic, June 2019. https://www.theatlantic.com/magazine/archive/2019/06/trump-racism-comments/588067/.

Green, Steve. "White Supremacists Meet in Idaho." United Press International, July 12, 1986.

Greene, Bryan. "Created 150 Years Ago, the Justice Department's First Mission Was to Protect Black Rights." Smithsonian Magazine, July 1, 2020. https://www.smithsonianmag.com/history/created-150-years-ago-justice-departments-first-mission-was-protect-black-rights-180975232/.

Griffin, Robert S. The Fame of a Dead Man's Deeds: An Up-Close Portrait of White Nationalist William Pierce. n.p, 2001; rev. ed. 2018. https://archive.org/stream/FameOfADeadMans

DeedsRobertS.Griffin/Fame%20of%20a%20Dead%20Man%27s%20Deeds%20-%20Rob
ert%20S.%20Griffin_djvu.txt.

Grimm, Elizabeth Arsenault, and Joseph Stabile. "Confronting Russia's Role in Transnational White Supremacist Extremism." *Just Security*, February 6, 2020. https://www.justsecurity
.org/68420/confronting-russias-role-in-transnational-white-supremacist-extremism/.

Gross, Jenny. "How Finland Is Teaching a Generation to Spot Misinformation." *New York Times*, January 10, 2023.

Grow, Kory. "Charles Manson: How Cult Leader's Twisted Beatles Obsession Inspired Family Murders." *Rolling Stone*, August 9, 2019. https://www.rollingstone.com/feature/charles
-manson-how-cult-leaders-twisted-beatles-obsession-inspired-family-murders-107176/.

Guilhot, Nicolas. "Why Pandemics Are the Perfect Environment for Conspiracy Theories to Flourish." *Conversation*, April 6, 2020. https://theconversation.com/why-pandemics-are
-the-perfect-environment-for-conspiracy-theories-to-flourish-135475.

Guinn, Jeff. *Waco: David Koresh, the Branch Davidians, and a Legacy of Rage.* New York: Simon & Schuster, 2023.

Guskin, Emily. "A Wide Majority of Americans Are Concerned About Politically Motivated Violence." *Washington Post*, November 4, 2022.

Guynn, Jessica. "Trump Believes QAnon Claim It's Fighting Pedophiles, Refuses to Disavow Extremist Conspiracy Theory." *USA Today*, October 15, 2020.

"GW Extremism Tracker." George Washington Program on Extremism (no date). https://
extremism.gwu.edu/sites/g/files/zaxdzs5746/files/DecGWET2022-4.pdf.

Haass, Richard. *The Bill of Obligations: The Ten Habits of Good Citizens.* New York: Penguin, 2023.

Haberman, Maggie, and Charlie Savage. "Trump, Lacking Clear Authority, Says U.S. Will Declare Antifa a Terrorist Group." *New York Times*, June 10, 2020.

Hackett, George, and Pamela Abramson. "Skinheads on the Rampage." *Newsweek*, September 7, 1987.

Haley, Claire. "Stone Mountain: Carving Fact from Fiction." Atlanta History Center. November 18, 2022. https://www.atlantahistorycenter.com/blog/stone-mountain-a-brief-history/.

Hanna, Jason, and Darran Simon. "The Suspect in Poway Synagogue Shooting Used an Assault Rifle and Had Extra Magazines, Prosecutors Said." CNN, April 30, 2019. https://edition.cnn.com/2019/04/30/us/california-synagogue-shooting-investigation
/index.html

Hall, Andy. "Secret War: 'Patriots' Have Loose Ties to Rightists Nationwide." *Arizona Republic.* December 21, 1986.

Hall, Charles W. "Former Neo-Nazi Had Troubled MD Past." *Washington Post*, February 26, 1987.

Hall, Madison, et al. "At Least 1,003 People Have Been Charged in the Capitol Insurrection So Far. This Searchable Table Shows Them All." *Insider*, December 7, 2022. https://www.insider
.com/all-the-us-capitol-pro-trump-riot-arrests-charges-names-2021-1.

——. "465 Rioters Have Pleaded Guilty for Their Role in the Capitol Insurrection So Far. This Table Is Tracking Them All." *Insider*, December 7, 2022, https://www.insider.com/capitol
-rioters-who-pleaded-guilty-updated-list-2021-5.

Hamm, Mark. S. "Tragic Irony: State Malfeasance and the Oklahoma City Bombing Conspiracy." *The Critical Criminologist*, 1998. http://sun.soci/niu/~critcrim/CC/hamm98.htm.

——. *Terrorism as Crime: From Oklahoma City to Al-Qaeda and Beyond*. New York: New York University Press, 2007.

Hamm, Mark S., and Ramón Spaaij. *The Age of Lone Wolf Terrorism*. New York: Columbia University Press, 2017.

Harris, Art. "Evader's End." *Washington Post*, June 5, 1983.

Hartmann, Margaret. "Turns Out the Secret Service Repeatedly Defied Trump on January 6." *Intelligencer*, October 12, 2022. https://nymag.com/intelligencer/2022/10/secret-service -repeatedly-defied-trumps-orders-on-january-6.html.

Hay, Andrew. "Kansas Militia Men Blame Trump Rhetoric for Mosque Attack Plan." Reuters, October 30, 2018.

Hébert, Keith S. "Ku Klux Klan in Alabama from 1915-1930." *Encyclopedia of Alabama*, March 30, 2023. https://encyclopediaofalabama.org/article/ku-klux-klan-in-alabama-from -1915-1930/.

Helling, David, Judy Thomas, and Mark Morris. "Records Suggest That F. Glenn Miller Jr. Was Once in Witness Protection Program." *Wichita Eagle*, April 15, 2014.

Hendrix, Steve. "He Always Hated Women. Then He Decided to Kill Them." *Washington Post*, June 7, 2019.

Hermansson, Patrik. "The British Hand: New Extreme Right Terror Cell Exposed." *Hope Not Hate*, September 27, 2020. https://hopenothate.org.uk/2020/09/27/british-hand/.

Herrera, Sebastian, and Sarah E. Needleman. "Live Stream of Germany Shooting Turns Spotlight to Amazon's Twitch." *Wall Street Journal*, October 10, 2019.

Hepworth, Shelley, Vanessa Gezari, Kyle Pope, Cory Schouten, Carlett Spike, David Uberti, and Pete Vernon. "Covering Trump: An Oral History of an Unforgettable Campaign." *Columbia Journalism Review*, November 22, 2016.

Hewitt, Christopher. *Understanding Terrorism in America: From the Klan to Al Qaeda*. London: Routledge, 2003.

Hill, Fiona. "The Kremlin's Strange Victory." *Foreign Affairs*, November/December 2021. https://www.foreignaffairs.com/articles/united-states/2021-09-27/kremlins-strange -victory.

Hoffman, Bruce. "American Right-Wing Extremism." *Jane's Intelligence Review* 7, no. 7 (July 1995).

——. "Back to the Future: The Return of Violent Far-Right Terrorism in the Age of Lone Wolves." *War on the Rocks*, April 2, 2019. https://warontherocks.com/2019/04/back-to-the -future-the-return-of-violent-far-right-terrorism-in-the-age-of-lone-wolves/.

——. *Inside Terrorism*. New York: Columbia University Press, 2017.

——. *Recent Trends and Future Prospects of Terrorism in the United States*. R-3618. Santa Monica, CA: RAND Corporation, May 1988.

Hoffman, Bruce, and Jacob Ware. "The Accelerating Threat of the Political Assassination." *War on the Rocks*, August 24, 2022. https://warontherocks.com/2022/08/the-accelerating -threat-of-the-political-assassination/.

——. "Is 3-D Printing the Future of Terrorism?" *Wall Street Journal*, October 25, 2019.

———. "July 22: A Pivotal Day in Terrorism History." *War on the Rocks*, July 22, 2021. https://warontherocks.com/2021/07/july-22-a-pivotal-day-in-terrorism-history/.

———. "The Terrorist Threat from the Fractured Far Right." *Lawfare*, November 1, 2020. https://www.lawfareblog.com/terrorist-threat-fractured-far-right.

Hoffman, Bruce, Jacob Ware, and Ezra Shapiro. "Assessing the Threat of Incel Violence." *Studies in Conflict and Terrorism* 43, no. 7 (April 2020): 565–87.

Holthouse, David. "Several High-Profile Racist Extremists Serve in the U.S. Military." Southern Poverty Law Center, August 11, 2006. https://www.splcenter.org/fighting-hate/intelligence-report/2006/several-high-profile-racist-extremists-serve-us-military.

Holpuch, Amanda. "US Capitol's Last Breach Was More Than 200 Years Ago." *Guardian*, January 6, 2021.

Homayun, Shamim. "An Ordinary Man with Extraordinary Values: Haji-Daoud, a Victim of the Christchurch Terror Attacks." *Stuff*, March 18, 2019. https://www.stuff.co.nz/national/111364502/an-ordinary-man-with-extraordinary-values-hajidaoud-a-victim-of-the-christchurch-terror-attacks.

Houghtaling, Ellie Quinlan. "Revealed: Secret Service Knew of Disturbing Neo-Nazi Threats Before Jan. 6." *Daily Beast*, September 22, 2022. https://www.thedailybeast.com/secret-service-knew-of-disturbing-neo-nazi-threats-before-jan-6-capitol-riot.

Howard, Philip N., Bharath Ganesh, Dimitra Liotsiou, John Kelly, and Camille François. *The IRA, Social Media, and Political Polarization in the United States, 2012–2018*. Oxford: University of Oxford, 2019.

Hsu, Spencer S. "Video Released of Garage Meeting of Proud Boys, Oath Keepers Leaders." *Washington Post*, May 24, 2022.

Hsu, Spencer S., and Hannah Allam. "Landmark Oath Keepers Verdict Hobbles Group, but the Movement Lives On." *Washington Post*, December 3, 2022.

Hsu, Spencer S., Peter Hermann, and Emily Davies. "Two Arrested in Assault on Police Officer Brian D. Sicknick, Who Died After Jan. 6 Capitol Riot." Washington Post, March 21, 2021.

Hsu, Spencer S., and Dan Morse. "Christopher Krebs Sues Trump Campaign, Lawyer Joe diGenova for Defamation." *Washington Post*, December 8, 2020.

Huie, William Bradford. "The Shocking Story of Approved Killing in Mississippi." *Look*, January 1956. http://www.shoppbs.pbs.org/wgbh/amex/till/sfeature/sf_look_confession.html.

Hull, Anne. "Randy Weaver's Return from Ruby Ridge." *Washington Post*, April 30, 2001.

"Intelbrief: White Supremacists and the Weaponization of the Coronavirus (COVID-19)." Soufan Center, March 25, 2020. https://thesoufancenter.org/intelbrief-white-supremacists-and-the-weaponization-of-the-coronavirus-covid-19/.

International Association of Chiefs of Police. *Terrorist Trends: The Quarterly Intelligence Reporter*. Alexandria, VA: IACP, 1985.

Irving, Doug. "Lesson Plans for Middle School Teachers to Help Improve Media Literacy Among Students." *RAND Review*, September–October 2022. https://www.rand.org/pubs/corporate_pubs/CPA682-13.html.

Itkowitz, Colby. "Trump Falsely Claims Jan. 6 Rioters Were 'Hugging and Kissing' Police." *Washington Post*, March 26, 2021.

Jackson, Charles O. "William J. Simmons: A Career in Ku Kluxism." *Georgia Historical Quarterly* 50, no. 4 (December 1966).

Jackson, Robert L. "Militant Relives Idaho Tragedy for Senators." *Los Angeles Times*, September 7, 1995.

Jackson, Robert L., and Ronald J. Ostrow. "Law in War on Far-Right Sect: White Supremacists Tied to Western Crime Spree." *Los Angeles Times*, January 21, 1985.

Jackson, Sam. "The Long, Dangerous History of Right-Wing Calls for Violence and Civil War." *Washington Post*, September 11, 2020.

——. *Oath Keepers: Patriotism and the Edge of Violence in a Right-Wing Antigovernment Group.* New York: Columbia University Press, 2020.

Jacobs, Sally. "The Radicalization of Timothy McVeigh." *Tulsa World*, June 10, 1995.

Jalonick, Mary Clare. "Jan. 6 Panel Shutting Down After Referring Trump for Crimes." Associated Press, January 2, 2023.

Jansen, Bart. "'Elephant in the Room': Police Grapple with Charges Against Officers in Jan. 6 Capitol Attack." *USA Today*, May 3, 2022.

Jany, Libor. "Minneapolis Police Say 'Umbrella Man' Was a White Supremacist Trying to Incite George Floyd Rioting." *Star Tribune*, July 28, 2020.

Jenkins, Brian M. "Five Reasons to Be Wary of a New Domestic Terrorism Law." *The Hill*, February 23, 2021. https://thehill.com/opinion/national-security/540096-what-exactly-is-the-definition-of-terrorism-and-four-other-reasons.

——. "International Terrorism: A New Mode of Conflict." In *International Terrorism and World Security*, ed. David Carlton and Carlo Schaerf. London: Croom Helm, 1975.

Jenkins, Brian Michael, Sorrel Wildhorn, and Marvin M. Lavin. *Intelligence Constraints of the 1970s and Domestic Terrorism: Executive Summary.* R-29239-DOJ. Santa Monica, CA: RAND Corporation, December 1982.

——. *Intelligence Constraints of the 1970s and Domestic Terrorism.* Vol. 1: *Effects on the Incidence, Investigation, and Prosecution of Terrorist Activity.* N-1901-DOJ. Santa Monica, CA: RAND Corporation, December 1982.

Jensen, Michael A., and Sheehan Kane. "QAnon-Inspired Violence in the United States: An Empirical Assessment of a Misunderstood Threat." *Behavioral Sciences of Terrorism and Political Aggression*, 2021.

Jimson, Robert. "How the FBI Smashed White Supremacist Group the Order." CNN, August 21, 2018.

Jin, Beatrice. "Biden Signed a New Hate Crimes Law—but There's a Big Flaw." *Politico*, May 20, 2021. https://www.politico.com/interactives/2021/state-hate-crime-laws/.

Johnson, Daryl. *Hateland: A Long, Hard Look at America's Extremist Heart.* Amherst, NY: Prometheus, 2019.

——. "I Warned of Right-Wing Violence in 2009. Republicans Objected. I Was Right." *Washington Post*, August 21, 2017.

Johnston, David Cay. "William Pierce, 69, Neo-Nazi Leader, Dies." *New York Times*, July 24, 2002.

Jones, James L. "Extremists Don't Belong in the Military." *Atlantic*, October 17, 2020. https://www.theatlantic.com/ideas/archive/2020/10/extremists-dont-belong-military/616763/.

Jones, Seth G., Catrina Doxsee, Grace Hwang, and Jared Thompson. "The Military, Police, and the Rise of Terrorism in the United States." Center for Strategic and International Studies, April 12, 2021. https://www.csis.org/analysis/military-police-and-rise-terrorism-united-states.

Jones, Seth G., Catrina Doxsee, Nicholas Harrington, Grace Hwang, and James Suber. "The War Comes Home: The Evolution of Domestic Terrorism in the United States." Center for Strategic and International Studies, October 22, 2020. https://www.csis.org/analysis/war-comes-home-evolution-domestic-terrorism-united-states.

Jouvenal, Justin. "Va. Teen Accused of Killing Girlfriend's Parents to Be Tried as an Adult." *Washington Post*, September 24, 2019.

Jupskås, Anders Ravik, and Eviane Leidig, eds. "Knowing What's (Far) Right: A Compendium." *C-REX*, 2020. https://www.sv.uio.no/c-rex/english/groups/compendium/c-rex-compendium-print-version.pdf.

"Juror Falls in Love with Ex-defendant." *The Oklahoman*, September 13, 1988.

Kael, Pauline. *For Keeps*. New York: Plume/Penguin, 1996.

Kanno-Youngs, Zolan, and Nicole Hong. "Biden Steps Up Federal Efforts to Combat Domestic Extremism." *New York Times*, April 4, 2021.

Kaplan, Jeffrey. "Right-Wing Violence in North America." In *Terror from the Extreme Right*, by Tore Bjorgo. London: Frank Cass, 1995.

Katz, Rita. *Saints and Soldiers: Inside Internet-Age Terrorism, from Syria to the Capitol Siege*. New York: Columbia University Press, 2022.

——. Violent Protests Are a Neo-Nazi Fever Dream Come True." *Daily Beast*, September 3, 2020. https://www.thedailybeast.com/violent-protests-are-a-neo-nazi-fever-dream-come-true.

Keller, Jared. "Navy Vet Allegedly Planned to Bomb Hospital Over Government's COVID-19 Response." *Military.com*, April 16, 2020. https://www.military.com/daily-news/2020/04/16/navy-vet-allegedly-planned-bomb-hospital-over-governments-covid-19-response.html.

Kelly, Meg, and Elyse Samuels. "Who Caused the Violence at Protests? It Wasn't Antifa." *Washington Post*, June 22, 2020.

Kelsey, Tim. "The Oklahoma Suspect Awaits Day of Reckoning." *Sunday Times*, April 21, 1996.

Kennard, Matt. *Irregular Army: How the US Military Recruited Neo-Nazis, Gang Members, and Criminals to Fight the War on Terror*. London: Verso, 2015.

Kenworthy, Tom. "Anti-Government Writings in McVeigh's Car, Agent Says." *Washington Post*, April 29, 1997.

——. "FBI Agents Testify About Guns, Fertilizer at Home of Nichols." *Washington Post*, November 18, 1997.

Kessler, Glenn, Salvador Rizzo, and Meg Kelly. *Donald Trump and His Assault on Truth: The President's Falsehoods, Misleading Claims, and Flat-Out* Lies. New York: Scribner, 2020.

Kifner, John. "The Gun Network: McVeigh's World—a Special Report. Bomb Suspect Felt at Home Riding the Gun-Show Circuit." *New York Times*, July 5, 1995.

——. "McVeigh's Mind." *New York Times*, December 31, 1995.

Kiely, Eugene, and Rem Rieder. "Trump's Repeated False Attacks on Mail-In Ballots." *FactCheck*, September 25, 2020. https://www.factcheck.org/2020/09/trumps-repeated-false-attacks-on-mail-in-ballots/.

"Killer Spent Two Weeks Planning School Attack." *The Local*, March 8, 2016. https://www
.thelocal.se/20160308/killer-spent-two-weeks-planning-school-attack.

Kime, Patricia. "Trial Date Set for Coast Guard Officer Who Allegedly Maintained 'Hit List.'"
Military.com, August 22, 2019, https://www.military.com/daily-news/2019/08/22/trial-date
-set-coast-guard-officer-who-allegedly-maintained-hit-list.html.

King, Wayne. "Links of Anti-Semitic Band Provoke 6-State Parley." *New York Times*, December 27, 1984.

——. "Neo-Nazi Is Focus of Searching by F.B.I." *New York Times*, August 18, 1986.

——. "20 Held in 7 States in Sweep of Nazis Arming for 'War' on U.S." *New York Times*,
March 3, 1985.

Kirsner, Scott. *Inventing the Movies: Hollywood's Epic Battle Between Innovation and the Status Quo, from Thomas Edison to Steve Jobs*. CinemaTech, 2008.

Klanwatch//Militia Task Force. *False Patriots: The Threat of Antigovernment Extremists*. Montgomery, AL: Southern Poverty Law Center, 1996.

Knudson, Thomas J. "Right-Wing Group Accused of Bank Robbery Plot." *New York Times*,
December 17, 1986.

Koehler, Daniel. "A Threat from Within? Exploring the Link Between the Extreme Right and
the Military." *International Centre for Counter-Terrorism—The Hague*, September 2019.
https://icct.nl/wp-content/uploads/2019/09/ICCT-Koehler-A-Threat-from-Within
-Exploring-the-Link-between-the-Extreme-Right-and-the-Military.pdf.

Kois, Dan. "They Were Out for Blood." *Slate*, January 8, 2021. https://slate.com/news-and
-politics/2021/01/was-there-a-plan-for-hostages-or-killings-at-the-capitol.html.

Kopplin, Gerald. "Suspected White Supremacist to Face Bank Robbery Charges." United Press
International, February 24, 1987.

Kunzelman, Michael. "Capitol Rioters' Social Media Posts Influencing Sentencings." Associated Press, December 11, 2021. https://apnews.com/article/media-prisons-social-media
-capitol-siege-sentencing-0a60a821ce19635b70681faf86e6526e.

Kuzmenko, Oleksiy. "'Defend the White Race': American Extremists Being Co-Opted by
Ukraine's Far-Right." *BellingCat*, February 15, 2019.

Kwong, Jessica. "Robert Bowers Gab Before Synagogue Shooting: 'Screw Your Optics, I'm
Going In.'" *Newsweek*, October 27, 2018.

Kydd, Andrew H., and Barbara F. Walter. "The Strategies of Terrorism." *International Security* 31, no. 1 (Summer 2006).

Laqueur, Walter, and Christopher Wall. *The Future of Terrorism: ISIS, Al-Qaeda, and the Alt-
Right*. New York: Thomas Dunne, 2018.

Lavin, Talia. *Culture Warlords: My Journey into the Dark Web of White Supremacy*. New York:
Hachette, 2020.

Lee, Jennifer. "Confronting the Invisibility of Anti-Asian Racism." Brookings Institution,
May 18, 2022. https://www.brookings.edu/blog/how-we-rise/2022/05/18/confronting-the
-invisibility-of-anti-asian-racism/.

Legal Information Institute. "Antiterrorism and Effective Death Penalty Act of 1996 (AEDPA)."
Cornell Law School. https://www.law.cornell.edu/wex/antiterrorism_and_effective_death
_penalty_act_of_1996_(aedpa).

León, Concepción de. "Tom Metzger, Notorious White Supremacist, Dies at 82." *New York Times*, November 12, 2020.

Lennard, Katherine. "Old Purpose, 'New Body': *The Birth of a Nation* and the Revival of the Ku Klux Klan." *Journal of the Gilded Age and Progressive Era* 14, no. 4 (October 2015).

Leonard, Ben. "'Practically and Morally Responsible': McConnell Scorches Trump—but Votes to Acquit." *Politico*, February 13, 2021. https://www.politico.com/news/2021/02/13/mcconnell-condemns-trump-acquitted-469002.

Levin, Brian. "Exclusive: Interview with Professor Who Extensively Studied Alleged Wisconsin Mass Killer." *Huffington Post*, August 7, 2012. https://www.huffpost.com/entry/exclusive-interview-with_b_1751181.

Levitas, Daniel. *The Terrorist Next Door: The Militia Movement and the Radical Right*. New York: Thomas Dunne, 2002.

Lewis, Mark, and Sarah Lyall. "Norway Mass Killer Gets the Maximum: 21 Years." *New York Times*, August 24, 2012.

Lewis, Rebecca. "Alternative Influence: Broadcasting the Reactionary Right on YouTube." *Data & Society*, September 18, 2018. https://datasociety.net/library/alternative-influence/.

Liebelson, Dana. "Inside the Unraveling of Las Vegas Shooting Spree Suspect Jerad Miller." *Mother Jones*, June 9, 2014.

Lii, Jane H. "After 15 Days, Search for Bodies Is Coming to an End." *New York Times*, May 4, 1995.

Lindemann, Albert S. *The Jew Accused: Three Anti-Semitic Affairs (Dreyfus, Beilis, Frank), 1894–1915*. Cambridge: Cambridge University Press, 1993.

Linder, Douglas O. "The Ruby Ridge (Randy Weaver) Trial: An Account." University of Missouri Kansas City School of Law. https://www.famous-trials.com/rubyridge/1152-home.

Linzer, Lori, and David Rosenberg. *Vigilante Justice*. New York: Anti-Defamation League, 1997.

Lister, Tim. "The Nexus Between Far-Right Extremists in the United States and Ukraine." *CTC Sentinel* 13, no. 4 (April 2020). https://ctc.usma.edu/the-nexus-between-far-right-extremists-in-the-united-states-and-ukraine/.

Los Angeles Times. "Obituaries: William P. Gale." *Los Angeles Times*, May 4, 1988.

Lovan, Dylan. "'Whites Don't Shoot Whites,' Suspected Gunman Told Man After Killing 2 Black Customers at Kentucky Kroger." *Chicago Tribune*, October 25, 2018.

Lowles, Nick. "Order of Nine Angles." *Hope Not Hate*, February 16, 2019. https://hopenothate.org.uk/2019/02/16/state-of-hate-2019-order-of-nine-angles/.

Macdonald, Andrew [William L. Pierce]. *The Turner Diaries*. 2nd ed. Arlington, VA: National Vanguard, 1985.

MacFarquhar, Neil. "Defendant in Plot to Kidnap Michigan Governor Is Sentenced to Six Years." *New York Times*, August 25, 2021.

——. "Oklahoma City Marks 25 Years Since America's Deadliest Homegrown Attack." *New York Times*, April 19, 2020.

MacFarquhar, Neil, Alan Feuer, and Adam Goldman. "Federal Arrests Show No Sign That Antifa Plotted Protests." *New York Times*, June 11, 2020.

MacFarquhar, Neil, and Thomas Gibbons-Neff. "Air Force Sergeant with Ties to Extremist Group Charged in Federal Officer's Death." *New York Times*, June 16, 2020.

Macklin, Graham. "The El Paso Terrorist Attack: The Chain Reaction of Global Right-Wing Terror." *CTC Sentinel* 12, no. 11 (December 2019). https://ctc.usma.edu/el-paso-terrorist-attack-chain-reaction-global-right-wing-terror/.

Madhani, Aamer. "Treasury to Designate Wagner Transnational Criminal Group." Associated Press, January 20, 2023. https://apnews.com/article/united-states-government-russia-b4a22b4e4ecc7c2b588e5719c05ba871.

Mallonee, Sue, Sheryll Shariat, Gail Stennies, et al. "Physical Injuries and Fatalities Resulting from the Oklahoma City Bombing." *JAMA: Journal of the American Medical Association* 276, no. 5 (August 7, 1996).

Marche, Stephen. *The Next Civil War: Dispatches from the American Future.* New York: Avid, 2022.

Martin, Nick R. "Radio active." *The Informant,* July 29, 2020. https://www.informant.news/p/radio-active.

Marx, Karl, and Frederick Engels. *Manifesto of the Communist Party.* 1848. Chicago: Charles H. Kerr & Co., 1906.

Mathias, Christopher. "Exclusive: Army Investigating Soldier's Alleged Leadership In Neo-Nazi Terror Group." *Huffington Post,* May 3, 2019. https://www.huffpost.com/entry/atomwaffen-division-army-soldier-investigation-corwyn-storm-carver_n_5ccb5350e4b0e4d7572fde38.

——. "Exclusive: Phrase 'White Nationalists' Cut from Measure to Screen Military Enlistees." *Huffington Post,* December 19, 2019. https://www.huffpost.com/entry/senate-removes-white-nationalists-from-military-bill-aimed-at-screening-for-extremists_n_5dfab39be4b0eb2264d3a18d.

——. "Exposed: Military Investigating 4 More Servicemen for Ties to White Nationalist Group." *Huffington Post,* April 27, 2019. https://www.huffpost.com/entry/white-nationalists-military-identity-evropa_n_5cc1a87ee4b0764d31dd839c.

Maulbetsch, Erik. "Denver Police Seized Assault Rifles from Anti-Government Gun Activists at Friday Night Protest." *Colorado Times Recorder,* May 31, 2020.

McAllister, Toni. "Arson and Hate Crime Suspected in Escondido Mosque Fire." *Times of San Diego,* March 24, 2019.

McAuliffe, Terry. *Beyond Charlottesville: Taking a Stand Against White Nationalism.* New York: Thomas Dunne, 2019.

McCann, Anthony. *Shadowlands: Fear and Freedom at the Oregon Standoff—a Western Tale of America in Crisis.* New York: Bloomsbury, 2019.

McCoy, Max. "Speaking of White Supremacists, Remember These Boys Who Did Not Make Kansas Proud." *Kansas Reflector,* October 4, 2020.

McDaniel, Michael. "Arizona Attorney General Finds Logistical and Legal 'Concerns' After Election Probe." *Courthouse News Service,* April 6, 2022. https://www.courthousenews.com/arizona-attorney-generals-election-investigation-finds-logistical-and-legal-concerns/.

McGrath, Ben. "The Movement: The Rise of Tea Party Activism." *New Yorker,* January 24, 2010.

McLellan, Dennis. "Ganging Up: 'Skinhead' Groups of White Youths Appear on Rise." *Los Angeles Times,* November 30, 1987.

McManamy, Rob. "Oklahoma Blast Forces Unsettling Design Questions." *Engineering News Record* 234, no. 17 (May 1, 1995).

McPherson, James. *Battle Cry of Freedom: The Civil War Era.* New York: Oxford University Press, 1988.

"McVeigh Admits Planting Okla. City Bomb." Reuters, February 28, 1997.

"The McVeigh Jury Speaks." *New York Times*, June 3, 1997.

Meddis, Sam. "Neo-Nazis Weakened, FBI Says." *USA Today*, February 18, 1985.

Melle, Ingrid. "The Breivik Case and What Psychiatrists Can Learn from It." *World Psychiatry* 12, no. 1 (2013).

Menendez, Pilar. "'Fuck All of You!': Capitol Rioter Raises Hell During Off-the-Rails Court Hearing." *Daily Beast,* May 6, 2021. https://www.thedailybeast.com/landon-kenneth -copeland-utah-man-charged-with-assaulting-police-during-capitol-riots-loses-it-in -court.

——. "McConnell Unleashes on 'Shameful' Trump—Moments After Voting 'Not Guilty.'" *Daily Beast*, February 13, 2021. https://www.thedailybeast.com/mitch-mcconnell-unleashes -on-shameful-trumpmoments-after-voting-to-acquit-in-impeachment-trial.

Mettler, Katie, and Paul Duggan. ""Two Accused of Plotting Racial 'Civil War' Are Sentenced to 9 Years Each in Federal Prison." *Washington Post*, October 28, 2021.

Michael, George. "Blueprints and Fantasies: A Review and Analysis of Extremist Fiction." *Studies in Conflict and Terrorism* 33, no. 2 (February 2010).

——. *Confronting Right-Wing Extremism and Terrorism in the USA.* London: Routledge, 2003.

Michel, Lou, and Dan Herbeck. *American Terrorist: Timothy McVeigh and the Oklahoma City Bombing.* New York: ReganBooks, 2001.

——. "Could the Oklahoma City Bombing Have Been Prevented?" *Tulsa World*, April 13, 2020. https://tulsaworld.com/news/local/could-the-oklahoma-city-bombing-have-been -prevented/article_11601cef-6e5b-55ae-9cb0-bc92b36af02c.html.

——. "How Oklahoma City Bomber Timothy McVeigh Changed the Fringe Right." *Buffalo News*, April 19, 2020.

Miller, Cassie. "The 'Boogaloo' Started as a Racist Meme." *SPLC: Hatewatch*, June 5, 2020. https://www.splcenter.org/hatewatch/2020/06/05/boogaloo-started-racist-meme.

——. "White Supremacists See Coronavirus as an Opportunity." Southern Poverty Law Center, March 26, 2020. https://www.splcenter.org/hatewatch/2020/03/26/white-supremacists -see-coronavirus-opportunity.

Miller, Michael E. "Hunting Black Men to Start a 'Race War.'" *Washington Post*, December 27, 2019.

Miller-Idriss, Cynthia. *Hate in the Homeland: The New Global Far Right.* Princeton, NJ: Princeton University Press, 2020.

Money, Luke. "Newport Man Accused of Murdering Blaze Bernstein Denies Hate Crime." *Daily Pilot*, August 22, 2018.

Morlin, Bill. "Former Butler Associate, Klan Leader Remain at Large." *Spokesman-Review Spokane Chronicle*, April 25, 1987.

Movement Advancement Project. *Policy Spotlight: Hate Crimes Law.* Boulder, CO: July 2021. https://www.lgbtmap.org/file/2021-report-hate-crime-laws.pdf.

Mudde, Cas. *The Far Right Today.* Cambridge: Polity, 2019.

Muirhead, Russell, and Nancy L. Rosenblum. *A Lot of People Are Saying: The New Conspiracism and the Assault on Democracy.* Princeton, NJ: Princeton University Press, 2020.

Murphy, Brett, Will Carless, Marisa Kwiatkowski, and Tricia L. Nadolny. "A 2009 Warning About Right-Wing Extremism was Engulfed by Politics. There Are Signs It's Happening Again." *USA Today,* January 27, 2021.

Nagourney, Adam. "A Defiant Rancher Savors the Audience That Rallied to His Side." *New York Times,* April 23, 2014.

Narea, Nicole. "Why Progressives Are Lining Up Against New Criminal Penalties for Domestic Terrorism." *Vox,* March 22, 2021. https://www.vox.com/22343959/criminal-law-domestic-terrorism-capitol-riot-congress.

"Nazi Court to Try First Foreign Jew for 'Rassenschande.'" *Jewish Telegraphic Agency,* November 3, 1935. https://www.jta.org/archive/nazi-court-to-try-first-foreign-jew-for-rassenschande.

Nelson, Libby. "'Why We Voted for Donald Trump': David Duke Explains the White Supremacist Charlottesville Protests." *Vox,* August 12, 2017. https://www.vox.com/2017/8/12/16138358/charlottesville-protests-david-duke-kkk.

Ness, Immanuel. *Encyclopedia of American Social Movements,* vol. 4. London: Routledge, 2015.

Neiwert, David A. *Alt-America: The Rise of the Radical Right in the Age of Trump.* New York: Verso, 2017.

——. *In God's Country: The Patriot Movement and the Pacific Northwest.* Pullman: Washington State University Press, 2019.

Neumann, Elizabeth. "Far-Right Extremists Went Mainstream Under Trump. The Capitol Attack Cements His Legacy." *USA Today,* February 15, 2021.

Nunn, Joseph. "The Posse Comitatus Act Explained." Brennan Center for Justice, October 14, 2021. https://www.brennancenter.org/our-work/research-reports/posse-comitatus-act-explained.

Obama, Barack. *A Promised Land.* New York: Viking, 2020.

OCA National Center. "COVID-19 and the Rise in Anti-Asian Hate." *OCA Advocate,* n.d. https://www.aapihatecrimes.org/facts.

"The Oklahoma Bombing Conspirators." http://law2.umkc.edu/faculty/projects/ftrials/mcveigh/conspirators.html.

Olmos, Sergio. "'The Timothy McVeighs Are Still There': Fears Over Extremism in US Military." *Guardian,* January 10, 2022.

Oltermann, Philip. "Erase and Forget: New Documentary Reveals Life Story of the Real Rambo." *Guardian,* February 13, 2017.

"1 big thing: Scoop . . . Trump Blames Antifa for Riot." *Axios,* January 12, 2021. https://www.axios.com/newsletters/axios-sneak-peek-1c44d7d7-d31e-4879-bff1-11965803be69.html.

Oosting, Jonathan. "FBI Informant: Facebook Led Me to Infiltrate Plot to Kidnap Gretchen Whitmer." *The Bridge* (Michigan), March 5, 2021. https://www.bridgemi.com/michigan-government/fbi-informant-facebook-led-me-infiltrate-plot-kidnap-gretchen-whitmer.

Oney, Steve. *And the Dead Shall Rise: The Murder of Mary Phagan and the Lynching of Leo Frank.* New York: Pantheon, 2003.

Pandith, Farah, and Jacob Ware. "Teen Terrorism Inspired by Social Media Is on the Rise. Here's What We Need to Do." *NBC News THINK*, March 22, 2021. https://www.nbcnews .com/think/opinion/teen-terrorism-inspired-social-media-rise-here-s-what-we -ncna1261307.

Paul, Kari, Luke Harding, and Severin Carrell. "Far-Right Website 8kun Again Loses Internet Service Protection Following Capitol Attack." *Guardian*, January 15, 2021.

Pearson, Naomi E. "Fringe Religion and the Far-Right: Dangerous Behavior Patterns Among Christian Millennialists." *Inquiries Journal* 11, no 3 (Fall 2019). http://www.inquiriesjournal .com/articles/1761/fringe-religion-and-the-far-right-dangerous-behavior-patterns -among-christian-millennialists.

Peltz, Jennifer. "Marine Veteran Among Two Proud Boys Facing Federal Conspiracy Charges in Capitol Riot." *Marine Corps Times,* January 31, 2021.

Perez-Pena, Richard. "The Terror Conspiracy: The Charges; A Gamble Pays Off as the Prosecution Uses an Obscure Nineteenth-Century Law." *New York Times*, October 2, 1995.

Perliger, Arie. *American Zealots: Inside Right-Wing Domestic Terrorism*. New York: Columbia University Press, 2020.

——. *Challengers from the Sidelines: Understanding America's Violent Far-Right*. West Point, NY: Combatting Terrorism Center, November 2012.

Perry, Kimball. "Mo. Executes White Supremacist Serial Killer Franklin." *USA Today*, November 20, 2013.

Peterson, Iver. "White Supremacists Meet in Quest for Homeland." *New York Times*, July 14, 1986.

Pfeiffer, Rick. "Oklahoma City Bombing Quickly Linked to Timothy McVeigh 25 Years Ago." *Lockport Union Sun & Journal*, April 19, 2020.

Peiser, Jaclyn. "Twitter Bans Steve Bannon for Video Suggesting Violence Against Fauci, FBI Director Wray." *Washington Post*, November 6, 2020.

Phelps, Timothy M. "Dylann Roof Tried to Kill Himself During Attack, Victim's SonS." *Los Angeles Times*, June 20, 2015.

Philipps, Dave. "White Supremacism in the U.S. Military, Explained." *New York Times*, February 27, 2019.

Philips, John W. *Sign of the Cross: The Prosecutor's True Story of a Landmark Trial Against the Klan*. Louisville, KY: Westminster John Knox, 2000.

Pidd, Helen. "Anders Breivik 'Trained' for Shooting Attacks by Playing *Call of Duty*." *Guardian*, April 19, 2012.

Pieslak, Jonathan. *Radicalism and Music: An Introduction to the Music Cultures of al-Qa'ida, Racist Skinheads, Christian-Affiliated Radicals, and Eco-Animal Rights Militants*. Middletown, CT: Wesleyan University Press, 2015.

Pierannunzi, Carol. "Thomas E. Watson (1856–1922)." *Georgia Encyclopedia: History & Archeology, Late Nineteenth Century, 1877–1900*, July 14, 2020. https://www.georgiaencyclopedia .org/articles/history-archaeology/thomas-e-watson-1856-1922.

Piggott, Stephen. "White Nationalists and the So-Called 'Alt-Right' Celebrate Trump's Victory." Southern Poverty Law Center, November 9, 2016. https://www.splcenter.org

/hatewatch/2016/11/09/white-nationalists-and-so-called-alt-right-celebrate-trumps
-victory.

Pilcher, James. "Charlottesville Suspect's Beliefs Were 'Along the Party Lines of the Neo-Nazi Movement,' Ex-Teacher Says." *USA Today*, August 13, 2017.

Pitt, David. "One Iowa Man in Capitol Riot Released, Other Remains in Jail." *U.S. News & World Report*, January 19, 2021.

Pomerantsev, Peter. *This Is Not Propaganda: Adventures in the War Against Reality.* New York: PublicAffairs, 2019.

Porter, Caroline, Ben Kesling, and Nathan Koppel. "Shooter Linked to Hate Group." *Wall Street Journal*, August 6, 2012.

Post, Jerrold. "Psychological and Motivational Factors in Terrorist Decision-Making: Implications for CBW Terrorism." In *Toxic Terror: Assessing Terrorist Use of Chemical and Biological Weapons*, ed. Jonathan B. Tucker. Cambridge, MA: MIT Press, 2000.

Post, Jerrold, Cody McGinnis, and Kristen Moody. "The Changing Face of Terrorism in the 21st Century: The Communications Revolution and the Virtual Community of Hatred." *Behavioral Sciences & the Law* 32, no. 3 (2014).

Potok, Mark. "Extremism and the Military." Southern Poverty Law Center, August 11, 2006. https://www.splcenter.org/fighting-hate/intelligence-report/2006/extremism-and -military.

——. "The Year in Hate and Extremism." Southern Poverty Law Center, March 4, 2013. https:// www.splcenter.org/fighting-hate/intelligence-report/2013/year-hate-and-extremism.

Price, Michelle L., and Scott Sonner. "Army Reservist, Navy and Air Force Vets Plotted to Terrorize Vegas Protests, Prosecutors Charge." *Military Times*, June 4, 2020. https://www .militarytimes.com/news/your-military/2020/06/04/army-reservist-navy-and-air-force -vets-plotted-to-terrorize-vegas-protests-prosecutors-charge/.

"Proud Boy." *ADL Backgrounder*, January 23, 2020. https://www.adl.org/proudboys.

"Public-Private Partnerships for Local P/CVE Position Paper." Strong Cities Network, n.d. https://strongcitiesnetwork.org/en/wp-content/uploads/sites/5/2019/03/WG3_position _paper_final.pdf.

Reid, T. R. and Mary Thornton. "Aryan Group, Jail Gangs Linked: FBI Reports on White Supremacist Organization." *Washington Post*, December 18, 1984.

Reid, T. R., Mary Thornton, and Doug Vaughan. "'Neo-Nazis' Inspire White Supremacists." *Washington Post*, December 26, 1984.

Reitman, Janet. "How Did a Convicted Neo-Nazi Release Propaganda from Prison?" *Rolling Stone*, May 25, 2018. https://www.rollingstone.com/politics/politics-news/how-did-a -convicted-neo-nazi-release-propaganda-from-prison-628437/.

Reeves, Jay. "Rudolph Gets 2 Life Terms in Abortion Clinic Attack." *Washington Post*, July 19, 2005.

Rhodes, Tom. "Man Charged with Oklahoma Bombing 'Had Klan Links.'" *Times*, March 21, 1997.

Richards, Imogen. "A Dialectical Approach to Online Propaganda: Australia's United Patriots Front, Right-Wing Politics, and Islamic State." *Studies in Conflict and Terrorism* 42, nos. 1–3 (January–March 2019).

Ricks, Bob. "Crimes of the Century: Oklahoma City." CNN, August 11, 2013. http://www.cnn.com/TRANSCRIPTS/1308/11/cotc.01.html.

Riley, Kevin Jack, and Bruce Hoffman. *Domestic Terrorism: A National Assessment of State and Local Preparedness.* MR-505J. Santa Monica, CA: RAND Corporation, 1995.

Riley, Tonya. "Political Extremists Are Using YouTube to Monetize Their Toxic Ideas." *Mother Jones,* September 18, 2018. https://www.motherjones.com/politics/2018/09/political-extremists-are-using-youtube-to-monetize-their-toxic-ideas/.

Rizzo, Tony. "Federal Hate-Crime Charges, State Charges Likely in Overland Park Shootings." *Kansas City Star,* May 16, 2014.

Robertson, Derek. "How an Obscure Conservative Theory Became the Trump Era's Go-To Nerd Phrase." *Politico,* February 25, 2018. https://www.politico.com/magazine/story/2018/02/25/overton-window-explained-definition-meaning-217010/.

Romell, Rick. "Shooter's Odd Behavior Did Not Go Unnoticed." *Milwaukee Journal Sentinel,* August 6, 2012.

Roose, Kevin. "A Mass Murder of, and for, the Internet." *New York Times,* March 15, 2019.

——. "'Shut the Site Down,' Says the Creator of 8chan, a Megaphone for Gunmen." *New York Times,* August 4, 2019.

Rosenberg, Howard. "Neo-Nazis Cloud the Utah Air: 'Aryan Nations' to Debut Over Tiny Salt Lake City Station." *Los Angeles Times,* November 24, 1987.

Rosenfeld, Megan. "Dodge City Showdown Racist, Anti-Semitic Radio Broadcasts Alleged." *Washington Post,* May 7, 1983.

Ross, Jeffrey Ian, ed. *Religion and Violence: An Encyclopedia of Faith and Conflict from Antiquity to the Present.* London: Routledge, 2015.

Russakoff, Dale, and Serge F. Kovaleski. "An Ordinary Boy's Extraordinary Rage." *Washington Post,* July 2, 1995.

"Ryan Kelly of the *Daily Progress,* Charlottesville, Va." Pulitzer Prizes, February 24, 2023. https://www.pulitzer.org/winners/ryan-kelly-daily-progress.

Satariano, Adam. "British Ruling Pins Blame on Social Media for Teenager's Suicide." *New York Times,* October 1, 2022.

Scherr, Sonia. "Hate Groups Claim Obama Win Is Sparking Recruitment Surge." Southern Poverty Law Center, November 6, 2008. https://www.splcenter.org/hatewatch/2008/11/06/hate-groups-claim-obama-win-sparking-recruitment-surge.

Schlatter, Evelyn A. *Aryan Cowboys: White Supremacists and the Search for a New Frontier, 1970–2000.* Austin: University of Texas Press, 2006.

Schogol, Jeff. "White Supremacist Group Leader Is Former Marine Corps Recruiter." *Marine Corps Times,* August 15, 2017. https://www.marinecorpstimes.com/news/2017/08/15/white-supremacist-group-leader-is-former-marine-recruiter/.

Scigliano, Eric. "He Was Not Following Orders." *Seattle Weekly,* October 9, 2006.

Schmid, Alex, and Janny De Graaf. *Violence as Communication: Insurgent Terrorism and the Western News Media.* Beverly Hills, CA: Sage, 1982.

Schuster, Henry, with Charles Stone. *Hunting Eric Rudolph: An Insider's Account of the Five-Year Search for the Olympic Bombing Suspect.* New York: Berkley, 2005.

Seal, Thomas. "U.K. Is Toughening Up Online Harms Bill, Culture Secretary Says." *Bloomberg*, November 23, 2021. https://www.bloomberg.com/news/articles/2021-11-23/u-k-is-toughening-up-online-harms-bill-culture-secretary-says.

Segal, David. "The Pied Piper of Racism: William Pierce Wants Young People to March to His Hate Records." *Washington Post*, January 12, 2000.

Seierstad, Åsne. *One of Us: The Story of Anders Breivik and the Massacre in Norway.* New York: Farrar, Straus & Giroux, 2015.

Seymour, Cheri. *Committee of the States: Inside The Radical Right.* Mariposa, CA: Camden Place Communications, 1987.

Shane III, Leo, and Megan McCloskey. "Sikh Temple Shooter was Army Veteran, White Supremacist." *Stars and Stripes*, August 6, 2012.

Sharpe, Tanya Telfair. "The Identity Christian Movement: Ideology of Domestic Terrorism." *Journal of Black Studies* 30, no. 4 (March 2000).

Sherman, Amy. "Fact Check: Did Trump Vote by Mail for the 2020 Election?" *Austin American-Statesman*, January 15, 2022. https://www.statesman.com/story/news/politics/politifact/2022/01/15/fact-check-did-trump-vote-mail-2020-election/6516078001/.

Signer, Michael. *Cry Havoc: Charlottesville and American Democracy Under Siege.* New York: PublicAffairs, 2020.

Simi, Pete, and Robert Futrell. *American Swastika: Inside the White Power Movement's Hidden Spaces of Hate.* Lanham, MD: Rowman & Littlefield, 2015.

Simon, Jeffrey. *Lone Wolf Terrorism: Understanding the Growing Threat.* Amherst, MA: Prometheus, 2016.

Simon, Steven, and Jonathan Stevenson. "How Can We Neutralize the Militias?" *New York Review of Books*, August 19, 2021. https://www.nybooks.com/articles/2021/08/19/how-can-we-neutralize-militias/.

——. "The Real Fallout from the Mar-a-Lago Search." *Politico*, August 19, 2022. https://www.politico.com/news/magazine/2022/08/19/fallout-mar-a-lago-search-00052799.

——. "These Disunited States." *New York Review of Books*, September 22, 2022. https://www.nybooks.com/articles/2022/09/22/these-disunited-states-steven-simon-jonathan-stevenson.

Simmons, Bill. "Defendants All Acquitted in Sedition Trial." *Journal News* (White Plains, NY), April 8, 1988.

Simpson, William Gayley. *Which Way Western Man?* https://booksrun.com/9780937944165-which-way-western-man-2nd-edition.

Sims, Patsy. *The Klan.* New York: Dorset, 1978.

Singer, P. W., and Emerson T. Brooking. *Like War: The Weaponization of Social Media.* Boston: Eamon Dolan/Houghton Mifflin Harcourt, 2018.

Singer, P. W., and Michael McConnell. "Want to Stop the Next Crisis? Teaching Cyber Citizenship Must Become a National Priority." *Time*, January 21, 2021. https://time.com/5932134/cyber-citizenship-national-priority/.

Singular, Stephen. *Talked to Death: The Life and Murder of Alan Berg.* New York: Beech Tree, 1987.

"Six Hurt in 'Anti-Refugee' Hotel Arson Attack." *The Local*, April 7, 2016. https://www.thelocal .de/20160407/six-hurt-in-anti-refugee-hotel-arson-attack.

"*Small Arms Survey* Reveals: More Than One Billion Firearms in the World." *Small Arms Survey*, June 18, 2018. https://www.smallarmssurvey.org/sites/default/files/resources/SAS -Press-release-global-firearms-holdings.pdf.

Smith, Brent L. *Terrorism in America: Pipe Bombs and Pipe Dreams*. Albany: State University of New York Press, 1994.

Smith, Laura. "Armed Resistance, Lone Wolves, and Media Messaging: Meet the Godfather of the 'Alt-Right.'" *Timeline*, November 6, 2017. https://timeline.com/louis-beam-white -supremacy-history-20d028315d.

Solotaroff, Paul. "He Spent 25 Years Infiltrating Nazis, the Klan, and Biker Gangs." *Rolling Stone*, January 30, 2022. https://www.rollingstone.com/culture/culture-features/fbi -infiltrator-nazis-kkk-biker-gangs-1280830/.

Sommer, Will. "A QAnon Devotee Live-Streamed Her Trip to N.Y. to 'Take Out' Joe Biden." *Daily Beast*, April 30, 2020. https://www.thedailybeast.com/a-qanon-devotee-live-streamed -her-trip-to-ny-to-take-out-joe-biden.

Sonne, Paul, and Missy Ryan. "As He Tackles Extremism, Lloyd Austin Draws on Military's Experience Dealing with 1995 Racially Motivated Murders." *Washington Post*, January 31, 2021.

Southern Poverty Law Center. "Antigovernment Movement." https://www.splcenter.org /fighting-hate/extremist-files/ideology/antigovernment.

——. "Elmer Stewart Rhodes." https://www.splcenter.org/fighting-hate/extremist-files /individual/elmer-stewart-rhodes.

——. "FBI Point Man Robert Blitzer Discusses Agency's Work with Extremist Groups." *Intelligence Report*, December 15, 1998.

——. "Fighting Hate." https://www.splcenter.org/fighting-hate.

——. "Frazier Glenn Miller." https://www.splcenter.org/fighting-hate/extremist-files /individual/frazier-glenn-miller.

——. "Larry Pratt." https://www.splcenter.org/fighting-hate/extremist-files/individual/larry -pratt.

——. "Louis Beam." https://www.splcenter.org/fighting-hate/extremist-files/individual/louis -beam.

——. "Louis Beam: In His Own Words." 2015. https://www.splcenter.org/fighting-hate /intelligence-report/2015/louis-beam-his-own-words.

——. "Oath Keepers." https://www.splcenter.org/fighting-hate/extremist-files/group/oath -keepers.

——. "'Patriot' Conspiracy Theorist Jack McLamb Dies." January 13, 2014. https://www .splcenter.org/hatewatch/2014/01/13/patriot-conspiracy-theorist-jack-mclamb-dies.

——. "Proud Boys." https://www.splcenter.org/fighting-hate/extremist-files/group/proud -boys.

——. "Remaking the Right." *Intelligence Report*, November 12, 2003. https://www.splcenter .org/fighting-hate/intelligence-report/2003/remaking-right.

——. "Sovereign Citizens Movement." https://www.splcenter.org/fighting-hate/extremist
-files/ideology/sovereign-citizens-movement.

——. "Ten Days After: Harassment and Intimidation in the Aftermath of the Election."
November 29, 2016. https://www.splcenter.org/20161129/ten-days-after-harassment-and
-intimidation-aftermath-election.

——. "*The Turner Diaries*, Other Racist Novels, Inspire Extremist Violence." *Intelligence
Report*, October 14, 2004. https://www.splcenter.org/fighting-hate/intelligence-report/2004
/turner-diaries-other-racist-novels-inspire-extremist-violence.

——. *The Year in Hate & Extremism 2021*. Montgomery, AL: Southern Poverty Law Center,
2022. https://www.splcenter.org/sites/default/files/splc-2021-year-in-hate-extremism-rep
ort.pdf.

——. "William Pierce." https://www.splcenter.org/fighting-hate/extremist-files/individual
/william-pierce.

——. "William Pierce: A Political History." https://www.splcenter.org/fighting-hate
/intelligence-report/2015/william-pierce-political-history.

Spagat, Elliot, and Julie Watson. "John Earnest—Physics Teacher's Son, Celebrated Pianist,
8chan User, Synagogue Shooting Suspect." Associated Press, April 30, 2019.

Spencer, Hawes, and Richard Pérez-Peña. "Murder Charge Increases in Charlottesville Protest Death." *New York Times*, December 14, 2017.

Spilde, Tony. "Changing Lives—in 15 Seconds." *Bismarck Tribune*, February 9, 2003. https://
bismarcktribune.com/news/local/changing-lives-in-15-seconds/article_d1e97691-ea36
-5a7a-978b-cc529942b019.html.

——. "From Mild to Madness," *Bismarck Tribune*, February 9, 2003. Excerpted at https://
murderpedia.org/male.K/k/kahl-gordon.htm.

Squire, Megan. "Monetizing Propaganda: How Far-right Extremists Earn Money by Video
Streaming." WebSci '21: 13th International ACM Conference on Web Science in 2021,
June 21–25, 2021. https://arxiv.org/pdf/2105.05929.pdf.

Stack, Liam. "Wildlife Refuge Occupied in Protest of Oregon Ranchers' Prison Terms." *New
York Times*, January 2, 2016.

Steinhauer, Jennifer. "Veterans Fortify the Ranks of Militias Aligned with Trump's Views."
New York Times, September 11, 2021.

Stern, Jessica. "The Covenant, the Sword, and the Arm of the Lord" [1985]. In *Toxic Terror:
Assessing Terrorist Use of Chemical and Biological Weapons*, ed. Jonathan B. Tucker. Cambridge, MA: MIT Press, 2000.

——. *Terror in the Name of God: Why Religious Militants Kill*. New York: ecco/HarperCollins,
2003.

Stern, Jessica, and J. M. Berger. *ISIS: The State of Terror*. New York: HarperCollins, 2015.

——. "Smart Mobs, Ultraviolence, and Civil Society: ISIS Innovations." *Lawfare*, March 23,
2015. https://www.lawfareblog.com/smart-mobs-ultraviolence-and-civil-society-isis-inn
ovations.

Stern, Kenneth S. *A Force Upon the Plain: The American Militia Movement and the Politics of
Hate*. New York: Simon & Schuster, 1996.

Stern, Samantha, Jacob Ware, and Nicholas Harrington. "Terrorist Targeting in the Age of Coronavirus." *International Counter-Terrorism Review* 1, no. 3 (June 2020), https://www.ict.org.il/Article/2562/Terrorist_Targeting_in_the_Age_of_Coronavirus.

Stock, Catherine McNicol. *Rural Radicals: Righteous Rage in the American Grain.* Ithaca, NY: Cornell University Press, 1996.

Suall, Irwin, et al. *ADL Special Report: Shaved for Battle: Skinheads Target America's Youth.* New York: Anti-Defamation League of B'nai B'rith, November 1987.

Suall, Irwin, and David Lowe. "The Hate Movement Today: A Chronicle of Violence and Disarray." *Terrorism* 10, no. 4 (1987).

Sullivan, Cheryl. "White Supremacists. Neo-Nazi Drive to Recruit US Youth Has Some Success Among 'Skinheads.'" *Christian Science Monitor*, August 14, 1987.

Sullivan, Dan. "Experts: One-Time Neo-Nazi Charged in Double Murder Has Autism, Schizophrenia." *Tampa Bay Times*, December 19, 2019.

Sun Staff. "A look Inside the Lives of Shooters Jerad Miller, Amanda Miller." *Las Vegas Sun*, June 9, 2014.

Sutherland, John. "Goodbye, Good Riddance." *Guardian*, July 29, 2002.

Tabor, James D., and Eugene V. Gallagher. *Why Waco? Cults and the Battle for Religious Freedom in America.* Berkeley: University of California Press, 1995.

Taylor, Helen. "Domestic Terrorism and Hate Crimes: Legal Definitions and Media Framing of Mass Shootings in the United States." *Journal of Policing, Intelligence, and Counter Terrorism* 14, no. 3 (2019).

Thackeray, Lorna. "The Freeman Standoff." *Billings Gazette*, March 25, 2006.

Times Wire Services. "Extremist Admits Gang's Racial Attack." *Los Angeles Times*, July 30, 1987.

Thomas, Elise. "Qanon Deploys 'Information Warfare' to Influence the 2020 Election." *Wired*, February 17, 2020. https://www.wired.com/story/qanon-deploys-information-warfare -influence-2020-election/.

Thomas, Jo. "At Bomb Trial, Tearful Stories of Terrible Day." *New York Times*, April 26, 1995.

——. "For First Time, Woman Says McVeigh Told of Bomb Plan." *New York Times*, April 30, 1997.

——. "Friend Says McVeigh Wanted Bombing to Start an 'Uprising.'" *New York Times*, May 13 1997.

——. "In a Letter, McVeigh Told of Shifting to 'Animal.'" *New York Times*, May 9, 1997.

——. "McVeigh Jury Decides on Sentence of Death in Oklahoma Bombing." *New York Times*, June 14, 1997.

——. "Officer Describes His Arrest of a Suspect in the Oklahoma City Bombing." *New York Times*, April 29, 1997.

——. "Political Ideas of McVeigh Are Subject at Bomb Trial." *New York Times*, June 11, 1997.

Thomas, Jo, and Ronald Smothers. "Oklahoma City Building Was Target of Plot as Early as '83, Official Says." *New York Times*, May 20, 1995.

Thompson, A. C., Ali Winston, and Jake Hanrahan. "Ranks of Notorious Hate Group Include Active-Duty Military." *ProPublica*, May 3, 2018. https://www.propublica.org/article /atomwaffen-division-hate-group-active-duty-military.

Thompson, Jared. "Examining Extremism: The Boogaloo Movement." Center for Strategic and International Studies, June 30, 2021. https://www.csis.org/blogs/examining-extremism/examining-extremism-boogaloo-movement.

Thorpe, Ryan. "Homegrown Hate." *Winnipeg Free Press*, August 16, 2019. https://www.winnipegfreepress.com/local/homegrown-hate-547510902.html.

Thrush, Glenn, and Michael Levenson. "Pair Is Charged with Plotting to 'Destroy Baltimore' by Attacking Electrical Grid." *New York Times*, February 6, 2023.

Timberg, Craig. "Gallows or Guillotines? The Chilling Debate on TheDonald.win Before the Capitol Siege." *Washington Post*, April 15, 2021.

——. "Trump's Comments on Conspiracy Theory Are Celebrated: 'This Was the Biggest Pitch for QAnon I've Ever Seen.'" *Washington Post*, October 16, 2020.

Toy, Eckard. "'Promised Land' or Armageddon? History, Survivalists, and the Aryan Nations in the Pacific Northwest." *Montana: The Magazine of Western History* 36, no. 3 (Summer 1986).

Treverton, Gregory F. *Intelligence for an Age of Terror.* New York: Cambridge University Press, 2009.

"Trump Praises QAnon Supporters: 'I Understand They Like Me Very Much.'" *Axios*, August 19, 2020. https://www.axios.com/trump-praises-qanon-supporters-i-understand-they-like-me-very-much-42146fb3-bd69-4943-8e80-2f0bcf4b0b17.html.

"Trump Tried to Grab Steering Wheel to Go to U.S. Capitol Jan 6—Witness." Reuters, June 28, 2022.

Tuma, Andrea Prado, and Alice Huguet. *Engaging Youth with Public Policy: Middle School Lessons to Counter Truth Decay.* TLA387-1. Santa Monica, CA: RAND Corporation, 2022. https://www.rand.org/pubs/tools/TLA387-1.html#overcoming-covid19-what-scientists-know-and-what-policy-can-tell-us.

Turner Lee, Nicol, James Seddon, Brooke Tanner, and Samantha Lai. "Why the Federal Government Needs to Step Up Efforts to Close the Rural Broadband Divide." Brookings Institution, October 4, 2022. https://www.brookings.edu/research/why-the-federal-government-needs-to-step-up-their-efforts-to-close-the-rural-broadband-divide/.

Turner, Wallace. "3 in Racist Group Held on Counterfeiting Charges." *New York Times*, October 4, 1986.

"Two Years and Thousands of Voices: What Community-Generated Data Tells Us About Anti-AAPI Hate." Stop AAPI Hate. https://stopaapihate.org/year-2-report/.

United Press International. "6 Gunmen Hold Up Brink's Truck and Escape with Sacks of Loot." *New York Times*, July 20, 1984.

——. "Neo-Nazi David Tate, Who Is Serving a Life Prison Sentence." March 3, 1986.

——. "Seven Reputed 'Skinheads' Indicted." February 19, 1988.

——. "Terrorism Charges Dropped Against Reputed Skinhead Leader." December 1, 1987.

Van Dyke, Nella, and Sarah A. Soule. "Structural Social Change and the Mobilizing Effect of Threat: Explaining Levels of Patriot and Militia Organizing in the United States." *Social Problems* 49, no. 4 (November 2002).

Verhovek, Sam Howe. "F.B.I. Agent to Be Spared Prosecution in Shooting." *New York Times*, June 15, 2001.

Verini, James. "The Paradox of Prosecuting Domestic Terrorism." *New York Times Magazine*, February 8, 2023.

Vigdor, Neil. "Man Charged with Making Death Threats to Nancy Pelosi in Coronavirus Rant." *New York Times*, March 26, 2020.

———. "Man Who Killed Two in Racial Attack at Kroger Gets Life." *New York Times*, December 18, 2020.

Villarreal, Daniel. "Navy Kicks Out Alleged Recruiter for Neo-Nazi Group Atomwaffen Division After Investigation." *Newsweek*, April 17, 2020.

Vogels, Emily A. "Some Digital Divides Persist Between Rural, Urban and Suburban America." Pew Research Center, August 19, 2021. https://www.pewresearch.org/fact-tank/2021/08/19/some-digital-divides-persist-between-rural-urban-and-suburban-america/.

Vollers, Maryanne. "Inside Bomber Row." *Time*, November 5, 2006. http://content.time.com/time/subscriber/article/0,33009,1555145,00.html.

Wakin, Daniel J. "Richard G. Butler, 86, Founder of the Aryan Nations, Dies." *New York Times*, September 9, 2004.

Walter, Jess. *Ruby Ridge: The Truth and Tragedy of the Randy Weaver Family.* New York: Harper Perennial, 2002.

Walter, Barbara F. *How Civil Wars Start—and How to Stop Them.* New York: Crown, 2022.

Walters, Jerome. *One Aryan Nation Under God: How Religious Extremists Use the Bible to Justify Their Actions.* Naperville, IL: Sourcebooks, 2001.

Wang, Amy B. "'ALL LIVES SPLATTER': Sheriff's Office Apologizes for Facebook Post of Car Hitting Protesters." *Washington Post*, September 12, 2017.

Warchol, Glen. "Coeur d'Alene Bombing Suspects Arraigned." United Press International, October 1, 1987.

Ware, Jacob. "Fighting Back: The Atomwaffen Division, Countering Violent Extremism, and the Evolving Crackdown on Far-Right Terrorism in America." *Journal for Deradicalization* 25 (Winter 2020/21), https://journals.sfu.ca/jd/index.php/jd/article/view/411.

———. "Siege: The Atomwaffen Division and Rising Far-Right Terrorism in the United States." *International Centre for Counter-Terrorism—The Hague*, July 2019. https://icct.nl/publication/siege-the-atomwaffen-division-and-rising-far-right-terrorism-in-the-united-states/.

———. "The Violent Far-Right Terrorist Threat to American Law Enforcement." CFR.org, January 24, 2023. https://www.cfr.org/blog/violent-far-right-terrorist-threat-american-law-enforcement.

Watts, Clint. *Messing with the Enemy: Surviving in a Social Media World of Hackers, Terrorists, Russians, and Fake News.* New York: Harper, 2018.

Weiner, Rachel. "After Renouncing White Supremacist Ideology, Virginia Man Sentenced to Year in Prison." *Washington Post*, February 28, 2020.

Weiner, Rachel, Jasmine Hilton, and Dan Morse. "Duo Accused of Neo-Nazi Plot to Target Maryland Power Stations." *Washington Post*, February 6, 2023.

Wells, Ida B. *Southern Horrors and Other Writings: The Anti-Lynching Campaign of Ida B. Wells, 1892–1900.* 2nd ed. Ed. Jacqueline Jones Royster. Boston: Bedford/St. Martin's, 2016.

"What Is the National Alliance? National Alliance Goals." https://natall.com/about/what-is
    -the-national-alliance/.

"Why Countering Violent Extremism Programs Are Bad Policy." Brennan Center for Justice,
    September 9, 2019. https://www.brennancenter.org/our-work/research-reports/why
    -countering-violent-extremism-programs-are-bad-policy.

"William Simmons of Ku Klux Klan; First Imperial Wizard of the Organization Dies—Left It
    in 20's After a Row Responsible for Founding Law-Abiding, He Claimed." *New York Times*,
    May 22, 1945.

Williams, David C. "The Militia Movement and Second Amendment Revolution: Conjuring
    with the People." *Digital Repository @ Maurer Law*, Law Library, University of Indiana,
    1996. https://www.repository.law.indiana.edu/facpub/633.

Wilson, Bernie. "URGENT—3 Linked to Aryan Nations Arrested." Associated Press, Octo-
    ber 3, 1986.

Wilson, Jason. "Republican Matt Shea 'Participated in Act of Domestic Terrorism,' Says
    Report." *Guardian*, December 20, 2019.

Wilson, T. K. *Killing Strangers: How Political Violence Became Modern*. Oxford: Oxford Uni-
    versity Press, 2020.

Wofford, Ben. "The GOP Shut Down a Program That Might Have Prevented Dallas and Baton
    Rouge." *Politico*, July 24, 2016. https://www.politico.com/magazine/story/2016/07/gop
    -veteran-radicalization-dhs-dallas-baton-rouge-214089/.

Wolf, Cam. "The New Uniform of White Supremacy." *GQ*, August 17, 2017. https://www.gq.com
    /story/uniform-of-white-supremacy.

Wolfe, Jan. "'He Invited Us': Accused Capitol Rioters Blame Trump in Novel Legal Defense."
    Reuters, February 2, 2021.

Woo, Elaine. "Richard Butler, 86; Supremacist Founded the Aryan Nations." *Los Angeles Times*,
    September 9, 2004.

Woodruff Swan, Betsy. "'The Intelligence Was There': Law Enforcement Warnings Abounded
    in the Runup to Jan. 6." *Politico*, October 7, 2021. https://www.politico.com/news/2021/10
    /07/law-enforcement-warnings-january-6-515531.

Woodruff Swan, Betsy, and Natasha Bertrand. "'Domestic Terrorist Actors' Could Exploit
    Floyd Protests, DHS Memo Warns." *Politico*, June 1, 2020. https://www.politico.com/news
    /2020/06/01/dhs-domestic-terrorists-protest-294342.

Woodward, C. Vann. *Tom Watson: Agrarian Rebel*. Oxford: Oxford University Press, 1963.

Wright, Stuart A. *Patriots, Politics, and the Oklahoma City Bombing*. Cambridge: Cambridge
    University Press, 2007.

Yaccino, Steven, and Dan Barry. "Bullets, Blood and Then Cry of 'Heil Hitler.'" *New York
    Times*, April 14, 2014.

Yellow Horse, Aggie J., Russell Jeung, Richard Lim, Boaz Tang, Megan Im, Lauryn Higashi-
    yama, Layla Schweng, and Mikayla Chen. "Stop AAPI Hate National Report, 3/19/20–
    6/30/21." Stop AAPI Hate. https://stopaapihate.org/wp-content/uploads/2021/08/Stop
    -AAPI-Hate-National-Report-Final.pdf.

Zahler, Andrew. "Aryan Nations: Summary." *Spokesman-Review* (Spokane, WA), n.d.

Zapotosky, Matt. "Terrorism Laws May Apply If People Intentionally Spread Coronavirus, Justice Dept. Says." *Washington Post*, March 25, 2020.

Zeleny, Jeff. "Secret Service Guards Obama, Taking Unusually Early Step." *New York Times*, May 4, 2007.

Zeskind, Leonard. *Blood and Politics: The History of the White Nationalist Movement from the Margins to the Mainstream*. New York: Farrar, Straus and Giroux, 2009.

Zitser, Joshua. "Pro-Trump Lawyer Lin Wood Insists He Is Not Insane After Tweeting That Mike Pence Should Face Execution by Firing Squad." *Insider*, January 2, 2021. https://www.businessinsider.com/pro-trump-lawyer-l-lin-wood-tweets-that-pence-executed-2021-1.

TELEVISION, RADIO, FILMS, AND VIDEO

Ainsley, Julia. "Extremists Discussed Plans to 'Remove Democratic Lawmakers': FBI-Homeland Security Bulletin." *NBC News*, March 3, 2021. https://www.nbcnews.com/news/us-news/extremists-discussed-plans-remove-democratic-lawmakers-fbi-homeland-security-bulletin-n1259467.

Allam, Hannah. "'Boogaloo' Is the New Far-Right Slang for Civil War." *All Things Considered*, National Public Radio, January 10, 2020. https://www.npr.org/2020/01/10/795366630/boogaloo-is-the-new-far-right-slang-for-civil-war.

American Mutoscope & Biograph Co. *Light Cone: Distribution, Exhibition, and Conservation of Experimental Film*. https://lightcone.org/en/group-4-american-mutoscope-biograph-co.

Augenstein, Neal. "Prosecutors Use Hitler Image Texted to Mother in James Alex Fields Murder Trial." WTOP, December 4, 2018. https://wtop.com/virginia/2018/12/prosecutors-seek-to-use-hitler-image-texted-to-mother-in-james-alex-fields-murder-trial/.

Benen, Steve. "Trump Promotes Barrage of QAnon Content Via Social Media Platform." MSNBC, August 30, 2022, https://www.msnbc.com/rachel-maddow-show/maddowblog/trump-promotes-barrage-qanon-content-social-media-platform-rcna45526.

Blankstein, Andrew, Tom Winter, and Brandy Zadrozny. "Three Men Connected to 'Boogaloo' Movement Tried to Provoke Violence at Protests, Feds Say." *NBC News*, June 3, 2020. https://www.nbcnews.com/news/all/three-men-connected-boogaloo-movement-tried-provoke-violence-protests-feds-n1224231.

BBC News. "Donald Trump Wants 'Total' Halt to Muslims Coming to US—BBC News." YouTube video, December 9, 2015. https://www.youtube.com/watch?v=mo_nYQ6ItWM&ab_channel=BBCNews.

Bennett, Kate, and Evan Perez. "Nation's Top Coronavirus Expert Dr. Anthony Fauci Forced to Beef Up Security as Death Threats Increase." CNN, April 2, 2020. https://www.cnn.com/2020/04/01/politics/anthony-fauci-security-detail/index.html.

Biden, Joe. "Joe Biden for President: America Is an Idea." YouTube video, April 25, 2019. https://www.youtube.com/watch?v=VbOU2fTg6cI&ab_channel=JoeBiden.

Bradner, Eric. "Alt-Right Leader: 'Hail Trump! Hail Our People! Hail Victory!'" CNN, November 22, 2016. https://www.cnn.com/2016/11/21/politics/alt-right-gathering-donald-trump/index.html.

Brennpunkt: Philips vei til terror. Episode 1: 10. august 2019. NRK TV. https://tv.nrk.no/serie /brennpunkt-philips-vei-til-terror/sesong/1/episode/1/avspiller.

British Pathé. "40,000 Ku Klux (1925)." YouTube video. April 13, 2014. https://www.youtube.com /watch?v=BnI8SUQPB4k.

Browne, Ryan, and Barbara Starr. "US Military Official: 50 ISIS Foreign Fighters Captured Since November." CNN, December 12, 2017. https://www.cnn.com/2017/12/12/politics/isis -foreign-fighters-captured-syria-iraq/index.html.

Burns, Gus. "Accused Whitmer Kidnapping Plotters Attended BLM Rally to Protect Protest- ers from Police, Attorney Says." MLive, March 5, 2021. https://www.mlive.com/public -interest/2021/03/accused-whitmer-kidnapping-plotters-attended-blm-rally-to-protect -protesters-from-police-attorney-says.html.

Canadian Broadcasting Company (CBC). "The Survivalists; Shopping for Doomsday." The Fifth Estate, 1981. https://www.youtube.com/watch?v=oYHUiL9HI5g.

"Capitol Rioters' Causes of Death Released; Capitol Officer's Still 'Pending.'" Fox 5 Washing- ton DC, April 7, 2021. https://www.fox5dc.com/news/capitol-rioters-cause-of-death -information-released-capitol-officers-cause-of-death-pending.

Carrega, Christina. "Two Self-Proclaimed Members of 'Boogaloo Bois' Charged with Attempt- ing to Support Hamas." CNN, September 6, 2020. https://www.cnn.com/2020/09/04 /politics/boogaloo-hamas/index.html.

Chappell, Bill. "Trump Pardons Ranchers Dwight and Steven Hammond Over 2012 Arson Conviction." NPR, July 10, 2018. https://www.npr.org/2018/07/10/627653866/president -trump-pardons-ranchers-dwight-and-steven-hammond-over-arson.

Cillizza, Chris. "Newt Gingrich Thinks Members of the January 6 Committee Should Be Threatened with Jail Time." CNN, January 24, 2022. https://www.cnn.com/2022/01/24 /politics/newt-gingrich-jail-time/index.html.

CNBC Television. "President Donald Trump: White Supremacist Group Proud Boys Should 'Stand Back and Stand By.'" YouTube video, September 30, 2020. https://www.youtube.com /watch?v=JZk6VzSLe4Y&ab_channel=CNBCTelevision.

CNN. "Donald Trump Doubles Down on Calling Mexicans 'Rapists.'" YouTube video, June 25, 2015. https://www.youtube.com/watch?v=Jaz1Jos-cL4&ab_channel=CNN.

Cohen, Marshall. "Trump Spreads New Lies About Foreign-Backed Voter Fraud, Stoking Fears of a 'Rigged Election' This November." CNN, June 22, 2020. https://www.cnn.com/2020 /06/22/politics/trump-voter-fraud-lies-fact-check/index.html.

——. "Trump Versus US Intelligence on Russian Election Interference." CNN, July 19, 2018. https://www.cnn.com/2018/07/18/politics/trump-versus-us-intelligence-on-russian -election-interference/index.html.

Collins, Ben, and Brandy Zadrozny. "In Trump's 'LIBERATE' Tweets, Extremists See a Call to Arms." NBC News, April 17, 2020. https://www.nbcnews.com/tech/security/trump-s -liberate-tweets-extremists-see-call-arms-n1186561.

Collins, Ben, Brandy Zadrozny, Tom Winter, and Cork Siemaszko. "Whitmer Conspiracy Alle- gations Tied to 'Boogaloo' Movement." NBC News, October 8, 2020. https://www.nbcnews .com/tech/tech-news/whitmer-conspiracy-allegations-tied-boogaloo-movement-n1242670.

Czachor, Emily Mae, and Nicole Sganga. "2 Suspects Arrested for Conspiring to Attack Baltimore Power Grid, Officials Say." *CBS News*, February 6, 2023. https://www.cbsnews.com /news/baltimore-power-grid-attack-plot-fbi-suspects-arrested-sarah-beth-clendaniel -brandon-russell/.

Date, Jack. "Feds Charge 3 Self-Identified 'Boogaloo' Adherents Plotting Violence at Black Lives Matter Protest." *ABC News*, June 3, 2020. https://abcnews.go.com/ABCNews/feds-charge -identified-boogaloo-adherents-plotting-violence-black/story?id=71059377.

——. "Mail Bomber Cesar Sayoc Obsessed with Trump, Fox News, Chilling New Court Filings Show." *ABC News*, July 23, 2019. https://abcnews.go.com/US/mail-bomber-cesar-sayoc -obsessed-trump-fox-news/story?id=64500598.

Doble, Anna. "Norway's Lost Leaders." Channel 4, July 26, 2011. https://www.channel4.com /news/norways-lost-leaders.

Donnelly, Frank. "The Day QAnon and the NYC Mafia Collided: It's Been 3 Years Since the Murder of Mob Boss Francesco Cali and Uncertainty Surrounds Case." *SI Live*, March 25, 2022. https://www.silive.com/crime-safety/2022/03/the-day-qanon-and-the-nyc-mafia -collided-its-been-3-years-since-the-murder-of-francesco-cali-and-questions-remain .html.

Elliott, Debbie. "Remembering Birmingham's 'Dynamite Hill' Neighborhood." National Public Radio: Code Sw!tch, July 6, 2013. https://www.npr.org/sections/codeswitch/2013/07/06 /197342590/remembering-birminghams-dynamite-hill-neighborhood.

"Embedded: The Terrorist." NPR, October 30, 2019. https://www.npr.org/transcripts/774437718 and https://podcasts.google.com/feed/aHRocHM6Ly9mZWVkcy5ucHIub3JnLzUxMDM xMS9wb2RjYXNoLnhtbA/episode/ZmU3ZGYxOTktY2VkZSooNmYiLThhYjAtOWUx MzZlOGY5NjBi?sa=X&ved=0CAUQkfYCahcKEwjgmvuqqrn_AhUAAAAAHQAAAA AQQQ.

Eradicate Hate Global Summit. "Undercover in the Far Right." YouTube video, September 21, 2022, https://www.youtube.com/watch?v=2awTHrqByOo&ab_channel=EradicateHate GlobalSummit.

"Expert on the Effect of 'Cascading Terrorism.'" MSNBC, June 29, 2016. https://www.msnbc .com/morning-joe/watch/expert-on-the-effect-of-cascading-terrorism-715100739718.

"Facebook: New Zealand Attack Video Viewed 4,000 Times." BBC, March 19, 2019. https:// www.bbc.com/news/business-47620519.

Fantz, Ashley, Joe Sutton, and Holly Yan. "Armed Group's Leader in Federal Building: 'We Will Be Here as Long as It Takes.'" CNN, January 4, 2016. https://www.cnn.com/2016/01 /03/us/oregon-wildlife-refuge-protest/.

Feather, Andrew. "FBI: Suspect in Whitmer Kidnapping Had History of Violent, Threatening Social Media Posts." WWMT, October 29, 2020. https://wwmt.com/news/local/fbi-suspect -in-whitmer-kidnapping-had-history-of-violent-threatening-social-media-posts.

"Florida Neo-Nazi Leader Gets 5 Years for Having Explosive Material." NBC News, January 9, 2018. https://www.nbcnews.com/news/us-news/florida-neo-nazi-leader-gets-5-years -having-explosive-material-n836246.

Frontline. "Documenting Hate: New American Nazis." PBS, February 4, 2020. https://www .pbs.org/wgbh/frontline/film/documenting-hate-new-american-nazis/.

———. "McVeigh Chronology." PBS, n.d., https://www.pbs.org/wgbh/pages/frontline /documents/mcveigh/mcveigh3.html.

"Getting Away with Murder." *American Experience*. https://www.pbs.org/wgbh/americ anexperience/features/emmett-biography-roy-carolyn-bryant-and-jw-milam/.

Gonzales, Richard. "Florida Man Who Mailed Bombs to Democrats, Media Gets 20 Years in Prison." NPR-WAMU 88.5, August 5, 2019, https://www.npr.org/2019/08/05/748420957 /cesar-sayoc-florida-man-who-mailed-bombs-to-democrats-and-media-gets-20-years.

Gregorian, Dareh, and Phil Helsel. "GOP Candidate for Florida House Is Booted from Twitter After Post About Shooting Federal Agents." *NBC News*, August 19, 2022. https://www .nbcnews.com/politics/2022-election/gop-candidate-florida-house-booted-twitter-post -shooting-federal-agent-rcna44020.

Hagstrom, Anders, and Courtney De George. "Mehmet Oz calls John Fetterman to Officially Concede Pennsylvania Senate Race." *Fox News*, November 9, 2022. https://www.foxnews.com /politics/mehmet-oz-calls-john-fetterman-officially-concede-pennsylvania-senate-race.

Halloran, Liz. "What's Behind the New Populism?" National Public Radio, The Tea Party In America, February 5, 2010. https://www.npr.org/templates/story/story.php?storyId =123137382.

"Hearing on Challenge to Rep. Marjorie Taylor Greene's Candidacy." C-SPAN, April 22, 2022. https://www.c-span.org/video/?519623-101/hearing-challenge-rep-marjorie-taylor -greenes-candidacy.

Hellgren, Mike. "FBI Arrest U.S. Army Veteran, 2 Other Suspected White Supremacists on Federal Firearms Charges in Maryland." CBS Baltimore, January 16, 2020. https://baltimore .cbslocal.com/2020/01/16/alleged-members-racially-motivated-extremist-group-the-base -face-firearms-alien-related-charges/.

Hétu, Marie-Hélène. "How Alexandre Bissonnette—and Other Mass Shooters—Could Be Stopped Before They Kill." CBC, October 19, 2019. https://www.cbc.ca/news/canada /alexandre-bissonnette-mass-shooters-1.5326201.

Holcombe, Madeline. "Pipe Bomb Suspect Writes to Judge That the 16 Devices He Mailed Were Only Meant for Intimidation." CNN, April 3, 2019. https://www.cnn.com/2019/04/03/us /cesar-sayoc-letter-to-judge/index.html.https://www.pbs.org/newshour/show/how -concerned-is-the-military-about-insider-threats-in-the-national-guard.

Homeland Security Committee Events. "Confronting the Rise in Anti-Semitic Domestic Terrorism, Part II." YouTube video, February 26, 2020. https://www.youtube.com/watch?v =BTOW8iWoR2E&ab_channel=HomelandSecurityCommitteeEvents.

Honningsøy, Kirsti Haga, and Kristine Ramberg Aasen. "Du har allerede drept pappaen min, jeg er for ung til å dø." NRK, July 24, 2011. https://www.nrk.no/norge/_jeg-er-for-ung-til-a -do_-1.7725593.

"How Concerned Is the Military About Insider Threats in the National Guard?" *PBS News-Hour*, January 18, 2021. https://www.pbs.org/newshour/show/how-concerned-is-the -military-about-insider-threats-in-the-national-guard.

"Illinois Now Requires Media Literacy Instruction in its High School Curriculum." WGLT, September 14, 2022. https://www.wglt.org/2022-09-14/illinois-now-requires-media-literacy -instruction-in-its-high-school-curriculum.

"In Old California (1910)." *Silent Era*. January 21, 2007. http://www.silentera.com/PSFL/data/I /InOldCalifornia1910.html.

"Interview with "Stephen Jones, McVeigh former lawyer." Associated Press Archive, June 10, 2001. https://www.youtube.com/watch?v=PBN1aOrhxi8.

Kamel, Zachary, Mack Lamoureux, and Ben Makuch. "'Eco-Fascist' Arm of Neo-Nazi Terror Group the Base Linked to Swedish Arson." *Vice*, January 29, 2020. https://www.vice.com /en/article/qjdvzx/eco-fascist-arm-of-neo-nazi-terror-group-the-base-linked-to-swedish -arson.

Kleefeld, Eric. "Tea Party Activist and Senate Candidate: 'If We Don't See New Faces, I'm Cleaning My Guns and Getting Ready for the Big Show.'" *Talking Points Memo*, January 26, 2010. https://talkingpointsmemo.com/dc/tea-party-activist-and-senate-candidate-if-we -don-t-see-new-faces-i-m-cleaning-my-guns-and-getting-ready-for-the-big-show-video.

Krieg, Gregory. "14 of Trump's Most Outrageous 'Birther' Claims—Half from After 2011." CNN, September 16, 2016. https://www.cnn.com/2016/09/09/politics/donald-trump-birther.

Kunzelman, Michael, and Jari Tanner. "He Led a Neo-Nazi Group Linked to Bomb Plots. He Was 13." *ABC News*, April 11, 2020. https://abcnews.go.com/US/wireStory/led-neo-nazi -group-linked-bomb-plots-13-70099974.

Lamoureux, Mack, and Ben Makuch. "Member of a Neo-Nazi Terror Group Appears to Be Former Canadian Soldier." *Vice*, August 2, 2018. https://www.vice.com/en/article/7xqe8z /member-of-a-neo-nazi-terror-group-appears-to-be-former-canadian-soldier.

"Las Vegas Shooting Couple Had Been Booted from Bundy Ranch as 'Too Radical.'" *ABC News*, June 10, 2014. https://abcnews.go.com/US/rampaging-couple-booted-bundy-ranch-radical /story?id=24067414.

"Law: Full Text of Eric Rudolph's Confession." NPR, April 14, 2005. https://www.npr.org /templates/story/story.php?storyId=4600480.

Lee, Amber, and KTVU Staff. "DePape in Bizarre Phone Call to KTVU Says He Should Have Been 'More Prepared.'" Fox 2 KTVU, January 27, 2023. https://www.ktvu.com/news/depape -in-bizarre-phone-call-to-ktvu-says-he-should-have-been-more-prepared.

Lybrand, Holmes, and Hannah Rabinowitz. "Oath Keeper Testifies About Mass of Guns Alleg-edly Stored Near DC on January 6." CNN, October 12, 2022. https://www.cnn.com/2022 /10/12/politics/oath-keeper-guns-dc-january-6.

Makuch, Ben, and Mack Lamoureux. "Neo-Nazi Terror Leader Said to Have Worked with U.S. Special Forces." *Vice*, September 24, 2020. https://www.vice.com/en/article/k7qdzv/neo -nazi-terror-leader-said-to-have-worked-with-us-special-forces.

Makuch, Ben, Mack Lamoureux, and Zachary Kamel. "Neo-Nazi Terror Group Harbouring Missing Ex-Soldier: Sources." *Vice*, December 5, 2019. https://www.vice.com/en_ca/article /8xwwaa/neo-nazi-terror-group-harbouring-missing-ex-soldier-patrik-mathews -sources.

Martinez, Lui. "Inside Look at How 25,000 National Guardsmen Are Arriving in Washing-ton, DC." *ABC News*, January 16, 2021. https://abcnews.go.com/Politics/inside-25000 -national-guardsmen-arriving-washington-dc/story?id=75299202.

"Maryland Neo-Nazis Accused of Discussing Bringing Firearms to Pro-gun Rally in Virginia." Fox 5, January 16, 2020. https://www.fox5atlanta.com/news/maryland-neo-nazis-accused -of-discussing-bringing-firearms-to-pro-gun-rally-in-virginia.

McCausland, Jeff. "Inside the U.S. Military's Battle with White Supremacy and Far-Right Extremism." *NBC News*, May 25, 2019. https://www.nbcnews.com/think/opinion/inside-u-s-military-s-battle-white-supremacy-far-right-ncna1010221.

McKay, Hollie. "Antifa Arrests Coming, Concerns Over Riots Heading to Suburbia, Government Source Says." *Fox News*, June 2, 2020. https://www.foxnews.com/us/antifa-arrests-coming-riots-suburbs.

Merica, Dan. "Trump Condemns 'Hatred, Bigotry, and Violence on Many Sides' in Charlottesville." CNN, August 13, 2017. https://www.cnn.com/2017/08/12/politics/trump-statement-alt-right-protests/index.html.

Moxley, Elle. "Why KCUR Refers to the Accused JCC Shooter as Frazier Glenn Cross." KCUR: NPR in Kansas City, March 4, 2015. https://www.kcur.org/community/2015-03-04/why-kcur-refers-to-the-accused-jcc-shooter-as-frazier-glenn-cross.

"Musk Lifts Donald Trump's Twitter Ban." BBC, November 20, 2022. https://www.bbc.com/news/world-us-canada-63692369.

Naylor, Brian. "Read Trump's Jan. 6 Speech, a Key Part of Impeachment Trial." NPR: WAMU 88.5, February 10, 2021. https://www.npr.org/2021/02/10/966396848/read-trumps-jan-6-speech-a-key-part-of-impeachment-trial.

NBC News. "Trump's Full, Heated Press Conference on Race and Violence in Charlottesville (Full)." YouTube video, August 15, 2017. https://www.youtube.com/watch?v=QGKbFA7HW-U&ab_channel=NBCNews.

New York Times. "Day of Rage: How Trump Supporters Took the U.S. Capitol." YouTube video, July 1, 2021. https://www.youtube.com/watch?v=jWJVMoe7OYo&ab_channel=TheNewYorkTimes.

Noakes, Jeremy. "Hitler and 'Lebensraum' in the East." BBC, March 30, 2011. https://www.bbc.co.uk/history/worldwars/wwtwo/hitler_lebensraum_01.shtml.

"Norway Killer Breivik Tests Limits of Lenient Justice System." *Voice of America News*, January 22, 2022. https://www.voanews.com/a/norway-killer-breivik-tests-limits-of-lenient-justice-system/6407441.html.

Noyes, Dan, and Amanda del Castillo. "Federal Officer Shooting Suspects Steven Carrillo, Robert Justus 'Came to Oakland to Kill Cops,' FBI Says." ABC 7, June 17, 2020. https://abc7news.com/steven-carrillo-robert-alvin-justus-jr-pat-underwood-killed-oakland/6250277/.

"Olathe, Kansas, Shooting Suspect 'Said He Killed Iranians.'" BBC, February 28, 2017. https://www.bbc.com/news/world-us-canada-39108060.

Owen, Tess. "The U.S. Military Has a Boogaloo Problem." *Vice*, June 24, 2020. https://www.vice.com/en/article/xg8g87/the-us-military-has-a-boogaloo-problem.

——. "White Supremacists Built a Website to Doxx Interracial Couples—and It's Going to Be Hard to Take Down." *Vice*, May 13, 2020, https://www.vice.com/en/article/n7ww4w/white-supremacists-built-a-website-to-doxx-interracial-couples-and-its-going-to-be-hard-to-take-down.

Pérez de Acha, Gisela, Kathryn Hurd, and Ellie Lightfoot. "'I Felt Hate More Than Anything': How an Active Duty Airman Tried to Start a Civil War." *Frontline*, April 13, 2021, https://www.pbs.org/wgbh/frontline/article/steven-carrillo-boogaloo-bois-active-duty-airman-incite-civil-war/.

Qazi, Shereen. "40 Years After Escaping War, Afghan Killed in Christchurch Mosque." *Al Jazeera*, March 16, 2019. https://www.aljazeera.com/news/2019/3/16/40-years-after-escaping-war-afghan-killed-in-christchurch-mosque.

Rachel Maddow Show. "Transcript 8/14/17: White America Has a Chronic Nazi Problem." MSNBC. http://www.msnbc.com/transcripts/rachel-maddow-show/2017-08-14.

Reilly, Ryan J. "Court Document in Proud Boys Case Laid Out Plan to Occupy Capitol Buildings on Jan. 6." *NBC News*, June 15, 2022. https://www.nbcnews.com/politics/justice-department/court-document-proud-boys-case-laid-plan-occupy-capitol-buildings-jan-rcna33755.

"Rep. Rodney Davis: "This Would Have Been a Massacre" If Not for Capitol Police." CBS Chicago, June 14, 2017. https://chicago.cbslocal.com/2017/06/14/rep-rodney-davis-this-would-have-been-a-massacre-if-not-for-police/.

Rogers, Alex, and Manu Raju. "McConnell Blames Trump but Voted Not Guilty Anyway." CNN, February 13, 2021. https://www.cnn.com/2021/02/13/politics/mitch-mcconnell-acquit-trump/index.html.

Romo, Vanessa. "Washington Legislator Matt Shea Accused of 'Domestic Terrorism,' Report Finds." NPR—WAMU 88.5, December 20, 2019. https://www.npr.org/2019/12/20/790192972/washington-legislator-matt-shea-accused-of-domestic-terrorism-report-finds.

Schuster, Henry. "Lone Wolves: Solitary Threats Harder to Hunt." CNN, February 1, 2005, http://www.cnn.com/2005/US/02/01/schuster.column/index.html.

Seitz-Wald, Alex. "Republicans Who Questioned the 2020 Results Are Bringing Back an Old Norm: Admitting Defeat." *NBC News*, November 10, 2022. https://www.nbcnews.com/politics/2022-election/republicans-questioned-2020-results-are-bringing-back-old-norm-admitin-rcna56486.

Seldin, Jeff. "Trump Renews 'Rigged Election' Claim Against All Evidence." Voice of America, November 13, 2020. https://www.voanews.com/2020-usa-votes/trump-renews-rigged-election-claim-against-all-evidence.

Seno, Tommy De. "Obama's to Blame for the Birther Movement." *Fox News*, July 29, 2009. https://www.foxnews.com/opinion/obamas-to-blame-for-the-birther-movement.

——. "Why Did Rudolph Do It? Question Lingers After Plea Deal Reached." CNN, April 11, 2005. http://www.cnn.com/2005/US/04/11/schuster.column/index.html.

Siegel, Benjamin. "DHS Whistleblower Testifies Before House Intelligence Committee." *ABC News*, December 11, 2020. https://abcnews.go.com/Politics/dhs-whistleblower-testifies-house-intelligence-committee/story?id=74675983.

Simone, Daniel De, Andrei Soshnikov, and Ali Winston. "Neo-Nazi Rinaldo Nazzaro Running US Militant Group the Base from Russia." BBC, January 24, 2020. https://www.bbc.com/news/world-51236915.

Simone, Daniel De, and Ali Winston. "Neo-Nazi Militant Group Grooms Teenagers." BBC, June 21, 2020. https://www.bbc.com/news/uk-53128169.

Smith, Terrance. "Trump Has Longstanding History of Calling Elections 'Rigged' If He Doesn't Like the Results." *ABC News*, November 11, 2020. https://abcnews.go.com/Politics/trump-longstanding-history-calling-elections-rigged-doesnt-results/story?id=74126926.

Spring, Marianna. "'Stop the Steal': The Deep Roots of Trump's 'Voter Fraud' Strategy." *BBC News*, November 23, 2020. https://www.bbc.com/news/blogs-trending-55009950.

Sprunt, Barbara. "7 GOP Senators Voted to Convict Trump. Only 1 Faces Voters Next Year." NPR, February 15, 2021. https://www.npr.org/sections/trump-impeachment-trial-live -updates/2021/02/15/967878039/7-gop-senators-voted-to-convict-trump-only-1-faces -voters-next-year.

"Teenage Neo-Nazis Jailed Over Terror Offences." BBC, June 18, 2019. https://www.bbc.com /news/uk-48672929.

"Thomas George Harrelson." *Unsolved Mysteries*. https://unsolvedmysteries.fandom.com/wiki /Thomas_Harrelson.

"Ty Hardin: Biography." *IMDb*. https://www.imdb.com/name/nm0362249/bio.

Vespa, Maggie. "'Go Back to Saudi Arabia': Muslim, Black Communities Watching MAX Attack Trial Closely." KGW8, February 18, 2020. https://www.kgw.com/article/news/local /trimet-attack/portland-max-trial-jeremy-christian-black-muslim-communities/283 -cd14e46c-f47a-4308-8bd0-239b6f26eb36.

"Victor Davis Hanson: Democrats 'Live Apartheid, Segregated Existences.'" *Fox News*, July 26, 2022. https://www.foxnews.com/video/6310049745112.

Wagner, Laura. "Accused Planned Parenthood Shooter: 'I'm a Warrior for the Babies." NPR, December 9, 2015. https://www.npr.org/sections/thetwo-way/2015/12/09/459116186/planned -parenthood-shooter-im-a-warrior-for-the-babies.

"'We Put Up One Heck of a Fight': Walker Concedes Senate Runoff to Warnock." Fox 5 Atlanta, December 7, 2022. https://www.fox5atlanta.com/news/herschel-walker-concession-speech -georgia-senate-runoff-warnock.

Westervelt, Eric. "Off-Duty Police Officers Investigated, Charged with Participating in Capi- tol Riot." National Public Radio Criminal Justice Collaborative, January 15, 2021. https://www.npr.org/2021/01/15/956896923/police-officers-across-nation-face-federal -charges-for-involvement-in-capitol-ri.

"White Supremacy in the Military." C-SPAN, February 11, 2020. https://www.c-span.org/video /?469238-1/white-supremacy-military.

Williams, Pete. "Gunman Who Attacked Florida Yoga Studio Gave Off Decades of Warning Signs, Secret Service Finds." *NBC News*, March 15, 2022. https://www.nbcnews.com/politics /politics-news/gunman-attacked-florida-yoga-studio-gave-decades-warning-signs -secret-rcna19883.

Winsor, Morgan. "2009 vs. 2017: Comparing Trump's and Obama's Inauguration Crowds." *ABC News*, January 25, 2017. https://abcnews.go.com/Politics/2009-2017-comparing-trumps -obamas-inauguration-crowds/story?id=44927217.

Wolf, Z. Byron. "Trump's Defense of the 'Very Fine People' at Charlottesville White Nation- alist March has David Duke Gushing." CNN, August 15, 2017. https://www.cnn.com/2017 /08/15/politics/donald-trump-david-duke-charlottesville.

Wu, Katherine J. "Radical ideas Spread Through Social Media. Are the Algorithms to Blame?" *NOVA*, March 28, 2019. https://www.pbs.org/wgbh/nova/article/radical-ideas-social-media -algorithms/.

INDEX